D1831269

MEDICAL JURISPRUDENCE

MEDICAL JURISPRUDENCE

VOLUME - 1

P. S. Kapoor
MBBS, MS, PCMS (Ex)

©Author
All rights reserved. No part of this work may be reproduced, stored, adapted, or transmitted in any form or by any means, electronic, mechanical, photocopying, micro-filming recording or otherwise, or translated in any language, without the prior written permission of the copyright owner and the publisher. The book is sold subject to the condition that it shall not, by way of trade or otherwise, be lent, resold, hired out, or otherwise circulated without the prior publisher's written consent in any form of binding or cover other than that in which it is published.

The views and opinions expressed in this book are author(s) own and the facts reported by them have been verified to the extent possible, and the publishers are not in any way liable for the same.

First Published, 2018

Published by

Kalpaz Publications
C-30, Satyawati Nagar,
Delhi – 110052
E-mail: kalpaz@hotmail.com
Ph.: 9212142040

Printed at: G. Print Process, Delhi

Cataloging in Publication Data—DK
Courtesy: D.K. Agencies (P) Ltd. <docinfo@dkagencies.com>

Kapoor, P. S., author.
Medical jurisprudence / Dr P.S. Kapoor.
volumes cm
Includes bibliographical references.
ISBN 9789386397584 (set: HB)
ISBN 9789386397591 (Vol-I: HB)

1. Medical laws and legislation—India. I. Title.

KNS1520.K37 2018 | DDC 344.54041 23

CONTENTS

PART - I

FORENSIC MEDICINE

PART - II

MEDICAL JURISPRUDENCE

PART - IV

APPENDIX

Dedicated
to
The Memory of My Father

PREFACE

This book has been written primarily for the medical students, medical officers and lawyers, especially those dealing with medico-legal problems. A Registered Medical Practitioner should have sufficient knowledge of laws and ethical aspects of Good Medical Practice, in order not to conflict with it during his/her professional practice. For that he/she ought to be familiar with various Acts, Rules and Regulations that are in force or else he/she may find himself/herself inadvertently contravening these and courting trouble and also amounting to professional misconduct attracting disciplinary action by the authorities. For that reason, provision of laws relating to medical practice in undergraduate/graduate curriculum should be seriously considered.

Medical jurisprudence benefits immensely both the medical and the legal field of work. A better understanding and cooperation has resulted and has facilitated a smoother working of both disciplines.

Medical jurisprudence connotes legal aspect of medical practice, that does not involve its curative aspect alone, but also is concerned with its legal nee medico-legal aspect relating to doctor-patient relationship, doctor-state relationship, with respect to doctor's duties, obligation to his/her patients apart from legal aspect of medical practice including. misconduct, medical negligence, malpractices, etc. State Medicine envisages proper code of conduct of Registered Medical Practitioners, to guide and regulate their professional activities, to protect the community at large from quacks and charlatans against malpractice.

Medical Jurisprudence has emerged as a speciality, stressing on the social and legal aspects of medical discipline. Medical practice has become systematised and regulated under rules and regulations of State Authorities including. Medical Council, infringement of which will invite explanation, if not punishment.

It is a speciality in which the Medical Practitioners have got to be aware of their duties and responsibilities, encompassing the legal aspect of the medical practice in their own interest.

This book is intended to serve as a useful reference, on widely accepted technics currently available for finding causes, clinical diagnosis and investigations of common disorders. The contents of this book are presented as separate sections, any one of which is complete in itself i.e. Forensic medicine, State Medicine (Medico-legal system), and Medical Ethics, have been described fully.

Specific references are included as a guide to further study. The evaluation of new medical concepts and advances in determining causes, diagnosis, investigation and Judgments, has been a constant challenge. Medical progress and space limitations are the deciding factors.

This book aims to help the medical students to have sufficient knowledge of Forensic Medicine and State Medicine (Medico-legal) in their preparation for examination, and in order not to conflict with it during his/her subsequent future medical practice, and for that he/she ought to be familiar with various Acts and rules and regulations, that are in force, failing that may find himself/herself inadvertently contravening these and courting unnecessary trouble and also amounting to professional misconduct attracting disciplinary action by the State Authorities.

Special chapters on medical aberrations, poisoning, medical offences and penalties, legal systems, legal procedures, Acts and Laws, Sections, important Medico-legal Judgments, Medical Ethics and Questionnaires for helping students in their preparation for examination. Recent Judgments (changes) in Criminal Procedure Code and IPC, relevant to medical profession have received special attention.

I have made endeavoured throughout to mention the authorities whose work I have made use of, but I should like to express here my appreciation of the fact that it is the work of others which gives this book any value it may have.

Dr P.S. Kapoor

ACKNOWLEDGEMENT

I wish to express my appreciation to Miss Komal Kapoor, Miss Arshpreet Kaur, Ms Anju, and Miss Deepa for their skilful assistance with the manuscript and electronic information with outstanding accuracy and reliability, meeting every deadline calmly and successfully. Without their help the job would have been many times more difficult.

I would like to acknowledge the help received from Mr Jagdeep Kapoor and Ms Rita Kapoor, in the form of useful suggestions and moral support. It is heartening to acknowledge the enthusiasm and encouragement gained at each step from dearest Isaac.

I am indebted to Drs C.N.Malla, S. K. Madan, Rajinder Singh, H.V. Jindal, S. Saggar, Vaneet Gupta, Ram Kumar, Vandana Sabharwal and Advocates Mandeep Sajjan, RL Batta Vikas Chowdhary and L. K. Thakur, who have offered special suggestions, comments and corrections. Lastly, I am highly thankful to the management of PGI Library and British Library and Hindustan Times, for acess to the medical and law books, journals and press articles.

Dr P.S. Kapoor

ABBREVIATION

A

Ab	–	antibody
ABC	–	airway, breathing, circulation
ACNG	–	actus curiae neminem gravabit
AICLR	–	all India court legal report
AIIMS	–	all India institute of Medical Sciences
AILER	–	all India Legal Empowered Report
AP	–	anteroposterior
ASAP	–	as soon as possible
AYUSH	–	ayurveda, unani, sidhi, homeopathy

B

b.d.	–	bis die (twice daily)
BP	–	blood pressure
B/L	–	bilateral
BRHC	–	bachelor of rural health and care
BRMS	–	bachelor of rural medicine and surgery
BMA	–	British Medical Association
BMJ	–	British Medical Journal

C

Ca	–	carcinoma
CE	–	cross-examination
CHF	–	congestive heart failure
CNS	–	central nervous system
CO	–	carbon monoxide
CO_2	–	carbon dioxide
COHb	–	carboxyhemoglobin
CC	–	criminal complaint
CCC	–	civil and criminal contempt

CCP – civil and criminal proceeding
CFI – court of first instance
CI – coroner‘s inquest
COC – contempt of court
CPC – civil procedure code
Cr C – criminal court
CrPC – criminal procedure code
CPA – Consumer Protection Act
C.P.J. – Consumer Protection Judgment
CSF – cerebrospinal fluid
CST – Civil Service Tribunal
CT – criminal trial
CVA – cerebrovascular accident
CVD – cardiovascular disease
CXR – chest X-ray
CEA – Clinical Establishment Act

D

DB – decomposed body
D & C – dilatation and curettage
DCA – drugs and cosmetic act
DD – dying declaration
dL – decilitre
DOT – directly observed treatment
DNA – deoxyribonucleic acid
DPA – Dowry Prohibition act
DT – delirium tremens

E

ECA – European Court of Auditors
ECFTA – European Court of Free Trade Association
ECG – electrocardiogram
ECHR – European Court of Human Rights
ECJ – European Court of Justice
E.D. – emergency department
EEG – electro-encephalography
e.g. – for example
EJC – extra-judicial confession

EPA – Environment Protection Act
ETOH – exposure to occupational hazards

F

FB – full bench
FH – family history

G

g – gram (s)
GA – general anesthesia
GIT – gastrointestinal tract
GP – general practitioner

H

HCO3 – bicarbonate
H2CO3 – carbonate
HDL – high density lipoprotein
Hg – mercury
HIV – human immunodeficiency virus
HMCS – her majesty's court service
hr – hour

I

ICC – International Criminal Court
ICJ – International Court of Justice
ICP – intracranial pressure
ICS – intercostal space
ICU – intensive care unit
i.e. – that is
ILO – International Labour Organisation
IMA – Indian Medical Association
IMC – Indian Medical Council
INTERPOL – International Crime Police Organisation
IPC – Indian Penal Code
ITA – Income Tax Act
ITPA – Immoral Traffic Prevention Act
ITR – Income Tax Rules

J

JJ – juvenile justice
JO – juvenile offender

K

kg – kilogram
kL – kilolitre

L

L – litre
LA – local anaesthesia
LAT – lateral
LMP – last menstrual period
Lt – left
LSD – lysergic acid diethylamide

M

max – maximum
mEq/L – milliequivalents per litre
mg – milligrams
MBBS – Bachelor of Medicine and Bachelor of Surgery
MCI – Medical Council of India
ME – medical evidence
MHA – mental health act min minute/minutes
MJ – medical jurisprudence
mL – millilitre
mm Hg – millimetres of mercury
mmol – millimoles
MO – medical officer
mU – million units
MN – medical negligence
MR – mens rea
MTP – Medical Termination of Pregnancy

N

NCHRH – National Commission of Human Resources for Health
NDPSA – Narcotic Drugs and Psychotropic Substances Act
NHS – national health service
NICU – neonatal intensive care unit
NSA – National Security Act
NSAIDs – nonsteroidal anti-inflammatory drugs
NT – narco test

O

OA – oaths act
OBS – organic brain syndrome
o.d.i. – omni die (once daily)
OPD – out-patients department
OT – oath-taking

P

PA – Poisons Act
$PaCO_2$ – partial pressure of carbon dioxide (arterial)
PaO_2 – partial pressure of oxygen (arterial)
PCA – prevention of cruelty to animals
PCRA – Protection of Civil Rights Act
PDA – prevention of disruptive activities
PDPPA – Prevention of Damage to Public Property Act
PGIMER – post-graduate institute of medical education and research
PHC – primary health centre
PHRA – Protection of Human Rights Act
PI – police inquest
PO – per os (orally/by mouth)
PNDT – pre-natal diagnostic techniques
P/R – per-rectum
PMA – post-mortem appearance
PMR – post-mortem report
PTA – post-traumatic amnesia
PUO – pyrexia of unknown origin
P/V – per vaginum
PWDVA – Protection of Women from Domestic Violence Act

Q

Q – quantum
q.d.s. – (qds) quater in die summendus (four times daily)
q.i.d. – quarter in die (4 times a day)

R

RA – rheumatoid arthritis
RCR – recent clinical report

RE – re-examination
RTI – right to information
RNTCP – revised national TB control programme
RRC – rarest of rare case
RS – remission of sentence
RW – resiled witness
S s.c.(S/c) – subcutaneously
S.C.C. – supreme Court Cases
SCSTA – Schedule Castes and Scheduled Tribes Act
SE – secondary evidence
SE (S/E) – side-effect(s)
s – second(s)
SSM – sputum smear microscopy stat immediately
SS – suspension of sentence
ST – speedy trial
STD – sexually transmitted disease

T

TADA – terrorist and disruptive activities
TB – tuberculosis
t.d.s.(TDS) – ter in die sumendus (three times daily)
t.i.w. – three times per week
THO – transplantation of human organs
U u/U/IU – unit ug microgram
U.O.I. – Union of India
URC – upper respiratory catarrh
UTI – urinary tract infection
USS – ultrasound (ultrasonography) study

V

VS – volunteering statement
VL – vicarious liability

W

WHO – World Health Organisation
Wit – witness
Wk(s) – week(s)
WS – written statement

wt – weight

WTO – World Trade Organisation

X

XT – xenopus test

Y

y – year(s)

CHAPTER - 1

INTRODUCTION

MEDICAL JURISPRUDENCE (SYN. FORENSIC/OR LEGAL MEDICINE)

Definition: Is defined as the application of medical science to the legal problems. It deals with the subject related to the principles of knowledge of medicine to purpose of Law and is typically involved in cases concerning blood relationship, mental illness, injury, or death resulting from violence.

Introduction: The discipline of medical jurisprudence and state medicine dates back to earliest medical history by dint of merit to guide and regulate medical profession and practice. In the past relation between medicine and law were by means of magic, superstition and religion. Science being in developing stage, was unable to assist in this subject. The evidence of witness was substituted by the law oriented miracles as explanation, superstition as a proof, confession as admission of guilt and torture (including Sexual torture). Hippocratic writings (Hippocrates in the Aegen, 460-375 BC) rejected the magic of "primitive medicine" and superstition, and laid the foundations of modern medicine, and laid down a code to be followed by a medical professional, so called "Hippocratic Oath", still sworn by each and every new doctor, as a pre-requisite to start medical career. In India, Charak and Susruta, followed almost the same principle, by recommending for proper medical teaching, training, duties and responsibilities, privileges and status in the society for doctors, governed by the professional norms and conduct (prescribed rules). Any violation of these norms and conduct, would held the doctor responsible and liable for his/her misconduct. Moreover, any practice by the unqualified persons (quacks) was strongly condemned. Thus, the State Medicine (regulated medical practice) was introduced long before Dr Stanford Emerson Chille (1949) who prescribed it as specialised branch of medicine dealing with medico-legal aspects. Currently the medical practice has become systematised and regulated under rules and regulations of governing body (Medical Council), violation of which may call for disciplinary action. Now-a-days people at large have become aware of their rights and privileges as per the consumer protection act, and may claim damage for the injury suffered, to be assessed by the Consumer Court. This in term is the assessment of level of medical care provided by the doctor to his/her patient

Relationship: State medicine envisages good medical practice that sets out the principles and values on which good practice is based, and these principles together describe medical professionalism in action. The guidance is addressed to doctors, but it is also intended to let the public know what they can expect from doctors. Currently the Medical Practitioner is required to have sufficient medico-legal knowledge, so as not to conflict with it during his/her medical practice.

"Medico-Legal" is the term, which incorporates the basics of two inter-related professions i.e. Medicine and Law. Everybody talks about the law but few, aside from lawyers, judges and law teachers, have more than the vaguest notion of what constitutes law. The average lawman often has about as much accurate information about the law as he has about medicine-or life on Venus. And, unfortunately, two professional groups suffer from more ignorance of law and medicine than is good for them. Lawyers, at least those who do not constantly deal with medical issues in their legal practice, know very little about the medical profession and its problems; physicians frequently comprehend too little about the law and how it affects them in the practice of their profession. Medico-legal experts can provide a link between these two professions for their smooth and effective functioning in a scientific manner. The physician meets the law at every turn. He confronts it when, as the treating doctor, he is subpoenaed as a witness in a personal injury lawsuit; he meets it when his aid is sought as an expert in connection with a claim that another member of his profession has been negligent and when he is faced in his office or clinic by a narcotic addict, a man with a gunshot wound, or a young couple seeking a blood test. He is face-to-face with the law when he is required to render an aggravating array of governmental reports or to preserve physical evidence for the benefit of a law enforcement agency. The physician, in fact, finds a great deal of the law intensely irritating, often because he is not absolutely clear as to its purpose. The following subjects deal with all the above aspects of Law and medicine:

Medical jurisprudence

Forensic Medicine

Toxicology

Medical jurisprudence: It is the application of medical science to legal problems. It is typically involved in cases concerning blood relationship, mental illness, injury, or death resulting from violence. Autopsy is often used to determine the cause of death, particularly in cases where foul play is suspected. Post-mortem examination can determine not only the immediate agent of death (e.g. gunshot wound, poison), but may also yield important contextual information, such as how long the person has been dead, which can help trace the killing.

Autopsy: Autopsy is the systematic examination of a cadaver for study or for determining the cause of death. Autopsy means "see for yourself". It is a special surgical operation, performed by specially trained physicians, on a dead body. Its purpose is to learn the truth about the person's health during life, and how the person really died. Autopsies, also known as necropsies, post mortems, or post mortem examinations, use many methodical procedures to determine the aetiology and pathogenesis of diseases, for epidemiologic purposes, for establishment of genetic causes, and for family counsel. There are many advantages to getting an autopsy. Even when the law does not require it, there is always something interesting for the family to know. Post-mortems may be performed at the request of the authorities in cases of unexplained and suspicious death or where a physician did not attend death. In other circumstances post-mortem examination may be performed only with the consent of the deceased's family or with permission granted by the person himself before death. These examinations are more frequently being used for the acquiring of organs and tissues for transplantation. Valuable medical information can be learned from a post-mortem examination. Legionnaire's disease, for example, was discovered as a result of autopsies, and improved safety standards have resulted from the examination of the bodies of crash victims.

The autopsy deals with the particular illness as evidenced in one individual and is more than simply a statistical average. Every autopsy is important to expose mistakes, to delimit new diseases and new patterns of disease, and to guide future studies. Morbidity and mortality statistics acquire accuracy and significance when based on careful autopsies. The autopsy procedure itself has changed very little during the twentieth century. It is a detailed examination of a body and each of its part, not only superficially but also through various tests on tissue in labs. Its purpose is to learn the truth about the person's health during life, and how the person really died. Apparently, autopsies are being performed with decreasing frequently. Where earlier in the century as many as half of all bodies had autopsies performed, now only 5-10 per cent of corpses undergo the procedure. Generally, an autopsy is only done when there is some cause of doubt as to the cause of death, although the family of the deceased can always request an autopsy even if the hospital doesn't think it necessary.

Benefits of Medical Jurisprudence

The introduction of medical jurisprudence has immensely benefited both the medical and the legal field of work. A better understanding and cooperation has resulted and has facilitated a smoother working of both disciplines. Previously unsolvable cases are now solved with ease with the development of the field of medical jurisprudence. It covers in its ambit the provision of evidence for a wide range and scope of cases. It can be used to determine the Paternity of a child and also be employed in determining the identity of human bodies, which have been mutilated beyond recognition in accidents like bomb blasts, factory explosions etc. In the field of Evidence Laws, it can be appropriated to solve cases involving murder, rape etc. Medical Jurisprudence techniques like autopsy can also be employed to discover important facts vital to the case after the person has died.

However, despite their vast benefits to the field of law, medical jurisprudential techniques are not treated as primary evidence till date.

The present Indian Evidence Act continues to treat technical findings, such as the results of DNA tests, as expert evidence. This situation will continue till a legislation is drafted and enacted by the Parliament. Under Section 45 of the Indian Evidence Act, 1872, it has been, inter alia, provided that, when the court has to form an opinion upon a point of science, or art, or as to identity of handwriting or finger impression, the opinions upon the point of persons specially skilled in science or art or any question as to identity of handwriting or finger impressions are relevant facts and such persons are called experts. The expression opinions upon a point of science of persons specially skilled in science is capable of application to all future advances in science which enable an expert opinion on a point.

Due to the heavy misuse and lack of knowledge of the courts as regards scientific evidence, they are hesitant in applying these techniques. In order to determine whether scientific evidence is admissible, the court may consider-

(1) whether the principle or technique has been or can be reliably tested,

(2) whether it has been subjected to peer review or publication,

(3) its known or potential rate of error,

(4) whether there are standards or organisations controlling the procedures of the technique,

(5) whether it is generally accepted by the community, and

(6) whether the technique was created or conducted independently of the litigation.

The situation appears hearty only as regards autopsy reports, which have been given the status of documentary evidence under the Indian Evidence Act. The merit attached to them, however, remains subjective and varies from case to case. The complete benefit of these medical jurisprudential techniques can be enjoyed only by an enactment recognising these techniques as primary evidence, giving it the credit it deserves.

Forensic medicine is a specialised branch of medicine related to the methods for finding out about a crime (an integral component of Criminal Justice System). It is used in the pursuit of justice in a Court proceeding. It has also become increasingly important in cases involving rape. Modern techniques use such specimens as semen, blood, and hair samples of the criminal found in the victim's bodies, which can be compared to the defendant's genetic makeup through a technique known as DNA fingerprinting; this technique may also be used to identify the body of a victim.

The establishment of serious mental illness by a licensed psychologist can be used in demonstrating incompetence to stand trial, a technique which may be used in the insanity defense, albeit infrequently.

Applications of Forensic Medicine: Range from Rape, child abuse, murder and deaths from civil rights violations (Torture).

Principles of Forensic Medicine:

- *Identification of a dead body or an individual (suspected accused):* by DNA fingerprinting, dental analysis, narco test.
- *Crime scene analysis:* by inspection/search, circumstantial evidence and laboratory evidence.
- *Audio-visual:* by Photography, audio-visual recordings, mobile phone video. Identification of weapons (Firearms, bullets, explosives, sharp tools, sticks, stones etc.) used in the crime.
- *Documentary evidence:* by documents (handwriting, counterfeiting, forgery).

- *Psychiatry and Profiling:* by analysing mental disorders and inspecting the crime scene to analyse the personality profile of the accused/ offender.

DNA Fingerprinting:

DNA fingerprinting or DNA profiling or any of the several similar techniques for analysing and comparing DNA from separate sources are used especially in law enforcement to identify suspects from hair, blood, semen, or other biological materials found at the scene of a violent crime. It depends on the fact that no two people, save identical twins, have exactly the same DNA sequence, and that although only limited segments of a person's DNA are scrutinised in the procedure, those segments will be statistically unique. The DNA samples of the culprit can be obtained from the scene of crime itself. For example, blood samples from a scene of murder or samples of seminal fluids deposited on the clothes or furniture or in the body of the victim of rape can be used to acquire a sample of the culprits DNA. These samples can be compared with those taken from a possible suspect in the case.

DNA evidence, apart from its use in criminal law to determine the killer or the rapist, is also employed for various other purposes. Amongst its varied applications, Paternity testing, Personal identification (of a mutilated body or skeletal remains), study of the evolution of the human population and study of inherited diseases like Alzheimers disease etc. are included.

The success rate in solving complex cases in Criminal Law has greatly increased after the discovery and use of DNA evidence technologies. The introduction of DNA evidence in the field of Criminal law has particularly facilitated convictions in the matters involving the offence of Rape.

Technique of DNA:

Rape: First samples of the seminal fluids found at the scene of crime by the investigating officer are analysed. If this is not available, then samples of the seminal fluid are extracted from the victims body itself. The DNA from this sample is then compared with the DNA sample taken from the accused. If the report establishes that these samples match, then this acts as evidence in the court proving rape.

Murder: As regards the offence of murder, DNA samples that are collected from the blood, mucous, saliva, skin, hair samples etc, found on the crime scene are employed to extract the DNA sample. This provides for a very effective technique to nail the culprit. DNA testing should be viewed against the fact that the growing citizen concern over crime is not merely about mounting statistics. It is also over the detectives' inability to solve many gruesome crimes. The question that is often asked is how far the police are equipped to handle investigations using modern science and technology, and how far does the current law of evidence in the country recognise evidence gathered from such tests. There is more than a trace of popular cynicism over police willingness to spurn third degree methods in favour of scientific investigation. It is mainly in this context that many critics of police performance raise the issue of DNA profiling frequently.

Exoneratting innocent: Apart from its use to nail the culprit, Post-conviction DNA Testing is also a very effective method to exonerate the innocent. The sophisticated technology makes it possible to obtain conclusive results in cases in which the previous testing had been inconclusive. Post-conviction testing will be requested not only in cases in which the DNA testing was never done but also in cases in which more refined technology may result in an indisputable answer.

Feature of DNA: The remarkable feature of DNA is that individuals leave at least traces of it almost everywhere. A few of the everyday objects handled by us, such as pens, telephones, mugs and keys are some of the things that require attention from a crime investigator. A variety of offences such as murder, rape, armed robbery; extortion and drug trafficking yield themselves to the application of DNA collection and testing.

Observation by the National Institute of Justice (NIJ) of US' Justice Department:

According to a study by the National Institute of Justice (NIJ) of the United States' Justice Department, there are many unusual sources of DNA evidence that need to be explored by an investigator. These include saliva found on the flap of an envelope containing a threat letter, spittle collected from the sidewalk where a suspect in a sexual assault case was under surveillance and blood collected from a bullet that had injured an assailant himself in a case of murder.

Collection of samples at a scene of crime requires some skill and observance of basic rules of hygiene. There are two dangers here. One is that, as in the case of hand fingerprints, there is a distinct possibility of several persons having left their DNA behind in a scene of crime. The need, therefore, is to identify all visitors and collecting their samples also (apart from those of the victim/suspect). This assiduous process can try an officer's patience. Secondly, DNA samples are extremely susceptible to contamination. It is essential that the technicians collecting the sample adopt all precautions that a surgeon would while performing a critical surgery. Any slackness could render the entire operation wasteful and susceptible to easy picking of holes by the defense counsel during a trial.

Application of DNA Fingerprinting in:

Civil cases	: Paternity dispute	: Imran Khan's paternity test
	Blue dress case	: Bill Clinton–Ex President of USA
Criminal cases	: Rape case	: Swami Premanandaji in rape case
	Rape and paternity dispute case	: Madhumita murder case
	Murder cases	: Rajiv Gandhi–Ex Prime Minister of India, murder case by a human bomb. Tandoor murder case (Delhi).

Circumstantial Evidence (CE)

Prior to the use of DNA evidence, matters involving the offence of rape could be solved primarily by circumstantial evidence only. It was very difficult for the victim of rape to prove the offence in the absence of either circumstantial evidence or an eyewitness, which was very rare. Since, the introduction of the DNA evidence, this has been greatly simplified.

Application of Circumstantial evidence in:

Criminal cases	: Rape and Murder	: Rameshbhai Chandubhai Rathod v/s State of Gujarat (2009)(3) RCR (Criminal) 619
	Sodomy and Murder	: Shakula v/s State (2009) (5) CR (Criminal) 941 (Delhi) (DB).

Narco Test (NT) : To be conducted on a suspected accused in rape and / or murder cases.

Application of Narco test in:

Criminal cases	: Rape and Murder	: Shashi kidnapping and murder case (2007).

Toxicology:

Definition: Is defined as the science and medical study of poisons and their noxious effects. A poison is a substance, which, when introduced into the body even in relatively small quantity, acts chemically, may be capable of causing death or serious side effects, in an individual of average health.

References

1. An Experienced Teacher: Poisons. Notes on Medical Jurisprudence and Toxicology. Current Publishers, Calcutta, 1965, pp. 163-177.
2. Baldwa, M: Introduction to Forensic Science and Scientific Investigations of crime. The Doctor's People, Vol. II, Issue-8, 06-07, 2010, New Delhi.

3. Bluglass, R.: A guide to the Mental Health Act, Churchill Livingstone, Edinburgh, 1983.
4. Goodman, LS and Gilman, A: General Principles of Toxicology. The Pharmacological Basis of Therapeutics. The Macmillan Co. New York, 1960. Appendix II, pp. 1777-1780.
5. Martin, T., and Burgess, J.: Dreisbach's Handbook of Poisoning, 13th ed., Parthenon Publishing, Carnforth, 2001.
6. Mayfield, D., McLeod, G., and Hall, P.: The CAGE questionnaire; validation of a new alcoholism screening instrument, American Journal of Psychiatry, 131, 1123:3, 1974.
7. Medical Defence Union and Royal College of Nursing of the United Kingdom. Joint Memorandum. Safeguards against wrong operations, Medical Defence Union, London, 1978.
8. Mukherjee, JB: Legal Aspect of Medical Practice. JIMA Vol. 97, No. 11, 461-474, Nov. 1999, Calcutta.
9. National Institute of Justice (NIJ) of US' Justice Department.
10. Sneha Venkataramani, Law Student, I.P. Law School.

PART - I

FORENSIC MEDICINE

CHAPTER - 2

MEDICAL ABERRATIONS

MEDICAL ABERRATIONS

- Death
- Wounds
- Sexual and Allied Disorders
- Sexual Perversions
- Sexual Offences
- Pregnancy (Medico-legal Aspect)
- Delivery (Medico-legal Aspect)
- Abortion (Medico-legal Aspect)
- Infanticide
- Psychiatric Disorders

DEATH

Definition: Is defined as complete and permanent cessation of respiration and circulation. Currently many doctors define death in terms of brain activity, as the heart and lungs can be kept working by resuscitation (CPM) measures, whereas the person/animal is considered clinically dead, in the absence of brain activity (electrical).

Etiology: Natural

- Un-natural: Accidental, Suicidal and Homicidal.

Mode : Multi organs failure: Heart, lungs, brain, kidneys, liver i.e. Sequence of events of death (Asphyxia, Syncope, Anuria, Coma) e.g.

- Asphyxia - for a minute or so
- Loss of consciousness due to lack of oxygen

- Respiratory centre (initially excited) fails within another minute or so
- Vasomotor centre (initially maintains vasoconstriction) fails, causing
- Peripheral vasodilatation
- Hypotension
- Heart beat weakens
- Cardiac output ceases
- Ventricular fibrillation - develops (irrecoverable)
- Renal failure - anuria
- Coma
- Death.

Diagnosis: Early Signs:

- Breathless
- Pulseless, B.P. – nil
- Heart sounds - absent
- Temperature – loss of temperature and cooling of body
- Eyes - cornea opaque, hazy or cloudy
    - Reflexes – loss of corneal, papillary and conjunctival reflexes
    - Movements - absent
- Skin- pale, lustreless, cold, clamy, loss of elasticity

Late Signs:

- Cadaveric lividity (P.M. Stain)
- Rigor mortis
- Putrefaction
- Adipocere
- Mummification

Early (Systemic or Somatic) Death:

- Complete cessation of activity of Multiple Organs (brain, heart and lungs):
- Cessation (complete and continuous) of respiration for > 3-5 mts.
- Cessation (complete and continuous) of circulation for > 5 mts.

- Ocular (eye) changes
- Skin: dermatological changes
- Cooling of body due to loss of temperature
- Muscles: flaccidity

Late (Molecular) death:

Late (Molecular or cellular) death of the body tissues, following few hrs. of early (Systemic death).

- Cadaveric lividity
- Rigor mortis: appears first in the involuntary muscles followed by in the voluntary muscles

  Sequence:- Eyelids, face and lower jaw
  - Muscles of back of the neck and trunk
  - Upper limbs, front of neck and chest
  - Muscles of abdomen and lower limbs
- Decomposition/or putrefaction
- Adipocere/or Saponification
- Mummification

Table 2.1: Pathogenesis of Death

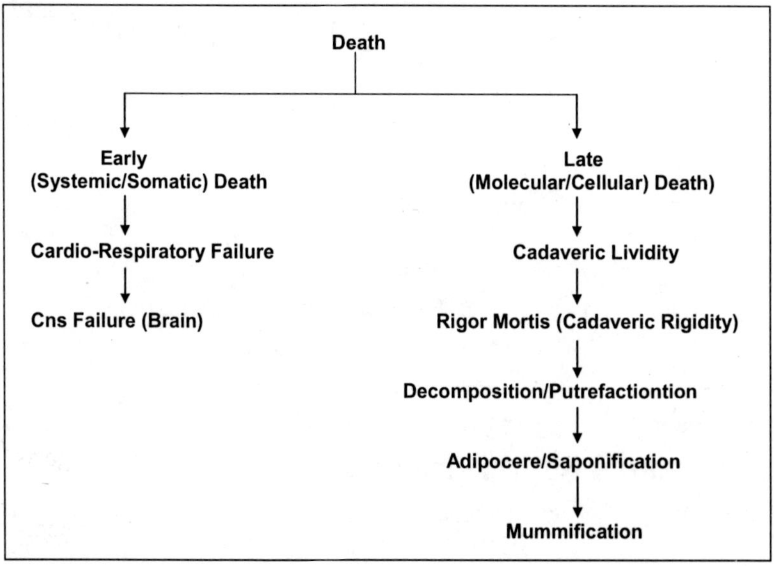

Medico-legal aspect: In UK (England and Wales) and India:

- That when a person dies, certain legal formalities ought to be completed.
- That in case of death of a person within 2/52 of receiving medical treatment, the concerned doctor is to issue a medical certificate stating the death's cause.
- That in suspected cases the Coroner/Magistrate is to be informed. He may order a post-mortem examination, to find the clinical cause of death.
- That there may have to be an Inquest i.e. the Coroner/Magistrate is to inquire an unnatural or suspected death.
- That the Registrar of Births and Death, issues a Death Certificate, on the basis of medical certificate issued by the doctor (certifying death).
- That the death certificate is required in claiming:
- Life Insurance policies and National Insurance benefits
- Property/estate rights 25

POST-MORTEM (PM CALORICITY)

Definition: After death there is rise of body temperature for an hr or so, instead of coming down.

Pathogenesis: Activity of micro-organisms present in body fluids and tissues, and progressive chemical changes

Etiology:

Infective:	Tetanus, Small-Pox, Cholera, Rheumatic fever, Hepatitis, Liver abscess
Traumatic:	Head injury, Spine injury
Toxic:	Strychnine poisoning
CNS:	Meningitis

Diagnosis: Temperature: raised for an hr. or so.

CADAVERIC LIVIDITY (PM STAINING)

Etiology: Stasis of blood in the capillaries of the dependent parts of the body following CVS failure (cessation of heart action).

Pathogenesis: Stasis of blood in the capillaries, results in distension of the capillaries (External and Internal hypostasis) of the dependent parts of the body (surface and internal organs/tissues).

Duration of P. M. Staining: 4-10 hrs. (till onset of putrefaction)

Diagnosis: External hypostasis: P.M. Staining on the dependant parts of the body (back, buttocks, limbs):

- Areas of discoloration (purple and red)

Internal hypostasis: P.M. staining on the internal organs/tissues (posterior cerebral lobes of brain, posterior surfaces of lungs, stomach, liver, kidneys) occupying the dependent position after death.

Exception: P.M. Staining – less marked in:

- Hemorrhagic death
- Anaemic persons

Medico-legal aspect:

- That it is a positive sign of death
- That it indicates time period, since death
- That it helps in finding the cause of death on the basis of colour:
- Red: normal
  - Crimson: burns
  - Pink: poisoning (CO, CO_2, snake)
  - Brown: poisoning (Phosphorus)
  - Violet: asphyxia.

CADAVERIC MUSCULAR CHANGES (Table 2-2):

TABLE 2.2: CADAVERIC MUSCULAR CHANGES

Stage	*Duration Hrs.*	*Limbs*	*Joints*	*Muscles response to external stimulus*
1st	1-6	Soft and flabby	Relaxed	Responding
2nd	24-48	Cold and stiff	Stiff	Responding
3rd	Variable	Soft and flabby	Flaccid	Not responding

Stages: 1st stage: Stage of primary relaxation:

Duration: 1-6 hrs.

Limbs: soft and flabby

Joints: relaxed

Muscles: responding (contractile) to external stimulus

2nd stage: Stage of stiffness (Rigor mortis):

Duration: 1-2 hrs. (fully established). Remains so for about 24-48 hrs.

Limbs: cold and stiff

Joints: stiff

Muscles: responding (contractile) to external stimulus

3rd stage: Stage of flaccidity leading to decomposition (Putrefaction):

Limbs: soft and flabby

Joints: relaxed

Muscles: not responding (non-contractile) to external stimulus

Medico-legal aspect:

- That it is a positive sign of death
- That it indicates time period, since death

CADAVERIC SPASM:

Definition: Is defined as a process in which muscles contracting before death, become stiff and rigid soon after death, bypassing the initial stage of relaxation.

Etiology: Continuation of muscle contraction after death due to overexertion or hyper excitement.

Pathogenesis: Instantaneous rigor mortis.

Factors hastening Cadaveric Spasm:

Traumatic: concussion – esp. in children

Infective: Tetanus, hydrophobia

Toxins/Poisons: Strychnine

Asphyxia: Drowning and hanging

Psychological: over-excitement

Diagnosis: - Attitude of body: stiff and rigid, adopted at the time of death, is maintained after death for couple of hrs.

- Body: warm and stiff

Medico-legal aspect:

- That to ascertain time of death
- That to ascertain mode of death
- That to ascertain the attitude of the body at the time of death

RIGOR MORTIS

Definition: Is defined as the cadaveric rigidity

Etiology: Dehydration of muscles due to decomposition and disappearance of A.T.P.

Pathogenesis: Coagulation of muscle plasma and formation of lactic acid, that accumulates into the muscle fibres, followed by disorganisation of muscle fibres with putrefaction (due to breaking down of myosin of muscle fibres).

Factors hastening Rigor mortis:

Age – Childhood and old age

Fatigued muscles – lightening, cholera, tetanus, opium, strychnine poisoning

Weather – warm and moist air

Cold – prolongs the duration

Factors delaying Rigor mortis:

Age - Adults

Active and strong healthy muscles

Weather – dry and cold air

Heat – shortens the duration

Medico-legal aspect:

- That it is a positive sign of death
- That it indicates time period, since death
- That it indicates mode of death
- That it helps in finding the cause of death

PUTREFACTION (DECOMPOSITION):

Definition: Is defined as the process of decay in a dead person/animal, following rigor mortis, and is characterised by foul smell, discolouration of the skin & blisters or bullae formation.

Etiology: Infective: Bacterial (Intestinal) infection

Pathogenesis: (Table 2.3) After death, the intestinal bacteria multiply and spread throughout the body at an alarming rate, causing putrefaction (decomposition) of internal organs due to release of proteolytic enzymes (Table 2.4):

TABLE 2.3: PATHOGENESIS OF PUTREFACTION

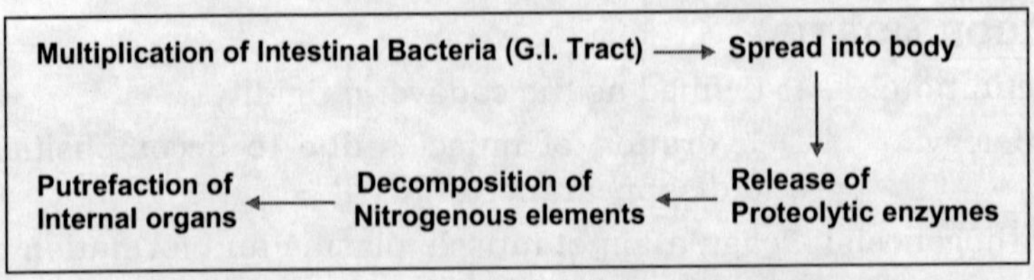

Table 2.4: Putrefaction of Internal Organs

Early Putrefying		***Late Putrefying***	
Head	: Brain of child, Brain of adult	Chest	: Lungs Heart
Neck	: Larynx Trachea	Abdomen	: Urinary bladder, Kidneys
Abdomen	: Stomach, Intestine, Liver, Spleen Uterus (pregnant)		Pancreas, Prostate, Uterus, Blood vessels Uterus (virgin)

Note: Putrefaction of prostate and virgin uterus may take couple of months, thus help in identifying the sex of dead body. Factors affecting Putrefaction (Table 2.5):

Table 2.5: Factors Affecting Putrefaction

Factors	*Accelerates (Favours)*	*Slows (Retards)*
Temperature	> 38 degrees centigrade	< 0 degree centigrade > 100 degree centigrade
Season	Summer	Winter
Air	Moist air	Dry air, tight coffin, Burial in dry soil
Age	New-born, Infants, Children	Old person bodies
Built	Flabby, fatty, obese bodies	Weak, emaciated bodies
Poisons	Opium, HCN	Arsenic, Strychnine, Phosphorus
Light	Darkness	Ultraviolet rays

Diagnosis: Skin:-discolouration of skin over right iliac region (postural), face, front of neck and chest, within few hrs.

Eyes:

- Eyeballs: soft and bulging
- Cornea: hazy and hard

Skull: oozing of liquefied brain through sutures (gaped)

Odour: foul

Pleural effusion

Pericardial effusion

Gas collection:

- Abdomen distension (ballooning)
- Discharging of frothy blood from the mouth and nostrils
- Eyes: bulging
- Anus: gaping, faeces expelled
- Rectum: prolapsed
- Uterus: prolapsed

Blisters/or bullae formation

Maggots/larvae appear (hatching of fleas eggs) – esp. on exposed parts of the body

Nails and Hairs: loosen

Soft parts: start splitting after 3-6 days e.g. burst abdomen and thorax

Internal Organs: (Table 3-4)

Medico-legal aspects:

- That to ascertain time of death
- That to ascertain mode of death
- That to ascertain the attitude of the body at the time of death

Adipocere (Saponification):

Definition: Is defined as a dead body transformed into a permanent waxy or cheese like substance, characterised by disagreeable odour, greyish or dark brownish colour and greasy feel, retaining its shape and form.

Etiology:
- Weather: Cold, wet climate
- Region: Common in - cold countries
  - warm and wet (Tropical) countries
- Watery grave/cess pools: dead bodies lying submerged in water
- Adipocere time: Cold weather: 3-12 months
  Warm and wet: 2-3 weeks.

Pathogenesis: Transformation of subcutaneous fats and bone marrows, into a waxy/or cheese like permanent substance (Adipocere), due to hydrogenation of the pre-existing fat (Olein), to higher fatty acids (Palmitic, Hydro-stearic and Staeric), and these acids mix to form the substance – Adipocere.

Diagnosis:
- Appearance of body: waxy/or cheese like, greyish or dark brown, retaining shape and form
- Feel: soft
- Odour: disagreeable
- Weight: lighter – floats in water
- Internal organs: un-effected
- Burns: with a luminous flame.

Medico-legal aspect:

- That to ascertain the place of death
- That to ascertain the cause of death
- That to recognise the features after death.

Mummification (Dead flesh):

Definition: Is defined as a dead flesh (formless, shrivelled mass).

Etiology: Weather: Hot, dry climate with dusty, hot wind.

Region: Common in sandy deserts of Asia and Africa.

Custom (Ritual): As an art of mummification by embalming the dead body (Ancient Egyptian Art).

Mummification time: Un-known. May be up to 2 yrs.

Pathogenesis: Dead bodies exposed to intense Sun's rays and hot dusty winds (of deserts) resort to shrivelling/ or dessication (due to loss of body fluids) rather than undergoing decomposition.

Diagnosis:

- Skin: dry, shrivelled, leathery, black or rusty brown in colour, adherent to underlying bones
- Internal organs: shrivelled into a dry, thick mass (inseparable)
- Odourless.

Medico-legal aspect:

- That to ascertain the place of death
- That to ascertain the cause of death
- That to recognise the features after death.

Factors Ascertaining (Determining) Time period (Post Death):

- Body temperature: warm or cool
- Rigor mortis: present or absent
- P.M. Staining: present or not
- Mode of digestion of stomach contents:

  - food rich in carbohydrates – leaves stomach by 6 hrs., while,

  - animal proteins rich food leaves stomach 5 hrs.

- Bladder: full (sleeping period) or empty (awake)
- Bowel: full (sleeping period) or empty (awake)
- Dress (clothes) worn:
  - well dressed (working, travelling, partying),
  - night gown, sleeping apparels.

MODES OF DEATH:

Types:
- Cerebro-vascular failure: Coma, Stroke (CVA)
- Cardio-vascular failure: Syncope
- Respiratory failure: ARDS, Acute Respiratory failure.

COMA:

Definition: Coma is defined as complete loss of consciousness (for a long time) from which the patient cannot be aroused, even by the most painful stimuli.

Etiology: Intra or Extra-cranial

Intracranial: Traumatic: head injuries

Cerebrovasacular accidents (CVA)

Raised intracranial pressure (ICP) CNS infections

Convulsive disorders (disturbed brain electrical activity): epilepsy

Reduced cerebral blood flow

Neoplastic: Intracranial tumors

Extracranial: Traumatic: RSA e.g. multiple injuries

Endocrinal: Diabetic ketoacidosis, hypoglycemia, uremia, hepatic coma, hypercapnia, hypercalcemia, hypothyroidism

Cardio-vascular: MI, hypotension, hemorrhage, shock

Renal failure encephalopathy

Osmolarity disorders: hyponatremia

Drugs misuse: barbiturates, narcotics, tranquilizers

Alcohol abuse

Toxins: endogenous toxins

Physical agents exposure e.g. hypo/hyperthermia, burns, electric shock, Poisons e.g. snake bite.

Diagnosis: Case-History: interrogate patient, his relatives, friends, to find out cause. Physical examination: signs of underlying cause.

PM findings: External:

- Head:
  - Scalp wounds may be found,
  - Skull fractures with extravasation of blood, spinal fluid and lacerated brain tissues,
- Signs of multiple injuries: may be found

Internal:

- Brain: injuries or congestion of brain may be found
- Heart: right side full while left side is usually found empty
- Other organs: found congested

Medico-legal aspects:

- That to ascertain time of death
- That to ascertain mode of death
- That to ascertain the attitude of the body at the time of death

STROKE (CEREBRO-VASCULAR ACCIDENT):

Definition: Is defined as a focal neurological disorder due to a pathologic process (coronary hemorrhage/or block). In majority of cases the onset is abrupt with rapid evolution.

Etiology: Thrombosis

Embolism

Hemorrhage

Hypertension

Syncope.

Risk factors: Ageing

High fat content in the blood, obesity

Sedentary life – lifestyle changes

Diabetes mellitus

Smoking

Alcohol abuse

Diagnosis:

S/S Sudden onset of signs and symptoms:
Hyperesthesia,
Limpaired speech,
Headache,
Neck rigidity,
Fever,
Vomiting
Loss of consciousness
Death.

PM findings:- Brain: extravasation of blood, blood clots may be found on the surface of brain or in its substances
- Heart: left side is usually empty
- Other organs: found congested.

Medico-legal aspects:

- That to ascertain time of death
- That to ascertain mode of death
- That to ascertain the attitude of the body at the time of death

SYNCOPE (syn. FAINTING):

Definition: Syncope Is defined as a sudden transient loss of consciousness with associated loss of postural tone, whereas faintness is defined as impending loss of consciousness (pre-syncope), with lack of muscular strength.

Etiology: Reduced cerebral blood supply (transient interruption) – due to:

A. Vasovagal (vasodepressor) and neutrally mediated: mid/post acts e.g. sneezing, coughing, swallowing, defecation, micturition.
B. Sympathectomy – due to antihypertensives use
C. Orthostatic: hypovolemia, diabetic ketoacidosis, alcohol, infection, drugs – antihypertensives, opiates, nitrates, and elderly patients
D. Carotid sinus syncope
E. Hypovolemia – G.I.Tract hemorrhage

F. Cardiovascular disorders causing reduced cardiac output:

- Obstructive: Pulmonary stenosis, pulmonary embolism, pulmonary hypertension, aortic stenosis, mitral stenosis
- Myocardial: Acute Myocardial infarction
- Pericardial: Cardiac tamponade
- Arrhythmic:
- Bradyarrhythmias: AV block – 2nd and 3rd degree, Stokes-Adams syndrome, sinus bradycardia, carotid sinus, glossopharyngial neuralgia
- Tachyarrhythmias: Supraventricular tachycardia, ventricular tachycardia and ventricular fibrillation

G. Cerebrovascular disorders e.g. CVA, cerebral ischemia, anemia

H. Emotional disorders e.g. anxiety, stress, fear, hysteria, sad news

I. Unexplained syncope – 50 per cent of patients.

Pathogenesis: Impairment of brain metabolism due to hypotension with transient reduction of cerebral blood flow.

Diagnosis: History taking and thorough physical examination – crucial to diagnosis.

S/S:
- Nausea,
- Yawning,
- Anxious appearance,
- Restlessness,
- Palpitation,
- Breathing – slow and feeble
- Perspiration, face – pale, cold, moist,
- Blurring of vision,
- Epigastric distress,
- Muscular weakness,

- Hypotension,
- Sudden loss of consciousness
- Death.

PM findings:
- Brain: empty and contracted
- Heart: Pre-rigor stage: flabby and full
  Rigor mortis stage: all chambers empty and contracted
  Putrefaction stage: blood in the right chambers
- Other internal organs: normal.

Medico-legal aspects:

- That to ascertain time of death
- That to ascertain mode of death
- That to ascertain the attitude of the body at the time of death

Adult Respiratory Distress Syndrome (ARDS)(syn. Shock/ Pump Lung)

Definition: It is defined as a condition characterised by injury to the alveolar epithelial and endothelial barriers of the lung, interalveolar exudation and interstitial edema.

Etiology: Traumatic - RSA with shock
Fat embolism
Aspiration – gastric contents, water with near drowning
Inhalation – noxious gases, smoke
Pneumonia – bacterial/viral
Heart-lung perfusions.

Pathogenesis: Trauma etc. leads to leakage from pulmonary capillary, alveolar exudation, interstitial edema, impaired perfusion ventilation, rigid lungs.

Diagnosis: Dyspnea
Cyanosis
Respiration - grunting
Hypotension
Shock
Death.

PM findings: External:

- Face: cyanosed
- Eyes: protruding and congested
- Lips, nose: livid
- Tongue: protruding

—Frothy discharge – from mouth and nostrils

- Rigor mortis.

Internal:

- Brain: congested
- Trachea and larynx: congested
- Lungs: congested, emphysematous
- Heart: left side empty
- Other organs: congested.

Medico-legal aspects:

- That to ascertain time of death
- That to ascertain mode of death
- That to ascertain the attitude of the body at the time of death

Acute Respiratory Failure:

Etiology: Airway obstruction:

- Acute bronchitis
- Acute asthma
- Acute emphysema

Restrictive defects:

- Pleural effusion
- Pneumothorax
- Pneumonia
- Fibrosis – interstitial

Deformities of Chest wall:

- Congenital/acquired - scoliosis, kyphosis
- Traumatic – flail chest
- Drugs - Opiates overdose

ARDS/ALI.

Diagnosis: Dyspnea,

Headache,

Restlessness,

Palpitation
Dizziness,
Confusion,
Unconscious,
Coma,
Death.

PM findings: External:

- Face: cyanosed
- Eyes: protruding and congested
- Lips, nose: livid
- Tongue: protruding
- Frothy discharge – from mouth and nostrils
- Rigor mortis.

Internal:

- Brain: congested
- Trachea and larynx: congested
- Lungs: congested, emphysematous
- Heart: left side empty
- Other organs: congested.

Medico-legal aspects:

- That to ascertain time of death
- That to ascertain mode of death
- That to ascertain the attitude of the body at the time of death

TABLE 2.6: ETIOLOGY OF SUDDEN DEATH

Cause	***Disorder***
Traumatic	RSA Fall from a height Direct violence (Fights)
Respiratory	Acute Respiratory failure Acute Glottis Acute Diphtheria Acute Pneumonia Acute Pneumothorax Acute Hemothorax Acute Bronchial Asthma

Cardiovascular	Acute Myocardial Infarction (MI) Acute Coronary Artery Disease Acute Left Ventricular Failure Acute Pulmonary Edema Acute Hypertension (Hypertensive Crisis) Acute Aortic Aneurysm Acute Myocarditis Acute Endocarditis Atrial Septal Defect (ASD)
Nervous system	Cerebrovascular Accident (CVA) : -Thrombosis, Embolism or Hemorrhage Acute Meningitis Brain Abscess, Brain tumors
G.I. Tract	Acute Pancreatitis Acute Intestinal Obstruction Acute Appendicitis (Burst appendix) Acute Hepatitis Upper G.I. Tract Hemorrhage Tumor–carcinoma
Genito-Urinary Endocrinal	Acute Renal Failure Acute Ectopic Gestation Diabetic Coma Acute Thyroid Crisis Acute Adrenal Syndrome
Psychological	Acute Depression Acute Schizophrenia Anorexia Nervosa Alcohol abuse, Drug Abuse
Toxins	Poisons
Miscellaneous	Starvation, Cold, Heat, Burns, Scalds, Asphyxia

DEATH FROM TOTAL STARVATION:

Definition: Is defined as failure to eat on the part of adolescents or young adults, mostly females, deliberately starving themselves to death.

Etiology: A weight reduction regimen

Psychological – Anorexia nervosa

Pathogenesis: Total starvation leads to:

- breakdown of fats mainly, but may also lead to,
- excessive breakdown of protein,
- decreased ECF volume (due to Sodium loss),
- hepatic necrosis (due to weight loss),
- accelerated weight loss (represents fluid loss due to ketonemia).

Diagnosis: Female - mostly

Acute hunger pangs (lasting for 36-48 hrs.), followed by thirst

Epigastric pain

Emaciation (depletion of subcutaneous fat):

- sunken eyes,
- cadaveric look,
- prominent cheek bones,
- lips – dry and cracked,
- skin – dry, wrinkled, rough, pale,
- hairs – dry and lustreless,
- prominent ribs,
- limbs girth diminished,
- abdomen retracted,

Weight loss - accelerated

Temperature – subnormal

Constipation – followed by diarrhea till death

Urine – scanty and turbid

Edema - feet

PM findings:

External examination:

Body – emaciated

Hairs – dry and lustreless

Odour - foul smelling

Skin – dry, shrivelled, ulcerated

Eyes – sunken, dry and open

Cheeks – prominent cheek bones

Tongue – dry, furred or coated

Neck – elongated

Abdomen - retracted

Muscles – soft, pale and wasted

Internal examination:

Brain – normal or soft

Meninges – congested

Heart – contracted, muscles flabby, chambers empty

Lungs – collapsed, pale or congested

Stomach – contracted, empty or contains undigested meals, taken just before death

Small intestine – contracted and empty, thinner walls

Large intestine – contains hard fecal matter

Liver – contracted, necrosed

Gall-bladder – distended with dark stained bile

Pancreas – contracted

Spleen – contracted

Kidneys – contracted

Urinary bladder – empty

Medico-legal aspect:

- That whether starvation had been the cause of death ?
- That what would have been the cause of starvation ?

  Whether due to criminal neglect by the legal protectors (parents of infants, children of old, bed ridden, invalid parents) or starvation death due to some medical/surgical ailment.
- That whether the starvation had been:
- Suicidal: common amongst neurotics (anorexia nervosa), hysterical, manics, lunatics, political prisoners
- Homicidal: poverty – starvation of family members, illegitimate infants, dowry - mother-in-law starving her daughter-in-law.
- Accidental: famine, ship wreck; mine or aeroplane accidents

DEATH FROM PHYSICAL AGENTS

Agents: Cold injuries:
- Hypothermia

Heat injuries:
- Heat exhaustion
- Heat stroke
- Burns

Asphyxia:
- Drowning:
- Caisson disease
- Suffocation
- Strangulation
- Throttling
- Hanging

Shock:
- Electric shock

Irradiation:
- Acute ionizing radiation

References.

DEATH FROM HYPOTHERMIA (syn. COLD INJURY)

Etiology: Exposure to prolonged/or extreme cold weather (wind, rain, chill)

Unconsciousness

Alcohol abuse

Drug abuse – sedatives.

Risk factors: Age – infants and old persons

Exposure – prolonged

Vital power – fatigue, exhaustion, intoxication and powerty.

Pathogenesis: Cold exposure leads to - vasoconstriction, skin temp < 25°C, slowing of metabolism, increased demand for oxygen, cyanosis, tissue necrosis.

Diagnosis: Skin: cold, clammy, pale/cyanotic, skin patches (Frost-bite, Chilblain or Trench foot)

Temp < 25°C (77°F)

Shivering

Hypotension, bradycardia
Stupor, Coma
Death.

PM findings: Skin – pale with dark red patches on exposed portions of the body
Brain – congested, ventricles filled with blood (serum)
Heart – congested
Lungs – congested
Other internal organs – congested

Medico-legal aspect:

- That whether the death was due to hypothermia?
- That whether death was accidental, suicidal or homicidal ?
- That how long the dead body exposed to cold?

DEATH FROM HEAT EXHAUSTION (syn. HEAT PROSTATION)

Etiology: Heat exposure. Patients with cardiac, cerebral, systemic disorders, are more prone to heat exhaustion.

Pathogenesis: Heat exposure leads to water and salt depletion, resulting in collapsed peripheral circulation.

Diagnosis: Muscular weakness, muscle cramps, dizziness, headache, Skin – cold, pale, perspiration
Oliguria
Tachycardia
Hypotension
Shock
Death – from heart failure.

PM findings: Rigor mortis – appears earlier and passes off rapidly
Cadaveric lividity – well marked
Brain – congested, ventricles filled with blood (serum)
Meninges - congested
Heart – congested, right chambers filled with dark blood, left side empty
Lungs – congested
Other internal organs – congested

Medico-legal aspect:

- That whether the death was due to heat exhaustion?
- That whether death was accidental, suicidal or homicidal ?
- That how long the dead body exposed to heat?

DEATH FROM HEAT STROKE (syn. SUNSTORKE)

Definition: Is defined as a condition due to failure of the heat-regulating mechanism, resulting in heat gained by the body from the surrounding atmosphere more than the heat lost, thereby causing death.

Mode: Exposure to hot weather

Affects mostly the elderly, alcoholics, weak, cardiac patients.

Pathogenesis: Sudden failure of heat-regulating system.

Diagnosis: High fever – temperature (Rectal) > 42 °C.

Sweating – absent.

Headache, nausea, vomiting, vertigo, convulsions, unconsciousness.

Skin – hot, dry, flushed.

Pulse fast, weak, and irregular.

Hypotension.

Shock

Death – may be accidental or homicidal (infanticide).

PM findings: Rigor mortis – appears earlier and passes off rapidly

Cadaveric lividity – well marked

Brain – congested, ventricles filled with blood (serum)

Meninges - congested

Heart – congested, right chambers filled with dark blood, left side empty

Lungs – congested

Other internal organs – congested

Medico-legal aspect:

- That whether the death was due to heat stroke?
- That whether death was accidental, suicidal or homicidal ?
- That how long the dead body exposed to heat?

DEATH FROM BURNS and SCALDS

Burns are due to dry heat, whereas scalds are due to moist heat.

Etiology: Heat: Gas flame, steam, hot water
Chemicals: Acids, alkalies (caustic soda)
Electricity
Radiation.

Diagnosis: Erythema with or without blisters
Discharging wounds
Shock – due to fluid loss
Infection
Scars
Death.

Evaluation of Burn Injury: By considering:

Area of body surface involved: By Rule of Nines i.e.

- Head and Neck = 9%
- Arms = 18%
- Legs front = 18%
- Legs back = 18%
- Trunk front = 18%
- Trunk back = 18%
- Genitalia = 1%

Depth of burn:

- Partial thickness burn
- Full thickness burn.

Mode of death:

Early:

- Asphyxia (suffocation): due to inhalation of smoke or fumes
- Shock: due to hypovolemia
- Coma: due to brain failure

Intermediate:

- Traumatic
- Inflammatory: Acute Meningitis, Acute Bronchitis, Acute Pneumonia
- Exhaustive Dehydration
- Toxemic

Late:

- Multiple Organ Failure

Medico-legal aspect:

- That what was the mode of death?
- That whether death was accidental, suicidal or homicidal ?
- That how long the dead body exposed to Burns?
- That to determine whether the resulted injury produced (extent of burnt surface) is:
- mild : < 1/3rd
- severe : 1/3rd
- grievous (fatal) : 2/3rd or 1/2

DEATH FROM ASPHYXIA:

Modes: Drowning, Caisson disease, Suffocation, Strangulation, Throttling and Hanging.

DEATH FROM DROWNING

Definition: Is defined as a violent asphyxia death, resulting from airway obstruction by submersion of mouth and nostrils under water or any fluid medium, thereby preventing air from entering lungs.

Incidence: Drowning is the third leading cause of accidental death in the USA. Children and young adults are mostly the victims, esp. the males.

Etiology: Accidental:
- Non-swimmers entering/falling into deep water,
- Swimmers due to their rashness,
- Children fall into a well, pond or tank, while playing nearby,
- Ladies fall in a well, pond or rivulet, while washing clothes,

- Intoxicated person, epileptic or lunatic person fall into water.

Suicidal: - By jumping into a well, pond, swimming pool, rivulet or river.

Homicidal: - common amongst infants and children (esp. Illegitimate),
- In adults:
- visible marks (ante-mortem) of violence on the body, hands and feet tied with ligature/band, heavy weight tied to the body (to keep it submerged under water).

Risk factors:- Lack of swimming training
- Avoiding to use the personal floating devices e.g. inflated tubes
- Absence of swimming instructors
- Use of high speed boats
- Alcohol abuse while swimming or boating
- Mental disorders: victims – epileptics, hysterics, depressives.

Sequence of events in drowning:
- Victim falls into the water
- Sinks down to a depth, proportionate to the velocity gained at the time of fall and as per the specific gravity of the body (depending on the relative proportion of fat, bone, muscles and other tissues)
- Immediate death: may occur due to shock or syncope, Alt.:
- Rises up: due to panicky/struggling movements of limbs
- Cries and shouts for help: thereby:

  - gulps water into his larynx – causing violent cough – that expels little air from the lungs, being replaced by water drawn into lungs,

  - gulps water into stomach
- Specific gravity of body – increases
- Re-sinking of the victim

- Re-rising: due to movements of the limbs
- Convulsive movements (automatic respiratory effort): draws more water into his lungs
- Repetition of sinking and rising: till the whole air is expelled from the lungs
- Exhausted
- Death.

Mode of death:

- Asphyxia - for a minute or so
- Loss of consciousness due to lack of oxygen
- Respiratory centre (initially excited) fails within another minute or so
- Vasomotor centre (initially maintains vasoconstriction) fails, causing
- Peripheral vasodilatation
- Hypotension
- Heart beat weakens
- Cardiac output ceases
- Ventricular fibrillation - develops (irrecoverable)
- Multiple organ failure
- Death – occurs within 2-5 mts.

Pathogenesis:

Dry drowning:

- At autopsy victims have been found without any evidence of water aspiration in the lungs.
- Death occurs due to asphyxia - as a result of reflex laryngospasm and airway obstruction (glottis closure).

Wet drowning:

- Drowning is further complicated by aspiration of water (containing solutes and solids) into the airway causing airway obstruction, asphyxia, and death.

Diagnosis: - Depends upon many factors including amount and type of aspirated water and speed and effectiveness of treatment

- Clinically there is not any significant difference between fresh water (hypotonic) and salt (sea) water (hypertonic) drowning, as per CPR (common for both) is concerned.

S/S: Fresh water drowning:

- Asphyxia, metabolic acidosis, hypervolemia, hemodilution, hemolysis
- Death occurs from ventricular fibrillation or respiratory failure.

Salt water drowning:

- Asphyxia, metabolic acidosis, pulmonary edema, hypovolemia, renal failure
- Death occurs from myocardial ischemia (anoxia).

PM findings: Marked signs of asphyxia found, until and unless death occurs due to head injury (concussion), shock or syncope, immediately following submersion.

External examination:

Body: cool, early decomposed

Marks of violence (in case of direct violence): bruises, abrasions visible

Signs of asphyxia:

- Face: pale, livid lips, tongue protruded, frothy mouth and nostrils
- Eyes: congested conjunctivae, dilated pupils
- Ears: ruptured tympanum (ear drum)
- Skin: Goose flesh
- Hands: clenched
- Penis and scrotum: retracted
- Rigor mortis: appears early

Internal examination:

- Brain: congested
- Larynx, trachea and bronchi: may contain froth, foreign body (mud or sand)
- Lungs: distended with blood stained frothy fluid
- Pleural cavity: contains watery fluid transudes
- Heart: right side full, while left side found empty

- Stomach: contains water, mud or sand etc.
- Intestines: contain water, mud or sand etc.
- Liver: congested
- Spleen: congested
- Kidneys: congested
- Ears: middle ear contains water (+ ve sign of death).

Duration of Floatation of dead body:

depends on:

- Weather:
  - floats earlier in summer (early putrefaction) than in winter
- Quality of water:
  - floats earlier in polluted, shallow or saline water (early decomposition)
- Built of body:
  - floats earlier in case of:
    - women and fatty persons (fat – lighter),
    - Infants and children (bones – lighter)

Factors interrupting floatation of dead body:

- Heavy weight tied to the body
- Body tied to some fixed object underneath water
- Body entangled in weeds, plants or roots, underneath water
- Body entrapped in a sunken (sea, river, lake) ship, aeroplane, car etc.

Medico-legal aspect:

- That whether the death was due to drowning ?
- That whether death was accidental, suicidal or homicidal ?
- That how long the dead body had been floating ?

DEATH FROM CAISSON (syn. DECOMPRESSION) DISEASE

Etiology: - Occupational disorder, prevalent in divers (who work under water, generally work in caissons –

a steel chamber, filled with compressed air in which the divers are placed and sunk in deep waters)

- Sports injury e.g. sport of scuba.

Pathogenesis: Firstly at low depths, respiratory gases under pressure, move into blood and tissues, which block the supply to various parts of the body, thus further diving into deeper depths, the gases in the blood and tissues, escape due to lower external pressure.

Diagnosis: Initially there may not be much discomfort except:

- Nausea, vomiting
- Headache, dizziness/or vertigo, visual disturbances, tinnitus
- Dyspnea
- Bradycardia
- Serious effects appear later on (during rapid decompression) e.g.
- Arthralgia
- Cyanosis
- Bradycardia
- Weakness/or paralysis
- Unconsciousness, coma
- Death.

Medico-legal aspect:

- That whether the death was due to Caisson disease ?
- That how long the victim had been exposed to compressed air ?

DEATH FROM SUFFOCATION

Definition: Is defined as death resulting from lack of air to breath.

Etiology: Airway obstruction by means of:

- a foreign body, saliva/vomit aspiration,
- closure of mouth and nostrils by hand (smothering), by pillows, quilts, clothes, towels etc.

Traumatic - pressure on the chest and abdomen by RSA and fall of heavy weight

Inhalation: of irrespirable gas e.g. carbon monoxide, carbon dioxide, sewer gas, vapours of sulphuric or nitric acids

Infective: diphtheria, peri-tonsillar abscess

Electric shock

Epileptic fit.

Mode: Asphyxia

Pathogenesis: Interrupted breathing, resulting in hypoxemia, brain damage, death.

Fatal period: 4-5 mts.

PM findings: Accidental suffocation:

- Flattening of nose, cyanosed face, open eyes, livid lips, protruded tongue, froth per mouth or per nasal

Suicidal: suffocation:

- Stuffing the mouth and throat with cloth, straw or hair balls
- Evidence of gas inhalation

Homicidal suffocation:

- Evidence of violence e.g. bruises, abrasions and scratches round about lips, cheeks, nose and mouth, injury marks on the chest & other parts of the body may be found.

Medico-legal aspects:

- That whether the cause of death is suffocation?
- That whether it is accidental, suicidal or homicidal?

DEATH FROM STRANGULATION

Definition: Is defined as a violent form of asphyxia death, resulting from airway obstruction, at the level of neck, by means other than the body weight or of the hand

Mode: Violence:

- Throttling: by pressing with hands
- Ligature: by pressing (tying) with a cord, cloth etc.

- Sticks: by pressing with sticks (one stick in front and another behind neck.

Diagnosis: Complete airway obstruction:

- Unconscious
- Death.

Incomplete airway obstruction:

- Face: swollen, cyanosed.
- Mouth and nose: discharging of blood stained froth
- Hands: clenched; nails – bluish colouration.

Modes:

- Asphyxia
- Asphyxia + Apoplexy
- Apoplexy
- Syncope
- Death.

PM findings: External examination:

Face: swollen, cyanosed, lips - livid

Eyes: eyeballs – protruding; conjunctiva – congested; pupils - dilated

Mouth and nostrils: discharging of blood stained froth

Hands: clenched

Genitals: turgid

Urine and feces: discharge

Ligature mark:

- pale or reddish, abraded, depressed, circular mark, on the neck, corresponding to the ligature width

Stick mark: bruises, lacerations of muscles, fractured bones

Internal examination:

Neck: - lacerated muscles, sheath and blood vessels,
- fractured vertebrae – esp. In infants

Larynx, trachea and bronchi – found congested

Chest: ribs – may be found fractured

Lungs: congested, emphysematous, frothy

Heart: Right one full while left one found empty

Other organs: found congested.

Medico-legal aspects:

- That whether the cause of death is strangulation?
- That what had been the mode of strangulation?

DEATH FROM THROTTLING

Definition: Throttling is to hold someone's throat very tightly, so as to make it difficult or impossible for him/her to breathe.

Mode: Manual compression of the neck by hand's grip.

Etiology: Homicidal.

Pathogenesis: Compression causes Airway obstruction by complete closure of the glottis (forcing base of tongue upwards and backwards against posterior pharyngeal wall). There might be injury of the superior laryngeal branch of vagus nerve, causing respiratory failure.

Diagnosis: Victims: mostly children, females or weak persons.

Fingers marks:

When pressed from front by the murderer, using his/her right hand:

- Thumb impression on the right side and four fingers on the left side of the victim's neck.

  Exception: murderer may be a left hander or might have used gloves)

Scratches, bruises:

- on the victim's neck, cheeks, nose and other parts of the body.

Chest: fractured ribs may be found.

D/d:

- Suicidal strangulation – rare, but may be possible

  Throttling – never suicidal
- Accidental strangulation – rare, but may be possible, while,

  Throttling – never suicidal
- Homicidal strangulation – favourable, with visible violence marks.

PM findings:- Fingers marks on the neck

- Scratches, bruises on the victim's neck, cheeks, nose and other parts of the body
- Chest: fractured ribs may be found.

Medico-legal aspect:

That whether the death had been caused by throttling ?

That whether death – accidental, suicidal or homicidal ?

That whether signs of violence present or not ?

DEATH FROM HANGING

Definition: Is defined as the action of killing someone by putting a rope around his/her neck and thereby dropping him/her, resulting in asphyxial death, whereby the constricting force may be the body weight.

Material used: rope, curtain cloth, wires, sarees, dhotis, turbans, belts or chains.

Modes of death:

Obstructive:

- Airway obstruction (Asphyxia): due to tongue being pushed upwards and backwards against the posterior pharyngeal wall
- Venous obstruction (Apoplexy): due to compression of the neck veins
- Airway obstruction and venous obstruction: commonest mode of death
- Arterial obstruction (Syncope): due to compression of the carotid arteries

Traumatic:

- Fracture-dislocation of the 2nd cervical vertebra: Judicial (Hang-man) hanging due to pressing/ cutting of medulla (paralysis of vital centres)
- Shock: due to pressing of the vagus nerve (vaso-vagal phenomenon).

Fatal period: - Immediate death: Judicial (Hang-man) hanging

- Very quick death (within 5-7 mts): Airway obstruction (Asphyxia)
- Slow death: Apoplexy.

PM findings: External examination:

- Ligature mark on the neck: depends on type of the cord, girth of the cord, weight of the victim and period of suspension.
  The mark may be circular, depressed, hard, dry.
- Neck: elongated
- Face: pale, swollen, decomposed
- Eyes: open, fixed, protruded, pupils dilated
- Mouth and nostrils: frothy discharge
- Lips: livid
- Tongue: protruded
- Hands: clenched
- Genitals: congested, swollen, discharge from the urethra

Internal examination:

- Fracture-dislocation of the cervical spine (C-2)
- Blood vessels (Carotid): may be lacerated
- Larynx, trachea and epiglottis: found congested
- Lungs: found congested
- Heart: right side is full, while left side is found empty
- Other internal organs:
  - found congested.

D/d: A. Ante-mortem v/s Post-mortem hanging (Table 2-7)

TABLE 2.7: ANTE-MORTEM v/s POST-MORTEM HANGING

SIGNS	ANTEMORTEM	POST-MORTEM
Face	Swollen, cyanosed	Cyanosis of face, lips, ears
Eyes	Congested	Normal
Mouth and Nostrils	Frothy discharge	No discharge
Tongue	Protruded	Not protruded
Ligature mark	High up in the neck, oblique, interrupted	Low down in the neck, circular, continuous
Knot	Tied on side of neck, ecchymosis	Tied on front of neck
Penis	Erection, seminal discharge	Erection and discharge absent

TABLE 2.8: SUICIDAL v/s HOMICIDAL HANGING

SIGNS	SUICIDAL	HOMICIDAL
History	Unsuccessful suicidal attempts	Absent
Signs of Violence	No evidence	Present
Signs of Struggle	Absent	Present
Place of hanging	Doors, windows locked from inside	Doors, windows locked from outside
Face	Bloated, cyanosed	Cyanosis of face, lips, ears
Eyes	Congested	Normal
Mouth & Nostrils	Frothy discharge	No discharge
Tongue	Protruded	Not protruded
Ligature mark	High up in the neck, oblique, interrupted	Low down in the neck, circular, continuous
Knot	Tied on side of neck, ecchymosis	Tied on front of neck
Hands	Not tied	Tied
Penis	Erection, seminal discharge	Erection and discharge absent

Medico-legal aspect:

- That whether the death had been caused by hanging?
- That whether death – accidental, suicidal or homicidal ?
- That whether signs of violence present or not ?
- That whether the hanging had been ante-mortem or post-mortem ?

DEATH FROM ELECTRIC SHOCK

Definition: Electric shock is dangerous to heart as it may cause ventricular fibrillation, resulting in death.

Mode: Touching a live wire, electric appliances (wet unearthed fridge/water cooler, washing machine/fans/motors etc.).

Diagnosis: Unconsciousness, or myalgia, headache, fatigue, irritation

Skin – cold and cyanotic

Pulseless

Respiration – absent

Hypotension

Ventricular fibrillation

Coma

Death may occur:

- Immediate death – due to ventricular fibrillation
- Late death – due to systemic infection.

Medico-legal aspect:

- That whether the death had been caused by electric shock?
- That whether death – accidental, suicidal or homicidal?
- That whether signs of violence present or not?

DEATH FROM ACUTE IONIZING RADIATION

Mode: Exposure to ionizing radiation e.g.

- Natural sources:
  - Radon (alpha particle)
  - Cosmic rays,
  - Earth's radionuclides,
  - Body's radioactive elements
- Man-made sources:
  - Diagnostic X-Ray
  - Nuclear medicine
  - Nuclear reactor accidents,
  - Nuclear weapon detonations,
  - Accidental ingestion of radionuclides.

Pathogenesis: The harmful effects of radiation depend upon degree of exposure i.e. quantity, type of radiation and duration of exposure. Many types of injury occur following exposure to ionizing radiation, esp. injury to genetic apparatus of the nucleus following structural alterations of DNA and chromosomes.

Diagnosis:

- Nausea, vomiting, anorexia
- Pain abdomen, diarrhea, dehydration
- Weakness, prostration
- Erythema, epidermolysis,

- Anaemia, ulcerative colitis, pneumonitis
- Sterility, miscarriage, foetal death
- Bone marrow depression, leucopenia
- Death.

Medico-legal aspect:

- That whether the death had been caused by ionizing radiation ?
- That whether death – accidental or homicidal?

WOUNDS

Definition: Is defined as a break in the continuity of skin or mucous membrane, due to injury. It may be a cut, puncture, contusion (caused by a blow), abrasion (graze) or laceration (tear). Cuts tend to bleed. Puncture or stab wounds usually cause damage to internal organs with subsequent internal bleeding.

Classification:

Surgical:
- Incised Wounds
- Lacerated Wounds
- Penetrating Wounds
- Contused Wounds
- Poisoned Wounds
- Gunshot Wounds

Medicolegal: Mechanical injuries:
- Abrasions
- Bruise or Contusion
- Wounds: Incised, lacerated, penetrating, contused, poisoned, gunshot
- Closed injuries: Injuries to internal organs without any external injury

Burn injuries:
- Burns
- Scalds
- Electricity and lightening injuries.

Pathological:
- Mild/Slight wounds
- Severe wounds
- Fatal/dangerous wounds
- Grievous wounds.

Age of the Wounds:

- Scabs formation: within a day in case of abrasions
- Colour changes: from the periphery 1-2 days in case of bruises
- Inflammation: commences within 2-3 days in case of simple wounds
- Healing: occurs within a week in case of scalp wounds
- Exudation of blood: within 1-3 days in case of a fracture
- Granulation tissues: appear after a week
- Tooth injury: bleeding stops within few hrs. Cavity of the socket fills up within a week.

Nature of Wounds:

Types: Accidental, suicidal or homicidal.

Factors: Position, number, direction, circumstantial evidence

Position:

- Suicidal wounds: mostly found on the front and left side of the body, on account of easily accessible parts e.g. left arm and left thigh. The direction of wound in case of upper limb is from above downwards and inwards, while in case of lower limb is from below up and inwards. The inflicted wounds are usually superficial ending in a tail and mostly parallel. Self-inflicted wounds are mostly made with malafide intentions (false charge of assault). A suicidal site may be homicidal but not the vice versa. In a case of suicide, the weapon is found grasped in the hand of victim on account of cadaveric spasm.
- Accidental wounds: lacerated and contused wounds on the forehead are mostly accidental in nature. Wounds caused by RSA are very common these days.
- Homicidal wounds: may be found on any part of the body including on the part inaccessible to own's body e.g. back. Deep stab wounds, lacerated and contused on the forehead, limbs

and back are mostly homicidal. Severe incised wounds on the wrist, throat, breasts, genitals are mostly found to be homicidal. In case the right handed assailant attacks the victim from front, wounds are mostly inflicted on the left side of victim's body while a left handed assailant inflicts wounds on right side of victim's body. Gunshot wounds may be found on any part of the body, fired from a close or distant range. In homicidal case hair, cloth etc. belonging to assailant may be found grasped in the victim's hand.

Number: Suicidal wounds: mostly multiple
Accidental wounds: mostly multiple
Homicidal wounds: mostly single.

Direction: - Suicidal wounds: mostly directed from above downwards and inwards in case of upper parts of the body, while in case of lower parts of the body the direction is usually from below upwards and inwards. Suicidal stab and gunshot wounds on the chest are usually from right to left direction.

- Accidental wounds: mostly contused and lacerated and found on any part of the body, esp. on exposed parts. No particular direction is found in case of accident wound. Extensive body injuries (wounds) may occur in case of a fall from a height e.g. shipyards, railway and in case of RSA.
- Homicidal wounds: mostly multiple. Homicidal stab wounds are mostly from below upwards. They may have any direction and are mostly deep and extensive.

Circumstantial evidence at site of accident:

- Suicidal: doors and windows found locked from inside, and in case the weapon found grasped in the victim's hand due to cadaveric spasm. Finger prints of the victim on the weapon found near the body confirms the suicide. In case the body is found on a railway track without scratches and dragging marks may suggest suicide. In cut-throat wound, the hands may be found near the throat, outside the bed-sheets or blanket.

- Accidental: doors and windows found locked from inside, and injuries might have occurred due to fall. In case the body is found on a railway track without scratches and dragging marks, may suggest accident.
- Homicidal: doors locked from outside may suggest homicide. The weapon is mostly not found on/or near the body. The weapon may be found distorted and may bear the finger prints of the assailant and blood stains of the victim. Signs of struggle may be observed in the surroundings i.e. bed, furniture, kitchnet, washroom. Foot-prints or finger marks of assailant/s may be observed. In cut-throat wound, the hands may be hidden under the bed sheets or blankets. Clothes of victim may be torn or stained with blood, mud or grease.

INCISED WOUNDS:

Etiology: Injury by a sharp cutting instrument e.g. knife, razor, safety razor blades, saw blade, sword, axe.

M.O.I.: Direct trauma: Striking, sawing and drawing

Types:

- Accidental: inflicted by razor, safety razor blades, knife, fish-knife, on any part of the body esp. hands and fingers. Self-inflicted wounds are mostly slight in nature and found in accessible parts of the body. These are more or less parallel to each other and are mostly self-inflicted to blame someone with malafide intentions.
- Suicidal: wounds deeper at beginning and shallow at the end called tailing (scratch) inflicted by razor, knife, mostly self-inflicted on the wrists, throat, abdomen and chest. The tail reflects which hand been used.
- Homicidal: wounds of greater severity, inflicted by knife, razor blade, axe, sword or daos, mostly on the neck, chest, abdomen or head. They may

also be seen on victim's hand or forearm, while attempting to ward off the attack. The tail reflects the relative positioning of the attacker and the victim.

Instruments:- Light cutting: razor, knife – by means of striking, drawing or sawing

- Heavy cutting: swords, axes, choppers
- Curved: sickles, daos

PM findings:- Hemorrhage

- Wound:
- Shape: spindle
- Size: length > breadth and depth
- Edges: clean-cut, regular, everted, or Irregular and inverted (neck and scrotum)
- Gaping: more in case of division of underneath muscles

Medico-legal aspect:

That whether the wounds are accidental, suicidal or homicidal

LACERATED WOUNDS:

Etiology: Inflicted by a hard and blunt instrument e.g. swords, axes, daos and choppers.

M.O.I.: Direct trauma – striking, tearing

RSA

Industrial accidents

Fall from a height on a sharp object

Types:

- Accidental: inflicted by fall from a height, RSA, on any part of the body esp. hands and fingers
- Suicidal: wounds very rare, self-inflicted by lunatics on the wrists, throat, abdomen and chest
- Homicidal: wounds of greater severity, inflicted by hard and blunt weapons e.g. axe, sword or daos, mostly on the neck, chest, abdomen or head

Instruments: Hard and blunt: swords, axes, choppers

Curved: sickles, daos

PM findings: - Hemorrhage < in an incised wound

- Wound:
- Shape: spindle
- Size: length > breadth and depth
- Edges: irregular, ragged and inverted
  Tissues: torn and not cut as in incised wounds
- Bruises or contusions: of adjacent parts
- Prone to infections e.g. Tetanus, Gas gangrene, infective organisms.

Medico-legal aspect:

- That whether the wounds are lacerated ones ?
- That whether the wounds are accidental, suicidal or homicidal ?

PENETRATING (PUNCTURED) WOUNDS:

Etiology: Inflicted by sharp pointed instruments e.g. knives, daggers, rifle bayonets, swords, peck-axes, arrows, sickles broken glass pieces, nailings or sharp horns of wild animals.

M.O.I.: Direct trauma – striking, tearing
RSA
Industrial accidents
Fall from a height on a sharp object

Types: - Accidental: inflicted by fall on a sharp projecting object, RSA, needle-pricks on any part of the body esp. hands and fingers

- Suicidal: wounds very rare, self inflicted by lunatics on the accessible parts of the body e.g. wrists, throat, abdomen and chest
- Homicidal: wounds of greater severity, inflicted by on the neck, chest, abdomen or head.

PM findings:- Hemorrhage – external and internal

- Wound: notoriously deceptive. Penetrating wounds of the abdomen may be symptomless until internal hemorrhage or peritonitis reveals injured blood vessels or viscera.
- Edges: clean-cut or ragged and inverted at entrance and averted at exit site

- Tissues: torn and not cut as in incised wounds
- Bruises or contusions: of adjacent parts.

Medico-legal aspect:

- That whether the wounds are penetrating or punctured one ?
- That whether the wounds are accidental, suicidal or homicidal ?

CONTUSED WOUNDS:

Etiology: RSA

M.O.I.: Direct trauma – striking
RSA
Industrial accidents
Fall from a height

Types:
- Accidental: inflicted by fall from a height, RSA, on any part of the body esp. back and buttock-shands and fingers
- Suicidal: wounds very rare, self-inflicted by jumping from a height, on the accessible parts of the body e.g. wrists, throat, abdomen and chest
- Homicidal: wounds of greater severity, inflicted by on the neck, chest, abdomen or head.

PM findings:
- Hemorrhage
- Wound: may be symptomless until internal hemorrhage or peritonitis reveals injured blood vessels, muscles or viscera.
- Edges: ragged and averted
- Tissues: pressed
- Bruises or contusions: of adjacent parts.

Medico-legal aspect:

- That whether the wounds are contused one ?
- That whether the wounds are accidental, suicidal or homicidal ?

POISONED WOUNDS:

Etiology: Inflicted by bites of wasps or bees, dog, cat, horse, camel, jackal, snake or human beings.

Types:
- Accidental: common amongst picknickers inflicted by bites of wasps or bees, dog, cat,

horse, camel, jackal, snake or human beings, on the exposed parts e.g. face, neck, arms, legs

- Suicidal: self-inflicted by handling (disturbing) wasps, bees, dog, cat, horse, camel on the accessible (exposed) parts of the body e.g. hands, fingers, arms, legs, face and neck
- Homicidal: inflicted by exposing (forcing) to poisonous snakes, scorpions, wasps, bees, ferocious dogs.

Cause of death:

- Anaphylactic shock
- Vasomotor collapse

PM findings:- Hemorrhage – external and internal

- Wound: notoriously deceptive. Penetrating wounds of the abdomen may be symptomless until internal hemorrhage or peritonitis reveals injured blood vessels or viscera.
- Edges: clean-cut or ragged and inverted at entrance and everted at exit site
- Tissues: torn and not cut as in incised wounds
- Bruises or contusions: of adjacent parts.

Medico-legal aspect:

- That whether the wounds are penetrating or punctured one ?
- That whether the wounds are accidental, suicidal or homicidal ?

GUNSHOT WOUNDS:

Etiology: Inflicted by sharp projectiles discharged from firearms.

Motives: Suicidal:

- Depression, feeling of shame, remorse, anger, failure in examination
- Domestic conflicts
- Disappointed love affairs
- Insanity

Homicidal:

- Property disputes

- Disputable sexual affairs:
  - murder of wife for adultery or infidelity
  - murder of a girl or young woman after rape
  - murder of an elderly woman before rape
  - murder of a woman followed by Necrophilia or Necrophagia (sexual perversions)
  - murder of illegitimate new born babies
  - murder of new born babies for inheritance.

M.O.I.: Depends on:

- projectile's type: at the time of impact
- projectile's velocity: at the time of impact
- projectile's distance: of the firearm from the victim at the moment of discharge
- projectile's angle: at which the projectile struck the body.

Types of Projectiles: round and cone shaped bullets.

- Round bullets: inflict greater damage, with bruising and lacerations of adjoining parts
- Conical bullets: inflict wounds of entry and exit, without any bruising or laceration

Velocity of Projectiles: high and low velocity bullets.

High velocity bullets: clean, circular, punched out opening at the entry, with splintering of the intervening bone

Distance of Projectiles: close to or at a distance from the victim's body.

- Close to body: at the entry, the adjacent area is lacerated and blackened, single entry
- At a distance: at the entry, no laceration or blackening of adjacent area,
  - 30 to 90 cm.: single entry, adjacent area blackened
  - 180 cm.: central entry surrounded by multiple openings made by pellets
  - 360 cm.: multiple openings made by pellets.

Angle of projectiles: direct: inflict greater damage, while at angle inflict lesser damage.

Scattering of pellets: depend on:

- Size of the firearm
- Distance of the firearm from the victim's body
- Powder's charging.

Types:

- Accidental: inflicted on any part of the body – self-inflicted always on front, but on any part of the body when inflicted by another person
- Suicidal: wound self-inflicted on the accessible parts of the body e.g. temple, inside the mouth, under the chin or chest, blackening of the adjacent area
- Homicidal: inflicted on any part of the body, multiple wounds of greater severity. Mostly the firearm is missing from the site of violence, and may be fired from a close or distance range.

Cause of death:

- Hemorrhage: external (revealed) and internal (concealed)
- Shock
- Injury to vital organs e.g. heart, lungs, liver, spleen, brain, blood vessels

PM findings:- Case circumstances

- Nature of violence
- Hemorrhage – external and internal
- Wound:
  - Type: accidental, suicidal or homicidal
  - Number: single or multiple
  - Size: length, breadth, depth and direction
  - Edges: clean-cut or ragged and inverted at entrance and everted at exit site
  - Tissues: torn and not cut as in incised wounds
  - Bruises or contusions: of adjacent parts
  - Garments: stained and torn

TABLE 2-9: ANTE-MORTEM v/s POST-MORTEM WOUNDS

	Ante-mortem Wounds	Post-mortem Wounds
Hemorrhage	Severe - arterial	Slight - venous
Blood	Clotted	Not clotted
Wound	Edges - gape, stained	Edges – do not gape, not stained
Tissues	Inflammed	Non-inflammed

CIRCUMSTANTIAL EVIDENCE (CE):

Definition: Is defined as an important factor in determining the murderer, motive, victim, place of murder and the type of weapon used in the crime.

Evidence: Doors and windows found bolted/closed from inside: suggestive of suicide

Doors and windows found bolted/closed from outside: suggestive of homicide

Body found on railway tracks: suggestive of accident, suicide or homicide

Weapon: found near the body, may be blood stained

Weapon: not found near the body – suggestive of homicide.

Medico-legal aspect:

- That whether the death sustained by firearm?
- That whether the wounds are accidental, suicidal or homicidal?
- That what about the age of the injury?

MEDICOLEGAL WOUNDS:

MECHANICAL INJURIES:

ABRASIONS

Definition: Is defined as an area on the surface of the skin, damaged or injured by being rubbed too hard.

Etiology: Direct violence: finger nails or teeth bite

RSA

PM findings: Bruise may be antemortem or post-mortem:

Antemortem bruises:

- Injured part swollen and discolored

- Extravastion of blood and infiltration in tissues.

Poat-mortem bruises:

- Injured part mostly not swollen and discoloured, even with major violence.

Medico-legal aspect:

- That whether the abrasions are due to slight or major violence ?
- That whether the abrasions accidental, suicidal or homicidal ?

BRUISE or CONTUSION

Definition: Is defined as surface discolouration and swelling resulting from a blow or pressure. Also being called as contusion. Bruises are mostly simple wounds.

Etiology: Direct violence: fist, blows or kicks: hit by a stick, brick or stone RSA.

Pathogenesis: Lacerartion of soft tissues (subcutaneous tissues or blood vessels etc.), leading to exravasation of blood.

Types: Superficial bruise: occurs at the seat of violence within a short time of injury (few mts). It may appear much earlier if the skin involved is thin (eyelids, nipple, scrotum and back of hands).

- Deep bruise: occurs away from the seat of violence mostly after a period of few days.

Examples: black eye produced by a blow on the face or a fall on the vertex.

Site and extent: depend on:

- Severity of violence
- Vascularity of the injured part
- Blood vessels: arteriosclerosed vessels rupture easily
- Looseness of adjoining tissues

Shape: depend on shape of the used weapon:

- irregular – by a stone
- elongated – by a lathi/stick blow
- round – by a hammer strike

Age: depends on colour changes of the extravasated blood:
- red – immediately after the injury
- violet/blue – 3rd day
- green – 5th day
- yellow – 7th day
- fades away: 14th day

PM findings:- No signs of bleeding: dry surface
- No signs of inflammation: no scab formation

Medico-legal aspect:
- That whether the bruises are due to slight or major violence ?
- That whether the bruises are accidental, suicidal or homicidal ?

That whether the bruises are antemortem or post-mortem?

CLOSED INJURIES (Injuries to internal organs without any external injury)

Definition: Is defined as an injury without any visible external wounds.

Etiology: Direct violence: blows; hitting with a stick, base ball, mob lynching RSA

Fall from height

Pathogenesis:

Chest injuries: heart and lungs injuries, due to fractured ribs or compression

Abdomen injuries: liver, spleen, kidneys

Pelvis injuries: urinary bladder, urethra, genitals injuries

Spine injuries: PIVD, fracture dislocations of spine

Limbs: closed fractures, dislocations, sprains.

PM findings: External examination: no visible external wounds.

Internal examination:

Chest injury: fractured ribs may be found, tearing heart or/and lungs

Abdomen injury:

- Liver rupture: commonest injury due to its large size and relatively unprotected
- Splenic rupture: relatively unprotected, large size
- Kidneys: target esp. In back injuries.

Pelvis injury:

- Urinary bladder: injured esp. If full at the time of injury
- Urethra: edematous
- Genitals: edematous, hemorrhagic

Limbs injury:

- Fractures, dislocations, swellings
- Spine injury: fractured, dislocatied or fracture-dislocation

Pelvic injury.

Medico-legal aspect:

- That whether the injuries are closed wounds, involving internal organs ?
- That whether the injuries are accidental, suicidal or homicidal ?
- That whether injuries are the cause of death?

BURNS and SCALDS

Definition: Burns: Is defined as an area on the surface of the skin, damaged or injured by the dry heats - radient heat, a flame, electric current, acid throwing, caustics, or by friction e.g. rubbing too hard of hands against hard/rough objects.

Scalds: Is defined as a burn caused by moist heats - hot liquid or steam.

Etiology:

- Direct violence: acid throwing, attack with a burning flame, gun-powder, coal-mines explosions
- Dry heat: radiant heat, flame, electric current
- Wet heat – hot liquid or steam
- Occupation hazard: rubbing too hard of hands against hard/rough objects, common in blacksmiths, farmers
- RSA.

TABLE 2.10: BURNS v/s SCALDS

	Burns	Scalds
Cause:	Dry heats – flame, radiant heat, electric current	Moist heats – hot liquid, steam
Blisters:	Absent	Present
Singeing: of hairs	Present	Absent
Skin:	Bleaching or Present scorching	Absent
Marks:	Heat marks above and at site of heat application	Below and at site of heat application. Vesicles along line of liquid trickling

Grades: 1st degree (slight): redness alone

2nd degree (severe): vesication alone

3rd degree (grievous): destruction/death of the part.

Ante-mortem v/s Post-mortem (Burn injuries): Table (2.11):

TABLE 2.11: ANTE-MORTEM v/s POSTMORTEM (BURN INJURIES)

	Ante-Mortem	Post-Mortem
Skin (line of redness:	Present - encircling the Injured (burnt) part	Absent
Vesication:	Present - containing serous fluid. Base of vesication - red, inflamed, septic	Absent
Inflammation	Present	Absent
Internal organs	Congested, hemorrhagic	Roasted, smelly
Ulceration	Presnt	Absent
Mucous membranes:	Bright red due to CO	Absent

PM findings: External appearance:

- Clothings: to be removed with great caution and examined for: evidence of acid, petrol, kerosene and any other combustible product
- Skin colour: - red produced by highly heated metallic object
  - white: produced by the radiant heat
  - black: produced by gun-powder, coal-mines explosions, kerosene oil

- Odour: characteristic smell produced by kerosene oil
- No signs of bleeding: dry surface
- No signs of inflammation: no scab formation
- Age: ascertained from number of teeth and centres of ossification
- Identity (ID): assisted by presence of foreign bodies e.g. artificial tooth/teeth, jewellery etc. In the ash left over in extremely burnt bodies.

Internal appearance;

Skull: may be fractured and burst open

Brain and meninges: inflamed and congested, extravasation of blood

Neck: larynx, trachea and bronchial tubes congested and frothy – asphyxia death

Chest: pleural congestion with serious effusion, lungs congested and inflamed, Heart congested filled with cherry red coloured blood due to inhalation of CO_2

Abdomen: stomach and intestine inflamed, Peyer's patches ulcerated, hepatomegaly, splenomegaly, kidneys - signs of nephritis and haemorrhages.

Medico-legal aspect:

- That whether the burn injuries are accidental, suicidal or homicidal?
- That whether the burn injuries are ante-mortem or post-mortem?

ELECTRICITY and LIGHTENNG INJURIES

Definition: Is defined as an area on the surface of the skin, damaged or injured by the electric current (direct or alternating).

Etiology:
- Direct electric current – much less dangerous
- Alternating current – more dangerous.

Grades: Flash (arcing) burns

Flame (clotting) burns

Direct heating.

Pathogenesis:

Electrochemical cutaneous burns

PM findings: External appearance:

- Clothings: to be removed with great caution and examined for: evidence of electric shock
- Skin: lesions – sharply demarcated, round or oval, grey inflammed areas, sloughing
- odour: absent
- No signs of bleeding: dry surface
- Age: ascertained from number of teeth and centres of ossification
- Identity (ID): assisted by presence of foreign bodies e.g. artificial tooth/teeth, jewellery etc. In the ash left over in extremely burnt bodies.

Internal appearance ;

Skull: may be fractured and burst open

Brain and meninges: inflamed and congested, extrava-sation of blood

Neck: larynx, trachea and bronchial tubes congested and frothy

Chest: pleural congestion with serious effusion, lungs congested and inflamed, Heart congested filled with blood

Abdomen: stomach and intestine inflamed, Peyer's patches ulcerated, hepatomegaly, splenomegaly, kidneys - signs of nephritis and haemorrhages

Medico-legal aspect:

- That whether the death sustained by electric burns?
- That whether the burn injuries are accidental, suicidal or homicidal?
- That whether the burn injuries are ante-mortem or post-mortem?

PATHOLOGICAL WOUNDS:

Mild/Slight wounds:

Definition: Are defined as wounds that heal in shorter time, without immobilising a person from his/her work for > 2-3 wks.

Severe wounds:

Definition: Are defined as wounds that heal in longer time, thereby immobilising a person for > 3 wks.

Fatal/Dangerous wounds:

Definition: Are defined as wounds that prove fatal due to resulting serious complications e.g. Gas gangrene, Tetanus, Chest wounds (stab).

Grievous wounds:

Definition: Are defined as wounds that cause a permanent damage, loss of a part, or immobilisation for > 3 wks. These wounds have medico-legal importance.

REGIONAL INJURIES:

SCALP WOUNDS

Wounds: Abrasions, hematoma, contused, incised or lacerated.

MOI:
- Fall on a hard object
- Direct violence: severe blow on the head with a hard and blunt object, sharp cutting weapons.

Types: Suicidal, accidental or homicidal wounds.

Accidental:
- Mode: fall on a hard object
- Site: usually top of the head
- Number: usually single, occasionally multiple
- Depth: usually deeper
- Blood tricking: oozing
- Signs of struggle: absent.

Suicidal:
- Weapon: usually found present at the site
- Site: anyone (top, side, back or front)
- Number: usually multiple severe wounds
- Depth: abrasions, hematoma, contused, lacerated or incised wounds
- Blood trickling: vertically down the back
- Signs of struggle: usually absent
- Clothings: usually stained with blood.

Homicidal
- Weapon: usually heavy sharp cutting weapons, found absent from the crime

- Site: usually on the top
- Number: usually multiple severe lacerated or incised wounds
- Death: usually instantaneous
- Blood trickling: vertically down the back
- Signs of struggle: usually visible
- Clothings: usually stained with blood.
- Cause of death: usually hemorrhage and/or brain injury.

Medico-legal aspect:

- That whether the injuries are abrasions, hematoma, contused, incised or lacerated wounds?
- That whether the injuries are accidental, suicidal or homicidal?
- That whether injuries are the cause of death?

SKULL WOUNDS

Wounds: Abrasions, hematoma, contused, incised or lacerated, fracture of skull

MOI:
- Fall on a hard object
- Direct violence: severe blow on the head with a hard and blunt object, sharp cutting weapons

Types: Suicidal, accidental or homicidal wounds

Accidental:
- Mode: fall on a hard object
- Site: usually top of the head
- Number: usually single, occasionally multiple
- Depth: usually deeper
- Blood tricking: oozing
- Fracture: usually found
- Signs of struggle: absent.

Suicidal:
- Weapon: usually found present at the site
- Site: anyone (top, side, back or front)
- Number: usually multiple severe wounds
- Depth: abrasions, hematoma, contused, lacerated or incised wounds

:
- Blood trickling: vertically down the back.

- Signs of struggle: usually absent
- Clothings: usually stained with blood.

Homicidal:
- Weapon: usually heavy sharp cutting weapons, found absent from the crime
- Site: usually on the top
- Number: usually multiple severe lacerated or incised wounds
- Death: usually instantaneous
- : Blood trickling: vertically down the back
- Fracture: closed or open, depressed or elevated, comminuted, bursting
- Signs of struggle: usually visible
- Clothings: usually stained with blood.
- Cause of death: usually hemorrhage and/or brain injury.

Medico-legal aspect:

- That whether the injuries are abrasions, hematoma, contused, incised or lacerated, fracture of skull?
- That whether the injuries are accidental, suicidal or homicidal?
- That whether injuries are the cause of death?

BRAIN WOUNDS

Wounds: Abrasions, hematoma, contused, incised or lacerated, fracture of skull.

MOI:
- Fall on a hard object
- Direct violence: severe blow on the head with a hard and blunt object, sharp cutting weapons

Types: Suicidal, accidental or homicidal wounds

Accidental:
- Mode: fall on a hard object
- Site: usually top of the head
- Number: usually single, occasionally multiple
- Depth: usually deeper
- Blood tricking: oozing
- Fracture: usually found
- Signs of struggle: absent.

Suicidal:
- Weapon: usually found present at the site
- Site: anyone (top, side, back or front)
- Number: usually multiple severe wounds
- Depth: abrasions, hematoma, contused, lacerated or incised wounds
- Blood trickling: vertically down the back
- Signs of struggle: usually absent
- Clothings: usually stained with blood.

Homicidal:
- Weapon: usually heavy sharp cutting weapons, found absent from the crime
- Site: usually on the top
- Number: usually multiple severe lacerated or incised wounds
- Death: usually instantaneous
- Blood trickling: vertically down the back
- Fracture: closed or open, depressed or elevated, comminuted, bursting
- Signs of struggle: usually visible
- Clothings: usually stained with blood
- Cause of death: usually hemorrhage and/or brain injury.

Medico-legal aspect:

- That whether the injuries are hematoma, contused, incised or lacerated, fracture of skull?
- That whether the injuries are accidental, suicidal or homicidal?
- That whether injuries are the cause of death?

FACIAL WOUNDS

Wounds: Abrasions, hematoma, contused, incised or lacerated.

MOI:
- RSA, fall downstairs
- Direct violence:
  - severe blow on the face with fist, hitting with a hard and blunt object
  - sharp cutting weapons, gouging off the eyes with fingers or sharp objects
  - sports injury: boxing, martial arts.

Types: Suicidal, accidental or homicidal wounds.

Accidental:
- Mode: fall on a hard object
- Site: usually front – nose, lips, eyes, side - ear
- Number: usually single, occasionally multiple
- Depth: usually deeper
- Blood tricking: oozing
- Fracture: usually found
- Signs of struggle: absent.

Suicidal:
- Weapon: usually found present at the site
- Site: anyone (front, or side)
- Number: usually multiple severe wounds
- Depth: abrasions, hematoma, contused, lacerated or incised wounds
- Blood trickling: vertically down the cheek.
- Signs of struggle: usually absent
- Clothings: usually stained with blood.

Homicidal:
- Weapon: usually heavy sharp cutting weapons, found from the crime
- Site: usually front or side
- Number: usually multiple severe lacerated or incised wounds
- Death: usually instantaneous
- Blood trickling: vertically down the cheek
- Fracture: nasal, orbital, maxilla, mandible, closed or open
- Signs of struggle: usually visible
- Clothings: usually stained with blood
- Cause of death: usually hemorrhage and/or brain injury.

Medico-legal aspect:

- That whether the injuries are abrasions, hematoma, contused, incised or lacerated, fracture of nose, mandible or maxilla ?
- That whether the injuries are accidental, suicidal or homicidal ?
- That whether injuries are the cause of death?

NECK WOUNDS

Wounds: Abrasions, hematoma, contused, incised or lacerated, fracture of spine.

MOI:
- RSA, fall on a hard object
- Direct violence: severe blow on the neck with a hard and blunt object, sharp cutting weapons, judicial hanging or hanging by long dropping.

Types: Suicidal, accidental or homicidal wounds.

Accidental:
- Mode: RSA, fall on a hard object
- Site: usually lower part more so on one side
- Number: usually single, occasionally multiple
- Depth: usually deeper
- Blood tricking: oozing
- Fracture: usually found
- Signs of struggle: usually present.

Suicidal:
- Weapon: usually found present at the site
- Site: anyone (top, side, back or front)
- Number: usually multiple severe wounds
- Depth: abrasions, hematoma, contused, lacerated or incised wounds

:
- Blood trickling: vertically down the back
- Signs of struggle: usually absent
- Clothings: usually stained with blood.

Homicidal:
- Weapon: usually heavy sharp cutting weapons, found from the crime site
- Site: usually front or sides
- Number: usually multiple severe lacerated or incised wounds
- Death: usually instantaneous

:
- Blood trickling: vertically down the front, back or side.
- Fracture, fracture dislocation: closed or open, comminuted, bursting
- Signs of struggle: usually visible
- Clothings: usually stained with blood.

- Cause of death: usually from shock, syncope, asphyxia, hemorrhage, air embolism, pneumonia, and/or spinal cord injury.

Medico-legal aspect:

- That whether the injuries are abrasions, hematoma, contused, incised or lacerated, fracture of skull ?
- That whether the injuries are accidental, suicidal or homicidal ?
- That whether injuries are the cause of death?

CUT THROAT WOUNDS

Dangers: Usually dangerous on account of involvement of adjoining unprotected vital structures. Main dangers are:

- hemorrhage from torn carotid artery and jugular veins
- asphyxia from torn larynx and trachea
- Death: occurs from asphyxia.

Types: Suicidal, accidental or homicidal wounds.

Suicidal:

- Weapon: usually sharp cutting weapons
- Site: above Pomum Adami
- Direction: usually with the head extended - more or less transverse
- Position: wound on the side of neck lies facing the hand used e.g. on the right side when left hand used and vice versa
- Number: usually single, may be multiple – amongst these on may be the severe wound.
- Depth: wound deeper at the start, but tails off at the end
- Blood trickling: vertically down the front or side of neck, in case of standing or sitting posture.
- Signs of struggle: absent.
- Clothings: usually intact.

Accidental:

- Weapon: usually sharp cut glass in case of RSA and fall from height over sharp object
- Site: not specific

- Direction: not particular
- Number: usually multiple
- Depth: usually deeper
- Clothings: usually torn and stained.

Homicidal:
- Weapon: usually heavy sharp cutting weapons, found absent from the crime
- Site: usually below Pomum Adami
- Direction: from down upwards or horizontal
- Position: horizontal and from left to right by right handed assailant, while horizontal and from right to left by left handed assailant
- Number: usually multiple severe wounds dividing soft tissues upto vertebrae
- Death: usually instantaneous
- Blood trickling: vertically down the back
- Signs of struggle: usually visible
- Clothings: usually cuts in the clothing found.

Medico-legal aspect:

: Cause of death: usually from shock, syncope, asphyxia, hemorrhage, air embolism, pneumonia, and/or spinal cord injury.

SPINE and SPINAL CORD WOUNDS

Wounds: Abrasions, hematoma, contused, incised or lacerated, fracture of spine.

MOI:
- RSA, fall on a hard object
- Direct violence: severe blow on the neck or lower back, with a hard and blunt object, sharp cutting weapons.

Types: Suicidal, accidental or homicidal wounds.

Accidental:
- Mode: fall on a hard object
- Site: usually cervical, dorso-lumbar or upper lumbar
- Number: usually single, occasionally multiple
- Depth: usually deeper
- Blood tricking: oozing
- Fracture: usually found
- Signs of struggle: absent.

Suicidal:
- Weapon: usually found present at the site
- Site: front or side
- Number: usually multiple severe wounds
- Depth: abrasions, hematoma, contused, lacerated or incised wounds

:
- Blood trickling: vertically down the front or back
- Signs of struggle: usually absent
- Clothings: usually stained with blood.

Homicidal:
- Weapon: usually heavy sharp cutting weapons, found absent from the crime
- Site: anywhere (back, side or front)
- Number: usually multiple severe lacerated or incised wounds
- Death: usually instantaneous

:
- Blood trickling: vertically down the back
- Fracture, fracture dislocation: closed or open, comminuted, bursting
- Signs of struggle: usually visible
- Clothings: usually stained with blood
- Cause of death: usually hemorrhage and/or cord injury.

Medico-legal aspect:
- That whether the injuries are abrasions, hematoma, contused, incised or lacerated, fracture of spine?
- That whether the injuries are accidental, suicidal or homicidal ?
- That whether injuries are the cause of death?

CHEST WOUNDS

Wounds: Abrasions, bruises, contused, incised, penetrating or perforating, lacerated, rib fractures.

MOI:
- RSA, fall from a height, fall of a heavy weight
- Direct violence: severe blow on the chest with fist or a hard and blunt object, stab wounds from sharp cutting weapons or broken ribs, bullet or explosive.

Types: Suicidal, accidental or homicidal wounds, simple or compound wounds.

Accidental:
- Mode: RSA, fall from a height, fall of a heavy weight
- Site: usually front of the chest wall
- Number: usually single, occasionally multiple
- Depth: usually deeper
- Blood tricking: oozing
- Fracture: ribs usually found
- Signs of struggle: absent.

Suicidal:
- Weapon: usually found present at the site
- Site: anyone (front, side or back)
- Number: usually multiple severe wounds
- Depth: abrasions, hematoma, contused, lacerated or incised wounds
- Blood trickling: vertically down the front
- Signs of struggle: usually absent
- Clothings: usually stained with blood.

Homicidal:
- Weapon: usually heavy blunt or sharp cutting weapons, at the crime site
- Site: usually the front
- Number: usually multiple severe lacerated or incised wounds
- Death: usually instantaneous
- Blood trickling: vertically down the front
- Fracture: closed or open, depressed or elevated, comminuted, bursting
- Signs of struggle: usually visible
- Clothings: usually stained with blood
- Cause of death: usually hemorrhage, shock and cardio-pulmonary failure.

Medico-legal aspect:

- That whether the injuries are abrasions, hematoma, contused, incised or lacerated, fracture of ribs?
- That whether the injuries are accidental, suicidal or homicidal?
- That whether injuries are the cause of death?

ABDOMEN WOUNDS

Wounds: Abrasions, bruises, contused, incised, penetrating or perforating, lacerated, fracture pelvis.

MOI:
- RSA, fall from a height, fall of a heavy weight
- Direct violence: severe blow on the abdomen with a fist or hard and blunt object, sharp cutting weapons.

Types:
- Suicidal, accidental or homicidal wounds
- Penetrating or non-penetrating wounds.

Accidental:
- Mode: RSA, fall from a height, fall of a heavy weight
- Site: usually front
- Number: usually single, occasionally multiple
- Depth: usually deeper
- Blood tricking: oozing
- Fracture: usually absent
- Signs of struggle: absent.

Suicidal:
- Weapon: usually found from the crime site
- Site: usually front
- Number: usually multiple severe wounds
- Depth: abrasions, hematoma, contused, lacerated or incised wounds

:
- Blood trickling: vertically down the front
- Signs of struggle: usually absent
- Clothings: usually stained with blood.

Homicidal:
- Weapon: usually heavy sharp cutting weapons, found absent from the crime
- Site: usually on the top
- Number: usually multiple severe lacerated or incised wounds
- Death: usually instantaneous from penetrating wounds

:
- Blood trickling: vertically down
- Fracture: closed or open
- Signs of struggle: usually visible

- Clothings: usually stained with blood.
- Cause of death: usually hemorrhage and/or brain injury.

PM findings: External appearance:

- Clothings: to be removed with great caution and examined for: evidence of violence, staining with blood, semen, vomitus etc.
- Skin: colouration, dry or moistlesions, sloughing etc.
- odour: present or absent
- Signs of bleeding: present or absent
- Age: ascertained from number of teeth and centres of ossification
- Identity (ID): assisted by presence of foreign bodies e.g. artificial tooth/teeth, jewellery etc. In the ash left over in extremely burnt bodies.

Internal appearance:

Skull:

- may be fractured – simple or compound, comminuted, depressed or raised, guttered or bursting
- brain injury : compressed, hemorrhage – extradural or sub-dural Brain and meninges:
- Injuries: lacerated, penetrating or perforating, incised wounds
- hemorrhage: extradural, subdural, and/or intracerebral
- compressed, inflamed and congested, extravasation of blood.

Face:

- wounds: bitting, cutting of nose, cheeks, lips, ears, lacerated or incised
- teeth: dislocated or uprooted

Neck:

- wounds: abrasions or bruises (throttling), lacerated (judicial hanging or hanging) incised, punctured
- larynx, trachea and bronchial tubes congested and frothy.

Spine and Spinal cord:

- fractures and fracture dislocations: cervical, lower dorsal or dorso lumber
- spinal cord injury: C2 – fatal due to injured medulla and cord.

Chest:

- heart: penetrating or punctured (stabbing, bullet) wounds – fatal, congested
- ribs: fractures
- pleural congestion with serious effusion, lungs congested and inflamed.

Abdomen:

- wounds: non-penetrating (RSA, fall from a height) or penetrating (sharp cutting objects, tools, bullets)
- extravasation of blood: may be present in the muscles or cellular tissues
- Rupturing: of internal organs may be found.

Stomach:

MOI: - Non-perforating: RSA, fall from a height, blow with a fist or a stick
- Perforating: stab or gunshot wounds, fall from a height over a sharp object, corrosive poisons – strong acids/alkalies.

Site: usual sites are pyloric antrum, anterior surface near the lesser curvature

Rupture: spontaneous

Death: usually from shock, hemorrhage or peritonitis.

Intestines:

MOI:-Non-perforating: RSA, fall from a height, blow with a fist/a stick, kick
- Perforating: stab or gunshot wounds, fall from a height over a sharp object, corrosive poisons – strong acids/alkalies.

Site: usual sites are anterior surface of duodenum, jejunum and ileum

Rupture: usually intra- or extraperitoneal

Death: usually from shock, hemorrhage or peritonitis.

Liver:

MOI:-Non-perforating: RSA, fall from a height, blow with a fist or a stick

- Perforating: stab or gunshot wounds, fall from a height over a sharp object, fractured ribs

Site: usual sites are right lobe – outer surface and lower border

Rupture: spontaneous

Death: usually from shock, hemorrhage or peritonitis.

Spleen:

MOI: - Non-perforating: RSA, fall from a height, blow with a fist or a stick

- Perforating: stab or gunshot wounds, fall from a height over a sharp object, diseased or enlarged spleen.

Site: usual site is inner surface (because of thinnest capsule)

Rupture: spontaneous – accidental

Death: usually from shock, hemorrhage or peritonitis.

Kidneys:

MOI: - Non-perforating: RSA, fall from a height, blow with a fist or a stick

- Perforating: stab or gunshot wounds, fall from a height over a sharp object, fractured rib.

Site: usual site is blows upon the loin or blows from in front or crush injuries

Rupture: usually complete tear of kidney, partial or complete avulsion from its pedicle. Tears of renal parenchyma follow the lines of uriniferous tubules

Death: usually from shock, hemorrhage, peritonitis or suppuration due to extravasation of urine.

Urinary bladder:

MOI:-Non-perforating: RSA, fall from a height, blow with a fist or a stick

- Perforating: stab or gunshot wounds, fall from a height over a sharp object, fracture pelvis.

Site: usual intraperitoneal

Rupture: usually extraperitonal (80 per cent) while intraperitoneal (20 per cent)

Death: usually from shock, hemorrhage or peritonitis from extravasation of urine in the peritoneal cavity.

Uterus:

MOI: - Non-perforating: RSA, fall from a height, blow with a fist or a stick

- Perforating: stab or gunshot wounds, fall from a height over a sharp object, corrosive poisons – strong acids/alkalies.

Site: usual sites are Caesarean or operational scars

Rupture: spontaneous during delivery

Death: usually from shock, hemorrhage, peritonitis or septicemia.

Vagina:

MOI:-Fall on a projectile object

- Sexual violence (forcible rape - esp. on minor girls)
- Criminal abortion – introducing of stick, a sharp object, corrosive agent
- Obstructed labour

Site: usual sites are walls

Rupture: spontaneous

Death: usually from shock, hemorrhage septic cellulitis.

Vulva:

MOI: - Fall on a projectile object

- Sexual violence (forcible rape - esp. on minor girls, by penetration of a large sized penis)

- Criminal abortion – introducing of stick, a sharp object, corrosive agent (inflicted as a punishment/management for adultery and infidelity)
- Obstructed labour

Site: anywhere

Rupture: spontaneous

Death: usually from shock, hemorrhage or septic cellulitis.

Urethra:

MOI: - Fall on a projectile object, fracture pelvis
- Sexual violence (forcible rape - esp. on minor girls, by penetration of a large sized penis)
- Criminal abortion – introducing of stick, a sharp object, corrosive agent
- Obstructed labour

Rupture: spontaneous

Death: usually from shock, hemorrhage or septic cellulitis.

Penis

MOI: - Accidental: fall astride a projecting object, cycling accidents
- Direct violence – kicking, hitting with a stick/ baseball, sexual violence
- Perforating: stab or gunshot wounds, fall from a height over a sharp object

Site: usual sites are bulbous urethra and membranous (intra-pelvic)

Rupture: spontaneous

Death: usually from shock, hemorrhage or peritonitis due to extravasation of urine.

Medico-legal aspect:

- That whether the injuries are complete or incomplete, penetrating or perforating, lacerated, fracture of spine or pelvis?
- That whether the injuries are accidental, suicidal or homicidal?
- That whether injuries are the cause of death?

Teses:

MOI: - Accidental: fall astride a projecting object, cycling accidents, straining at stool, lifting a heavy weight and coitus

- Direct violence – kicking, hitting with a stick/ baseball, sexual violence
- Perforating: stab or gunshot wounds, fall from a height over a sharp object

Predisposing factors: usually inversion of the testis and rarely torsion of the testis.

Rupture: usually the testis may be found protruding through the injured scrotum. Rarely the closed rupture of the testis from blows.

Death: usually from shock, hemorrhage or peritonitis due to extravasation of urine.

References

1. Chatton, J Milton: Disorders due to Physical Agents. Current Medical Diagnosis and Treatment, Lang Med Publications, Japan, 1975.
2. Orlowski, JP: Drowning, near drowning, and ice water drowning (editorial) JAMA 260:390, 1988.
3. Wallace, JF: Drowning and Near-Drowning. Principles of Internal Medicine. 12th ed, Vol. 2:2200-02.
4. Artz, CP, Moncrief JA: The Treatment of Burns. Saunders, 1969.
5. Baxter, CR: Emergency treatment of burn injury. Ann Emerg Med 17:1305,1988.
6. Hunt, J et al: Acute electrical burns: Current diagnostic and therapeutic approaches to management. Arch Surg 115:434, 1980.
7. Mettler, Jr FA, Mosely, Jr RD: Medical effectes of Radiation.

   Orlando. Florida. Grune and Stratton. 1985, pp. 1-288.
8. Strauss, RH, Prockop, LD: Decompression sickness among scuba divers. JAMA 223:637, 1973.

9. Rains, AJH and Capper, WM et al: Ulceration and Gangrene. Bailey and Love's Short Practice of Surgery, H.K. Lewis and Co. Ltd., London, 1965.
10. Chatterjee, CC, Banerjee, PK: Caisson Disease. Human Physiology, 5th ed. Books and Allied Pvt. Ltd., Calcutta, 1963.
11. Experienced Teacher: Notes on Medical Jurisprudence and Toxicology.
Current Publishers, Calcutta, 1965, 13. 69

SEXUAL and ALLIED PROBLEMS:

- IMPOTENCE
- STERILITY
- FRIGIDITY
- VIRGINITY

IMPOTENCE (syn. ERECTILE DYSFUNCTION):

Is a major quality of life issue for an increasing healthy ageing population.

Definition: Impotence is defined as complete inability to perform sexual act to premature ejaculation, where as erectile dysfunction (ED) is defined as Inability to achieve or maintain an erection adequate for sexual satisfaction. Incapacity on the part of the male to impregnate

Prevalence: Common in men >40 yrs. of age. Prevalence and severity increases with age.

Etiology: Psychological: anxiety, shame, fear or failure

Marital disharmony

Organic disorders: diabetes mellitus, endocrinal disorders, spinal cord disorders, disseminated sclerosis, hypertension, alcohol and drug abuse, malformations and deformities of penis and testis e.g. absence of penis, hypospadius, absence of testicles, undescended testis

Drugs: anti-hypertensive, anti-depressants, phenothizines.

Diagnosis: Erection – Primary ED: never had an erection

Secondary ED: moderate or incomplete erection

Ejaculation - premature

Libido – lack of sexual drive

Sexual satisfaction – decreased or absent.

Investigation: Blood sugar, Urine analysis.

Medico-legal Aspect:

- That Divorce can be claimed/granted legally on the basis of impotence.

STERILITY (syn.Infertility)

Definition: Is defined as an inability of female to produce offspring (incapacity on the part of the female to conceive). Sterility and impotency may be present in the same person or may exist separately in male and female.

Sterility mainly referred to females, while impotence to males.

Etiology: May be an organic or functional defect in the man or woman

Psychological: anxiety, fear, hysterical fits, faulty conception knowledge

Malformation of genitalia: absence of vagina, uterus, ovaries

Diseases: Vaginitis, cervicitis, salpingitis, leucorrhoea.

Medico-legal Aspect:

- That to nullify marriage and divorce
- That to contest adultery or an unnatural sexual offence
- That to contest paternity in an inherited case
- That to claim rights over the property, left by the husband of an issueless woman.

FRIGIDITY:

Definition: Is defined as an inability of a woman to derive pleasure from sexual relations. The early stages of intercourse are pleasurable, but the woman does not achieve an orgasm.

Etiology: Psychological:

- a dislike or actual abhorrence of it
- poor sexual technique e.g. lack of arousal or clitoral stimulation by her partner
- conscious or unconscious feelings of guilt and fear related to sex
- fear of pregnancy
- feelings of hostility (marital disharmony)

Dyspareunia

Vaginismus.

Medico-legal Aspect:

- That to nullify marriage and divorce

VIRGINITY:

Definition: A woman is called a virgin, who never had any sexual intercourse.

Virginity is defined as a state or fact of being a virgin.

Defloration is defined as loss of virginity.

Signs of Virginity:

Extra-genital:

- Breast: round, firm and elastic
- Nipple: small, pointed, surrounded by pink areola

Genitals:

- Mons pubis: cushion of fat in front of pubic symphysis, covered with short curly hair
- Labia majora: rounded, firm, elastic and in close contact with each other, covered on lateral surface by short curly hair
- Labia minora: small, soft, thin, elastic, pink coloured and in close contact, visible only on drawing them apart
- Clitoris: rudimentary
- Vestibule: narrow, smooth, almond shaped
- Fourchette and posterior commissure: intact
- Urethral orifice: puckered
- Vaginal orifice: slit-like, closed by the hymen and hidden by labia minora
- Hymen: a crescentic or circular fold of connective tissue covered with skin, closes in the vaginal orifice, leaving a small aperture

An intact hymen is considered as sure sign of virginity, as it ruptures at the first coitus, resulting in slight bleeding. Post labor it is torn up completely and thereby represented by tags of skin – so called caruncule hymenales.

Exceptions: Besides sexual intercourse, hymen may be ruptured due to:-

- Trauma: - Accidental fall on a projected object, with legs wide apart

- Sports injuries e.g. jumping, horse-riding
- Sexual torture e.g. introducing a foreign body into vagina
- Masturbation with the help of foreign bodies
- Infection: U.T.I.

Signs of Defloration (Loss of Virginity):

Extra-genital:

- Breast: enlarged and pendulous
- Nipple: enlarged

Genitals:

- Mons pubis: covered with long, coarse hair
- Labia majora: laxed without touching each other,
- Labia minora: enlarged and in loose contact with each other
- Clitoris: enlarged
- Vestibule: elongated and laxed
- Fourchette and posterior commissure: ruptured
- Urethral orifice: puckered
- Vaginal orifice: loosened
- Vaginal walls: dilated
- Hymen: ruptured.

Medico-legal aspect:

- That whether the said woman is virgin or not?
- That whether defloration is because of rape?
- That whether defloration is because of an accident?
- That whether defloration is base of defamation?
- That whether defloration is base of divorce?
- That whether defloration is base of nullity of marriage?

SEXUAL PERVERSIONS (DEVIATIONS)

Definition: Perversions comprise deviations in the aim of sexual satisfaction, or in the selection of a sexual partner, that are considered as unnatural and unacceptable. As long as activities in sexual foreplay are intended as a prelude to vaginal intercourse, they cannot be presumed as perversions.

Etiology: Family discords

Parental attitudes – behavioural problems e.g. dominance, rejection, unrealistic expectations, overcriticism, discrimination, unfavourable comparison etc.

Early sex experience

Environmental factors – school/college, prison

Experience (+ve/-ve)–with same/or opposite sex.

TYPES OF PERVERSIONS:

HOMOSEXUAL: Sexually attracted to a person of the same sex. When a partner of the same sex is preferred (Gay–a man sexually attracted to other man;

Lesbian–a woman sexually attracted to other woman). Homosexuality is relatively common these days, and social and legal attitudes toward homosexuality have markedly changed recently. But in general male homosexual's threat to boys, is not greater than male heterosexual's to girls.

BISEXUALS: Sexually attracted to both male and female.

Those having relationships with either sex, and frequently are homosexuals who have been denying his/her homosexual preference.

Bisexuality often ends by stabilising a sexual preference.

TRANSSEXUALISM: Someone who wants to be or look like a person of the opposite sex. An attempt to deny and reverse the biological sex and to achieve an opposite sex Identification. The transsexual male attempts to assume interests, dress, behaviour of opposite sex.

PEDOPHILIA: When a child is chosen/preferred as the sexual outlet.

GERONOPHILIA: When an elderly partner is chosen/preferred.

INCESTUOUS: Relationship between close relatives e.g. between father and daughter, mother and son, brother and sister, due to marital discords or family problems and modern cultural influences.

NECROPHILIA: Sexual intercourse with a dead body.

VOYEURISM: Sexual gratification by looking at a nude body or a sexual act.

EXTRAGENITAL INTERCOURSE: Anal or oral sex.

EX IBITIONISM: Sexual gratification by exposure of one's body or genitals to the opposite sex e.g. indecent exposure versus striptease

TRANSVESTISM: Someone who enjoys dressing like a person of the opposite sex.

Sexual gratification (masturbation, orgasm) by wearing clothes, make up, of opposite sex.

PORNOGRAPHISM: Sexual gratification (excited) by watching magazines, posters, calenders, movies, showing bikini clad girls, a nude body or sexual act.

SADOMASOCHISM:

Definition: Sexual gratification by inflicting or experiencing pain e.g. the sadist bites, flogs, injures or ill-treats the partner in a very violent manner. Death may occur in extreme acts e.g. he/or she may commit a murder (lust murder). Sometimes, after committing a murder, the sadist performs carnal intercourse on her – so called Necrophilia. He may even tear out her genitals or other organs and eat her flesh to gratify his sexual desire – so called Necrophagia.

Diagnosis: Sexual drive: increased/or decreased libido

Sexual satisfaction: deviations e.g. decreased/ or absent

Variations: in the choice of sexual partner, objects and practices.

MASOCHISM: Opposite of sadism.

Definition: Is defined as the sexual gratification, obtained by being physically tortured or bitten by the woman, he loves.

FETICHISM: Observed only in males.

Definition: Is defined as the sexual gratification, obtained by the sight of certain body parts of the woman or her belongings e. g. Lingerie, nighties, saree-blouse or swimsuit.

BESTIALITY:

Definition: Is defined as an offence where sexual intercourse is with an animal (tamed animals e.g. she-goat, she-ass, cow, bitch, duck etc., due to deprivation of other outlets and psychological disorders.

Diagnosis: Semen–from the vagina of the animal. Matting of the surrounding hairs with the discharge. Hair of the animal–may be observed on the body/cloth of the accused.

Investigation: P/V examination of the animal–for spermatozoa (+ve sign)

Hairs of the animal–for presence of spermatozoa.

Offence: Unnatural sexual offence against tamed innocent animals.

Penalty: Imprisonment along with fine.

Medico-legal aspect:

- That certain sexual perversions are punishable in most civilised countries, and doctors have no immunity.
- That the major complications are usually conflict with society and its laws.

SEXUAL OFFENCES (OFFENCES and PENALTY):

SEXUAL ABUSE:

Many cases of sexual abuse never come to light. Victims can often feel ashamed and too scared to report it, fearing it could make a situation worse. Any form of sexual activity that's against your will constitutes as sexual abuse. This includes bodily contact (such as sexual kissing, touching, fondling of genitals or penetration-oral, anal, or vaginal) and genital exposure (flashing), verbal pressure for sex and sexual exploitation through pornography or prostitution.

CONSENT FOR SEXUAL ACT OR BEHAVIOUR:

Definition: Is defined as an offence that often revolves around consent.

It's all about permission (or agreement). This is something that must be clearly established between two people before any kind of sexual act or behaviour. If an individual is accused of a sex offence, they must show that they reasonably believed consent had been given by the other person.

SEXUAL OFFENCES IN INDIA:

- Assault/Torture
- Moral turpitude
- Sodomy
- Rape
- Molestation: The Act makes it an offence for any male or female to Intentionally touch/fondle another person sexually without his or her consent.
- Pregnancy
- Surrogacy

SEXUAL OFFENCES IN UK:

- Assault
- Rape and other offences against children under 13
- Child sex offences
- Abuse of position of trust
- Familial child sex offences
- Offences against persons with a mental disorder impeding choice
- Care workers for persons with a mental disorder
- Indecent photographs of children
- Exploitation of prostitution
- Amendments relating to prostitution
- Trafficking
- Preparatory offences
- Sex with an adult relative
- Other offences
- Exposure
- Voyeurism

- Intercourse with an animal
- Sexual penetration of a corpse
- Sexual activity in a public lavatory

Offence: The Sexual Offences Act 2003 governs sex laws in the UK.

Under this Act, it is an offence for any male to penetrate with his penis the vagina, anus or mouth of a female or male without their consent.

Penalty: A person found guilty of this offence could be sent

Offence: Assault by penetration.

The Act makes it an offence for any male or female to penetrate the vagina or anus of another person without their consent. The offence is committed where the penetration is by a part of the body e.g. a finger or anything else e.g. a bottle for sexual intent.

Penalty: A person found guilty of this offence could be sent to prison for 10 yrs.

Offence: Assault/Molestation.

The Act makes it an offence for any male or female to intentionally Touch/fondle another person sexually without his or her consent.

Penalty: Under Section 3 of the Act, a person found guilty of this offence could be sent to prison for a maximum of ten years.

Offence: Causing sexual activity without consent.

It is an offence to cause or encourage another person to engage in sexual activity without his or her consent.

Penalty: If penetration is involved then a person found guilty of this offence could be sent to prison for life.

If no penetration is involved then a person found guilty of this offence could be sent to prison for up to ten years.

SEXUAL TORTURE/ASSAULT

Definition: Sexual torture/assault is as old as human civilisation and has been prevalent since ancient times in one form or other.

Types:

- Mental: forced nakedness, humiliations, abuses, threats and forced to witness others being sexually tortured/assaulted.
- Physical: molestation/assault of victim by the tormentor or by using an Animal for physical contact with the victim.

Objectives/Motives:

- Forceful confession–misused as legal proof.
- Personal vendetta-by torturing individual or his family members.
- To pollute (defile) the race.
- To satiate-sexual starvation of soldiers at war by assaulting women of enemy.
- Ethnic conflicts.
- Personality disorder-sexual assault of men/ women in custody by a mentally deranged person.
- Misuse of custodial power-by sexual assault of victims in custody.
- Distortion of the personality - victim tortured to develop helplessness, loss of self-confidence, and worthlessness.
- To extract information.
- Family violence (domestic/or marital violence), child abuse, sexual harassment, rape, kidnapping, hostage taking and terrorist act and pornography etc. Should also be viewed as human right violation as its repercussions are far reaching in society.

Modus operandi:

: Psychological:

- Verbal abuses, threats, and humiliation, publically
- Undressing (nudity) in front of opposite sex esp. fair sex

- Being photographed in compromising positions.
- Forced to masturbate in front of others.
- Forced to watch sexual torture/assault of others.
- Forced to perform sexual torture/assault on other colleague victims.

Physical:

- Introduction of chillies, irritants etc. into eyes, mouth, vagina, or anus.
- Introduction of ants, rats, insects, etc. into vagina, or anus.
- Penetration of vagina, anus by batons, rods, handle bars, candles etc
- Plucking of nails, fingers, teeth, toes by instruments.
- Use of burning cigarettes on sensitive parts (genitals, breasts etc.).
- Electrical shocks – given to sensitive parts.
- Mutilation of breasts, genitals, buttocks etc.

Sexual:

- Fondling, squeezing, kissing/sucking of breasts, buttocks, genitalia.
- Raped by person of same/opposite sex.
- Sexual assault (Rape etc.) by animals e.g. trained dogs, monkeys.

Medico-legal aspect:

- That sexual torture/assault punishable in most civilised countries.
- That the major complications are usually conflict with society and its laws.
- That to prevent these sexual torture/assaults:
- Public awareness-to condemn these barbarous, uncivilised acts and fight against torture.
- Media support–esp. for women's rights, curbing domestic violence.
- Police and administration's support–for implementation of law strictly.
- Motivation of National Commission for Women and ILO.

- Medical organisations participation-should spread the ethical principles that address human right and their violations.
- Motivation of Employers (Public and Private)–to set up women cells in order to curb sexual exploitation at their working places.
- Motivation of every physician to realise his/her duty to protest his/her fellow citizen against violation of his right.

(*Source:* Tokyo declaration, 1975)

Doctors and Torture:

Definition: A doctor may be involved illegally in the process of torture/assault directly or indirectly, either voluntarily (a human right activist) or under compulsion from the society, government or terrorists. He may participate unwillingly or unintentionally or may participate directly with malafide intentions.

Medico-legal aspect:

- That certain sexual perversions are punishable in most civilised countries, and doctors have no immunity.
- That the major complications are usually conflict with society and its laws.

MORAL TURPITUDE

Definition: Is not defined anywhere.

Parvesh v/s State of Haryana (2009) (4) RCR (Criminal) 470 (P&H)

- This term if used in law for centuries–Sexual crimes would fall within scope of moral turpitude, but sexual offences are not the only offences involving moral turpitude–There are other offences also which within term moral turpitude. AIR (1959) Allahabad 71 relied.
- Abrasions of the glans penis and prepuce, esp. on the frenulum.

Signs of sodomy on the Passive agent:

- Signs of struggle (forced act without consent) e.g. scratches, abrasions, bruises or lacerations of the anus–esp. If the passive agent is a young boy/or girl

- Stains: of blood, semen or both per anus or on the cloth
- Discharge: of pus (gonorrhoea) per anus or on the cloth.

Investigation: Anal swab and smear–for detection of spermatozoa (+ve sign) and pus cells (gonococci) Urethral discharge-for detection of pus cells (gonococci).

Offence: Both agents (active and passive) with their consent are liable to punishment under law, while only the active agent is liable to punishment if this act is done without the consent of passive agent

Penalty: Imprisonment, fine or both.

RAPE

Definition: Is defined as an offence by a man to illegally, penetrate with his penis (sexual intercourse), the vagina, anus or mouth of a female (own wife < 15 yrs., or any other girl < 16 yrs. or with any other woman > 16 yrs. of age), against her will or without her consent or with her consent, (taken by following unlawful means :-

- Personification–as her husband
- Blackmailing–on the pretext of treating her disease by act of sexual Intercourse, or on the pretext of marrying her.
- Mentally retarded or lunatic woman
- Drug abuse–under the influence of intoxicating or sedatives
- Torture–physical or mental (threat of death) e.g. to force someone to have sex, especially by using violence. Sexual intercourse with a prostitute, without her consent shall also be considered as rape, irrespective of being paid money or remuneration for the act.

Age of consent for sexual intercourse:

: In India:

A person cannot be held criminally responsible for his act of performing sexual intercourse on:

Own wife–at or above 15 yrs. Of age (the consent is presumed to have been given at the time of marriage)

Other woman–at or above 16 yrs.

Age of Male: A child < 12 yrs. of age (immature) cannot be held criminally responsible for rape.

Age of female: No age is exempted from rape. Maximum number of rapes committed on females between age of 6 to 30 yrs.

Diagnosis: History of the illegal act:

- Date, time, place
- Name and address (if known) of the accused person/s and victim
- Position of the parties
- Whether the victim resisted or shouted for any help
- Whether menstruating at that time
- Whether the victim was in full senses/ or intoxicated
- Whether the victim is feeling dysurea

A. Examination of the Victim:

Pre-examination precautions (essential requirements):

- A written warrant from the Magistrate or an Authorised Officer, is essential prior to examination of the victim. No warrant is required, in case the victim approaches the doctor directly.
- Identity of the victim (raped female)–by the escorting policeman/woman and by the legal guardian of the victim.
- The victim and her guardian–are apprised in details about the results of examination that may favour or oppose them in the court and that they have the option of not to submit for examination
- Consent–written consent of the victim (or of the legal guardian of a minor below 12 yrs. of age).

  Unconscious/or intoxicated victim–no consent of the victim is required, but with the permission of the legal guardians of the victim.

Precautions (requirements) during examination:

- Presence of a female attendant or her husband or legal guardian
- Undressing of the victim–done only by herself, female doctor/attendant
- Adequate light, suitable place and lithotomy position are essential

Examination: of clothes worn by the victim for evidence of struggle e.g. torn, stained of dust, blood and semen.

Body injuries:

Inflicted by the accused person/s:

- Mouth and cheeks: scratches, abrasions and bruises–inflicted on victim by the accused, to prevent the victim from crying or shouting for help.
- Neck: scratches, abrasions and bruises.
- Breasts: ecchymosis, bruises and nail or teeth marks.
- Arms: scratches, abrasions and bruises–resulted from forcible holding of the victim's arms by the accused, so as to prevent the victim's struggle and resistance.
- Thighs (esp. Upper and inner part): scratches, abrasions and bruises–resulted from an attempt by the accused to keep the victim's thighs apart.

Inflicted by the struggle:

- Scratches, abrasions and bruises resulting from forcible holding down of the arms by the accused, to prevent victim's struggle and resistance.

  Site: back, buttocks, arms and legs.
- Blood and semen stains–samples (scrapings) taken from vagina, vulva and thighs, are to be sent for laboratory testing.
- Pubic hairs–matted together with blood or semen
- Genitals: for evidence of violence:
- Labia majora–oedematous and tendered
- Vulva–red, abraded, bruised, oedematous and

tendered. There may be slight oozing of blood.

- Vagina–hot, dilated, abraded, bruised, oedematous and tendered.
- Hymen–ruptured with torn edges, oedematous and tendered.
- Perineum–oedematous and tendered. May be lacerated in children.
- P/V discharge of blood or pus.

Investigation: Vaginal swab and smear–for detection of spermatozoa (+ve sign) and pus cells

Urethral discharge-for detection of pus cells (gonococci).

B. Examination of the accused/s:

- Consent: written consent of the accused to be taken, or a warrant from the Magistrate or an Authorised Officer, for examination of the accused.
- Of clothes worn by the accused for evidence of struggle e.g. torn, stained of dust, blood and semen.
- Signs of struggle.
- Signs of recent intercourse:
- Abrasions of the glans penis and prepuce, esp. on the frenulum.

Medico-legal aspect:

- That whether the rape victim including wife, comes under the permissible age of consent or not ?
- That whether the consent of sexual intercourse obtained prior to actual act obtained or not ?
- That whether the consent obtained prior to actual act or afterwards ?
- That whether a man can commit rape on an alert, healthy woman ?
- That whether a man can commit rape on a sleeping woman ?

SODOMY

Definition: Is defined as an anal intercourse by a man

(active agent) with another man or woman (passive agent). Both agents (active and passive) with their consent are liable to punishment under law, while only the active agent is liable to punishment if this act is done without the consent of passive agent.

Diagnosis: Signs of sodomy on the Active agent:

- Consent: written consent of the accused to be taken, or a warrant from the Magistrate or an Authorised Officer, for examination of the accused.
- of clothes worn by the accused for evidence of struggle e.g. torn, stained of dust, blood and semen.
- Signs of struggle.
- Signs of recent intercourse:
- Abrasions of the glans penis and prepuce, esp. on the frenulum.

Signs of sodomy on the Passive agent:

- Signs of struggle (forced act without consent) e.g. scratches, abrasions, bruises or lacerations of the anus–esp. If the passive agent is a young boy/or girl
- Stains: of blood, semen or both per anus or on the cloth
- Discharge: of pus (gonorrhoea) per anus or on the cloth.

Investigation: Anal swab and smear–

for detection of spermatozoa (+ve sign) and pus cells (gonococci)

Urethral discharge-for detection of pus cells (gonococci).

Offence: Both agents (active and passive) with their consent are liable to punishment under law, while only the active agent is liable to punishment if this act is done without the consent of passive agent.

Penalty: Imprisonment, fine or both.

PREGNANCY (Medico-legal Aspect)

Diagnosis:

S/S: Presumptive, probable and positive:

Presumptive (Subjective) Signs: observed by the patient herself e.g.:

- Amenorrhea
- Morning sickness–nausea and vomiting. May be absent in some cases
- Mammary changes:
  - conscious of pricking and tingling sensations in early pregnancy (2/52),
  - feeling of fullness and enlargement–5/52 onwards
  - nipple: enlarged, erectile and darker in colour
  - areola–pigmentation during 10/52
  - extraction of colostrum–16/52 onwards.
- Abdominal changes–progressive enlargement of the abdomen, pigmentation and striae gravidarum
- Quickening–first feeling by the mother of the fetus movements in the uterus (commonly observed during 12-24 weeks. May be absent in some cases.
- Frequency of micturition–due to bladder irritation (observed commonly during early and last weeks of pregnancy).
- Nervous symptoms e.g. depravities of appetite, longings for spicy or sour Foods, temperament or peevishness.

Probable (Objective) Signs: elicited by the doctor on examination e.g.:

- Changes in Uterus size: uterus enlarges rapidly, steadily and uniformly.

  Progressive rising of fundus level, as per pregnancy progress.
- Change in Uterus consistency:
  - Rasch's sign: in early weeks, the uterus becomes soft and elastic.

- Hegar's sign: detection (6th to 10th week) by bimanual examination of a soft, compressible area between the cervix below and the elastic body of the uterus above.
- Braxton Hicks's sign: to recognise intermittent uterine contractions (the uterus growing hard and firm) passing over the uterus every 10-15 minutes, felt from 12th week onwards.
- Changes in the Cervix: softening of the cervix and its increased secretion.
- Changes in the Vagina:
  - Jacqemier's sign: blue discolouration of the vaginal mucosa due to congestion.
  - Kluge's sign: varicosity of the veins at the lower end of the vagina.
- Ballottement: tossing of the foetus inside the uterus by two methods i.e.
  Internal and external ballottement (elicited during 16th to 28th week).

Positive Signs:

- Foetal movements: felt by the mother by mid-term. Also felt on palpation and auscultation (as kicks or taps against the uterine wall)
- Foetal heart beat: detectable (faint sound) from 20th week onwards
- Uterine soufflé: soft, blowing murmur, heard on either side of the uterus, from 10th week onwards.
- Radio-diagnosis:
  - Plane X-ray Abdomen (C/I before 28th week, unless an immediate diagnosis of pregnancy is considered imperative)
  - to confirm the age of the foetus – by detecting the degree of ossification of the bones
- Ultrasound study:
  - to detect presentation and position of the foetus

- to confirm presence of twins

D/d: Early months of pregnancy to be differentiated from:

- Chronic metritis
- Fibroids – interstitial or submucosal
- Hematometra
- Spurious pregnancy–experienced by the neurotic women

Late months of pregnancy to be differentiated from:

- Uterine and Adenexal tumors

All of the presumptive and probable signs and symptoms of pregnancy can be caused by other disorders and all the clinical and pathological tests indicative of pregnancy may be positive in the absence of conception.

Investigation:

Pregnancy tests:

Biological Hormone tests: depend on the presence of chorionic gonadotrophic hormones in the urine. These tests are performed on the mouse, rabbit and sheep.

- **Aschheim–Zondek test:** depends on the recognition of the presence of chorionic gonadotrophic hormone in the pregnant woman's urine.

  Positive results obtained as early as 2/52 after conception.

  Method: 0.5 c.c. of pregnant woman's urine (morning) is injected daily for three days into an immature female mice, killed on the 4th day.

  Result: the ovaries are examined for any congestion, enlargement and rapid luteinisation (Hemorrhagic) of the ovaries.

  Disadvantage: the test takes a long time (4-5 days).

Fallacies: test also positive in:

- Ectopic gestation
- Hydatidiform mole
- Tumor: Chorion-carcinoma

- **Friedman's test:** a modified test being performed on virgin female rabbits.

  Advantage: the test takes a short time (36 hrs.)

  Method: 10 c.c. of pregnant woman's urine (morning) are injected IV into an immature female rabbit, twice at 12 hrs. interval, killed on the 3rd day.

  Result: the ovaries are examined for any congestion, enlargement and rapid luteinisation (Hemorrhagic) of the ovaries.

  Advantage: the test takes a short time (36 hrs.).

Hogben's test: urine is injected into a female Xenopus toad.

Result: Positive test–the toad ovulates within 25 hrs. and visible egg production occurs.

Male-toad test: urine is injected into a male toad and fluid is then extracted from the cloaca.

Result: Positive test–sperms are found in the cloacal fluid, and the result available in 2-4 hrs. Time, and the test is 98 per cent reliable.

Clinical Pregnancy tests (highly accurate):

- Estrogen withdrawal bleeding test:
- Estradiol 2 mg and Progesterone 20 mg IM: bleeding occurring within 5 days rules out pregnancy.

Immunodiagnostic Pregnancy tests (Positive from 40th day of LMP):

- Hemagglutination inhibition test (Pregnosticon).

  Method: human chorionic gonadotrophin injected into a rabbit may result in the production of antibodies. The pregnant woman's urine (inhibits the reaction between antibody and red cells) is added to specially treated sheep's red cells and such rabbit serum.

  Result: - clumping–indicates the woman is not pregnant,

  - No clumping–woman is pregnant

  Advantage: the test takes a very short time (2 hrs.).

- **Agglutination inhibition test (Gravindex):**

  Method: similar to above test, except latex particles with adsorbed HCG used in place of red cells. The pregnant woman's urine is added to HCG antigen (latex particles) and such rabbit serum.

  Result: - clumping – indicates the woman is not pregnant,

  - No clumping – woman is pregnant

  Advantage: the test takes a very short time (3 mts.)

Medico-legal aspect:

- That in case of alleged illegitimacy, paternity of the child may have to be determined by: consideration of the resemblance of the child's features with the said father, reported in the case ; blood grouping and DNA matching of the alleged father and child.
- That a pregnant woman – demands compensation from a person, alleged to be the father of the child.
- That a woman after her husband's death, feigns to be pregnant, in order to be entitled to the estate left over by her deceased husband on behalf of the prospective heir.
- That a pregnant woman can claim greater compensation in case of her husband's death in an aeroplane or railway accident.
- That a pregnant woman, files a case in the Court for breach of marriage, against a person
- That in cases of attempted Criminal abortion or Infanticide, esp. When forced on a woman by a person (s).
- That the motive of alleged suicide or murder may be suspected in case of a pregnant widow or an unmarried girl.
- That an unmarried woman, a widow or a woman deserted by her husband, desires to absolve herself from the alleged charges of adultery levelled against her for her pregnancy.

- That a pregnant woman cannot be sentenced to rigorous imprisonment or condemned to death, until she delivers the child and the child becomes 6/12 old.

  In India: recognition of animation is accepted, the moment the spermatozoa unites with the ovum

  In UK: recognition of animation is accepted, from 'quickening' onwards.
- That a husband files a divorce case (disputed legitimacy) on the ground:
  - that the child born is not his child (born after an average period of gestation i.e. 280 days)
  - that the child born is not his child (born within a short time of the marriage or within a short time of the couple living together, after years of separation).
- That in case of disputed legitimacy, a woman claims a child born after the death of her husband, had been conceived by the said late-husband.
- That a woman allegedly claims a child (born long after husband's death) to be legitimate.
- That in case of disputed legitimacy, paternity may be proved by means of:
- Blood grouping, and DNA testing of the alleged father
- That the child may be a suppositious child (allegedly claimed by a woman as her own, though in reality not belonging to her) accepted, the Dddb.

DELIVERY (Medico-legal Aspect)

Medico-legal aspect:

- That in case of disputed legitimacy
- That in case of feigned delivery of the child
- That in case of alleged criminal abortion and infanticide
- That in case of alleged concealment of child's birth
- That in case of disputed chastity

Diagnosis: Recent delivery:

In a living (primipara) woman:

- Appearance: composed, languished, sunken eyes, pigmented eye-lids
- Tachycardia
- Temperature: slightly raised.

Note: In a living (multipara) woman: - Above said signs may be absent.

- Odour: the body smells of a puerperal odour.
- Breasts: full, enlarged, firm, containing colostrum/or milk.

  Nipples: turgid.

  Areola: dark.
- Abdomen: soft, lax and flabby, skin – wrinkled with marks i.e. linea albicantes
- Uterus:
  - Post-delivery: a flabby mass palpable, extending up to umbilicus
  - Post-delivery (after 2-3 days): a hard mass (of cricket ball size) palpable above symphysis pubis (up to 2/52)
  - Uterine contractions (intermittent)–normally palpable up to 5th day.
- Cervix: soft, patulous, lips torn/or lacerated transversally.
- Internal os: normally closes within 24 hrs.
- External os: admits two fingers for few days, then one finger for 1/52 and closes in 2/52.

  Note: in a multipara, the external os is round with a central dimple.
- Vulva: edematous, may be bruised and lacerated.
- Perineum: edematous and may be lacerated.
- Labia majora: edematous, congested, may be bruised and tendered
- P/V: lochial discharge of peculiar odour

In a dead woman: Besides above-said signs:

- Autopsy findings are:

- Uterus: enlarged, flabby, wrinkled, dark coloured Intra-uterine placental site (placental sinuses).
- Ovaries and fallopian tubes: edematous and congested, intra-ovarian corpus luteum

Remote delivery:

In a living woman:

- Breasts: enlarged, lax and tender

  Nipples: erect

  Areolas: dark
- Abdomen: lax with marks i.e. linea albicantes
- Cervix: ragged
- Vagina: patulous, gaping and no rugae
- Labias: majora and minora separated apart
- Perineum: lacerated

In a dead woman: besides above-said signs:

- Uterus: enlarged, big cavity, thickened walls and heavier

ABORTION or MISCARRIAGE (Medico-legal Aspect)

Medico-legal aspect:

- That the aborted woman was actually pregnant or not, or
- That the woman was quick with the child or not
- That an attempt to abortion was resorted to or not
- That the consent of woman was taken before the act, or not
- That woman's death was due to abortion, or its attempt
- That child's death was due to abortion, or its attempt.

Definition: Is defined as the termination of pregnancy at any time and by any means prior to the attainment of viability (sufficient development of the foetus) by the foetus i.e. prior to 28th week. Also called a miniature labour.

Types: Spontaneous, Induced and criminal (septic):

SPONTANEOUS ABORTION: due to:

- Traumatic–RSA, falls
- CVS disorders–Hypertension, Rheumatic heart disease, CHF
- Diabetes mellitus
- Endocrinal disorders – Thyrotoxicosis
- Infective – viral, venereal
- Undernourishment
- Age - advanced
- Metabolic – Cervical cancer
- Chemical toxins

INDUCED ABORTION:

- By Authorised Medical Practitioners
- By Unauthorised persons illegally and under unhygienic conditions

Indications: Legally:

- Medical complications–threatening life of mother
- Genetic disorders of the fetus
- Psychological–lunatic mother
- Family planning: opted by the married women/ couple
- Rape case
- Minor girl
- Illegally:

  Unfair medical practice–monetary factor (to earn money)

Methods: During 1st trimester: Surgical methods e.g. D&C or D&E

Medical methods

During 2nd trimester: Surgical methods e.g. Hysterotomy

Medical methods

CRIMINAL (SEPTIC) ABORTION:

Definition: Is defined as an expulsion of the product of conception, at any stage of gestation, by an unauthorised person (s) illegally and under unhygienic conditions

Motives:
- To avoid shame and disgrace:

  That to get rid of the child following illicit intercourse in following cases:
  - Pregnant unmarried girls or women,
  - Pregnant widows, deserted by their husbands (living separately)
- To control family size:
  - Pregnant married women, as a family planning measure
- To grab family property/estate:
  - That an alleged heir to the property of her husband, may procure the abortion of the woman, thereby declaring her as issueless

Methods: General:
- That by resorting to stressful exercises e.g. cycling, horse riding, running, jumping, dancing or lifting of heavy weights
- That by resorting to kicks or blows on the abdomen
- That by knidding or firmly massaging of the abdomen, or by tightly compressing the lower abdomen
- That by resorting to bleeding, by applying leeches to the vulva, perineum or inner aspects of upper parts of thighs.

Local:
- Induction of labour by the Rupture of membranes by means of:
  - That by Introducing a uterine sound, catheter, rod, handle bar or a stick, into the uterus, by rupturing the membranes
- introducing abortifacient drugs (ergot, quinine, posterior pituitary extract)
- introducing irritants (lead, mercury, arsenic, caustics)
- introducing hormones (estrogens) by IV or IM routes

- Introducing electric current–to initiate sudden uterine contractions to expel the products.

S/S:
- Status: commonly unmarried girls or widows
- Physic: unhealthy, weak or mentally unsound girls/women
- Violence marks: on the abdomen and thighs
- Foreign bodies: parts of alleged abortion instruments e.g. sticks, handle bars etc. left inside the vagina or uterus
- Genitals:
- Vagina and cervix: bruises, abrasions or lacerations,
- Infection: fever, pain abdomen, foul smelling discharge per vaginum

Rules for examination:

Pre-examination requirements (essential):
- That warrant (orders) from the Magistrate or designated officer
- That Identification (ID) of the woman
- That written consent of the woman
- That presence of the husband or a female attendant
- That undressing of the woman should be done by the woman herself or by the accompanying female attendant.

INFANTICIDE (Medico-legal Aspect)

Medico-legal aspect:
- That the offence is committed to get rid of an illegitimate child
- That infanticide is legally considered as murder (homicide)
- That the offence is punishable under Section 302 I.P.C.
- That penalty is death sentence, or life imprisonment with fine.

Definition: Is defined as the killing (murder-Homicidal) of a newly born child.

Offence: In India: within 15 days
In UK: 12 months.

Motives: Illegitimacy

- To avoid shame and disgrace: that to get rid of the child following illicit intercourse in following cases:
- Pregnant unmarried girls or women,
- Pregnant widows, deserted by their husbands (living separately).

Parental poverty:

- Pregnant married women (esp. in poverty) for a family planning measure.

Inheritance:

- To grab family property/estate: that an alleged heir to the property of her husband, may procure the abortion of the woman, thereby declaring her as issueless.

Fanatism:

- To resort to illegal religious fanatism e.g.
  - Killing the infant with a sharp weapon (sword etc.)
  - Killing the infant, under influence of religious fanatics for purposes e.g. curing a chronic illness, to ward off influence of evil spirits, to promote business, to achieve success in examinations/job interviews
  - Throwing the infant in water (river, gutter or well)
  - Throwing the infant in front of a running train or religious vehicle
  - Throwing the infant from roof tops, mountains.

Sex preference:

- To kill the female infant because of parent's poverty
- To kill the male infant by an enemy of the parents (to take revenge).

Examination:

Dead body of the Infant:

- To ascertain the age at birth and after birth: by measuring the length and weight of the dead body

  Hiss's formula: Length in inches = double the number of months

  Average weight of a new born is 3-3.5 kg
- To ascertain the age of fetus in-utero: viable or not
- To ascertain whether still born or dead born.

  Still born (born dead): born after 28 weeks of gestation, without any signs of life and did not cry. Commonly found in an illegitimate pregnancy.

  Etiology: Immaturity

  Dead born: signs of mummification and maceration:

  Mummification: dry and shrivelled due to deficient blood and liquor amnii

  Maceration: edematous, skin peeled off, peculiar smelling
- To ascertain the state of the umbilical cord
- To ascertain whether born full term
- To ascertain whether the child born alive (as per witness's evidence and autopsy report) and that:
- how long it was alive ?
- what caused the death ?
- since when he died ?
- To ascertain the maturity of the child
- To ascertain whether the child belongs to the alleged woman.

Autopsy:
- To ascertain whether the child was born alive,
- To ascertain the cause of death,
- To ascertain the intra-uterine age of the fetus.

Viability:
- A viable child is one, who may survive (independent existence) apart from mother.
- Viability age: 180 to 210 days (3-6 months)

SURROGACY (Medico-legal Aspect)

Medico-legal aspect:

: - Commercial exploitation of poor, helpless persons, by the companies.
- Health hazards, faced by the poor, unhealthy, unaware surrogate mothers.
- Violation of agreement between the surrogate mother and the parents pursuing surrogacy.

Definition: Is defined as the procedure through which a couple or a person can motivate another woman to lend her womb to bear and deliver a child. This process starts by placing a fresh or frozen sperm clinically in the uterus of the surrogate mother (a woman who has a baby for another woman who is unable to give birth, and then gives her the baby after it is born).

Allowed: In following Countries (Alphabetically):

Argentina, Australia, Belgium, Brazil, Canada, China, Colombia, Cyprus, Czech Republic, Denmark, Egypt, England, France, Germany, Hong Kong, India, Indonesia, Ireland, Israel, Italy, Japan, Kazakhstan, Korea Republic of, Lebanon, Luxembourg, Malaysia, Mexico, Netherland, New Caledonia, New Zealand, Norway, Papua New Guinea, Peru, Phillipines, Russian Federation, Saudi Arabia, Scotland, Singapore, Slovenia, Spain, Sweedon, Swaziland, Taiwan, Turkey, United States, Venezuela, Wales.

VOX-POPULI:

OPPOSING SURROGACY:

Public: - ASU students debate pros and cons of egg donation:

Many companies target students with offers of earning thousands of dollars for donating something your body produces naturally, that some say the lucrative market for egg donation brings with it certain health risks that need to be considered. (2012-03-01T06:43:05Z).

- Surrogacy in India: According to a survey conducted in 2011, pregnancy outsourcing is a 20 billion rupee industry in India (Amy Gold).
- Women's rights being violated in India's surrogacy Capital:

  A study by the New Delhi based Centre for Social Research (CSR) has pointed to a grave violation of the woman's rights at India's surrogacy hub. (2012-03-02T17:10)
- Surrogacy Motherhood Ethical or Commercial:

  CSR calls on Centre to clear ART Bill to protect woman acting as surrogate mothers (2012-03002T17:10).
- Male-headed households: "all surrogate mothers" in Anand belonged to male-headed households (Anand in Gujarat).

FAVOURING SURROGACY:

Public: Sisters create extra-special first with a small pink bundle of joy. 2012-02-29T

12:32:14Z: The Canberra Times:

The birth, laboured by Mrs. Chiodo's sister Bernadette Marfre, 36, was the first by a surrogate mother in Victoria, since the law changed two yrs. ago to make surrogacy available Victorians with a legal structure to support it.

Agencies: Bill Handle, Director of Centre for Surrogate Parenting (CSP):

- Become a parent:
- Become a Surrogate:
- Gay Parenting:

Joan Barnes, President of TASC:

Surrogacy should only be entered into with the understanding that all the screening, emotional support, medical, legal, and communication guidelines are in place and handled by professional trained in their specific field whether it is done independently with the help of an agency. In fact, many surrogacy agencies offer services which may be purchased on an "a la carte" basis for couples who already have located their surrogates. These services may include but are not limited to screening and psychological evaluation of all parties, medical screening, background checks, local services for contracts and birth certificate issuance procedures etc. Or, you may seek to locate and hire each of the above disciplin independently, assembling your own surrogacy team to assist you with the process. In any event, assure yourself that you are in compliance with the applicable laws in the State and Country where you implement your arrangement.

If you chose this "road less travelled" of surrogacy, please seek guidance and support from experts who can make this a happy and successful experience for all.

(Joan Barnes, mother of two children born through gestational surrogacy via independent assurance).

TASC–Online Support:

Grouping:

- Egg donors only (ED-L): Is a unique group that offers support for women who are currently undergoing egg donation, considering donating or have donated in the past (231 members till 03/03/2012).
- Moms via Egg donation (MVED-L): Is an online support group for women, who are attempting to or have already become mothers via Egg Donation.
  (493 members).
- Parents Pursuing Surrogacy (PPS-L): Is a support group for couples, who are pursuing surrogacy to build their family after experiencing infertility. Parents who have children via surrogacy are also welcome to join (272 members).
- Embryo Adoption (EA-L): Is a support group just for people who are interpreted in building their families via donated embryos (140 members).

- Fertility (F-L): Is a support group that offers the latest information and support for women who are 40+ and attempting to build or add to their family.

  (367 members).
- Parents through Assisted Reproduction Technology (ART): Is a group of people who have come together to share parenting advise and discuss the issues related to raising children born via assisted reproduction (146 members).
- Surrogate Mothers only (SM-L): Is a unique support group only for women who are surrogate to mothers both as traditional seven gestational surrogates, and for women who are considering becoming one for another couple.

  (184 members).
- Parents via Sperm donation (PVSD-L): Is a online support group for couples who are considering using or who have used donor sperm to build their family.

  (154 members).
- Adoption (ADOPT-L): Is for people who are interested in adoption, whether they are potential and/or parents via adoption, both mothers and adoptees. The list is jointly supported by the communities of adopting. (119 members).
- Pregnant At Last Society (PALS-L): Is a support group for women who have become pregnant after a history of infertility with use of donor egg, donor embryos, or surrogacy. (207 members).

  Jagajeet Singh, Director in-charge of a Surrogacy Home:
- Money paid for the delivery
- Money paid for the Surrogate mother's food, lodging and medical care.

ORDER A LA CARTE:

Surrogacy in India has finally been corporatised, moving out of small mom and pop clinics ruled by the buyer's market to companies that offer fixed prices to surrogate for each eventuality and ensure medicare and delivery at an empanelled multi-specialty hospital, such as Max Super-Specialty, Sir Ganga Ram Hospital, and the Fortis Group of Hospitals. Apart from getting paid and treatment costs, surrogates are put up in a home where their boarding and lodging is taken care of.

Example: Sheikh is one of six women living away from their families in one such surrogacy home in West Delhi's Janakpuri, run by Wyzax Surrogacy.

Consultants (WSC), which offers all surrogacy solutions, including a home for the surrogates, legal consultancy, IVF treatment and delivery.

Vivek Kohli, Director, Wyzax Surrogacy Consultants (WSC): "Having the women live together helps us monitor their health, nutrition and hygiene aspects more closely. WSC diversified from medical tourism to concentrate on surrogacy two years. ago, and thereby established first surrogacy home in Delhi, and within 18 months, ten couples have taken babies home, and have a database of more than 80 surrogates, and an average of fifty queries a month, majority (90 per cent) of which are from foreigners.

Jagatjeet Singh, Director in-charge of a Surrogacy Home:

- Money paid for the delivery.
- Money paid for the Surrogate mother's food, lodging and medical care.

"The surrogates are grouped together, depending on their cultural and eating preferences (vegetarian or non-vegetarian). Their families may visit them whenever they like and the women may go home, although home visits being discouraged during the first trimester (critical phase of pregnancy)".

Apart from Janakpuri, Wyzax Surrogacy Services, have a home in Loni and another near Sir Ganga

Ram Hospital, and single room homes in Hari Nagar for women, who prefer to stay with their families.

Living off on Rent:

Like Sheikh, all the five other women at the Janakpuri home are married, with children, an essential pre-requisite for signing up as children, are a sign of "proven fertility":

- Sushma Ravi (name changed), 24, has two children, and is residing here with her extended family's blessing. Everyone from her joint family, supported her, for this good deed (daan/charity) to help someone in need. The surrogate mother also gets payment for her children's education.
- Parveen: 30 yrs. old, has been surrogating, in order to support her husband, a taxi-driver, in setting up business (getting their own taxi), and to provide better education and life to their children.
- Parvesh: Life in the surrogate home is comfortable e.g. sitting, chatting and watching TV, whole day.
- Sushma: Will not miss the baby are carrying (baby's not mind to keep).

India's, Rent-A-Womb Bill:

Assisted Reproductive Technology (Regulation) Bill and Rules, 2008:

- That the Bill legalises commercial surrogacy, stating that the surrogate mother can get "monetary compensation" for carrying the child in addition to health-care and treatment expenses during pregnancy. The surrogate mother has to relinquish all parental rights over the child once the amount is transferred. Birth certificates will be in name of genetic parents.
- That the surrogate mother should be between 21 and 45 yrs.
- That no surrogate mother can undergo an embryo transplant more than three times.

- That single parents can also have children using a surrogate mother.
- That all foreigners seeking infertility treatment in India, have to first register with their respective embassy. They will have to disclose/state, with whom the child should be entrusted to, in case the genetic parent dies.

PSYCHIATRIC DISORDERS (Medico-legal Aspect)

INSANITY (syn. EMOTIONAL and MENTAL DISORDERS)

Definition: Is defined legally as an insane person considered to be incapable of moral judgment and of managing his property and affairs.

Types:
- Congenital: Amentia - Idiocy, imbecility, cretinism
- Traumatic: Head injury, Brain trauma
- Inflammatory: Encephalitis, General paralysis of insane (Syphilis of CNS), Intracranial infections, systemic infections
- Endocrinal: Diabetic
- Degenerative: Senile dementia, Alzheimer's disease
- Neurotic: Anxiety, phobic, hysterical, Acute depression, suicide, mania
- Psychotic: Schizophrenia
- Functional: Testamentary (will), criminal responsibility
- Organic Brain Syndrome: Illusions, Delusions, Hallucinations, Obsessions, Impulses
- Feigned insanity
- Alcoholism: Alcohol abuse
- Drug abuse

Medico-legal aspect:
- That whether the person is insane or not ?
- That whether the insanity is true or feigned ?

AMENTIA (syn. MENTAL RETARDATION)

Definition: Is defined as mental deficiency.

Types:
- Idiocy
- Imbecility
- Cretinism

Idiocy: - a congenital state of defective mental development.

Diagnosis: - state of being an idiot
- devoid of will power, initiative power, memory, emotion
- unable to express himself/herself, but may cry or make gestures
- unable to protect himself/herself.

Imbecility: a congenital state of defective mental development.

Diagnosis: - state of being non-idiot
- unable to manage his/her own affairs
- dangerous to society

Cretinism: - a congenital state of defective mental development.

Diagnosis: - state of being an idiot
- deformities or arrested growth.

Medico-legal aspect:
- That whether the person is insane or not ?
- That whether the insanity is true or feigned ?

DEMENTIA (SENILE DEMENTIA)

Definition: Is defined as a disorder affecting the brain and memory, and gradually the patient loses the ability to think and behave normally. It is the progressive dementing illness in which the histological findings are the same as those in Alzheimer's disease.

Etiology: Traumatic - head injury
Infective
Metabolic
Vascular
Degenerative
Neoplastic - cerebral tumors.

Diagnosis: Age–disease of elderly e.g. usually begins over the age of 70
Sex–females > in males
Intellectual ability – markedly declined
Amnesia - memory loss
Delusions – depressive/manic mood

Depression – transient

Anxiety, Irritability

Hallucinations

Epileptic fits

Death–due to infection or general vegetative decay.

Investigation: CBC

Blood sugar

Blood cholesterol

Urine analysis

X-ray skull

EEG.

Medico-legal aspect:

- That whether the person is insane or not ?
- That whether the insanity is true or feigned ?

ALZHEIMER'S DISEASE (DEMENTIA)

Definition: Is a clinical syndrome characterised by acquired loss of cognitive and emotional abilities (loss of memory and cognitive functioning) that impairs with daily living activities, and as the illness progresses, it results in various behavioural and psychiatric symptoms. It is an elderly disease and that prevalence increases exponentially with age. More specifically the prevalence doubles with every five-year increase in age.

Etiology: Traumatic - head injury

Infective-cerebral infection, tuberculosis, syphilis

Vascular - arteriosclerosis of cerebral arteries

Malnutrition – deficiency of vitamin B12 and folic acid, cholinergic

Alcohol abuse

Endocrinal disorders – diabetes mellitus, estrogen depletion

Emotional – stress, anxiety, shock

Toxic – amyloidosis, glutamate

Metabolic disorders–brain tumors.

Risk factors: Senility, female sex, less education, family history of dementia, Down's syndrome, stroke, hypertension, heart disease, hyperlipidaemia, Thyroid disorders, hydrocephalus.

Protective factors:

Anti-oxidants e.g. vitamin E, C, turmeric etc.

Estrogen supplements

Anti-inflammatory drugs e.g. NSAIDs

Education and social status e.g. higher education and healthy status.

Diagnosis: Age > 60 yrs.

Loss of memory and inability to co-ordinates ideas with words.

Impaired daily living activities

Behavioural and psychiatric disturbances

Family history of dementia

Malnourishment

Investigation: Complete hemogram, ESR

Serological tests for syphilis:

- Complement fixation (Wassermann)
- Flocculation (VDRL)

Serum proteins, serum cholesterol, serum electrolytes

BUN, blood glucose

CSF examination.

Medico-legal aspect:

- That whether the person is insane or not ?
- That whether the insanity is true or feigned ?

ACCUTE DEPRESSION

Definition: It is defined as a feeling of sadness, that makes one feels extremely unhappy about a hopeless future, so that he/she can not live a normal life.

Etiology: Primary depression due to endogenous events:

- restlessness, feelings of guilt, loneliness and hopelessness, anorexia, loss of weight and insomnia

Secodary depression due to:

- organic brain syndromes, schizophrenia, drug reactions

Reactive depression due to exogenous events:

- Stress, anger, guilt, loss of a person, job or status, ignoring someone or something.

Diagnosis: According to Diagnostic and Statistical Manual of Psychiatric Disorders (DSM) diagnosis of a major depressive disorder requires presence of at least 5 out of following 13 signs/symptoms present for 2/52:

- Presence of depressed/or irritable mood nearly every day for most of the days–mild sadness to deep gloom
- Markedly diminished interest or pleasure in activities enjoyed earlier
- Anorexia
- Insomnia - loss of sleep or decreased/increased sleep
- Psychomotor agitation or retardation
- Lethargy - fatigue/or loss of energy–getting easily fatigued
- Feelings of worthlessness, hopelessness or inappropriate guilt
- Lack of satisfaction
- Loss of libido
- Impaired concentration-loss of concentration or indecisiveness
- Loss of weight
- Recurrent thinking about contemplating suicide or death
- Reluctance to speak.

Medico-legal aspect:

- That whether the person is insane or not ?
- That whether the insanity is true or feigned ?

SUICIDE

Definition: A possible danger in depression and the psychiatrist should make a careful assessment of this risk e.g. a broken home in childhood, a depressed parent with fears of harming his/her child. Is a psychiatric emergency and should be admitted to the hospital immediately.

Etiology: An intentional or voluntary determination to end one's life. Willingness to die initiates within the person. Presence of a known or hidden reason forces one to end one's life alternatives, other choices/or options – being not considered prior suicide.

Risk factors:

Age: suicide rates increase with age

Sex: male – more prone to commit suicide

Marital status: single, never married, divorcee or widowed

Occupation: unemployed

Psychiatric patients

Past history of suicidal attempt

Schizophrenia

Alcohol dependence

Family: unresponsive, isolated.

Diagnosis: Past history of suicidal attempt/attempts

Suicidal thoughts, intent, plans

Depression.

Medico-legal aspect:

- That whether the person is insane or not ?
- That whether the insanity is true or feigned ?

ACUTE MANIA

Definition: Is defined as a very strong feeling for something/someone, and for that he behaves in a stupid or dangerous way. There may be brief periods of depression lasting for only few seconds. These patients are overactive, overtalkative and overcheerful. They start many projects but never manage to complete them.

Etiology: Unknown

Excitement, stress, depression, surgery or infection–aggravate mania.

Diagnosis: Common in young adults

Attacks are often recurrent, and last for a few weeks or a few months

Flight of ideas–based on chance association including similar sounds

Irritability, irresponsibility

Elevated mood–marked cheerfulness to wild Hilary, hallucinations

Depression–very short period

Exhaustion

Intercurrent infection.

Investigation: CBC

Serum electrolytes

Renal function tests.

Medico-legal aspect:

- That whether the person is insane or not ?
- That whether the insanity is true or feigned ?

ACUTE SCHIZOPHRENIA

Definition: Is a serious mental disorder characterised by abnormal thinking, disturbed emotions, and disruption of communication links with others, unbased on real happenings around.

Etiology: Unknown.

Diagnosis: Agitation, unhappiness, frustration, disappointment, emotional imbalance:

- Thought disorder: normal steady progress of thought may be interrupted and the train of thought then starts again on a new track.
- Formal thought disorder: Patient is able to form concepts and make generalisations but includes too much and his thought is illogical. Thus, unusual combinations of ideas occur.
- Perceptual disorders: Presence of hallucinations (voices, visual, pain, touch, pressure and sexual sensations), which are perceptions without a relevant object in the external world.
- Emotional disorders: Depression, anxiety, elation, bewilderness. There is change of emotional expression.

- Motor and Behavioural disorders: Experience of passivity in which the patient has the experience that his/her thoughts, actions or emotions are not his own, but they are forced upon him/her by some external power.

Medico-legal aspect:

- That whether the person is insane or not ?
- That whether the insanity is true or feigned ?

EPILEPTIC (SEIZURE) INSANITY

Definition: A brain seizure or convulsion is characterised by an abrupt onset of transient alterations in the cortical electrical discharge, manifested clinically by a change in level of consciousness or by a motor, sensory, psychic, or autonomic symptom.

Etiology:

Organic brain disease

Head injury

Cerebrovascular accidents (CVA)

Brain infections

Hypoglycemia

Hypocalcemia

Uremia

Intoxications.

Types:

Partial or focal seizures:

- Simple partial seizure
- Complex partial (Psychomotor) seizures
- Secondary generalised seizures

Primary generalised seizures:

- Grand mal (Tonic-clonic) seizures
- Petit mal (Absence) seizures
- Febrile seizures
- Myoclonic seizure
- Atonic seizure

Status epilepticus (Recurrent seizures with/without intervals).

Diagnosis: Partial or focal seizures:

A. Simple partial seizure:

Consciousness: fully preserved during seizure

Seizure: may be motor, sensory, autonomic or psychic in type

Motor activity: twitching of one part of the body,

Sensory symptoms: paresthesia, vertigo, hallucinations

Autonomic and psychic symptoms: fear, anger, hallucinations

Jacksonian seizures: clonic convulsions in thumb/or greater toe, mouth's corner, and may soon involve the whole side (generalised)

EEG: regular spike discharges with intervening irregular discharges.

B. Complex partial (Psychomotor) seizures:

Consciousness–impaired, symptomology is complex

Aura: unusual sensation (smell of burning rubber, wood), abrupt emotional stress, illusions, hallucination

Motor activity disturbances: automatisms

Amnesia: for events taking place during seizure

EEG: unilateral/or bilateral spikes, sharp/or slow waves discharges.

C. Secondary generalised partial seizures:

Consciousness: loss of consciousness

Motor activity: convulsive

Aura: twitching, eye deviation, aphasia

EEG: shows presence of a postictal focal neurological deficit.

Primary Generalised seizures:

A. Grand mal (Tonic-clonic seizure):

Consciousness: sudden loss of consciousness

Aura: A typical aura may herald a major seizure e.g. spasm of a limb, turning of head and eyes, numbness, due to an irritating focus in the opposite prefrontal region

Tonic phase: contraction of respiratory muscles, followed by:

- Clonic convulsions of whole body

- Fall to the ground and emit a cry
- Frothing at the mouth
- Tongue bitting, bruises
- Loss of bladder and bowel control
- Pupils dilated, deep reflexes absent
- Dyspnea and cyanosis

EEG: Tonic phase: shows low voltage fast activity

Clonic phase: shows bursts of sharp waves with slow waves during pauses.

B. Petit mal (Absence seizures):

Consciousness: sudden, brief losses of consciousness, without loss of postural control. Seizures last for few seconds. Consciousness returns as suddenly as it was lost

Motor activity: without any convulsive motor activity

EEG: shows brief 3 Hz spike and wave discharges

C. Febrile seizures:

Age–infancy and early childhood

S/S–convulsive movements with fever

EEG: shows spasms and hypoarrhythmia

D. Myoclonic seizure:

Consciousness: fully preserved during seizure

Motor activity: convulsive movement–sudden and brief, involve part/or whole body

EEG: shows polyspike and wave discharges/or sharp and slow waves.

E. Atonic seizure:

Consciousness–briefly impaired and without any post-ictal confusion

Motor activity: postural muscle tone – sudden and brief

EEG: shows polypikes and slow waves.

Status epilepticus:

Prolonged/or repetitive seizures without a period of recovery between attacks – may occur with all forms of seizures, frequently of serious import.

Comatosed patients apt to become exhausted, hyperthermic and may die

EEG: shows polyspike and wave discharges/or sharp and slow waves.

Investigation: EEG

Skull X-rays

CSF analysis

Blood glucose and calcium

Brain scan.

Medico-legal aspect:

- That whether the person is insane or not ?
- That whether the insanity is true or feigned ?

Will (syn. TESTAMENTARY CAPACITY):

Definition: Is defined as the capacity of a person to make a valid will. A will is considered as the last act of giving gift or properties to others by a person before his/her death.

Medico-legal aspect:

Criteria:

- He/she must be a major.
- He/she must be fully conscious and sane, at the time of executing the will.
- He/she must fully understood the implications of his action.
- He/she must have complete knowledge of his/her assets (properties etc.).
- He/she must execute the will, in the presence of at least two persons including one of them being a medical person, both of these witnesses must attest the executed will.

An insane person may execute the will during lucid interval.

The will is considered invalid under following circumstances:

- Executed under pressure/influence
- Extreme age and poor health (incapable of understanding the will)
- An insane person
- Fully drunk or under drug influence.

CRIMINAL RESPONSIBILITY

Definition: Is legally defined as the liability of a person for his/her act of omission, and that a person at the age of discretion is sane and accountable for acts and deeds, until and unless the contrary is proved. The onus of proving rests upon the person putting up the plea of insanity.

Medico-legal aspect:

- In general a person is responsible for a criminal act done by him/her,
- Exception:
- A child < 7 yrs. of age
- A child 7- 12 yrs. of age – may be liable with an offence (to be decided by the Magistrate)
- Lunatics (except during lucid interval)
- An intoxicated person.

ORGANIC BRAIN SYNDROME (OBS):

Definition: Organic brain syndrome include delirium, confusional states, and clouded consciousness.

Diagnosis: Cognitive impairment:

- disorientation,
- impaired sensation and perception,
- Impaired capacity for recall and recent memory,
- impaired thinking and logical reasoning.

Conative impairment

Types: Illusion, Delusion, Hallucination, Obsession, Delirium, Impulse, and Lucid interval.

ILLUSION

Definition: Is defined as a false sense-impression of something actually present.

Illusions are mostly visual, but may be audible or olfactory.

Diagnosis:
- A rope may be thought to be a snake
- An object (hanging overcoat) may be thought to be a ghost in semi-dark

- A fire-cracker may be audible as a fire arm shot
- A cellar air may be smelt of a grave.

Medico-legal aspect:

- That in illusion false belief can be removed by proving the falsity or absurdity of the same.

DELUSION

Definition: Is defined as a false belief in something that has a real existence, but the belief is false to the fact. The delusion persists even after the falsity is clearly explained.

Medico-legal aspect:

- That in delusion false belief cannot be removed by any amount of proof or argument.

HALLUCINATION

Definition: Is defined as a vivid perception, while someone is awake of something that is non-existent in reality. Hallucinations are mostly visual, but may be audible, tactile, olfactory or gustatory.

Medico-legal aspect:

- That in hallucination, there is no object present
- That in hallucination, there is mainly a false belief in connection with any of the special sense.

OBSESSION

Definition: Is defined as an extreme, unhealthy interest in something, or worry about something, that stops a person from thinking about anything else. There are ideas (constant or frequent) due to some irresistible or impulse in the mind of a person, who is aware of the absurdity of the same. The person is unable to drive them away from the mind.

Example:

- A person repeatedly pulls down the lock, to make sure the lock is actually locked, after locking with the key.
- A person locks the door, but after sometime inspects this, to make sure the door is locked.

Medico-legal aspect:

That whether the person is suffering from obsessive neurosis ?

- That whether the person is sane or insane ?

DELIRIUM

Definition: Is defined as an acute mental disorder characterised by clouding of consciousness i.e. the patient is excited, restless, confused, disorientated, visually hallucinated and very frightened. These delusions may become so aggravated that the patient underestimate the environment and tries to escape from his supposed persecutors and and in haste may jump out of a window and accidentally kills/or injures himself/herself.

Medico-legal aspect:

- That whether the person suffering from mental disorder (delirium) ?
- That whether the offence committed–accidental?

IMPULSE

Definition: Is defined as a sudden strong irresistible desire to perform something, without any motive or thinking about the consequences of the actions.

Example:
- Suicidal and homicidal
- Sexual
- Kleptomania (impulse to steal)
- Pyromania (impulse to set fire)

Medico-legal aspect:

- That whether the person having above-said impulses is suffering from acute mania, ementia or epilepsy ?

LUCID INTERVAL

Definition: Is defined as a temporary period (time of sanity in madness) of returning to normal mental form, and may occur during the course of a mental disorder.

Example:

- An insane person may make a will during this lucid interval.

- Dying declaration of a person with head injury, may be recorded during this lucid interval.

Medico-legal aspect:

- That whether a person recording his will, is absolutely normal or not?
- That whether the criminal has committed the offence in a normal condition or not ?

FEIGNED INSANITY (syn. ASSUMED INSANITY)

Definition: Is defined as an insanity, whereby a person feigns insanity with a motive.

Motive: Civil case:

- A person feigns insanity in order to avoid any contract or business transaction
- Army and Police officials often feign insanity in order to justify their leave or resignation (to avoid harsh duties) when not permitted to do so.

Criminal case:

- A criminal feigns insanity to escape penalty
- A Medical officer – may be summoned to declare whether a person is insane or not.

D/d: True insanity and a feigned insanity may be differentiated (Table 2.12):

- by observing the person for a period not more than 2/52, or
- under the orders of the Magistrate, may be detained for up to a period of 30 days (period of observation of the signs and symptoms, by the Medical Officer, daily at different and odd hrs.).

TABLE 2.12: TRUE INSANITY v/s FEIGNED INSANITY

Factors	***True Insanity***	***Feigned Insanity***
Motive	Without any motive	With a motive
Onset	Gradual	Sudden
Exciting factors	Present	Absent
Expression	Facial expression with vacant look	Normal
S/S	Uniform	Not-uniform
Habits	Dirty and filthy	Pretends to be dirty and filthy

NEUROSES

Definition: Defined as an emotional or mental disorder accompanied by obsessional (excessive anger, anxiety, jealousy, or a phobia–unreasoned fear or hatred) behaviour, without any logic/reason.

Types: Anxiety neurosis

Phobic neurosis

Anorexia nervosa

Hysterical neurosis

Obsessive neurosis.

ANXIETY NEUROSIS

Definition: Defined as a feeling of being worried about an event that may happen or may have happened and keep on thinking about it all the time. What may be trivial for one person may be overwhelming to another who is vulnerable in a certain way.

Etiology: Response to a threatening life situation e.g. maladjusted attempt to resolve internal conflicts i.e. unresolved, childhood problems e.g. insecurity, dependency, hostility, need for affection, intimacy, depression, disturbed occupational, social or domestic environment.

Diagnosis: Anxiety, fear, tension, restlessness, palpitations, tremor of hands, breathlessness, dryness of the mouth, headache, dizziness, depression, perspiration, diarrhea, indigestion, fatigue, muscle cramps, hypertension, tachycardia, memory–disturbance, polyuria, sleep disturbances.

Medico-legal aspect:

- That whether the person is having anxiety neurosis or not ?
- That whether the anxiety is true or feigned ?
- That whether the person responds well or not to a life threatening situation.

PHOBIC NEUROSIS

Definition: Defined as a strong unreasonable condition in which patient is usually anxious, but also have an abnormal fear of something (claustrophobia).

Etiology: Fear, apprehension, guilt.

Diagnosis: Anxiety

Abnormal fear (claustrophobia):

- Fears of animals-fear of snake, dog, cat, lion etc.
- Obsessive fears - fear of being infected, fear of school
- Hysterical fears-fear of being alone in house, fear of travelling alone.

Medico-legal aspect:

- That whether the person is suffering from phobic neurosis or not ?
- That whether the phobia is true or feigned ?

ACUTE HYSTERICAL NEUROSIS

Etiology: Is a condition in which the patient suddenly feels very nervous, anxious, excited and is unable to control his/her emotions.

Hysteria is not the same as malingering (consciously feigns illness) as the hysteric is unaware of the motivation of the symptom.

Diagnosis: Patient has a tendency to be indifferent to the queries and relates manifestation in a detached manner.

Psychological conflict–being partly solved by the adoption of physical symptoms, without any organic base.

Conversion symptoms:

- Physical: thyrotoxicosis, hypoglycemia
- Psychological: amnesia, pseudo-dementia, anxiety, abnormal behaviour–difficulties with others, depression.

Medico-legal aspect:

- That whether the person is suffering from hysterical neurosis or not ?
- That whether the hysteria is true or feigned ?

OBSESSIVE NEUROSIS

Definition: Defined as an extreme unhealthy interest in something or worry too much about something, or repeat particular actions again and again (compulsion to action from which patient cannot free himself/herself, although he/she realises that it is senseless, or at least that it is persisting and dominating without cause.

Etiology: Anxiety, fear, tension, unhealthy interest, worry, compulsion.

Diagnosis: Obsessions: constantly recurring thoughts e.g. fear of hitting someone.

Compulsions: repetitive actions e.g. need to re-check the things they have already done, rituals of locking door and so on. Patient is forced to do something against his will.

Depression.

Medico-legal aspect:

- That whether the person is suffering from obsessive neurosis or not ?
- That whether the obsession is true or feigned ?

ANOREXIA NERVOSA

Definition: Defined as a mental disorder in which young women, stop eating as they believe themselves fat and want to loose weight to be thin.

Etiology: Age–common in younger persons

Dieting–for anxiety over weight gain

Exercise – excessive

Vomiting – self induced

Abuse-of laxatives, appetite suppressants, diuretics

Depression.

Diagnosis: Failure to eat–sometimes eat well, but in secret make themselves vomit

Vomiting

Depression–fear of gaining weight

Hypotension

Loss of weight, starvation to death.

Investigation: To check for hypoglycemia and hypokalemia.

Medico-legal aspect:

- That whether the person is suffering from anorexia nervosa or not ?

- That whether the anorexia nervosa is true or feigned ?

ALCOHOLISM (syn. ALCOHOL ABUSE)

Definition: An alcohol addict may be defined as one who has lost control over his drinking and has a compulsion to keep on drinking with resultant deterioration of emotional, social and work activities.

Etiology: Any social or cultural factor which leads to the rapid excessive consumption of alcohol will tend to cause alcohol addiction.

Reasonably stable persons who are exposed to an alcoholic environment may become addicted.

Some tense anxious individuals may begin drinking to allay anxiety and depression and then become addicts.

Psychological individuals may drink heavily as part of their generally disorganised behaviour and finally become addicted to alcohol.

Diagnosis: Blackout–temporary loss of memory

Loss of tolerance to alcohol

Tremors

Obsessive drinking–secret drinking

Craving for alcohol–for that he will lie, steal, or cheat to get it.

Medico-legal aspect:

That whether the person is alcohol addict or not?

That whether he/she has consumed alcohol or not ?

That whether the person be held responsible for a criminal act ?

That whether the person is capable of taking care of himself/herself ?

ACUTE ALCOHOL POISONING (INTOXICATION)

Definition: Acute alcohol poisoning may vary from intoxication to profound comatosed condition. and the condition depends on tolerance, amount ingested and absorbed.

Etiology:
- Inhalation of alcohol vapour
- Ingestion of alcohol
- Absorbed–applied over burns or large wounds

Diagnosis: History of alcohol abuse

Euphoria, disinhibition, mild co-ordination problems

Confusion, impaired consciousness–may progress to anaesthesia

Mood liability, impaired judgment, sexual or aggressive impulses

Speech-slurred

Nystagmus, ataxia,

Pupils–normal or dilated

Respiration–slow and noisy

Tachycardia

Skin–cold and clamy, hypothermia

Stupor, coma, death.

MLD: 60-150 ml (measured in terms of absolute alcohol).

Lethal period: 6-12 hrs. (may be less or more).

PM findings: Alcoholic smell: from mouth, nose, gastric contents, lungs, brain and bladder

Rigor mortis: prolonged

Internal organs: congested

Heart: right side full, while left one empty

Decomposition: retarded.

Medico-legal aspect:

- That whether the person is suffering from alcohol poisoning or not ?
- That whether the person be held responsible for a criminal act ?
- That whether the person is capable of taking care of himself/herself ?

DRUG ABUSE

The drug addict is one who is psychologically or physically dependent on a drug, He intends to increase the dose, develops some tolerance of its toxic effect and has an overwhelming need to continue taking it. In certain cases, physical dependence and marked tolerance are the outstanding features, while in others the dependence appears to be more psychological than physical.

Triad of drug addiction:

- Psychological craving or dependence in procurement of the drug
- Physical dependence with withdrawal symptoms on stopping of drug
- Tolerance – need to increase the dose to obtain desired effects.

Addictive drugs include:

- Narcotics:

Drugs: - Natural narcotics: Morphine and opium alkaloids e.g. morphine, codein, heroin

- Synthetic narcotics: mepridine
- Sedatives and Hypnotics or Tranquilizers:

Drugs: Barbiturates, alcohol, bromide, paraldehyde, chloral hydrate

- Psychedelics (Hallucinogens):

Drugs: Phenylalanine: norepinephrine, dopamine

Tryptophan: serotonin

- Stimulants:

Drugs: Cocaine, amphetamines, hashish, marihuana.

Diagnosis: Gait–defective

Tremors

Headache, heaviness (clouding) of head, visual disturbances

Nausea, vomiting, diarrhea.

Investigation: To induce withdrawal symptoms – by:

- Withdrawal of the drug
- Inj. Morphine antagonist.

Medico-legal aspect:

- That whether the person is drug addict or not ?

- That what type of drug he/she has consumed ?
- That whether the person be held responsible for a criminal act ?
- That whether the person is capable of taking care of himself/herself ?

NARCOTIC ABUSE

Action: Narcotic causes relief from pain, stupor, sleep.

Drugs: Morphine and opium alkaloids e.g. codein, heroin, mepridine (pethidine).

S/E: Addiction or dependence – if repeatedly used and ultimately results into tolerance, Pneumonia, infection, peripheral neuritis.

Diagnosis: Confusion, stupor, euphoria, aggressive behaviour

Speech – slurred, impaired

Miosis/or mydriosis

Drowsiness, sleep, coma, death.

Withdrawal S/S:Restlessness, irritability, dysphoria, bodyaches, anxiety, perspiration, lacrimation, flushes, nausea, vomiting, tachycardia, hypertension

Medico-legal aspect:

- That whether the person is narcotic addict or not ?
- That what type of narcotic he/she has consumed?
- That whether the person be held responsible for a criminal act ?
- That whether the person is capable of taking care of himself/herself ?

PSYCHEDELICS (HALLUCINOGENICS) ABUSE

Action: Psychedelics produce behavioural and psychological effects (Bad Trips).

Drugs: Phenylalanine: norepinephrine, dopamine.

Tryptophan: serotonin, lysergic acid diethylamide (LSD).

S/E: Addiction or dependence–if repeatedly used and ultimately results into tolerance.

Intoxication: Sympathomimetic effects:

- Mydriosis, hyperflexia, tachycardia, hypertension

- Feeling of tension, crying, laughing
- Visual illusions and hallucinations, fear of ego distruption
- Disorientation of time sense and distortion of all perceptions, mood lability
- Feeling of detachment and a sense of destiny and control
- Loss of memory and impaired motives, loss of interest in competition.
- Eratic behaviour: Injury or death by jumping from a height, thinking one's ability to fly.

Medico-legal aspect:

- That whether the person is psychedelic addict or not ?
- That what type of psychedelic he/she has consumed ?
- That whether the person be held responsible for a criminal act ?
- That whether the person is capable of taking care of himself/herself ?

MARIHUANA ABUSE

Properties: Marihuana is a lipoid soluble non-nitrogenous oleoresin, extracted from cannabis sativa/indica, a hemp plant.

Action: Marihuana induces somatic or psychic changes, when smoked or ingested

Types/Drugs:
- Charas, hashish: resinous exudate of flowering tops - most potent
- Bhang: dried leaves and flowering shoots
- Ganja: resinous mass from leaves.

S/E:
- Addiction or dependence–if repeatedly used and ultimately results into tolerance
- Pneumonia, infection, peripheral neuritis.

Diagnosis: Perception: altered time

Conjunctival injection

Emotions: loosened

Memory: impaired

Psychotomimetic effects occur with high doses:

- Confusion, stupor, euphoria, aggressive behaviour
- Insanity: mania, dementia, melancholia
- Halucination and delusion

  Speech: slurred, impaired

  Miosis/or mydriosis

  Drowsiness, sleep, coma

  Death occurs rarely.

Medico-legal aspect:

- That whether the person is marihuana addict or not ?
- That what type of marihuana he/she has consumed ?
- That whether the person be held responsible for a criminal act ?
- That whether the person is capable of taking care of himself/herself ?

References

1. Goodman, LS, and Gilman, A (editors):General Principles of Toxicology. The Pharmacological Basis of Therapeutics, 4th ed. Macmillan, New York, 1960.
2. An Experienced Teacher: Notes on Medical Jurisprudence and Toxicology. Current Publishers, Calcutta, 1965.
3. Brophy, James J, and Krupp, Marcus A, Chatton. Milton J (editors): Psychiatric Disorders. Lange Medical Publications, Japan, 590-638, 1975.
4. Reid, HA, Jhekaston, RDG. The management of snakebite. Bull WHO 63:885-95, 1983.
5. Russell FE. Snake venom poisoning. Philadelphia. JB Lippincot Co. 291-300, 1980.
6. Saitz R, O'Malley S: Pharmacotherapies for alcohol abuse. Med Clin North Am 81:881-907, 1997.
7. Schorling, JB, Buchsbaum, DG: Screening for alcohol and drug abuse. Med Clin North Am 81:845-65, 1997.
8. Basu, D, Singh, J: Drug and Alcohol Abuse: General Physician's Perspective. JIMA 103: 88-98, 2005.
9. Goel, SP: Common poisonings and their management in children. CMJ India 11: 7-14.
10. Ghai, OP, Piyush, G: Poisonings and accidents. Essential Pediatrics 640-41, 2004.

11. Steentoft, A: Fatal digitalis poisoning. Acta pharmacol 32:353, 1973.
12. Wyatt, JP, Illingworth, RN, Robertson, CE, Clancy, MJ, Munro, PT: Poisoning. Oxford Handbook of Accident and Emergency Medicine 174-202, 2005.
13. Varma, A, Gaur, KJBS, Bhatia, P: Mushrooms and poisoning. JIMA 109: 826-828, 2011, 108.

CHAPTER - 3

TOXICOLOGY

POISONS OR TOXINS

Definition

Types of poisons

Medico-legal classification of poisoning

Rules observed in a poisoning case

Diagnosis: Signs and symptoms

Laboratory analysis

Postmortem (PM) findings

Medico-legal aspects

Classification of Poisons:

- Corrosives:
  - Acids poisoning
  - Alkalies poisoning
- Irritants:

Irritants (Chemical):

- Carbolic Acid (Phenol) poisoning
- Oxalic Acid poisoning
- Copper sulphate poisoning
- Arsenic poisoning
- Mercury poisoning
- Copper Sulphate poisoning
- Lead poisoning
- Phosphorus poisoning

Irritants (Vegetable):

- Castor seeds (Ricinus Communis) poisoning

- Croton seeds (Jamalgota) poisoning
- Marking nuts (Semecarpus Anacardium) poisoning.
- Akdo (Calotropis gigantean and Procera)
- Chitra (Plumbago Zeylanica) poisoning
- Rati (Abrus Precatorius) poisoning

Irritants (Mechanical):

- Glass powder poisoning
- Diamond dust poisoning
- Pins/thorns/needles poisoning.

Irritants (Animal):

- Snake poisoning
- Scorpion poisoning
- Wasp and Bees poisoning

Neurotics:

Central Nervous System (CNS) Depressants:

- General Anesthetics:
    - Ether poisoning
    - Chloroform poisoning
    - Gas Anesthetics: Nitrous oxide poisoning
- Narcotics (Natural):
    - Opium poisoning
    - Morphine poisoning.
- Narcotics (Synthetic):
    - Mepridine poisoning).
- Nonnarcotics (Analgesics and Antipyretics):
    - Salicylates poisoning
    - Colchicine poisoning
    - Acetanilid poisoning.
- Hypnotics (Inebrients):
    - Alcohol (ethyl) poisoning
    - Alcohol (methyl) poisoning.
- Hypnotics and Sedatives:
    - Barbiturate poisoning
    - Chloral hydrate poisoning.

Central Nervous System (CNS) Stimulants:

- Strychnine poisoning,

- Caffeine poisoning
- Aminophylline poisoning.

Autonomic Stimulating Agents:

- Parasympathomimetics:
  - Pilocarpine poisoning
  - Muscarine (Mushrooms) poisoning.
- Sympathomimetics:
  - Amphetamine poisoning
  - Ephedrine poisoning.

Autonomic Blocking Agents:

- Cholinergic Blocking Agents:
  - Atropine poisoning.
- Adrenergic Blocking Agents:
  - Ergot Alkaloids
- Skeletal Muscles and Autonomic Ganglia Inhibitors:
  - Curare poisoning

Noxious Gases and Vapours:

- Carbon monoxide (CO) poisoning
- Carbon dioxide (CO_2) poisoning
- Sewer/or Drain gas poisoning
- Coal gas (CO + CO_2) poisoning
- Hydrocyanic acid poisoning
- Cyanide poisoning.

Local Anesthetics:

- Cocaine poisoning
- Procaine poisoning
- Lignocaine poisoning
- Cardiac Glycosides:
  - Digitalis poisoning
  - Anticoagulants poisoning.
- Cytotoxic drugs poisoning:
  - Alkylating agents poisoning
  - Antimetabolites poisoning
  - Antihormonal poisoning
  - Vinca alkaloids
  - Antineoplastic antibiotics poisoning.

Miscellaneous poisonings:

- Detergents poisoning:

Soaps, detergents, antiseptics poisoning

- Disinfectants and Germicides poisoning

  Formaldehyde poisoning

  Chlorine poisoning

  Iodine poisoning

  Boric acid poisoning.

Insecticides and Arachnicides (Pesticides) poisoning

  Chlorophenothane (DDT) poisoning

  Fluorides (Insect powder) poisoning

  Phosphates (Organic) poisoning.

Rodenticides poisoning

  Barium poisoning

  Fluoroacetate poisoning.

Antihelminthics poisoning

  Carbon tetrachloride poisoning

  Aspidium (Mali-Fern) poisoning.

Amebicidal agents poisoning

  Emetine poisoning.

Industrial poisoning

  Heavy metals

  Arsenic poisoning

  Antimony poisoning

  Mercury poisoning

  Lead poisoning

  Cadmium poisoning

  Manganese poisoning

  Zinc poisoning

  Gold poisoning

  Silver poisoning

  Bismuth poisoning

  Thallium poisoning.

  Beryllium poisoning

  Paint thinner poisoning.

Household poisoning

  Food poisoning.

Definition: Poison Is defined as a substance, that on absorption or by direct contact, and acting chemically, causes injury to body or death. It is a difficult task to differentiate between medicine and poison. Overdosage of almost all drugs, is poisonous. A medicine given in large dose may produce poisonous effect, whereas a poison given in smaller dose (therapeutic) may be considered as a medicine.

TYPES of POISONS:

As per routes of administration:

1. Ingested poisons:
   - Acids or alkalies (corrosives)
   - Kerosene oil, petrol, paint thinner, copper sulphate.
2. Inhaled poisons: Volatile acids, fumes, gases – chlorine, fluorine, vehicle exhaust gases.
3. Eye contamination poisons: Acids, alkalies, fumes.
4. Skin contamination poisons: Acids, alkalies, fumes, lead.
5. Drugs (over-dosage).
6. Bites/sting: Snake, scorpion, insect, ant bite poisons.

CLASSIFICATION of POISONING (MEDICO-LEGAL):

Accidental: (Un-intentional):

- By mistake e.g. swallowing of poisons – esp. by young children
- By curiosity
- By spontaneous activity
- By innocence – esp. children
- By habit – putting into mouth each and every objects- by children
- By negativism and imitation
- By snake bite, scorpion bite, wasp, bee sting
- By over-dosage
- By self medication or from mistaking a drug for another one.

Suicidal: (Self killing - intentional):

Suicide by drugs and noxious gases is common.

- Opium tops the list, followed by arsenic, barbiturates, carbon monoxide, copper sulphate.

Homicidal: (Murder): was more prevalent in the past than at present. The rapid improvements made in the science of toxicology have discouraged homicidal form of criminal offence.

- Arsenic tops the list, followed by aconite, opium, cyanide, snake bite.

Stupefication: Patient behaves like a stupid. The aim is to rob or to rape.

- Chloral hydrate mixed with alcohol – used for stupefication.

RULES OBSERVED IN A POISONING CASE:

- Insist for presence of another medical pracitioner or better send the patient to the hospital
- Inform the police and the relatives of the patient
- Preserve the vomited matter, urine, fecal matter, if any, and hand over to the police
- Do not issue death certificate and insist for a post-mortem examination.

Diagnosis: Follow the following steps in a suspected case of poisoning:

- Interrogate: the patient, guardian of a minor, accompanying relative/s or attendants/persons, police official, concerning the presence of poison in the environment.
- History in detail and physical examination.
- Laboratory analysis of vomitus, urine, stools, excreta, damaged viscera.

Signs and Symptoms:

Appearance:

- Anorexia, asthenia, loss of weight

GITract:

- Breath odour
- Nausea, vomiting, diarrhea
- Salivation, dryness of mouth

- Gums–black or blue line
- Abdominal pain
- Hematemesis, melena
- Jaundice

Respiratory:
- Cough
- Respiration – rapid/slow
- Dyspnea
- Cyanosis
- Pulmonary edema.

CVS:
- Palpitation
- Dyspnea
- Tachycardia/bradycardia
- Hypotension/hypertension

CNS:
- Headache, drowsiness, depression
- Hallucinations, delirium, convulsions
- Coma.

Eyes:
- Vision – blurred/coloured
- Pupils – dilated/contracted
- Disc - pale.

Ear, Nose and Throat (ENT):
- Tinnitus
- Deafness
- Vertigo.

Genitourinary:
- Polyuria
- Anuria
- Menstrual disturbances
- Sexual impairment: libido – decreased.

Endocrinal:
- Breast enlargement

Skin:
- Rash

- Corrosion
- Staining
- Cyanosis
- Perspiration: increased
- Jaundice
- Loss of hair.

Neuromuscular:

- Muscle weakness/or paralysis
- Muscle twitching.

Laboratory analysis: of vomitus, urine, stools, excreta, damaged viscera.

Specific tests:

Urine: Salicylate or phenothiazine tranquilizer ingestion:

- Phenistix test.

  Result: +ve confirms salicylate or phenothiazine tranquilizer poisoning.

  Bromide or Iodine ingestion:

- Add few drops of fuming nitric acid and 5 ml of chloroform to 10 ml of urine

  Mix slowly and let stand for 3 mts.

  Result: Chloroform settles at the bottom and assumes pink color for iodides or yellow color for bromides.

Gastric: - Iron ingestion:

  Test: dilute the gastric contents or vomitus with water. Filter and to the filtrate add 1 ml of 10 per cent potassium ferrocyanide sol.

  Result: An intense blue colour confirms presence of ferrous salts.

POST-MORTEM EXAMINATION (PM findings):

External examination:

- Any evidence of violence e.g. injury marks.
- Head:
- scalp wounds may be found.
- skull fractures with extravasation of blood, spinal fluid and lacerated brain tissues.
- signs of multiple injuries: may be found.

- Pupils: dilated or pin point.
- Any evidence of poison e.g. corrosion marks over the face: chin, angles of the mouth, nose, ears, on the hands or body.
- Any evidence of foreign body in the natural orifices.

Internal examination:

- Abdomen: to be examined first in a suspected case of poisoning:
- Stomach: note for:
  - any typical odour e.g. of alcohol, ether, chloroform, kerosene oil, carbolic acid, opium, phosphorus, copper sulphate.
  - any typical appearance of the contents.
- any discolouration of the mucous membrane:
  - yellow: in arsenic and nitric acid poisoning,
  - black: in sulphuric acid poisoning,
  - grey: in hydrogen perchlorate
  - any ulceration or perforation of mucous membrane - due to corrosion.
- Upper GITract: any marks of corrosion in the mouth, throat, esophagus
- Other organs: found soft and opaque.

Analysis of Preserved viscera, blood and urine:

Viscera: In suspected cases of poisoning, certain viscera, are to be sent for the laboratory analysis e.g. stomach alongwith its contents, portion of small intestine, duodenum and jejunum, liver, kidneys, uterus, ovaries, fallopian tubes, vagina, lungs, brain and spinal cord, hairs, nail, teeth, and some earth samples from the grave's floor.

Preservation:

Viscera: To be preserved in wide mouthed jars with lids. Stomach, liver and kidneys are sent mostly in one jar, while uterus and its appendages are to be preserved in a separate jar, and same in case of any foreign body.

Blood and urine: to be preserved in glass phials.

Preservative:

- Rectified spirit: universal preservative.
- NaCl: alcohol, carbolic acid, paraldehyde, phosphorus poisonings.
- No preservative: blood and urine.
- No formalin: as it may harden the viscera, thereby difficulty in extraction of poison.

Precautions:- Preservative fluid: to be sufficient to submerge the tissue.

- Air-space: to be left above the preservative level, to save the jar from cracking by the emitting putrefactive gases.
- Jar's lid: to be tied firmly, sealed (medicolegal) and labelled (name, age, sex, religion, CR No., nature of content, place of post-mortem, area's Police Station, signature with designation.

Transportation: Samples are to be sent:

- 1st one to be registered to the Chemical Examiner,
- 2nd one to be posted to the police station, and
- 3rd one retained by the RMO.

Analysis:

- Pre-death: - analysis of vomitus, food articles, urine, blood
- Post-death: - analysis of stomach and intestinal contents
- analysis of stomach, intestine, liver, kidneys and other viscera
- analysis of urine.

Medico-legal aspects:

- That to ascertain time of death.
- That to ascertain mode of death.
- That to ascertain the attitude of the body at the time of death.

CORROSIVES POISONING:

ACIDS POISONING

Properties: The strong mineral acids are currently employed as germicidal or antiseptic agents. These acids exert primarily a local corrosive effect on the skin or mucous membrane.

Classification:

- Strong mineral acids: Hydrochloric, sulphuric and nitric acids.
- Weak acids: Acetic and citric acids.

Poisoning: Occurs due to corrosive action, depending upon the concentration.

Etiology:

- Accidental: mostly accidental, esp. In children.
- Suicidal: rarely used.
- Homicidal:- forced ingestion: rarely due to strong colour and smell.
- vitriollage common.

Routes of administration:

- Ingestion: intentionally (suicidal) or unintentionally (by mistake)
- Inhalation–of acid fumes
- Skin contamination (through intact or broken skin)–by vitriollage or industrial mishap.

Pathogenesis:

- Corrosive effect on the skin or mucous membrane
- Circulatory collapse
- Pulmonary edema.

Diagnosis: G.I. Tract:

- Severe burning pain in the throat and upper G.I. Tract
- Thirst
- Vomiting of blood
- Difficulty in breathing
- Difficulty in swallowing
- Difficulty in speaking

Local:

- Disfiguration of skin and mucous membrane in and around the mouth

Shock, death may occur within hrs.

MLD: 1 ml of acid.

Lethal time: 1-24 hrs.

PM findings:

- Marks: black or brown corrosion marks over the mucous membrane of the upper GI Tract.
- Stomach: highly inflammed, perforated.

- Doudenum: corrosion marks.
- Other viscera: congested.

Laboratory analysis: of vomitus, urine, stools, excreta, damaged viscera.

Medico-legal aspect:

- That whether death is accidental, suicidal or homicidal ?
- That whether the cause of death was due to mineral acid poisoning ?
- That whether the case is that of vitriollage (vitriol throwing) i.e. throwing of acid by the accused person over the face of the victim, with malafide intentions ?
- That whether the case is that of criminal abortion: rarely used to procure criminal abortion ?

ALKALIES POISONING

Properties: The strong alkalies are currently employed as germicidal or antiseptic (detergents) agents. These alkalies exert primarily a local corrosive effect on the skin or mucous membrane.

Classification: Caustic soda, potash, ammonia. The strong alkalies are common ingredients of household cleansing compounds, confirmed by their soapy texture.

Poisoning: Occurs due to corrosive action, depending upon the concentration.

Etiology:

- Accidental: mostly due to wide domestic use.
- Suicidal: sometimes used.
- Homicidal: rarely due to strong colour and smell.

Diagnosis:

GI Tract:

- Severe burning pain in the throat and upper G.I. Tract
- Thirst
- Vomiting of blood
- Difficulty in breathing
- Difficulty in swallowing
- Difficulty in speaking

Local:

- Disfiguration of skin and mucous membrane in and around the mouth Shock, death may occur within hrs.

MLD: 1 ml of acid.

Lethal time: 1-24 hrs.

PM findings:
- Marks: black or brown corrosion marks over the mucous membrane of the upper GI Tract.
- Stomach: highly inflammed, perforated.
- Doudenum: corrosion marks.
- Other viscera: congested.

Laboratory analysis: of vomitus, urine, stools, excreta, damaged viscera.

Medico-legal aspect:

- That whether death is accidental, suicidal or homicidal ?
- That whether the cause of death was due to strong alkalis poisoning ?

IRRITANTS (CHEMICALS) POISONING:

CARBOLIC ACID (PHENOL) POISONING

Properties: Phenol is both bactericidal and fungicidal agent. It is composed of colourless crystals with a peculiar aromatic odour.

Poisoning: Occurs due to corrosive action.

Etiology:
- Accidental: mostly due to wide use of phenol as an antiseptic.
- Suicidal: sometimes used.
- Homicidal: rarely due to strong colour and smell.

Route of administration: Oral.

Pathogenesis:

- Acts as a corrosive agent locally and remotely,
- Acts as a narcotic poison affecting CNS and CVS.

Diagnosis:
- Local action: Skin - burning sensation, tingling, numbness, cold sweat
- G.I. Tract: Burning sensation in the upper GI Tract i.e. mouth, throat, and stomach, thirst

- Nausea, vomiting, acute abdominal pain
- Muscle cramps
- Oliguria
- Unconsciousness
- Respiratory and circulatory failure
- Death occurs due to respiratory failure.

MLD: 8 to 15 g.

Lethal time: Few mts. to 24 hrs.

PM findings:
- Skin: white or yellow stained.
- Marks: white or grey marks over the mucous membrane of the upper GI Tract.
- Stomach: inflammed, perforated, odour of carbolic acid emitting.
- Doudenum: congested.
- Other viscera: congested.

Laboratory analysis: of vomitus, urine, stools, excreta, damaged viscera.

Medico-legal aspect:

- That whether death is accidental, suicidal or homicidal ?
- That whether the cause of death was due to Carbolic acid poisoning ?

OXALIC ACID POISONING:

Properties: Is a powerful local irritant and the oxalate ion is toxic because it precipitates ionized calcium.

Uses:
- Oxalate salts are extensively used in laboratory procedures to prevent the coagulation of blood in vitro (as anti-coagulants) by precipitating ionized calcium.
- Used as a component of bleaching powder by the washer man/woman to remove ink/or iron stains.
- Used in printing industry.

Poisoning: Occurs due to corrosive action.

Etiology:
- Accidental: due to its close resemblance to Magnesium/or Zinc sulphate.
- Suicidal: rare due to its unpleasant taste.

- Homicidal: rare, due to its strong acid taste.

Diagnosis: Onset: quick.

S/S:
- burning sensation in the upper GI Tract i.e. mouth, pharynx, esophagus, stomach, intestine.
- Suffocation.
- Nausea, vomiting, diarrhea, acute abdominal pain.
- Oxaluria, hematuria, renal colic.
- Narcotic effect - remote and serious:
- Numbness, anesthesia of tips of fingers/toes, sciatica, or shooting pain in the loins.
- Convulsions, coma.
- Death occurs due to cardiac failure.

MLD: 4 g.

Lethal time: Few mts. to 2 hrs.

PM findings:
- Marks: white bleached marks over the mucous membrane of the upper GI Tract.
- Stomach: congested and contains a brownish acidic fluid.
- Doudenum: congested.
- Other viscera: congested.

Laboratory analysis: of vomitus, urine, stools, excreta, damaged viscera.

Medico-legal aspects:

- That whether death is accidental, suicidal or homicidal ?
- That whether the cause of death was due to Oxalic acid poisoning ?

COPPER SULPHATE (BLUE VITRIOL) POISONING

Properties: Copper sulphate is a metallic irritant and an astringent.

Poisoning: Occurs due to corrosive action.

Etiology:
- Suicidal–as easily available without permit.
- Homicidal–unsuitable for homicidal poisoning, due to its deep blue colour and an unpleasant metallic taste.

- Accidental–may occur in young children, mistakenly sucking it as a lozenge.

Diagnosis:
- Onset: symptoms appear within 15-20 mts after consumtion
- Strong metallic taste, thirst, salivation
- Sensation of constriction in the throat, headache
- Burning acute pain in the stomach
- Nausea, vomiting–bluish/greenish vomitus, diarrhea
- Jaundice–due to fatty degeneration of liver
- Oliguria
- Convulsions, paralysis, coma
- Death–may occur within 1-3 days, earlier in children.

MLD: 30 g.

Lethal time: Few hrs. to 3 days.

PM findings:
- Skin: yellow stained.
- Upper GI Tract: the mucous membrane of the upper GI Tract, stained blue or green.
- Stomach: highly inflammed, perforated, stained blue or green
- Doudenum: perforated
- Liver: fatty degeneration
- Other viscera: congested.

Laboratory analysis: of vomitus, urine, stools, excreta, damaged viscera.

Medico-legal aspect:
- That whether death is accidental, suicidal or homicidal ?
- That whether the cause of death was due to Copper sulphate poisoning ?

ARSENIC POISONING

Properties: It is a colourless, odourless, tasteless, highly cytotoxic agent, present in pesticides (insecticides spray on fruits and vegetables) and chemicals (rat poisons).

Poisoning: Occurs due to corrosive action.

Etiology:
- Accidental: very rare, may be ingested accidentally by children.
- Suicidal: amongst drug of choice.
- Homicidal: favourite of murderers (easy to obtain):-
  - To get rid of the enemy.
  - To get rid of the husband/wife, by the wife/husband, instigated by her/his Paramour.
  - To get rid of a person for monetary (money or estate) gain.
  - To get rid of a person by his/her jilted lover.

Pathogenesis: Arsenic is one of most potent capillary poisons. The capillaries dilate and allow escape of plasma, resulting in marked hypotension, circulatory failure, shock.

Diagnosis:
- Constriction of throat
- Difficulty in swallowing
- Pain abdomen
- Nausea, vomiting, diarrhea
- Muscle cramps–due to disturbed electrolytes of body fluids
- Thirst due to fluid loss
- Shock:
- skin becomes cold, clammy, pale
- pulse – rapid and weak
- hypotension
- respiration–depressed

Coma and death may occur.

MLD: 0.1-0.2 g.

Lethal time: 1- 24 hrs.

PM findings: External:
- Signs of dehydration: sunken eyes and prominent cheek bones.

Internal:

GI Tract:
- Marks: red inflammed marks over the mucous membrane of the upper GI Tract.

- Stomach: highly inflammed, perforated (rare), contents dark brownish.
- Doudenum: congested.

Heart: sub-endocardial hemorrhage

Other viscera: congested.

Laboratory analysis: of vomitus, urine, stools, excreta, damaged viscera.

Medico-legal aspects:

- That whether death is accidental, suicidal or homicidal ?
- That whether the death has been due to consumption of arsenic ?

MERCURY POISONING

Properties: Mercurial compounds are of great pharmacological and toxicological importance, and are being employed as germicides, cathartics, diuretics, antisyphilitics etc. Mercury is frequently the cause of industrial and household poisoning.

Poisoning: Occurs due to corrosive action.

Types: Acute and chronic mercury poisoning.

ACUTE MERCURY POISONING

Etiology: Accidental or suicidal:

- Oral ingestion of highly dissociated inorganic preparations.
- Commonly caused by mercuric chloride.

Pathogenesis: Mercury is a protein precipitant, affecting mucous membranes of mouth, pharynx, stomach, renal damage, distortion of electrolyte pattern and the distribution of body fluids.

Diagnosis:
- A strong metallic taste is felt in the mouth
- Ashen grey appearance of mouth and pharynx
- Feeling of constriction and choking in the throat
- Burning sensation, extending from mouth down to stomach
- Severe abdominal pain
- Thirst

- Nausea, vomiting, diarrhea (profuse bloody)
- Electrolyte and body fluids imbalance
- Anuria
- Skin rash
- Muscle cramps
- Shock, death–mainly due to renal failure.

MLD: 0.7 g.

Fatal Period: 3-5 days.

PM findings:
- Marks: ashen-grey corrosion marks over the mucous membrane of the upper GI Tract (mouth and pharynx).
- Stomach: mucous membrane: ashen-grey appearance and inflammed.
- Doudenum: highly inflammed.
- Colon: highly inflammed.
- Other viscera: congested.

Laboratory analysis: of vomitus, urine, stools, excreta, damaged viscera.

Medico-legal aspect:

- That whether death is accidental, suicidal or homicidal ?
- That whether the death has been due to consumption of mercury ?

CHRONIC MERCURY POISONING

Etiology:
- Exposure to mercury for longer period i.e. industries utilising mercury.
- Medicinal use.

Diagnosis:
- Stomatits
- Colitis
- Anorexia
- Peripheral neuritis
- Anemia
- Skin disorders
- Renal damage
- Depression, insomnia, hallucinations
- Death.

PM findings: Marks: ashen-grey corrosion marks over the mucous membrane of the upper GI Tract (mouth and pharynx).

- Stomach: mucous membrane: ashen-grey appearance and inflammed.
- Doudenum: congested.
- Colon: congested.

Other viscera: congested.

- Liver: fatty changes.
- Kidneys: congested, swollen, fatty changes.
- Heart: congested, fatty changes.

Laboratory analysis: of vomitus, urine, stools, excreta, damaged viscera.

Medico-legal aspect:

- That whether death is accidental, suicidal or homicidal ?
- That whether the death has been due to consumption of mercury ?

LEAD POISONING

Properties: Lead is a slow acting and subtle, but powerful poison.

Poisoning: Occurs due to corrosive action.

Etiology: Lead poisoning is mostly chronic because of slow absorption.

- Exposure in industry: Lead is inhaled in dusts or fumes i.e. workers exposed to lead mining, smelting, and refining.

  Printers, painters–also prone to lead poisoning
- Household Poisoning: Contaminated drinking water with lead in piping supply.

Diagnosis: - Appearance: patient is moody, restive, and excited in early stages.

- Skin: pallor, ashen face
- Lips–pale
- Gums: blue line (Burtonian line)–seen on the margin of gums
- Tongue: coated

- Breath: foul and offensive
- Taste: metallic
- Nausea, vomiting, anorexia, constipation
- Abdominal colic
- Jaundice
- Headache, dizziness, irritability, insomnia
- Muscle fatigue
- Hypotension.

Investigation: Urine – scanty, positive for lead, trace of albumin

TLC and DLC: Increase in reticulocytes.

MLD: 0.5 g.

Lethal time: 1-3 days.

PM findings:
- Marks: mucous membrane of the upper GI Tract-congested.
- Blue lead line on the gum margin.
- Stomach: congested.
- Doudenum: congested.
- Brain: encephalopathy, proliferative meningitis
- Other viscera: congested.

Laboratory analysis: of vomitus, urine, stools, excreta, damaged viscera.

Medico-legal aspect:

- That whether death is accidental, suicidal or homicidal ?
- That whether the cause of death was due to Lead poisoning ?

PHOSPHORUS (ELEMENTAL) POISONING

Properties: Is a non-metallic local irritant and systemic toxin that acts on the liver, kidneys, muscles, bones and CVS.

Poisoning: Occurs due to corrosive action.

Types: Acute or chronic.

Forms:
- Red or non-crystalline, does not oxidise in air (non-volatile) and nontoxic.
- Yellow or crystalline, preserved under water as it oxidise in air (volatile) and is toxic.

Etiology:
- Accidental: common amongst manufacturers of fire works and matches.
- Suicidal: may be taken with suicidal intention.
- Homicidal: unsuitable due to unpleasant smell and, taste.

Route: Inhalation, ingestion, or direct contact.

Diagnosis:
- Onset: within a few mts.
- Pain: burning type in the upper G.I.Tract
- Nausea, vomiting, diarrhea
- Breath: garlic odour and luminous in the dark
- Vomitus: garlic odour and luminous in the dark
- Tongue: coated, garlic taste
- Hemorrhages: epistaxis, purpuric spots underneath skin, hematuria, menorrhagia.
- Jaundice
- Hepatomegaly and splenomegaly
- Pulse: feeble, irregular
- Restlessness, insomnia, headache, convulsions
- Coma
- Death due to cardiovascular collapse

MLD: 50 mg of yellow phosphorus

Lethal time: Few hrs. to few days.

PM findings:
- Odour: garlic
- Skin: petichial hemorrhages underneath skin
- Stomach: mucous membrane stained yellow or ash grey.

  Gastric contents: garlic odour and luminous in the dark
- Heart: may show fatty degeneration
- Liver: hepatomegaly or atrophic liver
- Spleen: splenomegaly
- Bones: necrosis of bones, esp. of upper and lower jaw.

Laboratory analysis: of vomitus, urine, stools, excreta, damaged viscera.

Medico-legal aspects:

- That whether death is accidental, suicidal or homicidal ?
- That whether the cause of death was due to phosphorus poisoning ?

KEROSENE POISONING

Poisoning: from ingestion.

Etiology:
- Accidental: common amongst children
- Suicidal: as easily available.
- Homicidal: rare.

Diagnosis:
- Nausea, vomiting, thirst, salivation
- Burning pain in the throat
- Breath: smells of kerosene oil
- Headache, drowsiness, vertigo, loss of memory
- Burning acute pain in the stomach
- Pulse: weak and irregular
- Pulmonary edema
- Respiratory distress
- convulsions
- Coma
- Death – may occur within 1-3 days, earlier in children.

MLD: 10-50 ml.

Lethal time: within few hrs.

PM findings:
- Skin: pale or cyanosed
- Upper GI Tract: the mucous membrane of the upper GI Tract, inflammed.
- Stomach: highly inflammed, perforated
- Doudenum: congested
- Liver: fatty degeneration
- Other viscera: congested.

Laboratory analysis: of vomitus, urine, stools, excreta, damaged viscera.

Medico-legal aspect:

- That whether death is accidental, suicidal or homicidal ?

- That whether the cause of death was due to kerosene oil poisoning ?

IRRITANTS (VEGETABLE) POISONING:

IRRITANT OIL CATHARTICS:

CASTOR BEANS (RICINUS COMMUNIS) POISONING

Properties: These beans contain a highly toxic protein (abumin), so called ricin. Castor oil is commonly used as a cathartic.

Poisoning: Acts like a snake venom. Hypersensitive persons may develop an acute allergic reaction/fatal anaphylactic shock.

Etiology: Accidental: common amongst children.

Suicidal: common because of easy availability

Homicidal: rare.

Diagnosis: Burning pain in the mouth, thirst

Nausea, vomiting, diarrhea, pain abdomen (colicky)

Skin: cold clammy

Breathing: slow and weak

Pulse: feeble and rapid

Shock: anaphylactic type

Hemoglobinuria, oliguria

Coma

Death.

MLD: 1 bean.

Lethal time: within hrs. to few days.

PM findings: External:

- Signs of dehydration: sunken eyes and prominent cheek bones.

Internal:

GI Tract:

- Marks: red inflammed marks over the mucous membrane of the upper GI Tract.
- Stomach: highly inflammed, perforated (rare), contents dark brownish.
- Doudenum: congested.

Heart: sub-endocardial hemorrhage

Other viscera: congested.

External:

- Skin: cyanotic, dehydrated,

Internal-Internal: organs: inflammed, congested.

Laboratory analysis: of vomitus, urine, stools, excreta, damaged viscera.

Medico-legal aspect:

- That whether death is accidental, suicidal or homicidal ?
- That whether the cause of death was due to castor beans poisoning ?

CROTON OIL SEEDS (JAMALGOTA) POISONING

Properties: These seeds yield croton oil, which is the most drastic (highly irritant) of all cathartics.

Poisoning: The oil is very irritant on account of its content of croton resin.

Etiology: Accidental: habitual use of cathartics

Suicidal: rare

Homicidal: very rare.

Diagnosis: Burning pain in the mouth, thirst

Nausea, vomiting, diarrhea (watery/or bloody), pain of abdomen, tenesmus

Skin: itching, redness, vesication

Breathing: slow and weak.

Pulse: feeble and rapid

Hypotension

Unconsciousness

Coma

Death.

MLD: 1 g (20 drops).

Lethal time: within hrs. to few days.

PM findings: External:

- Signs of dehydration: sunken eyes and prominent cheek bones.

Internal:

GI Tract:

- Marks: red inflammed marks over the mucous membrane of the upper GI Tract.

- Stomach: highly inflammed, perforated (rare), contents dark brownish.
- Doudenum: congested.

Heart: sub-endocardial hemorrhage

Other viscera: congested.

Laboratory analysis: of vomitus, urine, stools, excreta, damaged viscera.

Medico-legal aspect:

- That whether death is accidental, suicidal or homicidal ?
- That whether the cause of death was due to croton oil poisoning ?

MARKING NUTS (SEMECARPUS ANACARDIUM) POISONING

Propeties: These nuts yield the toxic juice, which acts as an irritant poison, and is being applied to the os uteri to induce criminal abortion.

Poisoning: Irritant poisoning.

Etiology: Accidental: misuse by the quacks in the treatment of syphilis

Suicidal: rare

Homicidal: very rare.

Diagnosis: Nausea, vomiting, diarrhea, pain abdomen

Skin: itching, bruise, blisters

Eyes: ophthalmia

Breathing: slow and weak.

Unconsciousness

Coma

Death.

Laboratory analysis: of vomitus, urine, stools, excreta, damaged viscera.

MLD: 150 grs.

Lethal time: within 24 hrs.

PM findings: External:

- Marks: red inflammed marks at the hair root.

Internal:

GI Tract:

- Marks: red inflammed marks over the mucous membrane of the upper GI Tract.
- Stomach: highly inflammed, perforated (rare), contents dark brownish.
- Doudenum: congested.

  Heart: sub-endocardial hemorrhage

  Other viscera: congested.
- Internal organs: inflammed, congested.

Laboratory analysis: of vomitus, urine, stools, excreta, damaged viscera.

Medico-legal aspect:

- That whether death is accidental, suicidal or homicidal ?
- That whether the cause of death was due to marking nut poisoning ?

AKDO/MADAR (CALOTROPIS GIGANTEA AND PROCERA) POISONING

Properties: It yields a milky juice, which acts as an irritant poison.

Misuse:

- to induce criminal abortion by introducing into the uterus
- to cause infanticide by ingestion
- to cause animal poisoning by introducing into the rectum.

Poisoning: The active principle is a yellow resin.

Etiology: Accidental: misuse

Suicidal: rare

Homicidal: very rare.

Diagnosis: GI Tract:

Burning pain in the throat, salivation, stomatitis, acrid bitter taste, Acute abdominal pain, vomiting, diarrhea

Breathing: slow and weak.

Convulsions

Coma

Death.

Laboratory analysis: of vomitus, urine, stools, excreta, damaged viscera.

MLD: 100 grs.

Lethal time: Within few hrs.

PM findings: External:

- Marks: red inflammed marks at corners of the mouth.

Internal:

GI Tract:

- Marks: red inflammed marks over the mucous membrane of the upper GI Tract.
- Stomach: inflammed, perforated (rare), contents dark brownish.
- Doudenum: congested.

Other viscera: congested.

- Internal organs: inflammed, congested.

Laboratory analysis: of vomitus, urine, stools, excreta, damaged viscera.

Medico-legal aspect:

- That whether death is accidental, suicidal or homicidal ?
- That whether the cause of death was due to akdo/madar poisoning ?

CHITRA (PLUMBAGO ZEYLANICA) POISONING

Properties: It yields a milky juice, which acts as an irritant poison.

Misuse:

- to induce criminal abortion by introducing into the uterus
- to cause infanticide by ingestion
- to cause animal poisoning by introducing into the rectum.

Poisoning: The active principle is a yellow resin.

Etiology: Accidental: misuse

Suicidal: rare

Homicidal: very rare.

Diagnosis: GI Tract:

Burning pain in the throat, salivation, stomatitis, acrid bitter taste

Acute abdominal pain, vomiting, diarrhea

Breathing: slow and weak.

Convulsions

Coma

Death.

Laboratory analysis: of vomitus, urine, stools, excreta, damaged viscera.

MLD: 100 grs.

Lethal time: Within few hrs.

PM findings: External:

- Marks: red inflammed marks at corners of the mouth.

Internal:

GI Tract:

- Marks: red inflammed marks over the mucous membrane of the upper GI Tract.
- Stomach: inflammed, perforated (rare), contents dark brownish.
- Doudenum: congested.

  Other viscera: congested.
- Internal organs: inflammed, congested.

Laboratory analysis: of vomitus, urine, stools, excreta, damaged viscera.

Medico-legal aspect:

- That whether death is accidental, suicidal or homicidal ?
- That whether the cause of death was due to chitra poisoning ?

RATI (ABRUS PRECATORIUS) POISONING

Properties: The seeds yield a milky juice, made into a paste, hardened and shaped into needles, stabbed into the buttock, which acts as an irritant poison.

Misuse: - as oral contraceptive (pills)

- to cause animal poisoning by introducing into the rectum.

Poisoning: The active principle is Abrin (toxalbumin) analogous to snake venom.

Etiology: Accidental: misuse

Suicidal: rare

Homicidal: very rare.

Diagnosis: GI Tract:

Burning pain in the throat, salivation, stomatitis, acrid bitter taste

Acute abdominal pain, vomiting, diarrhea

Breathing: slow and weak.

Convulsions

Coma

Death.

Laboratory analysis: of vomitus, urine, stools, excreta, damaged viscera.

MLD: 100 grs.

Lethal time: Within few hrs.

PM findings: External:

- Marks: red inflammed marks at corners of the mouth.

Internal:

GI Tract:

- Marks: red inflammed marks over the mucous membrane of the upper GI Tract.
- Stomach: inflammed, perforated (rare), contents dark brownish.
- Doudenum: congested.

Other viscera: congested.

- Internal organs: inflammed, congested.

Laboratory analysis: of vomitus, urine, stools, excreta, damaged viscera.

Medico-legal aspect:

- That whether death is accidental, suicidal or homicidal ?

- That whether the cause of death was due to Rati poisoning ?

WHITE OLEANDER (NERIUM ODORUM) POISONING

Properties: All parts of the plant are poisonous.

Misuse: - to induce criminal abortion by ingestion or local application on uterus.

Poisoning: The active principle is Nerin (glucosides). Is a cerebro-cardiac poison.

Etiology: Accidental: misuse

Suicidal: rare

Homicidal: very rare.

Diagnosis: GI Tract:

Burning pain in the throat, salivation, difficult in swallowing

Acute abdominal pain, vomiting, diarrhea

Breathing: stertorous

Pulse: rapid

Muscle spasms, lock-jaw

Convulsions

Coma

Death from heart failure.

Laboratory analysis: of vomitus, urine, stools, excreta, damaged viscera.

MLD: 250 grs.

Lethal time: Within 1-2 days.

PM findings: External:

- Marks: red inflammed marks at corners of the mouth.

Internal:

GI Tract:

- Marks: red inflammed marks over the mucous membrane of the upper GI Tract.
- Stomach: inflammed, perforated (rare), contents dark brownish.
- Doudenum: congested.

Other viscera: congested.

- Internal organs: inflammed, congested.

Laboratory analysis: of vomitus, urine, stools, excreta, damaged viscera.

Medico-legal aspect:

- That whether death is accidental, suicidal or homicidal ?
- That whether the cause of death was due to white oleander poisoning ?

YELLOW OLEANDER (CERBERA THEVETIA) POISONING

Properties: All parts of the plant are poisonous.

Misuse: - to induce criminal abortion by ingestion or local application on uterus.

Poisoning: The active principle is Cerberin and Thevetin. Is a cerebro-cardiac poison.

Etiology: Accidental: misuse

Suicidal: rare

Homicidal: very rare.

Diagnosis: GI Tract:

- Burning pain in the throat, dryness of the mouth
- Acute abdominal pain, vomiting, diarrhea

Headache, vertigo

Pupils: dilated

Breathing: stertorous

Pulse: feeble, slow

Skin: cold clammy

Muscle spasms

Faintness

Convulsions

Coma

Death from heart failure.

Laboratory analysis: of vomitus, urine, stools, excreta, damaged viscera.

MLD: 10 seeds.

Lethal time: Within 1-2 days.

PM findings: External:

- Marks: red inflammed marks at corners of the mouth.

Internal:

GI Tract:

- Marks: red inflammed marks over the mucous membrane of the upper GI Tract.
- Stomach: inflammed, perforated (rare), contents dark brownish.
- Doudenum: congested.

Other viscera: congested.

- Internal organs: inflammed, congested.

Laboratory analysis: of vomitus, urine, stools, excreta, damaged viscera.

Medico-legal aspect:

- That whether death is accidental, suicidal or homicidal ?
- That whether the cause of death was due to yellow oleander poisoning ?

ACONITE (Liniment) POISONING

Properties: All parts of the aconite plant are poisonous, while its root is commonly used for poisoning. It is mainly used for homicidal purpose. Is a cerebro-cardiac depressant. It first stimulates, then paralyses the sensory and secretive nerves.

Poisoning: Is the drug of choice these days. Arrows poisoned with aconite liniment, are commonly used by hilly tribes and aborigins, to kill the enemies/ animals.

Drinking of poisoned water with aconite root may be fatal.

Etiology: Accidental: ingestion of poisoned water, tincture aconite.

Suicidal: common, as being easily available and sweet taste.

Homicidal: commonly used, as being easily available, sweet taste, destroyed rapidly in the viscera, and detection of poisoning is difficult.

Diagnosis: - G.I. Tract:

- Burning followed by numbness and tingling of the mouth, throat
- Nausea, vomiting, diarrhea, pain abdomen
- Pulse: slow, irregular
- Respiration: shallow
- Hypotension
- Cardiac:
- Chest pain: pre-cordial region
- Heart rate: increases
- Extra-systoles
- Neurological: Headache, fatigue, malaise and drowsiness, muscular weakness
- Psychological: confusion, disorientation, aphasia, hallucinations and delirium, convulsions
- Vision: Often blurred, white halos may appear on dark objects
- Skin: cold clammy
- Shock
- Death from cardiac or respiratory failure.

Laboratory analysis: of vomitus, urine, stools, excreta, damaged viscera.

MLD: 1 g.

Lethal time: 1-4 hrs.

PM findings: - Marks: mucous membrane of the upper GI Tract – shows signs of irritation.

- Stomach: signs of irritation e.g. congested and inflammed, fragments of roots may be present.
- Doudenum: signs of irritation e.g. congested and inflammed.
- Other viscera: congested e.g. congested and inflammed.

Laboratory analysis: of vomitus, urine, stools, excreta, damaged viscera.

Medico-legal aspect:

- That whether the death is accidental, suicidal or homicidal ?

- That whether the death has been due to aconite poisoning ?
- That whether the death has been due to aconite poisoning (aconite used with alcohol to increase its intoxicating power) ?

STIMULANT EXPECTORANTS:

TURPENTINE OIL (SPIRITS OF TURPENTINE) POISONING

Properties: Is a volatile oil distilled from turpentine (Gum turpentine), soluble in oils and alcohol but not in water. It acts as a cutaneous counter-irritant, used as a liniment, as a stupe (relieving abdominal distention), and as an expectorant.

Also being used in paint industry as a solvent.

Poisoning: The oil is an irritant poison from ingestion or inhalation.

Etiology: Accidental: by misuse and as an industrial hazard

Suicidal: rare

Homicidal: very rare.

Diagnosis: Burning pain in the mouth, thirst

Nausea, vomiting, diarrhea, pain abdomen (colicky)

Delirium, excitement, ataxia

Skin: itching, redness

Breathing: slow and weak.

Pulse: feeble and rapid

Hypotension

Pneumonitis

Albuminuria, hematuria, dysuria

Unconsciousness

Coma

Death.

Laboratory analysis: of vomitus, urine, stools, excreta, damaged viscera.

MLD: 15 ml for children, 150 ml for adults.

Lethal time: within hrs. to few days.

PM findings: External:

- Signs of dehydration: sunken eyes and prominent cheek bones.

Internal:

GI Tract:

- Marks: red inflammed marks over the mucous membrane of the upper GI Tract.
- Stomach: highly inflammed, perforated (rare), contents dark brownish.
- Doudenum: congested.

Heart: sub-endocardial hemorrhage

Other viscera: congested.

Laboratory analysis: of vomitus, urine, stools, excreta, damaged viscera.

Medico-legal aspect:

- That whether death is accidental, suicidal or homicidal ?
- That whether the cause of death was due to turpentine oil poisoning ?

IRRITANTS (MECHANICAL):

Poisoning: Irritants poisoning.

Types: Dust: diamond, silicon

Metallic: pins, hair pins, needles, razor blades, coins

Powder: glass

Etiology: Accidental: common amongst industrial workers and children

Suicidal: rare

Homicidal: very rare.

Diagnosis: GI Tract:

- Burning sensation in the throat
- Pain abdomen (colicky), vomiting, diarrhea

Respiratory:

- Breathing: slow and weak.

Unconsciousness

Coma

Death.

Lethal time: Few hrs. to few days.

PM findings: External:

- Signs of perforated abdomen/intestines: distended abdomen

Internal:

GI Tract:

- Marks: red inflammed marks over the mucous membrane of the upper GI Tract.
- Stomach: highly inflammed, perforated (common), contents dark brownish.
- Doudenum: congested.

Other viscera: inflammed, congested.

Medico-legal aspect:

- That whether death is accidental, suicidal or homicidal ?
- That whether the cause of death was due to irritants (mechanical) poisoning ?

GLASS POWDER POISONING

Poisoning: Irritants poisoning.

Etiology: Accidental: common amongst industrial workers and children

Suicidal: rare

Homicidal: very rare.

Diagnosis: GI Tract:

- Burning sensation in the throat
- Pain abdomen (colicky), vomiting, diarrhea

Respiratory:

- Breathing: slow and weak.

Unconsciousness

Coma

Death.

Laboratory analysis: of vomitus, urine, stools, excreta, damaged viscera.

Lethal time: Few hrs. to few days.

PM findings: External:

- Signs of perforated abdomen/intestines: distended abdomen.

Internal:

GI Tract:

- Marks: red inflammed marks over the mucous membrane of the upper GI Tract.
- Stomach: highly inflammed, perforated (common), contents dark brownish.
- Doudenum: congested.

Other viscera: inflammed, congested.

Laboratory analysis: of vomitus, urine, stools, excreta, damaged viscera.

Medico-legal aspect:

- That whether death is accidental, suicidal or homicidal ?
- That whether the cause of death was due to glass powder poisoning ?

DIAMOND POISONING

Poisoning: Irritants poisoning.

Types: Dust: diamond

Jewellery: diamond

Etiology: Accidental: common amongst industrial workers (dust inhalation)

Suicidal: common amongst women (Jewellery–ingestion of diamond)

Homicidal: very rare.

Diagnosis: GI Tract:

- Burning sensation in the throat
- Pain abdomen (colicky), vomiting, bloody diarrhea

Respiratory:

- Breathing: slow and weak.

Unconsciousness, convulsions

Coma

Death.

Laboratory analysis: of vomitus, urine, stools, excreta, damaged viscera.

Lethal time: within few hrs.

PM findings: External:

- Signs of perforated abdomen/intestines: distended abdomen.

Internal:

GI Tract:

- Marks: red inflammed marks over the mucous membrane of the upper GI Tract.
- Stomach: highly inflammed, perforated (common), contents dark brownish.
- Doudenum: congested.

Other viscera: inflammed, congested.

Laboratory analysis: of vomitus, urine, stools, excreta, damaged viscera.

Medico-legal aspect:

- That whether death is accidental, suicidal or homicidal ?
- That whether the cause of death was due to diamond poisoning ?

PINS/NEEDLES/THORNS POISONING

Poisoning: Irritants poisoning.

Types: Metallic: pins, hair pins, needles, razor blades, rusted coins, thorns

Etiology: Accidental: common amongst children

Suicidal: rare

Homicidal: very rare.

Diagnosis: GI Tract:

- Burning sensation in the throat
- Pain abdomen (colicky), vomiting, bloody diarrhea

Respiratory:

- Breathing: slow and weak.

Unconsciousness

Coma

Death.

Laboratory analysis: of vomitus, urine, stools, excreta, damaged viscera.

Lethal time: Few hrs. to few days.

PM findings: External:

- Signs of perforated abdomen/intestines: distended abdomen.

Internal:

GI Tract:

- Marks: red inflammed marks over the mucous membrane of the upper GI Tract.
- Stomach: highly inflammed, perforated (common), contents dark brownish.
- Doudenum: congested.

Other viscera: inflammed, congested.

Laboratory analysis: of vomitus, urine, stools, excreta, damaged viscera.

Medico-legal aspect:

- That whether death is accidental, suicidal or homicidal ?
- That whether the cause of death was due to pin/needle/thorn poisoning ?

IRON POISONING

Poisoning: Irritants poisoning.

Mode: Ingestion of large doses.

Etiology: Accidental: common amongst infants and children

Suicidal: rare

Homicidal: very rare.

Diagnosis: GI Tract:

- Burning sensation in the throat
- Nausea, vomiting, bloody diarrhea, pain abdomen (colicky)

Respiratory:

- Breathing: slow and weak.

Pulse: rapid and weak

Hypotension

Pallor or cyanosis

Hematemesis, malena

Pulmonary edema

Unconsciousness

Coma
Death.

Laboratory analysis: of vomitus, urine, stools, excreta, damaged viscera.

MLD: 5-10 g.

Lethal time: 24-48 hrs.

PM findings: External:

- Signs of perforated abdomen/intestines: distended abdomen.

Internal:

GI Tract:

- Gastroenteritis: hemorrhagic (red inflammed marks over the mucous membrane of the upper GI Tract) due to corrosion.
- Stomach: highly inflammed, perforated (common), contents dark brownish.
- Doudenum: congested.
- Hepatic injury

Other viscera: inflammed, congested.

Laboratory analysis: of vomitus, urine, stools, excreta, damaged viscera.

Medico-legal aspect:

- That whether death is accidental, suicidal or homicidal ?
- That whether the cause of death was due to iron poisoning ?

IRRITANTS (ANIMALS) POISONING:

SNAKE POISONING or OPHITOXEMIA (Ophidia-snake or serpent)

Properties: The venom of poisonous snakes may be predominantly neurotoxic or hemotoxic (cytotoxic). It is a clear, amber coloured, acidic fluid.

Types: Poisonous (venomous) snakes: < 10 per cent: Sea snakes, viper, krait or karait, cobra, rattle snake, and copperhead snake.

Non-poisonous snakes: > 90 per cent: Grass snakes.

Poisoning: Occurs due to neurotoxic or hemotoxic action.

Etiology: Accidental: mostly accidental amongst picknickers

Suicidal: old custom of committing suicide (Queen Cleopatra's suicide)

Homicidal: a mode of torture/revenge.

Pathogenesis: Venom (Toxin): - neurotoxin: paralytic effect

- hemotoxin: hemolytic effect.

Diagnosis:

S/S: depend upon the type of toxin injected during the bite e.g.

Neurotoxin: Onset: within 10-15 mts. of the bite.

Pain: severe burning type.

Nausea, vomiting, weakness, feeling of intoxication.

Pupils: contracted, reacting to light.

Gait: staggering.

Speech: inco-ordination.

Mouth and nostrils: frothy, excessive salivation.

Paralysis: of voluntary muscles.

Breathing: slow and weak.

Death: due to respiratory failure (paralysis of medullary respiratory centre).

MLD: 15-40 mg.

Lethal time: - within 30 mts. to 24 hrs. of the bite.

- may be immediate due to shock.

Hemotoxin: Onset: 60 mts. of the bite (may be delayed)

Pain: persistent

Salivation: absent

Mouth and nostrils: frothy.

Hemorrhages: subconjunctival, epistaxis, hemoptysis, petichial under skin, hematuria.

Pupils: dilated, non-reacting to light.

- Site: mostly hand or foot.
- Swelling: of the bitten part.
- Oozing of hemolyzed blood from the punctured wounds.

Death: due to cardiovascular failure.

MLD: 30 mg.

Lethal time: 01-7 days.

PM findings: Bite marks: 2 marks of 1-2 cm. Depth.

Bitten part: edematous, discoloured, cellulosed.

Blood: oozing from bitten wounds.

Mouth and nostrils: frothy in case of neurotoxin.

Internal organs: hemorrhagic in case of hemotoxin.

Laboratory analysis: of vomitus, urine, stools, excreta, damaged viscera.

Medico-legal aspect:

- That whether death is accidental, suicidal or homicidal ?
- That whether the death occurred due to snake poisoning ?

SCORPION POISONING

Properties: The scorpion bite may prove lethal because of its strong hemolytic toxin.

Poisoning: Occurs due to hemolytic action.

Etiology: Accidental: mostly accidental amongst picknickers

Suicidal: old custom of committing suicide

Homicidal: a mode of torture/revenge.

Pathogenesis: Venom (Toxin): hemotoxin (hemolytic effect).

Diagnosis: Onset: within 10-15 mts. of the bite

Pain: severe burning with local irritation

Nausea, vomiting, diarrhea, weakness, giddiness

Speech: inco-ordination

Mouth and nostrils: frothy

Breathing: slow and weak

Tachycardia

Hypotension

Convulsions

Death: due to cardiovascular failure

MLD: 10-30 mg.

Lethal time: - within 30 mts. to 24 hrs. of the bite.

- may be immediate due to shock.

PM findings:- Bitten part: edematous, discoloured, cellulosed
- Blood: oozing from bitten wounds
- Mouth and nostrils: frothy
- Internal organs: congested.

Laboratory analysis: of vomitus, urine, stools, excreta, damaged viscera.

Medico-legal aspect:

- That whether death is accidental, suicidal or homicidal ?
- That whether the death occurred due to scorpion poisoning ?

SPIDER POISONING

Poisoning: Hypersensitive persons may develop an acute allergic reaction/fatal anaphylactic shock.

Etiology: Accidental: common amongst picknickers, exposed to wasp, bees, esp. during the warmer months

Homicidal: very rare.

Diagnosis: Pain, swelling, itching.

Breathing: slow and weak.

Shock: anaphylactic type.

Hemoglobinuria.

Coma

Death.

PM findings: - Marks: black or brown sting marks.
- Internal organs: inflammed, congested.

Laboratory analysis: of vomitus, urine, stools, excreta, damaged viscera.

Medico-legal aspect:

- That whether death is accidental, suicidal or homicidal ?
- That whether the cause of death was due to Spider poisoning ?

WASP, BEE-STING POISONING

Poisoning: Hypersensitive persons may develop an acute allergic reaction/fatal anaphylactic shock.

Etiology: Accidental: common amongst picknickers, exposed to wasp, bees, esp. during the warmer months

Homicidal: very rare.

Diagnosis: Pain, swelling, itching.

Breathing: slow and weak.

Shock: anaphylactic type.

Hemoglobinuria.

Coma

Death.

PM findings: - Marks: black or brown sting marks.

- Internal organs: inflammed, congested.

Laboratory analysis: of vomitus, urine, stools, excreta, damaged viscera.

Medico-legal aspect:

- That whether death is accidental, suicidal or homicidal ?
- That whether the cause of death was due to Wasp/Bee poisoning ?

CATERPILLAR POISONING

Poisoning: Hypersensitive persons may develop an acute allergic reaction/fatal anaphylactic shock.

Etiology: Accidental: common amongst picknickers, exposed to Caterpillar esp. during the warmer months

Homicidal: very rare.

Diagnosis: Pain, swelling, redness, itching

Breathing: slow and weak.

Shock: anaphylactic type.

Hemoglobinuria.

Coma

Death.

PM findings: - Marks: black or brown sting marks.

- Internal organs: inflammed, congested.

Laboratory analysis: of vomitus, urine, stools, excreta, damaged viscera.

Medico-legal aspect:

- That whether death is accidental, suicidal or homicidal ?
- That whether the cause of death was due to Caterpillar poisoning ?

NEUROTICS POISONING:

CNS DEPRESSANTS: -

GENERAL ANESTHETICS:

Definition: Intravenous anesthesia with barbiturates has largely replaced inhalation anesthesia, on account of less rates of mortality and morbidity.

Types: Intravenous:

- Ultrashort-acting barbiturates: Thiopental Sodium.

Inhalation:

- Volatile liquids: Ethyl ether, vinyl ether, chloroform, trichloroethylene.
- Gases :Nitrous oxide-oxygen mixtures, ethylene, cyclopropane.

BARBITURATES POISONING: Described under Hypnotics and Sedatives.

ETHER POISONING

Properties: It is a clear, volatile, inflammable and explosive, with an ethereal odour and a pungent taste. It is marketed in dark, tightly stoppered bottles.

Ether was once the most widely used general anesthetic, although it has now been largely replaced by other agents e.g. trichloroethylene, cyclopropane and halothane, nitrous oxide-oxygen mixtures, and ultrashort-acting barbiturates (sod. pentothal) for induction anesthesia.

Poisoning: Ether is not safe to be used for procedures lasting more than an hour, due to excessive salivation, liver damage, and difficult to use at high altitudes and in hot climates, due to its extreme volatility.

Pathogenesis: Is more irritating than chloroform to the respiratory tract, because a higher concentration is required in the inspired air for general anesthesia. Most of acute anesthetic deaths occur in stage II, due to irregular breathing, resulting in sudden changes in the concentration of anesthetic in the body.

Etiology: Accidental: mostly accidental: overdose or used as stupefying agent

Suicidal: rarely suicidal because of its unpleasant smell and taste

Homicidal: very rare.

Diagnosis: Irritation of the upper part of G.I.Tract, causing:

- Nausea, vomiting, salivation, headache, palpitation
- Skin–cold and clammy, pallor and cyanotic
- Face–cyanosed
- Pupils-dilated
- Respiration–shallow or stertorous
- Pulse– slow, feeble, irregular
- Hypotension
- Death–may occur due to respiratory failure or cardiac arrest.

MLD: 2-4 drs. (10-20 ml).

Lethal time:
- During induction, or
- Within hrs. or days after its induction.

PM findings:
- Odour: strong nauseating odour of ether
- URC: throat and trachea are congested and contain frothy saliva
- Lungs: congested, edematous and emits strong odour of ether
- Upper GI Tract: highly inflammed and congested
- Stomach: highly inflammed and congested
- Doudenum: congested
- Other viscera: congested.

Laboratory analysis: of vomitus, urine, stools, excreta, damaged viscera.

Medico-legal aspect:

- That whether the death is accidental, suicidal or homicidal ?

- That whether the death has been due to ether poisoning ?

CHLOROFORM POISONING

Properties: Is a volatile liquid with strong aromatic smell.

Poisoning: It has largely been abandoned as general anesthetic, because of its greater toxicity (hepatotoxic). Sudden cardiac arrest resulting in death, may occur during the induction phase of the chloroform anesthesia, due to faulty administration or surgical maneuvers started before anesthesia is sufficiently deep.

Etiology: Accidental–prolonged anesthesia with chloroform.

Diagnosis:
- Burning pain in the upper GI Tract-mouth, throat, and stomach.
- Nausea, vomiting, jaundice.
- Gastric - tone, motility, and secretion depressed and emptying time delayed.
- Skin–cold and clammy.
- Face – cyanosed.
- Pupils - dilated
- Respiration–slow.
- Pulse – rapid, feeble, irregular
- Hypotension
- Oliguria
- Liver–fatty degeneration, cirrhosis due to prolonged anesthesia
- Death–may occur due to respiratory or cardiac failure.

MLD: 4-6 drs. (20-30 ml).

Lethal time: 4-6 hrs.

PM findings:
- Smell of chloroform
- Mucous membrane of upper GI Tract: congested and inflammed.
- Stomach: highly inflammed, perforated.
- Doudenum: corrosion marks.
- Other viscera: corrosion marks.

Laboratory analysis: of vomitus, urine, stools, excreta, damaged viscera.

Medico-legal aspect:

- That whether the death is accidental, suicidal or homicidal ?
- That whether the death has been due to Chloroform poisoning ?

TRICHLOROETHYLENE

Properties: It is a clear, colourless, volatile liquid, non-inflammable and nonexplosive, with a characteristic odour resembling that of chloroform. It is marketed in sealed 1 ml glass tubes, dark, tightly stoppered bottles.

Uses: As an analgesic for minor surgical procedures (debridement of wounds, I/D of abscesses, orthopedic manipulations, biopsy, dental surgery, obstetrics and minor surgery), and for relief of pain in angina pectoris and trigeminal neuralgia.

Poisoning: Trichloroethylene is not safe to be used for procedures lasting more than an hour, due to excessive salivation, liver damage, and difficult to use at high altitudes and in hot climates, due to its extreme volatility.

Pathogenesis: Is more irritating than chloroform to the respiratory tract, because a higher concentration is required in the inspired air for general anesthesia. Most of acute anesthetic deaths occur in stage II, due to irregular breathing, resulting in sudden changes in the concentration of anesthetic in the body.

Etiology: Accidental: mostly accidental: overdose or used as stupefying agent

Suicidal: rarely suicidal because of its unpleasant smell and taste

Homicidal: very rare.

Diagnosis: GI Tract: Irritation of the upper part of G.I.Tract, causing:

- Nausea, vomiting, salivation, headache, palpitation

Skin–cold and clammy, pallor and cyanotic
Face–cyanosed
Pupils-dilated
Respiration–shallow or stertorous
Pulse–slow, feeble, irregular
Hypotension
Hepatic damage
Cardiac arrhythmias
Death from cardiac arrest.

Laboratory: Urine analysis

MLD: 5 ml.

Lethal time: - During induction, or
- Within hrs. or days after its induction.

PM findings: - Odour: strong nauseating odour of ether
- URC: throat and trachea are congested and contain frothy saliva
- Lungs: congested, edematous and emits strong odour of ether
- Upper GI Tract: highly inflammed and congested
- Stomach: highly inflammed and congested
- Doudenum: congested
- Other viscera: congested.

Laboratory analysis: of vomitus, urine, stools, excreta, damaged viscera.

Medico-legal aspect:

- That whether the death is accidental, suicidal or homicidal ?
- That whether the death has been due to trichloroethylene poisoning ?

GAS ANESTHETICS:

Gases: Nitrous oxide-oxygen mixtures, ethylene, cyclopropane.

NITROUS OXIDE (Laughing gas) POISONING

Properties: Is the oldest of the inhalation anesthetics. Is a colourless, odourless, and tasteless gas. Is marketed in blue coloured steel cylinders, as a colourless liquid under pressure of 30 atmosphere, returnable to gas form on release of pressure. Is higly soluble in blood, carried as such in the blood (does not combine with hemoglobin), exhaled as such (unchanged). Fatal explosions may occur with ether/ethylene-nitrous oxide mixtures.

Poisoning: Nitrous oxide causes anoxia (avoidable) during induction of general anesthesia.

Factors governing safe induction of general anesthesia:

- Special Boyle's Apparatus for induction of general anesthesia.
- Experienced anesthesist
- Low anesthetic potency: requires preanesthetic medication, curare, or other agents.
- Inhalation of mixtures of nitrous oxide and oxygen: adequate concentration of oxygen (20 per cent) must be combined with the nitrous oxide.

Etiology: Accidental: use of undiluted/ or high concentrations of nitrous oxide.

Diagnosis: Anoxia:

- Headache, nausea, vomiting, giddiness, numbness, tinnitus, exhibits exhilaration or bursts into laughter, hallucinations.
- Tachycardia
- Respiration: deep and rapid
- Hypertension
- Pupils: dilated
- Skin: cyanotic
- Coma, convulsions
- Death due to respiratory failure.

MLD: 88:12 mixture of nitrous oxide and oxygen inhaled continuously.

Lethal time: > 2 mts.

PM findings: Circumstantial evidence:

- victim is mostly found under doubtless circumstances.

Externally:

Skin and mucous membrane: cyanotic

Internally:

- GI Tract: mucous membrane is congested
- Lungs: congested and edematous
- Other viscera: congested.

Laboratory analysis: of vomitus, urine, stools, excreta, damaged viscera.

Medico-legal aspect:

- That whether death was accidental, suicidal or homicidal ?
- That whether death was due to asphyxia ?
- That whether death was due to nitrous oxide poisoning ?

ETHYLENE POISONING

Properties: Is an unsaturated olefin hydrocarbon. Is a colourless, water soluble gas, having a sweet taste and odour, itself nonexplosive and noninflammable, but is explosive and inflammable when mixed with oxygen of certain concentrations.

It is marketed in compressed form in metallic cylinders, returnable to gas form on release of pressure.

Uses: Ethylene-oxygen mixtures produce satisfactory anesthesia (rapid and safe induction, minimal struggle, rapid recovery, and minimal postoperative complications).

Poisoning: Ethylene causes anoxia (avoidable) during induction of general anesthesia.

Factors governing safe induction of general anesthesia:

- Special Boyle's Apparatus for induction of general anesthesia.
- Experienced anesthesist
- Low anesthetic potency: requires preanesthetic medication, curare, or other agents.
- Inhalation of mixtures of ethylene and oxygen: adequate concentration of oxygen (20 per cent) must be combined with the ethylene.

Etiology: Accidental: use of undiluted/ or high concentrations of ethylene.

Diagnosis: Anoxia:

- Headache, nausea, vomiting, giddiness, numbness, tinnitus.
- Tachycardia,
- Respiration: deep and rapid
- Hypertension
- Pupils: dilated
- Skin: cyanotic
- Coma, convulsions
- Death due to respiratory failure.

MLD: 90 : 10 mixture of ethylene and oxygen inhaled continuously.

Lethal time: > 2 mts.

PM findings: Externally:

Skin and mucous membrane: cyanotic

Internally:

- GI Tract: mucous membrane is congested
- Lungs: congested and edematous
- Other viscera: congested.

Laboratory analysis: of vomitus, urine, stools, excreta, damaged viscera.

Medico-legal aspect:

- That whether death was accidental, suicidal or homicidal ?
- That whether death was due to asphyxia ?
- That whether death was due to ethylene poisoning?

CYCLOPROPANE POISONING

Properties: Is a colourless gas, with pleasant odour resembling petroleum ether, and having a pungent taste. Is marketed in metallic cylinders, as a liquid under pressure, returnable to gas form on release of pressure. Is explosive and inflammable).

Uses: Cyclopropane-oxygen mixtures produce satisfactory anesthesia (rapid and safe induction, minimal struggle, rapid recovery, and minimal postoperative complications).

Poisoning: Cyclopropane causes anoxia (avoidable) during induction of general anesthesia.

Factors governing safe induction of general anesthesia:

- Special Boyle's Apparatus for induction of general anesthesia.
- Experienced anesthesist
- Low anesthetic potency: requires preanesthetic medication, curare, or other agents.
- Inhalation of mixtures of cyclopropane and oxygen: adequate concentration of oxygen (20 per cent) must be combined with the cyclopropane.

Etiology: Accidental: use of undiluted/ or high concentrations of cyclopropane.

Diagnosis: Anoxia:

- Headache, nausea, vomiting, giddiness, numbness, tinnitus.
- Respiration: deep and rapid
- Atelectasis
- Pulse: volume changes
- Hypertension
- Cardiac arrhythmias
- Pupils: dilated
- Skin: cyanotic
- Coma, convulsions
- Death due to cardiac failure.

MLD: 90:10 mixture of cyclopropane and oxygen inhaled continuously.

Lethal time: > 2 mts.

PM findings: Externally:

Skin and mucous membrane: cyanotic

Internally:

- GI Tract: mucous membrane is congested
- Lungs: congested and edematous
- Other viscera: congested.

Laboratory analysis: of vomitus, urine, stools, excreta, damaged viscera.

Medico-legal aspect:

- That whether death was accidental, suicidal or homicidal ?
- That whether death was due to asphyxia ?
- That whether death was due to cyclopropane poisoning ?

NARCOTICS (Natural and Semisynthetic Alkaloids):

OPIUM POISONING

Source: Opium is obtained from the milky exudates/ juice of the incised unripe seed capsules of the poppy plant Papaver somniferum, indigenous to Asia Minor and being cultivated in other countries including China, India, Egypt and Turkey.

Opium is the drug of choice in suicide, as the death is painless.

Alkaloids: The pharmacologically active constituents of opium are alkaloids:

Natural alkaloids:

- Phenanthrene: Morphine, Codeine
- Benzyliso-quinoline: Narcotine, Papaverine

Semisynthetic alkaloids:

- Diacetylmorphine: Heroine (Heroin)
- Ethylmorphine: Dionine
- Apomorphine

Properties: Is a light brown, bitter, fine powder, available for clinical use in tablet, capsule, or pill form.

Routes of administration:

- Ingestion: accidental (victims mostly children).
- Direct contact: local application to a wound.
- Injectable: s.c. Inj. of morphine.
- Per rectal: as enema, or suppository.
- Per vaginal.

Poisoning: Occurs from clinical overdosage, or from attempts at self-destruction (addiction).

Etiology: Accidental: common amongst unattended children

Suicidal: old custom of committing suicide

Homicidal: rarely used because of its bitter taste, colour and smell.

Pathogenesis: Opium exerts narcotic action, manifested by analgesia, sleep, and respiration depression.

Diagnosis: - Onset: ½ to 1 hr.

S/S: - Sense of well being, hallucination, restlessness – headache, giddiness, drowsiness and lethargy

- Pupils: myosis (pinpoint contraction)
- Face: pale
- Lips: livid
- Skin: cod, clammy
- Pulse: slow, irregular
- Hypotension Reflexes: absent
- Skeletal muscles: flaccid
- Coma
- Death occurs due to respiratory failure and may also be due to shock, pulmonary edema or aspirated pneumonia.

MLD: 2 g

Lethal time: 12-24 hrs.

PM findings: - Signs of asphyxia e.g. lividity of lips, lobule of ears, finger tips and nails.

- Mouth and nostrils: frothy.
- Stomach: mucous membrane congested, contents emit oder of opium.
- Doudenum: congested.
- Other viscera: congested.

Laboratory analysis: of vomitus, urine, stools, excreta, damaged viscera.

Medico-legal aspect:

- That whether death is accidental, suicidal or homicidal ?
- That whether the death occurred due to opium poisoning ?

MORPHINE POISONING

Properties: Is an important phenanthrene alkaloid of opium. It is a white, bitter, fine powder, available for clinical use in tablet and sterile aqueous solution for parenteral use.

Salts: Morphine sulphate and Morphine hydrochloride.

Poisoning: Occurs from clinical overdosage, or from attempts at self-destruction (addiction).

Types: Acute and Chronic Morphine Poisoning.

ACUTE MORPHINE POISONING

Poisoning: Occurs from clinical overdosage, or from attempts at self-destruction (addiction).

Etiology: Accidental: from clinical overdosage.

Suicidal: from attempts at self-destruction.

Homicidal: rarely used.

Routes of administration:

- Parenteral: Inj. of morphine
- Oral: tablets.

Pathogenesis: Morphine exerts narcotic action, manifested by analgesia, sleep, and respiration depression.

Diagnosis:

- Nausea, vomiting
- Headache, depression, asleep or stuporous
- Respiratory depression
- Pulse–fast and weak
- Pinpoint pupils
- Convulsions
- Shock
- Coma, death–due to respiratory failure.

Laboratory analysis: of vomitus, urine, stools, excreta, damaged viscera.

MLD: 60-250 mg.

Lethal time: 01-12 hrs.

PM findings:

- Signs of asphyxia e.g. lividity of lips, lobule of ears, finger tips and nails.
- Mouth and nostrils: frothy.
- Stomach: mucous membrane congested, contents emit oder of opium.

- Doudenum: congested.
- Other viscera: congested.

Laboratory analysis: of vomitus, urine, stools, excreta, damaged viscera.

Medico-legal aspect:

- That whether death is accidental, suicidal or homicidal ?
- That whether the death occurred due to morphine poisoning ?

CHRONIC MORPHINE POISONING (OPIUM ADDICTION)

Etiology: Habitual smoking, IV (Addicts–for euphoria, thrill).

Diagnosis: Addict–shabbily dressed, cunning, malicious, degenerate criminal (due to disturbed financial, nutritional, social position).

Withdrawal Symptoms:

- Expresses craving and need for the drug
- Feeling of sickness, apprehensive, irritable
- Indulgence in criminal activities–theft, violence–to obtain drug
- Deep sleep (yen) followed by
- Restlessness, miserable, sweating, tremor
- Muscular weakness, depression
- Nausea, vomiting, colic
- Hypertension
- Headache, delirium
- Death–may occur due to cardiovascular failure.

PM findings:
- Signs of asphyxia e.g. lividity of lips, lobule of ears, finger tips and nails.
- Mouth and nostrils: frothy.
- Stomach: mucous membrane congested, contents emit oder of opium.
- Doudenum: congested.
- Other viscera: congested.

Laboratory analysis: of vomitus, urine, stools, excreta, damaged viscera.

Medico-legal aspect:

- That whether death is accidental, suicidal or homicidal ?
- That whether the death occurred due to morphine poisoning ?

NARCOTICS (SYNTHETIC):

MEPERIDINE (PETHIDINE) POISONING:

Properties: Is a white, crystalline, bitter powder, non-irritating to the GI Tract.

Poisoning: Occurs from clinical overdosage, or from attempts at self-destruction (addiction). The main manifestation of mepridine poisoning is CNS depression.

Etiology: Accidental: from clinical overdosage.

Suicidal: from attempts at self-destruction.

Homicidal: rarely used.

Routes of administration:

- Parenteral: Inj. of mepridine
- Oral: tablets.

Pathogenesis:

Diagnosis:
- Nausea, vomiting
- Headache, depression, asleep or stuporous
- Flushing of face, sweating, dryness of the mouth
- Vision: blurring
- Corneal reflex: abolished
- Urticaria
- Muscular weakness
- Respiratory depression
- Convulsions
- Coma
- Death may occur from respiratory failure.

MLD: 1-2 g.

Lethal time: 01-12 hrs.

PM findings: - Signs of asphyxia e.g. lividity of lips, lobule of ears, finger tips and nails.

- Mouth: dry
- Stomach: mucous membrane congested.
- Doudenum: congested.
- Other viscera: congested.

Laboratory analysis: of vomitus, urine, stools, excreta, damaged viscera.

Medico-legal aspect:

- That whether death is accidental, suicidal or homicidal ?
- That whether the death occurred due to mepridine poisoning ?

NON-NARCOTICS (ANALGESICS AND ANTIPYRETICS):

Drugs: Mild pain:

- Salicylates-Sodium salicylate, salicylic acid, acetyl salicylic acid (Aspirin)
- p-Aminophenols: Acetaminophen (Paracetamol), phenacetin
- Colchicine, aminopyrine, acetanilide
- NSAIDs
- Antimalarials: Quinine and Cinchona alkaloids

Moderate pain:

- Weak opioids alone, or in conjunction with mild analgesics
- Codein + paracetamol
- Dihydrocodeine + parcetamol
- Tramadol + paracetamol

Severe pain:

- Strong opioids: Morphine, fentanyl, methadone, phenazocine, tramadol. mepridine (pethidine).

Neuropathic pain:

- Corticosteroids: Dexamethasone, betamethasone

SALICYLATES POISONING

Properties: Salicylic acid is a white crystalline powder, sweetish/acrid taste, and odourless. It is highly irritating to skin and mucosa (destroys epithelial cells) of GI Tract.

Derivatives of salicylic acid:

- Esters of salicylic acid: aspirin, sodium and ammonium salicylate.
- Esters (salicylatye) of organic acid.

Compounds:- Salicylic acid, acetylsalicylic acid (aspirin), sodium salicylate, methyl salicylate (oil of Wintergreen), phenyl salicylate.

Poisoning: Occurs due to irritant action. All the salicylates cause the same type of poisoning.

Etiology:

- Accidental– overdosage (in the treatment of acute rheumatic fever)
- Idiosyncrasy: untoward response to salicylate
- Suicidal.

Pathogenesis: Acid-base disturbances (respiratory alkalosis followed by metabolic acidisis), hypoprothrombinemia, and gastroenteritis.

Diagnosis:

- Headache, dizziness, tinitis, impaired hearing, dimness of vision
- Nausea, vomiting, diarrhea, thirst, abdominal pain
- Cold, clammy skin, sweating, skin eruptions
- Epistaxis, bleeding from gums, retinal hemorrhage, hematuria
- Confusion, drowsiness, delirium, convulsions, coma
- Death–may occur due to respiratory or circulatory failure.

MLD: Lethal dose: variable with the preparation of salicylate.

- Acetylsalicylic acid or Sod. Salicylate: 10-30 g may cause death in adults.
- Methyl salicylate: considerably < Sod salicylate.

  Children: 4 ml of methyl salicylate may be fatal.

Lethal time: 1-5 days.

PM findings:

- Skin: petechial hemorrhages
- Marks: black or brown corrosion marks over the mucous membrane of the upper GI Tract.

- Stomach: highly inflammed, perforated.
- Doudenum: corrosion marks.
- Brain: diffuse encephalopathy
- Other viscera: corrosion marks.

Laboratory analysis: of vomitus, urine, stools, excreta, damaged viscera.

Medico-legal aspect:

- That whether death is accidental, suicidal or homicidal ?
- That whether the cause of death was due to salicylate poisoning ?

ACETAMINOPHEN (PARACETAMOL) POISONING

Properties: Is a valuable central analgesic, good antipyretic but weak anti-inflammatory agent.

Poisoning: Acute and chronic.

Route: Ingestion (Tablet and suspension form)

Etiology: Accidental: from clinical overdosage.

Suicidal: rarely used.

Pathogenesis: Exerts a variety of pharmacological actions, besides toxic effects.

Diagnosis: GI Tract:

- Nausea, vomiting, diarrhea, dyspepsia, epigastric pain

Skin: urticaria

Pulse: rapid and weak

Hepatotoxicity

Muscular weakness

Dizziness, convulsions, coma.

Death from respiratory failure.

Investigation: Measurement of plasma paracetamol as an emergency measure.

MLD: > 4 g

Lethal time: Within 24 hrs.

PM findings: GI Tract:

- mucous membrane of the upper GI Tract congested.

- Stomach: mucous membrane highly congested.
  Skin: dry, rashes
  Liver: damage
  Kidneys: fatty nephritic
  Other viscera: congested.

Laboratory analysis: of vomitus, urine, stools, excreta, damaged viscera.

Medico-legal aspects:

- That whether the death is accidental, suicidal or homicidal ?
- That whether the death has been caused by paracetamol poisoning ?

COLCHICINE POISONING

Properties: Is a water soluble yellowish powder, clinically available as tablets and injection.

Uses: Colchicine still has no rival for the relief of acute attacks of gout.

Poisoning: Acute and chronic.

Route: Ingestion and parenteral.

Etiology: Accidental: from clinical overdosage.
Suicidal: rarely used.
Homicidal: rarely used.

Pathogenesis: Exerts a variety of pharmacological actions, besides toxic effects.

Diagnosis: GI Tract:

- Nausea, vomiting, diarrhea, epigastric pain, throat burning,

Urinary tract injury:

- hematuria, oliguria
  Skin: urticaria
  Pulse: rapid and weak
  Muscular weakness, paralysis
  Dizziness, convulsions, coma.
  Death from respiratory failure.

MLD: 6-30 mg

Lethal time: 24-48 hrs.

PM findings: GI Tract:

- black or brown corrosion marks over the mucous membrane of the upper GI Tract.
- Stomach: mucous membrane highly congested, perforated

Skin: cold clamy

Kidneys: fatty nephritic

Other viscera: congested.

Laboratory analysis: of vomitus, urine, stools, excreta, damaged viscera.

Medico-legal aspects:

- That whether the death is accidental, suicidal or homicidal ?
- That whether the death has been caused by colchicine poisoning ?

ACETANILID POISONING

Properties: Known as coal-tar antipyretic. Is a white crystalline powder, available as powder, tablet, or capsule.

Poisoning: Acute and chronic. Death may result from either.

Etiology: Accidental: from clinical overdosage.

Suicidal: rarely from attempts at self-destruction

Homicidal: rarely used.

Diagnosis: Cyanosis: is the cardinal sign.

Spectroscopic examination of the blood: to confirm methemoglobin

Anemia, weakness, loss of weight

Breathing: shortness

Jaundice, urticaria

Oligurea or anuria

CNS stimulation: excitement, delirium, followed by depression and stupor.

Convulsions, collapse, coma

Death – sudden

MLD: Variable (as much as 30 g).

Lethal time: Sudden or may be delayed for several days.

PM findings: External: marked cyanosis of skin, fingernails.

Internal:

GI Tract: bluish colouration of the mucous membrane of the upper GI Tract.

- Stomach: highly inflammed, perforated.
- Doudenum: corrosion marks.
- Other viscera: corrosion marks.

Medico-legal aspects:

- That whether the death is accidental, suicidal or homicidal ?
- That whether the death has been caused by acetanilide poisoning ?

ANILINE POISONING

Properties: Known as cloth-marking ink. Is a colourless oily liquid with a characteristic odour. Is purely of toxicological importance.

Poisoning: Acute and chronic. Death may result from either.

Etiology: Accidental: from inhalation of aniline vapours, from ingestion of the chemical, or from skin absorption.

Suicidal: rarely from attempts at self-destruction

Homicidal: rarely used.

Diagnosis: Cyanosis: is the cardinal sign.

Spectroscopic examination of the blood: to confirm methemoglobin

Anemia, weakness, loss of weight

Breathing: shortness

Jaundice, urticaria

Oligurea or anuria

CNS stimulation: excitement, delirium, followed by depression and stupor.

Convulsions, collapse, coma

Death–sudden

MLD: Variable (as much as 30 g).

Lethal time: Sudden or may be delayed for several days.

PM findings: External: marked cyanosis of skin, fingernails.

Internal:

GI Tract: bluish colouration of the mucous membrane of the upper GI Tract.

- Stomach: highly inflammed, perforated.
- Doudenum: corrosion marks.
- Other viscera: corrosion marks.

Laboratory analysis: of vomitus, urine, stools, excreta, damaged viscera.

Medico-legal aspects:

- That whether the death is accidental, suicidal or homicidal ?
- That whether the death has been caused by aniline poisoning ?

NSAIDs POISONING

Properties: There is considerable individual variation in tolerance and response to NSAIDs. The main differences between NSAIDs are in the incidence and type of side effects. These should never be combined.

Poisoning: Occurs from clinical overdosage, or from attempts at self-destruction

Etiology: Accidental: from clinical overdosage.
Suicidal: from attempts at self-destruction.
Homicidal: rarely used.

Routes of administration:

- Oral: Tablet, capsule, suspension: Ibuprofen, ketoprofen, diclofenac, indomethacin, naproxen, piroxicam, nimesulide, celecoxib, azapropazone, mefanamic acid, aceclofenac.
- Parenteral:
  - IM: Diclofenac,
  - IV: Parecoxib
  - Intra-articular: Hyaluronates

Diagnosis: GI Tract:

- Nausea, vomiting, diarrhea, epigastric pain, constipation
- Headache, dizziness, drowsiness

- Skin rash, edema
- Respiratory depression
- Pulse–fast and weak
- Hypotension
- Convulsions
- Shock
- Coma, death–due to respiratory failure.

MLD: 200 mcg.

Lethal time: 01-12 hrs.

PM findings:
- Signs of asphyxia e.g. lividity of lips, lobule of ears, finger tips and nails.
- Mouth and nostrils: frothy.
- Stomach: mucous membrane congested, contents emit odour of opium.
- Doudenum: congested.
- Other viscera: congested.

Laboratory analysis: of vomitus, urine, stools, excreta, damaged viscera.

Medico-legal aspect:

- That whether death is accidental, suicidal or homicidal ?
- That whether the death occurred due to NSAIDs poisoning ?

QUININE AND CINCHONA ALKALOIDS POISONING

Properties: Quinine is the chief alkaloid of cinchona, exracted from the bark of cinchona tree. Is a white, crystalline, odourless, intensely bitter, water soluble powder

Cinchona alkaloids: Levorotatory: quinine and cinchonidine

Dextrorotatory: quinidine and cinchonine

Cinchona is rarely used currently.

Poisoning: Occurs from clinical overdosage, or from idiosyncrasy.

Quinine and cinchona alkaloids have similar toxic reactions.

Etiology: Accidental: from clinical overdosage to idiosyncrasy.

Suicidal: from attempts at self-destruction.

Homicidal: rarely used.

Routes of administration:

- Oral: tablet and capsule.
- IM and s.c.: injection painful and may cause abscess formation
- IV: for cerebral or pernicious malaria.

Diagnosis: Cinchonism syndrome:

GI Tract:

- Nausea, vomiting, diarrhea, pain abdomen

CNS:

- Headache, fever, excitement, apprehension, confusion, delirium

Ears: hearing impaired, tinnitus, vertigo

Eyes: vision disturbed: blurred vision, photophobia, diplopia, mydriasis

Respiratory depression

Pulse – fast and weak

Hypotension

Skin: cold and cyanotic, rashes

Renal damage, anuria, uremia

Purpura

Hepatitis

Convulsions

Shock, coma

Death from cardiorespiratory failure.

Laboratory: Urine analysis: proteinuria, hemoglobinuria, casts

MLD: 1 g.

Lethal time: 01-12 hrs.

PM findings: External:

Skin: cold and cyanotic

GI Tract upper: congested

- Stomach: mucous membrane congested

- Doudenum: congested.
- Other viscera: congested.

Laboratory analysis: of vomitus, urine, stools, excreta, damaged viscera.

Medico-legal aspect:

- That whether death is accidental, suicidal or homicidal ?
- That whether the death occurred due to quinine poisoning ?

TRAMADOL POISONING

Properties: Is a weak against at all types of opioid receptors with some selectivity for neuroreceptors. Is a good analgesic, without any drug dependence.

Is an important phenanthrene alkaloid of opium. It is a white, bitter, fine powder, available for clinical use in tablet and sterile aqueous solution for parenteral use.

Poisoning: Occurs from clinical overdosage, or from attempts at self-destruction.

Etiology: Accidental: from clinical overdosage.

Suicidal: from attempts at self-destruction.

Homicidal: rarely used.

Routes of administration:

- Parenteral: Inj. of tramadol
- Oral: tablet and capsule.

Diagnosis:
- Nausea, vomiting
- Headache, asleep or stuporous
- Respiratory depression
- Pulse – fast and weak
- Convulsions
- Shock
- Coma, death – due to respiratory failure.

MLD: 0.5 g.

Lethal time: 01-12 hrs.

PM findings:
- Signs of asphyxia e.g. lividity of lips, lobule of ears, finger tips and nails.
- Mouth and nostrils: frothy.

- Stomach: mucous membrane congested, contents emit odour of opium.
- Doudenum: congested.
- Other viscera: congested.

Laboratory analysis: of vomitus, urine, stools, excreta, damaged viscera.

Medico-legal aspect:

- That whether death is accidental, suicidal or homicidal ?
- That whether the death occurred due to tramadol poisoning ?

FENTANYL POISONING

Properties: Is a potent synthetic opioid analgesic, having rapid onset of action, acting for a short duration. It is available for clinical use in sterile aqueous solution for parenteral use.

Poisoning: Occurs from clinical overdosage, or from attempts at self-destruction

Etiology: Accidental: from clinical overdosage.
Suicidal: from attempts at self-destruction.
Homicidal: rarely used.

Routes of administration:

- Parenteral: Inj. of fentanyl.

Diagnosis:
- Nausea, vomiting
- Headache, depression, asleep or stuporous
- Respiratory depression
- Pulse–fast and weak
- Hypotension
- Convulsions
- Shock
- Coma, death–due to respiratory failure.

MLD: 200 mcg.

Lethal time: 01-12 hrs.

PM findings:
- Signs of asphyxia e.g. lividity of lips, lobule of ears, finger tips and nails.
- Mouth and nostrils: frothy.

- Stomach: mucous membrane congested, contents emit odour of opium.
- Doudenum: congested.
- Other viscera: congested.

Laboratory analysis: of vomitus, urine, stools, excreta, damaged viscera.

Medico-legal aspect:

- That whether death is accidental, suicidal or homicidal ?
- That whether the death occurred due to fentanyl poisoning ?

HYPNOTICS (INEBRIENTS):

ACUTE ALCOHOL (ETHYL) POISONING (INTOXICATION):

Poisoning: Acute alcohol poisoning may vary from intoxication to profound comatosed condition and the condition depends on tolerance, amount ingested and absorbed. The main manifestation of ethyl alcohol poisoning is CNS depression and GI Tract irritation.

Etiology:
- Inhalation of alcohol vapour
- Ingestion of alcohol
- Direct contact: applied over burns or large wounds

Strength: per cent of alcoholic beverages:
- Beer: 5-7 per cent
- Gin: 10-15 per cent
- Wine: 15-20 per cent
- Whisky: 30-40 per cent
- Brandy: 40-45 per cent
- Rum: 45-70 per cent

Diagnosis:

Alcohol intoxication:
- History of alcohol abuse
- Euphoria, disinhibition, mild co-ordination problems.
- Confusion, impaired consciousness–may progress to anesthesia

- Mood liability, impaired judgment, sexual or aggressive impulses
- Speech-slurred
- Nystagmus, ataxia,
- Pupils–normal or dilated
- Respiration–slow and noisy
- Tachycardia
- Skin–cold and clamy, hypothermia
- Nausea, vomiting, gastritis
- Headache, confusion, euphoria, ataxia
- Slurred speech
- Impaired judgement
- Sexual-aggressive behaviour (In Shakespeare's Macbeth e.g.

  Alcohol provokes the desire but it takes away the performance).
- Coma and death.

Withdrawal syndrome:

- Tremors of hands, tongue, eyelids
- Nausea, vomiting, headache, insomnia, hallucinations
- Hypotension–orthostatic.

Delirium tremens:

- Disorientation, confusion, agitation
- Hallucinations
- Seizures
- Death may occur due to fat embolism or cardiac arrhythmias.

MLD: 60-150 ml (measured in terms of absolute alcohol).

Lethal time: 6-12 hrs. (may be less or more).

PM findings: Alcoholic odour: from mouth, nose, gastric contents, lungs, brain and bladder.

Rigor mortis: prolonged.

Internal organs: congested.

Heart: right side full, while left one empty.

Decomposition: retarded.

Laboratory analysis: of vomitus, urine, stools, excreta, damaged viscera.

Medico-legal aspect:

- That whether the person is suffering from alcohol poisoning or not ?
- That whether the person be held responsible for a criminal act ?
- That whether the person is capable of taking care of himself/herself ?
- That whether the concentration of alcohol in the exhaled air, blood, urine, or saliva determined or not ?

METHYL ALCOHOL (syn. Methanol, Machinery Spirit) POISONING

Properties: Is widely used in industry as a solvent. It has no therapeutic use, but mainly of toxicological interest.

Poisoning: Occurs from its ingestion or from industrial exposure.

Poisoning occurs due to combination of the following factors:

- CNS depression.
- Retinal cell damage and metabolic acidosis due to production of formic acid.

Routes: Occurs from its ingestion or from industrial exposure

Diagnosis:

- Nausea, vomiting, abdominal pain.
- Headache, dizziness
- Dyspnea
- Bradycardia
- Skin: cold clammy
- Blindness.
- Delirium, convulsions, coma.
- Death may occur in severe case.

MLD: 30-60 ml.

Investigation: Blood and urine contain methanol and formic acid.

Albuminuria and acetonuria.

PM findings: - Stomach: brown colouration of the mucous membrane, with congestion.
- Liver: hepatomegaly or cirrhotic.
- Pancreas: extensive necrosis.
- Heart: enlarged, fatty degeneration.
- Lungs: edematous.
- Brain: edematous.
- Other viscera: congested.

Laboratory analysis: of vomitus, urine, stools, excreta, damaged viscera.

Medico-legal aspect:

- That whether the death is accidental, suicidal or homicidal ?
- That whether the death has been due to consumption of methyl alcohol ?

HYPNOTICS AND SEDATIVES:

BARBITURATES POISONING

Definition: Barbiturates are amongst the most common offenders in accidental and suicidal poisoning.

Types: Acute intoxication: poisoning
Chronic intoxication: addiction

Pathogenesis: Barbiturates are central nervous system depressants, frequently used by physicians. The central depressant action produces calmness, sleep, inhibit convulsions, and results in basal or complete surgical anaesthesia. The physiological and psychological changes produced by a toxic amount of any member of this class of drugs.

Routes: Occurs from its ingestion or from parenteral (injudicious) use.

Etiology: Accidental:

- may occur from overdose, esp. in drug addicts (injudicious use)
- Idiosyncrasy may cause intoxication
- automatism

- abuse: as sedative/hypnotic drug
- anesthesia (general) complication

Suicidal: with suicidal intent (fashionable and aristocratic poison)

Homicidal: as a mode of capital punishment to criminals.

Diagnosis:
- Excitement, delirium, hallucinations
- Depression, drowsiness, confusion
- Headache, nausea, vomiting
- Respiratory depression
- Skin: cold, clammy, cyanotic
- Pupils: constricted, later on dilated
- Coma
- Death occurs from respiratory failure due to paralysis of respiratory centre.

MLD: 0.5-2.0 g.

Lethal time: Within an hour.

PM findings:
- Skin: cyanotic
- Stomach: congested
- Doudenum: congested
- Other viscera: congested
- Presence of barbiturate in the gastric contents, blood, urine, or in the viscera (esp. brain and liver).

Laboratory analysis: of vomitus, urine, stools, excreta, damaged viscera.

Medico-legal aspect:

- That whether the death is accidental, suicidal or homicidal ?
- That whether the death has been due to barbiturate poisoning ?
- That whether the barbiturate identified in the viscera, blood, or urine ?

CHLORAL HYDRATE POISONING

Properties: It is the oldest and still one of the best hypnotic available, used mainly as a sedative and soporific.

Uses:
- Employed in patients undergoing withdrawal of morphine, alcohol, or barbiturate.
- Employed in cases with delirium tremens.
- Employed for narcoanalysis and narcolepsy.
- Employed in the management of eclampsia.

Poisoning: Acute and chronic types.

Etiology: Accidental: mostly accidental: overdose or used as stupefying agent

Suicidal: rarely suicidal

Homicidal: very rare.

Diagnosis: Burning pain: in the upper G.I. Tract

Nausea, vomiting

Deep stupor

Vasodilatation

Hypotension

Hypothermia

Respiration: slow

Cyanosis

Pupils: pin-point

Delirium

Death from respiratory failure.

MLD: 10-30 g.

Lethal time: 5-10 hrs.

PM findings:
- Marks: black or brown corrosion marks over the mucous membrane of the upper GI Tract.
- Odour: smell of chloral hydrate.
- Stomach: mucous membrane highly inflammed, eroded.
- Doudenum: congested.
- Other viscera: congested.
- Fatty degeneration: of liver, heart and kidneys, in chronic cases.

Laboratory analysis: of vomitus, urine, stools, excreta, damaged viscera.

Medico-legal aspect:

- That whether the death is accidental, suicidal or homicidal ?

- That whether the death has been due to Chloral hydrate poisoning ?

BROMIDE POISONING

Properties: It is the oldest and still one of the best hypnotic available, used mainly as a sedative and soporific.

Uses:
- Employed in patients undergoing withdrawal of morphine, alcohol, or barbiturate.
- Employed in cases with delirium tremens.
- Employed for narcoanalysis and narcolepsy.
- Employed in the management of eclampsia.

Poisoning: Acute and chronic types.

Etiology: Accidental: mostly accidental: overdose or used as stupefying agent

Suicidal: rarely suicidal

Homicidal: very rare.

Diagnosis: Burning pain: in the upper G.I.Tract

Nausea, vomiting

Deep stupor

Vasodilatation

Hypotension

Hypothermia

Respiration: slow

Cyanosis

Pupils: pin-point

Delirium

Death from respiratory failure.

Laboratory analysis: of vomitus, urine, stools, excreta, damaged viscera.

MLD: 10-30 g.

Lethal time: 5-10 hrs.

PM findings:
- Marks: black or brown corrosion marks over the mucous membrane of the upper GI Tract.
- Odour: smell of chloral hydrate.
- Stomach: mucous membrane highly inflammed, eroded.
- Doudenum: congested.

- Other viscera: congested.
- Fatty degeneration: of liver, heart and kidneys, in chronic cases.

Laboratory analysis: of vomitus, urine, stools, excreta, damaged viscera.

Medico-legal aspect:

- That whether the death is accidental, suicidal or homicidal ?
- That whether the death has been due to Bromide poisoning ?

PARALDEHYDE POISONING

Properties: It is the oldest and still one of the best hypnotic available, used mainly as a sedative and soporific.

Uses:
- Employed in patients undergoing withdrawal of morphine, alcohol, or barbiturate.
- Employed in cases with delirium tremens.
- Employed for narcoanalysis and narcolepsy.
- Employed in the management of eclampsia.

Poisoning: Acute and chronic types.

Etiology: Accidental: mostly accidental: overdose or used as stupefying agent
Suicidal: rarely suicidal
Homicidal: very rare.

Diagnosis: Burning pain: in the upper G.I.Tract
Nausea, vomiting
Deep stupor
Vasodilatation
Hypotension
Hypothermia
Respiration: slow
Cyanosis
Pupils: pin-point
Delirium
Death from respiratory failure.

MLD: 10-30 g.

Lethal time: 5-10 hrs.

PM findings: - Marks: black or brown corrosion marks over the mucous membrane of the upper GI Tract.

- Odour: smell of chloral hydrate.
- Stomach: mucous membrane highly inflammed, eroded.
- Doudenum: congested
- Other viscera: congested.
- Fatty degeneration: of liver, heart and kidneys, in chronic cases.

Laboratory analysis: of vomitus, urine, stools, excreta, damaged viscera.

Medico-legal aspect:

- That whether the death is accidental, suicidal or homicidal ?
- That whether the death has been due to paraldehyde poisoning ?

MARIHUANA (CANNABIS) POISONING

Properties: Marihuana is a lipoid soluble non-nitrogenous oleoresin, extracted from cannabis sativa/indica, a hemp plant.

Action: Marihuana induces somatic and psychic changes, when smoked or ingested.

Types/Drugs:-Charas, hashish: resinous exudate of flowering tops - most potent

- Bhang: dried leaves and flowering shoots
- Ganja: resinous mass from leaves.

S/E:

- Addiction or dependence – if repeatedly used and ultimately results into tolerance,
- Pneumonia, infection, peripheral neuritis.

Diagnosis: Perception: altered time

Conjunctival injection

Emotions: loosened

Memory: impaired

Psychotomimetic effects occur with high doses:

- Confusion, stupor, euphoria, aggressive behaviour
- Insanity: mania, dementia, melancholia

- Hallucination and delusion

Speech: slurred, impaired

Miosis/or mydriosis

Drowsiness, sleep, coma,

Death occurs rarely.

Laboratory analysis: of vomitus, urine, stools, excreta, damaged viscera.

Medico-legal aspect:

- That whether the person is marihuana addict or not ?
- That what type of marihuana he/she has consumed ?
- That whether the person be held responsible for a criminal act ?
- That whether the person is capable of taking care of himself/herself ?

SEDATIVES AND TRANQUILISERS:

Drugs: Benzodiazepines: Chlordiazepoxide, alprazolam, diazepam, lorzepam

Phenothiazines: Chlorpromazine, promazine, trifluoperazine

Butyrophenones: Haloperidol

BENZODIAZEPINES POISONING:

Drugs : Chlordiazepoxide, alprazolam, diazepam, lorzepam

Actions: Hypnosedative, anxiolytic, muscle relaxant, and anticonvulsant.

Routes: Occurs from its ingestion or from parenteral (injudicious) use.

Etiology: Accidental:

- may occur from overdose, esp. in drug addicts (injudicious use)
- Idiosyncrasy may cause intoxication
- abuse: as sedative and tranquiliser drug

Suicidal: with suicidal intent (fashionable and aristocratic poison)

Homicidal: rare.

Diagnosis:
- Anxiety, insomnia, tremor
- Headache, nausea, vomiting
- Perspiration, tinnitus
- Anorexia, loss of body weight
- Respiratory depression
- Skin: cold, clammy, cyanotic
- Pupils: constricted, later on dilated
- Coma
- Death occurs from respiratory failure.

MLD: Relatively safe drugs, even large overdoses are seldom fatal.

Lethal time: Within an hour.

PM findings:
- Skin: cyanotic
- Stomach: congested
- Doudenum: congested
- Other viscera: congested

Laboratory analysis: of vomitus, urine, stools, excreta, damaged viscera.

Medico-legal aspect:

- That whether the death is accidental, suicidal or homicidal ?
- That whether the death has been due to benzodiazepine poisoning ?

PHENOTHIAZINES POISONING

Drugs: Chlorpromazine, promazine, trifluoperazine

Actions: Antipsychotic and anxiolytic.

Routes: Occurs from its ingestion or from parenteral (injudicious) use.

Etiology: Accidental:

- may occur from overdose, esp. in drug addicts (injudicious use)
- Idiosyncrasy may cause intoxication
- abuse: as sedative and tranquiliser drug

Suicidal: with suicidal intent (fashionable and aristocratic poison)

Homicidal: rare.

Diagnosis:
- Drowsiness, faint, weakness, depression
- Headache, nausea, vomiting, epigastric distress
- Hypothermia
- Tachycardia, hypotension
- Anorexia, loss of body weight
- Respiratory depression
- Skin: cold, clammy, cyanotic
- Muscular weakness
- Jaundice, urticaria
- Coma
- Death occurs from respiratory failure.

MLD: 0.5-2 g.

Lethal time: Within an hour.

PM findings:
- Skin: cyanotic
- Stomach: congested
- Doudenum: congested
- Other viscera: congested

Laboratory analysis: of vomitus, urine, stools, excreta, damaged viscera.

Medico-legal aspect:
- That whether the death is accidental, suicidal or homicidal ?
- That whether the death has been due to phenothiazine poisoning ?

CCNTRAL NERVOUS SYSTEM (CNS) STIMULANTS:

STRYCHNINE POISONING

Properties: Is a CNS stimulant, acting mainly on the anterior horn cells of the spinal cord.

It is followed by depression.

Poisoning: Strychnine poisoning is not rare. May result from ingestion or injection.

Etiology: Accidental poisoning: is common in children due to consumption of sugar coated cathartic pills containing strychnine

Suicidal poisoning: rare now as CNS depressants being favoured now.

Homicidal: very rare.

Diagnosis: CNS stimulation:

- Convulsions, muscle spasms, hyperesthesia, twitching type of contractions
- Sensations: touch, smell, and taste, become more acute.
- Hypertension
- Appetite: increases

CNS depression:

- Respiratory failure due to medullary failure
- Peripheral nerves: transmission of impulses to skeletal muscles depressed.
- Drowsiness, sleep, coma.

Death: from medullary paralysis due to excessive stimulation and apnea.

MLD: 0.5 to 2.0 grs.

Lethal time: - During administration, or

- Within hrs. or days after its administration.

PM findings: - Marks: black or brown corrosion marks over the mucous membrane of the upper GI Tract.

- Stomach: highly inflammed, perforated.
- Doudenum: corrosion marks.
- Other viscera: corrosion marks.

Laboratory analysis: of vomitus, urine, stools, excreta, damaged viscera.

Medico-legal aspect:

- That whether the death is accidental, suicidal or homicidal ?
- That whether the death has been due to strychnine poisoning ?

CAFFEINE POISONING

Properties: Is a CNS stimulant, acting mainly on the cerebral cortex, medulla, and spinal cord. It is the most powerful amongst methylated xanthines.

Poisoning: Caffein poisoning is not rare. May result from ingestion or injection.

Etiology: Accidental poisoning: mostly accidental-overdose or prolonged use.

Suicidal poisoning: rare.

Homicidal: very rare.

Diagnosis: CNS stimulation:

- Excitement, restlessness, insomnia, delirium, convulsions.
- Visual disturbances – flashes of light.
- Auditory disturbances – ringing in the ears.
- Skeletal muscles spasms.

CVS effects:

- Tachycardia
- Hypertension

GI Tract:

- Gastritis, peptic ulcer
- Death – due to respiratory failure.

MLD: 10 g.

Lethal time: - Within hrs.

PM findings: GI Tract:

Stomach: congested, perforated

Other viscera: congested

Laboratory analysis: of vomitus, urine, stools, excreta, damaged viscera.

Medico-legal aspect:

- That whether the death is accidental, suicidal or homicidal ?
- That whether the death has been due to caffeine poisoning ?

AMINOPHYLLINE POISONING

Properties: Is a CNS stimulant. It is available as white or pale granules with bitter taste and ampoules for injection. Is a valuable adjunct in the management of status asthmaticus.

Poisoning: Aminophylline poisoning is not rare. May result from ingestion or injection.

Etiology: Accidental poisoning: mostly accidental: overdose or prolonged use.

Suicidal poisoning: rare.

Homicidal: very rare.

Diagnosis: CNS stimulation:

- Headache, dizziness, restlessness, insomnia, delirium, convulsions.
- Visual disturbances–flashes of light.
- Auditory disturbances–tinnitus.
- Skeletal muscles spasms.

CVS effects:

- Palpitation, chest pain
- Hypertension

GI Tract:

- Nausea, vomiting, diarrhea.

Death–due to respiratory failure.

MLD: 10 g.

Lethal time: - Immediate or within hrs.

PM findings: GI Tract:

Stomach: congested, perforated

Other viscera: congested

Laboratory analysis: of vomitus, urine, stools, excreta, damaged viscera.

Medico-legal aspect:

- That whether the death is accidental, suicidal or homicidal ?
- That whether the death has been due to aminophylline poisoning ?

DRUGS ACTING ON AUTONOMIC EFFECTOR CELLS:

Autonomic Stimulating Agents:

- Drugs stimulating structures innervated by cholinergic nerves (Parasympathomimetics)
- Drugs stimulating structures innervated by adrenergic nerves (Sympathomimetics)

Autonomic Blocking Agents:

- Drugs inhibiting structures innervated by postganglionic cholinergic nerves

- Drugs inhibiting structures innervated by adrenergic nerves (Adrenergic Blocking Agents)
- Drugs inhibiting skeletal muscles and autonomic ganglia.

DRUGS STIMULATING STRUCTURES INNERVATED BY CHOLINERGIC NERVES (PARASYMPATHOMIMETICS):

PILOCARPINE POISONING

Properties: Are the fruits of fungus, some of which are edible while others are non-edible (poisonous). Its poisoning is a common, but poorly recognised.

Poisoning: Caused by potent amnatoxins: muscarine, phalline, agaricine, hydrazines, ibotenic acid, corpine, and orellanine. These block the DNA synthesis, while others block the neuromuscular junction.

Types:
- Rapid type (mycetismus nervosus): caused by Amanita muscaria, which yields the alkaloid muscarine
- Delayed type (mycetismus choleriformis): caused by Amanita phalloides, which yields the alkaloids phalloidine and amanitine.

Etiology:

Accidental: - accidental ingestion of poisonous mushrooms

Suicidal: - easiest and shortest mode of committing suicide

Homicidal: - mode of executing criminals
- mode of taking revenge.
- mode of professional poisoning

Diagnosis: Rapid type (within few mts. to 2 hrs.):

Muscarinic effects:
- Bronchospasm, marked lacrimation, salivation, sweating, miosis, dyspnea watery diarrhea, abdominal cramps, vasodilatation, hypotension, headache, bradycardia, headache, confusion, tremors, cardiovascular collapse, coma, death may occur within a few hrs.

Delayed type (within 24 hrs.):

GI Tract symptoms:

- Nausea, vomiting, diarrhea, abdominal pains, blood stained stools/vomitus, thirst, marked dehydration, liver damage, jaundice.

Kidney damage effects:

- Oliguria or anuria ensues

Peripheral vascular damage effects:

- Hypotension, bradycardia, cyanosis

Histaminic effects:

- Flushing, bronchoconstriction

Neurotoxic effects:

- Peripheral neuropathy, numbness, autonomic symptoms

Psychotropic effects:

- Hallucinations, delusion, depression

Hepatic failure

Renal failure

Coma, death.

Investigation:- Blood estimation of amatoxins by RIA and capillary zone electrophoresis

- LFT: marked elevation of ALT and AST
- Prothrombin time and INR: deranged
- RFT: BUN and serum creatinine: elevated
- Gastric lavage analysis of the toxins
- ECG: features of myocarditis.

MLD: Unknown.

Lethal time: Rapid type: within a few hrs.

Delayed type: within a week.

PM findings: External:

- Skin: dry, pale, dehydrated
- Hapatmegaly.

Internal:

- GI Tract: stomach and dudenum congested.
- Liver: damaged
- Kidneys: damaged
- Other viscera: congested

Laboratory analysis: of vomitus, urine, stools, excreta, damaged viscera.

Medico-legal aspects:

- That whether the death is accidental, suicidal or homicidal ?
- That whether the death has been caused by pilocarpine poisoning ?

MUSHROOMS (MUSCARINE) POISONING

Properties: Are the fruits of fungus, some of which are edible while others are non-edible (poisonous). Its poisoning is a common, but poorly recognised.

Poisoning: Caused by potent amnatoxins: muscarine, phalline, agaricine, hydrazines, ibotenic acid, corpine, and orellanine. These block the DNA synthesis, while others block the neuromuscular junction.

Types:
- Rapid type (mycetismus nervosus): caused by Amanita muscaria, which yields the alkaloid muscarine
- Delayed type (mycetismus choleriformis): caused by Amanita phalloides, which yields the alkaloids phalloidine and amanitine.

Etiology:
Accidental: - accidental ingestion of poisonous mushrooms
Suicidal: - easiest and shortest mode of committing suicide
Homicidal: - mode of executing criminals
- mode of taking revenge.
- mode of professional poisoning

Diagnosis: Rapid type (within few mts. to 2 hrs.):

Muscarinic effects:

- Bronchospasm, marked lacrimation, salivation, sweating, miosis, dyspnea watery diarrhea, abdominal cramps, vasodilatation, hypotension, headache, bradycardia, headache, confusion, tremors, cardiovascular collapse, coma, death may occur within a few hrs.

Delayed type (within 24 hrs.):

GI Tract symptoms:

- Nausea, vomiting, diarrhea, abdominal pains, blood stained stools/vomitus, thirst, marked dehydration, liver damage, jaundice.

Kidney damage effects:

- Oliguria or anuria ensues

Peripheral vascular damage effects:

- Hypotension, bradycardia, cyanosis

Histaminic effects:

- Flushing, bronchoconstriction

Neurotoxic effects:

- Peripheral neuropathy, numbness, autonomic symptoms

Psychotropic effects:

- Hallucinations, delusion, depression
  Hepatic failure
  Renal failure
  Coma, death.

Investigation:- Blood estimation of amatoxinsby RIA and capillary zone electrophoresis

- LFT: marked elevation of ALT and AST
- Prothrombin time and INR: deranged
- RFT: BUN and serum creatinine: elevated
- Gastric lavage analysis of the toxins
- ECG: features of myocarditis.

MLD: Unknown.

Lethal time: Rapid type: within a few hrs.

Delayed type: within a week.

PM findings: External:

- Skin: dry, pale, dehydrated
- Hapatmegaly.

Internal:

- GI Tract: stomach and dudenum congested.
- Liver: damaged
- Kidneys: damaged
- Other viscera: congested

Laboratory analysis: of vomitus, urine, stools, excreta, damaged viscera.

Medico-legal aspects:

- That whether the death is accidental, suicidal or homicidal ?
- That whether the death has been caused by mushroom poisoning?

DRUGS STIMULATING STRUCTURES INNERVATED BY ADRENERGIC NERVES (SYN. SYMPATHOMIMETICS, PSYCHOTOMIMETICS):

Drugs: - Epinehrine (adrenaline), levarterenol (norepinephrine, noradrenaline), ephedrine, amphetamine, phenylepherine, isoproterenol

Natural: Marihuana, ibogaine

Semisynthetic: LSD (lysergic acid diethylamide),

Synthetic: DMT (dimethyltryptamine), DET (diethyltryptamine), Mescaline

Amhetamine, Ephedrine.

Drugs: Phenylalanine: norepinephrine, dopamine.

Tryptophan: serotonin, lysergic acid diethylamide (LSD).

EPINEPHRINE (ADRENALINE) POISONING

Properties: Is a CNS stimulant (stimulation of adrenergic nerves).

Routes:

- Oral: available as white or pale, crystalline, odourless powder
- s.c.: sterile solution 1:1000 (0.1 per cent) 1 ml ampuls and 5-30 ml vials
- IM: in oil (0.2 per cent)
- IV: rarely used. Dose: not to be > 0.25 mg
- Intracardiac:
- Oral inhalation: aqueous sol. (1 per cent), delivered by nebulizer or atomizer.

Poisoning: Is not rare. May result from ingestion or injection.

Intoxication frequently occurs in its clinical use.

Etiology: Accidental poisoning: mostly accidental: overdose or prolonged use.

Suicidal poisoning: rare.

Homicidal: very rare.

Diagnosis: CNS effects:

- Fear, anxiety, headache, dizziness, restlessness, insomnia, delirium
- Visual disturbances–flashes of light.
- Auditory disturbances–tinnitus.
- Skeletal muscles spasms

Cerebral hemorrhage

CVS effects:

- Palpitation, chest pain, pallor
- Hyportension
- Cardiac arrhythmias

Respiratory distress

GI Tract:

- Nausea, vomiting, diarrhea.

Shock

Death – due to cardio-respiratory failure.

MLD: 5-20 mg.

Lethal time: - Immediate or within hrs.

PM findings: GI Tract:

Stomach: congested, perforated

Other viscera: congested

Laboratory analysis: of vomitus, urine, stools, excreta, damaged viscera.

Medico-legal aspect:

- That whether the death is accidental, suicidal or homicidal ?
- That whether the death has been due to epinephrine poisoning ?

PSYCHOTOMIMETIC AGENTS POISONING

Actions: Psychotomimetic.

Poisoning: Amotivational syndrome.

Routes: Occurs from its ingestion or from parenteral (injudicious) use.

Etiology: Accidental:

- may occur from overdose, esp. in drug addicts (injudicious use)
- Idiosyncrasy may cause intoxication

Suicidal: with suicidal intent (fashionable and aristocratic poison)

Homicidal: rare.

Diagnosis:
- Anxiety, restlessness, dizziness, insomnia, tremor
- Nausea, vomiting, diarrhea, dry mouth
- Perspiration, palpitation, headache
- Chest pain
- hypertension/hypotension
- Anorexia, loss of body weight
- Respiratory depression
- Skin: cold, clammy, cyanotic
- Pupils: constricted, later on dilated
- Convulsions, coma
- Death occurs from brain hemorrhage.

MLD: 30-120 mg.

Lethal time: Within an hour.

PM findings:
- Skin: cyanotic
- Stomach: congested
- Doudenum: congested
- Other viscera: congested

Laboratory analysis: of vomitus, urine, stools, excreta, damaged viscera.

Medico-legal aspect:

- That whether the death is accidental, suicidal or homicidal ?
- That whether the death has been due to psychotomimetic poisoning ?

PSYCHEDELICS (HALLUCINOGENICS) ABUSE

Action: Psychedelics produce behavioural and psychological effects (Bad Trips).

Drugs: Phenylalanine: norepinephrine, dopamine.
Tryptophan: serotonin, lysergic acid diethylamide (LSD).

S/E: Addiction or dependence–if repeatedly used and ultimately results into tolerance.

Intoxication: Sympathomimetic effects:

- Mydriosis, hyperflexia, tachycardia, hypertension
- Feeling of tension, crying, laughing,
- Visual illusions and hallucinations, fear of ego distruption
- Disorientation of time sense and distortion of all perceptions, mood lability
- Feeling of detachment and a sense of destiny and control
- Loss of memory and impaired motives, loss of interest in competition.
- Eratic behaviour: Injury or death by jumping from a height, thinking one's ability to fly.

Laboratory analysis: of vomitus, urine, stools, excreta, damaged viscera.

Medico-legal aspect:

- That whether the person is psychedelic addict or not ?
- That what type of psychedelic he/she has consumed ?
- That whether the person be held responsible for a criminal act ?
- That whether the person is capable of taking care of himself/herself ?

MARIHUANA ABUSE

Properties: Marihuana is a lipoid soluble non-nitrogenous oleoresin, extracted from cannabis sativa/indica, a hemp plant.

Action: Marihuana induces somatic or psychic changes, when smoked or ingested.

Types/Drugs: - Charas, hashish: resinous exudate of flowering tops-most potent

- Bhang: dried leaves and flowering shoots
- Ganja: resinous mass from leaves.

S/E:
- Addiction or dependence–if repeatedly used and ultimately results into tolerance,
- Pneumonia, infection, peripheral neuritis.

Diagnosis: Perception: altered time

Conjunctival injection

Emotions: loosened

Memory: impaired

Psychotomimetic effects occur with high doses:
- Confusion, stupor, euphoria, aggressive behaviour
- Insanity: mania, dementia, melancholia
- Hallucination and delusion

Speech: slurred, impaired

Miosis/or mydriosis

Drowsiness, sleep,

Coma,

Death occurs rarely.

Laboratory analysis: of vomitus, urine, stools, excreta, damaged viscera.

Medico-legal aspect:
- That whether the person is marihuana addict or not ?
- That what type of marihuana he/she has consumed ?
- That whether the person be held responsible for a criminal act ?
- That whether the person is capable of taking care of himself/herself ?

AUTONOMIC BLOCKING AGENTS:

DRUGS INHIBITING STRUCTURES INNERVATED BY POSTGANGLIONIC CHOLINERGIC NERVES:

BELLADONNA ALKALOIDS POISONING:

Natural:
- Atropa belladonna (deadly nightshade) yields atropine and hyoscyamine

- Datura stramonium (thorn-apple) yields atropine and hyoscyamine
- Hyoscyamus niger (henbane) yields scopolamine (hyoscine)
- Scopola carniolica yields scopolamine.

Synthetic:
- Atropine methynitrate
- Homatropine (tropine+mandelic acid).

ATROPINE POISONING

Properties: Is the main belladonna alkaloid, which inhibits structures innervated by the postganglionic cholinergic nerves (autonomic blocking agent). It is available as readily soluble salt, in powder or tablet form for oral, and ampoules for s/c or I/V injection.

Poisoning: Atropine poisoning is not rare. May result from ingestion or injection.

Intoxication frequently occurs in its clinical use.

Etiology: Accidental poisoning: mostly accidental: overdose or prolonged use. Infants and young children are susceptible.

Suicidal poisoning: rare.

Homicidal: very rare.

Diagnosis: GI Tract:
- Mouth: dryness, burning sensation, thirst, difficulty in swallowing
- Abdomen: distention

Pupils: dilated, non-reacting

Vision: blurred, and photophobia

Skin: dry, flushed, hot, rash – over face, neck and trunk

Fever

Pulse: weak

CNS stimulation:
- Headache, dizziness, restlessness, insomnia, delirium, convulsions.
- Auditory disturbances – tinnitus.

- Muscular incoordination
- Gait: disturbed

CVS effects:

- Palpitation, chest pain
- Tachycardia
- Hyportension

Death occurs due to respiratory failure.

MLD: 100 mg.

Lethal time: - Immediate or within hrs.

PM findings: External:

- Skin: dry and flushed

Internal:

- GI Tract: upper GI Tract dry, uvula and glottis edematous
- Stomach: congested
- Other viscera: congested.

Laboratory analysis: of vomitus, urine, stools, excreta, damaged viscera.

Medico-legal aspect:

- That whether the death is accidental, suicidal or homicidal ?
- That whether the death has been due to atropine poisoning ?

SCOPOLAMINE (HYOSCINE) POISONING

Properties: Is one of the main belladonna alkaloids, which inhibits structures innervated by the postganglionic cholinergic nerves (autonomic blocking agent). It is available as 2.5 mg oral tablets and injections (vials).

Indications: - as a sedative and tranquiliser for agitated and restless patients

- as a preanesthetic agent (combined with barbiturate or morphine) to overcome laryngospasm
- as an antispasmodic agent (combined with amphetamine) in the therapy of spasmodic torticollis.

Poisoning: Scopolamine poisoning is not rare. May result from ingestion or injection.

Intoxication frequently occurs in its clinical use.

Etiology: Accidental poisoning: mostly accidental: overdose or prolonged use. Infants and young children are susceptible.

Suicidal poisoning: rare.

Homicidal: very rare.

Diagnosis: GI Tract:

- Mouth: dryness, burning sensation, thirst, difficulty in swallowing
- Abdomen: distention, constipation

Urinary retention

Pupils: dilated, non-reacting

Vision: blurred, and photophobia

Skin: dry, flushed, hot, rash – over face, neck and trunk

Fever

Pulse: weak

CNS stimulation:

- Headache, dizziness, restlessness, insomnia, delirium, convulsions.
- Auditory disturbances – tinnitus.
- Muscular incoordination
- Gait: disturbed

CVS effects:

- Palpitation, chest pain
- Tachycardia
- Hyportension

Death occurs due to respiratory failure.

MLD: 100-500 mg.

Lethal time: - Immediate or within hrs.

PM findings: External:

- Skin: dry and flushed

Internal:

- GI Tract: upper GI Tract dry, uvula and glottis edematous

- Stomach: congested
- Other viscera: congested.

Laboratory analysis: of vomitus, urine, stools, excreta, damaged viscera.

Medico-legal aspect:

- That whether the death is accidental, suicidal or homicidal ?
- That whether the death has been due to scopolamine poisoning ?
- That whether scopolamine had been employed to obtain confession from criminals ?

DATURA (thorn-apple) POISONING

Properties: Is one of the main belladonna alkaloids, which inhibits structures innervated by the postganglionic cholinergic nerves (autonomic blocking agent). All parts of the plant are toxic, but mostly the seeds and leaves are used for the purpose of poisoning. They yield the alkaloids hyoscine, hyosciamine, and traces of atropine. Active principle is daturine.

Poisoning: Datura poisoning is not rare. May result from ingestion of food (lentils, bread, veg/non-veg curry) stuffed with datura seeds/leaves, smoking of cigarette/biri stuffed with datura, adulterated alcohol with datura.

Etiology: Accidental poisoning: mostly accidental: overdose or prolonged use. Infants and young children are susceptible.

Suicidal poisoning: rare.

Homicidal: very rare.

Diagnosis: CNS stimulation:

- Headache, dizziness, restlessness, insomnia, delirium, convulsions.
- Auditory disturbances – tinnitus.
- Muscular incoordination
- Gait: disturbed.

GI Tract:

- Mouth: dryness, burning sensation, thirst, difficulty in swallowing

- Abdomen: distention, constipation
  Urinary retention
  Pupils: dilated, non-reacting
  Vision: blurred, and photophobia
  Skin: dry, flushed, hot, rash – over face, neck and trunk
  Fever
  Pulse: weak

CVS effects:
- Palpitation, chest pain
- Tachycardia
- Hyportension

Death occurs due to respiratory failure.

Investigation: Urine for testing of the active principle (daturine):
- yields atropine on heating, or by treating with alkalies.

MLD: 100-150 seeds (20-30 grs.).
Fatal dose of daturine is 0.5-2.0 grs.

Lethal time: Within 24 hrs.

PM findings: External:
- Skin: dry and flushed
- Pupils: widely dilated

Internal:
- GI Tract: upper GI Tract dry, uvula and glottis edematous
- Stomach: congested, may contain datura seeds
- Other viscera: congested.

Laboratory analysis: of vomitus, urine, stools, excreta, damaged viscera.

Medico-legal aspect:
- That whether the death is accidental, suicidal or homicidal ?
- That whether the death has been due to datura poisoning ?
- That whether urine had been tested for the presence of active principle ?

Drugs inhibiting structures innervated by adrenergic nerves (Adrenergic Blocking Agents):

ERGOT ALKALOIDS POISONING (ERGOTISM)

Properties: Are potent adrenergic blocking agents, besides exerting nonadrenergic actions such as vasoconstriction, central depression of vasomotor reflexes, and central vagal stimulation.

Alkaloids: Amino acid alkaloids:

- Ergotamine tartrate: 0.5-1.0 mg tablets and 1.0 mg/ml injection.

Amine alkaloids:

- Ergonovine maleate: 0.2-0.5 mg tablets and 0.2-0.5 mg/ml injection.
- Lysergic acid-diethylamide (LSD): powder for oral use.

Uses: Treatment of Essential hypertension (medical sympathectomy)

Treatment of Migraine (as vasodilator)

Treatment of Peripheral vascular disease:

- Raynaud's disease (as vasodilator)

Treatment of Bronchial asthma (as bronchodilator)

Obsterical indications (as an oxtocic agent):

- to induce labour at term,
- to control post-partum hemorrhage,
- to aid and hasten the normal involution of the uterus during pueroerium, and
- to induce uterine contraction post-caesarean section.

Diagnostic indications:

- Pheochromocytoma (to diagnose the tumor).

Poisoning: Is not rare. May result from clinical overdosage or injudicious use of the drug.

Etiology: Accidental: - accidental overdosage or injudicious use of the drug

Suicidal: - rarely used

Homicidal: - mode of executing criminals

Pathogenesis: Curare produces highly selective paralysis of motor end-plates in skeletal muscle and also paralyzes autonomic ganglion cells.

Diagnosis:
- Onset of symptoms:-within a few sec. of injection of curare
- Hypoxia: due to depression of respiration
- Bronchospasm
- Pulse: weak
- Hypotension
- Circulatory collapse
- Unconsciousness
- Asphyxial convulsions
- Death occurs due to anoxia secondary to peripheral respiratory arrest.

MLD: 6-26 mg.

Lethal time: few sec. (may be within hrs.).

PM findings: External:
- Skeletal muscles: paralytic

Internal:
- Stomach: congested.
- Doudenum: congested.
- Other viscera: congested.

Laboratory analysis: of vomitus, urine, stools, excreta, damaged viscera.

Medico-legal aspects:
- That whether the death is accidental, suicidal or homicidal ?
- That whether the death has been caused by ergot poisoning ?

LYSERGIC ACID-DIETHYLAMIDE (LSD) POISONING

Properties: Is a semisynthetic amine alkaloid of ergot, which is of interest only because of its central action (highly specific psychic alterations).

Poisoning: May result from injudicious use of the drug.

Etiology: Accidental: -accidental overdosage or injudicious use of the drug

Suicidal: -rarely used

Homicidal: -rarely used.

Pathogenesis: Produces highly specific psychic alterations.

Diagnosis: Psychic alterations:

- Visual perceptions disturbed: visual hallucinations and illusions
- Feeling of detachment and a sense of destiny and control
- Ego function: prolonged disintegration
- Loss of memory
- Motive deficits: dropping out
- Passivity: marked
- Avoidance of competition
- Erratic behaviour: amotivational syndrome
- Incidence of spontaneous abortions: higher
- Pulse: weak
- Hypotension
- Circulatory collapse
- Unconsciousness
- Asphyxial convulsions
- Death occurs due to anoxia secondary to peripheral respiratory arrest.

MLD: 0.5 mcg/kg body weight.

Lethal time: few sec. (may be within hrs.).

PM findings: External:

- Skeletal muscles: paralytic

Internal:

- Stomach: congested.
- Doudenum: congested.
- Other viscera: congested.

Laboratory analysis: of vomitus, urine, stools, excreta, damaged viscera.

Medico-legal aspects:

- That whether the death is accidental, suicidal or homicidal ?
- That whether the death has been caused by LSD poisoning ?

DRUGS INHIBITING SKELETAL MUSCLES and AUTONOMIC GANGLIA (SKELETAL MUSCLES and AUTONOMIC GANGLIA INHIBITORS):

CURARE POISONING

Properties: It is a highly selective paralytic agent of motor ene-plates in skeletal muscle, and the agent also paralyzes autonomic ganglion cells. It is available as a sterile aqueous solution in 10 ml vials.

Uses:
- Curare is an adjuvant in surgical anesthesia.
- Curare is employed to prevent trauma in the Electroshock therapy of psychiatric disorders
- Curare is employed to aid in endoscopy
- Curare is employed as a muscle relaxant during reduction of fractures and dislocations
- Curare is employed as muscle relaxant in tetanus
- Curare is employed as an aid in diagnosing Myasthenia gravis.

Poisoning: Atropine poisoning is not rare. May result from clinical overdosage or injudicious use of the drug.

Etiology: Accidental: - accidental overdosage or injudicious use of the drug

Suicidal: - rarely used

Homicidal: - mode of executing criminals

Pathogenesis: Curare produces highly selective paralysis of motor end-plates in skeletal muscle and also paralyzes autonomic ganglion cells.

Diagnosis:
- Onset of symptoms: -within a few sec. of injection of curare
- Hypoxia: due to depression of respiration
- Bronchospasm
- Hypotension
- Circulatory collapse
- Asphyxial convulsions
- Death occurs due to anoxia secondary to peripheral respiratory arrest.

Lethal time: few sec. to few mts. (may be within 3 hrs.)

PM findings: External:

- Skeletal muscles: paralytic
- Stomach: congested.
- Doudenum: congested.
- Other viscera: congested.

Laboratory analysis: of vomitus, urine, stools, excreta, damaged viscera.

Medico-legal aspects:

- That whether the death is accidental, suicidal or homicidal ?
- That whether the death has been caused by curare poisoning ?

NOXIOUS GASES AND VAPOURS (INHALENTS):

Properties: - That inhalents are substances whose chemical vapours are inhaled to produce euphoric, disinhibiting and exciting effects.

CARBON MONOXIDE (CO) POISONING:

Properties: Carbon monoxide is a gas produced by incomplete burning of organic matter.

It has no therapeutic value, but highly toxic.

Poisoning: Carbon monoxide poisoning causes large number of accidental and suicidal deaths from its inhalation.

Factors governing poisoning of carbon monoxide:

- Gas concentration in the inspired air
- Exposure duration
- Respiratory minute volume
- Tissues oxygen demand
- Cardiac output
- Hb concentration.

Etiology: Accidental: use of gas or coal burning heaters in an unvented room resulting in deaths.

Suicidal: exhaust fumes inhalation for commiting suicide

Pathogenesis: CO + Hb = Carboxyhemoglobin–causing tissue anoxia.

Diagnosis: Anoxia: correlated with carboxyhemoglobin concentration:

- Headache, nausea, vomiting, giddiness, faintness, unconsciousness, cyanosis,
- Syncope, collapse,
- Tachycardia,
- Respiration: Chyene-Stokes
- Coma, convulsions
- Death due to respiratory failure.

MLD: 70-80 per cent of blood saturation (carboxyhemoglobin concentration).

Lethal time: - Immediate or within hrs.

PM findings: Circumstantial evidence:

- victim is mostly found under doubtless circumstances.

Externally:

- Cyanotic, or cherry red (bright red skin, fingernails and mucous membrane)

Internally:

- GI Tract: mucous membrane is highly congested
- Lungs: congested and edematous
- Other viscera: congested.

Decomposition of body: retarded

Laboratory analysis: of vomitus, urine, stools, excreta, damaged viscera.

Medico-legal aspect:

- That whether death was accidental, suicidal or homicidal ?
- That whether death was due to asphyxia ?
- That whether death was due to carbon monoxide poisoning ?

CARBON DIOXIDE (CO_2) POISONING

Properties: Carbon dioxide is an odourless and colourless gas produced by the oxidation of carbon. Available as a compressed gas in metallic cylinders or in solid form (snow, dry ice).

Poisoning: Carbon dioxide poisoning occurs from its inhalation.

Etiology: Accidental: Mostly accidental:

- Use of gas or coal burning heaters in an unvented room
- Inhalation of fumes from deep wells
- Inhalation of fumes in a burning house

Inhalation of gas from coal mines

Suicidal:-inhalation of exhaust fumes for commiting suicide

Homicidal:-inhalation of fumes by the victim, locked in a burning room.

Diagnosis: Respiratory:

- hyperpnea followed by hypocapnea

Circulatory:

- heart rate increased
- palpitation
- vasodilatation

CNS:

- depression, headache, dizziness, unconsciousness, convulsions

Skin: cold, clammy

Vision: diminished

Death occurs from asphyxia or suffocation (glottis spasm).

PM findings: That of asphyxia:

Externally:

Face: pale, livid and edematous

Tongue: protruded

Mouth and nasal: frothy

Pupils: dilated

Internally:

- Stomach: highly inflammed, congested
- Doudenum: congested
- Heart: right side full, left side empty
- Other viscera: congested.

Decomposition of body: retarded

Laboratory analysis: of vomitus, urine, stools, excreta, damaged viscera.

Medico-legal aspect:

- That whether death was accidental, suicidal or homicidal ?
- That whether death was due to asphyxia or suffocation ?
- That whether death was due to carbon dioxide poisoning ?

SEWER GAS POISONING

Properties: It is a mixture of gases (H_2S, CO_2, and Nitrogen).

Etiology: Accidental: mostly accidental e.g. common amongst workers used to clear the drain pipes.

Pathogenesis: The gas contains: CO_2, H_2S and Nitrogen. Nitrogen constituent causes de-oxidation, resulting in asphyxia, while H_2S is the most fatal constituent.

Diagnosis:
- Nausea, vomiting, headache, giddiness, faintness, unconsciousness, cyanosis, convulsions.
- Death occurs due to asphyxia.

PM findings: That of asphyxia:

Circumstantial evidence:

- victim is mostly found under doubtless circumstances.

Externally:

- Cyanosis: cherry red (bright red skin, fingernails and mucous membrane)

Internally:

- GI Tract: mucous membrane is highly congested
- Lungs: congested and edematous
- Other viscera: congested.

Decomposition of body: retarded.

Laboratory analysis: of vomitus, urine, stools, excreta, damaged viscera.

Medico-legal aspect:

- That whether death was accidental, suicidal or homicidal ?
- That whether death was due to asphyxia ?
- That whether death was due to sewer gas ?

COAL GAS POISONING

Properties: It is a mixture of gases–CO is the most fatal constituent.

Etiology: Accidental : Use of gas or coal burning heaters in an unvented room resulting in deaths.

Suicidal: Exhaust fumes inhalation for commiting suicide.

Pathogenesis: CO + Hb = Carboxyhaemoglobin–causing tissue anoxia.

Diagnosis: Nausea, vomiting, headache, giddiness, faintness, unconsciousness, cyanosis, death occurs due to asphyxia.

PM findings: That of asphyxia:

Circumstantial evidence:

- victim is mostly found under doubtless circumstances.

Externally:

- Cyanosis: cherry red (bright red skin, fingernails and mucous membrane)

Internally:

- GI Tract: mucous membrane is highly congested
- Lungs: congested and edematous
- Other viscera: congested.

Decomposition of body: retarded.

Laboratory analysis: of vomitus, urine, stools, excreta, damaged viscera.

Medico-legal aspect:

- That whether death was accidental, suicidal or homicidal ?
- That whether death was due to asphyxia ?
- That whether death was due to coal gas poisoning?

HYDROCYANIC (PRUSSIC ACID) POISONING

Properties: Hydrocyanic acid and the cyanides result in death due to inactivation of the respiratory enzyme, thereby inhibiting oxygen consumption by the tissues.

Poisoning: Is one of the most fast acting deadly poisons. It has no therapeutic value, but highly toxic. Potassium Cyanide (KCN) is a lethal inorganic cyanide salt.

Etiology: Accidental: -accidental exposure to vapours in Industry

- cattle grazing on grass and plants rich in cyanophoric glycosides, used as a fumigating agent (insecticide)

Suicidal: - easiest and shortest mode of committing suicide

Homicidal: - mode of executing criminals

- mode of taking revenge.

Pathogenesis: Produces cytotoxic anoxia by reversibly inhibiting cellular oxidizing enzyme (cytochrome oxidase).

Diagnosis: Cyanide Poisoning:

- Onset of symptoms: - within a few sec. of ingestion of cyanide compounds
- within a few mts. of inhalation of vapours of the ion
- Headache, giddiness, hyperpnea, palpitation, cyanosis, and unconsciousness
- Asphyxial convulsions
- Death

MLD: 30 minim of HCN.

60 minim of bitter almond.

Lethal time: few sec. to few mts. (may be within 3 hrs.)

PM findings: That of asphyxia:

Circumstantial evidence:

- victim is mostly found under doubtless circumstances.

Externally:

- Cyanosis or cherry red (bright red skin, fingernails and mucous membrane)

- Mouth and nasals: frothy
- Pupils: dilated.

Internally:

- Veins: engorged with fluid blood
- GI Tract: mucous membrane is highly congested
- Lungs: congested and edematous
- Other viscera: congested.

Decomposition of body: retarded.

Laboratory analysis: of vomitus, urine, stools, excreta, damaged viscera.

Medico-legal aspects:

- That whether the death is accidental, suicidal or homicidal ?
- That whether the death has been caused by Hydrocyanic poisoning ?

CYANIDE POISONING

Properties: Cyanide results in death due to inactivation of the respiratory enzyme, thereby inhibiting oxygen consumption by the tissues.

Poisoning: Is one of the most fast acting deadly poisons. It has no therapeutic value, but highly toxic. Potassium Cyanide (KCN) is a lethal inorganic cyanide salt.

Etiology:
Accidental: - accidental exposure to vapours in Industry
Suicidal: - easiest and shortest mode of committing suicide
Homicidal: - mode of executing criminals
- mode of taking revenge.

Pathogenesis: Produces cytotoxic anoxia by reversibly inhibiting cellular oxidizing enzyme (cytochrome oxidase).

Diagnosis:
- Onset of symptoms: - within a few sec. of ingestion of cyanide compounds
- within a few mts. of inhalation of vapours of the ion
- Headache, giddiness, hyperpnea, palpitation, cyanosis, and unconsciousness

- Asphyxial convulsions
- Death.

MLD: 30 minim of KCN

Lethal time: few sec. to few mts. (may be within 3 hrs.)

PM findings: That of asphyxia:

Circumstantial evidence:

- victim is mostly found under doubtless circumstances.

Externally:

- Cyanosis or cherry red (bright red skin, fingernails and mucous membrane)
- Mouth and nasals: frothy
- Pupils: dilated.

Internally:

- Veins: engorged with fluid blood
- GI Tract: mucous membrane is highly congested
- Lungs: congested and edematous
- Other viscera: congested.

Decomposition of body: retarded.

Laboratory analysis: of vomitus, urine, stools, excreta, damaged viscera.

Medico-legal aspects:

- That whether the death is accidental, suicidal or homicidal ?
- That whether the death has been caused by cyanide poisoning ?

BENZENE POISONING

Properties: Benzene is toxic when it gains access to the body by inhalation of vapours, ingestion, or by contact with the skin.

Uses: Employed in as solvent in rubber, dyes, leather, paint, munitions industries, and in dry cleaning establishments.

Poisoning: Acute or chronic.

Etiology: Accidental: from exposure to vapours in Industry, or from accidental ingestion, or from contact with the skin.

Suicidal: common

Homicidal: rare.

Diagnosis: CNS:

- Headache, giddiness, excitement, restlessness, depression.

GITract:

- Nausea, vomiting, anorexia

Bone marrow depression.

CVS:

- Palpitation, cyanosis, unconsciousness

Asphyxial convulsions

Death from respiratory failure.

MAC: 35 ppm.

Lethal time: 5-10 mts.

PM findings: That of asphyxia:

Circumstantial evidence:

- victim is mostly found under confirmed circumstances.

Externally:

- Cyanosis
- Mouth and nasals: frothy.
- Pupils: dilated.

Internally:

- Veins: engorged with fluid blood
- GI Tract: mucous membrane is highly congested
- Lungs: congested and edematous
- Other viscera: congested.

Decomposition of body: retarded.

Laboratory analysis:

- of vomitus, urine, stools, excreta, damaged viscera.

Medico-legal aspects:

- That whether the death is accidental, suicidal or homicidal ?
- That whether the death has been caused by benzene poisoning ?

HYDROGEN SULPHIDE POISONING

Properties: Hydrogen sulphide (H_2S) is a colourless, inflammable, highly toxic, local irritant gas, encountered in sewers and clinical laboratories.

Uses: Used in/or as a by-product of industrial processes e.g. production of sulphur dyes and carbon disulphide, rayon, and the refining of high-sulphur petroleum products.

Action: Produces a histotoxic anoxia, by combining with the metallic components of oxidative enzymes.

Poisoning: Symptoms of poisoning variable with the inhaled concentrations of hydrogen sulphide.

Etiology: Accidental: from exposure to vapours in Industry, or from accidental contact with the skin.

Suicidal: rare.

Homicidal: very rare.

Diagnosis: CNS:

- Headache, nausea, giddiness, restlessness, dyspnea, hyperpnea

  Eyes: conjunctivitis

  Skin: dermatitis.

Respiratory:

- Pharyngitis, bronchitis, pneumonia, asphyxial convulsions.

CVS:

- hypotension, unconsciousness

  Death from respiratory failure.

MAC: 20 ppm.

Lethal time: within mts.

PM findings: That of asphyxia:

Circumstantial evidence:

- victim is mostly an industrial worker.

Externally:

- Cyanosis
- Mouth and nasals: congested
- Pupils: dilated.

Internally:

- Veins: engorged with fluid blood
- Upper respiratory tract: congested and inflammed
- Lungs: congested and edematous
- Other viscera: congested.

Decomposition of body: retarded.

Laboratory analysis: of vomitus, urine, stools, excreta, damaged viscera.

Medico-legal aspects:

- That whether the death is accidental, suicidal or homicidal ?
- That whether the death has been caused by hydrogen sulphide poisoning ?

LOCAL ANESTHETICS:

COCAINE POISONING

Properties: Is a white, bitter drug. It is a powerful cortical stimulant, as well as a local analgesic. Due to its addicting potency, its use is controlled by the Narcotic Regulations Act.

Poisoning: Acute poisoning from cocaine is not rare, because of the wide use of cocaine as a local anesthetic agent and the considerable individual variation in susceptibility to the drug.

Etiology: Accidental: mostly accidental: overdose or used as stupefying agent

Suicidal: rare

Homicidal: very rare.

Diagnosis: Symptoms mostly pertain to CNS:

- Excited, restless, anxious, confused
- Reflexes: hyperactive
- Burning pain in the upper part of G.I.Tract
- Nausea, vomiting, salivation, headache, palpitation
- Skin – cold and clammy
- Face – cyanosed
- Pupils - dilated

- Respiration – slow, irregular, Cheyne-Stokes respiration
- Pulse – slow, feeble, rapid
- Hypotension
  Delirium, convulsions
- Death – may occur due to respiratory failure or cardiac arrest.

MLD: 2-4 drs. (10-20 mg).

Lethal time:- During administration, or
- Within hrs. or days after its administration.

PM findings:- Marks: multiple scars/abscesses at the site of injection.
- Nasal perforated.
- Pupils: dilated.
- Mucous membrane of upper G.I.Tract: congested and inflammed
- Other viscera: congested.

Laboratory analysis: of vomitus, urine, stools, excreta, damaged viscera.

Medico-legal aspect:
- That whether the death is accidental, suicidal or homicidal ?
- That at whether the death has been due to cocaine poisoning ?

LIGNOCAINE (syn. LIDOCAINE, XYLOCAINE) POISONING

Properties: Is an aminoacyl amide.

Indications: Is a versatile local anesthetic for:
- infiltration anesthesia in concentration of 0.5-2 per cent, with or without adrenaline (epinephrine).
- nerve block, epidural, caudal in concentration of 0.5-2 per cent.
- spinal anesthesia for surgery of 5 per cent (Lignocaine Heavy 5 per cent).
- topical application to mucous membranes (urethral, vaginal, anal) of 2-4 per cent.

- hemorrhoids, dentistry, proctoscopy, sigmoidoscopy ointment of 5 per cent.
- introduction of catheters, probes into stomach, esophagoscopy of 2 per cent.
- ventricular arrhythmias of 2 per cent (Lidocaine/Xylocard).
- Incision drainage of abscess of spray (lignocaine 100 mg+ethanol 28 per cent/ml).

Poisoning: Acute poisoning from lignocaine is not rare, because of the wide use of lignocaine as a local anesthetic agent and the considerable individual variation in susceptibility to the drug.

Etiology: Accidental: mostly accidental: overdose.

Suicidal: rare

Homicidal: very rare.

Diagnosis: S/S mostly pertain to CNS stimulation and depression of cerebral medulla:

- Headache, dizziness, visual disturbances, anxious, confused
- Reflexes: hyperactive
- Burning pain in the upper part of G.I.Tract
- Nausea, vomiting, salivation, headache, palpitation
- Skin: cold and clammy
- Face: cyanosed
- Pupils: dilated
- Vision: blurred
- Respiration: depression
- Bradycardia
- Cardiac arrhythmias
- Hypotension
- Joints: chondrolysis
- Delirium, convulsions
- Death–may occur due to respiratory failure or cardiac arrest.

MLD: 1-2 g

Lethal time:- During administration, or

- Within hrs. or days after its administration.

PM findings:
- Marks: multiple scars/abscesses at the site of injection.
- Nasal perforated.
- Pupils: dilated.
- Mucous membrane of upper G.I.Tract: congested and inflamed
- Other viscera: congested.

Laboratory analysis: of vomitus, urine, stools, excreta, damaged viscera.

Medico-legal aspect:
- That whether the death is accidental, suicidal or homicidal ?
- That at whether the death has been due to lignocaine poisoning ?

DIGITALIS AND ALLIED CARDIAC GLYCOSIDES:

DIGITALIS POISONING

Properties: Digitalis and certain closely allied cardiac glycosides exert a powerful action on themyocardium, unrivalled for the management of CHF.

Poisoning: Many of the toxic reactions of digitalis are just extensions of its therapeutic effects i.e. poisoning occurs due to continued ingestion of the drug in amounts greater than are destroyed or eliminated. A non-toxic digitalis does not exist.

Etiology: Accidental: mostly accidental: overdose or prolonged use.

Suicidal: rare

Homicidal: very rare.

Diagnosis:
- G.I.Tract:
- Nausea, vomiting, diarrhea, anorexia, pain abdomen, are the earliest features of digitalis poisoning
- Pulse: slow, irregular
- Respiration: breathing slow and sighing
- Hypotension

- Cardiac:
- Chest pain: pre-cordial region
- Heart rate: increases
- Extra-systoles
- Arrhythmias: Paroxysmal tachycardia, atrial tachycardia, ventricular tachycardia, ventricular fibrillation
- Neurological: Headache, fatigue, malaise and drowsiness, muscular weakness
- Psychological: confusion, disorientation, aphasia, hallucinations and delirium, convulsions
- Vision: Often blurred, white halos may appear on dark objects
- Skin: Rashes, Eosinophilia
- Shock
- Death from ventricular fibrillation

MLD: 3 g.

PM findings:- Marks: mucous membrane of the upper GI Tract–shows signs of irritation.
- Stomach: signs of irritation.
- Doudenum: signs of irritation.
- Other viscera: congested.

Laboratory analysis: of vomitus, urine, stools, excreta, damaged viscera.

Medico-legal aspect:

- That whether the death is accidental, suicidal or homicidal ?
- That whether the death has been due to digitalis poisoning ?

ANTICOAGULANTS POISONING

Agents: Dicumarol, biscoumacetate, phenindione and warfarin.

Properties: Dicumarol, biscoumacetate, phenindione and warfarin, inhibit the formation of prothrombin in the liver, thereby inhibit the clotting mechanism, resulting in hemorrhage from prolonged use.

Poisoning: Toxic reactions of anticoagulants are just extensions of their therapeutic use i.e. poisoning occurs from prolonged use.

Etiology: Accidental: mostly accidental: overdose or prolonged use.

Suicidal: rare

Homicidal: very rare.

Diagnosis: Hemorrhage:

- Hemoptysis, hematemesis, hematuria, hemarthrosis, hemorrhages into organs, menorrhagia, bleeding per rectum, bruises.

Hepatomegaly, jaundice

Skin rash

Nausea, vomiting, diarrhea, anorexia, pain abdomen

Pulse: slow, irregular

Respiration: breathing slow and sighing

Hypotension

Neurological: Headache, fatigue, malaise and drowsiness, muscular weakness

Psychological: confusion, disorientation, aphasia, hallucinations and delirium, convulsions

Vision: Often blurred, white halos may appear on dark objects

Shock

Death from cardiac arrest.

Laboratory: Prothrombin concentration: low

RBC count: low

MLD: Dicumarol and warfarin: 0.1 g,

Biscoumacetate: 0.6 g

Phenindion: 0.2 g

PM findings: - Marks: mucous membrane of the upper GI Tract– shows signs of irritation.

- Stomach: signs of irritation.
- Doudenum: signs of irritation.
- Other viscera: congested.

Medico-legal aspect:

- That whether the death is accidental, suicidal or homicidal ?
- That whether the death has been due to anticoagulants poisoning ?

CYTOTOXIC DRUGS POISONING

Drugs: Alkylating agents, antimetabolites, vinca alkaloids, antineoplastic antibiotics, hormonal (antiestrogens and antiandrogen) drugs.

Properties: Cancer chemotherapeutic drugs exert cytotoxic actions against cellular proliferation and cell nucleus of the bone marrow, mucosa and skin.

Poisoning: Toxic reactions of cytotoxic drugs are just extensions of their therapeutic use i.e. poisoning mainly bone marrow depression, occurs from misuse/or prolonged use.

Etiology: Accidental: overdose or prolonged use.

Diagnosis: GI Tract:

- Nausea, vomiting, stomatitis, constipation

Fever, local pain

Alopecia

Skin: dermatitis

Pulse: slow, irregular

Respiration: breathing slow and sighing

Hypotension

Neurological: Headache, fatigue, malaise and drowsiness, muscular weakness

Psychological: depression, disorientation, aphasia

Convulsions

Death from cardiac arrest.

Laboratory: CBC (TLC and DLC, hematocrit, Hb and platelet count)

ECG: show changes of cardiac toxicity e.g. S-T segment and T wave abnormalities, systolic time interval changes, high resting pulse.

MLD: Variable as per the cytotoxic drug

PM findings: External:

- Emaciated
- Skin: dry

Internal:

- Stomach: congested
- Doudenum: congested
- Other viscera: congested.

Laboratory analysis: of vomitus, urine, stools, excreta, damaged viscera.

Medico-legal aspect:

- That whether the death is accidental, suicidal or homicidal ?
- That whether the death has been due to cytotoxic drugs poisoning ?

ALKYLATING AGENTS POISONING

Agents: Cyclophosphamide, chlorambucil, mustine, busulphan, melphalan.

Properties: Alkylating agents exert cytotoxic actions against cellular proliferation and cell nucleus of the bone marrow, mucosa and skin.

Poisoning: Toxic reactions are just extensions of their therapeutic use i.e. poisoning mainly bone marrow depression, occurs from misuse/or prolonged use.

Etiology: Accidental: overdose or prolonged use.

Diagnosis: GI Tract:

- Nausea, vomiting, stomatitis, constipation

  Fever, local pain

  Alopecia

  Skin: dermatitis

  Pulse: slow, irregular

  Respiration: breathing slow and sighing

  Hypotension

  Neurological: Headache, fatigue, malaise and drowsiness, muscular weakness

  Psychological: depression, disorientation, aphasia

  Convulsions

  Death from cardiac arrest.

Laboratory: CBC (TLC and DLC, hematocrit, Hb and platelet count)

ECG: show changes of cardiac toxicity e.g. S-T segment and T wave abnormalities, systolic time interval changes, high resting pulse.

MLD: Variable as per the cytotoxic drug

PM findings: External:

- Emaciated
- Skin: dry

Internal:

- Stomach: congested
- Doudenum: congested
- Other viscera: congested.

Laboratory analysis: of vomitus, urine, stools, excreta, damaged viscera.

Medico-legal aspect:

- That whether the death is accidental, suicidal or homicidal ?
- That whether the death has been due to alkylating agents drugs poisoning ?

ANTIMETABOLITES POISONING

Agents: Methotrexate, mercaptopurine, 5-fluorouracil, thioguanine.

Properties: Antimetabolites exert cytotoxic actions against cellular proliferation and cell nucleus of the bone marrow, mucosa and skin.

Poisoning: Toxic reactions are just extensions of their therapeutic use i.e. poisoning mainly bone marrow depression, occurs from misuse/or prolonged use.

Etiology: Accidental: overdose or prolonged use.

Diagnosis: GI Tract:

- Nausea, vomiting, diarrhea, stomatitis, constipation

Fever, local pain

Alopecia

Skin: dermatitis

Hepatomegaly
Amenorrhea, transient azoospermia
Pulse: slow, irregular
Respiration: breathing slow and sighing
Hypotension
Neurological: Headache, fatigue, malaise and drowsiness, muscular weakness
Psychological: depression, disorientation, aphasia
Renal failure
Convulsions
Death from cardiac arrest.

Laboratory: CBC (TLC and DLC, hematocrit, Hb and platelet count): anemia, leukopenia, thrombocytopenia
ECG: show changes of cardiac toxicity e.g. S-T segment and T wave abnormalities, systolic time interval changes, high resting pulse.

MLD: Variable as per the cytotoxic drug.

PM findings: External:
- Emaciated
- Skin: dry

Internal:
- Stomach: congested
- Doudenum: congested
- Other viscera: congested.

Laboratory analysis: of vomitus, urine, stools, excreta, damaged viscera.

Medico-legal aspect:
- That whether the death is accidental, suicidal or homicidal ?
- That whether the death has been due to intimetabolites drugs poisoning ?

ANTI HORMONAL AGENTS POISONING

Agents: Antiestrogens (letrozole, formestane, tamoxifen, fosfestrol (stilbestrol), Antiandrogens (bicalutamide, cyproterone)

Properties: Anti-hormonal agents exert cytotoxic actions against cellular proliferation and cell nucleus of the bone marrow, mucosa and skin.

Poisoning: Toxic reactions are just extensions of their therapeutic use i.e. poisoning mainly bone marrow depression, occurs from misuse/or prolonged use.

Etiology: Accidental: overdose or prolonged use.

Diagnosis: GI Tract:

- Nausea, vomiting, stomatitis, constipation

  Fever, local pain

  Alopecia

  Skin: dermatitis, tissue necrosis

  Pulse: slow, irregular

  Respiration: breathing slow and sighing

  Hypotension

  Neurological: Headache, fatigue, malaise and drowsiness, muscular weakness

  Psychological: depression, disorientation, aphasia

  Convulsions

  Death from cardiac arrest.

Laboratory: CBC (TLC and DLC, hematocrit, Hb and platelet count): anemia, leukopenia

ECG: show changes of cardiac toxicity e.g. S-T segment and T wave abnormalities, systolic time interval changes, high resting pulse.

MLD: Variable as per the cytotoxic drug

PM findings: External:

- Emaciated
- Skin: dry

Internal:

- Stomach: congested
- Doudenum: congested
- Other viscera: congested.

Laboratory analysis: of vomitus, urine, stools, excreta, damaged viscera.

Medico-legal aspect:

- That whether the death is accidental, suicidal or homicidal ?
- That whether the death has been due to antihormonal agents poisoning ?

VINCA ALKALOIDS POISONING

Agents: Vinblastine, vincristine, vindesine

Properties: Vinca alkaloids exert cytotoxic actions against cellular proliferation and cell nucleus of the bone marrow, mucosa and skin.

Poisoning: Toxic reactions are just extensions of their therapeutic use i.e. poisoning mainly bone marrow depression, occurs from misuse/or prolonged use.

Etiology: Accidental: overdose or prolonged use.

Diagnosis: GI Tract:

- Nausea, vomiting, stomatitis, constipation

Fever, local pain

Alopecia

Skin: dermatitis

Pulse: slow, irregular

Respiration: breathing slow and sighing

Hypotension

Neurological: headache, fatigue, malaise and drowsiness, muscular weakness

Psychological: depression, disorientation, aphasia

Convulsions

Death from cardiac arrest.

Laboratory: CBC (TLC and DLC, hematocrit, Hb and platelet count)

ECG: show changes of cardiac toxicity e.g. S-T segment and T wave abnormalities, systolic time interval changes, high resting pulse.

MLD: Variable as per the cytotoxic drug

PM findings: External:

- Emaciated
- Skin: dry

Internal:

- Stomach: congested
- Doudenum: congested
- Other viscera: congested.

Laboratory analysis: of vomitus, urine, stools, excreta, damaged viscera.

Medico-legal aspect:

- That whether the death is accidental, suicidal or homicidal ?
- That whether the death has been due to vinca alkaloids poisoning ?

ANTINEOPLASTIC ANTIBIOTICS POISONING

Agents: Bleomycin, mitomycin-c, thalidomide, gefitinib.

Properties: Antineoplastic antibiotics exert cytotoxic actions against cellular proliferation and cell nucleus of the bone marrow, mucosa and skin.

Poisoning: Toxic reactions are just extensions of their therapeutic use i.e. poisoning mainly bone marrow depression, occurs from misuse/or prolonged use.

Etiology: Accidental: overdose or prolonged use.

Diagnosis: GI Tract:

- Nausea, vomiting, stomatitis, constipation

Fever, local pain

Alopecia

Skin: urticaria, rash

Pulse: slow, irregular

Chest pain

Hepatomegaly

Respiration: breathing slow and sighing

Hypotension

Neurological: Headache, fatigue, malaise and drowsiness, muscular weakness

Psychological: depression, disorientation, aphasia

Convulsions

Death from cardiac arrest.

Laboratory: CBC (TLC and DLC, hematocrit, Hb and platelet count)

ECG: show changes of cardiac toxicity e.g. S-T segment and T wave abnormalities, systolic time interval changes, high resting pulse.

MLD: Variable as per the cytotoxic drug

PM findings: External:

- Emaciated
- Skin: dry

Internal:

- Stomach: congested
- Doudenum: congested
- Other viscera: congested.

Laboratory analysis: of vomitus, urine, stools, excreta, damaged viscera.

Medico-legal aspect:

- That whether the death is accidental, suicidal or homicidal ?
- That whether the death has been due to antineoplastic antibiotics poisoning?

MISCELLANEOUS POISONING:

DETERGENTS POISONING:

Compounds:
- Cationic: Soaps, detergents, antiseptics,
- Anionic: Laundary and dishwahing solutions–containing alkalies (caustic), or phosphate additives.

Properties: GI Tract irritants.

Poisoning: due to ingestion.

Etiology: Accidental: accidental ingestion esp. by young children

Suicidal: rarely from attempts at self-destruction

Homicidal: rare.

Pathogenesis: GI Tract poisoning (irritants).

Diagnosis: Nausea, vomiting, diarrhea, bronchitis, pulmonary edema, respiratory failure, convulsions, death.

MLD: 1-3 g.

Legal time: 1-4 hrs.

PM findings: GI Tract:

- Marks: black or brown corrosion marks over the mucous membrane of the upper GI Tract.
- Stomach: highly inflammed, perforated.
- Doudenum: corrosion marks.

Other viscera: corrosion marks.

Laboratory analysis: of vomitus, urine, stools, excreta, damaged viscera.

Medico-legal aspects:

- That whether the death is accidental, suicidal or homicidal ?
- That whether the death has been caused by detergents poisoning ?

DISINFECTANTS AND GERMICIDES POISONING:

Properties: Defined as compounds, lethal to all types of micro-organisms. The toxicity of these drugs for the host's tissues, must be weighed against its germicidal potency. It is difficult to measure toxicity.

Drugs/Compounds:

- Aldehydes: Formaldehyde, methanamine.
- Halogens: Chlorine, chloramine-T, halazone, iodine.
- Furan derivatives, nitrofurantoin, sulphur, sulphur dioxide, anthralin, betanaphthol, balsams, volatile oils, chlorophyll.

FORMALDEHYDE POISONING

Properties: Is a gas, readily soluble in water, extensively used as disinfectant.

Poisoning: The systemic actions of formaldehyde are toxic.

Etiology: Accidental: accidental exposure to vapours, or from ingestion of formalin.

Suicidal: rarely from attempts at self-destruction

Homicidal: rare.

Diagnosis: Eyes: Intense irritation of the eyes, conjunctivitis.

URC: Intense irritation of respiratory tract, bronchitis, pulmonary edema.

GI Tract: Intense irritation of mouth, throat, and GI Tract, nausea, vomiting, diarrhea.

Respiratory depression.

Cardiovascular collapse.

Convulsions, coma, death.

MLD: 60 ml.

Lethal time: within 1 hr.

PM findings: GI Tract:

- Marks: black or brown corrosion marks over the mucous membrane of the upper GI Tract
- Stomach: highly inflammed, perforated.
- Doudenum: corrosion marks.

Upper respiratory tract: congested

Other viscera: congested.

Laboratory analysis: of vomitus, urine, stools, excreta, damaged viscera.

Medico-legal aspects:

- That whether the death is accidental, suicidal or homicidal ?
- That whether the death has been caused by formaldehyde poisoning ?

CHLORINE POISONING

Properties: Is one of the most potent germicidal agent (Respiratory stimulant).

Poisoning: Acute and chronic.

Route: Inhalation of vapours, or ingestion.

Etiology: Accidental: accidental exposure to vapours, or from ingestion of formalin.

Suicidal: rarely from attempts at self-destruction

Homicidal: was the 1st gas used as a chemical weapon during World War I.

Diagnosis: Respiratory tract: Severe burning (irritation of the respiratory tract), laryngeal spasm, bronchitis, pulmonary edema.

Cyanosis: bluish face, lips and tongue
Neck veins: engorged
Skin: ashon colour
Respiration: rapid and deeper
Syncope, unconsciousness,
Death from pulmonary edema and cardiovascular failure.

MLD: Concentration of 1:1000

Lethal time: 5 mts.

PM findings: Respiratory tract:

- Bronchi : acute inflammation,
- Lungs: edematous,

Heart: right ventricle dilated.

GI Tract:

- Stomach: highly inflammed
- Doudenum: congested
- Other viscera: congested.

Laboratory analysis: of vomitus, urine, stools, excreta, damaged viscera.

Medico-legal aspects:

- That whether the death is accidental, suicidal or homicidal ?
- That whether the death has been caused by chlorine poisoning ?

IODINE POISONING

Properties: Is one of the oldest of the current antibiotics. It consists of greyish-black, brittle plates with a metallic luster and a characteristic odour of the breath.

Poisoning: Elemental iodine is more toxic than iodides. Iodine is higly corrosive.

Route: Inhalation of vapours, or ingestion.

Etiology: Accidental: common esp. In case of young children.

Suicidal: tincture of iodine is often taken with suicidal intent.

Homicidal: rare.

Diagnosis: GI Tract:

- staining: oral mucous membranes stained brown
- nausea, vomiting, diarrhea, thirst, burning in the pharynx and esophagus, abdominal pain.

Respiratory:

- asphyxiation from edema of the glottis
- aspiration pneumonia.

Shock

Death from circulatory collapse.

MLD: 2 g.

Lethal time: 1-48 hrs.

PM findings: Respiratory tract:

- Bronchi : acute inflammation,
- Lungs: edematous,

Heart: right ventricle dilated.

GI Tract:

- Stomach: highly inflammed
- Doudenum: congested
- Other viscera: congested.

Laboratory analysis: of vomitus, urine, stools, excreta, damaged viscera.

Medico-legal aspects:

- That whether the death is accidental, suicidal or homicidal ?
- That whether the death has been caused by iodine poisoning ?

BORIC ACID POISONING

Properties: Is a very weak germicidal agent, commonly used as household item in the form of ointments and irrigating solutions.

Poisoning: Occurs from misuse.

Route: From ingestion or skin application.

Etiology: Accidental: from misuse e.g. continued application of boric acid ointment to burned areas, or repeated washing of granulation tissue with boric acid solution.

Suicidal: rare.

Diagnosis: GI Tract:

- nausea, vomiting, diarrhea, thirst, burning in the pharynx and esophagus, abdominal pain.

Hypothermia

Skin: erythematous rash, desquamation

Headache, restlessness, weakness

Respiratory distress

Circulatory collapse

Shock

Death from circulatory collapse.

MLD: 10-20 g in adults and 5-6 g in infants.

Lethal time: within 5 days.

PM findings: External:

Skin: desquamated

Internal:

GI Tract:

- Stomach: highly inflammed
- Doudenum: congested
- Other viscera: congested.

Laboratory analysis: of vomitus, urine, stools, excreta, damaged viscera.

Medico-legal aspects:

- That whether the death is accidental, suicidal or homicidal ?
- That whether the death has been caused by boric acid poisoning ?

INSECTICIDES AND ARACHNICIDES (PESTICIDES) POISONING:

Drugs/Compounds:

: Chlorinated insecticides: -Chlorophenothane (DDT), benzene hexachloride, benzyl benzoate.

- Chlorophenothane (DDT): is a very valuable insecticide (agriculture and household).

  Medical use: treatment of pediculosis.
- Benzene hexachloride: is an arachnicide.

  Medical use: treatment of scabies.

- Benzyl benzoate: is an arachnicide.
  Medical use: treatment of scabies.
  Fluorinated insecticides: Fluorides (Insect powders).
  Phosphates Organic.

CHLOROPHENOTHANE (DDT) POISONING

Properties: Is one of the most potent insecticidal agent (agriculture and household).
Is non-volatile chlorinated hydrocarbon

Poisoning: Acute and chronic.

Action: CNS stimulant

Routes: Inhalation of vapours, or ingestion.

Etiology:
Accidental:
- accidental exposure to vapours from spraying in the fields of agriculture
- cattle grazing on grass and plants rich in DDT.

Suicidal:
- easiest and shortest mode of committing suicide

Homicidal:
- mode of executing criminals
- mode of taking revenge.

Diagnosis: Nausea, vomiting, diarrhea
Headache, tiredness, bodyaches, tremors
Skin: dermatitis
Convulsions, coma
Death

MLD: 10-20 g.

Lethal time: within 24 hrs.

PM findings:
- Marks: black or brown corrosion marks over the mucous membrane of the upper GI Tract.
- Stomach: highly inflammed, perforated.
- Doudenum: corrosion marks.
- Other viscera: corrosion marks.

Laboratory analysis: of vomitus, urine, stools, excreta, damaged viscera.

Medico-legal aspects:

- That whether the death is accidental, suicidal or homicidal ?

- That whether the death has been caused by DDT poisoning ?

FLUORIDES (Insect Powders) POISONING:

Properties: Is one of the most potent insecticidal agent (agriculture and household).

Is of interest because of its toxic properties.

Poisoning: Acute and chronic.

Action: Inhibits enzymatic activity, diminishes tissue respiration, and decreases oxygen consumption and lactic acid in the muscles.

Etiology: Accidental:
- accidental ingestion of insecticidal fluoride salts
- cattle grazing on grass and plants rich in insecticidal fluorides.

Suicidal: rare

Homicidal: very rare

Diagnosis: GI Tract:
- Nausea, vomiting, diarrhea, salivation, abdominal pain

Headache, tiredness, bodyaches, tremors

Hypotension

Pulse: rapid

Respiratory distress

Convulsive seizures, coma

Death from respiratory or cardiac failure.

Laboratoty: X-ray: Skeletal changes: increased opaqueness and width of the bones, seen in chronic fluoride poisoning.

MLD: 5 g.

Lethal time: within 24 hrs.

PM findings:
- Marks: black or brown corrosion marks over the mucous membrane of the upper GI Tract.
- Stomach: highly inflammed, perforated.
- Doudenum: corrosion marks.
- Other viscera: corrosion marks.

Laboratory analysis: of vomitus, urine, stools, excreta, damaged viscera.

Medico-legal aspects:

- That whether the death is accidental, suicidal or homicidal ?
- That whether the death has been caused by fluoride salts poisoning ?

PHOSPHATES (ORGANIC) POISONING

Properties: Are distributed all over the body. Is one of the most potent insecticidal agent (agriculture and household).

Is of interest because of its toxic properties.

Compounds: Pesticide sprays: Malathion, Parathion, Phosdrin, TEPP, OMPA.

Poisoning: Acute and chronic.

Action: Inhibits enzyme cholinestrase, resulting in continuous and excessive stimulation of parasympathetic nervous system.

Etiology: Accidental:
- by ingestion, inhalation, or direct contact (skin absorption) of organic phosphorus.
- cattle grazing on grass and plants rich in organic phosphorus by pesticide sprays.

Suicidal: rare

Homicidal: very rare

Diagnosis: GI Tract:

- Nausea, vomiting, diarrhea, salivation, abdominal pain

Headache, sweating, tiredness, bodyaches, tremors, blurred vision

Hypotension

Pulse: rapid

Respiratory distress

Pupils: contracted

Convulsive seizures, coma

Death from respiratory or cardiac failure.

Laboratoty: Estimation of red cell cholinesterase levels.

MLD: 1 g.

Lethal time: within 24 hrs.

PM findings:
- Marks: black or brown corrosion marks over the mucous membrane of the upper GI Tract.
- Stomach: highly inflammed, perforated, contents emit garlick odour.
- Doudenum: corrosion marks.
- Other viscera: corrosion marks.

Laboratory analysis: of vomitus, urine, stools, excreta, damaged viscera.

Medico-legal aspects:
- That whether the death is accidental, suicidal or homicidal ?
- That whether the death has been caused by organic phosphate poisoning ?

RODENTICIDES POISONING:

BARIUM POISONING

Properties: Is extremely toxic when absorbed.

Uses: As an opaque contrast medium for roentgenographic indications, and as an antidiarrheal and demulcent powder. Is used for the rodenticidal purpose.

Poisoning: Acute and chronic.

Action: Powerful muscular stimulation.

Etiology: Accidental: may occur as an industial hazard, or from the accidental use of a soluble barium salt in roentgenographic work.

Suicidal: common

Homicidal: rare.

Diagnosis: GI Tract:
- Nausea, vomiting, diarrhea, abdominal pain (colic), hematemesis

CVS:

Hypertension

Heart: irregularity

Pulse: rapid

CNS:

- Headache, sweating, tiredness, bodyaches, tremors

Respiratory distress

Convulsions

Coma

Death from cardio-respiratory failure.

Laboratoty:

MLD: 1 g.

Lethal time: within an hr.

PM findings: - Stomach: highly inflammed, perforated, contents dark red in colour.

- Doudenum: corrosion marks.
- Other viscera: corrosion marks.

Laboratory analysis: of vomitus, urine, stools, excreta, damaged viscera.

Medico-legal aspects:

- That whether the death is accidental, suicidal or homicidal ?
- That whether the death has been caused by barium poisoning ?

FLUOROACETATE POISONING

Properties: Is extremely toxic.

Uses: Is used as a rodenticidal agent.

Poisoning: Acute and chronic.

Action: Powerful muscular stimulation.

Etiology: Accidental: may occur as an industrial hazard.

Suicidal: rare.

Homicidal: very rare.

Diagnosis: GI Tract:

- Nausea, vomiting, diarrhea, abdominal pain (colic), hematemesis

CVS:

Hypertension

Heart: irregularity

Pulse: rapid

CNS:

- Headache, sweating, tiredness, bodyaches, tremors

Respiratory distress

Convulsions

Coma

Death from cardio-respiratory failure.

Laboratoty:

MLD: 100 mg.

Lethal time: within an hr.

PM findings:
- Stomach: highly inflammed, perforated, contents dark red in colour.
- Doudenum: corrosion marks.
- Other viscera: corrosion marks.

Laboratory analysis: of vomitus, urine, stools, excreta, damaged viscera.

Medico-legal aspects:

- That whether the death is accidental, suicidal or homicidal ?
- That whether the death has been caused by fluoroacetate poisoning ?

ANTHELMINTICS POISONING:

CARBON TETRACHLORIDE POISONING

Properties: Is a local irritant and cellular poison. It is used mainly as an anthelmintic, household cleaner, and as an industrial solvent, resulting in a high incidence of poisoning.

Poisoning: Acute and chronic types.

Etiology: Accidental: from oral ingestion of the compound or from inhalation of vapours.

Suicidal: rarely suicidal.

Homicidal: very rare.

Diagnosis: CNS:

Headache, dizziness, stupor, depression, unconsciousness

CVS:

Cardiovascular collapse

GI Tract:

Nausea, vomiting, diarrhea

Respiration: slow

Cyanosis

Liver damage: necrosis

Renal damage: nephrosis

Delirium

Death from respiratory failure.

MLD: 3 ml.

Lethal time: Within hrs.

PM findings:
- Marks: black or brown corrosion marks over the mucous membrane of the upper GI Tract.
- Stomach: mucous membrane highly inflammed, eroded.
- Doudenum: congested.
- Other viscera: congested.
- Fatty degeneration: of liver, heart and kidneys, in chronic cases.

Laboratory analysis: of vomitus, urine, stools, excreta, damaged viscera.

Medico-legal aspect:

- That whether the death is accidental, suicidal or homicidal ?
- That whether the death has been due to carbon tetrachloride poisoning ?

ASPIDIUM (MALE-FERN) POISONING

Properties: Aspidium Oleoresin, is an ether extract of the dried rhizomes, available as a thick, dark green liquid. Is an irritant poison.

Uses: It is used as an anthelmintic, mainly effective against tapeworms (Taenia and Diphyllobothrium).

Poisoning: Acute and chronic types.

Etiology: Accidental: overdose or hypersensitivity.

Suicidal: rare.

Homicidal: very rare.

Diagnosis: CNS:

Headache, dizziness, stupor, depression, unconsciousness

CVS:

Cardiovascular collapse

GI Tract:

Nausea, vomiting, bloody diarrhea, pain abdomen

Vision: amblyopia, or temporary blindness

Respiration: slow

Jaundice

Liver damage: necrosis

Renal damage: nephrosis

Muscle cramps, followed by convulsions.

Unconsciousness

Delirium

Death from cardio-respiratory failure.

Laboratory: Urine analysis: may show protein, red cells, and casts.

MLD: 4 g.

Lethal time: Within hrs.

PM findings:
- Marks: black or brown corrosion marks over the mucous membrane of the upper GI Tract.
- Stomach: mucous membrane highly inflammed, eroded.
- Doudenum: congested.
- Other viscera: congested.
- Fatty degeneration: of liver, heart and kidneys, in chronic cases.

Laboratory analysis: of vomitus, urine, stools, excreta, damaged viscera.

Medico-legal aspect:

- That whether the death is accidental, suicidal or homicidal ?
- That whether the death has been due to aspidium poisoning ?

AMEBICIDAL AGENTS POISONING

EMETINE POISONING

Properties: Emetine is a hydrated hydrochloride alkaloid, obtained from ipecac (Brazil root).

Uses: It is used as an amebicidal agent for treatment of amebic diarrhea, acute amebic dysentery, amebic abscesses, and amebic hepatitis.

Poisoning: Emetine causes local and systemic reactions.

Etiology: Accidental: overdose or hypersensitivity.

Suicidal: rare.

Homicidal: very rare.

Diagnosis: Local reactions:

- Aching, stiffness, muscular weakness, tenderness– at site of injection.

Systemic reactions:

GI Tract:

- Nausea, vomiting, bloody diarrhea, pain abdomen, malaena

CNS:

- Headache, dizziness, stupor, weakness, aching, stiffness, fatigue.

CVS:

Chest pain, dyspnea, tachycardia, hypotension

Vision: amblyopia, or temporary blindness

Respiration: slow

Jaundice

Liver damage: necrosis

Renal damage: nephrosis

Unconsciousness

Delirium

Death from cardiac failure.

Laboratory: ECG: flattening and inversion of T waves in all leads, prolonged PR and QT intervals, changed rhythm.

MLD: 1 g.

Lethal time: Within hrs.

PM findings: GI Tract:

- Corrosion marks over the mucous membrane of the upper GI Tract.
- Stomach: mucous membrane highly inflammed, eroded.
- Doudenum: congested.
- Other viscera: congested.
- Fatty degeneration: of liver, heart and kidneys, in chronic cases.

Laboratory analysis: of vomitus, urine, stools, excreta, damaged viscera.

Medico-legal aspect:

- That whether the death is accidental, suicidal or homicidal ?
- That whether ECG had been conducted or not prior to death ?
- That whether the death has been due to emetine poisoning ?

INDUSTRIAL POISONING

HEAVY METALS POISONING:

METALS: Arsenic, antimony, mercury, lead, cadmium, manganese, zinc, gold, silver, bismuth, thallium, beryllium.

ARSENIC POISONING: Described on page ....

ANTIMONY POISONING

Properties: Chemically antimony compounds are in many ways similar to that of the arsenicals.

Types:

- Inorganic compounds: toxic, never employed as drugs. Potassium antimonyl tartarate or tartar emetic is commonly used as a poison.
- Organic compounds: trivalent and pentavalent, employed as drugs, available as buff-coloured, odourless, amorphous, water soluble powder, marketed as ampuls for IM and IV injection.

Actions: Similar to those of arsenic.

Poisoning: Similar to those of arsenic. Occurs due to corrosive action.

Etiology:
- Accidental: may be ingested accidentally by children, or from careless therapeutic use of antimony containing drugs by the patients.
- Suicidal: rare.
- Homicidal: rare, as the element is not widely used in medicine or industry.

Pathogenesis: Antimony is more caustic than arsenic. Trivalent antimonials inhibit sulphydryl enzymes.

Diagnosis: GI Tract:
- Metallic taste, burning pain in the mouth
- Constriction of throat
- Difficulty in swallowing
- Pain abdomen
- Nausea, vomiting, diarrhea (hemorrhagic), thirst due to fluid loss

Muscle cramps–due to disturbed electrolytes of body fluids

Hepatitis

Nephritis: hemorrhagic

Shock (anaphylactic reaction):
- skin becomes cold, clammy, pale
- pulse–rapid and weak
- hypotension
- respiration–depressed

Coma and death may occur.

Investigation: ECG: P wave: increased amplitude, ST segment and T wave fused, Q-T interval increased.

MLD: 0.1 g.

Lethal time: 10-96 hrs.

PM findings: External:
- Signs of dehydration: sunken eyes and prominent cheek bones.

Internal:

GI Tract:
- Marks: red inflammed marks over the mucous membrane of the upper GI Tract.

- Stomach: highly inflammed, perforated (rare), contents dark brownish.
- Doudenum: congested.

Heart: sub-endocardial hemorrhage

Other viscera: congested.

Laboratory analysis: of vomitus, urine, stools, excreta, damaged viscera.

Medico-legal aspects:

- That whether death is accidental, suicidal or homicidal ?
- That whether the death has been due to consumption of antimony ?

MERCURY POISONING: Described on page 98.

LEAD POISONING: Described on page 122..

CADMIUM POISONING

Properties: Is a highly toxic metal used extensively as a rustproof plating for iron and steel articles, as a constituent of various alloys, and for numerous industrial purposes.

Action: Is a potent inhibitor of sulphydryl enzymes.

Poisoning: Industrial or household poisoning

Etiology: Accidental:
- from the inhalation of cadmium dusts/or cadmium oxide, or
- from the ingestion of cadmium salts

Suicidal: - rarely from attempts at self-destruction

Homicidal: - rarely used.

Pathogenesis:

Diagnosis: GI Tract:

- Nausea, vomiting, diarrhea, abdominal pain
- Hepatic failure
- Renal failure

Lungs: pulmonary edema, pneumonitis, lung damage

MLD: 40 mg.

Lethal time: Within 24 hrs.

PM findings: GI Tract:

- Marks: yellow band on the teeth, dental caries.
- Stomach: congested.
- Doudenum: congested.

Lungs: edematus, pneumonitic, extensively damaged.

Kidneys: damaged

Other viscera: congested

Laboratory analysis: of vomitus, urine, stools, excreta, damaged viscera.

Medico-legal aspects:

- That whether the death is accidental, suicidal or homicidal ?
- That whether the death has been caused by cadmium poisoning ?

MANGANESE POISONING

Definition: Is seldom used in therapeutics, and the main interest arises from the fact that the metal is the cause of industrial poisoning.

Properties: Potassium permanganate is a powerful oxidizing agent, is employed as an antiseptic and chemical antidote.

Poisoning: Neurological injury and liver damage (cirrhosis).

Etiology: Accidental: - accidental exposure to vapours in industry

Diagnosis: Neurological syndrome:

- Face: mask-like
- Voice: low and monotonous
- Tremors
- Muscular pains, rigidity
- Gait: spastic
- Reflexes: increased
- Ankle and plantar clonus
- Liver cirrhosis
- Pneumonia

MLD: 6 mg/cu mm.

Lethal time: within 24 hrs.

PM findings: GI Tract:

- Stomach: congested.
- Doudenum: congested.

Lungs: edematus, pneumonitic, extensively damaged.

Liver: damaged

Kidneys: damaged

Other viscera: congested.

Laboratory analysis: of vomitus, urine, stools, excreta, damaged viscera.

Medico-legal aspects:

- That whether the death is accidental, suicidal or homicidal ?
- That whether the death has been caused by manganese poisoning ?

ZINC POISONING

Properties: Clinically zinc is employed only for its local actions (astringents and antiseptics)

Zinc is a constituent of most foods and is necessary for the normal growth and development of both animals and plants.

Poisoning: Occurs due to precipitation of the protoplasm of the mucosa of the GI Tract.

Etiology:

- Accidental: - accidental exposure to zinc dusts in industry, or from careless medication.
- Suicidal: by ingestion of a soluble zinc salts in sufficient concentration.

Diagnosis:

- Skin: itching, argyria (bluish pigmentation).
- GI Tract: nausea, vomiting, diarrhea (hemorrhagic), and abdominal pain.
- Metal fume fever: fever, chills, leucocytosis.
- Kidneys: albuminurea, hematuria, renal failure.
- Liver: hepatitis, hepatic failure.
- CNS: depression, tremors, paralysis of limbs.
- Shock.
- Death.

MLD: 1 g.

Lethal time: Within 24 hrs.

PM findings: GI Tract:

- Mucous membrane of the upper GI Tract: inflammed, mouth discolouration
- Stomach: mucous membrane inflammed and hemorrhagic.
- Doudenum: mucous membrane inflammed and congested.

Skin: argyria.

Lungs: edematus, pneumonitic, extensively damaged.

Liver: damaged.

Kidneys: damaged.

Other viscera: congested.

Laboratory analysis: of vomitus, urine, stools, excreta, damaged viscera.

Medico-legal aspects:

- That whether the death is accidental or suicidal?
- That whether the death has been caused by zinc poisoning ?

GOLD POISONING

Properties: Clinically gold exerts no pharmacodynamic actions, while toxic reactions are many.

Poisoning: The main deterrence to the clinical use of gold salts is the high incidence of untoward reactions.

Etiology: Accidental: -accidental exposure to vapours in industry.

Diagnosis:

- Skin: itching, exfoliative dermatitis.
- Mucous membrane: stomatitis, pharyngitis, laryngitis, gastritis, colitis, and vaginitis.
- Hematopoietic organs: blood dyscrasias, thrombocytopenia, leucopenia, aplastic anemia, and agranulocytosis.
- Kidneys: albuminurea, hematuria, renal failure.
- Liver: hepatitis, hepatic failure.
- Brain: encephalitis.

- Peripheral neuritis.
- Convulsions
- Death may occur in 0.5 per cent.

MLD: Unknown.

Lethal time: Within 24 hrs.

PM findings: GI Tract:

- Mucous membrane of the upper GI Tract: inflammed, congested
- Stomach: mucous membrane inflammed and congested.
- Doudenum: mucous membrane inflammed and congested.

Skin: rash.

Lungs: edematus, pneumonitic, extensively damaged.

Liver: damaged.

Kidneys: damaged.

Other viscera: congested.

Laboratory analysis: of vomitus, urine, stools, excreta, damaged viscera.

Medico-legal aspects:

- That whether the death is accidental or suicidal?
- That whether the death has been caused by gold poisoning ?

SILVER POISONING:

Properties: Clinically silver is employed only for its local actions (antiseptic and germicidal).

Silver salts: Employed clinically are silver nitrate, silver picrate and silver lactate.

Poisoning: Occurs due to precipitation of the protoplasm of the mucosa of the GI Tract.

Etiology:
- Accidental:- accidental exposure to silver in industry, or from careless medication.
- Suicidal: by ingestion of a soluble silver salt in sufficient concentration.

Diagnosis: - Skin: itching, argyria (bluish pigmentation).

- Mucous membrane: stomatitis, pharyngitis, laryngitis, gastritis, colitis, and vaginitis.
- Hemorrhagic gastroenteritis.
- Hematopoietic organs: blood dyscrasias, thrombocytopenia, leucopenia, aplastic anemia, and agranulocytosis.
- Kidneys: albuminurea, hematuria, renal failure.
- Liver: hepatitis, hepatic failure.
- Shock
- Death.

MLD: 10 g.

Lethal time: Within 24 hrs.

PM findings: GI Tract:

- Mucous membrane of the upper GI Tract: inflammed, mouth discolouration
- Stomach: mucous membrane inflammed and hemorrhagic.
- Doudenum: mucous membrane inflammed and congested.

Skin: argyria.

Lungs: edematus, pneumonitic, extensively damaged.

Liver: damaged.

Kidneys: damaged.

Other viscera: congested.

Laboratory analysis: of vomitus, urine, stools, excreta, damaged viscera.

Medico-legal aspects:

- That whether the death is accidental or suicidal?
- That whether the death has been caused by silver poisoning ?

BISMUTH POISONING

Properties: Available as a white granular powder for oral administration, and as a sterile solution in water and as a sterile suspension in oil, for intramuscular injection.

Uses: Clinically bismuth is employed for its local demulcent, protective, antidiarrheal, and antispirochetal actions.

Poisoning: Causes local and systemic toxic reactions

Etiology:
- Accidental: from misuse.
- Suicidal: rare.
- Homicidal: very rare.

Diagnosis: Local reactions:
- Skin: pain, dermatitis (eruptions).

Embolism: oil embolism (IV inj.)

Systemic reactions:
- Mucous membrane: stomatitis, pharyngitis, laryngitis, gastritis, colitis, hemorrhagic gastroenteritis, and vaginitis.
- Jarisch-Herxheimer reaction (fatal).
- Headache, fever, arthralgia, malaise
- Kidneys: nephritis, anuria
- Liver: hepatitis, jaundice, hepatic failure.

Cardiovascular collapse
- Shock
- Death.

Laboratory: Urine analysis: albuminuria, casts, hematuria

LFT: Impaired.

MLD: 0.5 g.

Lethal time: Within 24 hrs.

PM findings: GI Tract:
- Mucous membrane of the upper GI Tract: inflammed, mouth discolouration
- Stomach: mucous membrane inflammed and hemorrhagic.
- Doudenum: mucous membrane inflammed and congested.

Skin: eruptions.

Lungs: edematus, extensively damaged.

Liver: damaged.

Kidneys: damaged.

Other viscera: congested.

Laboratory analysis: of urine, stools, excreta, damaged viscera.

Medico-legal aspects:

- That whether the death is accidental or suicidal?
- That whether the death has been caused by bismuth poisoning ?

THALLIUM POISONING

Properties: Is a highly toxic metal used as a depilatory, in the treatment of ringworm of the scalp in children.

Action: It has a marked action on the sympathetic nervous system, greatly augmenting the normal response to stimulation.

Poisoning: Industrial or household poisoning.

Etiology: Accidental: -from the accidental ingestion of thallium containing rat poisons, or industrial exposure.

Suicidal: - rare.

Homicidal: - rarely used for this purpose.

Diagnosis: GI Tract:

- Nausea, vomiting, diarrhea, severe abdominal pain

Mucosa: desquamation, hemorrhage,ulcerative stomatitis, gingival line.

Nervous system:

- Paresthesia: of hands and feet
- Peripheral polyneuritis
- Retrobulbar neuritis
- Ptosis, strabismus, mydriosis, facial palsy
- Speech: jumbled

Skin: eruptions, ecchymoses and patechiae

Hair: loss

Fever, lethargy

Hepatic failure

Renal failure

Lungs: pulmonary edema, pneumonitis, lung damage

Delirium, convulsions

Death from respiratory failure.

MLD: 1 g.

Lethal time: Within 12-24 hrs. in acute poisoning.

PM findings: GI Tract:

- Marks: yellow band on the teeth, dental caries.
- Stomach: congested.
- Doudenum: congested.

Lungs: edematus, pneumonitic, extensively damaged.

Kidneys: damaged

Other viscera: congested

Laboratory analysis: of vomitus, urine, stools, excreta, damaged viscera.

Medico-legal aspects:

- That whether the death is accidental, suicidal or homicidal ?
- That whether the death has been caused by thallium poisoning ?

BERYLLIUM POISONING

Properties: Is a highly toxic metal used extensively as a rustproof plating for iron and steel articles, as a constituent of various alloys, and for numerous industrial purposes esp. in the manufacturing of fluorescent lamps coated with a mixture of zinc, manganese, and beryllium silicates.

Poisoning: Industrial or household poisoning.

Etiology: Accidental:- from the inhalation of beryllium dusts/or fumes, or

- from the exposure of skin lesions (from cuts by broken fluorescent lamps) of workers to beryllium compounds.

Diagnosis: URC: nasopharyngeal and tracheobronchial irritation, causing:

- Cough: dry, becomes more severe and productive
- Chest pain: substernal
- Dyspnea: becomes severe to incapacitate the patient
- Cyanosis

- Fever

Lungs: pulmonary edema, pneumonitis, lung damage.

Anorexia and weight loss.

Death may occur from acute pneumonitis.

Investigation: CXR: diffuse increase in density of the lung fields or snowstorm appearance.

MLD: 40 mg.

Lethal time: Within 24 hrs. in acute poisoning.

PM findings: Nose and throat: congested.

Lungs: edematus, pneumonitic, extensively damaged.

Other viscera: congested

Laboratory analysis: of vomitus, urine, stools, excreta, damaged viscera.

Medico-legal aspects:

- That whether the death is accidental ?
- That whether the death has been caused by beryllium poisoning ?

PAINT THINNER POISONING

Poisoning: Occurs from inhalation.

Etiology: - Accidental: common amongst painters.

- Suicidal: rare.
- Homicidal: very rare.

Diagnosis:

- Nausea, vomiting, thirst, salivation
- Burning pain in the throat
- Breath: smells of kerosene oil
- Headache, drowsiness, vertigo, loss of memory
- Burning acute pain in the stomach
- Pulse: weak and irregular
- Pulmonary edema
- Respiratory distress
- Convulsions
- Coma
- Death–may occur within 1-3 days, earlier in children.

MLD: 10-50 ml.

Lethal time: within few hrs.

PM findings:- Skin: pale or cyanosed

- Upper GI Tract: the mucous membrane of the upper GI Tract, inflammed.
- Stomach: highly inflammed, perforated
- Doudenum: congested
- Liver: fatty degeneration
- Other viscera: congested.

Medico-legal aspect:

- That whether death is accidental, suicidal or homicidal ?
- That whether the cause of death was due to paint thinner poisoning ?

HOUSEHOLD POISONING:

BLEACHING SOLVENTS POISONING

Compounds: Bleaching solvents: Clorox, Purex, Sani-Clor.

Properties: Are irritants and corrosives to mucous membranes.

Poisoning: Cause irritation and corrosion of mucous membranes with edema of the pharynx and larynx.

Etiology:
Accidental: - may be ingested accidentally by children.
Suicidal: - common as freely available and shortest mode of committing suicide.
Homicidal: - rare.

Diagnosis: GI Tract:

- Nausea, vomiting, diarrhea, pain abdomen

Fever, headache,

Skin: rash

Nervous system:

Drowsiness, fatigue, tremors

Respiratory distress

Convulsions

Death from respiratory failure.

MLD: 15 ml.

Lethal time: Within 24 hrs.

PM findings: External:

Marks: corrosive marks over the mouth.

Skin: cyanosed, cold clammy.

Internal:

Pharynx and larynx: edematous.

Stomach: congested and perforated.

Duodenum: congested and perforated.

Other viscera: congested.

Laboratory analysis: of vomitus, urine, stools, excreta, damaged viscera.

Medico-legal aspects:

- That whether the death is accidental, suicidal, or homicidal ?
- That whether the death has been due to bleaching solutions poisoning ?

FOOD POISONING

Poisoning: Is defined as an acute illness resulting from ingestion of contaminated food.

Pandemic: Food poisoning should always be suspected if several people in the same place and at the same time suddenly develop syndrome of nausea, vomiting, diarrhea, and pain or tenderness in the abdomen.

Mode: Accidental: - contaminated food or drink ingested by children or poor people.

Suicidal: - rare.

Homicidal: - rare.

Etiology: Infective:

- Bacterial:
  - from toxin produced infection: Staphylococci, Clostridia botulinum, Escherichia coli, Vibrio cholera, Shigella sonnei
  - from food-born infection: Salmonella enteritis.
- Viral infections.

Food intolerance

Poisons:

- Inorganic: sodium nitrite
- Organic: mushroom, shellfish, poisonous toadstools or plants/berries
- Fruits and vegetables: sprayed with insecticides.

Pathogenesis: Bacteriae cause food to spoil (rot), and most of them produce poisonous toxin causing gastro-enteritis. Botulism is a serious, but rare form of food poisoning, due to a toxin (one of the deadliest poisons known), produced by the Clostridium botulinum.

Diagnosis: GI Tract:

- Nausea, vomiting, diarrhea, pain abdomen

Fever, headache

Skin: rash

Nervous system:

- Drowsiness, fatigue, dysphagia, dysphonia, tremors

Respiratory distress

Convulsions

Death from respiratory failure.

MLD:

- Nitrites: 2 g
- DDT 10-20 g.
- Thiocyanates 20 mg/dl

Mortality:

- Botulism toxin is usually fatal if untreated, inadequately treated, or lately treated.
- Vibrio cholera is usually fatal if untreated, inadequately treated, or lately treated.

PM findings: As per the causative agent:

Infective agent:

External:

Skin: dehydrated.

Internal:

- Pharynx and larynx: edematous.
- Stomach: congested and perforated.
- Duodenum: congested and perforated.
- Other viscera: congested.

Poisoning agent:

External:

Marks: corrosive marks over the mouth

Skin: cyanosed, cold clammy

Internal:

- Pharynx and larynx: congested
- Stomach: congested and perforated.
- Duodenum: congested and perforated.
- Other viscera: congested.

Laboratory analysis: of vomitus, urine, stools, excreta, damaged viscera.

Medico-legal aspects:

- That whether the death is accidental, suicidal, or homicidal ?
- That whether the death has been due to food poisoning ?
- That whether the death has been due to bacterial infection or a poison ?

References:

1. Goodman, LS, and Gilman, A (editors): General Principles of Toxicology. The Pharmacological Basis of Therapeutics, 4th ed. Macmillan, New York, 1960.
2. An Experienced Teacher: Notes on Medical Jurisprudence and Toxicology. Current Publishers, Calcutta, 1965.
3. Dreisbach Robert H, and Krupp Marcus, A, Chatton Milton, J (editors): Poisons. Lange Medical Publications, Japan, 916-945, 1975.
4. Reid, HA, Jhekaston, RDG. The management of snakebite. Bull WHO 63:885-95, 1983.
5. Russell, FE. Snake venom poisoning. Philadelphia. JB Lippincot Co. 291-300, 1980.
6. Saitz, R, O'Malley S: Pharmacotherapies for alcohol abuse. Med Clin North Am 81:881-907, 1997.
7. Schorling, JB, Buchsbaum, DG: Screening for alcohol and drug abuse. Med Clin North Am 81:845-65, 1997.
8. Ghai, OP, Piyush, G: Poisonings and accidents. Essential Pediatrics 640-41, 2004.
9. Wyatt, JP, Illingworth, RN, Robertson, CE, Clancy, MJ, Munro, PT: Poisoning. Oxford Handbook of Accident and Emergency Medicine 174-202, 2005, 209.

MEDICAL JURISPRUDENCE

MEDICAL JURISPRUDENCE

VOLUME - 2

P. S. Kapoor
MBBS, MS, PCMS (Ex)

KALPAZ

©Author

All rights reserved. No part of this work may be reproduced, stored, adapted, or transmitted in any form or by any means, electronic, mechanical, photocopying, micro-filming recording or otherwise, or translated in any language, without the prior written permission of the copyright owner and the publisher. The book is sold subject to the condition that it shall not, by way of trade or otherwise, be lent, resold, hired out, or otherwise circulated without the prior publisher's written consent in any form of binding or cover other than that in which it is published.

The views and opinions expressed in this book are author(s) own and the facts reported by them have been verified to the extent possible, and the publishers are not in any way liable for the same.

First Published, 2018

Published by

Kalpaz Publications
C-30, Satyawati Nagar,
Delhi – 110052
E-mail: kalpaz@hotmail.com
Ph.: 9212142040

Printed at: G. Print Process, Delhi

Cataloging in Publication Data—DK
Courtesy: D.K. Agencies (P) Ltd. <docinfo@dkagencies.com>

Kapoor, P. S., author.
Medical jurisprudence / Dr P.S. Kapoor.
volumes cm
Includes bibliographical references.
ISBN 9789386397584 (set : HB)
ISBN 9789386397607 (Vol-II : HB)

1. Medical laws and legislation—India. I. Title.

KNS1520.K37 2018 | DDC 344.54041 23

CONTENTS

PART - I

FORENSIC MEDICINE

PART - II

MEDICAL JURISPRUDENCE

PART - III

STATE MEDICINE

PART - II

MEDICAL JURISPRUDENCE

CHAPTER - 4

LEGAL PROCEDURES

LEGAL (CRIMINAL) PROCEDURES

- Judicial Inquest
- Police Inquest
- Exhumation
- PM Examination
- Summon
- Subpoena
- Oath-Taking
- Witness
- Evidence Recording
  - Examination-in-Chief
  - Cross-Examination
  - Re-Examination
- Medical Evidence:
  - Oral/Verbal evidence:

  Direct Evidence: Sensory- Visual (Eye witness),
  - Audible
  - Olfactory

  Indirect Evidence: Circumstantial/Associated Evidence
- Documentary Evidence:

  Dying Declaration

  Dying Deposition

  Medical Certificate of Illness, Insanity and Fitness

  Medical Certificate of Death

Medico-legal Reports: Accident/Injury Report
Post-Mortem Report
Age-Evidence Report
Rape, Abortion, Molestation Reports
Poisoning Report

- Witness:
  - Common/Ordinary Witness
  - Professional Witness:
    Medical Professionals,
    Finger-Print Experts
    Hand-Writing Experts
    Chemical Examiner Experts
    Arms and Ammunition Experts
  - Skilled Witness
- Identity:
  - Indications
  - Identifying (ID) factors

JUDICIAL INQUEST (JI):

Inquiry Officer: An official whose job is to discover the cause of someone's death, esp. if he/she died in a sudden or unusual way.

Eligibility:
- Coroner or Deputy Coroner, or
- Chief Judicial Magistrate (CJM) or
- Additional Chief Judicial Magistrate (ACJM).

Appointment: By the Government.

Jurisdiction : Is a Court of inquiry and not a Court for Trial.

Duties:
- To conduct an inquiry into an unnatural (accidental, suicidal or homicidal) death.
- To order for an examination of a dead body for ID and PM examination.
- To order for exhumation, in a suspected case of foul play–esp. poisoning (usually Arsenic poisoning), in order to confirm the identity of the dead body and to perform the autopsy.
- To order an inquiry into a sub-custodial death.
- To order any Medical Officer, to conduct the post-mortem examination.

- To summon the Medical Officer, who had attended the case, or had conducted the post-mortem examination.
- To appoint a Deputy Coroner or ACJM, as his/her replacement, due to unavoidable circumstances.

POLICE INQUEST (PI):

Police Officer: An officer who conducts the police inquiry in the presence of respectable, known persons of the locality.

Eligibility: An officer of the rank of Sub-Inspector or above.

Duties:
- To conduct an inquiry into an unnatural (accidental, suicidal or homicidal) death.
- To visit the dead body and to conduct an inquiry assisted by persons of the locality.
- To write a report mentioning the site of mishap, appearance of the body, body injuries, mode of injuries and the type of weapon used.
- To transfer/shift the body to the regional civil hospital for PM examination, to be conducted by the Medical Officer in charge or the Medical Officer appointed by the Coroner/Deputy Coroner or CJM/ACJM.
- To supply a copy of the PM report to the Coroner/ Deputy Coroner or CJM/ACJM.

EXHUMATION:

Definition: Is defined as a legally disinterment or digging out of a buried dead body from the grave, for the aim of identification and autopsy, with/or without chemical examination of viscera, in suspected cases of deaths.

Eligibility: Authorised officer, in presence of a Police officer, authorised by District Magistrate, Sub-Divisional Magistrate or any other authorised Magistrate.

Duties of MO: Medico-legal PM Examination, may be conducted at the site or at a nearby mortuary.

Time limit: India and UK: unlimited (No time limit)

France: 10 yrs, Scotland: 20 yrs, Germany: 30 yrs.

POST- MORTEM (PM) EXAMINATION:

Duties of MO:-To conduct the PM examination

- To write in detail the reports (external and internal findings) of wounds (number, site, size, shape, colour) and mode of inflicted injuries.
- To ascertain the cause of death and time of death.
- To supply copies of the PM findings to the Civil Surgeon and Superintendent of Police of the concerned district.

SUMMEN:

Definition: An official order by the Court of Law to an accused person or to a witness, whose presence is required in the Court. The signed and sealed summon is served by the Court, through police or Court staff.

SUBPOENA:

Definition: Is defined as a law to order (written) someone to come to a Court of Law and be a witness. The summoned person cannot leave the Court, without the permission of the concerned Judge/ or Magistrate.

Penality:
- Failing to attend: warrant may be issued against, to compel his/her presence in the court
- Non-compliance to summons in a:
- Civil case: liable to action for damages
- Criminal case: liable to fine or imprisonment, or both

Rules: To attend two courts on a particular day by a Medical Officer, then:
- The Criminal case would get priority over the Civil case, and
- The Higher Courts would get priority over the Lower Courts
- Same level Courts: Summon received earliest, to be attended first

Medical Officer, to inform the other court, that he is unable to attend.

OATH TAKING (OT):

Definition: Is defined as a solemn appeal to the God or somewhat holy or reverenced as witness or sanction of the truth of a statement. A witness is required to take an oath before deposition.

Example: "I solemnly affirm that I shall speak the truth, whole truth, nothing but truth and I conceal nothing, if anything false, so help me God."

WITNESS:
- Common/Ordinary Witness.
- Professional Witness: one who is an expert in his professional subject:

  Medical Professionals,

  Finger-Print Experts,

  Hand-Writing Experts,

  Chemical Examiner Experts,

  Arms and Ammunition Experts.
- Skilled Witness.
- Hostile Witness: one who gives false evidence with an ulterior motive.

EVIDENCE RECORDING (ER):

Definition: After taking an oath, evidence recording (deposition) of the witness starts

Procedure:
- Deposition of the witness
- Examination in Chief:
- Cross-Examination
- Re-Examination

Deposition of the Witness: That the witness narrates within his knowledge the facts in details, within his knowledge.

EXAMINATION-IN-CHIEF (EIC): by the prosecution side:

Prosecution: Prosecutor (State prosecutor or a lawyer engaged by the prosecution):
- Puts questions to the witness and elicits answers, which are recorded by the Court.

Observation:- Overrule: No leading questions are permissible and the Judge may overrule these

- Permits: The Judge may allow the leading questions, if being convinced that the witness is hostile.

CROSS-EXAMINATION (CE): by the defence side:

Defence: Defence (Defence lawyer engaged by the defence): The defence lawyer try his/her best to weaken the witness evidence, by:

Putting questions to the witness and thereby tries to prove before the Court that the evidence given by the witness unbelievable and false.

Observation: Permits: The Judge may allow the leading questions, if being convinced that the witness is hostile.

Overrule: The Judge may overrule the objection raised by the prosecutor for putting leading questions, if being convinced that the leading questions may be relevant to the case.

The Judge may not allow irrelevant questions to the witness.

Time-limit: Un-limited for cross-examination.

RE-EXAMINATION (RE): by the prosecution side:

Prosecution: - To clarify certain discrepancies made by during cross-examination by the witness.

Observation: Overrule: The Judge may disallow any question relevant to new subjects.

Permits: The Judge may allow prosecutor, to ask question relevant to new subjects and for that defence will be allowed another cross-examination.

Power: The Coroner, Judge, Magistrate or Jury may put/ask any question, at any level of trial.

MEDICAL EVIDENCE (ME):

Definition: Is defined as medical information,statements and objects that are given in a Court of Law, in order to prove that someone is guilty or not guilty.

Types: - Oral/Verbal evidence:

Direct Evidence: Sensory - Visual (Eye witness),

- Audible
- Olfactory

Indirect Evidence: Circumstantial/Associated Evidence

- Documentary Evidence:
  Dying Declaration
  Dying Deposition
  Medical Certificate of Illness and Insanity
  Medical Certificate of Fitness
  Medical Certificate of Death
  Medico-legal Reports: Accident/Injury Report
  Post-Mortem Report
  Age-Evidence Report
  Rape, Abortion, Molestation Reports
  Poisoning Report.

DYING DECLARATION (DD):

Definition: Is defined as a declaration/statement made by a dying person who does not survive the trial of the accused.

Admissible: Admitted as a documentary evidence in the Court of Law (Civil and Criminal).

Recording: Immediately on receipt of a serious patient in the A&E, the attending doctor on duty is to inform the Magistrate, for recording of dying declaration.

Eligibility: A Magistrate.

Exception: MO can record the dying declaration, If he/she considers that the serious patient may die before the arrival of the Magistrate

Non-eligible: A Police Officer cannot record a dying declaration.

Criteria:
- That MO should declare/certify the fitness (mental) of the person making dying declaration.
- That it should be recorded as per dying person's wordings.
- That it should not be dictated to the dying person (no leading suggestions).

- That after completion of the recording, it should be read over to the dying person, prior to his/her signing it.
- That dying declaration should be signed by two witnesses.

DYING DEPOSITION:

Definition: Is defined as a declaration/statement made by a dying person, being recorded by the Magistrate, in the presence of accused or his lawyer.

Admissible: Admitted as a more valuable evidence than the dying declaration, as the accused has the benefit of challenge and cross-examination.

Criteria: - That MO should declare/certify the fitness (mental) of the person making dying deposition.

IDENTITY

Definition: To recognise and correctly name someone, living or dead, or something.

Indications:-In living persons:

(A) Identification in:

Criminal cases of:

Apprehhended:

- Criminals,
- Murderers,
- Assaulters
- Rapists.

Civil cases of:

- Marriage disputes
- Inheritance disputes
- Disputed sex
- Missing persons
- Insurance claims

(B) As an ID proof in following criterias:

Financial criteria:

- To open Bank Account,
- To apply for loan
- To guarantee for someone's loan etc.

Licence criteria:

- To apply for driving licence
- To apply for passport
- To apply for ration card
- To apply for Arms licence.

Registration criteria:

- To apply for school/college admission
- To apply for professional registration
- To apply for membership of a club, society.

Travel criteria:

- To apply for Passport, Visa, Ticket
- To book a hotel accommodation
- To purchase certain items at the Airport custom free shops.
- Of dead bodies: identification of:

Known dead bodies:

- prior to post-mortem examination by the relatives, persons familiar with the dead person, or the accompanying police official.

  Unknown dead bodies: prior to PM examination by the Medical Officer, on the basis of information provided by the police official, in the form of fingerprint database and photographs, helpful in subsequent identification.

Identifying (ID) factors:

Age

Sex

Race and religion

Complexion

Features

External peculiarities

Hair-colour and texture

Eyes

Deformities

Biometric database

Fingerprints

Footprints
Occupation marks
Tattoo marks
Photographs
Clothing, ornaments and articles found on the body.

Age: Assessed by observing:

- Body built: well built in an adult male
- Height and weight: of valuable in case of fetus and new-borns.
- Teeth: Number:
  - Permanent: 32 in number (8 on each side of each jaw)
  - Deciduous: 20 in number (5 on each side of each jaw)
  - Eruption: Babies cut their
    1st milk teeth at the age of 5-6 months,
    2 upper teeth appear at the age of 7-8 months,
    4 more teeth appear at the age of 9-10 months, and so on, until there are 20 milk teeth, 2nd molar appear as last milk teeth at the age of about 24 months.
    3rd molars (Wisdom tooth) appear at the age of about 16-24 yrs.

Age-wise number of teeth:

At 12 months = 8 Deciduous teeth
At 15 months = 12 Deciduous teeth
At 18 months = 16 Deciduous teeth
At 24 months = 20 Deciduous teeth
At 09 yrs. = 12 Permanent teeth
At 12 yrs. = 24 Permanent teeth
At 16 yrs. = 32 Permanent teeth

Exception:	Pre-mature eruption:	in Congenital syphilis
	Delayed eruption:	in Rickets
Lower jaw:	assessed by observing angle of jaw:	
Age:	Infants:	obtuse angle
	Adults:	midway of upper and lower borders
	Elders:	nearer to upper border due to absorbed alveoli
Sex:	Male:	everted
	Female:	inverted
Ossification of bones:		assessed by observing X-rays of elbow, wrist and pelvis
Elbow:	Capitellum:	appears at the age of 2nd yr.
	Medial epicondyle:	appears at the age of
	Radial head:	appears at the age of 5th yr.
	Olecranon tip:	appears at the age of 10th yr.
	Trochlea:	appears at the age of 11th yr.
	Lateral epicondyle:	appears at the age of 12th yr.
Wrist:	Pisiform bone:	appears at the age of 10th yr.
	Lower ends of:	unite at the age of 16-17 yrs.
	Radius and Ulna	
Pelvis:	Iliac crest:	unite with the body at 18-24 yrs.
	Ischial tuberosity:	unite with Ischium at 20 yrs.

Medico-legal aspects:

Criminal responsibility:

< 7 yrs.: no criminal responsibility

7-12 yrs.: - to be decided by the Juvenile Court for offences of:

- Giving consent for a surgical procedure
- Kidnapping or abduction
- Sexual offences e.g. Rape, molestation, sexual perversion

< 14 yrs.: Illegible to be hanged

< 18 yrs.: Illegible for consent to marriage by a girl (Minor)

Illegible for consent to sexual intercourse by a girl

18 yrs.: Age for attaining majority for girls

Age for marriage registration of a girl

Age of consent for sexual intercourse by a wife

Age for girls for charging of kidnapping or abduction

21 yrs.: Age for attaining majority for boys

Age for marriage registration of a boy

Age of consent for sexual intercourse by a husband.

Sex: assessed by observing:

- Genitalia: Male: penis, testes, prostate gland

  Female: vagina, uterus, ovaries and fallopian tubes.

  Exception: - Hermaphrodites
  - Advanced putrefied bodies
  - Mutilated bodies
  - Skeleton only.
- Body built: well built in an adult male
- Facial hairs

- Breast developed – in an adult female
- Pomum adam – prominent in males
- Pubic hairs: Male: directed upwards
Female: directed downwards

Medico-legal aspects:

- Marriage
- Impotence, sterility
- Rape, molestation, sexual perversion
- Heritage, property disputes
- Employment in army, police, industry.

Race and Caste: assessed by observing:

Males:

Religious (customs) signs:

- Circumcision: a religious custom in Jews and Muslims
- Tuft of hair over occiput: a religious custom in Hindus
- Sacred thread worn over shoulder: by high caste Hindus
- Mark (Tilak) of red or white on forehead: by Hindus
- Ear-lobes pierced by rings: by Brahmin Hindus
- Turbons (Head gear) worn: by Sikhs, Muslims
- Beard flown: by Sikhs, Muslims
- Iron wristlet (Kara): by Sikhs.

Clothing:

- Pants, Knickers, Dhotis, Kurta-Payjamas: by Hindus
- Salwar Kameeze, Pants: by Muslims
- Pants, Knickers: by Christians.

Females:

Religious (customs) signs:

- Vermillion marks in hair: by married Hindu women
- Nasal ring in the left nasal ala: by Hindu girls/ women.

- Nasal ring in the nasal septum: by Muslim girls/women
- Bangles in the forearms: by Hindu girls/women
- Tattoo marks on forehead, chest, arm: by Hindu girls/women.

Clothing:

- Sarees, Salwar Kameeze, Jeans: by Hindu girls/women.
- Salwar Kameeze, Jeans, Gowns: by Muslim girls/women
- Jeans, Blouse-Skirts: by Christian girls/women.

Complexion: assessed by observing:

Skin complexion: fair, black, brown or faint yellow.

Features: assessed by observing:

A person may resemble to his/her parents, brothers or sisters, on account of features.

Exception: Decomposed (advanced) dead bodies.

Criteria: Resembling features of: nasal bridge, lips, ear lobes, colour of eyes (Iris).

External: assessed by observing:

peculiarities Birthmarks, moles, malformations, scars, occupational marks, tattoo marks, wounds etc.

Hair: Hair colour and texture: Black, brown, grey or white.

Eyes: Iris colour: black, brown, blue, green or grey.

Deformities: Congenital: Club foot (CTEV), CDH, Spina bifida, Kyphosis, Scoliosis, Hare lip, Cretin-dwarf, Gigantism, Polydactylism, Umbilical hernia.

Acquired: Post-polio paralytic, post-traumatic (Mal-united fractures), RA, OA, rheumatic and gout, amputation.

Biometric: Biometric database, is the currently, most reliable ID test.

Database Criteria: includes fingerprints, occupational marks, tattoo marks and facial photographs.

Fingerprints: assessed by:

- Galton system (Dactylography)

- Bertillon system (Bertillonage)
- Jaffrey system (DNA fingerprinting).

Footprinting: assessed by observing:
Footprints in the vicinity of place of violence

Occupation marks: Industrial: Lead marks,
Painters: Paint marks,
Coblers: Callosities on the hands
Farmers: rough hands.

Tatoo-marks: on the chest, arms, back, abdomen, legs, produced by injecting an insoluble dye into the skin, visible for about 10-20 yrs.

Photographs: To be taken by the photographer accompanying Police Official, and are reliable ID factor.

Clothing: To be handed over to the police for identification purpose.

Medico-legal aspects:

- To identify unknown or unclaimed bodies.

POST-MORTEM EXAMINATION (AUTOPSY)

Definition: Is defined as an examination of a dead body (Table 4.1).

Autopsy is the systematic examination of a cadaver for study or for determining the cause of death. Autopsy means "see for yourself". It is a special surgical operation, performed by specially trained physicians, on a dead body. Its purpose is to learn the truth about the person's health during life, and how the person really died. Autopsies, also known as necropsies, post-mortems, or post-mortem examinations, use many methodical procedures to determine the aetiology and pathogenesis of diseases, for epidemiologic purposes, for establishment of genetic causes, and for family counsel. There are many advantages to getting an autopsy.

Even when the law does not require it, there is always something interesting for the family to know. Post-mortems may be performed at the request of the authorities in cases of unexplained and suspicious death or where a physician did not attend death. In other circumstances post-mortem examination may be performed only with the consent of the deceased's family or with permission granted by the person himself before death. These examinations are more frequently being used for the acquiring of organs and tissues for transplantation. Valuable medical information can be learned from a post-mortem examination. Legionnaire's disease, for example, was discovered as a result of autopsies, and improved safety standards have resulted from the examination of the bodies of crash victims.

The autopsy deals with the particular illness as evidenced in one individual and is more than simply a statistical average. Every autopsy is important to expose mistakes, to delimit new diseases and new patterns of disease, and to guide future studies. Morbidity and mortality statistics acquire accuracy and significance when based on careful autopsies. The autopsy procedure itself has changed very little during the twentieth century. It is a detailed examination of a body and each of its part, not only superficially but also through various tests on tissue in labs. Its purpose is to learn the truth about the person's health during life, and how the person really died.

Apparently, autopsies are being performed with decreasing frequently.

Where earlier in the century as many as half of all bodies had autopsies performed, now only 5-10 per cent of corpses undergo the procedure.

Generally, an autopsy is only done when there is some cause of doubt as to the cause of death, although the family of the deceased can always request an autopsy even if the hospital doesn't think it necessary.

Indication:
- To determine the cause of death
- To identify or characterise the extent of disease/disorder that the person may have had

- To determine the effectiveness of a particular medical or surgical treatment
- To be helpful in Academic Institutions, for Teaching and Research aims.

Judicial Inquest: Following are empowered to order for PM Examination:

- Coroner or Deputy Coroner (in abscence of Coroner), or
- Chief Judicial Magistrate (CJM), or
- Additional Chief Judicial Magistrate (ACJM) in abscence of CJM.

Performer: PM examination is to be conducted by the Medical Officer Incharge (SMO) of the concerned hospital, or by a Pathologist, or by a Medical Officer appointed by the:

- Coroner/or Deputy Coroner, or
- Chief Judicial Magistrate (CJM)/or Additional Chief Judicial Magistrate (ACJM).

Duties of M.O.: - To conduct the PM examination

- To write in detail the reports (external and internal findings) of wounds (number, site, size, shape, colour) and mode of inflicted injuries
- To ascertain the cause of death and time of death
- To supply copies of the PM findings to the Civil Surgeon and Superintendent of Police of the concerned district.

Trial Court: of Session Judge or Additional Session Judge of the District.

Power:

- To deal with all types of un-natural deaths (suspected to be murder) under Section 302
- To deal with cases of grieveous injuries under Section 307
- To deal with cases of Rape under Section 376
- To summon the Medical Officer, who had attended the case, or had conducted the post-mortem examination.
- To record medical evidence.

Autopsy findings:

The first step is a gross-examination of the exterior for any abnormality or trauma and a careful description of the interior of the body and its organs.

This is usually followed by further studies, including microscopic examination of cells and tissues. Then the pathologist proceeds to the dissection, which consists of removing and examining carefully all parts of the body.

TABLE 4.1: PROFORMA: POST-MORTEM (AUTOPSY) REPORT

SURNAME.............................. FIRST NAME.............C.R. No..................
AGE/DOB............................ SEX..........................Date......................
SON/DAUGHTER/WIFE...
ADDRESS ....TEL.......................
D.O.RECEIT OF BODY..TIME...................
D.O. POST MORTEM...TIME...................
CAUSE OF DEATH...
Dr Incharge...

EXAMINATION

EXTERNAL EXAMINATION:

Appearance:	Built..................................	Deformity......................
Temperature:	Cold..................................	WARM..........................
Skin:	Colour..............................	Lustre.............Elasticity....
	PM Stain (Lividity)...	
	Rigor Mortis..	

Examination of different parts of the Body:

HEAD AND NECK:

Scalp:	Wounds..............................	Blood clots.......................
Skull:	Shape................................	Size.................................
	Wounds..............................	Fracture...........................
Odour:	Fowl/Toxic	
Hair:	Texture..............................	Lustre..............................
Eyes:	Sunken..............................	Lustre..............................
	Orbittal fracture................	Eyeballs tension...............
	Eye lids.............................	Conjunctiva.......................

(Cont'd...)

	Cornea.............................	Sclera..............................
	Iris..................................	Lens.................................
Reflexes:	Conjunctival......................	Pupillary......... Corneal.....
Ears:	Wounds............................	Colour..............................
Face:	Wounds............................	Fractures..........................
Mouth:	Cheeks.............................	Lips.................................
Tongue:	Protrusion.........................	Colour............ Wounds.....
Teeth and Gums:	Missing............................	Fracture...........................
Saliva/froath:	Mouth...............................	Nose............... Ears.........
Bleeding:	Mouth...............................	Nose............... Ears.........
Neck:	Prominent.........................	Deformity.........................
	Ligature mark....................	Finger marks....................
	Abrasions..........................	Bruises............................
	Contusions........................	Wounds............................
	Fractures..........................	Dislocations......................
Chest:	Shape of Chest..................	Breast..............................
	Bruises............................	Abrasions.........................
	Wounds............................	Fracture Ribs...................
Spine:	Deformity..........................	Prominence......................
	Fracture............................	Dislocation.......................
Abdomen:	Size..................................	Shape..............................
	Distension.........................	Wounds............................
Genitalia:		
Male:	Penis.................................	Scrotum.........Testicles......
Female:	External genitalia...	
Gynaecology and Obstetrics examination (To confirm Rape/Molestation):		
Breast:	Colour...............................	Pigmentation....................
	Nipple retraction................	Discharge from nipples......
	Bruises.............................	Abrasions.........................
	Wounds............................	Swelling...........................
Abdomen:	Bruises.............................	Abrasions.........................
	Wounds............................	Swelling...........................
Limbs: Upper and lower limbs:		
Inspection:	Shape...............................	Size..................................
	Built.................................	Muscle wastings...............
	Edema feet/thighs...	
Palpation:	Muscle tone.......................	Power..............................
	Reflexes............................	Sensations ....
	Edema ankles/thig............	Local tenderness ....
	Pulsations: Radial..............	Femoral ....

(Cont'd...)

	Posterior tibial	Dorsalis pedis ....
	Lymph nodes enlargement	
	Measurements	
Examination of a young child's body:		
	Height	Weight ....
	Head Cirf	Chest Cirf ....
	Midarm Cirf	Ant. Fontanelle ....
	Pallor	Cyanosis ....
INTERNAL EXAMINATION:		
Head and Neck:		
Brain and Meninges:	Wounds	Blood/Blood clots ....
	Congestion	Edema ....
Larynx and Trachea:	Wounds	Congestion ....
Glottis:	Wounds	Edema ....
Esophagus	Wounds	Edema ....
Chest:		
Lungs:	Wounds	Edema ....
Heart:	Wounds	Hemorrhage ....
	Right side	Left side ....
Abdomen:		
Liver:	Wounds	Edema ....
Gall bladder:	Wounds	Stones ....
Spleen:	Wounds	Edema ....
Stomach:	Wounds	Full/Empty ....
Intestines:	Wounds	Compressed ....
Kidneys:	Wounds	Urine extravasation ....
Bladder:	Wounds	Urine extravasation ....
Genitalia:		
Penis and Testis:	Wounds	Squeezing ....
Urethra:	Wounds	Urine extravasation ....
Vulva:	Wounds	Hemorrhage ....
Vagina:	Wounds	Hemorrhage ....
	Edema	Semen (Rape) ....
Bones and Joints:		
Limbs:	Fractures	Dislocations ....
	Wounds	Blood effusion ....

References:

1. Halder, S: Pathological post-mortem examination. JIMA Vol. 108 No. 09, 554, 2010.
2. Shrivastava et al: Profile of post-mortem cases conducted at a morgue of a tertiary care hospital in Kolkata. JIMA Vol. 108 No. 11, 730-733, 2010.

VIRTUAL AUTOPSY

Definition: This virtual autopsy system cuts, slices, spins, and magnifies images of the body, at the touch and spin of fingers, providing physician/surgeon, glimpses of every tissue, organ, fluid, and foreign body, without a single cut. Using a virtual knife, one can slice the body, remove layers of skin and muscles, to peek inside.

Performer: Dr Anders Persson, Director of the Centre for Medical Image Science and Visualisation at Linkoping University, Sweeden, invented this Visualisation.

Table, that looks like a large touch-sensitive LCD screen, mounted on four legs. According to Dr Persson, all this can be done with a wave of one's fingers, and Dr Persson does it with the enviable deftness of a gamer. The table uses real-time and stored images created using computed tomography.

(CT scans)-25000 slices across the body–done in less than 20 seconds, he explains.Since different tissues, bone, fluids, and foreign bodies, have different densities, the scanner's ray absorption varies. The software assigns them a density value and an NVIDiA graphics card–the kind used for high speed gaming – transfers the data 3-D images.

Blue: air pockets

Beige: soft tissues

Red: blood vessels

White: bones.

According to Dr Persson, dfferent types of injuries and trauma, such as drowning, strangulation and gnshot wounds are easier to identify through imaging than conventional scalpel autopsy e.g. cases of strangulation without external marks or bruising show up in autopsy imaging. He shows an image with blue marking in the throat tissue. The blue colour seen is gas, confirming it to be a strangulation case, and this evidence was accepted by the Court.

Next on display, is the image of a man with a knife stuck in his ribs–case of suicide and not of murder.

Detective: The Sweedish police, are already using the virtual-autopsy system to detect hidden evidence, such as air-pockets in the wrong place in the body or bone fractures in a burns victim. The biggest plus is that the system creates a permanent 3-D record, that can be studied, reviewed, archived, and transferred easily. Investigators can revisit the case anytime and look at the images again and again, says Dr Persson.

Another obvious advantage is that virtual autopsy allows investigation without destroying the body, a procedure considered distasteful, invasive or offensive by some cultures and faiths. Since autopsies are not always acceptable to people from the Muslim and Jewish faiths, the table drew a lot of interest at Arab Health Medical Congress, in Dubai, last month, says Lars Wettergren, Global partner manager, Sectra Imtec AB.

The technology is also being used in medical colleges to teach human anatomy without the need for cadavers. In hospitals, it is used for pre-operative planning and clinical diagnosis. It helps Surgeons choose the best treatment method before making the first cut, especially in the fields of orthopedics and sports medicine, says Dr Persson.

That apart, the table has made back-breaking medical education and forensics a lot more fun.

Indication:
- To determine the cause of death
- To identify or characterise the extent of disease/ disorder that the person may have had
- To determine the effectiveness of a particular medical or surgical treatment

- To be helpful in Academic Institutions, for Teaching and Research aims.

Advantages:
* Virtual dissection makes diagnosis, treatment and autopsy possible without cutting up the body.
* The Visualisation Table uses real-time and stored images created using CT scans–25000 slices across the body – in less than 20 sec.
* Since different tissues, bone, fluids and foreign objects have different densities, the softwear assigns them a density value and an NVIDiA graphics card:
- the kind used for high-speed gaming
- transforms the date into 3-D images.
* Using a Virtual knife, doctors and surgeons can slice the body, remove layers of skin and muscle to look inside.
* Creates a permanent 3-D record that can be studied, reviewed, archived and transferred easily.
* Cheaper, as it's less labour intensive.
* Used in medical education to teach anatomy without the need for cadavers.
* In hospitals, used for pre-operative planning and clinical diagnosis.

(*Source:* Sanchita Sharma, Health Editor, Hindustan Times, Dated: 21/02/2012).

CHAPTER - 5

LEGAL SYSTEM

THE INDIAN LEGAL SYSTEM

Supreme Court (Federal Court) of India

History: After its inauguration on January 28, 1950, the Supreme Court commenced its sittings in a part of the Parliament House. The Court moved into the present building in 1958. The building is shaped to project the image of scales of justice. The Central Wing of the building is the Centre Beam of the Scales. In 1979, two New Wings - the East Wing and the West Wing – were added to the complex. In all there are 15 Court Rooms in the various wings of the building. The Chief Justice's Court is the largest of the Courts located in the Centre of the Central Wing. The original Constitution of 1950 envisaged a Supreme Court with a Chief Justice and seven associate Judges-leaving it to the Parliament to increase this number. In the early years, all the Judges of the Supreme Court sat together to hear the cases presented before them. As the work of the Court increased and arrears of cases began to cumulate, Parliament increased the number of Judges from 8 in 1950 to 11 in 1956, 14 in 1960, 18 in 1978 and 26 in 1986. As the number of the Judges has increased, they sit in smaller Benches of two and three coming together in larger Benches of five and more only when required to do so or to settle a difference of opinion or controversy.

Constitution:

Constitution and Law Courts:

: Constituted into a Sovereign Democratic Republic, containing:

- Federal system with Parliamentary form of Government in the Union and the States,
- An independent judiciary,
- Guaranteed Fundamental Rights, and
- Directive Principles of State Policy containing objectives which though not enforceable in law are fundamental to the governance of the nation.

Sources of Law:

The principle source of law in India is the Constitution which, in turn, gives due recognition to statutes, case law and customary law consistent with its dispensations.

- Statues: are enacted by Parliament, State Legislatures and Union Territory Legislatures.
- Subordinate legislation: laws in the form of rules and regulations and by-laws made by Central and State Governments and local authorities like Municipal Corporations, Municipalities, Gram Panchayats and other local bodies. This subordinate legislation is made under the authority conferred or delegated either by Parliament or State or Union Territory Legislature concerned.

Power: The decisions of the Supreme Court are binding on all Courts within the territory of India. As India is a land of diversities, local customs and conventions which are not against statute, morality, etc. are to a limited extent also recognised and taken into account by Courts while administering justice.

The Supreme Court of India: is the highest court of the land.

Establishment: Established by Part V, Chapter IV of the Constitution of India.

Composition: Consists of the Chief Justice of India and associate Justices, appointed by the President of India.

Supreme Court Judges retire upon attaining the age of 65 yrs.

Eligibility for appointment:

- Must be a citizen of India, and
- Must have experience of five yrs. as a Judge of a High Court or of two or more such Courts in succession, or
- An Advocate of a High Court or of two or more such Courts in succession for at least 10 yrs, or

- A distinguished jurist, in the opinion of the President
- Ad-hoc Judge: Provisions exist for the appointment of a Judge of a High Court as an Ad-hoc Judge of the Supreme Court and for retired Judges of the Supreme Court or High Court to sit and act as Judges of that Court.

Criterias for Removal:

The Constitution seeks to ensure the independence of Supreme Court Judges in various ways.

- A Judge of the Supreme Court cannot be removed from office except by an order of the President passed after an address in each House of Parliament supported by a majority of the total membership of that House and by a majority of not less than two-thirds of members present and voting, and presented to the President in the same Session for such removal on the ground of proved misbehaviour or incapacity.
- Debarred: A person who has been a Judge of the Supreme Court may be debarred from practising in any court of law or before any other authority in India.

Role: According to the Constitution of India, the role of the Supreme Court of India is that of a federal court, guardian of the Constitution and the highest court of appeal.

Source of cases: It takes cases referred from Provincial High Courts.

Procedure: The proceedings of the Supreme Court are conducted in English only. Supreme Court Rules, 1966 are framed under Article 145 of the Constitution to regulate the practice and procedure of the Supreme Court.

Supreme Court Registry:

Composition: Consists of:

The Registrar General-one,

Registrars - three,

Additional Registrars-four,

Joint Registrars–twelve.

Appointment: Article 146 of the Constitution deals with the appointments of officers and servants of the Supreme Court Registry.

Attorney General:

Appointment: Appointed by the President of India under Article 76 of the Constitution and holds office during the pleasure of the President.

Eligibility: He/She must be a person qualified to be appointed as a Judge of the Supreme Court.

Role: It is the duty of the Attorney General for India to give advice to the Government of India upon such legal matters and to perform such other duties of legal character as may be referred or assigned to him by the President. In discharge of his functions, the Attorney General is assisted by a Solicitor General and four Additional Solicitors General.

Privilege: In the performance of his duties, he has:

- the right of audience in all Courts in India, and
- the right to take part in the proceedings of Parliament without the right to vote.

Supreme Court Advocates:

There are three categories of Advocates who are entitled to practise law before the Supreme Court of India:-

Senior Advocates:

Designation: designated as Senior Advocates by the Supreme Court of India or by any High Court. The Court can designate any Advocate, with his consent, as Senior Advocate by:

- virtue of his ability,
- standing at the Bar, or
- special knowledge or experience in law.

Non-entitlement: A Senior Advocate is not entitled to:

- appear without an Advocate-on-Record in the Supreme Court,
- appear without a junior in any other court or tribunal in India
- accept instructions to draw pleadings/or affidavits, advise on evidence or do any drafting work of an analogous kind in any court or tribunal in India, or
- undertake conveyancing work of any kind whatsoever but this prohibition shall not extend to settling any such matter as aforesaid in consultation with a junior.

Advocates-on-record:

Entitlement:

- Only these Advocates are entitled to file any matter or document before the Supreme Court.
- They can also file an appearance, or
- Act for a party in the Supreme Court.

Other Advocates:

Enrolment: These are on the roll of any State Bar Council maintained under the Advocates Act, 1961.

Entitlement: can appear and argue any matter on behalf of a party in the Supreme Court.

Non-entitlement: not entitled to file any document or matter before the Court.

High Courts of India (TABLE 5.1):

Jurisdiction: Are the principal civil courts of original jurisdiction in the state.

Composition: The High Court consists of The Chief Justice of High Court and associate Justices.

Role: Can try all offences including those punishable with death.

Source of cases: The work of most High Courts consists of Appeals from lowers courts and writ petitions in terms of Article 226 of the Constitution of India.

Table 5.1: High Courts of India

HIGH COURTS	*HEAD/CHIEF*
Andhra Pradesh	Chief Justice
Allahabad	Chief Justice
Bombay	Chief Justice
Chhattisgarh	Chief Justice
Delhi	Chief Justice
Gujarat	Chief Justice
Gauhati	Chief Justice
Himachal Pradesh	Chief Justice
Imphal	Chief Justice
Jammu and Kashmir	Chief Justice
Jharkhand	Chief Justice
Karnataka	Chief Justice
Kerala	Chief Justice
Madras	Chief Justice
Orissa	Chief Justice
Patna	Chief Justice
Punjab and Haryana	Chief Justice
Rajasthan	Chief Justice

DELHI HIGH COURT:

Delhi High Court

History: The High Court of Delhi was established on 31st October, 1966.

Initially, the High Court of Judicature at Lahore, which was established by a Letters Patent dated 21st March, 1919, exercised jurisdiction over the then provinces of Punjab and Delhi. This position continued till the Indian Independence Act, 1947 when the dominions of India and Pakistan were created. The High Courts (Punjab) Order, 1947 established a new High Court for the territory of what was then called the East Punjab with effect from 15th August, 1947. The India (Adaptation of Existing Indian Laws) Order, 1947 provided that any reference in an existing Indian Law to the High Court of Judicature at Lahore, be replaced by a reference to the High Court of East Punjab. The High Court of East Punjab started functioning from Shimla in a building called "Peterhoff". This building burnt down in January, 1981. Secretariat of the Punjab Government shifted to Chandigarh in 1954-55, the High Court also shifted to Chandigarh. The High Court of Punjab, as it is later came to be called, exercised jurisdiction over Delhi through a Circuit Bench which dealt with the cases pertaining to the Union Territory of Delhi and the Delhi Administation. In view of the importance of Delhi, its population and other considerations, Parliament thought it necessary to establish a new High Court of Delhi. This was achieved by enacting the Delhi High Court Act, 1966 on 5th September, 1966. By virtue of Section 3(1) of the Delhi High Court Act, the Central Government was empowered to appoint a date by a notification in the official gazette, establishing a High Court for the Union Territory of Delhi. The appointed date was 31st October, 1966. The High Court of Delhi initially exercised jurisdiction not only over the Union Territory of Delhi, but also Himachal Pradesh. The High Court of Delhi had a Himachal Pradesh Bench at Shimla in a building called Ravenswood. The High Court of Delhi continued to exercise jurisdiction over Himachal Pradesh until the State of Himachal Pradesh Act, 1970 was enforced on 25th January, 1971.

DISTRICT COURTS OF INDIA:

The District Courts consist of The Session Judge of District Court and associate Justices. They administer justice in India at a district level. These courts are under administrative and judicial control of the High Court of the State to which the district concerned belongs.

Jurisdiction: Are the principal civil courts of original jurisdiction in the district.

Composition: The highest court in each district is that of the District and Sessions Judge. The District Court consists of The Session Judge of District.

There are many other courts subordinate to the court of District and Sessions Judge. There is a three tier system of courts. On the civil side, at the lowest level is the court of Civil Judge (Junior Division).

On criminal side the lowest court is that of the Judicial Magistrate.

Civil Judge (Junior Division) decides civil cases of small pecuniary stake. Judicial Magistrates decide criminal cases which are punishable with imprisonment of up to five years.

Role: This is the principal court of civil jurisdiction. Sessions-triable cases are tried by the Sessions Court. It has the power to impose any sentence including capital punishment. Can try all offences including those punishable with death.

Civil Judge (Junior Division) decides civil cases of small pecuniary stake. Judicial Magistrates decide criminal cases which are punishable with imprisonment of up to five years.

Source of cases: The work of most District Courts consists of Appeals from lowers courts and writ petitions in terms of Article 226 of the Constitution of India.

DISTRICT COURTS OF DELHI:

Constitution: Delhi as a distinct legal entity was recognised by the Proclamation Notification No. 911 dated 17/09/1912, issued by the Governor General of India in Council.

Delhi Laws Act 1912: was enacted to enforce the existing laws in Delhi.

Judges:
- District and Session Judge
- Additional District Judge
- Additional Session Judge
- Special Judge
- Presiding Officer

Courts: Delhi State has six District Courts that function under the control of

Delhi High Court. The Courts are:
- Tis Hazari Courts
- Patiala House Courts
- Rohini Courts
- Dwarka Courts
- Saket Courts
- Karkardooma Courts

TIS HAZARI COURTS:

Tis Hazari Court

Constitution: Construction of Tis Hazari Courts Building started in 1953. The same was inaugurated on 19/03/1958 by the then Chief Justice of Punjab High Court-Mr A.N. Bhandari. All the civil courts and many criminal courts were housed in this building. Even today Tis Hazari continues to be the principal Court building in Delhi.

Courts: Following Courts are functioning at Tis Hazari Courts Complex:

- Courts of District and Session Judge
- Courts of Additional District Judges
- Courts of Additional Session Judges
- Courts of Special Judges
- Courts of Civil Judges
- Courts of Rent Controllers
- Courts of CMM/ACMM/MMs
- Children Courts.

PATIALA HOUSE COURTS:

Patiala House Courts Complex

Constitution: Patiala House Courts Complex was established in 1977. The Court Complex is situated in the palace of erstwhile Maharaja of Patiala near India Gate. The criminal Courts at Patiala House Courts Complex deal with cases pertaining to New Delhi, South and South-West Districts.

Courts: Following Courts are functioning at Patiala House Courts

Complex:

- Courts of District and Session Judge
- Courts of Additional District Judges
- Courts of Additional Session Judges
- Courts of Civil Judges
- Courts of Rent Controllers
- Courts of CMM/ACMM/MMs
- Motor Accident Claim Tribunals

ROHINI COURTS:

Rohini Court

Constitution: The building of Rohini Courts Complex completed in the year 2005. Currently cases pertaining to West and North-West District are dealt with at Rohini Courts Complex

Courts: Following Courts are functioning at Rohini Courts Complex:

- Courts of District and Session Judge
- Courts of Additional District Judges
- Courts of Additional Session Judges
- Courts of Special Judges
- Courts of Civil Judges
- Courts of Rent Controllers
- Courts of CMM/ACMM/MMs
- Courts of Motor Accident Claims Tribunal

DWARKA COURTS:

Dwarka Court

Constitution: Construction of Dwarka Courts Complex completed in 2008, and was inaugurated by Hon'ble Chief Justice of India Sh. K.G. Balakrishnan on 6th September 2008.

Dwarka Courts Complex is another modern operational District Courts Complex in Delhi.

Courts: Following Courts are functioning at Dwarka Courts Complex:

- Courts of District and Session Judge
- Courts of Additional District Judges
- Courts of Additional Session Judges
- Courts of Civil Judges
- Courts of Rent Controllers
- Courts of ACMM/MMs
- Motor Accident Claim Tribunal
- Family Courts

SAKET COURTS:

Saket Courts

Constitution: Saket Courts Complex started functioning on 28th August, 2010. The work of Civil and Criminal cases related to South Civil District and South and South East Police Districts, hitherto being taken up at Patiala House Courts Complex have been taken up with effect from the afforsaid date by the Courts of the respective districts at the new Court Complex at Saket.

Courts: Following Courts are functioning at Saket Courts Complex:

- Courts of District and Session Judge
- Courts of Additional District Judges
- Courts of Additional Session Judges
- Courts of Special Judges
- Courts of Civil Judges
- Courts of Rent Controllers
- Courts of CMM/ACMM/MMs
- Motor Accident Claim Tribunals

KARKARDOOMA COURTS COMPLEX:

Karkardooma Courts Complex

Constitution: Karkardooma Courts Complex started functioning in 1993.

The building of Karkardooma Courts Complex was completed in the year 1997-98. The Judicial Academy is also functioning from the Karkardooma Courts Complex for the time being till its own building is constructed. A residential block for Judicial Officers and Staff is also located alongwith the regular Court building.

Courts: Following Courts are functioning at Saket Courts Complex:

- Courts of District and Session Judge
- Courts of Additional District Judges
- Courts of Additional Session Judges
- Courts of Civil Judges
- Courts of Rent Controllers
- Courts of CMM/ACMM/MMs
- Motor Accident Claim Tribunals
- Children Courts
- Labour Courts
- Industrial Tribunals

DISTRICT COURTS OF MAHARASHTRA STATE

DISTRICT COURTS:

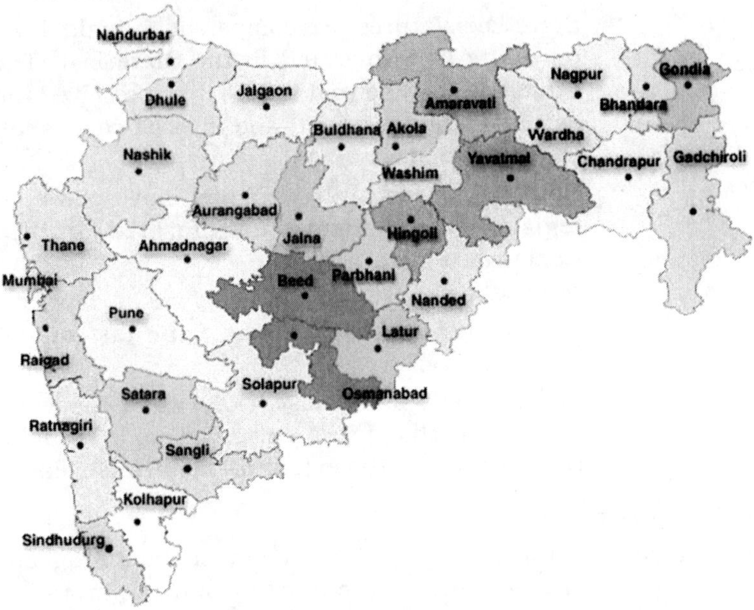

TRIBUNALS: A **tribunal (Table 5.2)** is a generic term for any body acting judicially, whether or not it is called a tribunal in its title. For example, an advocate appearing before a Court on which a single Judge was sitting could describe that judge as 'their tribunal'.

Table 5.2: Tribunals

Sl. No.	*No. Tribunals*
1.	Appellate Tribunal for Electricity
2.	AP Administrative Tribunal
3.	Central Administrative Tribunal
4.	Central Excise Ser. Tax App.
5.	Debt Rec. Trib., Coimbatore
6.	Debts Rec. Trib.I, Chennai
7.	Debts Rec. Trib. II, Chennai
8.	Intellectual Pro. App., Chennai
9.	Income Tax Appellate Trib.
10.	Railway Claims Tribunal

ENACTMENT OF LAWS:

Power:
- The Indian Parliament is competent to make laws on matters enumerated in the Union List.
- State Legislatures are competent to make laws on matters enumerated in the State List. The State law shall be void unless it has received the assent of the President, and in such case, shall prevail in that State.
- Both the Union and the States have power to legislate on matters enumerated in the Concurrent List.
- Parliament only has power to make laws on matters not included in the State List or the Concurrent List.
- In the event of inconsistency, laws made by Parliament shall prevail over law made by State Legislatures, to the extent of the inconsistency.

Applicability of Laws:

Jurisdiction: - Laws made by Parliament may extend throughout or in any part of the territory of India, and

Laws made by State Legislatures may generally apply only within the terrirory of the State concerned. Variations exist from State to State in provisions of law relating to matters falling in the State and Concurrent Lists.

Judiciary: - Inspite of adoption of a federal system and existence of Central Acts and State Acts in their respective spheres, a single integrated system of Courts to administer both Union and State laws, has been provided:

Supreme Court: At the apex of the entire judicial system, exists the Supreme Court of India under which are:

High Courts in each State or group of States, under which are:

- A hierarchy of Subordinate Courts.
- Panchayat Courts (Nyaya Panchayat, Panchayat Adalat, Gram Kacheri) also exist in some States,

to decide civil and criminal disputes of petty and local nature.

Jurisdiction: - Different State laws provide for different kinds of jurisdiction of courts.

Composition: -District and Sessions Judge: Each State is divided into judicial districts presided over by a District and Sessions Judge, which is the principal civil court of original jurisdiction. The Sessions Judge is the highest judicial authority in a district.

Power: Can try all offences including those punishable with death. Under his/her are:

- Civil Judiciary comprises Courts of civil jurisdiction, known in different States as Civil Judges, Sub-Judges and Munsifs.
- Criminal judiciary comprises the Chief Judicial Magistrates and Judicial Magistrates of First and Second Class.

THE UK LEGAL SYSTEM

Supreme Court of UK

History and Constitution

History: The United Kingdom was established in 1801 with the union of Great Britain and Ireland, but only achieved its present form in 1922 with the partition of Ireland and the establishment of the independent Irish Free State (later the Republic of Ireland).

In 1993, the UK joined the European Economic Community–currently called the European Union (EEU). Since then it has been an obligation/ requirement to incorporate European legislation into UK law, and recognise the jurisdiction of the European Court of Justice in matters of EU law.

Since 1993, the Labour Government, made any description of the UK legal system before then out of date, by devolving certain areas of government to the component countries of the UK:

- A separate Scottish Parliament, and
- A Welsh Assembly were established following referendums in the countries concerned.

Ireland already had its Assembly, although this was not in operation.

It is in the context of these new legislatures the English Parliament is often referred to as Westminster.

Human Rights Act 1988: The UK is a signatory of the European convention of Human Rights, and this has recently been incorporated into UK law with the passing of this Act. This Act allows for the provisions of the Convention to be applied directly by the UK courts.

The Ministry of Justice: was established in 2007 replacing the Department for Constitutional Affairs (DCA), which in turn replaced the Lord Chancellor's Department.

Duties: It is responsible for the courts, probation, prisons, criminal law and sentencing.

Constitution: There is no written constitution.

The United Kingdom of Great Britain and Northern Ireland consists of four countries forming three distinct jurisdictions each having its own court system and legal profession:

- England and Wales,
- Scotland, and
- Northern Ireland.

The Queen is the Head of State, although in practice supreme authority of the Crown is carried by the government of the day. The legislature is a bicameral Parliament.

The House of Commons consists of 659 Members of Parliament (MPs), elected by simple majority vote in a general election every five years, although the government has the right to call an election at any time before then, and in practice usually brings the date forward to secure electoral advantage.

The House of Lords until recently consisted of life peers, awarded peerages for public service, and a large number of hereditary peers, whose membership of the House of Lords depended on their aristocratic birth. The Labour Government has started the long-overdue process of reform of the House of Lords by abolishing the voting rights of all the hereditary peers apart from 92 who remain until the House is fully reformed. Proposals put forward by the Royal Commission on the Reform of the House of Lords have yet to be decided upon.

The Government is made up of the Prime Minister, formally appointed by the Queen, and who is normally the leader of the majority party in the House of Commons, and ministers with departmental responsibilities, of whom the Ministers of State form the Cabinet. The ministerial posts are the choice of the Prime Minister.

The constitutional law of the UK is regarded as consisting of statute law on the one hand and case law on the other, whereby judicial precedent is applied in the courts by judges interpreting statute law. A third element consists of constitutional conventions which do not have statutory authority but nevertheless have binding force. Much of the relationship between the Sovereign and Parliament is conventional rather than statutory.

COURT SYSTEM:

Legal system-In England, Wales and Northern Ireland

COURTS OF LAW: CIVIL COURTS and CRIMINAL COURTS:

- The UK Supreme Court
- The House of Lords (Supreme Court of Appeal)
- Law Lords (Presided by up to 13 Senior Judges)
- The High Court – 3 Divisions:
- Queen's Bench
- Family Division
- Chancery Division
- The Court of Appeal (Criminal Division and Civil Division)
- The Crown Courts (Queen's Bench Division)
- The Youth Courts
- The Magistrates' Courts
- The County Courts (for minor claims)
- The European Court of Justice
- The European Court of Human Rights
- Specialised Tribunals.

The Supreme Court:

Constitution: to replace the judicial function of the House of Lords with an independent appointments system, thereby making a constitutional separation between the legislature and the judiciary.

Role: The UK Supreme Court deals with:

- Civil and Criminal appeals from the Court of Appeal, or
- in some cases the High Court where the case involves a point of law or is of general public importance.
- Cases covered by European law (where European Legislation has not been implemented fairly by a

National Government), which may be referred to the European Court of Justice (ECJ), based in Luxembourg.

The House of Lords:

Constitution: Is the supreme court of appeal. Its judicial functions are quite separate from its legislative work, and cases are heard by up to 13 Senior Judges known as the Lords of Appeal in Ordinary, or Law Lords.

It shares its function as the supreme appellate court with. However, the Constitutional Reform Act 2005 provides for the establishment of a Supreme Court to replace the House of Lords as the Court of final appeal.

Role: The House of Lords deal with:

- appeals mainly from the Court of Appeal, or
- direct from the High Court, where the case involves a point of law or general public importance.
- Appeals are mostly about civil cases although the Lords do deal with some criminal appeals.

The High Court

Role: The High Court deals with:

- civil cases,
- hears appeals in criminal cases,
- hears appeals from the County Courts
- power to review the actions of individuals or organisations to make sure they have acted legally and justly

Divisions: The High Court has three divisions :-

1. The Family Division: deals with:

- complex defended divorce cases,
- dissolution of civil partnerships,
- wardship, adoption,
- domestic violence and so on.
- appeals from magistrates and county courts in matrimonial cases.

- Mentally ill matters i.e. In Northern Ireland, the Family Division also deals with the affairs of people who are mentally ill and simple probate matters.

2. **The Queens Bench Division:** deals with:
   - large and/or complex claims for compensation.
   - A limited number of appeals from magistrates courts or Crown Courts.
   - Reviewing the actions of organisations to see whether they have acted legally, and with libel and slander actions.
3. **The Chancery Division:** deals with:
   - trusts, contested wills, winding up companies, bankruptcy, mortgages, charities, contested revenue (usually income tax) cases etc.

   Non-family claims in Northern Ireland

   In Northern Ireland, the High Court can be used for a case if the value of the claim is > £15,000.

   Exception:
   - In some circumstances, a case > £15,000 can be remitted to the county court, and similarly,
   - A case < £15,000 may be transferred from the High Court to the county court.

The Court of Appeal (Civil and Criminal Division) in England and Wales:

Court of Appeal (Civil Division):

Role: The Court of Appeal deals with:

- Civil appeals from the High Court and the county court,
- Employment Appeal Tribunal and the Lands Tribunal.

Court of Appeal (Criminal Division):

Role: The Court of Appeal deals with:

- Criminal appeals including appeals against convictions in the Crown Court, and points of law referred by the Attorney General following acquittal in the Crown Court or where the sentence imposed was unduly lenient.

The Crown Court:

Role: The Crown Court deals with:

- More serious criminal offences which will be tried by the judge and jury.
- Appeals from the magistrates court-which are dealt with by a judge and at least two magistrates.
- Convictions in the magistrates' court that are referred to the Crown Court for sentencing Imprisonment and fines which are more severe in the Crown Court than in the magistrates' court.

The Youth Court

The youth court deals with:

- Young people who have committed criminal offences, and who are aged between 10 and 17. The Youth Court is part of the Magistrates Court and up to three specially-trained magistrates hear the case. If a young person is charged with a very serious offence, which in the case of an adult is punishable with 14 years imprisonment or more, the youth court can commit them for trial at the Crown Court.

Magistrate Court:

Jurisdiction: Is the lowest criminal courts, which deal with minor offences.

Role: The Magistrate Court deals with:

- criminal and some civil cases, and cases are dealt with either by justices of the peace, who are unqualified and who are paid only expenses, or by

District Judges (Magistrates Courts) who receive some payment.

- In Northern Ireland, cases are heard by paid magistrates only.
- Magistrates' courts usually only deal with cases which arise in their own area.
- In exceptional cases, they can deal with offences that occur in a number of areas, e.g. where

several burglaries have been committed across a number of areas.

Criminal cases in the Magistrate's Court:

- All criminal cases start in the magistrates' court.
- Some cases begin in the magistrates' court and then automatically go to the Crown Court for trial by jury.
- Other cases are started and finished in the magistrates' court. These are where the defendant is not entitled to trial by jury. They are known as summary offences. Summary offences involve a maximum penalty of six months imprisonment and/or a fine of up to £5,000 (£2,000 in Northern Ireland).
- Magistrates also deal with offences where the defendant can choose trial by jury but decides to have their case heard in the magistrates' court. If the defendant chooses trial by jury, the case will be passed on to the Crown Court.

Civil cases in the Magistrates' Court:

Magistrates can deal with a limited number of civil cases as follows:-

- Some civil debts e.g. arrears of income tax, national insurance contributions, council tax and VAT arrears, rates in Northern Ireland.
- Some matrimonial problems e.g. maintenance and removing a spouse from the matrimonial home.
- Welfare of children, for example, local authority care or supervision orders, adoption proceedings and residence orders.

The County Court

Jurisdiction:
- Civil cases (for minor claims) at 1st instance are heard in the County Courts the High Court.
- Civil cases which are dealt with by a judge or district judge.
- A case can be started in any county court but it may be transferred to the defendant's local

court, if the case is defended and the claim is for a fixed amount of money. The case will be transferred automatically by the court to the defendants local court (if the defendant is an individual not a company). In other cases the defendant can request its transfer.

- All claims arising from regulated credit agreements must be started in the county court, whatever their value.

Role: The County Court deals with:

- landlord and tenant disputes e.g. possession (eviction), rent arrears, repairs.
- Consumer disputes e.g. faulty goods or services.
- Personal injury claims (injuries caused by negligence), e.g. traffic accidents, falling into holes in the pavement, accidents at work.
- Undefended divorce cases and proceedings to end a registered civil partnership, but only in some county courts. In inner London the Principle registry of the family division in the Strand deals with undefended divorces and proceedings to end registered civil partnerships some domestic violence cases, but these may also be heard in the Magistrates Court.
- Race, sex and disability discrimination cases.
- Debt problems e.g. a creditor seeking payment.
- Employment problems e.g. wages or salary owing or pay in lieu of notice.
- Cases may be appealed from the County Court to the High court.

Rehearing of a County Court case in Northern Ireland

In Northern Ireland, there can be a rehearing of a county court case in the High Court and an appeal from there if the case is stated to the Court of Appeal.

Judicial Committee of the Privy Council:

Role: The Judicial Committee of the Privy Council deals with:

- hears cases from the British overseas territories and dependencies as well as some specialised domestic appeals.
- hears cases concerning questions relating to the powers and functions of the devolved legislatures. The 'devolution' function will be transferred to the new Supreme Court.

Specialised Tribunals:

Role: In addition to the courts there are specialised Tribunals, which hear appeals on decisions made by various public bodies and Government departments, e.g.:

- Employment,
- Immigration,
- Social security,
- Tax and land.

The Court Service also contains information on these.

Her Majesty's Court Service (HMCS):

Role: Is an agency of the DCA responsible for administration of the court system, and was established in 2005 under the Courts Act 2003, bringing together the separate agencies previously responsible for court administration.

The European Court of Justice

Role: The European Court of Justice (ECJ), based in Luxembourg, deals with:

- Referred problems covered by European law, where it may be found:
- that the European legislation has not been implemented properly by a national government,
- that there is confusion over its interpretation, or
- that it has been ignored.

Procedure:

- The aggrieved person must first pursue his/her case through the National legal system.
- The National Court can (and in some cases must) refer an issue to the ECJ for guidance (a ruling).

- The case is then sent back to the National Court to make a decision based on the ruling of the ECJ.

The European Court of Human Rights

Role: The European Court of Human Rights, based in Strasbourg, deals with:

- Referred cases in which a person thinks their human rights have been contravened and for which there is no legal remedy within the National legal system.

Reforms: Civil Courts:

There has been extensive reform of civil procedure in recent years i.e.

- Publication of a major report on Access to Justice by Lord Woolf in 1966,
- A completely new set of civil procedure rules were put into operation in 1999, as well as new legislation for modernising the courts and legal services.

Criminal Courts:

- The Legal Services Commission was created under the Access to Justice Act 1999 to provide a Community Legal Service and Criminal Defence Service and administer legal aid.
- A Criminal Courts Review is due to report on reform of the criminal justice System.
- **Magistrate Court:** Criminal cases are heard at first instance in the Magistrates' Court.
- **Crown Court:** more serious ones being heard in the Crown Court.
- **Court of Appeal (Criminal Division):** criminal appeals being heard in the Court of Appeal Criminal Division.
- **Consolidated Criminal Procedure Rules:** were introduced in 2005, as a result publication of **Review of the Criminal Courts** by Sir Robin Auld in 2001.
- The Constitutional Reform Act 2005 provides for the establishment of a Supreme Court to replace the House of Lords as the Court of final appeal.

Small claims cases

In England and Wales, a case will, if defended, be dealt with in one of three ways. The court will decide which procedure will apply and then allocate the case to the corresponding track. The three tracks are:-

- the small claims track
- the fast track
- the multi-track.

The small claims track is the usual track for claims with a value of £5,000 or less.

The procedure in the small claims track is simpler than in the other tracks and in most cases will the losing party not have to pay the other party's costs.

There is one track to small claims in Northern Ireland for claims with a value of £2,000 or less.

THE USA LEGAL SYSTEM

Supreme Court of USA

Constitution: Legal (Federal) system in the United States was created under Article III of the United States Constitution.

Branches of the Federal Government:

- The Judicial Branch,
- The Legislative Branch, and
- The Executive Branch.

FEDERAL COURT SYSTEM

THE SUPREME COURT OF THE UNITED STATES

Status: The Supreme Court is the highest court in the federal Judiciary.

Congress has established two levels of federal courts under the Supreme Court: the trial courts and the appellate courts.

Composition: The United States Supreme Court consists of:

- The Chief Justice of the United States, and
- Associate justices – eight (8)

Jurisdiction: The Supreme Court, at its discretion and within certain guidelines established by the Congress, hears a limited number of the cases it is asked to decide.

Those referred cases may be heard in the Federal or State Courts and they usually involve important questions about the Constitution or Federal law.

DISTRICT (TRIAL) COURTS:

Status: District courts are the trial courts of the federal court system.

Composition:- There are 94 federal judicial districts, including:

- The District of Columbia and Puerto Rico–at least 1 district in each State.
- Each district includes a Bankruptcy Court as a unit of the district court.

Jurisdiction: The district courts have jurisdiction (limits set by Congress and Constitution) to hear nearly all categories of federal cases, including both civil and criminal matters.

- the Virgin Islands, Guam, and the Northern Mariana Islands – have district courts that hear federal cases, including bankruptcy cases.
- Special Trial Courts: There are two special trial courts that have nationwide jurisdiction over certain types of cases.
- The Court of International Trade: addresses cases involving international trade and customs issues.

- The United States Court of Federal Claims has jurisdiction to hear:
- Monetary damages claims against the United States, disputes over federal contracts,
- Unlawful "taking" of private property by the Federal Government, and
- A variety of other claims against the United States.

APPELLATE COURTS:

Composition: The 94 judicial districts are organised into 12 regional circuits, each of which has a United States court of appeals.

UNITED STATES OF APPEALS:

Role: A court of appeals hears:

- Appeals from the district courts located within its circuit, and
- Appeals from decisions of Federal Administrative Agencies,
- Appeals (Nationwide jurisdiction) in specialised cases e.g. those involving patent laws and cases decided by the Court of International Trade and the Court of Federal Claims.

FEDERAL COURTS:

Establishment:-Article III of the Constitution invests the judicial power of the United States in the federal court system.

- Article III, Section 1 specifically creates the U.S. Supreme Court and gives Congress the authority to create the lower federal courts.
- Congress has used this power to establish the 13 U.S. courts of appeals, the 94 U.S. district courts, the U.S. Court of Claims, and the U.S. Court of International Trade. U.S. Bankruptcy Court and handle bankruptcy cases.

Magistrate judges handle some district court matters.

- Parties dissatisfied with a decision of a U.S. district court, the U.S. Court of Claims, and/or the U.S. Court of International Trade may appeal to a U.S. court of appeals.

- A party may ask the U.S. Supreme Court to review a decision of the U.S. Court of Appeals, but the Supreme Court usually is under no obligation to do so. The U.S. Supreme Court is the final arbiter of federal constitutional questions.

Selection: - **Under Article III, Section 1 of the Constitution, the Federal Judges**

- Are nominated by the President and confirmed by the Senate.
- They hold office during good behaviour, typically, for life.
- Through congressional impeachment proceedings, the Federal Judges may be removed from office for misbehaviour.

Jurisdiction: - Limited jurisdiction: The federal courts, thus, are courts of limited jurisdiction provided by the Congress or as identified by the Constitution because they may only decide certain types of cases as provided by the Congress or as identified in the Constitution.

- Federal courts also have jurisdiction over all bankruptcy matters, which Congress has determined should be addressed in federal courts rather than the state courts. Through the bankruptcy process, individuals or businesses that can no longer pay their creditors may either seek a court-supervised liquidation of their assets, or they may reorganise their financial affairs and work out a plan to pay off their debts. Although federal courts are located in every state, they are not the only forum available to potential litigants. In fact, the great majority of legal disputes in American courts are addressed in the separate state court systems.

Types of cases heard:

- Cases that deal with the constitutionality of a law;

- Cases involving the laws and treaties of the U.S.;
- Cases involving ambassadors and public ministers;
- Cases of disputes between two or more states;
- Cases of Admiralty law;
- Cases of Bankruptcy; and
- Cases of Habeas corpus issues.

Limit to diversity jurisdiction:

- only cases involving > $75,000 in potential damages may be filed in a Federal Court.
- Claims < $ 75,000 may be filed in a State Court. Moreover, any diversity jurisdiction case, regardless of the amount of money involved, may be filed in a State Court rather than in a Federal Court.

Procedure: Through the bankruptcy process, individuals or businesses that can no longer pay their creditors may either seek a court-supervised liquidation of their assets, or they may reorganise their financial affairs and work out a plan to pay off their debts.

THE STATE COURT SYSTEM

Establishment: The State Courts are established under constitution and laws of each state.

- The Supreme Court: is usually the highest court in a State.
- Courts of Appeals: Some States also have Intermediate Court of Appeals.
- State Trial Courts: So called Circuit or District Courts, under these appeals courts.
- Parties dissatisfied with the decision of the trial court may take their cases to the intermediate court of appeals.
- Parties have the option to ask the highest state court to hear the case.

- Some state court cases are eligible for review by the U.S. Supreme Court Selection: State court judges are selected in a variety of ways, incld.:
- By election,
- By appointment for a given number of years,
- By appointment for life, and
- By combinations of these methods, e.g., appointment followed by election.

Jurisdiction: Although federal courts are located in every state, they are not the only forum available to potential litigants. In fact, the great majority of legal disputes in American courts are addressed in the separate state court systems.

Types of cases heard:

The State Courts hear cases involving:

- family disputes (marriage, divorce and child custody matters,
- probate and inheritance issues (involving wills and estates)
- real estate questions, and juvenile matters; and
- most criminal cases, contract disputes, traffic violations, and personal injury.

Power: State Courts are the final deciders of state laws and constitutions. Their interpretations of federal law or the U.S. Constitution may be appealed to the U.S. Supreme Court.

The Supreme Court may choose to hear or not to hear such cases.

ARTICLE I COURTS

The Congress has created several Article I Legislative Courts, (Table 5.3) that do not have full judicial power.

The Judicial authority to be the final decider in:

- all questions of Constitutional law,
- all questions of federal law, and
- to hear claims at the core of habeas corpus issues.

Table 5. 3: Total Number of Judgeships

Judgeships	*Number*
Supreme Court	9
Court of Appeals	179
District Courts	678
Court of International Trade	9
Total	**875**

RULES AND POLICIES

Federal court rules and policies are essential in carrying out the mission of the federal Judiciary:

- The national policy-making body for the federal courts,
- The Judicial Conference of the United States,
- The Federal rules of practice that are used in all federal courts,
- The Code of Conduct for judges, which addresses matters of judicial ethics are essential to court operations and maintaining a fair and impartial federal judiciary.

DISTRICT COURTS

Constitution: The United States district courts are the trial courts of the federal court system, within limits set by Congress and the Constitution.

Jurisdiction: The district courts hear:

- Nearly all categories of federal cases, including both Civil and Criminal matters. The Jury selected amongst people, performs the jury duty that helps in deciding some of these cases.
- There are 94 federal judicial districts, including at least one district in each state.
- The District of Columbia and Puerto Rico and three territories of the United States—the Virgin Islands, Guam, and the Northern Mariana Islands–have district courts that hear federal cases, including bankruptcy cases.

BANKRUPTCY COURTS

Constitution: Bankruptcy courts are separate units of the district courts.

Jurisdiction: Federal courts have exclusive jurisdiction over bankruptcy cases, meaning a bankruptcy case cannot be filed in a state court.

SPECIAL TRIAL COURTS

Constitution: There are two special trial courts: Court of International Trade and United States Court of Federal Claims.

Jurisdiction: Special Trial Courts have nationwide jurisdiction over certain types of cases.

THE COURT OF INTERNATIONAL TRADE:

Jurisdiction: Hears cases involving International Trade and Customs issues.

THE UNITED STATES COURT OF FEDERAL CLAIMS:

Jurisdiction: Hears cases involving:

- claims for money damages against the United States,
- disputes over federal contracts,
- unlawful "takings" of private property by the federal government, and a variety of other claims against the United States.

COURTS OF APPEALS

Constitution: The 94 U.S. judicial districts are organised into 12 regional circuits, each of which has a United States Court of appeals.

Jurisdiction: A court of appeals hears:

- appeals from the district courts located within its circuit,
- appeals from decisions of federal administrative agencies,
- the Court of Appeals for the Federal Circuit has nationwide jurisdiction to hear appeals in specialised cases e.g. those involving patent laws and cases decided by the Court of International Trade and the Court of Federal Claims.

FEDERAL COURTS AND THE PUBLIC

Access: - With few exceptions, each step of the federal judicial process is open to the public, designed to inspire in the public a respect for the tradition and purpose of the American judicial process.

- Any American citizen, wishing to observe a court in session may go to the federal courthouse, check the court calendar, and watch a proceeding.
- Anyone may review the pleadings and other papers in a case by going to the clerk of court's office and asking for the appropriate case file.
- Exception: the Federal Courts, unlike most of the State Courts, generally do not permit television or radio coverage of trial court proceedings.
- Court dockets and some case files are available on the Internet through the Public Access to Court Electronic Records system (known as PACER).
- The right of public access to court proceedings is partly derived from the Constitution and partly from Court tradition.

Aim: Transparency : By conducting their judicial work in public view, the judges enhance public confidence in the courts, and thereby allow citizens to have first-hand knowledge about the Judicial system working.

Exception:
- In a few situations the public may not have full access to court records and court proceedings.
- In a high-profile trial, there may not be enough space in the courtroom to accommodate everyone who would like to observe.
- Access to the courtroom also may be restricted for security or privacy reasons, such as the protection of a juvenile or a reliable informant.
- Confidential records: certain documents (confidential business and juvenile records, and law enforcement reports) may be placed under seal by the judge, that are not available to the public.

CIVIL CASES/CRIMINAL CASES/BANKRUPTCY CASES/ THE APPEALS PROCESS

Procedure: A federal civil case involves a legal dispute between two or more parties.

Complaint: The plaintiff files a complaint with the Federal Court and "serves" a copy of the complaint on the defendant. The complaint describes the plaintiff's injury, explains how the defendant caused the injury.

Relief:
- A plaintiff asks the court to order relief, and
- may seek money to compensate for the inflicted injury, or
- may ask the court to order the defendant to stop the conduct that is causing the harm.

Observation: The court may order relief (settlement) or trial:
- Settlement: To avoid the expense of having a trial, judges encourage the litigants to try to reach an agreement resolving their dispute. In particular, the courts encourage the use of mediation, arbitration, and other forms of alternative dispute resolution, or "ADR," designed to produce an early resolution of a dispute without the need for trial or other court proceedings.
- Trial: If a case is not settled, the court will schedule a trial:
- Jury trial: the judge will explain the law that is relevant to the case and the decisions the jury needs to make. The jury is asked to determine whether the defendant is responsible for harming the plaintiff in some way, and then to determine the amount of damages that the defendant will be required to pay. In a civil case the plaintiff must convince the jury by producing evidence that the defendant is responsible for the harm the plaintiff has suffered from.
- Bench trial: If the parties waive their right to a jury, then the case will be heard by a judge without a jury and the judge will decide these issues.
- At a trial, witnesses testify under the supervision of a judge. By applying rules of evidence, the judge determines which information may be presented in the courtroom. To ensure that

witnesses speak from their own knowledge and do not change their story based on what they hear another witness say, witnesses are kept out of the courtroom until it is time for them to testify.

- As the questioning of a witness proceeds, the opposing attorney may object to a question if it invites the witness to say something that is not based on the witness's personal knowledge, is unfairly prejudicial, or is irrelevant to the case. The judge rules on the objection, generally by ruling that it is either sustained or overruled. If the objection is sustained, the witness is not required to answer the question, and the attorney must move on to his next question. The court reporter records the objections so that a court of appeals can review the arguments later if necessary.

  At the conclusion of the evidence, each side gives a closing argument.

Judgment:
- To order relief, and
- To order fine so as compensate for the inflicted injury,
- To order the defendant to stop harassing the plaintiff.

COURT REPORTER: Duties:

- Keeps a record of the trial proceedings.
- A deputy clerk of court also keeps a record of each person who testifies and marks for the record any documents, photographs, or other items introduced into evidence.

CRIMINAL CASES:

The Judicial process in a criminal case differs from a civil case in several important ways.

Procedure: Pre-trial: After a person is arrested, a pre-trial services or probation officer of the court immediately interviews the defendant and conducts an investigation of the defendant's background. The information obtained by the pre-trial services or probation officer will be used to help a judge to decide whether to release the defendant into the community pre-trial, and whether to impose restrictions on release.

Trial: At the beginning of a federal criminal case, the case is:

Defendant v/s U.S. Attorney General representing United States

Prosecutor: The U.S. Attorney General (represents United States)

Judge: The Grand jury, reviews evidence presented by the U.S. Attorney

General and decides whether there is sufficient evidence to require a defendant to stand trial.

Evidence: In a criminal trial, the burden of proof is on the government.

Defendants do not have to prove their innocence. Instead, the government must provide strong evidence to convince the jury of the defendant's guilt.

Observation: At an initial appearance, a judge advises the defendant of the charges filed, considers whether the defendant should be held in jail until trial, and determines whether there is probable cause to believe that an offense has been committed and the defendant has committed it. Defendants who are unable to afford counsel are advised of their right to a court-appointed attorney. The court may appoint either a federal public defender or a private attorney who has agreed to accept such appointments from the court. In either type of appointment, the attorney will be paid by the court from funds appropriated by Congress.

Parole: Defendants released into the community before trial may be required to obey certain restrictions imposed, such as home confinement or drug testing, and to make periodic reports to a pre-trial services officer to ensure appearance at trial.

Defence: Plea bargain: The defendant enters a plea to the charges brought by the U.S. attorney at a hearing known as an arraignment. Most defendants plead guilty rather than go to trial.

Judgment:
- If a defendant pleads guilty in return for the government agreeing to drop certain charges or to recommend a lenient sentence, the Judge may impose a sentence at that time, or the judge waits for the results of a presentence report, prepared by the court's probation officer, before imposing sentence. If a defendant is found not guilty, the defendant is released and the government may not appeal. Nor can the person be charged again with the same crime in a federal court. The Constitution prohibits defendant being tried twice for the same offence.
- If the defendant pleads not guilty, the judge will proceed to schedule a trial. If the verdict is guilty, the judge determines the defendant's sentence according to:
- special federal sentencing guidelines issued by the United States Sentencing Commission.
- The court's probation officer's report for the court that applies the sentencing guidelines to the individual defendant and the crimes for which he/or she has been found guilty.
- The reports of substance abuse testing and treatment programmes, job counselling, and alternative detention options.
- All relevant information that may be provided by the pre-trial services officer, the U.S. attorney, and the defense attorney.

Exception: In exceptional cases, the court may depart from the sentence calculated according to the sentencing guidelines.

Penality: Imprisonment (Time) and fine to be paid to the government, and restitution to be paid to the plaintiff. The court's probation officers assist the court in enforcing any conditions that are imposed as part of a criminal sentence.

BANKRUPTCY CASES

Federal courts have exclusive jurisdiction over bankruptcy cases. This means that a bankruptcy case cannot be filed in a state court.

The primary purposes of the law of bankruptcy are:

- To give an honest debtor a "fresh start" in life by relieving the debtor of most debts, and
- To repay creditors in an orderly manner to the extent that the debtor has property available for payment.

Procedure: Some bankruptcy cases are filed to allow a debtor to reorganise and establish a plan to repay creditors, while other cases involve liquidation of the debtor's property.

- A bankruptcy case normally begins by the debtor filing a petition with the bankruptcy court.
- A petition may be filed by an individual, by a husband and wife together, or by a corporation or other entity.
- The debtor is also required to file statements listing assets, income, liabilities, and the names and addresses of all creditors and how much they are owed.

Defence:

- The filing of the petition automatically prevents, or "stays," debt collection actions against the debtor and the debtor's property.
- As long as the stay remains in effect, creditors cannot bring or continue lawsuits, make wage garnishments, or even make telephone calls demanding payment.
- Creditors receive notice from the clerk of court that the debtor has filed a bankruptcy petition.

Observation:

- Some bankruptcy cases are filed to allow a debtor to reorganise and establish a plan to repay creditors.
- Other cases involve liquidation of the debtor's property. In many bankruptcy cases involving liquidation of the property of individual

consumers, there is little or no money available from the debtor's estate to pay creditors. As a result, in these cases there are few issues or disputes, and the debtor is normally granted a "discharge" of most debts without objection. This means that the debtor will no longer be personally liable for repaying the debts.

- In other cases, however, disputes may give rise to litigation in a bankruptcy case over such matters as who owns certain property, how it should be used, what the property is worth, how much is owed on a debt, whether the debtor should be discharged from certain debts, or how much money should be paid to lawyers, accountants, auctioneers, or other professionals.
- Litigation in the bankruptcy court is conducted in much the same way that civil cases are handled in the district court.

Judgment:
- There may be discovery, or
- Pre-trial proceedings, or
- Settlement efforts, or
- Trial.

THE APPEALS PROCESS

Procedure:
- Judicial review in cases involving certain federal agencies or programmes or disputes over Social Security benefits, may be obtained first in a district court rather than a court of appeals.
- In a civil case either side may appeal the verdict.
- In a criminal case, the defendant may appeal a guilty verdict, but the government may not appeal if a defendant is found not verdict guilty. Either side in a criminal case may appeal with respect to the sentence that is.
- In most bankruptcy courts, an appeal of a ruling by a bankruptcy judge may be taken to the district court. Several courts of appeals, however, have established a bankruptcy appellate panel consisting of three bankruptcy judges to hear appeals directly from the bankruptcy courts.

Re-appeal: In either situation, the party that loses in the initial bankruptcy appeal may then appeal to the court of appeals.

Appellant: - The losing party in a decision by a trial court in the federal system normally is entitled to appeal the decision to a federal court of appeals.

- A litigant who is not satisfied with a decision made by a federal administrative agency usually may file a petition for review of the agency decision by a court of appeals.
- The appellant presents legal arguments to the panel, in writing, in a document called a "brief", to persuade the judges that the trial court made an error, and that its decision should be reversed.

Defendant: - That the trial court decision was correct, or

- That any error made by the trial court was not significant enough to affect the outcome of the case.

Judgment: - Appeals are decided by panels of three judges working together.

- In some cases the decision may be reviewed by the Bench.
- The court of appeals makes its decision based on the record of the case established by the trial court or agency, if It does not receive additional evidence or hear witnesses.
- The court of appeals may review the factual findings of the trial court or agency, but typically may only overturn a decision on factual grounds if the findings were "clearly erroneous."
- The court of appeals decision usually will be the final in a case, unless it sends the case back to the trial court for additional proceedings, or the parties ask the U.S. Supreme Court to review the case.

Review: - The Supreme Court, normally does not grant review.

- The Supreme Court rarely agrees to review a case that involves an unusually important legal principle, or when two or more federal appellate courts have interpreted a law differently. Both the parties are required to file written briefs and the Court at its discretion may hear an oral argument instead of written briefs alone.

JURY SERVICE

Definition: Jury service is one of the most important civic duties one can perform.

The protection of rights and liberties in federal courts is mainly achieved through the teamwork of judge and jury.

Selection: The Jury is selected under Selection and Service Act. It lays down certain qualifications for eligibility to serve on a federal jury.

Types: Petit jury and Grand jury.

PETIT (TRIAL) JURY

Composition: Civil petit jury and Criminal petit jury.

Civil petit jury: Consists of 6-12 members.

Role:
- to listen to the evidence presented at a trial,
- to decide whether the defendant injured the plaintiff, or
- failed to fulfill a legal duty to the plaintiff, or
- to determine what the compensation or penalty should be.

Criminal petit jury: consists of 6-12 members.

Role: to decide whether the defendant committed the crime as charged.

Verdict: Verdicts in both civil and criminal cases must be unanimous, although the parties in a civil case may agree to a non-unanimous verdict. Jury's deliberations are conducted in private, out of sight and hearing of the judge, litigants, witnesses, and others in the courtroom.

Judgment: The sentence usually is awarded by a judge.

GRAND JURY

Composition: Consists of 16-23 members.

Role: plays a more specialised role.

Prosecutor: The United States attorney presents evidence to the Jury.

Verdict: The grand jury issues an indictment against the defendant, if it finds enough evidence, it will issue an indictment against the defendant.

Grand jury proceedings are not open for public observation.

References:

1. Grand Jury Handbook (pdf) October 2007 ed.
2. Trial Jury Handbook (pdf) October 2007 ed.

CANADA'S COURT SYSTEM

CANADA SUPREME COURT, OTTAWA

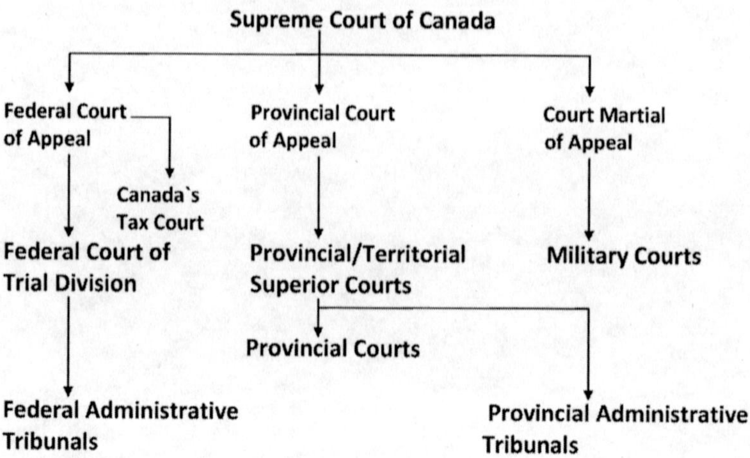

CANADA'S COURT SYSTEM:

Composition: Supreme Court of Canada
Federal Courts
Provincial (Territorial) Courts

Power: The Canadian constitution gives the federal government the exclusive right to legislate criminal law. This intricate interweaving of federal and provincial powers is typical of the Canadian constitution.

Federal Courts:

- Control over Criminal law

Provincial Courts:

- Control over Civil law

Jurisdiction: Federal Courts: The quite small system of federal courts only hear cases concerned with matters which are under exclusive federal control, such as federal taxation, federal administrative agencies, intellectual property and certain aspects of national security. The federal government appoints and pays for both the judges of the federal courts and the judges of the "superior-level" court of each province.

Provincial Courts: Over the administration of justice in their territory. Almost all cases, whether criminal or civil, start in provincial courts and may be eventually appealed to higher level. The provincial governments are responsible for appointing judges of the "inferior-level" court of each province.

COURT SYSTEM:

Categories: 4-level hierarchy–highest to lowest in terms of legal authority.

Constitution: Each court is bound by the rulings of the courts above them; however, they are not bound by the rulings of other courts at the same level in the hierarchy.

Exception: Civil courts in Quebec, in particular, are under no obligation to apply judicial precedent-the principal of *stare decisis*–which is the general rule elsewhere in Canada. This is because Quebec's civil law is entirely codified, while civil law in the other nine provinces grew out of the English common law.

SUPREME COURT OF CANADA

Constitution:- Under the Constitution Act, 1867, "General Court of Appeal for Canada" was established by the Federal Parliament.

- Under an Act of Parliament, 1875, the Supreme Court of Canada was established by the Liberal Government of Alexander Mackenzie.

Ammendments:

- In 1926, the Judicial Committee ruled that the Canadian Parliament lacked the jurisdiction to extinguish appeals to the Judicial Committee, as the right of appeal was founded in the royal prerogative and could only be terminated by the Imperial Parliament.
- In 1933, following the enactment of the Statute of Westminster, the federal Parliament passed legislation again abolishing the right of appeal in criminal matters.
- In 1935, the Judicial Committee upheld the constitutional validity of that amendment.
- In 1939, the federal government proposed a reference to the Supreme Court of Canada, asking whether the federal Parliament could terminate all appeals to the Judicial Committee. By a 4-2 decision, the Supreme Court held that the proposal was within the powers of the federal Parliament and would be constitutional. The question was then appealed to the Judicial Committee, but the hearing of the appeal was delayed by the outbreak of World War II.
- In 1949, Parliament passed an amendment to the *Supreme Court Act* which abolished all appeals, making the Court truly the Supreme Court. However, cases which had been instituted in the lower courts prior to the amendment could still be appealed to the Judicial Committee. The last Canadian appeal to the Judicial Committee was not decided until 1960.

Composition: The Court currently consists of Chief Justice of Canada, nine justices, and eight puisne justices.

Three of the nine justices are appointed from Quebec because of Quebec's use of civil law.

Role:
- To hear appeals of decisions from the Appellate Courts,
- To deliver references (occasionally) - the court's opinion on constitutional questions raised by the federal government.

Courts:
- Supreme Court of British Columbia
- Supreme Court of Newfoundland and Labrador (Court of Appeal)
- Supreme Court of Nova Scotia
- Supreme Court of Prince Edward Island (Trial Division)
- Supreme Court of Northwest Territories
- Supreme Court of Yukon Territory
- Court of Queen's Bench of Alberta
- Court of Queen's Bench of Manitoba
- Court of Queen's Bench of New Brunswick
- Court of Queen's Bench of Saskatchewan
- Court of Queen's Bench of Alberta
- Quebec Superior Court
- Nunavut Court of Justice.

APPELLATE COURTS of the PROVINCES and TERRITORIES

Constitution: These courts of appeal exist at the provincial and territorial levels and were separately constituted in the early decades of the twentieth century, replacing the former Full Courts-the old Supreme Courts of the provinces, many of which were then re-named Courts of Queens Bench.

Jurisdiction: These courts are Canada's equivalent of the Court of Appeal in England and the various State Supreme Courts and U.S. Courts of Appeals in the United States. Each of these Appellate Courts, is the Highest Court from its respective province or territory. Each Province's Chief Justice sits in the appellate court of that province.

Power: These appellate courts do not normally conduct trials or hear witnesses.

Role:
- To review decisions rendered by the superior-level courts.
- To deliver references when requested by a provincial or territorial government as the Supreme Court does for the federal government.

Courts:
- Court of Appeal of British Columbia
- Supreme Court of Newfoundland and Labrador (Court of Appeal)
- Court of Appeal of Nova Scotia
- Court of Appeal of Northwest Territories
- Court of Appeal of Manitoba
- Court of Appeal of New Brunswick
- Court of Appeal of Alberta
- Court of Appeal of Nunavut
- Court of Appeal of Ontario
- Supreme Court of Prince Edward Island (Appeal Division)
- Court of Appeal of Quebec
- Court of Appeal of Saskatchewan
- Court of Appeal of Yukon Territory

Status: These courts are Canada's equivalent of the Court of Appeal in England and the various State Supreme Courts and US Courts of Appeals in the USA. Each of these appellate courts is the highest court from its respective province or territory. Each province's Chief Justice sits in the appellate court of that province.

INFERIOR-LEVEL COURTS of the PROVINCES and TERRITORIES (INFERIOR COURTS)

Constitution: Established by the Province's Legislature under the Constitution Act, (1867) 92(14). Each province and territory in Canada has an "inferior" or "lower" trial court, usually called a Provincial (or Territorial) Court, to hear certain types of cases.

Jurisdiction: Limited. As courts of limited jurisdiction, their decisions are potentially subject to judicial review by the superior courts via the prerogative writs, but in most cases there are now well-established statutory rights of appeal instead.

Power: The Head of power provides the Province the power:

- To regulate the Constitution,
- To maintain and organise the Provincial Courts–Civil and Criminal Jurisdiction,
- To conduct procedure in Civil Matters in Civil and Criminal Courts

Role:

- To entertain small claims.
- To entertain municipal by-laws.
- To have limited civil jurisdiction, over small claims and certain family law affairs.
- To perform certain specialised roles e.g. hearing only criminal law matters, youth matters, family law matters, small claims matters, "quasi-criminal" offences (i.e., violations of provincial statutes), or bylaw infractions.
- To serve as an appeal division from the decisions of administrative tribunals.

Exception: In most of the Provinces: the Provincial Court is created as a

- Specific Court (main Criminal Court) by the Province, having jurisdiction over most of the criminal offences except for the most serious ones.

SUPERIOR-LEVEL COURTS OF THE PROVINCES AND TERRITORIES (SUPERIOR COURTS)

Constitution: Is a court of inherent jurisdiction. Historically, these are the descendants of the royal superior courts in England.

Jurisdiction: The Federal Court of Appeal and the provincial and territorial Courts of Appeal are all superior courts.

Power: The decisions of a superior court are not subject to review, unless a statute specifically provides for review or appeal. The term is not limited to trial courts.

Role:
- To entertain divorce petitions, civil lawsuits involving claims greater than small claims and criminal prosecutions for felonies (indictable offences).
- To perform a reviewing function for judgements from the local inferior courts and administrative decisions by provincial or territorial government entities such as labour boards, human rights tribunals and licensing authorities.

Exception:
- Some of these superior courts (like the one in Ontario) have specialised branches that deal only with certain matters such as family law or small claims.
- The Ontario Superior Court of Justice has a branch called the Divisional Court that hears only appeals and judicial reviews of administrative tribunals and whose decisions have greater binding authority than those from the "regular" branch of the Ontario Superior Court of Justice.
- Although the Supreme Court of British Columbia, may have the word "supreme" in its name, it is not necessarily the highest court in its respective province or territory.
- Most provinces have special courts dealing with small claims (lawsuits for less than a certain amount of money). These are typically divisions of the superior courts in each province. Parties often represent themselves, without lawyers, in these Courts.

FEDERAL COURTS

Constitution: In 1867, in addition to the Supreme Court of Canada, three civil courts were established by the federal Parliament under Section 100 of the Constitution Act.

Courts:
- Federal Court
- Federal Court of Appeal
- Tax Court of Canada

FEDERAL COURT OF CANADA

Jurisdiction:- To review administrative decisions by federal government bodies such as the immigration board and

- To hear lawsuits under the federal government's jurisdiction such as intellectual property and maritime law.
- To hear civil lawsuits brought against the federal government.
- To determine inter-jurisdictional legal actions between the federal government and a provinces, or between different provinces, provided the province in question has passed corresponding legislation granting the Federal Court jurisdiction over the dispute.
- In the aftermath of 9/11, Parliament enacted a number of laws to protect national security. The Federal Court has exclusive jurisdiction to determine many issues which arise under those laws relating to national security.
- Appeals lie from the Federal Court to the Federal Court of Appeal.

FEDERAL COURT OF APPEAL

Jurisdiction: The Federal Court of Appeal hears appeals from decisions rendered by the Federal Court, the Tax Court of Canada and a certain group of federal administrative tribunals like the National Energy Board and the federal labour board.

All judges of the Federal Court are ex-officio judges of the Federal Court of Appeal, and vice versa, although it is rare that a judge of one court will sit as a member of the other.

TAX COURT OF CANADA

Jurisdiction: - To hear disputes over federal taxes, primarily under the federal Income Tax Act, between taxpayers and the federal government.

- Appeals lie from the Tax Court to the Federal Court of Appeal.

MILITARY COURTS:

COURT MARTIAL APPEAL COURT OF CANADA

Courts:
- General Court Martial
- Standing Court Martial
- Summary Trial Hearings

Constitution: The Courts Martial are conducted and presided over by the military personnel and exist for the prosecution of military personnel, as well as civilian personnel who accompany military personnel, accused of violating the Code of Service Discipline, under National Defence Act (1985) R.S.C. Chapter N-5 The Court Martial Appeal Court is made up of civilian judges from the Federal Court, Federal Court of Appeal, and the superior courts of the provinces.

Jurisdiction: A complete code of military law applicable to persons under military jurisdiction.

Appeal: The decisions of the courts martial can be appealed to the Court Martial Appeal Court of Canada which, in contrast, exists outside the military and is made up of civilian judges.

SUMMARY TRIALS

Constitution: These hearings are similar to the former Law Magistrates' Courts.

Jurisdiction: Summary trials are adhoc hearings meant to dispense with minor service offenses. The Presiding Officer will have little formal legal training and is generally the service member's Commanding Officer.

TRIBUNALS:

FEDERAL AND PROVINCIAL ADMINISTRATIVE TRIBUNALS

Constitution: Established by statute, their adjudicators are usually appointed by government, and they focus on very particular and specialised areas of law. Some tribunals are established by federal law while others are established by provincial law. There are both federal and provincial tribunals for some subject matters such as unionised labour and human rights. Tribunals which have the power to decide questions of law may take into consideration the Canadian Charter of Rights and Freedoms.

Jurisdiction: Principle of stare decisis does not apply to tribunals e.g. a tribunal adjudicator could legally make a decision that differs from a past decision, on the same subject and issues, delivered by the highest court in the land. Because a tribunal is not bound by legal precedent, established by itself or by a reviewing court, a tribunal is not a court even though it performs an important adjudicative function and contributes to the development of law like a court would do.

SUPER TRIBUNALS: Is a small group of tribunals whose decisions must be appealed directly to the Federal Court of Appeal rather than to the Federal. These are listed in Subsection 28(1) of the *Federal Court Act* (R.S.C. 1985, Chapter F-7).

Examples: National Energy Board, Canadian International Trade Tribunal, the Competition Tribunal, the Canada Industrial Relations Board (i.e. federal labour board), the Copyright Board. These are quasi-judicial adjudicative bodies, which means that they adjudicate (hear evidence and render decisions) like courts, but are not presided over by judges.

Judicial review: Depending on its enabling legislation, a tribunal's decisions may be reviewed by a court through an appeal, viewing court may be required to show some deference to the tribunal if the tribunal possesses some highly specialised expertise or knowledge that the court does not have.

Procedure: The procedure is relatively less formal than that of a court. While relevant evidence is admissible, evidence which the adjudicator determines to have questionable reliability, or is otherwise questionable, is most likely to be afforded little or no weight.

Statutory Courts:

Constitution: The Supreme Court of Canada, the federal courts, the various appellate courts from the provinces and territories, and the numerous low-level provincial courts are statutory courts whose decision-making power is granted by either the federal parliament or a provincial legislature. These Courts are similar to non-judicial adjudicative bodies such as administrative tribunals, boards, and commissions, which are created and given limited power by legislation.

Jurisdiction: Limited by the terms of the statute. A statutory court cannot try cases in areas of law that are not mentioned or suggested in the statute. A statutory court cannot provide a type of legal remedy or relief that is not expressly or implicitly referred to in its enabling or empowering statute.

Judges:

Appointment: Are appointed and not elected. Judges of the Supreme Court of Canada, the federal courts, the appellate courts and the superior-level courts are appointed by the Governor-in-Council (by the Governor General on the advice of the Federal Cabinet).

Exception: Judges of the Ontario Superior Court of Justice are chosen not by Ontario's provincial government but upon recommendations of Her Majesty's Canadian Government.

Judicial appointments to judicial posts in the so-called "inferior" or "provincial" courts are made by the local provincial governments.

Court language: English and French are official languages of the Federal Government of Canada.

Constitution: Under the Constitution Act, 1867, either language may be used by any person or in any pleading or process in or issuing from any Court of Canada established by Parliament.

Jurisdiction: This constitutional guarantee applies to the Supreme Court of Canada, the Federal Court of

Appeal, the Federal Court, the Tax Court of Canada, and the Court Martial Appeal Court, to ensure that the federal courts are institutionally bilingual.

Exception: Right to use either language in the provincial and territorial courts varies. The Constitution guarantees the right to use either French or English in the courts of Quebec and New Brunswick. There is a statutory right to use either English or French in the courts of Ontario and Saskatchewan, and a limited right to use French in oral submissions in the courts of Alberta.

AUSTRALIAN LEGAL SYSTEM

COMMONWEALTH COURTS:

- **High Court of Austaralia**
- **Federal Court of Australia**
- **Family Court of Australia**
- **Federal Magistrates Court**
- **Industrial Relations Court of Australia**

SUPREME COURTS OF STATE AND TERRITORY:

- **Supreme Court of the Australian Capital Territory**
- **Supreme Court of the Northern Territory**
- **Supreme Court of Queensland**
- **Supreme Court of New South Wales**
- **Supreme Court of South Australia**
- **Supreme Court of Victoria**
- **Supreme Court of Tasmania**
- **Supreme Court of Western Australia**

HIGH COURT of AUSTRALIA:

Status: Is the highest Court of appeal in Australia.

Composition: Chief Justice and six other Judges.

Functions: - To decide disputes related to meaning of the Constitution i.e. to determine the constitutional powers of the Commonwealth Parliament in passing an Act (being challenged).

- To decide (finally) all types of appeals, including those related to State matters–interpretation of Criminal laws.

Jurisdiction: Two types of jurisdiction vested in the High Court, by the Australian.

Constitution: Origional jurisdiction and Appellate jurisdiction.

Origional jurisdiction:

Section 75: conferred by the constitution, pertaining to the following matters:

- Arising under any treaty.
- Affecting Consuls or representatives of other Countries.
- Affecting the Commonwealth of Australia/or a person, suing/or being sued on behalf of the Commonwealth of Australia, is a party.
- Arising - between States, or
  - between residents of different States, or
  - between a State and a resident of another State.
- Affecting an officer of the Commonwealth, including a Judge, facing a writ of mandamus or prohibition, or an injunction.

Section 76: conferred by the constitution, pertaining to the following matters:

- Arising under laws enacted by the Parliament

Appellate Jurisdiction:

Section 73: conferred by the constitution, pertaining to the hearing of appeals from judgments of:

High Court

Federal Courts

Courts discharging Federal jurisdiction

State Supreme Courts.

Consideration: To grant an application for leave to appeal from a judgment, the High Court may consider interests of Public as well as of Administration of Justice.

FEDERAL COURT of AUSTRALIA

Established: Established in 1977 (1st February 1977). Exists in each State, Australian Capital Territory and Northern Territory.

Composition: Federal Judges and Magistrates, without any specific qualification, are appointed by the current Government. However, as per laws laid down by the Commonwealth Parliament, criterias for appointment:

Federal Judge: to be a legal practitioner for 5 yrs., or to be a Judge of another Court.

Federal Magistrate: to be a legal practitioner for 5 yrs.

Family Court Judge: to be fully trained and experienced in family law matters.

Age: Federal Judges and Magistrates are appointed to the age of 70.

Power: To decide a dispute of the kind set out under sections 75 and 76.

Constitution: Chapter III of the Constitution (Judicature) under sections 71-80, provides for the Judicial Branch of the Commonwealth. It empowers the Commonwealth Parliament to establish:

- To establish the High Court of Australia.
- To create Federal Courts.
- To vest federal judicial power in State and Territory Courts.
- To appoint Federal Judges and Magistrates to the age of 70.
- To remove a Federal Judge or Magistrate, from office, on the basis of proved misconduct or incapacity.
- To guarantee the tenure and remuneration of a Federal Judge and Magistrate.
- To guarantee the independence of the Courts from the Legislative and Executive powers.

FAMILY COURT of AUSTRALIA

Status: Is a Specialist Court, dealing with family and child support.

Etablished: Established in 1977 (1st February 1977). Exists in each State, Australian Capital Territory and Northern Territory.

Jurisdiction: Exercises Original and Appellate jurisdiction thoughout Australia, Exception: Family Court of Western Australia, that:

- Is a State Court, funded by the Commonwealth Government.
- Judges in addition, hold Commissions, as Judges of the Family Court of Australia.
- Decides disputes related to family law and child support.

FEDERAL MAGISTRATES COURT

Status: Federal Magistrate Court deals, with less complex disputes under Commonwealth laws.

Established: Established in 2000 (July 2000).

Jurisdiction: Decides disputes related to family law and child support.

Deals with administrative and bankruptcy laws, ethical discrimination, workplace disputes, consumer protection law (CPL).

Shares jurisdiction with the Federal Court of Australia and Family Court of Australia.

INDUSTRIAL RELATIONS COURT of AUSTRALIA

Status: Industrial Relations Court of Australia, deals with industrial relations disputes.

Established: Established in 1994 (March 1994).

Jurisdiction: In May 1997, its jurisdiction was transferred to the Federal Court of Australia. Judges of the Industrial Relations Court, are in addition, Judges of the Federal Court, to perform latter Court's work, as full time Judges.

SUPREME COURTS

Status: The Supreme Courts of the States, Australian Capital Territory, Northern Territory, and Norfolk Island, are the highest State and Territory Courts.

Jurisdiction: The Supreme Courts of the States, the Australian Capital Territory, the Northern Territory, and

Norfolk Island:

- deal with prominent Civil and Criminal cases.
- hear appeals from judgments made by the lower State Courts, or single Judges of the Supreme Court.

STATE AND TERRITORY COURTS

Status: State and Territory Courts, are designated as Courts of summary Jurisdiction, that deal with cases governed by the State or Territory laws.

Established: Established by the Commonwealth Parliament.

Jurisdiction: Summary jurisdiction - deal with:

- Summary (ordinary) offences e.g. traffic violations and minor assaults.
- Civil cases (minor) e.g. minor claims against persons/or companies.
- Committal proceeds related to minor offences: to find out, whether there is any prima facie case to be determined by a Judge and Jury of a Supreme Court or an Intermediate Court, because Juries are not used in Courts of Summary Jurisdiction.

References:

Authorised by: Branch Head, Federal Courts Branch.

Maintainer: Federal Courts Branch.

Date Created: Thursday, 27 July 2006. Last Modified: Monday, 1 November 2010.

EUROPEAN COURT SYSTEM

EUROPEAN JUDICIAL SYSTEM:

Composition:- **European Court of Justice (ECJ)**
- **Court of First Instance (CFI)**
- **Civil Service Tribunal (CST)**
- **European Court of Human Rights (ECHR)**
- **European Court of Auditors (ECA)**
- **European Court of Free Trade Association (ECFTA)**

INTERNATIONAL JUDICIAL SYSTEM:

Composition:- **International Court of Justice (ICJ), The Hague Court**
- **International Labour Organisation (ILO)**
- **World Trade Organisation (WTO)**
- **International Criminal Court (ICC)**

NATIONAL JUDICIAL SYSTEM:

Jurisdiction: - Important and complex relationship between the European and National Courts of MS.
- No hierarchy and direct jurisdictional link between the European Courts and National Courts of MS (none of the European Courts has an appellate role in the National Courts).
- Effectiveness of the European Courts depends on their relationship with the National Courts.
- None of the European Courts (except to some extent the CFI) are available for direct litigation to private parties.

EUROPEAN COURT of JUSTICE (ECJ)

Status: The European Court of Justice (officially the Court of Justice) is the highest Court in the European Union (EU), in terms of European Union law. As a part of the Court of Justice of the European Union Institution, it is entrusted with interpreting EU law and ensuring its equal application across all EU member states (Assures uniform interpretation of Community law).

The Court was established in 1952 and is based in Luxembourg. It is composed of one judge per MS (currently 27 in number), although it normally hears cases in panels of 3, 5, or 13 Judges. The Court has been led by President Vassilios Skouris since 2003.

History:

- In 1952, the Court was established, by the Treaty of Paris (1951), as part of the European Coal and Steel Community. It was established with 7 Judges, allowing both representative of each of the 6 member states and being an unequal number of Judges in case of a tie.
- In 1967, the European Coal and Steel Community, the European Economic Community (EEC), and the European Atomic Energy Community (Euratom) merged to form an institute of two additional Communities.
- In 1993, the Maastricht Treaty was ratified, that created the European Union (EU). The name of the Court remained unchanged.

  The Court's power vested in the Community pillar (1st pillar).
- In 1997, The Amsterdam Treaty was sighned, that transferred issues from the 3rd pillar to the 1st pillar, prior to that these issues were settled amongst the member states.
- In 2009 (1st Dec.), the ECJ's name was changed (officially), from the Court of Justice of the European Communities, to the Court of Justice (in English), still the Court is referred as European Court of Justice (ECJ). The Court of First Instance, was renamed as the General Court.

Overview: The ECJ is the highest Court of the European Union in terms of Community law, but not National law. It is not possible to appeal the decisions of National Courts to the ECJ, but rather National Courts refer questions of EU law to the ECJ. However, it is ultimately for the National Court to apply the resulting interpretation to the facts of any given case, although only Courts of final appeal are bound to refer a question of EU law, when one is addressed. The Treaties give the ECJ, the power to consistent application of EU law across the EU as a whole. The Court also acts as an arbiter between the EU's Institutions and can annul the latter's legal rights, if it acts outside its powers.

Composition: 27 Judges, assisted by 8 Advocate-Generals. The Judges and Advocate-Generals are appointed by the common accord of the Governments of the MSs.

Powers:
- Differently described by different people:
- Motive for European Union (EU) integration, or
- Political Court interfering in National sovereignty.
- Enacted important EU law principles:
- Direct effect (VanGend en loos, Ratti, Von Colson, Marshall, Marleasing, etc.).
- Supremacy of EU law (Costa v. ENEL, Simmenthal).
- Recognition and incorporation of fundamental rights (Internationale Handelsgesellscoft, Nold).
- Requirement of the availability of remedies in the case of breach of EU lane (Francovich, Brasserie de Pecheur).
- Role of reason.
- Proportionality.
- Implied powers of the EC.

Location: Luxemberg.

Established: In 1952, based at Luxembourg.

Composition: 27 Judges, assisted by 8 Advocate-Generals. The Judges and Advocate-Generals.

Appointment: Appointed by the common accord of the Governments of the MSs, for a renewable period of six yrs. term by agreement between the Member States, which select them from persons of integrity.

Jurisdiction:- Preliminary rulings on EC law upon request by National Courts.

- Action against MS for failure to fulfil obligation.
- Action for annulment of regulations, directions, decisions by the EU Institutions.
- Action against EU Institutions for failure to act. The Amsterdam Treaty, explicitly conferred jurisdiction on the ECJ to check that Community Instruments respect fundamental rights and it extended the ECJ's jurisdiction to matters affecting the freedom and security of the people (limited powers for the ECJ in the intergovernmental 2nd and 3rd pillars).

Functions: Constitutional, civil, administrative and arbitration.

Advocate General:

Composition: Eight AGIs work for 27 Judges of the ECJ.

Qualification: No specialisation of the AGIs by subject matter.

Duties:
- Only one AG per case.
- Since 2003 (Nice), AG gives an opinion only if the ECJ considers that a case raises new points of law.
- AG opinions (advisory) not binding on ECJ, but very important for the development of EU law, because:
  - AG is the laboratory for the new interpretation of EU law.
  - AG helps the ECJ reshape its legal reasoning.
  - AG provides the substitute of double examination.
  - AG complements and completes decision of the ECJ.
  - AG provides the critical perspective internal to the ECJ–something like a dissenting opinion in common law court systems.

ECJ–Quasi Constitutional Court:

Role: The formal role of the ECJ and its exclusive power to ensure that in the interpretation and application of this Treaty, that law is observed (Art. 220) and to decide on the validity of instruments enacted by all other Institutions (the 1st pillar):

- Guardian of the objectives and the rules of law laid down in the treaties; appellate and final instance.
- Legality of the secondary legislation.
- Preservation of equilibrium of institutions.
- Determines division of constituencies between the EU and MS.
- Preliminary rulings ensures uniform application and interpretation of EU law.

ECJ – Rules and Actions:

- The basic rules of the ECJ and CFI (Art. 220-245).
- The rules of procedure of the Court set out in the statutes (attached to the Treaty as a Protocol) and the Rules of Procedure (drafted by the Court but approved by the Council.
- Actions before the ECJ could be divided into two types:
    - Judgments
    - Opinions.
- Two categories of Judgments:
    - Preliminary rulings (requested by National Courts (Art. 234).
    - Direct actions by EC institutions, MS or individuals.

ECJ - Preliminary Rulings:

- Judgments made upon requests by any National Court for interpretation of the treaty or secondary legislation 7 the questions on the validity secondary relations.
- When a question of EU law is raised by the National court in which there is no appeal under National law, the National Court is required to refer the matter to the ECT (Art. 234(3)).

- This is not a formal decision of a case and its subject matter, but would be a binding guideline for the National Court when decides the referred case.
- *Note:* after Treaty of Nice, the Statute allows the ECJ to entrust to the CFI, the responsibility for preliminary rulings in certain matters (this has not yet happened).

Importance of Preliminary Rulings:

- Opened the channel for litigation before the ECJ independent of the commission.
- Enhanced the position of individual in the system of EU law creating for them an access to the ECJ (it is not easy for individuals to get locus standi in direct actions–it is easier for individuals to raise cases in National Courts).
- Giving such an indirect access to individuals reduces the tension between the commission and MS (the commission does not need to confront MS in cases of non-compliance because individuals would do that before National Courts).
- Ensures the uniform interpretation of the EU law.
- Mechanism of indirect judicial review by the ECJ of National legislation for its compatibility with ECJ law (even though the ECJ has no formal power for judicial review of National legislation, the judgment indicates the extent to compatibility to National Courts).
- Gives legitimacy to ECJ and also gives National Courts the important role of enforcing EU law through sanctions available in National Systems giving the EU law "teeth".

Direct Actions:

Jurisdiction:- of the ECJ and CF to hear those cases could be established by the operation of law (Treaty) or by agreement of the parties.

- Jurisdiction established by the operation of law facilitates two basic categories of direct actions:

- Actions against the EU Institutions: review of the legality of Acts by the Institutions (Art. 230-231), challenge of a failure to act by the EU Institutions (Art. 232-233), and claims for liability for damage caused by the EU Institution (Art. 235, 238(2)), brought by another Institution, or by a MS, or individual.
- Enforcement actions against MS for failure to fulfill an obligation under the Treaty, brought usually by the commission (Art. 227-228) or by other MS (Art. 227-228-very rare) but not by individuals.

ECJ's Procedure:

- Admissibility of a case.
- Written procedure.
- Preliminary report of the Judge Rapporteur.
- Oral procedure–day in Court (hearing).
- Opinion of the AG–important but not binding on ECJ.
- Deliberation and judgment.
- Compliance and enforcement.

ECJ's Challenges:

- Linguistic: French is the official language in which the Court has to write judgments and opinions, but it is difficult to articulate sophisticated legal principles in a foreign language.
- Discrepency: More Judges appointed after the upgrading, but the number of AG's remain the same.
- Impairment: Potential of jeoparding the unity of the Court by increasing the number of Judges (discord at ECJ ref.: Microsoft antitrust case).
- Complexity of issues: Need for specialised Tribunals.
- Overburden: Possible increased number of cases due to upgrading and extension of the Court's jurisdiction.

- Overlapping: Potential overlap of jurisdiction with other International Tribunals.

COURT of FIRST INSTANCE (CFI):

Established: in 1989.

Composition: 27 Judges, without any Advocate General.

Status: Alleviates case load of ECJ.

Jurisdiction:- Direct actions brought by the natural of legal persons against community acts.

- Actions brought by MS against the Commission.
- Actions brought by MS against the Council dealing with matters of State aid, "Dumping" or acts by which Council exercises its implementing powers.
- Actions according to contracts (choice of jurisdiction).
- Actions for damages caused by the Community Institutions or their staff.
- Actions concerning Community trademarks.
- Has jurisdiction, subject to further appeal to the Court of Justice, on points of law, to deal with disputes between the commission and individuals, or businesses as well administrative disputes within the Institutions, between the commission and its staff (Table 5.4):

Table 5.4: Appeal

European Court of Justice ←	Appeal limited to questions of law. In exceptional cases, review of decisions by the Court of First Instance on appeals against Civil Service Tribunal.
Court of First Instance ←	Appeal limited to questions of law. Court of First Instance may decide case on appeal itself (depending on individual case.
Civil Service Tribunal	

Source: Anita B Frohlich – 2007-2008.

CIVIL SERVICE TRIBUNAL (CST):

Established: on November 2, 2004, by the Council decision.

Composition:- 7 Judges for the Tribunal appointed for a six yrs. renewable term, by the Council's decision of January 18, 2005; Chambers of 3 or 5 rarely full or 1 (so far 130 cases pending from 2005 and 46 cases pending since 2006)–they decide who will be the President of the Tribunal.

- The Council appointed is on the proposal of the special committee (7 former ECJ or CFI Judges) who reviewed the applications.
- A Judge must be a national of a MS and will know legal expert and the selection should reflect a broader geographical basis and legal cultures of the MS.

Jurisdiction:- Limited to staff cases (Art. 236). Hears disputes between the Community Institutions and their staff.

- The parties have to appeal to CFI within 2 months after the decision of the Civil Service Tribunal is rendered.

Judicial Method and Analysis of the Judgments:

- Teleological method of reasoning (justifies objectives of any provisions of EU law in the setting of the whole treaty scheme, arguments based on analogy, general principles or law, contextual harmonisation.
- Format and discourse patterned on the French model.
- Decisions are rather short, terse, offer condensed factual descriptions, often 3-8 pages, except in preliminary rulings.
- No dissenting or concurring opinions, only one decision for the whole Court.
- Every judgment has reference to the legal basis for the Court's jurisdiction and the reference to the legislation upon which the decision is made.
- No doctrine of State decises so precedents are mentioned but not referred to as to the legal

basis of a decision (AG refers to them as to the case or ECJ's jurisprudence).

Procedure Before the ECJ Direct Actions:

Written Procedure:

- Written application by a lawyer (in the language of the applicant).
- Service of the application on the defendant.
- Publication of the application in official journal.
- Defence
- Reply
- Rejoinder
- Preparatory inquiry.

Oral Procedure:

- Hearing
- AG opinion

Deliberation:- Only after AG delivers her/his opinion.

Judgment: - Always delivered in Franch.

Enforcement of Judgments:

- If the MS has not complied with a judgment, the commission may ask the ECJ to impose the fine on MS (since Maastricht Treaty):

  Greece-the 1st MS to be fined in July 2000; commission v. Hellenic Republic (C-387/97) to pay euro 20,000 for every day of delay in implementing the measures necessary to comply with the judgment.
- If damages are awarded against private individual, the winning party must seek enforcement before the appropriate National Court (Art. 244 and 256).
- If award has been given against the EU Institution, whose act has been declared void or who has failed to act, that Institution is required to take the necessary measures to comply with the judgment (Art. 233).

EUROPEAN COURT OF HUMAN RIGHTS (ECHR):

ECHR

Established: - In 1959, based at Strasbourg.

Function: - To deal with disputes arising out of infringements of the European Convention for Human Rights.

- The essence of the system is the right of individual petition against State (including their own), when an individual feels that she/he feels being a victim personally and directly of a violation of human rights and guarantees specified in the convention.
- Originally ECHR was assisted by the European Commission on Human Rights and then approaches the Court, which filtered all applications but Protocol 11 in 1998 changed the process; the ECHR became the full time Court dealing with applications (since 1999, number of cases has been increasing dramatically).
- Every MS of the convention has a Judge, but they do not represent their States; 6 yrs. Mandate; appointed by the Assembly of the Council of Europe.
- Judges are divided into 4 sections, and they sit in Chambers of 7 and Committees of 3.

Requirements:- An individual must be personally and directly victim of violation of the right specified in the convention (not a general statement)–individual does not need to be a National of a contracting party of the convention, but violation must be on the territory of the MS.

- All National remedies have to be exhausted and the application launched within six months from the final decision at the National level.

Procedure: - Application could be simply mailed to the Court, but must explain the fact, violations and remedies already used, no application fees; legal assistance preferable.

- Application goes to a section whose President appoints a Judge rapporteur.
- Mainly written proceedings, oral hearings very rare (and public).
- The Court would try to settle a dispute, if no settlement, if violations found "just satisfaction" will be awarded (in English and French);
- Dissenting and concurring opinions allowed.

Enforcement:- Committee of Ministers of the Council of Europe supervises execution of the award by the contracting party.

Jurisdiction: The Court acts as a collegial body: decisions are those of the Court rather than of individual judges; no minority opinions are given and indeed the existence of a majority decision rather than unanimity is never suggested.

Presidents of ECJ (Table 5.5):

Table 5.5: Presidents of European Court of Justice

President	*Country*	*Term*
Massimo Pilotti	Italy	1952-1958
Andreas Matthias Donner	Netherlands	1958-1964
Charles Leon Hammes	Luxembourg	1964-1967
Robert Lecourt	France	1967-1976
Hans Kutscher	Germany	1976-1980
Josse Mertens de Wilmars	Belgium	1980-1984
John Mackenzie-Stuart	United Kingdom	1984-1988
Gil Carlos Rodriguez Iglesias	Spain	1988-1994
Ole Due	Denmark	1994-2003
Vassilios Skouris	Greece	(7 October 2003-incubent) (term expires 31 October 2014)

EUROPEAN COURT OF AUDITORS (ECA):

Composition:- 27 members appointed for a six years term, by agreement between the Member States, after consultation with the European Parliament.

Jurisdiction:- To check that the revenue is received and expenditure incurred "in a lawful and regular manner" and that the community's financial affairs are properly managed.

- The Maastricht Treaty gave the Court of Auditors the status of a Community Institution, making it the 5th most important EU Institution.

INTERNATIONAL JUDICIAL SYSTEM:

INTERNATIONAL COURTS:

Composition:- International Court of Justice (ICJ), The Hague

- **International Criminal Court (ICC), The Hague**
- **International Labour Organisation (ILO)**
- **World Trade Organisation (WTO)**

History: International Courts are different from International Arbitration Forums.

Established: Are established by Treaties amongst Nations, or by the authority of an International Organisation e.g. United Nations (UN).

Courts: Permanent International Courts and Tribunals (ad hoc), excluding National Courts.

Permanent International Courts:

- International Court of Justice
- International Criminal Court
- Permanent Court of Arbitration
- Permanent Court of International Justice
- World Trade Organisation Dispute Settlement Body
- International Tribunal for the Law of the Sea

African:

- Court of Human and People's Rights
- Court of Justice for the Eastern and Southern Common Market

- Court of Justice for West African States Economic Community
- Court of Justice for East Africa
- Developmental Community Tribunal for Southern Africa.

American:

- Caribbean Court of Justice
- Eastern Caribbean Supreme Court
- Central American Court of Justice
- Court of Justice of the Andean Community
- Common Court of Justice of Aruba, Curacao, Sint Maarten, Bonaire, Sint Eustatius and Saba.
- Inter-American Court of Human Rights.

European and the Commonwealth of Independent States:

- Benelux Court of Justice
- European Court of Justice
- European Court of Auditors
- European Union Civil Service Tribunal
- European Court of Free Trade Association
- European Court of Human Rights
- European Commission of Human Rights
- Human Rights Chamber for Bosnia and Herzegovina.
- Economic Court of the Commonwealth of Independent States

Tribunals (ad hoc) : incld. Nuremberg and Tokyo, established in the post-World War II. Three such Courts, exist at the Hague, Netherlands :

- International Criminal Tribunal for the former Yugoslavia (ICTY).
- International Court of Justice (ICJ)
- International Criminal Court (ICC).

Jurisdiction: To deal with crimes committed in a civil war or during genocide.

Judges: Judges and high-level staff, are afforded diplomatic immunity, as per their governing authority.

Ad hoc Tribunals :

Ad hoc Arbitration Tribunals :

- Beagle Channel Court of Arbitration
- Iran-United States Claims Tribunal

Ad hoc Criminal Tribunals :

- International Military Tribunal, Nuremberg (1945-46)
- International Military Tribunal for the Far East (1946-48)
- International Criminal Tribunal for the ex-Yugoslavia (ICTY-93)
- International Criminal Tribunal for Rwanda (ICTR-since1994)
- International Residual Mechanism for Criminal Tribunals (will replace ICTR and ICTY, from 2012/2013).
- Special Panels of the Dili District Court (2000-2006).

Hybrid Tribunals :

- Special Court for Sierra Leone (since 2002)
- Extraordinary Chambers in the Courts of Cambodia (since 2003)
- Special Tribunal for Lebanon (since 2009).

INTERNATIONAL COURT OF JUSTICE

International Court of Justice

Established: In 1945, by the UN Charter.

Location: In The Hague (Peace Palace), Netherlands.

Function: Started functioning in 1946, as a successor to the Permanent Court of International Justice, with the same Statute of its predecessor.

- To settle legal disputes, submitted to it by the Member States (MS).
- To provide advisory opinions on legal queries, submitted to it by the authorised International agencies and the UN General Assembly.

Jurisdiction: Worldwide, 192 Member States.

Article 94 : empowers the UN to enforce all the UN members to comply with the decisions of the ICJ related to the members, failing that the matter may be referred to the UN Security Council for implementation of the action under Chapter XIV of the UN Charter :

Chapter XIV of the UN Charter : empowers the UN Security Council to enforce World Court rulings, subject to overruling by the veto power of the five permanent members (USA, UK, France, Russia, People's Republic of China).

Setback/drawback : A resolution on enforcement may be vetoed, in case the judgment of the ICJ, is directed against any one of the permanent member or its allies.

Examples :

- Nicaragua crisis : USA v/s Nicaragua : US's non-compliance of the ICJ's decision, by using the veto power.
- Syria Crisis : Arab League v/s Syria : Russia and China vetoed a UN Security Council resolution, that sought backing for an Arab League proposal to end the alleged bloodshed in Syria,by urging Syrian's President Assad (blaming opposition groups equally for the bloodshed) to pull troops from cities and allow a political transition to begin.

Judges: Articles 4-19 of the ICJ Statute : 15 Judges, elected to 9 yrs. term, by the UN General Assembly and the UN Security Council, from a list of Judges, nominated by the National Groups in the Permanent Court of Arbitration. Judges may be re-elected for upto two terms of three yrs. Each.

Article 6 of the ICJ Statute : Judges elected are of high moral character, highly qualified, and well competent in International law.

Article 16-18 of the ICJ Statute: Judicial independence specifically dealt with.

Dismissal : by a unanimous vote of the members (Judges) of the ICJ.

Judgments: May be joint judgments or individual ones (separate dissenting opinions).

Chambers: Articles 26-29 of the ICJ Statute : allow the Court to form smaller chambers (3-5 Judges), instead of full bench, to hear cases.

Types :

- Special Chambers : to hear special categories of cases
- Ad hoc Chambers : to hear particular disputes, and are more frequently convened.

Ad hoc Judges : Article 31 of the ICJ Statute : Judges sit on contentious cases, allowing any party to a contentious case to nominate a Judge of their choice.

Contentious Cases :

- USA v/s Canada : dispute over the course of the maritime boundary dividing US and Canada (Gulf of Maine Case).
- Tunisia v/s Libya : dispute over the delimitation of the continental shelf between them.
- US v/s Iran : dispute over the detention of American diplomats in Tehran (Iran), in violation of International law.
- Federal Republic of Yugoslavia v/s MS of NATO : dispute over the NATO's actions in the Kosovo War.
- Pakistan v/s India : dispute over the Kashmir, over alleged State terrorism against the people of Kashmir, in violation of the International law.

Hearing: In general, the Court has been successful in resolving border delineation and claims/counterclaims over the use of oceans and waterways. While the Court has resolved some of the claims by MS, the Court in general has refrained from entertaining contentious cases :

- that are political in nature
- that the Court lacks enforcement and compulsory jurisdiction, to hear Cases.

Article 36(1) : provides :

- The parties may refer cases to the ICJ (as special agreement or compromise), based on explicit consent rather than true compulsory jurisdiction (acceptable with Court's judgment).
- The Court's jurisdiction over matters specifically provided for, in Treaties and Conventions in force. Treaties mostly contain a compromise clause, for disputed resolution by the ICJ (not as effective as special agreement).

Example : Iran hostage crisis : Iran neither agreed to participate in the matter raised by the US proposed compromise clause, as per Vienna Convention on Diplomatic Relations, nor did it comply with the Court's judgment.

Article 36(2) : provides :

- MS to voluntarily declare optional clause, thereby accepting the Court's jurisdiction.

  Example : In 2002, US and Australia modified their declaration, to exclude disputes on maritime boundaries.

Article 36(5) : provides : Jurisdiction based on declarations made under the Permanent Court of International Justice's Statute.

Article 37 : provides : Transfers jurisdiction under any compromise clause in a Treaty, providing jurisdiction to the PCU.

Article 36 : provides : Jurisdiction based on tacit consent (forum prorogatum), That is the respondent accepts ICJ jurisdiction explicitly/or pleads on the merits.

Example : Corfu Channel case : UK v/s Albania (1949) : Albania accepted the ICJ's jurisdiction, to grant the Court's jurisdiction.

Advisory opinion :

Jurisdiction: Is the official declaration of the principal judicial organ of the UN.

Court's function available only to specified UN Bodies and Agencies.

The Court may decide and provide an opportunity to supportive MS and Organisations, to submit statements (oral or written).

The Court's advisory opinions are only consultative.

Aims : As a tool, by the UN Bodies and Agencies, to seek the Court's help, in deciding complex legal issues, under their respective mandates.

Character : The Court's advisory opinions are only consultative, influential and respectable. The Court's authoritative views on important issues of International law, reflect the Court's function of following the same rules and procedures, governing its own judgments delivered in contentious cases, submitted to it by the MS (Sovereign States).

Controversial:- That the questions asked may be controversial

- That the case before the Court in relity may be a contentious one.

Example: Nuclear Weapons Case.

INTERNATIONAL CRIMINAL COURT (Cour penale Internationale)

INTERNATIONAL CRIMINAL COURT, The HAGUE

Definition: Is a permanent Tribunal to prosecute individuals for genocide, crimes against humanity, war crimes, and the crime of aggression.

Location: The Hague, Netherland

Members: 120 MS.

Languages: English and French.

Establishment: Rome Statute adopted : 17 July 1998 Entered into force: 1 July 2002.

Law of Treaties: obliges these States to refrain from acts which would defeat the object and purpose of the Treaty.

Jurisdiction:

- That the accused is a national of a State party.
- That the alleged crime has taken place on the territory of State Party.
- That the case is referred to the Court by the UN Security Council.

- That when the National Courts are unwilling or unable to investigate or prosecute such crimes.

State Parties of the Roman Statute grants the Court jurisdiction over the :

- crimes of genocide,
- crimes against humanity,
- war crimes, and
- crime of aggression.

History:

1919: Paris Peace conference by the Commission of Responsibilities.

1937 : Geneva Conference by the League of Nations.

1948 : Nuremberg and Tokyo Tribunals by the International Court to deal with atrocities committed during World War II.

1998 : Rome Statute of the ICC was adopted by a majority vote (120 v/s 7 MS with 21 absentee).

2002 : Rome Statute became a binding treaty.

2002 : 1st Bench of 18 Judges elected by an assembly of States.

2005 : The Court issued 1st arrest warrant.

2006 : Pre-trial hearings held.

2010 : Kampala, Uganda : two amendments to the Rome Statute of the ICC, were adopted. The 2nd amendment concerns the definition of the aggression.

Structure: Governed by an assembly of States Parties.

Presidency, Judicial divisions, office of the Prosecutor, and the Registery.

Assembly: Of State Parties includes one member from each State Party, having one vote, and the decisions are mostly taken by consensus, otherwise by voting in case of differences in opinion.

Composition : President and 2 Vice Presidents elected by the MS, for a period of 3 yrs.

Session: Once per year, in New york or The Hague. The sessions are open to MS and NGOs.

Constitution: The Assembly :

- elects the Judges and the Prosecutors, - decides the Court's budget,
- adopts important texts (Rules of Procedure and Evidence),
- provides management oversight to the other organs of the Court.

Article 46: of the Rome Statute allows the Assembly, to remove from office, a

Judge or Prosecutor, who :

- Is found to have committed serious misconduct, or
- a serious breach of his/her duties, or
- is unable to perform the duties as per required by this Statute.

The State parties can not interfere in the Judicial functions of the Court.

Individual cases are settled by the Judicial division.

Presidency: Judges of the Court, elected by the fellow Judges, for a period of 3 yrs.

Composition:- President

- Vice Presidents – 1st and 2nd.

Functions: - Administration of the Court, besides office of the Prosecutor.

Judges: 18 Judges of the ICC, organised into 3 Chambers : Pre-trial Chamber, Trial Chamber, and Appeals Chamber. Judges are elected to the Court by the Assembly of States Parties, for a period of 9 yrs., without any re-election. Judges must be nationals of the State Parties to the Rome Statute.

Functions: Judicial functions of the Court.

Proseutor: The Assembly elects the Chief Prosecutor, assisted by one or more Deputy Prosecutors.

Function: To conduct investigations and prosecutions, independently.

The Prosecutor may open an investigation under 3 conditions :

- The Case is referred by a State Party.
- The case is referred by the UN Security Council, to address a threat to the International peace and security.
- The Pre-trial Chamber authorises, to open an investigstion based on information provided by an individual or NGOs.

Removal: Of Prosecutors decided by the Appeals Chamber, based on :

- committing serious misconduct, or
- breach of his/her duties, or
- unable to perform his/her duties.

Infrastructure of ICC :

- Headquarters of ICC : Officially the ICC Court is in The Hague.

  Netherlands, but the proceedings may be held anywhere.
- Liaison office in New York.
- Field offices in : Kampala, Bunia, Kinshasa, Abeche, and Bangui.
- Detention centre : Scheveningen branch of the Haaglanden Penal Institution, The Hague.

Trials: Are conducted under a hybrid Common law and Civil Law Judicial System. In camera trials are conducted, to protect the defendant, witnesses, and sensitive evidence.

Rights of the Accused: All persons are presumed innocent until proven guilty, beyond reasonable doubts, and establishes certain rights of the accused during trials i.e.:

- right to full information of the charges, levelled against him/her
- right to present evidence
- right to council: right to hire an appointed lawyer, free of charge

- right to confront witnesses against him/her.
- right to remain silent
- right to be present at the trial

Defence of the Accused: ICC has established an independent Office of Public Council for the Defence (OPCD) :

- to provide logistical support, advice and information to defendants and their councel
- to safeguard the rights of the accused during the trial.

CHAPTER - VI

OFFENCES AND PENALTIES

OFFENCES :

- **Abetment to Suicide**
- **Acid Attacks Trauma**
- **Agony of Senior Citizens**
- **Alcohol Abuse**
- **Child Abuse/Vulnerable Childhood/No Country for Children**
- **Domestic Violence (Intimate-partner violence)**
- **Doping**
- **Dowry**
- **Drug Abuse**
- **Environment Pollution**
- **Euthanasia**
- **Eve-teasing**
- **Homicide**
- **Honour Killing**
- **Medical Negligence :**
  - **Civil negligence**
  - **Criminal negligence**
  - **Implied understanding**
  - **Subtle/Complicated negligence**
  - **Liability**
  - **Act of commission**
  - **Act of omission**
  - **Actionable negligence**

- **Vicarious liability**
- **Contributory negligence**
- **Medical Terminatiom of Pregnancy (MTP) :**
  - **Abortion Policy in India**
  - **Critique of MTP Act**
  - **Mental Retardation and Multiple Disabilities**
  - **Moral turpitude**
  - **Pre-natal Sex Determination Test (PNDT)**
- **Psychological violence :**
  - **Sadists and Trolls**
- **Sexual Offences :**
  - **Sexual harassment at working place**
- **Sexual Offences in India :**
  - **Adultery**
  - **Rape**
  - **Child Abuse**
  - **Sexual Offences in UK**
  - **Sexual Offences in USA**
- **Sexual Violence (Physical) :**
  - **Sexual Abuse**
  - **Consent for Sexual Act or Behaviour**
  - **Sexual Assault**
  - **Sexual Torture**
  - **Sodomy**
- **Torture (Medico-legal Aspect) :**
  - **Doctors and Torture**
- **Torture (Psychological) :**
  - **Trolls/Sadists**
  - **Violence Against Medical Establishments**
  - **Violence against Women**
  - **Transplantation of Human Organs**

ABETMENT TO SUICIDE (Decriminalise suicide attempts)

Offence: That is to incite by encouragement or aid someone to commit suicide, which is wrong or illegal. In India-2011 (National Crime Records) about 1.35 lakh people took their own lives (372 suicides/

day i.e. 16 suicides/hr.). While social and financial factors have been the major causes to commit suicide, in case of females, emotional and personal being the primary reasons. Although the actual numbers may be much higher than these as the statistics only pertain to reported cases. Recently, an increasing trend of enacting publically, suicide threats (pressurising tactics) on minor subjects, in order to gain cheap publicity. Many a times, jilted lovers climb high rise buildings/water tanks, threatend to end their lives, thereby disturbing public's peace and tranquility. That in cases of hunger strikes, incldduding fast-unto-death, these tactics are resorted to pressurise concerned authority to concede to agitator/s demand/s. Mostly the intention of agitator n't to kill him/herself. Only in case of agitator's refusal to take meals and fluids and in case of imminent danger to life, he/she may be held under the Attempt to Suicide Act.

Courting trouble :

That the lust for power and everything that comes with it has been driving women to disaster. Lured by the majestic ways of the rich world of the high and mighty, many of them have been entering into forbidden liaisons only to realise, much later, that they have tied the knot with trouble. Some of them had to pay with their lives for attempts to break free from the shackles of a mundane middle-class existence.

Cases :

- Anuradha Bali, alias Fiza, who entered into a murky relationship with a Deputy CM Haryana, Chander Mohan, and hit the headlines, was just one of them whose love story ended in tragedy. Their marriage lasted only forty days, and nobody realised that she would end up like so many other victims of "forbidden love". Her maggot-infested body was found in a highly decomposed state in her house in SAS Nagar.

- Shivani Bhatnagar, Monika Kapila and Madhumita met the fatal end with hardly any difference, while Monica Bedi is the only exception.
- Shivani Bhatnagar
- Monika Kapila
- Madhumita
- Monica Bedi an actress–only exception, who managed to come out of the underworld after her alliance with don Abu Salem, and is now struggling to again find a foothold in Bollywood after serving her jail sentence.

Penalty : Punishable under Section 306-309 IPC: that whoever attempts to commit suicide and does any act towards the commission of such offence shall be punishable with simple imprisonment for a term which may extend to one year or with fine or with both. Thus, technically, suicide as such not a crime under the IPC Act, but it is only an attempt to commit suicide that is punishable.

Legally :
- SC in case of P Rathinam (1994): The Bench held that Section 309 of IPC deserves to be effected (void) from the statute book as it violate Article 21.
- SC in case of Gian Kaur (1996): The Constitutional Bench held that Article 21 of Constitution guarantees the right to life but not the right to die. The SC had only upheld the Constitutional validity of Section 309 of IPC, and did not conside the desirability of retaining the same in the IPC.
- Law Commission of India (18th): Humanisation and Decriminalisation of Attempt to Suicide 210th report (2008): also advocated for alising the suicide attempt.

International scenario:

That in many countries, attempt to commit suicide, regarded more as a manifestation of a perverted (diseased) mind, deserving treatment and care rather than an offence attracting punishment :

UK : The British Parliament in 1961, enacted the Suicide Act, whereby attempt to commit suicide ceased to be an offence.

India, Pakistan, Bangladesh, Malaysia,Singapore etc. : persisted with this undesirable law.

Vox-populi : H Kumar, Advocate: That an attempt to suicide indeed merits decriminalisation and hence omission from the penal statute. It is really unfortunate that attempt to commit suicide continues to be a penal offence under the IPC, despite the fact that when distressed people decide to terminate life prematurely, they require sympathy, counselling and appropriate treatment, and certainly not any punishment.

Reference : H Kumar: Decriminalise suicide attempts, HT, July, 2012.

ACID ATTACKS TRAUMA

Offence : Is a barbarian, monstrous, uncivilised, unpardonable crime, committed by accused on helpless victims mostly young innocent girls/ women. This inhuman crime has to be condemned forcefully by the society and deserves stringent punishment to the accused while full medical aid (free) and financial compensation to the victim and affected family.

Penalty : Acid attacks are registered under Section 307 (attempt to murder) or Section 326 (voluntarily causing grievous hurt) of the IPC. Under both sections maximum punishment is life sentence, but there is no minimum sentence.

Legal:

- V Ghai (Sr. Advocate Punjab and Haryana High Court, Chandigarh) : "There should be a provision for such cases under Section 307 and a minimum sentence of seven years. Law should be amended to match social reality."
- V Dadwal (Advocate Punjab and Haryana High Court, Ludhiana): "Touched upon the delay in conviction, usually adding to trauma of the

victim. Witnesses do not come for hearings due to social pressures. That is a big problem."

- T Singh (Advocate District Courts, Chandigarh): Courts rarely order compensation for victims in criminal cases. Victims' families have to file separate petitions to avail of the benefit.

The IPC was amended in 2013 to including a new Section 326A which deems acid attack as being punishable by imprisonment which shall not be less than 10 yrs but which may extend to life and with fine which may extend to Rupees 10 lakh, provided that any fine levied under this section shall be given to the person on whom acid has been thrown or administered.

Etiology : Jealousy:- dejected lovers, family members (relatives), buiseness rivals

Revenge:- sexual exploitations e.g. rape, molestation

Violence:- fights

Cheating:- financial frauds

Dowry: family members–mostly greedy husband and in-laws Property disputes

Errors : tragedy of errors

Psychological : Schizophrena, antisocial, sadism

Risks : Acids easily available in the market, without any licence

Easily thrown over the victim/s

Accused/s mostly go unnoticed after committing the crime

Legal flaws : long legal procedures, lack of evidence/witness little penality bail provision to accused, family pressures–mostly family reputation

Media : "Scarred Bodies, Wounded Souls":

It is the most insidious face of violence against women. Yet the scourage of acid attacks, an alarming trend in Punjab, Haryana and Himachal, remains invisible and hardly provokes the public outrage that dowry deaths and female feticide do. Victims of these revenge-wit-acid dedations, invariably by jilted lovers, are young and unmarried girls. Scarred, both physically and mentally, the survivors are condemned to a life-long horror of disfigured faces and limbs. As an HT investigation reveals, the victims are left to fend for themselves and need prolonged and expensive treatment. Worse, while some give up the fight against their tormentors altogether out of fear or frustration over the slow-moving wheel of justice, others are fighting a losing legal battle. Their scarred bodies–images of which may be disturbing to some readers–capture the searing trauma that words could never describe. It's time to faceup to the horrific reality and take steps to stamp out this diabolic crime. (Ramesh Vinayak, Resident Editor, Hindustan Times, June 8, 2012)

Case : "Our legal system is crippled. I have given up" :

Jyoti, Ambala : After loosing her father at the age of 12, Jyoti had somehow managed to rebuild her life by getting a job in a telecom company by the time she turned 19. By 22, she seemed to have found real love with a colleague.

"He put forth a marriage propsal, that was rejected by both's families. This angered the jilted lover, who threw acid on her on February 14, Valentine's day. Jyoti suffered burns on her face. Main problem is financial as well as disturbed family. So far, she has spent around ₹ 1.5 lakh, but there are boils on the face again.

"The Deputy Commissioner had promised me a job, but it has been more than a year and no assistance has come. Not even the Red Cross Society has helped. A private hospital in Karnal where I go for treatment had told me that ₹ 10,000, is the cost for the laser treatment per week. Her cousion's husband, helped, but still, they would not be able to afford the treatment."

A case was registered, but the attacker is out on bail at present. “With a salary of ₹ 6,000 from a private job in a telecom company, I have to get myself treatment, fend for the family and bear legal expenses. I have lost faith in the government, society and the media too. The legal system in this country is crippled.” I even thought of ending my life initially, but I can’t leave my mother alone,” she said, not morose but confident, having just completed her graduation through distance education. (Monica Sharma, HT)

Case : “jailed culprits live better” :

Mamta, Mandi : A jilted lover, Mahmud Magrub, threw acid on her on May 27.

Mamta suffered burns on her face and lost her vision, dashing her hopes of becoming a teacher. The main problem is financial as well as disturbed family.

The family of six is surviving on the pension of her ex-serviceman father Khem Chand, who said, “Even life imprisonment is no deterrent. The jailed culprit lead a better life as compared to the victims.”

The culprit has been lodged in the Nahan jail, serving a seven year sentence, his bail plea has been rejected by the HP High Court. (Bhawani Negi, HT)

Case : “Seeing her in such pain, we wished for her death” :

Prerna, Rohtak : The target was someone else, but a tragedy of errors led to Prerna suffering 40 per cent burns and being left with a severely disfigured face. Her friends–Yashika, the actual target, and Urwashi–too suffered burns but were lucky to escape severe injuries that have made Prerna an outcast of sorts.

Prerna’s mother, Monika, said “Just those vital two minutes made all the difference.” Wrapped in a bandage around her chin, Prerna has hardly any structured features, words don't come out of her mouth, but her eyes scream, anguished, searching for your face from behind thick glasses to see whether you are just another sympathiser from the neighbourhood. Those eyes tell a story, the story of June 18, 2011, when acid was thrown on Prerna, Yashika, both 14 at the time, and Urwashi, who was 15 then, by two boys in sector 3 of Rohtak.

Yashika's family believes one of their jealous relatives hired the acid throwers to disfigure her. Yashika's aunt is among the three arrests made so far in the case. After the State Police exonerated Rohan, one of the attackers identified by Prerna, the High Court ordered a CBI investigation on a petition by the victims on May 22. The HC has also directed the Haryana Government to pay ₹ 5 lakh as compensation to Prerna "too little too late". Her father said, more than ₹ 19 lakh has been spent on her 10 skin grafting surgeries, while nine more surgeries (each costing ₹ 2 lakh) being required to restore her face. "No one from the Government, media and public helped," said Monika, revealing in distress.

But why does she have to suffer ? She just happened to come in the line of fire," cried Prerna's mother.

Prerna (mistaken target) suffered burns on her face, chest and arms, while Yashika (actual target) got her back and arms badly burnt, and Urvashi suffered from the spills.

A year has lapsed since Prerna, a keen dancer and Kho-kho player, faced the horror. But troubles continue. Even now, she has to constantly remain indoor to avoid heat outside. Can't afford hospitalisation (₹ 6000 per day).

"Fast track Courts should be set up and a policy should be framed for the treatment as well," she added sobbing. And then came the anger. "For us, justice will be done when acid is poured on the culprits." (Monica Sharma, HT)

Case : "Life finished for volleyball player" :

Ritu Saini, Rohtak : Ritu's cousion Ram Niwas, out of jealousy is alleged to have hatched the conspiracy by hiring men, who threw acid on her on May 27.

Ritu suffered 20 per cent burns on her face, arms and chest. Her eye is endangered. The main problem is lacking money. Lakhs of rupees are required for skin graftings. For Ritu, it is a one sentence verdict: "My life is finished."

Police has arrested all the attackers and the conspirators.

Case : "I can make you pretty, not myself" :

Amandeep Kaur, Bathinda : A jited lover, Daljinder Singh, Aman's brother-in-law, alleged to have hatched the conspiracy by hiring men, who threw acid on her on January 31. Aman suffered 90 per cent burns on her face and lost her vision, now a living, walking life lesson (To be the object of someone's affection is a compliment. But when it turns to obsession, don't ignore the obvious signs of impending paranoia). The main problem is financial as well as disturbed family. Aman's future depends on donations. "The treatment will cost ₹ 20 lakh more, beyond their reach," rued Aman's father.

Police arrested the culprit, inspite of protests by both the families, to save the reputation as well as the sensitive relationships. Aman's family requested the Court to drop the case, but the Judge said, he would first like to see if Daljinder helps in Aman's treatment. (Kamaldeep Singh Brar, HT)

Case : "From beauty business to a life of loneliness" :

Sharanjit Kaur, Amritsar : A jealous sister-in-law, masterminded the attack–two unknown persons threw acid on her on August 18.

Sharanjit suffered burns on her face and right arm, dashing her hopes of running her business (beauty parlour). The main problem is financial as well as disturbed family. The incident left the family hapless. The beauty parlour closed down, the family took loans to pay for Sharanjit's treatment.

Police case continued for nearly two years. But the societal pressures forced a compromise. "The family decided to consider a settlement, as continuation of the case would spoil the life of their seven years. old niece." After the compromise everybody else has settled in their lives, but for Sharanjit, whose life has been spoiled by the unfortunate incidence. (Archna Matharui, HT)

Case : "Let me throw acid on him. That will be justice"

Rajwant Kaur, Ludhiana : Balkar Singh, a jealous, threw acid on Sandeep and Rajwant on April 1, 2007. While Sandeep (main target) succumbed on June 28, Rajwant suffered burns on her face and lost her eyesight. The main problem is financial (her father and sisters are daily wagers) as well as disturbed family–her parents have given up hope of a normal life for her. The police arrested Balkar, who is in jail facing trial for attempt to murder, but the case lingers. "This delay is rubbing salt on our wounds. We want justice," sobbed her mother. Rajwant burst out, "I'll tell you what justice is. I should be given permission to throw acid on Balkar's face. Only then he will realise what it's like to be a lifeless being, who just breathes, eats and drinks, and just exists, does not live." (Anshu Seth)

Case : "No clue who attacked me and why" :

Anu Bhola, Ropar : An unknown, masked man threw acid on her on January 27. Anu suffered burns on her face, neck, arms and back. The main problem is financial as well as disturbed family–her mother is the lone financial support as her father died four years ago. With a meagre monthly income of ₹ 2,500.

In reality, it was to support her mother that she had dropped out after BA-I and taken up a job as a helper in a hospital. "False promises of justice or medical aid were made but not a single person has helped.

The police used to come to her house initially but never made any breakthrough, blaming it a case of mistake identity. (Monica Sharma, HT)

Medical : Dr. Bholeshwar Prasad Mishra (Psychologist, DMCH, Ludhiana) : Acid attacks are "the most heinous" crime against women. "We need to inculcate tolerance in youngsters. Most attacks are by jilted lovers." Young victims go into deep depression. Due to high costs, not everyone can afford cosmetic surgery. Thus, counselling plays an important role in making them believe in themselves and took beyond the disfiguring."

Dr. Sanjeev Uppal (Cosmetic Surgeon, DMCH, Ludhiana) : "In most cases, the victims suffer 3rd degree burns, which even char bones.

Reconstruction is possible but complicated and expensive. It requires 8-12 surgeries and each costs around ₹ 50,000."

Police : Ishwar Singh (Police Commissioner, Ludhiana): Blamed the attackers 'criminal mentality'. "Their prime aim is to disfigure the faces of the victims, which leaves them scarred for life." On action he said, "We immediately register cases under the relevant sections, though I personally feel that these cases should be decided in fast-track Courts to expedite convictions. That will be an effective deterrent."

Government: Administration to aid of acid attack and rape victims :

Notification : The Chandigarh Administration

has notified a new scheme for providing financial assistance to acid attack victims, rape victims and to those who have suffered loss of life or injury in any criminal act.

Provision : The scheme would have a provision to provide maximum financial assistance of ₹ 5 lakh for loss of life, ₹ 3 lakh to victims who suffer loss of any body part resulting in permanent disability above 40 per cent, ₹ 3 lakh to those whose faces are disfigured in acid attacks and ₹ 2 lakh for rape victims.

Eligibility: Only those victims and their dependents would be eligible for grant of assistance who have not received any assistance for loss of life and injury under any other scheme of the central government or the administration.

Moreover, the scheme would also empower the State Legal Service Authority and the District Legal Services Authority, Chandigarh, to order for immediate first-aid facility or any other interim relief to the victim.

"The benefit will be made available free of cost and would not be adjustable against the amount of assistance. However, no request would be entertained after a period of three years. from the date of commission of crime." said MM Sabharwal, the Director Department of Public Relations, UT, Chandigarh.

AGONY OF SENIOR CITIZENS

Offence : In the past, elderly citizens usually lived with their children and grandchildren; currently this has changed, and the reality of today's children abandoning their parents is a common sight. It is agonising to think of the heartbreak elderly parents, who must have gone through when their children turned away and forsook them. With the gradual erosion of the joint family system, there have been many unfortunate cases of senior citizens facing lack of basic needs such as housing, as many instances of seniors being forcibly evicted from their own properties or being wrongfully denied unhindered access and enjoyment of their property by their children and/or relatives. Finally their hopes were crushed to the point that they breathed their last.

Factors : Children's point of views :

- That their working schedule hinders them sparing time for attending to elderly.
- That they have to look after the interests of their own wife and children.
- That they have to face the financial constraint, for looking after the elderly.
- That they have to take the side of their wives and children over their parents in family disputes.

Elderly's point of views :

- That they feel dejected in family disputes, when their children take the sides of their own wives and children, even while the elderly feel themselves on the right side.

That

- That they suffer financially after handing over property etc. to their children, and thereafter almost request/beg for money for their common needs.
- That they feel loneliness as their children don't spare time to chat/gossip etc with them esp. those living abroad

Penalty : Legal option :

- Under Maintenance and Welfare of Parents and Senior Citizens Act 2007 :

  Seeks to ensure that the elderly are not deprived of basics esp. housing. One of the main objects of the Act is to provide an institutional framework for the protection of life and property of elderly persons. There's a legal responsibility on children and relatives to maintain the senior citizen or elderly parent, in order to facilitate them with a normal life. This obligation applies to all Indian citizens, including those who lived abroad. Making matters worse is the fact that much of the elderly population doesn't know what they can do to procure sufficient support needed for themselves.

Section 23 of Act 2007: essentially enables an aggrieved senior citizen to reclaim ownership and/or possession of his/her property that had been earlier transferred by him/her. The term 'property' includes :

- both immovable and movable property.
- both ancestral and self-acquired property–both tangible and intangible property.

Eligibility: to seek relief under the Act, certain points to be kept in mind :

- senior citizens should have made the transfer of his/her property in favour of his/her offspring/ relative, post-enactment of Act 2007.
- Mode of transfer of the property can be gift, sale or long-term lease.
- senior citizen should have transferred his/her property to his/her offspring/relative, subject to the condition that the transferee would provide basic amenities and fulfil the essential needs of the senior citizen. For that, senior citizen may certainly include an explicit clause for setting out this condition in the gift/sale or lease deed.

Maintenance Tribunals : failure/refusal to comply: this clause in future by the transferee, the senior citizen may approach the special maintenance tribunals established under this Act, to seek legal relief. The Tribunal would first assess whether the requirements set out are fulfilled or not, in a particular case.

- In case requirements are fulfilled, then the transfer of property in question would be deemed as a transfer made by fraud, coercion or under undue influence due to the transferee's subsequent failure in fulfilling the clause of providing basic amenities to the senior citizen.

- An earlier transfer of property made by senior citizen in favour of his/her offspring/relative may also be declared void, in case the senior citizen desires so, and the transfer of property made by him/her shall be deemed to never have taken effect.
- In case senior citizen is unable to contact the maintenance tribunal, action may be taken on his/her behalf by voluntary organisations/ associations, or may be represented by a specially designated maintenance officer during the proceedings.
- Appeal : an appeal may be filed against the order of a maintenance tribunal, by an aggrieved senior citizen, within 60 days from the date of the order. To curb prolonged litigation, the appellate tribunal endeavours to decide the case within one month from the receipt of the senior citizen's appeal.

Non-legal option :

- Elderly parents and senior citizens, who don't like the legal option can reduce stress by concentrating on their hobbies and interests, like indulging in yoga, studying, playing cards or field games, music, visiting friends, watching movies, TV plays/movies. They can travel together or resume working life. The purpose is to make an effort to remain happy and stand firmly on their own feet, sparing their children venture into their own life.
- Senior citizen homes : Some elderly persons prefer/under compulsion, opt for senior citizen homes, where they live peacefully amongst other elderly persons, sharing their grief / joys, till the end of their lives. This may help in solving the problem of loneliness.

References: 1. R Krishan : The agony of loneliness. Sunset Boulevard, HT, February, 2014.

2. S Tyagi : Who will protect the rights of Senior Citizens, HT, March, 2014.

3. S Tyagi : Regret transferring your property ? Get it back, March, 1014.

ALCOHOL ABUSE

Offence : That alcohol abuse is a menace, particularly amongst the youth. Increase in underage drinking is a problem that needs to be curbed with participation of society. Law alone can't be enough to tackle the problem.

RP Upadhyaya, UT IGP, Chandigarh : That whatever help can be extended to women who are found drunk is always provided. They should also remain careful and refrain from being vulnerable.

A Gupta, Panchkula : That legally drinking age variable from State to State, and ranges from 18 to 25 yrs. while nobody cares about it. States cann't ban alcohol sale on account of revenue earned. Through surrogate advertising they are adopting tactics to lure vulnerable segment of customers, which is youth and women, keeping in their mind, profit as the only motive, Young boys and girls have given a new meaning to socialising. Taking advantage of this, pubs and night clubs keep on serving them till they are over-drunk and then uncontrolling their senses they create ruckus publically on roads or lie on roadside unattended, most often indulging in road accidents. Here arises the need for introspection.

S Negi, Panchkula : Drinking menace among teenagers–a blot on society :

Youths under the influence of alcohol wandering on streets in the night has become commonplace. "It's my life" attitude, not only deteriorating their health but also degrading society, culture and their lifestyle. The drunken teenagers often end up creating ruckus on roads by shouting, quarrelling or misbehaving with by-standers. The discotheque too indulges in marketing of alcohol by offering free drinks for girls and ladies, and on misbehaviour, they are left to fend for themselves on the roads by the bar-managers.

Penalty : Driving under the influence of alcohol (confirmed by alcoholmeter reading) is punishable in form of sentencing, fine or both. Also creating ruckus publically is punishable.

Remedy:
- Alcohol causes health issues.
- Drinking, the bane of society.
- Alcohol has potential to ruin a generation.
- Need for introspection.
- Need for counselling and awareness amongst teenagers.
- Need for awareness amongst youth about ill-effects of drinking.
- Need for pragmatic laws.
- Need for society's curb underage drinking.
- Need for saving youth from drinking menace.
- Need for banning teenage drinking.
- Need for parents acting as role models.
- Need for parents and teachers playing their part.
- Need for parents and Police saving youth from alcohol's blazing inferno.
- Need for collective effort.
- Availability of alcohol must be controlled.
- Prevention programmes must be encouraged.
- Matter of concern.
- Collective effort.

CHILD ABUSE/VULNERABLE CHILDHOOD/NO COUNTRY FOR CHILDREN

Preface : Child abuse is a catastrophe. It can only function as the end of one story and the beginning of another.

Issue : Safety of youngsters. As the Police struggle to crack the cases, incidents of kidnapping and subsequent murder of minor children, which have been coming to light at a regular interval, have put a question mark on the safety of children. In majority of cases parents of kidnapped children got ransom calls, and later on brutally murdered by the perpetrators for not fulfilling their unjustified/hefty demands.

Offence:

- Kidnapping for ransom of money, jealousy or revenge.
- Murders for jealousy or revenge.
- Kidnapping and murder for ransom of money, jealousy or revenge.
- Assault : physical torture or inflicting burn injuries.
- Monitory : making children blind or physically handicapped, for purpose of forced begging, and selling girls to brothels for illict purposes.
- High on drugs and liquor, prey on infant/young daugters.

Cases **Assault:**

- Roshan Lama (4) hospitalised with 20 per cent burns, inflicted by his neighbour by pouring a pot of boiling hot soup on his back. The reason–ongoing bickering with Roshan's father. (HTC)
- Raipur teen (12) committed suicide, after pinning blame on her allegedly cruel school teacher of frequently tormenting her. (HTC)
- Tripura girl, stripped and tied up for hrs.
- Patiala teen (3 months old), hospitalised with vaginal bleeding, inflicted by her alcoholic father by pushing a toothbrush into her vagina, just half-an-inch in size. The mother refused to lodge a police complaint to save the accused, and left the hospital, refusing even medication for the child.
- Patiala teen (9 months old), hospitalised with vaginal bleeding, inflicted by her drug-addict

father by pushing a carrot into her vagina, just half-an-inch in size. The mother refused to lodge a police complaint to save the accused, and left the hospital, refusing even medication for the child.

Sexual abuse : by close relatives, friends, or unknown persons luring teens :

- Bhilwara teen (14) raped by her adoptive father for more than three years.
- Kerala teen (13) raped by drug addict and alcoholic. dad, uncle and brother.

  The elder sister commited suicide after being similarly abused.
- Bangalore teen (4) allegedly sexually abused by her father's friend, has seventeen bite marks on her body. ((HTC)
- Patiala teen (5), hospitalised with vaginal tear inflicted by her alcoholic father by trying to penetrate her. The mother refused to lodge a police complaint against the accused in order to save the family honour, and the father is the only bread-winner.

Media:

- Kidnapping incidents are on the rise because of growing greed among people. Lust among people to get rich faster is leading to such crimes. People must go back to the old style of living and shun greed.

  (Dr. Inderjit Kaur, president, All India Pingalwara Charitable Society)
- In most kidnapping cases, personal enmity is involved. It is not a social problem but a law and order issue. Children are the easiest and most sensitive targets and incidents involving kidshurt parents emotionally the most. The police need to handle such cases in a better way.

  (Dr. BL Goel, director,Vidya Sagar Institute of Mental Health)
- Security of children needs to be ensued. To ensure safety of children, people should remain vigilant whether they are in the house or outside.

Police personnel need to be active and they should increase patrolling outside schools.

(A Mehra, principal, Spring Blossoms School)

- This is a serious law and order problem. The notorious persons have no fear of police and they commit such crimes. There is an urgent need that police instill fear among anti-social elements and then only such heinous crimes can be brought under control. (A Singh, investigator with PHRO)

Penalty : Punishable under various sections for the concerned offence/s e.g. for kidnapping, sexual abuse, under age labour, physical assault or murder etc.

DOMESTIC VIOLENCE:

Offence: - Domestic violence against women is a tradition of sorts. This system of relegating the women to the status of slaves has been evolved by men. Politicians are least bothered about the problems faced by these women in distress.

Penalty : Punishable under section 12 Rule 6, 13-B of the Domestic violence Act 2006 :

- That the Centre promulgated the Domestic Violence Act 2006, for protection of women facing regular domestic violence.
- That the act was enacted in October 2006.

Aims: - To protect the interest of the women from domestic violence by the husband or his family members (mother/father-in-law, sister/brother-in-law etc.)

Vox-populi: - That Rajit Tandi, a Dalit woman in Pithora, Chhatisgarh: walked out of her marriage, as her husband was an alcoholic and wife-beater, like most other in her village. She decided to realise women in her community speak up against domestic violence and turned activist. Today her women's groups put together plans to help sisters in distress (facing similar issues).

Held: - That use of words as nearly as possible here to in Section 12 and Rule 6 show that intention of

Legislature was not to reject complaint for not filing in the prescribed Form II.

Cases: - *Milan Kumar Singh* v/s *State of U.P.* (2009)(5) *RCR(Criminal)124 (Allahabad)*

Domestic Violence :

Suit:- That **c**omplaint lodged under the Act

Held:- That use of words as nearly as possible here to in Section 12 and Rule 6 show that intention of Legislature was not to reject complaint for not filing in the prescribed Form II.

Kulwinder Singh v/s State of Punjab (2009)(5) RCR(Criminal) 784(P&H)

Domestic Violence – Quashing of proceedings :

Held:- That on the intervention of the respectable, a compromise has been arrived at

- That a joint petition for mutual divorce under Section 13-B of the Hindu Marriage Act, has been filed.
- That where a compromise has been effected between the parties. Continuation of proceedings would be an abuse of the processing of Court.
- That impugned FIR and all subsequent proceedings quashed.

Reference : E Kaiser: Telling them not to tolerate domestic violence, HT March, 2014.

DOPING

Offence : An illegal practice of taking drugs, in order to improve one's performance in a sport.

Abuse : As per a NADA Official survey, cases of dopping are noticed in power sports such as athletics (in which abuse is more likely for a sprint (100 meter race) than a long distance (5000 meter) race, weightlifting, short put, javelin throw, hammer throw, wrestling, boxing, cycling, swimming and rowing etc.

Etiology : Lack of awareness amongst young sportspersons. Most of the time they indulge in doping as being advised by their trainer/or coach. Many of them (trainees) are clueless about the medical consequences.

Drugs : Stimulants : Methylhexaneamine

Steroids : Stanozolol, Nandrolone

Diuretics : Furosemide

THC : Marijuana.

All these drugs are prohibited by the World Anti-Dopping Agency.

S/S : Neurological : trembling of hands, impaired balance and coordination

Psychological : hallucinations, drowsiness, loss of concentration, insomnia, euphoria, restlessness, agitation, tenseness.

CVS: palpitation, tachycardia, arrhythmias, hypertension/hypotension

Skin: hyperthermia

GI Tract: anorexia, irritable bowl syndrome

Hepatic: dysfunction

Renal: dysfunction

Infirtility.

Laboratory : Blood and urine samples testing.

Complaint : Doping-related complaints received from the media and parents.

Penalty : First time offence can lead to a two-year ban from participation in the sport, while a second-time offence may lead to a life-time ban.

DOWRY PROHIBITION ACT

Offence : An Act to prohibit the giving or taking of dowry. That in this Act "Dowry" means any property or valuable security given or agreed to be given either directly or indirectly :

- by one party to a marriage to the other party to the marriage, or
- by the parent of either party to a marriage or by any other person, to either party to the marriage or to any other person, at or prior to or any time post-marriage, in connection with the marriage of the said parties, but does not include dower

or mahr in the case of persons to whom the Muslim Personal Law (SHARIAT) applies.

Comments: That the word "dowry" should be any property or valuable given or agreed to be given in connection with the marriage. The customary payments in connection with birth of child or other ceremonies are not involved within ambit of dowry.

- That any property given by parents of the bride need not in consideration of the marriage, it can even be in connection with the marriage and would constitute dowry.
- That poor people find it difficult to get their daughters married as they cannot afford the dowry, many a times prefer to sell their daughters as they do not have to give any dowry, plus they get money in return.
- That the skewed sex ratio in Haryana, Punjab and western UP has led to a flourishing trade in women, often bought for as little as Rs 5K.

Penalty:

- That any person demanding, directly or indirectly, from the parents or other relatives or guardians of a bride or bridegroom, as the case may be, any dowry, he/she shall be punishable with imprisonment for a term which shall not be less than six months, but which may extend to two years and with fine which may extend to ₹ 10K.
- That the court may consider adequate and special reasons to be mentioned in the judgment, awards a imprisonment for a term of less than six months.

Section : Under Section 498-A IPC and Section 3 of Dowry Prohibition Act.

Judgment: Satbir Singh v/s State of Punjab (2001) AIR 2828(SC) –

Held:

- That the word "dowry" should be any property or valuable given or agreed to be given in connection with the marriage. The customary payments in connection with birth of child or other ceremonies are not involved within ambit of dowry.

Judgment: **Rajeev v/s Ram Kishan Jaiswal (1994) Cri. LJ NOC 255 (ALL) –**

Held:
- That any property given by parents of the bride need not in consideration of the marriage, it can even be in connection with the marriage and would constitute dowry.

Judgment: **Prem Kumar v/s State of Rajasthan (2009) (1) RCR (Criminal) 850: (2009) (1) R.A.J. 524 (SC) : Section 2–Dowry death :**

Held:
- That to prove an offence under Section 304-B IPC, it is not required to be shown that there was agreement with regard to giving of dowry as mention under Section 304-B IPC.
- That offence under Section 304 B makes demand of dowry itself punishable.
- That when Section 304-B refers to "demand of dowry", it refers to the demand of property or valuable security as referred to in the definition of "dowry" under the Act.

Judgment: **K.U. Mariambi v/s P.A. Abdul Khader (2009) (5) RCR (Criminal) 889 (Karnataka) : Sections 3, 4 and 5 – IPC (1860), Sections 498-A and 506–Complaint case–Demand of dowry Investigation:**

Suit:
- That private complaint filed by the wife on the allegations of dowry harassment.
- That it is the duty of the Magistrate to record the statement of the complainant and her other witnesses to find out as to whether there is any prima facie case made out to proceed against the accused by investigating the same as per the provisions of Section 202 of the Cr.P.C.
- That complainant is to be allowed to prove her case.

Judgment: **K.U. Mariambi v/s P.A. Abdul Khader (2009) (5) RCR (Criminal) 889 (Karnataka) : Sections 3, 4 and 5 IPC (1860), Sections 498-A and 506–Demand of dowry :**

Suit:
- That Magistrate referred the matter to the police under Section 156(3) Cr.P.C.

- That accused agreed to repay amount before investigating officer and issued cheque.
- That Magistrate recorded a finding that amount paid to the husband was only a financial help to him and dismissed the complaint.

Held:
- That Order set aside
- That Magistrate was required to see only the prima facie case against the accused, not the evidence for conviction.
- That order passed by the Magistrate amounts to an order of acquittal by discarding the evidence of the complainant.
- That such a course is not permissible in law.
- That order of the Magistrate set aside.

Judgment: Kishangiri Mangalgiri Goswami v/s State of Gujarat (2009) (1) RCR (Criminal) 947 : (2009) (1) R.A.J. 675 (SC) : Section 3–Abetment of Suicide:

Suit:
- That accused (husband) sent letters to in-laws demanding ₹ 40,000-for purchase of house.
- That allegation of torture and harassment to wife demanding dowry.
- That defence evidence showed that accused had purchased valuable silver ornaments for the deceased and in his insurance policy, the deceased was shown to be his nominee.
- That accused himself had taken the deceased to the hospital.
- That letters were unsigned.

Held: That accused acquitted under Section 306 IPC, but convicted under Section 498-A IPC and Section 3 of Dowry Prohibition Act.

DRUG ABUSE

Offence : That drug abuse is a menace, particularly amongst the youth. Increase in underage drug abuse is a problem that needs to be curbed with participation of society. Law alone can't be enough to tackle the problem.

A Gupta, Panchkula : That legally drinking age variable from State to State, and ranges from 18 to 25 yrs. while nobody cares about it. States cann't ban alcohol sale on account of revenue earned. Through surrogate advertising they are adopting tactics to lure vulnerable segment of customers, which is youth and women, keeping in their mind, profit as the only motive. Young boys and girls have given a new meaning to socialising. Taking advantage of this, pubs and night clubs keep on serving them till they are over-drunk and then uncontrolling their senses they create ruckus publically on roads or lie on roadside unattended, most often indulging in road accidents. Here arises the need for introspection.

Drug abuse menace among teenagers–a blot on society :

- That youths under the influence of drugs, wandering on streets in the night has become commonplace. "It's my life" attitude, not only deteriorating their health but also degrading society, culture and their lifestyle. The drugged teenagers often end up creating ruckus on roads by shouting, quarrelling or misbehaving with by-standers. The discotheque too indulges in marketing of drugs by offering banned drugs, free drugs/drinks for girls and ladies, and on misbehaviour, they are left to fend for themselves on the roads by the bar-managers.

Drugs : That neither heroin nor smack, it's indigenous intoxicants ranging from capsules (Propoxyphene) to poppy husk, are most preferred by drug addicts (survey in drug addiction centres across Punjab State).

Priority : Addicts of capsules (Propoxyphene) top the chart with 29 per cent, followed by alcohol 14.9 per cent and bhukki (poppy husk) with 13.3 per cent, opium 4 per cent, cannabis 2 per cent, buprenorphine 2 per cent, brown sugar 2 per cent, inhalants (correction fluid) 1 per cent, cocaine 1 per cent, heroin 1 per cent, morphine 0.5 per cent and others 29 per cent.

Marital status : Majority of the patients were married (72.5 per cent), while 18.1 per cent were unmarried, about 9.4 per cent were separated/ divorced due to drug abuse.

Education : About 36.3 per cent were educated upto higher secondary, 18.43 per cent middle class, 13.53 per cent primary education, 11.8 per cent literate (can read and write), and 10.9 per cent illiterate. 5.6 per cent were graduate and 3.4 per cent postgraduates.

Penalty : That drug addiction is punishable in form of sentencing, fine or both. Also creating ruckus publically is punishable.

Remedy:

- Drug abuse causes health issues;
- Drugs abuse, the bane of society;
- Drug abuse has potential to ruin a generation;
- Need for introspection;
- Need for counselling and awareness amongst teenagers;
- Need for awareness amongst youth about ill-effects of drug abuse;
- Need for pragmatic laws;
- Need for society's curb underage drug abuse;
- Need for saving youth from drug abuse menace;
- Need for banning teenage drug abuse;
- Need for parents acting as role models;
- Need for parents and teachers playing their part;
- Need for parents and police saving youth from drug abuse's blazing inferno;
- Need for collective effort;
- Availability of drugs must be controlled;
- Prevention programmes must be encouraged;
- Matter of concern;
- Collective effort.

ENVIRONMENT POLLUTION (MEDICO-LEGAL ASPECT):

Offence : Is defined as an offence for contamination of environment (Air, water and land) with pollutants i.e. Bio-Medical Waste.

Etiology : Greenhouse gas emissions :

- Vehicular pollution
- Industrial pollution

Bio-Medical Waste generation (Schedule 1) :

- Human Wastes : body tissues, organs, wastes
- Animal Wastes : body tissues, organs, parts, carcasses, body fluid, blood and blood products, surgical waste, autopsy waste, animal house for research work, veterinary hospital, livestock farms, hatcheries.

Laboratory (Microbiology and Bio-technology) Waste:

- Specimens of micro-organisms
- Culture stocks
- Vaccines : live and attenuated

Sharp Waste :

- Needles, syringes, knives, scalpels, blades, glass, autoclaving/microwaving.

Discarded Medicines :

- Expired, contaminated and discarded medicines.

Solid Waste :

- Discarded tubes, catheters, intravenous sets, urine packs.

Liquid Waste :

- Disinfectants : waste from laboratory, OT, cleaning, washing.

Soiled Waste :

- Soiled cotton, dressings, plaster casts, linens, beddings, contaminated soiled packaging materials.

Chemical Waste :

- Biological chemicals, disinfectants, insecticides.

Risk factors:

- Cutting down trees and forests

- Mismanagement of Biological Waste Disposal.

Effects : Global Warming (Raising of Earth's temperature)

BMW : Colour Coding and Type of Container for BMW Disposal (Table 6-1: Scedule 2)

Disposal : Colour coding and type of Container for BMW Disposal (Table 6-1) :

TABLE 6.1: Schedule 2 (Colour Coding and Type of Container for BMW Disposal

Colour	***Yellow***	***Red***	***Blue/White***	***Black***
Container	Plastic Bag	Plastic Bag	Plastic Bag	**Plastic Bag**
Waste	Human, Animal	Soiled, Microbiology, Biotechnology	Soiled, Sharp, Solid	**Discarded medicines, Cytotoxic drugs Incineration ash**
Treatment Options	Incineration/ Deep burial	Autoclave/ Microwave/ Chemical Destruction/ Shredding	Autoclave/ Microwave/ Chemical/	**Disposal in secured landfill**

(*Source* : ENVIS-CENTRE, Department of Environment, Chandigarh, India).

EUTHANASIA (MERCY KILLING)

Definition : Is defined as an act or practice of putting painless death to people, who are very sick, especially in cases of incurable suffering, or very old, in order to stop them from suffering (the intentional killing by act or omission of a dependant human being for his/or her alleged benefit. (The key word here is "intentional").

Note: If death is not intended, it is not an act of euthanasia.

Classification :

- Active Euthanasia : Intentionally causing a person's death by performing an action such as by giving a lethal injection.

  Example : A lethal injection given to a patient with a terminal disease.

  Active euthanasia declared illegal by the Supreme Court of India, while allowing passive euthanasia vide SC Bench's verdict on 7th March 2011.

  Active euthanasia is permitted in countries such as Netherlands, Belgium and Switzerland.

- Passive Euthanasia : Intentionally causing death by withholding medical care, food and water of terminally ill patients.

  Example : Removing the Heart-Lung machine (Ventilator) from a patient in coma. The Supreme Court of India allows passive euthanasia.

  Passive euthanasia is allowed in :

  USA : in the States of Oregon, Montana and Washington.

- Voluntary euthanasia: When the person who is killed has requested to be killed.
- Non-voluntary: When the person who is killed made no request and gave no consent.
- Involuntary euthanasia: When the person who is killed made an expressed wish to the contrary.
- Assisted suicide: Someone provides an individual with the information, guidance, and means to take his or her own life with the intention that they will be used for this purpose. When it is a doctor who helps another person to kill themselves it is called "physician assisted suicide."

What Euthanasia is NOT: There is no euthanasia unless the death is intentionally caused by what was done or not done. Thus, some medical actions that are often labeled "passive euthanasia" are no form of euthanasia, since the intention to take life is lacking. These acts include not commencing treatment that would not provide a benefit to the patient, withdrawing treatment that has been shown to be ineffective, too burdensome or is unwanted, and the giving of high doses of pain-killers that may endanger life, when they have been shown to be necessary.

All those are part of good medical practice, endorsed by law, when they are properly carried out.

Factors Favouring Euthanasia :

Factors: - Unbearable pain

- Right to commit suicide
- Forced to stay alive.

Unbearable pain :

- May be the major argument in favour of euthanasia.
- Euthanasia advocates stress the cases of unbearable pain as the top criterias for euthanasia.
- Drawback : people are driven into a painless drugged (undignified) state and for that reason may require euthanasia (on demand).

Solution:
- Almost all types of pain can be eliminated fully and in unrelieved cases can be reduced significantly by providing adequate treatment and :
- By upgrading medical knowledge to healthcare professionals on these vital issues,
- By enlarging access to healthcare,
- By making aware patients about their consumer rights (to pain relief),
- By referring the patient to a specialist in pain management, for relief of pain as well as to alleviate emotional suffering and depression that may accompany pain.

Right to commit suicide factor :

- Euthanasia is not about the right to die. It's about the right to kill.
- Euthanasia is not about giving rights to the person who dies but, instead, is about changing the law and public policy to support the doctors, relatives and others, to end another person's life, directly and intentionally.
- People do have the power to commit suicide. Suicide and attempted suicide are not criminalised. Suicide is a tragic, individual act.
- Euthanasia is not about a private act. It's about letting one person facilitate the death of another. That is a matter of very public concern since it

can lead to tremendous abuse, exploitation and erosion of care for the most vulnerable people among us.

- Supreme Court of India on 7th March, 2011, recommended to the Parliament to consider decriminalising attempt to suicide, saying the provision had become anachronistic and the time has come when Section 309 IPC (attempt to commit suicide) should be deleted by the Parliament.
- US Supreme Court Backs Oregon Assisted Suicide Law (2006) :
- Supreme Court Holds Hearing on Assisted Suicide Dispute :
- Gonzales v/s Oregon (2005)
- Washington v/s Glucksberg Supreme Court Ruling (1997)
- Vacco v/s Quill Supreme Court Ruling (1997)

Forced to stay alive factor :

- That neither the law nor medical ethics permit force to keep a person alive against his/her wishes.
- That postponing death by any available means is violation of law and being cruel and inhumane.
- That at certain stage, continuing treatment on compassionate base, may be considered medically unwise.

Solution : That is the deciding time when all efforts should be made :

- To make the patient's remaining time comfortable, by alleviating pain and other discomforts (emotional suffering and depression).

ARGUMENTS FAVOURING EUTHANASIA:

Legal Fraternity :

- **The Supreme Court of India: "Active euthanasia declared illegal by the Supreme Court of India, while allowing passive euthanasia vide SC Bench's verdict on 7th**

March 2011. The SC made it clear that the guidelines for passive euthanasia (withholding medical treatment for terminally ill patients) would be in force until Parliament enacts a proper law."

- **Delhi High Court Judge RS Sodhi (Retd)** : "India allows capital punishment and the State is allowed to take one's life. Then why an individual who suffers extensively should not be allowed to say I have had enough?"
- **Delhi High Court Judge JD Kapoor (Retd)** : "Expressed similar views".
- **Sr. SC lawyer KTS Tulsi** : "The SC ruling with in-built safeguards has made the right to live more meaningful."

Legal expert Subash Kashyap : "It is good that the Apex Court has laid down certain guidelines and each plea for mercy killing will be decided on a case-by-case basis. If there was a general rule, there would have been misuse.

Legal Panel: Right to die :

Justice PV Reddi, The Law Commission's Chairman :

In April 2011, the Govt. Sought the Law Commission's views after the Supreme Court (SC) legalised passive euthanasia in the Shanbaug case and said its verdict will be the Law of the land until Parliament enacted a Law on the issue.

The Law Commission has sent a draft "Medical Treatment of terminally-ill patients (Protection of Patients and Medical Practitioners) Bill" to the Government, to initiate measures to enact a comprehensive law on passive euthanasia, subject to certain safeguards. "A competent adult patient has the right to insist that there should be no invasive medical treatment by way of artificial life-sustaining measures/treatment and such a patient, provided that the doctor is satisfied that the patient has taken an 'informed decision' based on free exercise of his/her will," the panel said. Should the patient not be in a position to take healthcare decisions due to an irreversible coma or is in a persistent vegetative state, the doctor's or relatives' decision to withhold or withdraw medical treatment is not final, the report stated.

But, active euthanasia remains a crime under Section 303 (murder) or 304 (culpable homicide not amounting to murder) of the Indian Penal Code (IPC), along with physician-assisted suicide under Section 306 IPC (abetment to suicide).

Medical fraternity: The divide is sharp. There are many experienced doctors who insist that:

'Quality' is more important than 'right to life' esp. In the case of Aruna Shanbaug, who has been living in a permanent vegetative state for the last 38 years.

Right to Die Organisations:

Amicus Curiae (Friend of the Court):

- "Passive euthanasia should be allowed. Right to life does not include right to live in a vegetative state."
- "End of violation of one's right to live with dignity."

Euthanasia Squads: Netherlands Evereniging Vooreen Vrijwillig Levenseinde (NVVE) "Right To Die":

London: Euthanasia squads offer death by delivery: A controversial mobile euthanasia programme has been launched in the Netherlands, sending specialised teams door-to-door to help patients end their lives, reports the Independent. The project which has provoked sharp criticism from doctors, is the brainchild of the Dutch's largely donor-funded pro-mercy killing group "Right to Die" NL (NVVE in Dutch). It follows the Government's 2002 decision to legalise euthanasia, making the Netherlands the first Country in the world to do so. Right to Die-NL, said it had received seventy phone calls from potential assisted suicide patients since the scheme was announced in early February, 2012. It said that its six tems expected to receive around 1,000 requests each year.

The organisation stressed that its mobile units were comprised of doctors and nurses, specially trained in performing assisted suicide at its clinic. It said the procedure involved injecting the patient with a sleep inducing drug and then with barbiturates to stop heart and lung function, according to the newspaper. (*Source* : ANS) Categories : NEWS Tags: Euthanasia Squads, NVVE, Right to Die.

Right to Die Families:

- A**IIMS data** : "Families of 10 out of 200 patients in a vegetative state have asked for active euthanasia. Many families, in fact, have refused to take such patients back."

Vox Populi:

- **Actor Hrithik Roshan** : "Euthanasia must be allowed in cases that merit it. But a strong system needs to be set in place." The actor recently played the role of a paraplegic magician Ethen, whose plea for euthanasia, only to be turned down by the court.

FACTORS OPPOSING EUTHANASIA:

Factors:

- Terminally ill factor
- Cost factor
- Involuntary factor
- Human life factor

Terminally ill factor:

The definition of "terminal" is controversial in case of Euthanasia i.e. :

- That a terminal illness may be any disorder, restricting life even for a day.
- That a terminal condition may be any disorder, resulting in death within a "relatively short time."

- That a terminal may be any disorder, resulting in death within a couple of months.
- That a terminally ill patient may not die for months/years, from the diagnosed disorder.
- That to simplify, terminal illness may be replaced with such titles as desperately ill, hopelessly ill, incurably ill, hopeless condition," or useless life.
- That assisted suicide may be a suicidal impulse resulting from terminal illness, unbearable pain, emotional stress or depression.

Cost factor- That recently greater emphasis has been placed on healthcare providers to curtail costs, thereby projecting euthanasia a means of cost containment, as many people have no medical insurance coverage.

- That the poor and minorities generally lack access to available pain control.
- That doctors are being offered cash incentives by the managed-care facilities for not providing required treatment to terminally ill patients.
- That by legalising euthanasia, doctors may be financially sound, by forcing/counselling, a seriously ill or disabled person, to choose to die rather than receive a long-term medical care.
- That the government may also have a cost consideration i.e. govt. may cut back on paying for medical care and treatment, thereby consider for choosing euthanasia.

Examples :

- That the State of Oregon announced plans to cut back on healthcare coverage for poor state residents.
- That in Canada, hospital stays are being shortened while, at the same time, funds have not been made available for home care for the sick and elderly.
- That Registered nurses are being replaced with less expensive Practical nurses.

- That patients are forced to endure long waits for many types of needed surgery.

Involuntary factor:

- That depressed/or dependant persons may be pressurised by financial, emotional and psychological factors to opt for euthanasia or assisted suicide, rather than to receive medical care.
- That persons favouring euthanasia, insist that voluntary euthanasia may not result in involuntary euthanasia.

Human life factor :

For Euthanasia :

- That it is better for terminally ill, depressed, emotionally stressed and financially unsound persons to opt for voluntary euthanasia, instead of guilty feeling of burden on dependants (cost and care factors).

Against Euthanasia :

- That with euthanasia no one's life is being saved - life is only taken.
- That euthanasia has been considered a crime since ages.
- That it is better help those suffering from unbearable pain, depression, emotional stress and financial crisis, by all available means, instead of pressurising them to opt for horrible/ disgusting euthanasia.

Vox Populi: - That "Nazi legislation and Hitler's ideas are reemerging in Europe via Dutch euthanasia laws and the debate on how to kill ill children."

Carlo Giovanardi. Italian Parliamentary Affairs Minister, March 2006

- That "Experience in The Netherlands, where there has been relatively little effort to improve pain and symptom treatment, suggests that legalisation of physician-assisted suicide might weaken society's resolve to expand services and resources aimed at caring for the dying patient."

Foley, 1995; Hendin, 1994 ..... from "Treatment of Pain at the End of life: A Position Statement from The American Pain Society."

- That "I can understand at the individual level that in some cases you wish it was all over with, but the problem is as a society you have to chose what's going to be your norm."... "We have this idea that what happens to me is nobody's business. The problem with euthanasia is it requires another person to do it, and it requires a complicit society to authorise it."

  Margaret Somerville, founding director of the McGill Centre for Medicine, Ethics and Law

- That "physician-assisted suicide, if it became widespread, could become a profit-enhancing tool for big HMOs." "...drugs used in assisted suicide cost only $ 40, but that it could take $ 40,000 to treat a patient properly so that they don't want the "choice" of assisted suicide. Wesley J. Smith, Sr. Fellow at the Discovery institute.

ARGUMENTS OPPOSING EUTHANASIA:

Legal Fraternity :

- **The Supreme Court of India : "is not in favour of active euthanasia that involves the use of lethal substances to end a patient's life."**
- SC lawyer Anand Grover : "Courts cannot decide such a sensitive issue. As per the Constitution, no one can take away anyone's life without a procedure established by law. It means there has to be a proper statute on the issue..."
- Advocate Pinky Anand : "I cannot countenance a position where one is allowed to end one's life. It is an area which must be left alone. Courts cannot take on such a difficult task..."

Legislators : **"Euthanasia can't be allowed in our country as it is still backward and emotional. It would**

lead to misuse" "Understandably, for the legislators, euthanasia, like life itself, is a grey area with too many conflicting views e.g. "The view of religious leaders".

Medical Fraternity :

Most of doctors, who publically, swear by the Hippocratic Oath :

"I will give no deadly medicine to anyone if asked, nor suggest any such counsel", oppose euthanasia.

Organisations :

- **"No one had the right to take one's life without a proper law on euthanasia in the country."**

Reference:

1. Sinha, B: Passive euthanasia allowed. Hindustan Times, March 08, 2011.
2. Prakash, S: 'DECRIMINALISE SUICIDE BIDS`. Hindustan Times, March 08, 2011.
3. Prakash, S: Legislators dither, apex court steps in. Hindustan Times, March 08, 2011.
4. Nair, HV: Legal fraternity divide on passive euthanasia. Hindustan Times, March 08.

EVE-TEASING

Offence : The menace of eve-teasing has reached to an alarming level. What to talk about public places, the offenders even reach the girls' house in order to physically harm the family. Whether she confronts the eve teaser or complains to the police, the hapless female finds herself at cross-roads and always at the receiving end.

Incidence : Such is the extent of sexual harassment, that even in a modern and educated society, the numbers only underline an ugly reality. For this campaign, institutional changes to ensure a safer place are to be major aim.

- That in the current era, more girls are working and move freely, yet majority of them face sexual harassment, and only minority find their workplace safe.

- That sexual harassment is rising in spite of new laws and public outrage.
- That girls are being sexually harassed in the public domain, yet this misbehaviour is not under public scrutiny.

Risk factors:- To use deserted roads, esp. late at night.

- To walk alone and not in groups.
- To ignore indescent remarks by the boys, as the girls prefer to suffer in silence. This way they embolden the eve-teasers and thereby encourage them to strike again.
- To avoid reporting to police about the eve-teasing.
- Mushrooming PG business.
- Discotheque culture.
- Vulnerable areas : Most of these incidents take place outside schools, colleges, university campuses and premises for private tutorials. Rehri markets (overcrowded) too are prone to eve-teasing incidents, with miscreants passing obscene remarks and even touching/molesting girls and young women in busy markets. Festivals and shopping fairs also witness eve-teasing incidents.

Eve-teasers profile :

Most eve-teasers are outsider students from neighbouring areas. The miscreants mostly zip around in their cars/motorbikes and pass lewd remarks at passing girls/women. In certain cases, colony residents too indulge in harassing girls/ women esp. Moving at late night hours. Many men still view women as inferior to them and cannot tolerate any reactions from them, as it hurts their male ego and the miscreants end up assaulting the victims. Senior citizens too indulge in eve-teasing. Cops too found guilty of act. Girls often fear backlash.

Grouse:

- Harassment of family post-complaint
- Fear of character assassination.

- Indecent cops
- Senior citizens teasing girls
- Financial status should not hinder action.

Penalty : Punishable under Section 294 of IPC, if they sing, recite or utter any obscene song or word in or near any public place to the annoyance of others.

Misuse : Male students voiced their apprehension that law could be misused, which in reality is very remote, as no sane girl/woman would like to involve herself unnecessarily and be under stress by lodging a false complaint. Also the case can't be registered without proper verification of the complaint.

Police : Fighting the menace of eve-teasing :

SSP, during an interaction with college students on eve-teasing, motivated the girls to become strong – physically and psychologically to combat the problem.

He sought cooperation and alertness from girls to minimise the incidence of crime against women and exorted them to fight for their right to dignified existence and fear-free atmosphere. He ensured that the offender would be dully punished, irrespective of his social or political stature. About the right reaction to a situation, he advised : Use intuition, couple it with intelligence and inform the police accordingly.

Q. One of the male students asked the SSP on what their reaction should be if girls pass comments ?

Ans. Responding to the question in a lighter way, the SSP said the boy should consider himself lucky if he received comments from a girl. (Naunihal Singh, SSP UT, Chandigarh)

Case: October 16: Police have arrested 3 miscreants, on the charge of eve-teasing and intimidation.

Case: Police have arrested 20 miscreants, incld. a home guard volunteer, on charge of eve-teasing from different parts of Chandigarh, in the past more than a week, while the PCR received more than 30 calls from victims of eve-teasing during this period.

Case: August 10: Satpal, a resident of Dadumajra colony, booked for eve-teasing and outraging modesty of a girl at dividing road of Sectors 37 and 38.

Case : August 23: Shekhar, a resident of Maloya village, booked for making obscene gestures and singing vulgar songs in front of a woman.

Case : September 16: Manoj Kumar and Ajay, residents of Vikas Nagar, Mauli Jagran, were arrested from Sector 17 Inter-state bus stand, for eve-teasing.

Case : September 30: Ranjit Singh, a resident of Sector 22, working as a driver, was arrested under Section 294 of IPC, after being spotted passing obscene remarks at girls near the Tribune roundabout by a police control room vehicle (PCR) deployed in the area.

Vox populi: While many feel the need for a stringent law to punish eve-teasers, most say police presence should be increased around educational institutions and other vulnerable points–Cops need to step up vigil.

Supportive of Police efforts :

* Principal Dr. Puneet Bedi was supportive of the efforts being made by the authorities to ensure safety of women. She said such endeavours enthuse in the public the spirit of oneness against crime, thereby making society fraternal,stronger and more goal-oriented.

(Dr. P Bedi, Chandigarh)

* Take strict action against eve-teasers :

The incidents of all types of crimes against women are on the increase because of the fast diminishing fear of law and police among the youths.

The police officials should hold periodical interaction with the girls, provide necessary protection and security to them and increase patrolling at strategic points. The cops should also take strict action against eve-teasers to inspire confidence among the girls. The police top-brass should introspect as to what has gone wrong in policing, resulting into spurt in crimes and decreasing fear of law. (PC Sanghi, Chandigarh)

* Introduce helpline for women to report eve-teasing:

  It is high time that the menace of eve-teasing is curbed. The police and local administration need to pull up their socks and take measures to check this heinous crime against women. Apart from increasing security near schools, college and bus stops, the police should introduce a quick response helpline for women so that they can promptly report such incidents. Undoubtedly, this will give a feeling of security and self-defence to girls, and encourage them to report such incidents. In addition to this, there is a need to ensure that eve-teasers are dealt with an iron hand, so **that they feel ashamed of their doing** and do not think about repeating their disgraceful act. (MB Dhamrait, Kharar)

* Girls' dressing sense provokes boys:

  One cannot blame the boys only. They are provoked because of girls' modern dressing sense. (B Bitu, Chandigarh)

* Society should support police initiative:

  Apart from encouraging women to come forward to report such incidents to the police, orientation programme for boys' colleges are also required to motivate them to desist from the evil and to make aware of consequences (registration of an FIR is sufficient to ruine one's carrier).. (SL Soni, Chandigarh).

* Need for social change :

  Social change is taking place fast in some spheres while traditional practices continue to be part of multifaceted persona. There have been living-in relationships, women are heading offices and industries, single women are adopting children, men take pride in looking after household activities like cooking and decorating their homes etc., best friends are no longer of the same gender, groups of boys and girls are travelling out together. Simultaneously, Indian culture is booming e.g. Karva Chauth richly drapes the markets and women, Raksha Bandhan load the brothers' wrists and honour, Tikka (Bhai Dooj) marks the foreheads with responsibility, and the bride ushers in her lavish Sangeet with 'Sheela ki Jawani'. Add to this mix the migrants, industrial workers and traditionalists who enjoy the item number, but maintain that female respectability is bound to her conduct and distance from men. What is a right in one setting becomes an invitation in another. But, neither the modernity nor the traditional challenges, the growing market for sexuality, the expression of power or the overriding individual needs collective responsibility. (Dr Rainuka Dagar, Chandigarh).

Remedy : Do's and Don'ts for Girls :

- Avoid use of deserted roads, easp. late at night.
- Avoid walking alone and walk groups, outside schools/colleges.
- Avoid ignoring indescent remarks by the boys, and prefer not to suffer in silence. This way do not embolden the eve-teasers and thereby encourage them to strike again.
- Girls must speak up and report to the police about eve-teasers' vehicle registration number.
- Girls to wear helmets for more safety.
- Avoid taking lift while walking alone.
- Dress up properly, in order to avoid lewd remarks from offenders with low thinking personality.

Countering the menace (Young women more assertive) :

- That the 1st move to secure women is the nature and extent of abuse must be understood and people sensitised that it is not just the brutal or the physical that is abuse, but its many forms included indecent behaviour, leering, kerb crawling, stalking. All of these are a violation, and should be unacceptable to any male or female.
- That reaction continues to remain focussed on brutalities of rape and molestation, while condoning abrasive, intrusive misconduct and even legitimising offensive violation as part of a natural sexuality.
- That if the culture of silence continues, accepting abuse of others and blaming modernity, media and victims themselves, an epidemic awaits.
- That Desperate situations demand desperate measures. So would it seem going by the rising number of eve-teasing incidents, and the way some of the city girls are countering the menace. Gone are the days when they would ignore obscene remarks or bear the insult quietly. The gen-next women like late-night partying, are well equipped to have their following ways:
- Some girls react to eve-teasing by raising voice or even using abusive language against miscreants.
- Carry products e.g. chilli powder, pepper spray, Swiss knives, needles, steel batons (short thin stick) or deodorants. These are some of the 'weapons' that are gaining popularity amongst the college-going girls.
- Carry a 'stungun', a weapon that momentarily disables a person with an electric shock.
- Martial art : gaining popularity amongst the teenagers. In fact, martial art to be made a compulsory subject for school and college girls and for all working girls, as one of the best safety measure.

Do's and Don'ts for Boys :

- Avoid eve-teasing as the punishment (registration of an FIR is sufficient to ruine one's carrier.
- Be a responsible citizen and behave like a Gentleman (one who behaves proper in presence of women). Always think the victim girl/woman to be someone's daughter or sister like yours own.

Stop the offenders from eve-teasing, by adopting:

- To persuading them not to indulge in this indescent behaviour.
- To note down the registration number of the offender's vehicle and report to the police for immediate action.
- To support the victim rather than the offenders.
- To accompany the girl walking alone at odd hrs. In a descent manner, to her destination.

HOMICIDE, ABORTION AND RELATED OFFENCES :

INDIA :

Section : 302 IPC: culpable homicide
304 IPC: case of murder
306 IPC: abetement to suicide
307 IPC: attempt to murder
308: attempt to commit culpable homicide

Section : 302 IPC: culpable homicide

Offence : Is defined as conduct that causes deliberately and illegally the death of a person, or an unborn child with which a female has been pregnant for more than 24 weeks (24/52), and rape and murder of a girl/woman.

Penalty:
- sentenced to life term with fine in majority of cases.
- sentenced to death in rarest of rare cases.

Section : 304 IPC.

Offence : Is defined as conduct that causes deliberately and illegally the death of a person, or an unborn child with which a female has been pregnant for more than 24 weeks (24/52), and rape and murder of a girl/woman.

Penalty: - sentenced to life term with fine in majority of cases.
- sentenced to death in rarest of rare cases.

Section : 304-A IPC:
Offence :
Penalty : - sentenced to term with fine.

Section : 306 IPC:
Offence : abetement to suicide.
Penalty : - sentenced to term with fine.

Section : 307 IPC:
Offence : attempt to murder.
Penalty : sentenced to term with fine.

Section : 308 IPC.
Offence : attempt to commit culpable homicide.
Penalty : sentenced to term with fine.

USA :

Offence : Homicide (murder).

ATRICLE 125

Section : 125.00 : Homicide - definition
Section : 125.05 : Homicide, abortion and related offenses–definitions of terms
Section : 125.10 : Criminally negligent homicide
Section : 125.11 : Aggravated criminally negligent homicide
Section : 125.12 : Vehicular manslaughter
Section : 125.13 : Vehicular Manslaughter in the 1st degree
Section : 125.14 : Aggravated vehicular homicide
Section : 125.15 : Manslaughter in the 2nd degree
Section : 125.20 : Manslaughter in the 1st degree
Section : 125.21 : Aggravated manslaughter in the 2nd degree
Section : 125.22 : Aggravated manslaughter in the 1st degree
Section : 125.25 : Murder in the 2nd degree
Section : 125.26 : Aggravated murder
Section : 125.27 : Murder in the 1st degree

Section : 125.40 : Abortion in the 2nd degree

Section : 125.45 : Abortion in the 1st degree

Section : 125.50 : Self-abortion in the 2nd degree

Section : 125.55 : Self-abortion in the 1st degree

Section : 125.60 : Issuing abortional articles

Section : 125.00 : Homicide

Offence : Is defined as conduct that causes the death of a person, or an unborn child with which a female has been pregnant for more than 24 weeks (24/52) under circumstances constituting murder :

- manslaughter in the 1st degree
- manslaughter in the 2nd degree
- criminally negligent homicide, abortion in the 1st degree or
- self-abortion in the 1st degree.

Section : 125.05 : Abortional Act :

Offence : Abortional Act : Is defined as an act committed upon or with respect to a female, whether by herself or by another person, whether she is pregnant or not, whether directly upon her body or by administration, taking or prescription of drugs or by any other manner, with intention to cause a miscarriage of such female.

Justifiable Abortional Act : Abortional Act is justifiable when committed upon a female with her consent by a Registered Medical Practitioner, acting : (a) under a reasonable belief that such is necessary to preserve her life, or (b) within twenty four wks. from the commencement of her pregnancy.

Section : 125.10 : Criminally Negligent Homicide :

Offence : Criminally Negligent Homicide : Is defined as a person guilty of criminally negligent homicide when, with criminal negligence, he/she causes the death of another person. Criminally Negligent Homicide is a class 'E' felony.

Section : 125.11: Aggravated Criminally Negligent Homicide :

Offence : Aggravated Criminally Negligent Homicide: Is defined as a person guilty of aggravated criminally negligent homicide when, with criminal negligence, he/she causes the death of a police officer/or peace officer. Aggravated Criminally Negligent Homicide is a class 'C' felony.

Section : 125.12 : Vehicular Manslaughter in the 2nd degree.

Offence : Vehicular Manslaughter in the 2nd degree : Is defined as a person guilty of vehicular manslaughter in the 2nd degree when he/she :

- commits the crime of criminally negligent homicide as per Section 125.10, and either.
- causes death of such other person by operation of a vehicle in violation of subdivision 2, 3 or 4 of Section 1192 of the vehicle and traffic law or by operation of a vehicle or public vehicle, in violation of paragraph (b), (c), (d) or (e) of subdivision 2 of Section 49 of the Navigation law, or –causes death of such other person by operation of a motor vehicle with a gross vehicle weight rating of more than 18K pounds which contains inflammable gas, radioactive materials or explosives in violation of subdivision 1 of Section 1192 of the vehicle and traffic law, and such inflammable gas, radioactive materials or explosives is the cause of death, by operation of a snowmobile in violation of paragraph (b), (c) or (d) of subdivision 1 of Section 25.24 of the parks, recreation and historic preservation law or by operation of all terrain vehicle as per paragraph (a) of subdivision 1 of Section 2281 of the vehicle and traffic law in violation of subdivision 2, 3 or 4 of Section1192 of the vehicle and traffic law.

Vehicular manslaughter in the 2nd degree is a class 'D' felony.

Section : 125.13:Vehicular manslaughter in the 1st degree:

Offence : Vehicular Manslaughter in the 1st degree : Is

defined as a person guilty of vehicular manslaughter in the 1st degree when he/she :

- commits the crime of vehicular manslaughter in the 2nd degree as per Section 125.12, and commits such crime while knowing or having reason to know that:

(a) his/her license or his/her privilege of operating a motor vehicle in another State or his/her privilege of obtaining a licence to operate a motor vehicle in another state is suspended or revoked and such suspension or revocation is based upon a conviction in such other State for an offense which would, if committed in that State, constitute a violation of any of the provisions of Section 1192 of the vehicle and traffic law, or

(b) his/her license or his/her privilege of operating a motor vehicle in the State or his/her privilege of obtaining a license issued by the commissioner of motor vehicles is suspended or revoked and such suspension or revocation is based upon either a refusal to submit to a chemical test pursuant to Section 1194 of the vehicle and traffic law or following a conviction for a violation of any of the provicions of Section 1192 of the vehicle and traffic law.

Vehicular manslaughter in the 1st degree is a class 'C' felony, either:

- causes death of such other person by operation of a vehicle in violation of subdivision 2, 3 or 4 of Section 1192 of the vehicle and traffic law or by operation of a vehicle or public vehicle, in violation of paragraph (b), (c), (d) or (e) of subdivision 2 of Section 49 of the Navigation law, or
- causes death of such other person by operation of a motor vehicle with a gross vehicle weight rating of more than 18K pounds which contains inflammable gas, radioactive materials or explosives in violation of subdivision 1 of Section

1192 of the vehicle and traffic law, and such inflammable gas, radioactive materials or explosives is the cause of death, by operation of a snowmobile in violation of paragraph (b), (c) or (d) of subdivision 1 of Section 25.24 of the parks, recreation and historic preservation law or by operation of all terrain vehicle as per paragraph (a) of subdivision 1 of Section 2281 of the vehicle and traffic law in violation of subdivision 2, 3 or 4 of Section 1192 of the vehicle and traffic law.

Vehicular manslaughter in the 2nd degree is a class 'D' felony.

Section : 125.14 : Aggravated vehicular homicide :

Offence : Aggravated vehicular homicide is defined as a person guilty of aggravated vehicular homicide when he/she engages in reckless driving as per Section 1212 of the vehicle and traffic law, and commits the crime manslaughter in the 2nd degree as per Section 125.12 of Article125, and either:

- commits such crimes while operating a motor vehicle while such person has .18 of 1 per cent or more by weight of alcohol in such person's blood as per chemical analysis of such person's blood, breath, urine or saliva made pursuant to the provisions of Section 1194 of the vehicle and traffic law.
- commits such crime while knowing or having reason to know that:

(a) his/her license or his/her privilege of operating a motor vehicle in another State or his/her privilege of obtaining a license to operate a motor vehicle in another state is suspended or revoked and such suspension or revocation is based upon a conviction in such other State for an offense which would, if committed in that State, constitute a violation of any of the provisions of Section 1192 of the vehicle and traffic law, or

(b) his/her license or his/her privilege of operating a motor vehicle in the State or his/her privilege of obtaining a licence issued by the commissioner of motor vehicles is suspended or revoked and such suspension or revocation is based upon either a refusal to submit to a chemical test pursuant to Section 1194 of the vehicle and traffic law or following a conviction for a violation of any of the provisions of Section 1192 of the vehicle and traffic law.

- has previously been convicted of violating any of the provisions of Section1192 of the vehicle and traffic law within the preceding 10 yrs., provided that, for the purposes of this subdivision, a conviction in any other State or jurisdiction for an offence which, if committed in that State, would constitute a violation of Section 1192 of the vehicle and traffic law, shall be treated as a violation of that law.
- causes the death of more than one other person.
- causes the death of one person and the serious physical injury of at least one other person, or
- has previously been convicted of violating any provision of Article 125 or Article 120 of that title involving the operation of a motor vehicle, or was convicted in any other State or jurisdiction of an offense involving the operation of a motor vehicle which, if committed in that State, would constitute a violation of Article 125 or Article 120 of that title. If it is established that the person operating such motor vehicle caused such death or deaths while unlawfully intoxicated or impaired by the use of alcohol or a drug, or by the combined influence of drugs or of alcohol and any drug or drugs, then there shall be a rebuttable presumption that, as a result of such intoxication or impairment by the use of alcohol or a drug, or by the combined influence of drugs or of alcohol and any drug or drugs, such person operated the motor vehicle in a manner that

caused such death or deaths, as required by this Section 125.14 and Section 125.12 of that Article.

Aggravated vehicular homicide is a class 'B' felony.

Section : 125.15 : Manslaughter in the 2nd degree.

Offence : Manslaughter in the 2nd degree is defined as a person guilty of manslaughter in the 2nd degree when :

(1) he/she recklessly causes the death of another person, or

(2) he/she commits upon a female an abortional act which causes her death, unless such abortional act is justifiable pursuant to subdivision 3 of Section 125.05, or

He/she intentionally causes or aids another person to commit suicide.

Manslaughter in the 2nd degree is a class 'C' felony.

Section : 125.20 : Manslaughter in the 1st degree.

Offence : Manslaughter in the 1st degree is defined as a person guilty of manslaughter in the 1st degree when:

(1) with intent to cause serious physical injury to another person, he causes the death of another person, or of a 3rd person, or

(2) with intent to cause the death of another person, he/she causes the death of such person or of a 3rd person under circumstances which do not constitute murder because he/she acts under the influence of extreme emotional disturbance, as per paragraph (a) of subdivision 1 of Section 125.25. The fact that homicide was committed under the influence of extreme emotional disturbance constitutes a mitigating circumstance reducing murder to manslaughter in the 1st degree and need not be proved in any prosecution initiated under this subdivision, or

(3) he/she commits on a female pregnant for more than 24 wks. an abortional act which causes her

death, unless such abortional act is justifiable pursuant to subdivision 3 of Section 125.05, or

(4) being 18 yrs. old or more and with intent to cause physical injury to a person less than 11 yrs. old, the defendant recklessly engages in conduct which creates a grave risk of serious physical injury to such person and thereby causes the death of such person.

Manslaughter in the 1st degree is a class 'B' felony.

Section : 125.21 : Aggravated manslaughter in the 2nd degree.

Offence : Aggravated manslaughter in the '2nd' degree is defined as a person guilty of aggravated manslaughter in the 2nd degree when:

- he/she recklessly causes the death of a police officer or public officer, where such officer was in the course of performing his/her official duties and the defendant knew or reasonably should have known that such victim was a police officer or public officer.

Aggravated manslaughter in the '2nd' degree is a class 'C' felony.

Section : 125.22: Aggravated manslaughter in the 1st degree.

Offence : Aggravated manslaughter in the '1st' degree is defined as a person guilty of aggravated manslaughter in the 1st degree when:

- he/she intentionally causes serious physical injury to a police officer or public officer, where such officer was in the course of performing his/her official duties and the defendant knew or reasonably should have known that such victim was a police officer or public officer, or
- he/she causes the death of such officer or another police officer or public officer, or
- with intent to cause the death of a police officer or public officer, where such officer was in the course of performing his/her official duties, and the defendant knew or reasonably should have

known that such victim was a police officer or public officer, or

- he/she causes the death of such officer or another police officer or public officer under circunstances which do not constitute murder because he/she acts under the influence of extreme emotional disturbance, as per paragraph (a) of subdivision 1 of Section 125.25.–the fact that homicide was committed under the influence of extreme emotional disturbance constitutes a mitigating circumstance reducing murder to aggravated manslaughter in the 1st degree or manslaughter in the 1st degree and need not be proved in any prosecution initiated under this subdivision.

Aggravated manslaughter in the '1st'degree is a class 'B' felony.

Section : 125.25 : Murder in the 2nd degree :

Offence : Murder in the 2nd degree is defined as a person guilty of murder in the 2nd degree when:

- he/she causes the death of such person or of a 3rd person except that :
- the defendant acted under the influence of extreme emotional disturbance, precluding a conviction of manslaughter in the 1st degree, or
- the defendant's conduct incld. causing or aiding without use of duress or deception, another person for abetment to suicide, or
- he/she recklessly engages in creating a grave risk of death to another person, or
- he/she causing death of a person alone or with help of one or more accused person/s, while attempting to commit robbery, burglary, kidnapping, arson, rape, sodomy, sexual abuse or aggravated sexual abuse in the 1st degree, or escape in the 2nd degree, or
- he/she was not carrying any deadly weapon or instrument capable of causing death or serious physical injury (Murder in the 2nd degree is a class A-I felony).

Section : 125.26 : Aggravated murder :

Offence : Aggravated murder is defined as a person guilty of aggravated murder when :

- he/she causes the death of such person or of an official (polce officer, peace officer, Court official, parole officer) performing his/her official duties
- he/she (defendant) was more than 18 yrs. Old, at the time of commission or the crime.
- the defendant acted under the influence of extreme emotional disturbance, precluding a conviction of manslaughter in the 1st degree, or
- the defendant's conduct incld. causing or aiding without use of duress or deception, another person for abetment to suicide, or
- he/she recklessly engages in creating a grave risk of death to another person
- he/she causing death of a person alone or with help of one or more accused person/s, while attempting to commit robbery, burglary, kidnapping, arson, rape, sodomy, sexual abuse or aggravated sexual abuse in the 1st degree, or escape in the 2nd degree
- he/she was not carrying any deadly weapon or instrument capable of causing death or serious physical injury (Aggravated murder is a class A-I felony).

Section : 125.27 : Murder in the 1st degree :

Offence : Murder in the 1st degree is defined as a person guilty of murder in the 1st degree when :

- he/she causes the death of such person or of a 3rd person (official (polce officer, peace officer, Court official, parole officer) performing his/her official duties
- he/she (defendant) was more than 18 yrs. Old, at the time of commission or the crime.
- the defendant acted under the influence of extreme emotional disturbance, precluding a conviction of murder in the 1st degree, or

- the defendant's conduct including causing or aiding without use of duress or deception, another person for abetment to suicide, or
- he/she recklessly engages in creating a grave risk of death to another person
- he/she causing death of a person alone or with help of one or more accused person/s, while attempting to commit robbery, burglary, kidnapping, arson, rape, sodomy, sexual abuse or aggravated sexual abuse in the 1st degree, or escape in the 2nd degree
- he/she was not carrying any deadly weapon or instrument capable of causing death or serious physical injury (Murder in the 1st degree is class A-I felony).

Section : 125.40 : Abortion in the 2nd degree

Offence : Self-abortion in the 2nd degree is defined as a female guilty of self-abortion in the 2nd degree when:

- he/she commits an abortional act upon a female, unless such abortional act is justifiable pursuant to subdivision 3 of Section 125.05. Abortion in the '2nd" degree is a class 'E' felony.

Section : 125.45 : Abortion in the 1st degree

Offence : Self-abortion in the 1st degree is defined as a female guilty of self-abortion in the 1st degree when:

- he/she commits upon a female pregnant for > 24 wks., an abortinal act which causes the miscarriage of such female, unless such abortional act is justifiable pursuant to subdivision 3 of Section 125.05.

Abortion in the '1st' degree is a class 'D' felony.

Section : 125.50 : Self-abortion in the 2nd degree

Offence : Self-abortion in the 2nd degree is defined as a female guilty of self-abortion in the 2nd degree when:

- being pregnant for > 24 wks., she commits or submits to an abortional act upon herself whichcauses her miscarriage, unless such abortional act is justifiable pursuant to subdivision 3 of Section 125.05.

Self-abortion in the '1st' degree is a class 'B' misdemeanor.

Section : 125.55 : Self-abortion in the 1st degree.

Offence: Self-abortion in the 1st degree is defined as a female guilty of self-abortion in the 1st degree when :

- being pregnant for > 24 wks., she commits or submits to an abortional act upon herself which causes her miscarriage, unless such abortional act is justifiable pursuant to subdivision 3 of Section 125.05.

Self-abortion in the '1st' degree is a class 'A' misdemeanour.

Section : 125.60 : Issuing abortional articles.

Offence : Issuing abortional articles is defined as a person guilty of issuing abortional articles when he/she manufactures, sells or delivers any instrument, article, medicine, drug or substance: with intent that the same be used in unlawfully procuring the miscarriage of a female.

Issuing abortional articles is a class 'B' misdemeanor.

HONOUR KILLING

Offence : Honour killing.

Penalty: - Cases of honour killings are registered under the offence of murder.

Amendment: "The Government has been engaged in the process to make changes in the criminal law, to deal with growing incidents of honour killings across the Country. However, its efforts so far seem to have failed to convince nearly half the States in the Country". 13 States yet to send views on proposed changes in the criminal laws laws to curb honour killings, esp. in Haryana, Rajasthan and UP. These three States have admitted in the Supreme Court that they have not prepared any specific legal framework to curb the menace. "There was no specific legal framework to address the problem of honour killings, but top police officials have issued directions to treat such cases seriously," the UP Government informed the Supreme Court. Rajasthan and Haryana cited administrative circulars issued by the state Governments to address the problem of honour killings. Another problem faced by the Centre is the lack of official data on honour killings.

"Cases of honour killings are registered under the offence of murder, therefore not possible to exactly pinoint such cases," said a Government official. States in favour : Assam, Bihar, Chhattisgarh, Delhi, Goa, Jammu and Kashmir, Madhya Pradesh, NE States, Rajasthan and U.P.

Non-committed : Andhra, Gujarat, Jharkhand, Karnataka, Kerala, Maharashtra, Odisha, Punjab, Uttarkhand, Opposed : Haryana.

MEDICAL NEGLIGENCE

Offence : Is defined as perceived and actual dereliction of duty e.g. deficient care/or attention, by a medical professional, causing injury or death of a patient. Medical negligence or medical malpractice comes under the purview of law of contracts e.g. breach of a legal duty to patient's care–meaning carelessness in a matter for which the law mandates carefullness. Any breach of this duty gives the patient/or relatives, a right to initiate legal action against the negligent doctor/hospital.

Decisions of British applicable and relied by Indian Judiciary:

Charles Worth and Percy on Negligence (Tenth Edition, 2001):

That as per current forensic speech, negligence has three meanings :

- a state of mind, in which it is opposed to intention;

- careless conduct; and
- the breach of duty to take care that is imposed by either common or statute law.

That all three meanings are applicable in different circumstances but anyone of them does not necessarily exclude the other meanings (Para 1.01).

That the essential components of negligence, as recognised, are three :

"duty", "breach" and "resulting damage" i.e.:

- the existence of a duty to take care, which is owed by the defendant to the complainant;
- the failure to attain that standard of care, prescribed by the law, thereby committing a breach of such duty; and
- damage, which is both causally connected with such breach and recognised by the law, has been suffered by the complainant (Para 1.23).

Classification:

- Civil negligence
- Criminal negligence.

Civil Negligence

Offences:
- That a patient/or relatives lodges the complaint in a Civil court against the doctor for realisation of damages or compensation from the doctor/ hospital, for the injury to/or death of the patient, as per the case, resulting from medical negligence.
- That a doctor lodges the complaint in a Civil Court for the realisation of his Professional dues from the patient/or relatives, who refuse to pay the same on the pretext of medical negligence on the part of the attending doctor during the course of treatment.

Suit:
- Suit under Consumer Protection Act (CPA)
- Suit for damages
- Suit for recovery under specific.

Judgment:
- Fine–compensation and costs, or
- No punishment.

Criminal Negligence

Definition : That a patient/or relatives lodges the complaint in a Criminal court against the doctor/hospital for the injury to/or death of the patient, as per the case, resulting from gross medical negligence (res ipsa loquitur).

Gross negligence (res ipsa loquitor) :

- That the thing speaks for itself i.e. negligence written over the face of the case facts.
- That negligence is palpable, easily deducible, requires very little proof and is very difficult to defend.
- That in certain circumstances no proof of negligence is required beyond the accident itself.

Defence : **Sections 80 and 88 of the IPC :** Contain defences for doctors accused of criminal liability.

- That under Section 80 (accident in doing a lawful act) nothing is an offence that is done by accident or misfortune and without any criminal intention or knowledge in the doing of a lawful act in a lawful manner by lawful means and with proper care and caution.
- That under Section 88 a person cannot be accused of an offence if he/she performs an act in good faith for the other's benefit, does not intend to cause harm even if there is a risk, and the patient has explicitly or implicitly given consent.

Observation:- That the amount and degree of negligence is a fector in determining liability.

However, certain elements must be established to determine criminal liability in any particular case, the motive of the offence, the magnitude of the offence, and the character of the offender.

- That a doctor can not be held responsible for a patient's death unless it is shown that he/she was negligent or incompetent, with such disregard for the life and safety of his patient that it amounted to a crime against the state.

Penalty : **Section 304-A of the IPC** (whoever causes the death of a person by a rash or negligent act amounting to culpable homicide).

Punishment : Imprisonment for a term of two years, with or without fine.

Implied Understanding :

Definition : That persons who offer medical advice and treatment implicitly state :

- that they have the skill and knowledge to do so.
- that they have the skill to decide whether to take a case, to decide the treatment, and to administer that treatment.

This is known as an "implied understanding" on the part of a medical professional.

Negligence : duties owed to the patient :

- That a person who holds himself oat as ready to give medical advice or treatment impliedly undertakes that he is possessed of skill and knowledge for the purpose.
- That such a person, whether he is a registered medical practitioner or not, who is consulted by a patient, owes him certain duties, namely, a duty of care in deciding whether to undertake the case; a duty of care in deciding what treatment to give: and a duty of care in his administration of that treatment.
- That a breach of any of these duties will support an action for negligence by the patient.

Subtle/Complicated Negligence :

Definition:

- That the doctor's role is judged by method of comparison with his peers, and the claims of negligence are proved/or disproved by expert opinions and witnesses. However, no human being is perfect and even the most renowned specialist could make a mistake in detecting or diagnosing the true nature of a disease.
- That a doctor can be held liable for negligence only if one can prove that he/she is guilty of a

failure that no doctor with ordinary skills would be guilty of if acting with reasonable care.

- That an error of judgement constitutes negligence only if a reasonably competent professional with the standard skills that the defendant professes to have, and acting with ordinary care, would not have made the same error.

Liability :

Definition : That certain conditions must be satisfied before liability can be considered.

The person who is accused must have commited an act of commission or omission :

- That this act must have been in breach of the person's duty
- That this must have caused harm to the injured person.
- That the complainant must prove the allegation against the doctor by citing the best evidence available in medical science and by presenting expert opinion.

Act of Commission :

Definition : That something committed by a doctor that other prudent, reasonable doctor with similar qualification and experience wouldn't do, under similar circumstances.

Examples:

- That performing radical mastectomy without histo-pathology evidence.
- That performing Appendectomy without proper investigations.
- That giving HT (hormonal therapy) in suspected case of breast malignancy.
- That giving Penicillin, ATS, or Lignocain without testing.
- That delayed ABC management in a serious accidental case.
- That delayed management of a suspected MI case.

- That issuing a death certificate without ascertaining its cause/identification.

Act of Omission :

Definition : That something omitted by a doctor that other prudent, reasonable doctor wouldn't have omitted to do under similar circumstances.

Examples:
- That non-performing of basic investigations e.g. hemogram, MP slide, urine analysis in a case of PUO.
- That non-performing of allergy test prior to giving Penicillin, ATS or Lignocain.

Actionable Negligence :

Definition : That following criterias liable for actionable negligence :
- That breach of doctor patient relationship.
- That breach of responsibility/duty by the doctor/ or his/her staff.
- That breach of duty–gross or act of commission/ or omission.
- That patient's damage caused by alleged act of negligence.

Vicarious Liability :

Definition : That one is liable to pay for others mistakes :
- That emphasises the need for "vicarious liability" coverage, which protects the owner/employer from being sued because of the actions of staff, members of group practice, other independent DCs and virtually any other healthcare provider of any health related service who leases or shares space in the office.
- That it is easy to accept the fact that owner/ employer is responsible for the actions of his/ her staff e.g. employees, CA or technician.
- That if one of them injures a patient, violates state regulations, or fails to protect a patient's privacy, the owner/employer will be held liable for any damages they do.

- That no matter how careful the owner/employer been in the hiring process, the actions of a staff member could trigger a lawsuit or board complaint.
- That's always been the "price" of having employees.
- That it is harder to accept the reality that you might also be held responsible for the actions of non-employees who happen to work in the same office.
- That the rules of vicarious liability can put the owner/employer at risk even if he/she has never seen the patient in question.
- That Dr. Leslie Wise said in an article for Institute for Chiropractic Ethics :
- That as professionals, in chiropractic practice, dealing with the public, we need to remember that there are occasions where we reap what others have sown.

Insurance Giant CNA explains to its policy holders :

- That when you have a professional practice, you can be held responsible for overseeing the patient care provided by associates, other licences, technicians, and everyone else even vaguely connected to your practice.
- That if an insured is sharing space (incld. subleasing their own space) with any other healthcare professional and there is or can be any perception of an association between the practitioners (no matter how remote) by the patient or lay public, it is virtually guaranteed both parties will be named in a claim by an injured patient."
- That this has become more of a problem in recent years, as many DCs have begun working in, or running, multidisciplinary offices. In some cases, the DC is legally considered to be an "agent" for physical therapists, massage therapists, acupuncturists, nutritionists, or other healthcare providers.

- That these other providers work often indirectly (usually as independent contractors or simply as tenants leasing space) with the DC, who can be held liable for their actions.
- That often, these other providers fail to obtain their own insurance policies and the DC is the one with the "deep pockets" when it comes to a lawsuit.
- That even if someone not held legally liable, it will still take hundreds of dollars in legal fees to remove him/her from the case.
- That in addition, the liability will increase if the other provider is authorised to perform procedures beyond scope of practice.
- That depends on one state (incld. PTs, nurses, nurse practitioners, and other providers).
- That is why most boards prohibit or strongly advise against employing or contracting with persons with licenses in ancillary medical disciplines outside of chiropractic.

New York State office of the Professions Advisory Bulletin:

- That it is not recommended that licencee's be the controlling entity in a practice with licencees in medicine or any other profession authorised to perform procedures beyond the scope of chiropractic licence.

CAN points out :

- That vicarious liability can occur even when no actual agency relationship exists.
- That if a patient comes to owner/employer' office but receives care from another person, that patient could sue owner/employer if there was an iota to assume that owner/employer ran the office, and had authority over the person providing care.

Example : Florida' case, simply because owner' name is on the door. It does not matter whether he/she, simply leasing the space to another doctor or provider.

- That he/she could be held responsible for the actions of any person in his/her office.
- That also keep in mind, too, that absentee owners may be subject to professional misconduct violations as well.
- That being not on site doesn't mean not at risk.
- That the same thing applies if one is in a partnership or group practice.
- That as a member of the group, could be faced with vicarious liability issues should any member of group practice be sued.
- That risk is greater if the treating doctor does not have an insurance policy of his or her own.
- That **medical profession** has a long history of vicarious liability exposure, since so many medical officers have group or shared-space practices.

Example : Arizona-based medical malpractice company warns its doctors of the problem with the example of a group of doctors sharing office space and employees.

- That there is no actual agency relationship between the doctors - they are just sharing the burden of common expenses.
- That a reasonable person coming into the office may view this as a group practice, the doctors may appear to have some type of agency relationship.
- That patient filing a medical malpractice lawsuit against one doctor in the group may, therefore, name the other doctors alleging vicarious liability.
- That in this case, the physicians named solely because of their apparent agency relationship may not have insurance coverage for this type of vicarious liability allegation.
- That obviously, anytime you have employees, or share space with other professions (whether or not you have authority over them) you increase your exposure to lawsuits and board complaints.

- That this doesn't necessarily mean need to avoid these situations, but need to protect yourself.

Prevention : For safety purpose follow the following:

- That prior to any type of space-sharing agreement, carefully consider your potential liability risks. It may make sense to discuss the issues with an attorney, even drawing up a contract outlining each person's responsibilities and specifically addressing malpractice insurance requirements.
- That secure proof of current practice insurance with the same limits as your own coverage from every healthcare provider–Dc, MT, PT, etc.–who works in proximity to you and has the potential to create a vicarious liability issue for you.
- That make sure your malpractice insurance policy does not exclude vicarious liability, and your insurance company will respond should this type of situation arise. Many policies offered specify that liability applies only to the listed licencee, offering no protection for these situations.
- That notify your insurance company of any situation in your practice that might result in vicarious liability (hiring independent contractors, leasing or sharing space, etc.).

Remedy : That it is better to take steps now to protect yourself, your family and your practice instead of finding out the hard way.

Contributory Negligence :

Definition : That when a patient doesn't comply with doctor's suggestions/advice, conncerning his/her management, the patient is responsible partially/ or completely for the final results.

Examples:
- Non-compliance of prescribed treatment
- Non-compliance of follow up
- Non-compliance of prescribed investigations.

Onus of proof :

- That is on the complainant (patient) alleging negligence.
- That this burden shifts to the defendant doctor/ or hospital :

Examples: - That circumstances where patient is without access to, as in O.T./ICU etc.

Prevention: - That following precautions to be taken by the negligent doctor :

- Behaviour–avoid provoking the patient/ attendants
- Avoid criticising colleagues
- Taking of additional opinions–esp. in doubtful cases.
- Never try to over do–remain within one's knowledge and facilities
- Taking of informed consent of the patient/ attendant
- Avoid/change of records
- Avoid issuing bogus certificates
- Avoid disclosing privileged information of the patient to anyone
- Expertise–efficiency, empathy
- Taking professional indeminity insurance.
- Registration with professional bodies e.g. Medical Council.

Observation:

- That a doctor is not guilty of negligence if he has acted in accordance with a practice accepted as proper by a responsible body of medical men skilled in that particular art.
- That in the realm of diagnosis and treatment there is ample scope of genuine difference of opinion and a doctor is not negligent merely because his conclusion differs from that of other professionally men.
- That the true test for establishing negligence in diagnosis or treatment on the part of a doctor is

whether he has been proved to be guilty of such failure as no doctor of ordinary skill would be guilty of acting with twelve ordinary care.

MEDICAL TERMINATION OF PREGNANCY (MTP)

Definition : That is defined as termination of pregnancy, by an Authorised Registered Medical Practitioner at a Registered Place, when the continuance of the pregnancy would involve :

- a risk to the life of the pregnant woman or of grave injury to her physical or mental health.
- a substantial risk that if the child was born, it would suffer from such physical or mental abnormalities to be seriously handicapped.
- pregnancy caused by rape, the anguish caused by such pregnancy shall be presumed to constitute a grave injury to the mental health of the pregnant woman.
- where any pregnancy occurs as a result of failure of any device or method used by any married woman or her husband for the purpose of limiting the number of children, the anguish caused by such unwanted pregnancy may be presumed to constitute a grave injury to the mental health of the pregnant woman.
- no pregnancy of a woman, who has not attained the age of 18 years, or, who, having attained the age of 18 years is a lunatic, shall be terminated except with the consent in writing of her guardian.

International Scenerio :

Australia: Imposed strict restrictions over abortion.

Canada: No governing laws/restrictions over abortion.

Europe: Abortion is legally allowed upto 12 weeks in most of the countries.

France: Abortion is legally allowed upto 12 weeks, except in cases of maternal complications (Acute Medical and Surgical Emergencies and mental trauma) and Genetic disorders of the fetus.

India: Only qualified doctors, under stipulated conditions, can execute an act of abortion on a woman in a clinic/or a hospital, that has been approved of performing the abortion. The Indian Abortion Laws fall under the ambit of MTP ACT, which was enacted by the Indian Parliament in 1971, and came into force from 1st April, 1972.

Netherlands : Abortion is legally allowed upto 21 weeks.

Sweden: Abortion is legally allowed upto 18 weeks.

U.K. : Prior to 1968 MTP ACT, abortion was illegal in UK. This ACT made abortion legal since then.

Amendments :

- In 1971 amendment of MTP ACT, made abortion legal upto 28 weeks in UK.
- In 1990, MTP ACT was amended by enacting the Human Fertilisation and Embryology ACT, which made abortion legal upto 24 weeks, except in cases of maternal complications (Acute Medical and Surgical Emergencies and Mental Trauma) and Genetic disorders of the fetus.

U.S.A.: Abortion is legally allowed upto 26 weeks.

Indication : MTP under following circumstances by an RMP at a registered place, as continuance of pregnancy would endanger the life of the pregnant woman.

Medical disorders :

- C.V.S.: Rheumatic heart disease, CHF, Congenital heart disease.
- Diabetes Mellitus : incidence of hydramnios, toxemia of pregnancy, Infections and pre-maturity increased.
- Infections : UTI, Syphilis, Gonorrhea, Herpes Genitalis, Small pox, and Acute Chicken pox.

- Endocrinal disorders: Thyrotoxicosis, Parathyroid disorders and Tetany.
- Psychological : Grave injury to her mental health- that if the child was born, it would suffer from serious mental or physical abnormalities.
- Genetic disorders : Often there is no specific treatment that can help the fetus until it is born. The aim is to provide the parents the choice to opt for abortion, instead of having a baby with a health problem or disability or may be possibility of stillbirth.

  Surgical disorders: Acute : appendicitis, Cholecystitis, Ectopic gestation would suffer from serious mental or physical abnormalities

  Miscellaneous :
- Sexual abuse :
- Pregnancy caused by rape–the agony caused by such pregnancy shall be presumed to constitute a grave mental injury.
- Pregnancy of a minor girl.
- Family planning failure : Pregnancy caused by failure of any device or contraceptive–used for the purpose of family planning (limiting no. of children).
- Prenatal diagnosis : To test for birth defects e.g. Down's syndrome, spina bifida, cleft palate, cystic fibrosis, osteitis fibrosa cystic.

Criteria (essential) for Authorised Medical Practitioners doing MTP :

- That she/he has a Diploma/or Degree in Obstetrics and Gynecology.
- That she/he has assisted > 25 MTPs.
- That she/he has worked for six months as an SHO in Obstetrics and Gynecology.
- That she/he has three years of practice in Obstetrics and Gynecology, with prior registration, to enactment of 1971 MTP ACT, or

- That she/he has one year of practice in Obstetrics and Gynecology, with registration after the enactment of 1971 MTP ACT.

Consent:
- That a written consent is essentially required, prior to performing the MTP by the Authorised Medical Practitioner, providing full information by the RMP to the woman undergoing MTP, that:
- She has been fully informed about all the options available to her.
- She has been fully informed about the procedure to be performed, possible risks involved during and after the procedure, and post-care.
- That for married woman-her own written consent is adequate. Her husband's consent not required.
- That for unmarried woman and above 18 yrs. of age-her own written consent is adequate.
- That below 18 yrs. of age-written consent of her guardian is required.
- That mentally unsound-written consent of her guardian is required.

Abortion Policy in India: Flaws (Lacune) and Challenges :

- That, In India, legalising abortion in 1971, has not yielded the expected results inspite of existing liberal policies and majority of women still resort to unsafe abortion, resulting in high morbidity and mortality. This is partly due to the little awareness of the legality of abortion amongst women, and many misconceptions about the law amongst the MTP providers. Thus, liberal abortion policies and legislation are not sufficient to ensure safe abortion services. In India, abortion policy is consistent with safeguarding reproduction rights as envisaged by the International agreements. It does not advocate abortion as a family planning measure. Rather it promotes the family planning services by preventing uneventful pregnancies and at the same time recognises the importance of providing safe, affordable, accessible and acceptable abortion services to women who need to terminate an unwanted pregnancy.

MTP ACT aims to regulate and ensure access to safe abortion care and defines 'when', 'where' and under 'what' conditions abortion is permissible.

- That the recent amendment to decentralise regulation of abortion care to the district level services, to encourage regulation of abortion facilities by minimising administrative delays.
- That while defining punitive measures to deter abortion facilities that provide unsafe abortion care, the ACT offers full protection to the Registered MTP providers from any legal proceedings for any injury caused to a woman seeking abortion.

Critique of MTP ACT :

Biased policy : That apparent 'over medication' and 'physician only' reflects a strong medical biased policy that ignores the socio-politico-religious aspects of abortion.

Restrictive policy: That unnecessary legal restriction imposed i.e. need for taking opinion of two doctors prior to conducting 2nd trimester MTP.

Woman's rights: That besides woman's right to seek safe abortion, her right to access safe abortion services, and information about the availability of these services and the ultimate responsibility of the State to provide such services, ought to be emphasised strongly.

Denial of abortion care: That denial of abortion care to woman in need on flimsy grounds e.g. conscientious objections.

Compel to lie: That the ACT may compel a woman to lie about the exact circumstances about her unwanted pregnancy.

Discriminate clause: That contraceptive failure clause applies only to married woman, and this discrimination ought to be corrected.

Imunity to Public sector abortion facilities: That as per Act the Public sector abortion facilities made immune to adhere to the quality and specific standards essential for abortion care, being expected from the private sector.

Lacking guidelines for Good Medical Practice: That the MTP providers continue to use old unsafe abortion practices e.g. sharp curettage, check curettage following a vacuum suction, general anesthesia, variable drug dosage schedules and protocols for abortion.

Amendment to MTP Rules and Regulations (June 2003): That as per amendment, there is illogical requirement for a Blood Bank within 5 Km distance of the abortion facility. This criteria may be reconsidered as desirable instead of enforcing as essential.

Overmedication and Restricted access: That overmedication and restricted access to safe abortion facilities.

Consensus on drug dosage and schedule: That there is no National consensus on drugs dosage and schedule.

Poor Training Policy: That there is lack of training avenues for private medical practitioners (Private Sector), desirous of providing abortion care.

Demarcation of PNDT ACT and MTP ACT: That there is a need to demarcate the aims and domains of these acts. These acts do not conflict or contradict each other, rather co-exist. Policy requires to ensure for measures to prevent sex selective abortion from affecting access to safe abortion care, for the genuine abortion seeker.

MENTAL RETARDATION (Mental defect) and MULTIPLE DISABILITIES

Definition : Is defined as subnormal intelligence due to defective brain development.

Types: - Borderline

- Mild
- Moderate
- Severe (Irreversible).

Etiology:
- Inherited
- Infective: German measles, HIV, HPV, syphilis, during early months of pregnancy
- Unmatched baby's Rhesus factor with the mother's.
- Childbirth injuries
- Endocrinal : Hypothyroidism
- Malnutrition.

D/d:
- Mental illness
- General emotional disorders.

Diagnosis:
- Irrevesible condition: in case of brain's damage
- Moderately handicapped : Intelligence : slow learners.

Medicolegal aspect :
- That whether the parents treat retarded children with extra understanding and patience ?
- That whether the retarded children of very low intelligence need special care in a mental hospital or special home for the mentally retarded, and whether concerned specialists, psychologists, or psychiatrists, have been consulted ?

Reference :
1. Brophy, JJ: mental Retardation, pp. 604. Current Medical diagnosis and treatment, Maruzen Ed., Tokyo, 1975.
2. Lock, S, Smith, A: Mental Retardation. pp. 412. Reader's Digest Family Health Guide, London, 1972.

MORAL TURPITUDE

Definition : Is non-defined subject.

Judgment: Parvesh v/s State of Haryana (2009)(4) RCR (Criminal) 470(P&H)

Moral turpitude–Meaning of the term moral turpitude is not defined anywhere–This term is used in law for centuries.

Held:
- That there is no hard and fast rule as to what constitutes 'moral turpitude'.
- That moral turpitude is not involved in every criminal act.
- That whether any particular conviction involves moral turpitude, may be a question of fact and frequently depending on surrounding circumstances.
- That it is difficult to determine what crimes involve moral turpitude.
- That there is a tendency to restrict the term to sexual crimes, but the meaning certainly is much broader.
- That sexual crimes fall within the scope of definition.
- That mere assault, causing hurt etc. does not or may not involve moral turpitude.
- That homicide may or may not involve moral turpitude depending upon the degree of the crime and so would be the position regarding attempted homicide.

Judgment : Parvesh v/s State of Haryana (2009)(4) RCR (Criminal) 470(P&H)
- That this term used in law for centuries.
- That sexual crimes would fall within scope of moral turpitude, but sexual offences are not the only offences involving moral turpitude.
- That there are other offences also within term moral turpitude.

Relied : AIR (1959) Allahabad 71.

PRE-NATAL SEX DETERMINATION TESTS (PNDT) ACT

Preface : In the past Medical Profession was considered as a noble profession–next only to the God Almighty. With the passing times, this image has been eroded on account of many factors e.g. malpractices, commercialisation leading to negligence, patient's mistrust, enforcing authorities to enact the PNDT Act. opposed/ resented by the medicos.

Judgment : Rajasthan Medical Council suspends 12 doctors, Jaipur, July, 2012:

Complaint : Sri Ganganagar's SDM filed cases against 11 doctors, in the Court of Chief Judicial Magistrate, for conducting sex determination tests in their clinics and hospitals.

RMC : Rajasthan Medical Council (RMC) suspended licences of 12 doctors allegedly conducting sex determination tests.

Vox populi : Chiranjeeb Kakoty, July, 2012 : shame, shame: "Suspension of licences is a vague phrase. Patients do not ask for licence of doctors prior, during or after consultation–at least I have never heard of it so far !!".

Doctors : Dr. Shambhu N Gupta: July, 2012: No one knows the causes of suspension of the Registration of doctors, by the RMC. The A ppropriate Authority (AA) neither given the notice nor heard the alleged doctors and the Court framed charges on the basis of AA's complaint only.

Vox-populi: - That the medical profession has become a profit-making business, with many bureaucrats and politicians also in connivance. The authorities have failed to keep a check on such errant doctors and hospitals. (SP Kansal, Chandigarh)

- That commercialisation and deteriorating moral standards in the society have had their effect on the medical profession too. Patients are equally guilty for the current scenario, by filing unnecessary medical litigation cases, in order to make a fast buck. The media has been instrumental in sensationalising and exaggerating incidents (SK Chawla, Chandigarh)

SEXUAL OFFENCES (OFFENCES AND PENALTY)

SEXUAL HARASSMENT OF WOMEN AT WORKPLACE (PREVENTION, PROHIBITION AND REDRESSAL) ACT, 2013

Definition : Is defined as an Act to provide for the protection of women against sexual harassment at workplace. Sexual harassment results in violation of the fundamental rights of a woman to equality under Articles 14 and 15 of the Constitution of India and her right to life and to live with dignity under Article 21 of the Constitution and right to practice any profession or to carry on any occupation, trade or business which incld. A right to a safe environment free from sexual harassment. The Act has replaced Vishaka guidelines.

International scenario :

- That the protection against sexual harassment and the right to work with dignity are universally recognised. Human Rights by International Conventions and Instruments such as Convention on the Elimination of all Forms of Discrimination against women, which has been ratified on 25 June, 1993 by the Government of India. Navi Pillay (UN High Commissioner for Human Rights) :

Aims:

- To provide protection not only to women who are employed but also to any woman who enters the workplace as a client, customer, apprentice, and daily wage worker or in an ad-hoc capacity. It also covers students, research scholars in Colleges/Universities and patients in Hospitals. It seeks to cover workplaces in the unorganised sectors.
- To provide an effective complaints and redress mechanism.
- To be mandatory for every employer to constitute a Local (internal).

  Complaints Committee (LCC) to be constituted by the designated District Officer at the District/ or Sub-district levels, depending on the need. The LCCs will enquire into the complaints of sexual harassment and recommend action to the employer or District Officer.

Forms : That sexual harassment at workplace constitutes:

- physical contact and advances
- a demand or request for sexual favours

- making sexually coloured remarks
- showing pornography
- any other unwelcome physical, verbal/non-verbal conduct of sexual nature.

Enactment : Vishaka case verdict (1997) : A three Judge bench headed by the then Chief Justice of India, JS Verma, had laid down a set of detailed guidelines mandating setting up of internal complaints committee headed by a woman in every organisation – government or private – to address the issue of sexual harassment of women employees at workplace. But the SC held that these directions (Vishaka guidelines) would be binding and enforceable in law until suitable legislation is enacted to occupy the field.

The Sexual Harassment of Women at Workplace (Prevention, Prohibition and Redressal) Act, 2013: The Parliament passed the new law, that is an improvement over the Vishaka guidelines as it also covers unorganised sector and domestic workers and expands the definition of 'workplace' to include many public and private organisations incld. educational institutions, sports institutes, stadium, hospitals employing more than ten workers, and even a house.

The Act provides for a mechanism in terms of internal and local complaints committees to be established by the employer and the appropriate government.

Jurisdiction : Extends to the whole of India.

Offence : Sexual harassment at workplace. Also the promise or threat to a woman's employment prospects or creation of hostile work environment as 'sexual harassment' at the workplace and expressly seeks to prohibit such acts.

Flaws : Members of the complaints committee might not always be independent of the influences of the management which has instituted it, and this esp. becomes a tricky issue if the offender in question is part of the top management.

Security : Though the bill is not foolproof, it at least provides a starting point of security.

But yes, every working woman should take the onus of her personal security and well-being at the work place.

Safeguards : That the bill provides for safeguards in case of false or malicious complaint of sexual harassment. However, merely inability to substantiate the complaint or give adequate proof would't make the complaint liable for punishment.

Precautions:- That women should express strong resistance to the smallest inappropriate gesture, action, word or speech. Otherwise the offender will assume that he has her consent and will progress to bigger offences.

- That women should learn to discern friendly behaviour from inappropriate behaviour and maintain certain boundaries with men at all times.

Example : Laugh and joke may be fine, but crude jokes are unpardonable.

Penalty : Employers who fail to comply with the provisions, will be liable to punishment with a fine which may extend to ₹ 50K.

Since there is a possibility that during the inquiry, the woman may be subject to threat and aggression, she has been given the option to seek relief in the form of transfer either of her own or the respondent or seek leave from work. The complaint committees are required to complete their inquiry within 90 days and a period of 60 days has been given to the Employer/ District officer for the implementation of the recommendations of the committee.

Accused person : held guilty :

- deduction of his salary @ 10 per cent PM for a period of one year or in lumpsum, or
- withdrawal of privileges and perks, or
- termination of service.

Safeguards : The bill provides for safeguards in case of false or malicious complaint of sexual harassment. A fine of ₹ 500 or 5 per cent of the salary of the complainant PM for a year. However, merely inability to substantiate the complaint or give adequate proof would't make the complaint liable for punishment.

Vox-populi : Ramesh Behl (Sr. Manager MNC, Gurgaon): The problem stems at 2 levels :

1st : That some women, who think there is nothing wrong in talking loosely and dressing provocatively. This category of women, more often than not, is not conscious of the fact that their conduct is likely to attract unwanted attention from male colleagues. Needless to say, however they are courting risk.

2nd : That certain women, who have ambitions but lack efficiency and knowledge of the job, they have been assigned to do. There have been women, who used their feminine guiles to manipulate career moves and hence became very susceptible to sexual harassment.

Raina Bhattacharjee (Psychological Therapist and Wellness Counsellor): From the woman's point of view, this alleged manipulation usually starts and stops with flirting. This means that more often than not, most women in this scenario might be fine going for an occasional lunch date or receiving a few flirtatious compliments, but they are uncomfortable and unwilling when it comes to anything beyond this. Unfortunately, however, most men cannot comprehend this unspoken firewall in terms of permissiveness and consequently these women soon find themselves in sticky situations. That women should express strong resistance to the smallest inappropriate gesture, action, word or speech. Otherwise the offender will assume that he has her consent and will progress to bigger offences. That women should learn to discern friendly behaviour from inappropriate behaviour and maintain certain boundaries with men at all times.

Example : Laugh and joke may be fine, but crude jokes are unpardonable. Flavia Agnes (Women's Rights Lawyer and Writer): The worst thing that may happen in such cases is that the women finds herself completely alone. She feels that if she complains, people will unduly and sceptically question her about her initial overtures. And when the situation becomes unbearable, women often resort to extreme measures like Geetika Sharma suicide case.

Members of the complaints committee might not always be independent of the influences of the management which has instituted it, and this esp. becomes a tricky issue if the offender in question is part of the top management.

Gauri Sharma (Journalist) : I couldn't believe I was being harassed.

Legal Speak : That accused's comments and embracing would fall within the definition of inappropriate conduct at workplace. A woman/ man in the organisation has a right to expect their company to be in compliance with the law (Adv. Naina Kapur).

Tania Banerjee (Journalist) : I left the publication disheartened.

Legal Speak : That feeling uncomfortable, she could have asked her boss to stop criticising her dress, or spoken to the HR (Adv. Seema Misra).

Mahima Singh (IT Professional) : I didn't complete my internship.

Legal Speak : That the actions of the team leader could fall within the definition of prohibited conduct under the law as an unwelcome and direct physical advance (Adv. Naina Kapur).

Preeti (HR Professional) : The girl's reputation is tarnished.

Legal Speak : That the unwelcome attempt by the organisation head to hug Preeti would fall within prohibited unwelcome physical conduct as per Vishaka guidelines for Sexual harassment of Working Women (prevention, prohibition and redressal) Act, 2013 (Adv. Naina Kapur).

Judgment : SC : Medha Kalwal Lele: October 20, filed a PIL, seeking its direction to expand the ambit of the historic 1997 verdict (Vishaka case) to include various other institutions. A bench headed by Justice RM Lodha said "lip service and hollow statements" are not enough to uplift the condition of women and asked the governments to put in place law to tackle the problem. The Court thus expanded the ambit of its historic 1997 Vishaka verdict, by directing regulating bodies and all the institutions affiliated to them to implement the guidelines framed in the Vishaka case of 1997 within two months.

Remedy : In orfer to check this heinous crime, following measures are suggested :

- Immediate filing of the FIR against the accused.
- Non-bailable warrants against the accused/s.
- Fast-track Courts, to decide the case at the earliest.
- Stringent punishment to the accused/s (Imprisonment plus fine).
- Full payment to the victim/s and their families incld. total cost of treatment and compensation for the disability or loss of life, to be recovered from the accused/s.
- Government to provide full protection to the victim and family.
- Public awareness and support in preventing this crime and providing help to the victim and affected family.
- Media exposure of this crime till the punishment to the accused as well as full compensation to the victim.

SEXUAL OFFENCES IN INDIA :

- Adultery

- Rape
- Child abuse (sex offences) -
- Causing sexual activity without consent
- Rape and other offences against children under 13
- Child sex offences
- Abuse of position of trust
- Familial child sex offences
- Offences against persons with a mental disorder impeding choice
- Care workers for persons with a mental disorder
- Indecent photographs of children
- Exploitation of prostitution
- Amendments relating to prostitution
- Trafficking
- Preparatory offences
- Sex with an adult relative
- Other offences :
- Exposure
- Voyeurism
- Intercourse with an animal
- Sexual penetration of a corpse
- Sexual activity in a public lavatory.

ADULTERY

Definition : That whoever has sexual intercourse with a woman who is and whom he knows or has reason to believe to be the wife of another man, without the consent or connivance of that man, such sexual intercourse not amounting to the offence of rape, is guilty of the offence of adultery.

Section : Under Section 497 of IPC: Adultery can be committed only by a man and not by a woman. Further Section 198 of IPC, 1973, allows a husband to bring charges against the man with whom his wife has committed adultery. But it explicitly denies the husband the right to charge his wife with adultery and also denies a woman the right to charge her husband with adultery.

Penalty : Punishable with imprisonment of either description for a term which may extend to five years, or with fine, or with both. That in such a case, the wife shall not be punishable as an abettor.

Law : That the basic rationale behind criminalising adultery is to protect the sanctity of the institution of marriage.

India :

Gender bias in Indian adultery law: has both supporters and critics :

The law in India is biased against men in as much as a woman cannot be prosecuted for adultery even when she is an abettor.

- That as per law adultery is only committed against the husband of the adulterous woman. A man can not level an adultery charge against the other man. The Indian law treats wives as their husbands' property and considers adultery as an offence that a man commits by trespassing upon the property (wife) of another. That is why she is not liable as an abettor.

  National Commission for Women (NCW): 2006, recommended decriminalising Adultery: maintained that there may be cases where a woman whose husband may have cheated on her, would still want to save her marriage. It had favoured making adultery a civil wrong. Women should not be punished for adultery, as they are victims and not offenders in such cases. Considering women's position in India, the NCW said Section 497 should not be made gender-neutral (M Shama Chairperson NCW).

- That any woman who has sex outside marriage, even if she is a rape victim, should be hanged. If any woman, married or unmarried, goes along with a man, with or without her consent, she should be hanged, said in an interview, when asked for a solution to end rapes (A Azmi, Maharashtra chief SP). But Azmi's family disowns remark "Farhan and me are deeply embarrassed and ashamed. We do not share this mindset, it's disrespectful to women, and if these statements are true, then it's sad (A Takia, Actress and Azmi's daughter-in-law).

- Judgment: Kalyani v/s Sailja: SC quashed the case of adultery registered against Andhra woman Kalyani at the instance of another woman Sailja who alleged that her husband was in illicit relationship with the former. While absolving Kalyani of criminal charges of adultery, the SC said: the provision is currently under criticism from certain quarters for showing a strong gender bias for it makes the position of a married woman almost as a property of her husband. But in terms of the law as it stands, it is evident from a plain reading of the Section 497 IPC that only a man can be prosecuted against and punished for the offence of adultery.
- Judgment: *Navy Commander KM Nanavati* v/s *businessman P Ahuja:* April 27, 1959, Nanavati shot dead Ahuja, for his illict relationship with his wife Sylvia. While Nanavati faced prosecution, Sylvia went scot free.

International :

USA : that the law on adultery variable from State to State, and even in States that regard it as an offence, the punishment is variable e.g.

- Michigan: adultery punishable with life imprisonment.
- Maryland: adultery punishable with just a fine of 10 US dollars. European Union Countries (including UK, Netherlands, Belgium, Finland and Sweden) adultery is not considered as an offence. But in Switzerland it is considered as illegal.

Islamic Countries: in many Islamic Countries, laws on adultery are enforced very strictly and wives are often punished more harshly than their husbands. In certain cases married women are considered guilty of adultery even when have been raped e.g.

- North Nigeria, 2001: Safiya, was sentenced to death by stoning by an Islamic Sharia Court. But the Islamic Appeal Court ruled that the act of adultery was committed prior to being declared as illegal.

Religions view: All religions generally disapprove of adultery and consider it a major sin.

- Christianity: That the Old Testament forbids adultery and the punishment is death sentence, while in the New Testament, Jesus describes it as a sin but refrains from punishment. In Judaism, the 7th commandment forbids adultery.

  But, a married man's relations with an unmarried woman was not considered adultery. Only a married woman's consensual sexual intercourse with another man amounted to adultery and both the woman and the man were considered guilty. The penalty for adultery is stoning for both man and woman.
- Islam: stresses that sexual relations should be restricted to marriage and for creation of a family. Pre-marital and extra-marital sex are considered sins. As per Islamic law, unless purged by punishment, sinners are likely to be punished after death.
- Hinduism: also disapproves of adultery, while certain Tantric branches including. Yogi Osho, believe in enlightenment through divine sex.
- Buddhism: also believe in that sexual intercourse may be used for higher spiritual development.

Reference : S Prakash, Fatal Attraction, HT December, 2013.

RAPE

Definition : That is defined as an offence by a man to illegally, penetrate with his penis (sexual intercourse), the vagina, anus or mouth of a female (own wife < 15 yrs., or any other girl < 16 yrs. or with any other woman > 16 yrs. of age), against her will or without her consent or with her consent, (taken by following unlawful means:-

- Personification–as her husband.
- Blackmailing–on the pretext of treating her disease by act of sexual intercourse, or on the pretext of marrying.
- Mentally retarded or lunatic woman.
- Drug abuse–under the influence of intoxicating or sedatives.
- Torture–physical or mental (threat of death) e.g. to force someone to have sex, especially by using violence.
- That sexual intercourse with a prostitute, without her consent shall also be considered as rape, irrespective of being paid money or remuneration for the act.

Deviate sexual intercourse :

- That the offence is committed where sexual conduct between the penis and the anus, the mouth and penis, or the mouth and the vulva.
- That the offence is committed where the penetration is by a part of the body e.g. a finger or anything else e.g. a bottle for sexual intent.
- That even an attempt is an offence.

Sexual contact :

- That the offence is committed where any touching of the sexual or other intimate parts of a person not married to the accused for the purpose of gratifying sexual desire of either party. It includes the touching of the victim by the accused, whether directly or through clothing.

Aggravated sexual contact :

- That the offence is committed whereby without any valid medical purpose, inserting a foreign object in the vagina, anus or urethra, causing physical injury.

Age of Male: A child < 12 yrs. of age (immature) cannot be held criminally responsible for rape.

Age of female; No age is exempted from rape. Maximum number of rapes committed on females between age of 12 to 30 yrs.

Diagnosis : History of the illegal act :

- date, time, place
- name and address (if known) of the accused person/s and victim
- position of the parties
- whether the victim resisted or shouted for any help
- whether menstruating at that time
- whether the victim was in full senses/ or intoxicated
- whether the victim is feeling dysurea.

A. Examination of the Victim :

Pre-examination precautions (essential requirements) :

- a written warrant from the Magistrate or an Authorised Officer, is essential prior to examination of the victim. No warrant is required, in case the victim approaches the doctor directly.
- identity of the victim (raped female) – by the escorting policeman/woman and by the legal guardian of the victim.
- the victim and her guardian – are apprised in details about the results of examination that may favour or oppose them in the court and that they have the option of not to submit for examination.
- consent – written consent of the victim (or of the legal guardian of a minor below 12 yrs. of age). Unconscious/or intoxicated victim – no consent of the victim is required, but with the permission of the legal guardians of the victim.

Precautions (requirements) during examination :

- presence of a female attendant or her husband or legal guardian.

Undressing of the victim – done only by herself, female doctor/attendant.

- adequate light, suitable place and lithotomy position are essential.

Examination: of clothes worn by the victim for evidence of struggle e.g. torn, stained of dust, blood and semen

Body injuries :

Inflicted by the accused person/s :

- mouth and cheeks : scratches, abrasions and bruises– inflicted on victim by the accused, to prevent the victim from crying or shouting for help.
- neck : scratches, abrasions and bruises.
- breasts : ecchymosis, bruises and nail or teeth marks.
- arms : scratches, abrasions and bruises – resulted from forcible holding of the victim's arms by the accused, so as to prevent the victim's struggle and resistance.
- thighs (esp. Upper and inner part) : scratches, abrasions and bruises resulted from an attempt by the accused to keep the victim's thighs apart.

Inflicted by the struggle :

- scratches, abrasions and bruises resulting from forcible holding down of the arms by the accused, to prevent victim's struggle and resistance.

Site : back, buttocks, arms and legs.

- blood and semen stains–samples (scrapings) taken from vagina, vulva and thighs, are to be sent for laboratory testing.
- pubic hairs–matted together with blood or semen
- genitals : for evidence of violence :
- labia majora–edematous and tendered
- vulva–red, abraded, bruised, edematous and tendered. There may be slight oozing of blood
- vagina–hot, dilated, abraded, bruised, edematous and tendered

- hymen–ruptured with torn edges, edematous and tendered
- perineum–edematous and tendered. May be lacerated in children
- P/V discharge of blood or pus.

Investigation : Vaginal swab and smear–for detection of spermatozoa (+ve sign) and pus cells Urethral discharge - for detection of pus cells (gonococci).

B. Examination of the accused/s :

- consent : written consent of the accused to be taken, or a warrant from the Magistrate or an Authorised Officer, for examination of the accused.
- of clothes worn by the accused for evidence of struggle e.g. torn, stained of dust, blood and semen.
- signs of struggle.
- signs of recent intercourse :
- abrasions of the glans penis and prepuce, esp. on the frenulum.

Medico-legal aspect :

- That whether the rape victim incld. wife, comes under the permissible age of consent or not ?
- That whether the consent of sexual intercourse obtained prior to actual act obtained or not ?
- That whether the consent obtained prior to actual act or afterwards ?
- That whether a man can commit rape on an alert, healthy woman ?-That whether a man can commit rape on a sleeping woman ?

Penalty : Laws and Penalty Internationally (Table 6.2).

Table 6.2: Rape laws (International)

	India	*UK*	*USA*
Law	Sexual intercourse with a woman against her will & and without her consent	Gender neutral law. Incld. penile penetration of vagina, anus or mouth of another person without consent	No National law. Each State has its own laws. Most States have broad definition of rape, genders and acts oriented
Penalty	Rigorous imprisonment State for a term extended to10 yrs. Maximum–life term	Maximum–life term	Variable–each

Child sex offences :

CHILD ABUSE/VULNERABLE CHILDHOOD/NO COUNTRY FOR CHILDREN

Definition : Child abuse is a catastrophe. It can only function as the end of one story and the beginning of another.

Issue : Safety of youngsters.

Abuse:
- Kidnapping for ransom of money, jealousy or revenge
- Murders for jealousy or revenge
- Kidnapping and murder for ransom of money, jealousy or revenge
- Assault: physical torture or inflicting burn injuries
- Monitory : making children blind or physically handicapped, for purpose of forced begging, and selling girls to brothels for illicit purposes.

Cases : **Kidnapping and Murder :**

- Gurkirat Singh (10) kidnapped on November 7 from Verka. Body found on November 16. As the Amritsar police struggle to crack the case, incidents of kidnapping and subsequent murder of minor children, which have been coming to light at a regular interval, have put a question mark on the safety of children. In majority of cases parents of kidnapped children got ransom calls, and later on brutally murdered by the perpetrators for not fulfilling their unjustified/ hefty demands.
- Sushant (11) kidnapped on June 12. Body found on June 20.
- Mohit Kapoor (11) kidnapped on October 26. Body found on October 27.
- Jagjit Singh (14) kidnapped on April 28. Body found at Bhuchchar village.

Assault :

- Roshan Lama (4) hospitalised with 20 per cent burns, inflicted by his neighbour by pouring a pot of boiling hot soup on his back. The reason–ongoing bickering with Roshan's father. (HTC)

- Raipur teen (12) committed suicide, after pinning blame on her allegedly cruel school teacher of frequently tormenting her. (HTC)
- Tripura girl, stripped and tied up for hrs.

Sexual abuse: by close relatives, friends, or unknown persons luring teens :

- Bhilwara teen (14) raped by her adoptive father for more than three yrs.
- Kerala teen (13) raped by drug addict and alcoholic. dad, uncle and brother. The elder sister commited suicide after being similarly abused.
- Bangalore teen (4) allegedly sexually abused by her father's friend, has 17 bite marks on her body. (HTC)

Media:

- Kidnapping incidents are on the rise because of growing greed among people. Lust among people to get rich faster is leading to such crimes. People must go back to the old style of living and shun greed.

  (Dr. Inderjit Kaur, president, All India Pingalwara Charitable Society)
- In most kidnapping cases, personal enmity is involved. It is not a social problem but a law and order issue. Children are the easiest and most sensitive targets and incidents involving kidshurt parents emotionally the most. The police need to handle such cases in a better way.

  (Dr. BL Goel, director,Vidya Sagar Institute of Mental Health)
- Security of children needs to be ensued. To ensure safety of children, people should remain vigilant whether they are in the house or outside. Police personnel need to be active and they should increase patrolling outside schools.

  (A Mehra, principal, Spring Blossoms School)
- This is a serious law and order problem. The notorious persons have no fear of police and

they commit such crimes. There is an urgent need that police instill fear among anti-social elements and then only such heinous crimes can be brought under control.

(A Singh, investigator with PHRO)

SEXUAL OFFENCES IN UK :

- Rape
- Assault
- Causing sexual activity without consent
- Rape and other offences against children under 13
- Child sex offences
- Abuse of position of trust
- Familial child sex offences
- Offences against persons with a mental disorder impeding choice
- Care workers for persons with a mental disorder
- Indecent photographs of children
- Exploitation of prostitution
- Amendments relating to prostitution
- Trafficking
- Preparatory offences
- Sex with an adult relative
- Other offences :
- Exposure
- Voyeurism
- Intercourse with an animal
- Sexual penetration of a corpse
- Sexual activity in a public lavatory:

SEXUAL OFFENSES IN USA :

Definitions of terms

Lack of consent

Limitation ; Defenses

Corroboration

Sexual misconduct

Rape in the 3rd degree

Rape in the 2nd degree
Rape in the 1st degree
Criminal Sexual Act in the 3rd degree
Criminal Sexual Act in the 2nd degree
Criminal Sexual Act in the 1st degree
Forcible touching
Persistent sexual abuse
Sexual abuse in the 3rd degree
Sexual abuse in the 2nd degree
Sexual abuse in the 1st degree
Aggravated sexual abuse in the 4th degree
Aggravated sexual abuse in the 3rd degree
Aggravated sexual abuse in the 2nd degree
Aggravated sexual abuse in the 1st degree
Course of sexual conduct against a child in the 1st degree
Course of sexual conduct against a child in the 2nd degree
Female genital mutilation
Facilitating a sex offense with a controlled substance
Sentencing
Predatory sexual assault
Predatory sexual assault against a child.

Definitions: Sexual intercourse :

- That the Act makes it an offence for any male or female to penetrate however slight, the vagina or anus of another person without their consent.

Deviate sexual intercourse :

- That the offence is committed where sexual conduct between the penis and the anus, the mouth and penis, or the mouth and the vulva.
- That the offence is committed where the penetration is by a part of the body e.g. a finger or anything else e.g. a bottle for sexual intent.
- That even an attempt is an offence.

Aggravated sexual contact :

- That the offence is committed whereby without any valid medical purpose, inserting a foreign object in the vagina, anus or urethra, causing physical injury.

Sexual contact :

- That the offence is committed where any touching of the sexual or other intimate parts of a person not married to the accused for the purpose of gratifying sexual desire of either party. It includes the touching of the victim by the accused, whether directly or through clothing.

Female :

- That any female not married to the accused e.g. lacking an existing relationship of husband and wife between the accused and the female, as recognised by law or
- That the existence of the relationship of husband and wife between the accused and the female recognised by law at the time the accused commits an offense, by means of forcible compulsion against the female, and the female and accused are living apart, pursuant to a valid and effective :
- order issued by a Court of competent jurisdiction which requires such living apart, or
- decree or judgment of separation or
- written agreement of separation subscribed by them.

Mentally disabled :

- That a person suffers from a mental disease or defect which renders him/her incapable of appraising the nature of his/her conduct.

Mentally incapacitated :

- That a person is rendered temporarily incapable of appraising or controlling his conduct owing to the influence of a narcotic or intoxicating substance administered to him without his consent, or to any other act committed upon him without his consent.

Physically helpless :

- That a person is unconscious or for any other reason is physically unable to communicate unwillingness to an act.

Forcible compulsion :

- That means to compel by either use of physical force or a threat, express or implied, which places a person in fear of immediate death or physical injury to himself, herself or another person, or in fear that he, she or another person will be kidnapped.

Foreign object :

- That any instrument or article which, when inserted in the vagina, penis or rectum, is capable of causing physical injury.

Lack of consent :

- That whether or not specifically stated, it is an element of every sexual offense, except the offense of consensual sodomy, the sexual act was committed without consent of the victim.

  That a person is deemed incapable of consent when he/she is :

  Less than 17 yrs. old or Mentally disabled or mentally incapacitated or Physically helpless or committed to the care and custody of the State Deptt. of Correctional Services or a hospital, and the accused is an employee, not married to the victim, knowing well about the victim's care and custody of such deptt.

Etiology :

- Forcible compulsion or
- Incapacity to consent or
- Sexual abuse or
- Rape in the 3rd degree or
- Sodomy in the 3rd degree

Limitation : Defences :

- That it is an affirmative defence that the defendent, at the time he/she engaged in the conduct constituting the offence, did not know of the facts or conditions responsible for such incapacity to consent because he/she was mentally disabled, mentally incapacitated or physically helpless.

- That conduct performed for a valid medical or mental healthcare purpose shall not constitute a violation of any section of Article 130.

Corroboration :

- That results solely from incapacity to consent because of the victim's mental defect, or mental incapacity, or an attempt to commit the same, solely on the testimony of the victim, unsupported by other evidence tending to :
- establish that an attempt was made to engage the victim in sexual intercourse, deviate sexual intercourse, or sexual contact, as the case may be, at the time of the occurrence, and
- connect the defendant yuth the commission of the offense or attempted offence.

Sexual misconduct (class A misdemeanour) :

- That a person is accused of sexual misconduct if :
- He/she engages in sexual intercourse with another person without such person's consent, or
- He/she engages in oral or anal sexual conduct with another person without such person's consent, or
- He/she engages in sexual conduct with an animal or a dead human body.

Rape in 3rd degree (class E felony) :

- That he/she engages in sexual intercourse with another person incapable of giving consent by reason of some factor other than being less than 17 yrs. old, or
- That being 21 yrs. old or more, he/she engages in sexual intercourse with another person less than 17 yrs. old, or

That he/she engages in sexual intercourse with another person without his/her consent, by reason of some factor other than incapacity to consent.

Rape in 2nd degree (class D felony) :

- That he/she engages in sexual intercourse with another person incapable of giving consent by reason of being mentally disabled or mentally incapacitated.
- That being 18 yrs. old or more, he/she engages in sexual intercourse with another person less than 15 yrs. old or

Rape in 1st degree (class B felony) :

- That he/she engages in sexual intercourse with another person :
- By forcible compulsion, or
- Incapable of giving consent by reason of being physically helpless, or
- Who is less than 11 yrs. old, or
- Who is less than 13 yrs. Old and the accused is 18 yrs. Old or more.

Criminal sexual act in 3rd degree (class E felony) :

- That he/she engages in oral or anal sexual conduct with another person incapable of giving consent by reason of some factor other than being less than 17 yrs. old, or
- Being 21 yrs. old or more, he/she engages in oral or anal sexual conduct with another person less than 17 yrs. old or
- He/she engages in oral or anal sexual conduct with another person without his/her consent by reason of some factor other than incapacity to consent.

Criminal sexual act in 3rd degree (class E felony) :

- That he/she engages in oral or anal sexual conduct with another person incapable of giving consent by reason of some factor other than being less than 17 yrs. old, or
- Being 21 yrs. old or more, he/she engages in oral or anal sexual conduct with another person less than 17 yrs. old or

- He/she engages in oral or anal sexual conduct with another person without his/her consent by reason of some factor other than incapacity to consent.

Criminal sexual act in 2nd degree (class D felony) :

- That he/she engages in oral or anal sexual conduct with another person incapable of giving consent by reason of some factor other than being less than 17 yrs. old, or
- Being 21 yrs. old or more, he/she engages in oral or anal sexual conduct with another person less than 17 yrs. old, or
- He/she engages in oral or anal sexual conduct with another person without his/her consent by reason of some factor other than incapacity to consent.

Criminal sexual act in 1st degree (class B felony) :

- That he/she engages in oral or anal sexual conduct with another person incapable of giving consent by reason of some factor other than being less than 17 yrs. old, or
- Being 21 yrs. old or more, he/she engages in oral or anal sexual conduct with another person less than 17 yrs. old, or
- He/she engages in oral or anal sexual conduct with another person without his/her consent by reason of some factor other than incapacity to consent.

Forcible touching (class A misdemeanour) :

- That a person is accused of forcible touching, intentionally, and for illegitimate purpose, forcibly touches (squeeze, grab, fondle or pinch) the sexual/intimate/private parts of another person for :
- purpose of gratifying the accused's sexual desire
- purpose of degrading/abusing such person.

Persistent sexual abuse (class E felony) :

- That a person is accused of persistent sexual abuse, when during the last 10 yrs. he/she convicted two/three times, in separate criminal transactions for which penalised on separate occasions of sexual abuse in the 3rd of section 130.55 or 2nd degree of section 130.60.

Sexual abuse in 3rd degree (class B misdemeanour) :

- That a person is accused of sexual abuse in the 3rd degree when he/she subjects victim to sexual contact without the victim's consent that in any prosecution under this section, it is an affirmative defence that :
- victim's lack of consent was mainly due to incapacity to consent for reason of being less than 17 yrs. old
- victim was more than 14 yrs. old, and – defendant was less than 5 yrs. older than victim.

Sexual abuse in 2nd degree (class A misdemeanour) :

- That a person is accused of sexual abuse in the 2nd degree when he/she subjects victim to sexual contact and when the victim is :
- incapable of consent by reason of some factor other than being less than 17 yrs. old, or - less than 14 yrs. old.

Sexual abuse in 1st degree (class D misdemeanour) :

- That a person is accused of sexual abuse in the 1st degree when he/she subjects victim to sexual contact :
- by forcible compulsion, or
- when the victim is incapable of consent by reason of being physical helpless, or when the victim is less than 11 yrs. old.

Aggravated sexual abuse in 4th degree (class E felony) :

- That a person is accused of aggravated sexual abuse in the 4th degree when he/she :
- inserts a foreign object in the vagina, penis, urethra or rectum of victim, and without victim's consent by reason of some factor other than being less than 17 yrs. old, or
- inserts a finger in the vagina, urethra, penis or rectum of victim resulting in physical injury to

victim, and when the victim is incapable of consent by reason of some factor other than being less than 17 yrs. old.

- That such a conduct performed for a valid medical reason does not violate the provisions of this section.

Aggravated sexual abuse in 3rd degree (class D felony) :

- That a person is accused of aggravated sexual abuse in the 3rd degree when he/she :
- inserts a foreign object in the vagina, penis, urethra or rectum of victim :
- by forcible compulsion, or
- when the victim is incapable of consent by reason of being physical helpless, or
- when the victim is less than 11 yrs. old.
- inserts a finger in the vagina, urethra, penis or rectum of victim resulting in physical injury to victim, and when the victim is incapable of consent by reason of being mentally disabled or mentally incapacitated.
- That such a conduct performed for a valid medical reason does not violate the provisions of this section.

Aggravated sexual abuse in 2nd degree (class C felony) :

- That a person is accused of aggravated sexual abuse in the 2nd degree when he/she :
- inserts a foreign object in the vagina, penis, urethra or rectum of victim :
- by forcible compulsion, or
- when the victim is incapable of consent by reason of being physical helpless, or
- when the victim is less than 11 yrs. old.
- inserts a finger in the vagina, urethra, penis or rectum of victim resulting in physical injury to victim, and when the victim is incapable of consent by reason of being mentally disabled or mentally incapacitated.

- That such a conduct performed for a valid medical reason does not violate the provisions of this section.

Aggravated sexual abuse in 1st degree (class B felony) :

- That a person is accused of aggravated sexual abuse in the 1st degree when he/she :
- inserts a foreign object in the vagina, penis, urethra or rectum of victim :
- by forcible compulsion, or
- when the victim is incapable of consent by reason of being physical helpless, or
- when the victim is less than 11 yrs. old.
- That such a conduct performed for a valid medical reason does not violate the provisions of this section.

Course of sexual conduct against a child in 1st degree (class B felony) :

- That a person is accused of course of sexual conduct against a child in the 1st degree when, over a period of time not less than 3 months, he/she :
- engages in 2 or more acts of sexual conduct, which incld. at least 1 act of sexual intercourse, deviate sexual intercourse or aggravated sexual contact, with a child less than 11 yrs. old, or
- being 18 yrs. old or more, engages in 2 or more acts of sexual conduct, incld. at least 1 act of sexual intercourse, deviate sexual intercourse or aggravated sexual contact, with a child less than 13 yrs. old.
- That a person may not subsequently prosecuted for any other sexual offence involving the same victim unless the other charged offence occurred outside the time interval charged under this section.

Course of sexual conduct against a child in 2nd degree (class D felony) :

- That a person is accused of course of sexual conduct against a child in the 2nd degree when, over a period of time not less than 3 months, he/she :

- engages in 2 or more acts of sexual conduct, with a child less than 11 yrs. old, or
- being 18 yrs. old or more, engages in 2 or more acts of sexual conduct with a child, less than 13 yrs. old.
- That a person may not subsequently prosecutes for any other sexual offence involving the same victim unless the other charged offense occurred outside the time interval charged under this section.

Female genital mutilation (class E felony) :

- That a person is accused of female genital mutilation when he/she :
- knowingly circumcises, exercises, or infibulates the whole or any part of the labia majora, minora or clitoris of the victim, less than 18 yrs. old, or
- being a parent, guardian or other person legally responsible and charged with the care or custody of a child less than 18 yrs. old, he/she knowingly consents to the circumcision, excision or infibulations of whole or part of such child's labia majora, minora or clitoris.
- That such circumcision, excision, or infibulations is not a violation of this section if such act is :
- performed by a Registered Medical Practitioner for the sake of deteriorating health of the child, or performed by a Registered Medical Practitioner, on the person in labour or post-partum, to save the deteriorating patient.
- such procedure is required as a matter of custom or ritual.

Facilitating sexual offence with controlled substance (class D felony) :

- That a person is accused of facilitating sexual offence with controlled substance when he/she :

- knowingly and unlawfully possesses a controlled substance and administers it to victim without his/her consent and with intent to commit such conduct against victim.
- commits or attempts to commit such conduct.

ARTICLE 263 : SEXUAL PERFORMANCE BY A CHILD

Use of a child in a sexual performance (class C felony) :

- That a person is accused of using a child in a sexual performance if :

  Knowing the character and content thereof he/she employs, authorises or induces a child less than 17 yrs. old to engage in a sesual performance or being a parent, legal guardian/custodian of such child, consents to the participation by such child in a sexual performance.

Promoting an obscene sexual performance by a child (class D felony) :

- That a person is accused of promoting an obscene sexual performance by a child when:- knowing the character and content thereof, he/she produces, directs or promotes any obscene performance incld. sexual conduct by a child less than 17 year old.

Possessing an obscene sexual performance by a child (class E felony) :

- That a person is accused of promoting an obscene sexual performance by a child when:- knowing the character and content thereof, he/she knowingly has in his/her possession/control any obscene performance incld. sexual conduct by a child less than 16 year old.

Promoting a sexual performance by a child (class D felony) :

- That a person is accused of promoting a sexual performance by a child when:- knowing the character and content thereof, he/she produces, directs or promotes any obscene performance incld. sexual conduct by a child less than 17 year old.

Possessing a sexual performance by a child (class E felony):

- That a person is accused of possessing a exual performance by a child when:- knowing the character and content thereof, he/she knowingly has in his/her possession/control obscene performance incld. sexual conduct by a child less than 16 year old.

Sexual performance by a child : Affirmative defences :

- That the defendant in good faith reasonably believed the person appearing in the performance was :
- 16 yrs. old or more, under section 11 or 16 of Article 263
- 17 yrs. old or more, under section 05, 10 or 15 of Article 263
- That the person accused was an employed librarian, motion picture projectionist, stage employee, spotlight operator or theatre assistant, who does not share receipts from the sale, rental or exhibition of promotion of sexual performance.

Proof of age of child :

- That section 25 of Article 263, becomes necessary by the Court or Jury, to determine the age of the child accused of participating in a sexual performance (juvenile rape or sodomy).

SEXUAL VIOLENCE (PHYSICAL) :

SEXUAL ABUSE

Definition : That any form of sexual activity that's against your will constitutes as sexual abuse. This includes bodily contact (such as sexual kissing, touching, fondling of genitals or penetration-oral, anal, or vaginal) and genital exposure (flashing), verbal pressure for sex and sexual exploitation through pornography or prostitution. Many cases of sexual abuse never come to light. Victims can often feel ashamed and too scared to report it, fearing it could make a situation worse.

CONSENT FOR SEXUAL ACT OR BEHAVIOUR

Definition:
- That is defined as an offence which often revolves around consent.
- That is all about permission/or agreement.
- That is something which must be clearly established between two persons before any kind of sexual act or behaviour.
- That is, if an individual is accused of a sex offence, it must be poved that consent had been given by the other person.

Offence : The Sexual Offences Act 2003 governs sex laws in the UK. Under this Act, it is an offence for any male to penetrate with his penis the vagina, anus or mouth of a female or male without their consent.

Penalty : A person found guilty of this offence could be sent to prison for life.

SEXUAL ASSAULT

Offence : Assault by penetration.

The Act makes it an offence for any male or female to penetrate the vagina or anus of another person without their consent. The offence is committed where the penetration is by a part of the body e.g. a finger or anything else e.g. a bottle for sexual intent.

Penalty : A person found guilty of this offence could be sent to prison for 10 yrs.

Offence : Assault/Molestation.

The Act makes it an offence for any male or female to intentionally touch/fondle another person sexually without his or her consent.

Penalty : Under Section 3 of the Act, a person found guilty of this offence could be sent to prison for a maximum of ten years.

Offence : Causing sexual activity without consent.

It is an offence to cause or encourage another person to engage in sexual activity without his or her consent.

Penalty:
- If penetration is involved then a person found guilty of this offence could be sent to prison for life.
- If no penetration is involved then a person found guilty of this offence could be sent to prison for up to ten years.

SEXUAL TORTURE

Sexual torture/assault is as old as human civilisation and has been prevalent since ancient times in one form or other.

Types:
- Mental : forced nakedness, humiliations, abuses, threats and forced to witness others being sexually tortured/assaulted.
- Physical : molestation/assault of victim by the tormentor or by using an Animal for physical contact with the victim.

Objectives/Motives :
- Forceful confession – misused as legal proof.
- Personal vendetta-by torturing individual or his family members.
- To pollute (defile) the race.
- To satiate - sexual starvation of soldiers at war by assaulting women of enemy.
- Ethnic conflicts.
- Personality disorder - sexual assault of men/ women in custody by a mentally deranged person.
- Misuse of custodial power - by sexual assault of victims in custody.
- Distortion of the personality - victim tortured to develop helplessness, loss of self confidence, and worthlessness, insane.
- To extract information.
- Family violence (domestic/or marital violence), child abuse, sexual harassment, rape, kidnapping, hostage taking and terrorist act and pornography etc. Should also be viewed as human right violation as its repercussions are far reaching in society.

Modus operandi :

Psychological :

- Verbal abuses, threats, and humiliation, publically
- Undressing (nudity) in front of opposite sex esp. fair sex.
- Being photographed in compromising positions.
- Forced to masturbate in front of others.
- Forced to watch sexual torture/assault of others.
- Forced to perform sexual torture/assault on other collegue victims.

Physical :

- Introduction of chillies, irritants etc. into eyes, mouth, vagina, or anus.
- Introduction of ants, rats, insects, etc. into vagina, or anus.
- Penetration of vagina, anus by batons, rods, handle bars, candles etc
- Plucking of nails, fingers, teeth, toes by instruments.
- Use of burning cigarettes on sensitive parts (genitals, breasts etc.).
- Electrical shocks – given to sensitive parts.
- Mutilation of breasts, genitals, buttocks etc.

Sexual :

- Fondling, squeezing, kissing/sucking of breasts, buttocks, genitalia.
- Raped by person of same/opposite sex.
- Sexual assault (Rape etc.) by animals e.g. trained dogs, monkeys.

Medico-legal aspect :

- That sexual torture/assault punishable in most civilised countries.
- That the major complications are usually conflict with society and its laws.
- That to prevent these sexual torture/assaults :

- Public awareness - to condemn these barbarous, uncivilised acts and fight against torture.
- Media support–esp. for women's rights, curbing domestic violence.
- Police and administration's support–for implementation of law strictly.
- Motivation of National Commission for Women and ILO.
- Medical organisations participation-should spread the ethical principles that address human right and their violations.
- Motivation of Employers (Public and Private) – to set up women cells in order to curb sexual exploitation at their working places.
- Motivation of every physician to realise his/her duty to protest his/her fellow citizen against violation of his right.

(*Source :* Tokyo declaration, 1975)

SODOMY

Definition : That an anal intercourse by a man (active agent) with another man or woman (passive agent).

Offence:
- That an anal intercourse by a man (active agent) with another man or woman (passive agent), with or without consent of passive agent.

Penalty:
- That both agents (active and passive) with their consent liable to punishment under law.
- That the active agent is liable to punishment if this act is done without the consent of passive agent.

Diagnosis : Signs of sodomy on the Active agent :
- Consent : written consent of the accused to be taken, or a warrant from the Magistrate or an Authorised Officer, for examination of the accused.
- Of clothes worn by the accused for evidence of struggle e.g. torn, stained of dust, blood and semen.
- Signs of struggle.
- Signs of recent intercourse :

- Abrasions of the glans penis and prepuce, esp. on the frenulum.

Signs of sodomy on the Passive agent :

- Signs of struggle (forced act without consent) e.g. scratches, abrasions, bruises or lacerations of the anus–esp. If the passive agent is a young boy/or girl.
- Stains : of blood, semen or both per anus or on the cloth.
- Discharge : of pus (gonorrhoea) per anus or on the cloth.

Investigation: Anal swab and smear–for detection of spermatozoa (+ve sign) and pus cells (gonococci) Urethral discharge - for detection of pus cells (gonococci).

Offence: - That an anal intercourse by a man (active agent) with another man or woman (passive agent), with or without consent of passive agent.

Penalty: - That both agents (active and passive) with their consent liable to punishment under law
- That the active agent is liable to punishment if this act is done without the consent of passive agent.

Judgment: - Imprisonment, fine or both.

TORTURE (MEDICO-LEGAL ASPECT)

Definition : An act of deliberate hurting someone in order to compel them to confess :

"Deliberate systematic or wanton infliction of physical/or mental injury or damage by one or more persons acting alone or on the orders of the higher authority, to force another person to disclose information/to make a forced confession, or for any other reason".

(*Source :* World Medical Association in its Tokyo Declaration, 1975)

Violation : Global issue of Concern-Human Rights Violation:

Torture is considered as an important human rights violation–a worldwide misuse of power. "Any act by which severe pain or suffering (physical or mental) inflicted intentionally on a person for purposes e.g. obtaining information or a confession, punishing him for an act he/she or a third person has committed/or is suspected of having committed, or intimidating/or coercing him for any reason based on discrimination of any kind, when such pain or suffering is inflicted by/or at the instigation of/or with the consent/or acquiescence of a public official/or another person acting in an official capacity, excluding pain of suffering inflicted from, inherent in or incidentals to lawful sanctions."

(*Source :* United Nations Convention, December 1991).

Motives:
- To extort a confession–misused as legal proof.
- To extract information.
- To punish a person.
- To suppress persons associated with tortured person (violent distortion).
- To torture/torment-prisoners, political opponents, by methods incld. water boarding etc.

Rehabilitation: Anti-torture and rehabilitation centre is in Copenhagen Denmark, where torture victims are rehabilitated and studies are carried out on the effects of torture. So many works are done but many objectives are still to be fulfilled.

DOCTORS AND TORTURE

Definition : That a doctor may be involved illegally in the process of torture/assault directly or indirectly, either voluntarily (a human right activist) or under compulsion from the society, government or terrorists. He may participate unwillingly or unintentionally or may participate directly with malafide intentions.

Motives:
- To assess victim's threshold to tolerate pain/suffering.
- To provide professional knowledge and skill to the tormentor.

- To monitor torture/assault by means of medical therapy.
- To suppress medical information deliberately while issuing medical certificates esp. death certificates, surgical or autopsy reports etc.
- To conceal/withhold information about incidence of abuses.
- To participate actively in administering torture/ assault.

Role of Doctors :

Ethical : That doctors in the government and military services are most vulnerable (under compulsions) to pressure from seniors, for these illegal acts.

Medico-legal aspect :

- That certain sexual perversions are punishable in most civilised countries, and doctors have no immunity.
- That the major complications are usually conflict with society and its laws..

TORTURE (PSYCHOLOGICAL) :

TROLLS /SADISTS

Definition : That both trolls and sadists feel glee at the distress of others. That they just want to have fun, and Internet is their playground, although it's just not funny anymore. That with increasing death and rape threats, bitter and incessant abuse and psychological torture that has even led some to suicides, and that hate trolling is currently a menacing activity carried out by the positively twisted, and the only way to fight back is to stand up to them. Trolls have always found place in popular culture since the later Nineties, and till recently was endured as a kind of pungent kick that came with the enriching, particularly experience that is the Imternet. But anyone who has been remotely active online, will know that TBAT just doesn't cut it anymore for the invective-laden, violent, hate-filled and often deeply terrifying comments that are doing the rounds these days. That troll is an imaginary creature in the ancient Scandinavian stories, like a very large or very small ugly person.

Vulnerable: That persons seen to sway opinion e.g. journalists, film critics, activists, stand-up comics, Twitter celebrities or public figures, are often the most vulnerable to it. Perhaps those who indulge in this derive a fake sense of power, aided by the anonymity the Internet provides (R Sardesai, editor-in-chief IBN7 network).

- Gender: while men are abused too, trolling is not entirely gender neutral and women get the rawest end of the deal. Men too mostly get abused with regard to their mothers and sisters, displaying a deep-seated patriarchal mindset. That men go after women with a sense of powerlessness because they feel unfulfilled somewhere. That with the changing social scenario, women are no longer dependent on men the way their mothers were. That's unsettling for them and thereby reacting with violence, both in real life and online.

  (S Bhaduri, Psychoanalyst).

Celebrity Trolls: That celebrities evoke scary levels of devotion among their fans, which translate into troll armies online. International: That different. Equally aggressive or sometimes more so, these fan bases work in unison against anyone, even other public figures, for what they feel is best for their idol. Examples:

- Justin Bieber: Beliebers-a rabid fan base, defend the teen idol's every action (DUIs, arrests, public fights etc.) and thrash anyone suggesting otherwise.
- Lady Gaga; during TV show, host Kelly Osborne criticised Gaga for missing a red carpet appearance, and Gaga's fans routinely called her fat and asked her to kill herself.
- Beyonce: her fan base often miffed with the singer for actions, they think she shouldn't do

e.g. her recent friendship with Kim Kardashian, which drew ire.

Web without name:- That same anonymity lies at the centre of abusive trolling. That in real life, interaction is aided by biological cues e.g. hurt, shame or anger which prevent us from being abusive in person. But this connect is missing in the online world. That it brings out the worst in human behaviour when a person is behind a computer or tablet screen. "The real world bears consequences. That the rules of good behaviour (whether formed), have't been implemented firmly (HK Arora, Psychologist).

- That absence of social cues also fails to generate empathy online, because that's what essentially enables people to identify with the pain and discomfort of others. That there is nothing to jolt his/her (Troll's) consciousness or tell how hurt one could be from his/her comments, which in turn makes one crueller, aggressive and animal like. That there is a delusional control over the medium where the abuser often feels that he/she can exit anytime without any harm.

  (S Bhaduri, Psychoanalyst).
- That democracy at home and school is important, as childen need to be made aware that there could be legal implications of their internet use. That enough emotional contact and sufficient education about the law can curb the misuse of Internet (H Shetty, HTC)).

Checks and Controls :

- That Internet abuse is a global phenomenon, many countries have evolved active laws to counter it. Young Internet users should guard against putting up content that could lead them in trouble under the IT Act. Parents should supervise net use.

  UK: apart from running several campaigns against cyber bullying, recently arrested two men, threatening rape and violence to a woman on twitter.

Winnipeg: online trolling correlates to narcissism, Machiavellianism (being deceitful and cunning), psychopathy, and sadism, with sadism being the most robust link (EE Buckels, University of Manitoba).

India: inspite of the law being fairly toothless, when it comes to online abuse, it does lay the responsibility on the agency to moderate the comments hosted on it. As per Section 75 of the IT Act, an agency hosting such abuse does become complicit in it, and has to exercise due diligence to remove it (P Duggal, SC lawyer). That while most news websites monitor comments, on Twitter a lot of vulgar hate speech continues to thrive. Currently the social network has a 'report tweet' feature, under which one can report abusive tweets, and for which there is a round-the-clock team to take care of the grievances. However, abuse continues to proliferate.

- Facebook: comparatively sees the least trolling, owing to the presence of a wide network of friends, pictures and family ready to judge you.
- Twitter: offers a lower degree of personalisation.
- Reddit: requires nothing more than an email ID to join, sees greater degree of abuse and hate speech.
- 4chan: public bulletin board, where anyone can post anonymously, is the dark space of Internet, where users goad others into suicide and serious self-harm e.g. 4chan users organised groups to goad teenaged girls to cut themselves in the name of teen pop musician Justin Bieber.

Offence:
- Thane: Jealous, a school girl created a fake online profile of her classmate, and posted obscene pictures of her on it.

Thane:
- Mumbai: a 22 year old chartered student, hacked into the e-taxation accounts of Anil Ambani, Salman Khan, Shah Rukh Khan, Sachin Tandulkar and MS Dhoni and others, out of

curiosity. That he was booked under Sections of the IT Act.

(*Source:* HTC).

Act : Indian IT Act does make provisions to prevent online abuse.

Section : under Section 66-A, sending abusive messages or adopting a menacing character over an electronic medium is punishable with three yrs. imprisonment and a fine. That action is taken only when an individual complaint being lodged at the local police station (cumbersome - abuse generally generated from anonymous accounts).

VIOLENCE AGAINST MEDICAL ESTABLISHMENTS

Definition : Public attacks on doctors have become more mainly as a result of grief once the patient dies and the relatives have to pay hefty amount as hospital charges.

In some cases, attacks are planned in such a way to frighten the hospital management and get the hospital charges waived or demand money as compensation. If the patient belongs to a dominant local caste or political party, then the hospital staff will have horrid time.

Penalty : Prevention of Violence and damage to Property Act 2012

Indian scenario:

"Any offence committed under the section shall be cognisable and non-bailable." Attack on doctors in Kerala may invite 3 years in jail, a fine of ₹ 50K,

July, 2012. Thiruvananthapuram: The State Assembly passed an Act, by which any attack against a duty bound doctor, a hospital or its staff would invite an imprisonment of upto 3 years and a fine of ₹ 50K. The offender will also be liable to pay to the hospital a compensation of twice the amount of the purchase price of medical equipment damaged and loss caused to the property as determined by the Court trying the offender.

Act : **PREVENTION OF VIOLENCE and DAMAGE TO PROPERTY ACT :**

THE PUNJAB PROTECTION OF MEDICARE SERVICE PERSONS AND MEDICARE INSTITUTIONS (PREVENTION OF VIOLENCE AND DAMAGE TO PROPERTY) ACT, 2008

(Punjab Act No. 26 of 2008) Department of Legal and Legislative Affairs, Punjab, Notification. The 30th October, 2008.

No. 29-Leg./2008.–The following Act of the Legislature of the State of Punjab received the assent of Governor of Punjab on the 10th October, 2008, and is hereby published for general information :

Definition : Defined as an Act to provide for the protection of Medicare Service Persons and Medicare Service Institutions in the State of Punjab and for prevention of violence and damage to the property and for the matters connected therewith or incidental thereto.

Enactment : Enacted by the Legislature of the State of Punjab in 2008 (30-10-2008) shall come into force at once, vide notification dated 30th October 2008.

Jurisdiction: Extends to the whole of Punjab State.

Definitions: In this Act, unless the context otherwise requires, -

(a) "Medicare Service Institution" means an institution, providing Medicare service either in the Medicare Service Institution or through Mobile Medical Unit or by arranging medical camps, which is under the control of the Central Government or the State Government or a local body including any private hospital having facility of treatment of the sick and used for their reception or stay, any private maternity home, where women are usually received and accommodated for the purpose of confinement and ante-natal and post-natal care in connection with the child birth or anything connected herewith, and any private nursing home used or intended to be used for the reception and accommodation of persons suffering from any sickness, injury or infirmity whether of body or mind, and providing of treatment of nursing or both of them and includes convalescent home ;

(b) "Medicare Service Person" in relation to a Medicare Service Institution, shall include, -

Registered Medical Practitioner, Registered Practitioner and Practitioner, working in a Medicare Service Institution :

- Nurse;
- Auxiliary Nurse and Mid-wife;
- Nurse-Dai;
- Trained-Dai;
- Medical Student;
- Nursing Student;
- Para Medical Worker; and
- Other staff or workers directly or indirectly engaged by a Medicare Service Institution for providing the required services;

Explanation–For the purpose of this Act, the expressions Registered Medical Practitioner, Medical Practitioner, Practitioner, Nurse, Auxiliary Nurse and Midwife and trained Dai, shall have the same meanings, as assigned to them in the Punjab Medical Registration Act, 1916, the Punjab Nurses Registration Act, 1932, the Punjab Ayurvedic and Unani Practitioners Act, 1963 and the Punjab Homeopathic Practitioners Act, 1965;

(c) "Medical Student" means a student, who is undergoing training or studies in Medical in medical profession;

(d) "Mobile Medical Unit" means an ambulance, equipped with medical equipment, used for providing medicare services;

(e) "Nursing Student" means a student, who is undergoing training or studies in nursing profession;

(f) "Offender" means any person, who either by himself or as a member or leader of a group of persons or organisation commits or attempts to commit or abets or incites the commission or violence;

(g) "Paramedical Worker" means a person, who assists the Medicare Service Person providing Medicare services;

(h) "Property" shall include both movable and immovable property; and

(i) "Violence" means any act, which causes or may cause any harm, injury or endanger life, obstruct or hinder any Medicare Service Person in the discharge of his duty in a Medicare Service Institution or damage to property in Medicare Service Institution. Prohibition of violence : Any act of violence against a Medicare Service Person or damage to property in a Medicare Service Institution, shall be prohibited.

Penalty : An offender, who commits any act in contravention of the provisions of this Act shall be punished with an imprisonment, which may extend to one year, or with fine, which may extend to ₹ 50,000, or with both.

Cognisance : Any offence committed under this Act, shall be cognisable and non-bailable and shall be triable by the Court of Judicial Magistrate of the First Class.

Recovery of : (1) In addition to the punishment as specified in Section 4, the Offender shall also be liable to pay a penalty of twice the amount of purchase price of medical equipment damaged or loss caused to the property, as may be determined by the Court referred to in Section 5.

(2) If the offender has not paid the penalty, imposed under sub-section (1) the same shall be recoverable as arrears of land revenue.

Derogation : The provisions of this Act shall be in addition to the provisions of any other law, for the time being in force.

THE HARYANA PROTECTION OF MEDICARE SERVICE PERSONS AND MEDICARE INSTITUTIONS ACT, 2009

(Haryana Act No. 14 of 2009) Haryana Government, Law and Legislative Department, Notification, The 26th March, 2009

No. Leg. 18/2009.–The following Act of the Legislature of the State of Haryana received the assent of Governor of Haryana on the 19th March, 2009, and is hereby published for general information :

Definition : defined as an Act to prohibit violence against Medicare Service Persons and damage to property in Medicare Service Institutions and for matters connected therewith or incidental thereto.

Enactment : Enacted by the Legislature of the State of Haryana in 2009 (19th March, 2009), shall come into force at once, vide notification dated 26-3-2009

Jurisdiction : Extends to the whole of Haryana State.

Definitions: In this Act, unless the context otherwise requires :

(a) "Medicare Service Institution" means an institution, used or intended to be used for the reception, accommodation, treatment and medicare of persons suffering from any sickness, injury or infirmity whether of body or mind and providing of treatment or nursing or both of them and includes maternity home, convalescent home, nursing home or hospital etc. owned or controlled either by the State Government or Central Government or any person or individual;

(b) "Medicare Service Person" in relation to a Medicare Service Institution, shall include, -

(i) Registered Medical Practitioners (including those having provisional registration);

(ii) Registered Nurses;

(iii) Medical Students;

(iv) Nursing Students;

(v) Para-Medical Workers.

Penalty : (1) Whoever, endangers the life of or causes any harm, injury, intimidation, obstruction or hindrance to any Medicare Service Person in the discharge of duty or damage to any property in Medicare Service Institution, commits an act of violence which shall be an offence under this Act.

(2) Whoever, either by himself or as a member or as a leader of a group of persons or organisation commits or attempts to commit or abets or incites the commission of offence, shall be punished with imprisonment for a term of three years and shall also be liable to a penalty of actual amount of purchase price of medical equipment damaged and loss caused to the property as may be determined by the competent Court.

Cognisable offence : The offence committed under Section 3 shall be cognisable and non-bailable.

Recovery as arrears of land revenue. If a person fails to pay the penal amount under Section 3, the said amount shall be recoverable as if it were arrears of land revenue.

Act not in derogation of any other law : The provisions of this Act shall be in addition to and not in derogation of the provisions of any other law, for the time being in force.

Power to make rules :

The State Government may, by notification in the Official Gazette, make rules for carrying out the purposes of this Act.

Every rule made under this Act shall be laid, as soon as may be, after it is made, before the House of State Legislative, while it is in session.

VIOLENCE AGAINST WOMEN

Definition : That is defined as any act of gender-based violence that results in, or is likely to result in, physical, sexual, or psychological harm or suffering to women, incld. threats of such acts, coercion or arbitrary deprivation of liberty, whether occurring in public or private life. It encompasses, but is not limited to, "physical, sexual and psychological violence occurring in the family, incld. battering, sexual abuse of female children in the household, dowry related violence, marital rape, female genital mutilation and other traditional practices harmful to women, non-spousal violence and violence related to exploitation; physical, sexual and psychological violence occurring within the general community, incld. rape, sexual abuse, sexual harassment and intimidation at work, in educational institutions and elsewhere; trafficking in women and forced prostitution; and physical, sexual and psychological violence perpetrated or condoned by the state, wherever it occurs. (Declaration on the Elimination of Violence against Women, adopted by the United Nations General Assembly, 1993).

Forms : Violence against women takes many forms, from the overt to the subtle.

WHO has adopted the following definitions of physical and sexual violence to aid in research and programming, concentrating on identifiable acts :

* Physical violence : perpetrators are looking for weak and easily submissive victims. A woman has been slapped, pushed, shoved, or had something (acid or foreign body) thrown at her, or had her hair pulled; hit with a fist or something else that could hurt; choked or burnt; threatened with or had a weapon used against her.
* Sexual violence : a woman has been physically forced to have sexual intercourse; had sexual

intercourse because she was afraid of what her partner might do; or forced to do something sexual she found degrading or humiliating.

* Psychological violence : though recognised as a serious and pervasive problem, emotional violence does not yet have a widely accepted definition.

  Example : a woman has been humiliated or belittled; been scared or intimidated purposefully.

* Domestic (Intimate-partner) violence : a woman has encountered any of the above types of violence, at the hands of an intimate partner or ex-partner; this is one of the most common and universal forms of violence experienced by women.

Indian scenario :

- That while many women made giant strides in their own fields, the issue of violence against women remains an enduring blot on Indian society.
- That the girl who died after that horrific gang-rape in Delhi seemed, for a while to bring about a real change in attitudes towards women, but only short-lived. The attacks on women in the Capital have not abated one bit. Even little girls have not been spared. In many cases, the perpetrators of rape and murder are those known to the victims. But the increasing violence against women is not only a Delhi phenomenon.
- That, in Kolkata, ruled by a woman Chief Minister, there have been instances of many rapes and murders of young women including a tribal panchayat sanctioned gang-rape. Each time the Chief Minister dismissed the allegations of rape as political plot against her government by her political opponents.
- That, in UP, almost daily there have been incidents of violence against women incld. rapes and murders of very young girls. Many women were raped during the Muzaffarnagar riots and live in fear in the relief camps, while

their assailants walk about scot-free. The rapes and murders of young women on their way home from work have risen many-fold.

- That in short, women's vulnerability has increased manyfold, while the strengthened laws have not really been a deterrent.
- That by and large, the safety of women has not been debated by our lawmakers who are too busy squabbling among themselves.
- That mushrooming of khap panchayats, which invariably pass anti-women verdicts, seems to have political sanction, although those passing such retrograde orders should have been behind bars.
- That the only hope, when the women will be able to make political parties listen through their franchise votes.
- That India ratified the United Nations Convention on Elimination of All Forms of Discrimination against Women (CEDAW) in 1993.
- That The Protection of Women from Domestic Violence Act, 2005, tries to be in line with this convention.

International scenario :

WHO multi-country study on women's health and domestic violence against women in 10 mainly developing Countries found that among women aged 15-49:

* 20 per cent of women and 5-10 per cent of men report being victims of sexual violence as children.
* Intimate-partner and sexual violence are mostly perpetrated by men against girls and women. Child sexual abuse affects boys and girls.
* 0.3-11.5 per cent of women reported experiencing sexual violence by a non-partner since the age of 15 yrs.
* 15 per cent of women in Japan and 71 per cent of women in Ethiopia reported physical and/or sexual violence by an intimate partner.

* First sexual experience for many women was reported as forced–17 per cent in rural Tanzania, 24 per cent in rural Peru and 30 per cent in rural Bangladesh.

(Prashant Chaudhary, HT January 06, 2013)

Remedy:
- That given the impression of a confident and strong person may catch the perpetrators off guard and the victim may be able to run away. Pushing him off (if he's closer than desirable), saying NO and STOP are setting boundaries.
- That the voice should be assertive and loud and words such as sorry, please, can you, could you, etc. have to be avoided. No smiling either! Most women try to be polite and smile when they feel uncomfortable. Always present yourself as a resolute, strong and unintimidated person. Your facial expression and body language should portray that as well.
- That for bystanders help, yell and tell them that you are being attacked. Many times the bystanders are reluctant to intervene fearing the attacker's motives. Failure to intimidate the attacker, change your tactic. Reason with him, for not ruining his carrier by rusting in a jail. That failure to convince him by reasoning, may force you to fight–by serious shouting, yelling, kicking, punching, elbowing, kneeing, scratching, eye gouging, bitting, well pretty much using everything you can do and what you have been practicing. The aim is to fight him hard, even if that means getting hurt in the process.
- That mandatory training of martial arts for self-protection for girls, women.

References:
1. VP Jacob : Fight your attacker tooth and nail, HT, March, 2014 :
2. The Editor : She will be heard through the ballot, HT, March, 2014.

TRANSPLANTATION OF HUMAN ORGANS

Definition : An illegal trading of human organs (removal, storage, transplantation, issuing an advertisement).

Offence : Both agents (active and passive) with their consent are liable to punishment under law, while only the active agent is liable to punishment if this act is done without the consent of passive agent.

Penalty : Imprisonment, fine or both, under section 19 of Transplantation of Human Organs Act, 1994.

Section 19 of Transplantation of Human Organs Act:

Complaint : Sonu Maheswari, a Bhatinda based social activist, complained to police, against Karnail Singh of Khera Jattan village, Patiala Distt., for advertising in a vernacular newspaper on 8th October, 2010, inviting persons for negotiations, related to buying or selling of kidneys. The police failed to take any action and did not register the case against the accused. The social activist moved the Court, following the police's refusal to book the advertiser. Finally, the complainant filed a public interest litigation (PIL) plea in the Punjab and Haryana High Court, on 8th August, 2011.

Offence : Issuing an advertisement in a Hindi Daily, inviting people, who wanted to buy or sell kidneys for negotiations.

Penality : The accused has been arrested on the orders of Punjab and Haryana High Court Complaint : Pankaj Rai (Retd. Major), a member of PBT, filed a criminal case against the doctors and Fortis hospital, Bangalore, following the illicit transplantation of pancreas that eventually resulted in the untimely death of his wife Seema Rai, in 2010. She died from septic shock, following a botched up surgery by the doctors of Fortis Hospital, to transplant pancreas without even obtaining the "informed consent", or explaining the risks involved to her and her husband.

Offence : Illegal Transplantation of Human Organs, with ulterior motive, and Medical Negligence.

Penalty : Cancellation of licence of Fortis Hospital, Bengaluru, and action against the accused doctors (PBT INDIA, 17th September, 2011).

CHAPTER - VII

ACTS AND LAWS

ACTS (CIVIL AND CRIMINAL) RELATED TO MEDICAL PROFESSION:

- **Civil and Criminal Proceeding**
- **Civil Procedure Code, 1908**
- **Consumer Protection Act (CPA), 1986**
- **Consumer Protection Act (CPA), 1995**
- **Clinical Establishment (Registration and Regulation) Act, 2010**
- **Consent**
- **Contempt of Courts Act, 1971**
- **Copyright Act, 1957**
- **Domestic Violence**
- **Dowry Prohibition Act, 1961**
- **Drugs and Cosmetics Act, 1940**
- **Drugs and Magic Remedies (Objectionable Advertisements) Act, 1954**
- **Dying declaration**
- **Environment Protection Act, 1986 :**
    - **Bio-Medical Waste (Management and Handling) Rules, 1998**
- **Fatal Accidents Act, 1855**
- **Immoral Traffic (Prevention) Act, 1956**
- **Medical Termination of Pregnancy (MTP) :**
    - **Medical Termination of Pregnancy Act, 1971**
    - **Medical Termination of Pregnancy Act, 2002**

- **Medical Termination of Pregnancy Regulations, 2003**
- **Mental Health Act, 1987**
- **Mental Retardation and Multiple Disabilities Act, 1999**
- **Narcotic Drugs and Psychotropic Substances Act, 1985:**
  - **Narco-Analysis**
- **Oaths Act, 1969**
- **Poisons Act, 1919**
- **Pre-natal Diagnostic Techniques (PNDT) Acts and Rules:**
  - **PNDT Act, 1994**
  - **PNDT Rules, 1996**
  - **PNDT Amendment Act, 2002**
  - **PNDT Amendment Rules, 2003**
- **Prevention of Food Adulteration Act, 1954**
- **Prevention of Violence and Damage to Property Act, 2008**

(The Punjab Protection of Medicare Service Persons and Medicare Institutions)

- **Prevention of Violence and Damage to Property Act, 2009**

(The Haryana Medicare Service Persons and Medicare Service Institutions)

- **Prohibition of Child Marriage Act, 2006**
- **Protection of Human Rights Act, 1993**
  - **National Human Rights Commission**
  - **State Human Rights Commissions**
- **Protection of Women from Domestic Violence Act, 2005**
- **Protection of Women against Sexual Harassment at Workplace Bill, 2007**
- **Protection of Women against Sexual Harassment at Workplace Bill, 2013**
- **Registration Act, 1908**
- **Registration of Births and Deaths Act, 1969**
- **Transplantation of Human Organs Act, 1994**

IMPORTANT ACTS AND RULES :

CIVIL AND CRIMINAL PROCEEDING :

Definition: - That Court shall not bring about a situation whereby a criminal proceeding would remain stayed.

- That where a Civil Proceeding as well as a Criminal Proceeding is pending, the latter shall get primacy.
- That a decision by a Criminal Court does not bind the Civil Court while a decision by the Civil Court binds the Criminal Court.

CIVIL PROCEDURE CODE, 1908 :

Definition: - That C.P.C. is a procedural law

- That it is "procedure" something designed to facilitate and further its ends
- That it is not a penal enactment for punishment and penalties
- That it is not a thing designed to trip people up.

Aims: - Scope and object of C.P.C. : all the rules of procedure are handmaid of justice.

CONSUMER PROTECTION ACT (CPA)-1986

Definition: - That CPA is to protect the interest of the user/or purchaser (consumer) of goods/or service, from exploitation by the seller/or service provider.

- That the act was passed by the Indian Parliament in 1986.

Aims: - To protect the interest of the consumer (purchaser/or consumer) of the goods/or service, from exploitation by the seller/or service provider.

CONSUMER PROTECTION ACT (CPA)-1995

Definition: - That to protect the interest of the consumer (purchaser/or consumer) of the goods/or service, from exploitation by the seller/or service provider.

- That currently the doctor-patient relationship has been commercialised to a great extent, resulting in rising trend in medical negligence.

Necessity:
- That Medical services were brought into the purview of CPA in 1995.
- That prior to CPA enactment, the aggrieved patient/or relatives had three alternatives for redressal of grievances i.e. to approach :
- the Civil Courts
- the Criminal Courts
- the Medical Councils.
- That so far justice to the patients has been denied due to reasons :
- Enormous delays
- Hectic and cumbersome Court procedures.
- Medical Councils have practically become toothless (powerless) and corrupt (malpractices).
- That is why the aggrieved and unsatisfied patients or their relatives demanded and have been approaching the Consumer Courts (established) these days with great expectations.

Expectations: That to expect Good Medical Practices from doctors e.g. :
- To make the patient's care, doctor's first concern
- To protect and promote the health of patients and the public
- To receive a good standard of practice and patient's care from doctors
- To provide the patients the information they want or need in a way they can understand
- To maintain healthy doctor-patient relationship.

Benefits:
- No Court fee or stamp duty
- No enormous delays and without any hectic and cumbersome procedures
- Simple procedure i.e. complaint can be filed in a specific format
- Speedy disposal of the case i.e. less time consuming.

Forums:
- District Consumer–at the lowest level
- State Consumer Commission–at the middle level

- National Consumer Commission–at the highest level
- Supreme Court–a final order passed by the National Consumer Commission is appealable to the Supreme Court.

Litigations : Medical Negligence is the base of all litigations against doctors under CPA.

Burden of Proof : The burden of proof is always on the complainant. He/she has to prove that the damage has been done due to the doctor's negligence and such negligence is the direct and proximate cause of the damage.

Resistance (Resentment) posed by Medical Profession :

Apprehension: A perceptible sense of fright is common amongst majority of the doctors due to following factors/reasons :

- Frivolous complaints may be lodged against the doctors either to harass or to black-mail them
- Inherent risk may always be there in any form of treatment
- Response of an individual may be variable from patient to patient e.g. a drug may be effective in one patient, while ineffective in another patient
- Speed of recovery is variable amongst each individual and may/or may not be dependant upon treatment alone, but also on the patient's strength
- Basic infrastructures e.g. Clinical laboratory, X-ray, Ventillator etc. may not be made available at every placel (mainly due to cost factor).

Defensive medicine :

- As a precautionary measure (safety purpose) many doctors have been opting for defensive medicine–aimed at avoiding medical negligence suits and hefty compensation claims, resulting in wastage of time and energy, besides wastage of financial and medical resources and delayed treatment of the patient (by advising investigations– many a times are not absolutely required).

Insurance coverage :

- These days many doctors (GPs and Specialists) esp. in the private sector have been opting for insurance cover, in order to prevent financial loss besides mental tension, resulting from various litigations relating to the medical negligence charges brought against them at Consumer Courts (Consumer Redressal Forum) and in Criminal Courts under Section 304-A of IPC Act.

Conclusion:- That there is hardly any reason for any honest doctor to entertain any fear if they are doing their jobs properly with amicable attitude towards their patients and their relatives.

- That Consumer Protection Act (CPA) has changed only the procedure of Law and not the principles of Law.
- That the doctors should rather welcome CPA.
- That doctors are also the consumers of various goods and professional services.

CLINICAL ESTABLISHMENT (REGISTRATION AND REGULATION) ACT 2010

Constitution: The Clinical Establishment Act 2010 (passed by both the houses of Indian Parliament) was enacted under Article 252 of the Constitution.

Definition : The Clinical Establishment is defined under Section 2(c) of the Act as :

(i) A hospital, maternity home, nursing home, dispensary, clinic, sanatorium or an institution by whatever name called that offers services, facilities requiring diagnosis, treatment or care for illness, injury, deformity, abnormality or pregnancy in any recognised system of medicine (Allopathy, Homeopathy, Ayurveda, Unani or Siddha), except the establishments run by the Armed Forces.

Explanation : That for the purpose of this clause "Armed Forces" means the forces constituted under the Army Act, 1950, and the Navy Act, 1957.

(ii) A place established as an independent entity or part of an establishment referred to in sub-clause (i), in connection with the diagnosis or treatment of diseases where pathological, bacteriological, genetic, radiological, chemical, biological investigations or other diagnostic or investigative services with the aid of laboratory or other medical equipment, are usually carried on, and established and administered or maintained by any person or body of persons, whether incorporated or not, and shall include a clinical establishment owned, controlled or managed by :

(a) The Government or a department of the Government ;

(b) A trust, whether public or private;

(c) A corporation (including a society) registered under a Central, Provincial or State Act, whether or not owned by the Government;

(d) A local authority;

(e) An individual doctor.

Jurisdiction:- That the Act was enacted by the Central Government under Article 252 of the Constitution for implementation in the :

- States of Arunachal Pradesh, Himachal Pradesh, Mizoram and Sikkim;
- Union Territories;
- Other States have a choice of implementing this legislation or enacting their own legislation on the subject;
- That Any place where a patient is examined or advised treatment, is a Clinical Establishment (CE) and has to be registered under this Act.
- That no free medical camps or eye camps can be held - as the place will not be registered;
- That no home visits can be made;
- That no home deliveries can be performed;
- That no mobile health clinics can be run – as the particular area may not be registered for the Act.

Aims:
- That registration is mandatory
- That the purpose of the Act is to provide for the registration and regulation of clinical establishments with a view to prescribe minimum standards of facilities and services, which may be provided by them i.e. :

(a) To prevent quackery :
- That under the Act, only qualified persons will be able to practice medicine
- That under the Act, even single practitioner shall be covered by CE
- That under the Act, registration of all clinical establishments, shall be mandatory.
- That to run an unregistered clinical establishment, shall be an offence.

(b) To abide by the principles of Good Medical Practice.
- That Good Medical Practice sets out the principles and values on which good practice is founded; these principles together describe medical professionalism in action.

Registration:
- That as per the Act, registration is mandatory for all clinical establishments.
- That the CE Act is governed by Sections 12(1), 12(2), 2(o) and 10:

Section 12(1): Under this section :
- That for registration and re-registration, it would be mandatory for all clinical establishments to fulfil the following criteria :
- That to prescribe the minimum standards of facilities and services
- That to prescribe the minimum requirement of personnel
- That to prescribe provisions for maintenance of records and reporting
- That to prescribe such other conditions.

Section 12(2): The clinical establishment shall undertake to provide within the staff and facilities available, such medical examination and treatment as may be required to stabilise the emergency medical condition of any individual who comes or is brought to such clinical establishment.

Conclusion : The Act provides that every CE will have to treat all types of emergency cases and provide treatment in order to stabilise it before referring to other hospital/institute.

Section 2(o): Under this section stabilisation has been defined in the Act as:

"to stabilise (with the grammatical variations and cognate expressions)" means, with respect to an emergency medical condition specified in clause (d), to provide such medical treatment of the condition as may be necessary to assure, within reasonable medical probability, that no material deterioration of the condition is likely to result from or occur during the transfer of the individual from a clinical establishment".

Conclusion : The Act provides that every CE will have to treat all types of emergency cases and provide treatment in order to stabilise it before referring to other hospital/institute.

Section 10 : The State Government by notification, shall appoint the District Registering Authority for each district for registration of clinical establishments.

Composition of District Registration Authority :

Chairperson : District Collector

Convenor : District Health Officer

Members (3) : On terms and conditions prescribed by Central Government.

Doctor's point of view : To avoid arbitrary punishment, one of the three nominated members of the District Registering Authority, should be a member from the legal profession on the lines of the similar provision under Section 21 of the Delhi Medical Council Act, 1997, and under Section 17(6) of the PNDT Act, 1994

Procedure for Registration :

- That registration is done by the District Registering authority (District Health Officer).

- That the Provisional registration issued within ten days of submission of application as prescribed, without any inquiry or inspection.
- That Provisional registration is renewable yearly.
- That the establishments existing before commencement of the Act will have to apply within a year and those started after the commencement of the Act, within six months of the date of their establishment.
- That the registration will be non-transferable.
- That Provisional registration will not be granted beyond two years from the date of notification of standards in case of establishments that existed before the notification of standards, and beyond six months of notification of standards in case of those established after the notification of standards.
- That Permanent registration will be granted for a period of five years, on submission of application along with fees and evidence of compliance with prescribed standards. The particulars of the applicant will be published for information and for any objections by the public within 30 days. If objections are received, the same will be communicated to the clinical establishment for a response within 45 days.

Penalty: - A fine of up to ₹ 5,00,000 (0.5 million) may be imposed by the District Registration Authority (notified by the State Government vide Section 10). meant for registration of clinical establishments.

Cancellation of Registration :

Section 32: - That the registration can be cancelled in case of any violation of :

32(1)(a)- the conditions of the registration are not being complied with; or

32(1)(b)- the person entrusted with the management of the clinical establishment has been convicted of an offence punishable under this Act,

- That means any offence even a minor one for which a monetary penalty is imposed will be a valid ground for cancellation.
- That the District Registering Authority is vested with quasi judicial powers and will decide about the punishment for offences under this Act and punishment is imposing of the monetary penalty and naturally penalty can only be imposed if one is convicted of the offence. This effectively means that if a penalty is levied that means conviction under the Act and it will be a valid ground for cancellation.

Doctor's point of view :

- That there is no room for even a single offence howsoever minor one.
- That the Act makes the practicing of medicine a zero margin profession!
- That a doctor commits even a minor non-clinical error like some shortcoming in record keeping and he/she is gone !
- That can a doctor work with free mind under such stressful conditions with a gun pointed to his/her head.
- That to compound the matters further, there is no provision for revocation of the cancellation, so once cancelled the doctor who is running his own hospital will have no alternative but to join some other hospital or start doing something else.

Offences and Punishments :

Section 42: - That running a clinical establishment without registration would be punishable for :

1st offence : a fine of ₹ 50 KA

2nd offence : a fine of ₹ 2 lakh

Subsequent offence : 5 lakh.

Serving in an unregistered clinical establishment: a fine of upto ₹ 25 KA. Wilful disobedience of any lawful direction or obstruction to lawful authority or refusal to submit any information asked for or giving false information knowingly : a fine of upto ₹ 5 lakh.

Section 44: - That contravention by a company (hospital) the person in charge of the operations/management: liable for action.

Section 45: - That the provisions of Section 44 and punishments would be equally applicable to Government Departments : liable for action.

Critical Analysis :

- That the old Acts for registration of hospitals/ nursing homes in nine States (mentioned in the Acts Schedule), made registration mandatory only for the hospitals and nursing homes (excluding private clinics, clinical laboratories, blood banks, imaging centres etc.) to get registered with the State Health Authorities.
- That the old Acts applicable only to the Allopathic establishments.
- That AYUSH–Ayurveda, Unani, Siddha, Homeopathy establishments were not covered by these old Acts.
- That the new Central Act is a blanket legislation making it mandatory for all establishments i.e. hospitals, nursing homes, private clinics, clinical laboratories, blood banks, imaging centres etc. of all systems–Allopathic as well as AYUSH), to get registered by a common single Registering Authority (District Registering Authority).
- That the Defence Services establishments (Army, Naval, Airforce, Police, BSF, CRPF) exempted from registration for unknown reasons.
- That some of the States allowed to continue with their old Legislations, thereby exempting registration to the private clinics, clinical laboratories, imaging centres of all systems and hospitals/nursing homes/dispensaries of non-allopathic systems (controversial/disputable part of the Act).

- That the Central and State Councils incld. the members from non-allopathic systems for dealing with non-allopathic (AYUSH) establishments.
- That the District Registration Authority does not incld. representation from non-allopathic systems.

Confirmity to the Standards :

- That conformity to the standards: time consuming factor to lay down the standards for so many different types of establishments pertaining to different systems of medicine.
- That monitoring the compliance with standards by millions of establishments requires a fleet of officials.
- That implementing/enforcing the standards to millions of establishments : a very cumbersome procedure.
- That fear of inspector raj and undue harassment: main resentment.

Schedule of Charges :

- That schedule of charges for services : to be decided by the State – a provision not palpable to the clinical establishments at all. The State can not and should not dictate the fees for the services/procedures provided by the clinical establishments.
- That every clinical establishment should have the right to determine the charges for the services provided by it.
- That while confirming to the prescribed minimum standards, there may be a lot of difference between the standards of facilities and expertise provided by the establishments, catering to the different locations, clients, standards/ tastes / expectations and paying capacity of clients.
- That every clinical establishment should have the right to determine the charges for the services provided by it.

Standard Treatment Guidelines issued by the Central Government :

- That the standard treatment protocols, in principle, help to ensure certain basic standards of treatment.
- That these protocols can be acceptable only as long as they are limited to broad principles, life threatening emergencies (CPR, anaphylactic shock, poisoning, treatment of snake-bite etc.) or treatment of major public health problems (such as AIDS, malaria, pulmonary tuberculosis).
- That physicians should have adequate freedom to decide as per their learning and experience, which modality of treatment to use in which situation in broad compliance with the protocols practised by the professional community– nationally and internationally.

Maintenance of EHR and EMR of every patient :

- That may be determined and issued by the Central or State Government. A good idea in principle, but a requirement, which is likely to be resented by the private clinics because of the added cost (of the system, software and the salary of the computer operator) as well as additional workload for busy clinicians.
- That many physicians esp. of Indian System of Medicine (ISM), may not be computer savvy at all.

Fear of Scrutiny :

- That physicians are worried most about scrutiny and exposure of their professional inadequacies, shortcuts, poor facilities, and mistakes as well as the harassment caused by the inspecting officials.
- That millions of private clinics, nursing homes/ hospitals, clinical laboratories etc. have been operating throughout the country, unknown, unregistered, thereby not subject to any scrutiny/ inspection/questioning by authorised authorities. There is no check over their facilities or standards and many of them giving care and treatment of dubious quality to the patients, often in utter disregard of the rules and regulations.

- That their fear is, once registered, they would no more be able to hide from the legal and professional scrutiny.

Public notice :

- That publishing the particulars of the clinical establishment for public comments is not a palpable idea.
- That purpose of publishing not clear, as the public will have no clue about the technical aspects/standards of the hospital esp. in case of the newly commissioned establishments. Also the local community or the rival establishments are unlikely to come forward with any meaningful comments.
- That periodic feedback/comments from public about the quality of services provided by the establishments can be important in case of already permanently registered establishments, as their renewal due after five long years.

Cancellation of Registration (Section 32) :

- That cancellation of registration in case of private clinics, clinical laboratories, nursing homes etc. may be possible, but in case of hospitals it may not be practically feasible idea in view of patients admitted for indoor treatment.
- That in case of repeated violations and reckless disregard for the safety of patients, exemplary penalties, to the tune of a yearly profit amount and/or imprisonment for the trustees/CEO/COO (if found negligent), may be more practical.

Treatment of life-threatening emergencies :

- That treatment in case of life-threatening emergencies remain the prime duty of every doctor, wherever, in whatever position or location. Shirking this responsibility or refusal to render necessary assistance in timely transportation of patient will be viewed as medical negligence liable to punishment.
- That non-payment of medical bills of treatment of emergency cases is a point of serious and

genuine concern of the medical community. The Act is silent on this aspect.

- That the concerned Authorities must redress the grievance to the satisfaction of medical professionals by following a mechanism of ensuring problem free reimbursement of bills. The liability may be borne by the insurance sector or by the Government itself.

Opposition/Resentment to Act by the Medical Fraternity (Doctor's point of view) :

The Act has evoked strong resentment from the medical fraternity. It opines :

- That, It is doubtful that this will improve the healthcare dramatically or that it will prove to be boon for the patients.
- That it will result in many-fold escalation in cost of treatment which an average person will find difficult to afford.
- That an ordinary person will suffer the most.
- That there are many objectionable clauses in the Clinical Establishment Act 2010, which will make the medical practice esp. by single or couple doctors in small setups almost impossible. The Act appears motivated to promote flourishing of only large corporate hospitals. Given the diversity of Indian Population, and clustering of medical facilities in different areas this appears to be a retrograde step which will in one stroke kill medical entrepreneurship.
- That no free medical camps or eye camps can be held, as the place will not be registered.
- That no home deliveries can be done.
- That no mobile health clinics can be run without registration in the particular area.
- That no provision has been made in the Act, stating that who will pay for the treatment ? Worst hit will be small clinics run by a single practitioner or a couple managing small hospitals/nursing homes.

- That doctors attain specialisations in very limited areas of their respective specialty. They are specialists in their own field and have a right to practice in their specialty. They cannot stabilise the patients of other specialties 'within the staff and the facilities available' in their clinical establishment.

  They cannot be forced to engage another specialist for emergency cases.

  The doctor will be caught in a Catch-22 situation i.e. if he treats the emergency case which he is not qualified to treat and God forbid, the patient dies, the doctor will be held guilty of negligence and if he doesn't treat, he will be liable for action under this Act.
- A General surgeon may have operated and established his practice only by managing haemorrhoids. Forcing him to stabilise a case of acute pancreatitis or to close down his establishment may deny the society of services of a competent surgeon.
- What will a Medical specialist do in case of a surgical emergency ?, or
- What will an Eye specialist do in case of a heart attack ?, or
- What will an Orthopaedic surgeon do in case of obstetric emergency ?
- That a patient who has suffered a heart attack requires primary angioplasty as best mode of treatment. Similarly a patient with vomiting of blood (Haemoptysis) is best handled by a facility providing endoscopy.

  Even very good medical centres will not have facilities for all the procedures. There will always be a risk of deterioration when patient is being sent to higher centre. But the risk of not doing angioplasty or endoscopy in appropriate situation is greater. This law will be a hindrance in good medical practice.
- That even, if the emergency case happens to be his own speciality, but the patient cannot be

stabilised, "within the staff and the facilities available" then what to do ? Patient cannot be referred because he is not 'stabilised' as per the Act. So what do you do?, just let the patient die? Without giving him a remote chance of survival if he could have been sent to a hospital better equipped to deal with such cases.

- That how can a single or couple doctors doing their practice in their own specialties in small centres, provide 24 hrs. emergency care in any other specialty? After notification of this Act, everyone will have to manage multi-specialties in his clinical establishment. For that huge investments required and the cost will have to be passed on to the patient. Forcing them to provide round the clock emergency care; free of cost, means they have to bear expenditure to hire minimum of four MBBS doctors, nurses, OT technicians, radiographers and lab technicians to provide round the clock services. That makes smaller hospitals/nursing homes unviable and it is a certainty that many smaller clinical establishments will close down.
- That to make it mandatory for all hospitals including OPD clinics to make arrangements to give guaranteed treatment to all emergency cases round the clock and that too without any provisions for recovering the cost of the treatment is neither feasible nor desirable and not acceptable. Accepting this will mean that all these small to medium hospitals/nursing homes will close down and only big corporate sector hospitals which can provide round the clock emergency services in all specialties will survive and then those will charge at exorbitant rates that even middle and upper middle class will find difficult to afford. Why not an emergency patient, approach a hospital that advocates providing 24 hr. Emergency services.
- That there are retired professors and senior doctors of medical/surgical specialties, who are

doyens in their field and now wish to practice in a limited fashion, providing only consultation or wish to operate on limited number of specialised cases. By bringing this Act, we force all doctors to become unpaid bonded labourers of the society with no freedom to regulate their working hrs. Effectively all establishments which desire to provide only limited services of their own specialty and within their resources will be forced to close down. This draconian law in effect states that an individual doctor cannot practice medicine unless he/she invests crores (millions) and works 24 hrs. For which patients may or may not pay.

- That a highly skilled doctor suffers a heart attack and is advised restricted professional activity and no stress. Under this Act, he/she has to retire by closing his/her clinical establishment because he/she will no longer be able to provide round the clock medical services to all emergencies. That again is society's loss, as it may deprive services of a trained professional who would have provided services–may be for a limited hrs.
- That the Act will become another avenue for corruption, because the punishments of far reaching consequences including cancellation of registration with no provision for its revocation will be awarded not by the courts but by the District Registration Authority, that will be inspecting prosecuting and Judging authority, all rolled into one !

  "Too much power is being vested into this Authority and Absolute power always corrupts"
- That the State has to provide right to health to all its citizens. The right to health of any citizen is against the State and not against fellow citizen even if he is a doctor.
- That this ill conceived idea will destroy the private healthcare sector which has so long been filling the vacuum created by the government abdicating its own fundamental duties to provide

affordable and accessible healthcare facilities to its citizens.

Does it help remove quackery ?

- That Para 34 allows inspection of unregistered premises only after giving proper notice (and adequate time for the quack to close shop and disappear). However, as per Para 33(1) no such notice is required to inspect a registered (legal) clinical establishment.

Section 2.1.1. of the Code of Ethics Regulations, 2002 :

(Indian Medical Council Professional Conduct, Etiquette and Ethics) :

"However for good reason, when a patient is suffering from an ailment which is not within the range of experience of the treating physician, the physician may refuse treatment and refer the patient to another physician".

It is of paramount importance to provide life-saving emergency treatment to citizens, such treatment is costly and does not come free and the treatment giver needs to be compensated through an appropriate mechanism that needs to be worked out by the government before the bill is made operative.

Advantages (Benefits) of the Act :

- That the Act is a positive development, if implemented in all the States in the form, broadly in line with the Central Act and Rules.
- That it would act as the first ever factual census of the number, category, speciality and location of all the physicians and all the medical establishments of all the systems of medicine in the country.
- That helpful in the countrywide planning and posting of physicians as well as healthcare establishments.
- That uptil now the Authorities do not know exactly how many of what category are available in a particular area.

- That Registration without any inspection or inquiry, based on the documents submitted by the establishment, should be encouraging for many private clinics, nursing homes to come forward and opt for registration.
- That it helps in isolating and identifying millions of quacks, playing havoc with the lives of people all over the country.
- That the system of registration will necessarily help in improving the standards of healthcare establishments within few years.
- That the system of registration will bring about some uniformity in the standards of care all over the country.
- That for maximum benefits and uniform effects, the Central Act should have been made applicable in all the States and Union Territories.
- That being a State subject, mandatory application is not possible. As most of the States enact their own legislations, there are variations in the provisions from State to State.
- That the important aspect is the speed of enactment and enforcement of legislation in the States. There should be no delays on any account.
- That for better implementation, lacunae are to be addressed and removed and the legislations made more friendly to the medical community.
- That the medical professionals also rise above the individual interests and keep in mind of larger public as well as professional interests.

(*Source:* Dr. SK Joshi, CEA 2010).

CONSENT :

Definition : An agreement between doctor/hospital and the patient/parents of a young child or an unconscious patient, for medical care.

Informed Consent

Definition : Is defined as an agreement between doctor and patient (parents in case of young child), whereby information in details, to be provided by the doctor the nature of disease/disorder, necessary investigations, treatment incld. type of surgery required, cost of treatment, any complication e.g. drug reaction, anesthesia or surgical complication, prospects of success, alternative treatment and prognosis.

Caution:
- Consent should not be given by a person under threat, misconception, mis-representation, unsoundness of mind and minors.
- Consent should be taken/given (in writing) in regional language of patient and doctor, and in the presence of a witness.
- It is not sufficient that the patient was fully informed about the consent, but is also essential that he/she has clearly understood it.

Penalty : The doctor/hospital is charged under Medical Negligence Act.

Legal issues pertaining to consent :

Inadequate explanation/information prior to treatment :

- **Failure to inform inherent risks :**

  Laws in :

  USA– The doctor is required to inform the patient about inherent risks.

  UK- Only substantial risks are to be informed/ disclosed.

  India- Only substantial risks are to be informed/ disclosed i.e. patient - is to be informed about the high risk of unpleasant result, ignoring the resulting psychological effect on him/her.

- **Failure to provide adequate advice and caution:**
- **Failure to provide promised treatment (as per informed consent).**

Implied Consent

Definition : Is defined as assumed consent e.g. the visit of a patient to a doctor's clinic, or hospital may be taken as agreeable to medical examination.

Express consent

Definition : Is defined as an oral or written permission, obtained for specific examination e.g. P/V or PR, and specific investigations/diagnostic procedures.

Offence : Negligence, and the doctor/hospital is charged under negligence act.

Judgment : **Pala Ram v/s State of Punjab (2009) 2 RCR (Criminal) 628 (P&H) :**

Medical Evidence and Ocular Evidence– If there is variance between the medical and ocular evidence, latter has to be accepted, provided it stands the test of Judicial scrutiny in the crucible of probabilities.

CONTEMPT OF COURTS ACT, 1971

Definition : Is defined as failure to obey or show respect toward a Court of Law.

Enactment : Enacted by the Parliament in 1971 (into force on 24-12-1971).

Jurisdiction : Extends to the whole of India.

Offence : Act to define and limit the powers of certain Courts in punishing contempts of Courts and to regulate their procedure in relation thereto.

Penalty : Imprisonment (simple) for a term which may extend to six months, or with fine which may extend to ₹ 2,000, or with both :

Provided that the accused may be discharged or the punishment awarded may be remitted on apology being made to the satisfaction of the Court. An apology shall not be rejected merely on the ground that it is qualified or conditional if the accused makes it bona-fide.

Types : Civil and Criminal.

- Civil contempt : means wilful disobedience to any judgment, decree, direction, order, writ or other process of a Court or wilful breach of an undertaking given to a Court.
- Criminal contempt : means the publication (whether by words, spoken or written, or by signs, or by visible representation, or otherwise)

of any matter or the doing of any other act what so ever which

- scandalises or tends to scandalise, or lowers or tends to lower the authority of, any court, or
- prejudices, or interferes or tends to interfere with, the due course of any judicial proceeding, or
- interferes, or tends to interfere with, or obstructs, or tends to obstruct, the administration of justice in any other manner.

COPYRIGHT ACT, 1957

Definition : Is defined as violation of copyright (the legal right to be the only maker or seller of a book, play, movie, or record for a specific time period.

Enactment : Enacted by the Parliament in 1957 (into force on 21-01-1958).

Jurisdiction : Extends to the whole of India.

Offence : Infringement of copyright /or other rights conferred by this Act :

- When any person, without a licence granted by the owner of the copyright violates the copyright act, he/she is committing an infringement of the act :
- produces/or reproduces the work, wholly or in parts e.g. reproduction in a book, journal, newspaper, magazine or in electronic form.
- Copying of literary work and thereby converting the work into dramatic work.
- Copying of musical work e.g. transcription of the musical work.

Penalty : 1st conviction : with imprisonment for a term of six months to three years and with fine of ₹ 50,000 to ₹ 2,00,000, or with both.

2nd or subsequent conviction : with imprisonment for a term of 1-3 years and with fine of ₹ 1,00,000 to ₹ 2,00,000 Plus confiscation of the stock for sale.

Offence : No infringement-made for any business or trade profit/gain.

Penalty : Imprisonment for a term < one year or a fine of < ₹ 1,00,000.

Offence : Misuse of Register of Copyright – making of false entries into this Register. Penalty : Imprisonment for a term – up to one year, or with fine, or with both.

Offence : Violation of Section 52–copying a sound recording or video filming.

Penalty : Imprisonment for a term - up to three years and with fine.

Cognisance : Only Court of Metropolitan Magistrate or Judicial Magistrate 1st class, shall of offence try such offence under this Act.

Appeals : Against orders of Magistrate : Any aggrieved person, by an order made under sub-section (2) of Section 64 or Section 66, may appeal to the court within thirty days, the appellate court may stay the execution of the order, pending disposal of appeal.

Against orders of Registrar of Copyrights/ and Board: Any aggrieved person, by an order made under sub-section (1) may appeal to the High Court within three months, provided no such appeal shall lie against a decision of the Copyright Board under Section 6.

DOMESTIC VIOLENCE

Definition : Is defined as an Act to provide for more effective protection of the rights of women guaranteed under the Constitution who are victims of violence of any kind occurring within the family and for matters connected therewith or incidental thereto.

Enactment : Enacted by the Parliament in 2005 (13-09-2005).

Enforcement: Came into force on 26-10-2006.

Jurisdiction : Extends to the whole of India, except the State of Jammu and Kashmir.

Offence : Clause :

(a) Harms, injures or endangers the life, safety, health or well-being, whether mental or physical, of the aggrieved person or tends to do so and includes causing physical, sexual, verbal, emotional and economic abuse ; or

(b) Harms, injures, harasses or endangers the aggrieved person with a view to coerce her or any other person related to her to meet any unlawful demand for any dowry or other property or valuable security ; or

(c) Threatens the aggrieved person or any person related to her by any conduct mentioned in clause (a) or clause (b).

Observation : Provided that before passing any order on an application, made by an aggrieved person, or a Protection Officer or any person on behalf of aggrieved person, the Magistrate shall take into consideration any domestic incident report received by him from the Protection Officer or the service provider.

Penalty : The Magistrate's orders :

Counselling orders :

- The Magistrate may direct the aggrieved person to undergo counselling with any member of a service provider–Restraining the respondent from dispossessing or disturbing the possession of the aggrieved person from the shared household.

Protection orders :

- To prohibit the respondent from committing any act of domestic violence.
- To prohibit the respondent from aiding or abetting in the commission of acts of domestic violence.
- To prohibit the respondent from entering the place of emplowment of the aggrieved person.
- To prohibit the respondent from attempting to communicate in any form, whatsoever, with the aggrieved person, including personal, oral or written or electronic or telephonic contact.

Residence orders :

- Directing the respondent to remove himself from the shared household.

- Restraining the respondent or any of his relatives from entering any portion of the shared household in which the aggrieved person resides.
- Restraining the respondent from alienating or disposing off the shared household or encumbering the same.
- Restraining the respondent from renouncing his rights in the shared household or except with the leave of the Magistrate; or

Monetary orders :

- under sub-section (1) of Section 12, the Magistrate may direct the respondent to pay monetary relief to meet the expenses incurred and losses suffered by the aggrieved person and any child of the aggrieved person as a result of the domestic violence. The respondent shall pay the monetary relief granted to the aggrieved person within the period specified in the order under sub-section (1).

Penalty : For breach of protection order by respondent :

Imprisonment which may extend to one year, or with fine which may extend to ₹ 20,000, or with both.

DOWRY PROHIBITION ACT, 1961

Definition : Is defined as an act by which any property or valuable security given or agreed to be given either directly or indirectly :-

- By one party (mostly Girl's side) to the marriage to the other party (mostly Boy's side) to the marriage.
- By the parent of either party to a marriage, or by any other person, to either party to the marriage or to any other person.

Before, at or after the marriage, in connection with the marriage of the said Parties.

Exception : Muslim Personal Law (Shariat) i.e. Dower or Maher in persons to whom this law is applicable.

Enactment : Enacted by the Parliament in 1961(20-05-1961).

Jurisdiction : Extends to the whole of India, except the State of Jammu and Kashmir.

Offence : Demanding Dowry : Any person demanding dowry directly or indirectly, from the parents or other relatives/guardians of a bride/or bridegroom, as the case may be.

Penalty : He/she shall be punishable with imprisonment for a term which shall not be less than six months, but which may extend to two years and with fine which may extend to ₹ 10,000.

Exception : The Court may impose a sentence of imprisonment for a term of less than six months, for adequate and special reasons to be recorded in the judgment.

Offence : Giving Dowry : Any person giving dowry directly or indirectly, to the parents or other relatives/guardians of a bridegroom/or bride, as the case may be.

Exception : Nothing in sub-section (1) shall apply to, or in relation to :-

- Presents which are given at the time of a marriage to the bride (without any demand having been made in that behalf) :

  Provided that such presents are entered in a list maintained in accordance with the rules made under this Act :

- Presents which are given at the time of a marriage to the bridegroom (without any demand having been made in that behalf) :

  Provided that such presents are entered in a list maintained in accordance with the rules made under this Act. Provided that where such presents are made by or on behalf of the bride or any person related to the bride, such presents are of a customary nature and the value thereof is not excessive having regard to the financial status of the person by whom, or on whose behalf, such presents are given.

Penalty : He/she shall be punishable with imprisonment for a term which shall not be less than five years and with fine which shall not be less than ₹ 15,000, or the amount of the value of such dowry, whichever is more.

Exception : The Court may impose a sentence of imprisonment for a term of less than five years, for adequate and special reasons to be recorded in the judgment.

DRUGS AND COSMETICS ACT, 1940

Definition : Is defined as an Act to regulate the import, manufacture, distribution and sale of drugs and cosmetics.

Enactment : 10/04/1940.

Jurisdiction : Extends to the whole of India.

Offence : Whoever, himself/herself or someone on his/her behalf, manufactures for sale or for distribution, or sells, or stocks or exhibits or offers for sale or distribution of any drug :

Penalty: - Under Section 320 of IPC, for causing grievous injury by any drug deemed to be adulterated under Section 17A or spurious under Section 17B.

Punishment : Imprisonment for a term which shall not be less than ten yrs., and may be extended for life imprisonment and with fine which shall not be less than ₹ 10,00,000 (1 million) or three times value of confiscated drugs, whichever is more.

Offence : Whoever, himself/herself or someone on his/her behalf, manufactures for sale or for distribution, or sells, or stocks or exhibits or offers for sale or distribution of any cosmetic :

Penalty: - Under Section 320 of IPC, for causing grievous injury by any cosmetic deemed to be spurious under Section 17D or adulterated under Section17E.

Punishment : Imprisonment for a term which may be extended to three yrs. and with fine which shall not be less than ₹ 50,000 or three times to value of the confiscated cosmetic, whichever is more. less than ₹ Ten lakh or three times value of confiscated drugs, whichever is more.

Offence : Non-disclosure of the name of the manufacturer.

Penalty : Under Section 18A or Section 24.

Punishment : Imprisonment for a term which may be extended to one yr., or with fine which shall not be less than ₹ 20,000 or with both.

Offence : Non-disclosure of information/not maintaining documents.

Penalty : Under Section 18A.

Punishment : Imprisonment for a term which may be extended to one yr., or with fine which shall not be less than ₹ 20,000 or with both.

DRUGS AND MAGIC REMEDIES ACT, 1954

Definition : Is defined as an Act to control the advertisement of drugs in specific cases, to prohibit the advertisement for specific purposes of remedies alleged to possess magic qualities, with provision for matters connected therewith.

Enactment : Enacted by the Parliament in 1954 (30/04/1954).

Jurisdiction : Extends to the whole of India, except the State of Jammu and Kashmir.

Offence: - Prohibition of advertisement of specific drugs to cure certain diseases and disorders.

- Prohibition of advertisement of magic remedies to cure certain diseases and disorders.

Penalty : Imprisonment upto 6 months, or with fine or with both, for 1st conviction Imprisonment upto 1 yr., or with fine or with both for subsequent conviction.

DYING DECLARATION ACT

Definition : Is defined as a statement made by a person prior to his/her death, that is admitted as a documentary evidence in a Court of Law.

Enactment : /05/1986).

Jurisdiction : Extends to the whole of India.

Penalty: - Conviction under Section 302 based on dying declaration

Arjun v/s state of U.P., 2009(5) RCR (criminal) 642 (Allahabad

- Acquition giving benefit of doubt

Jitender Kumar v/s State NCT of Delhi, 2009(5) RCR (Criminal) 931(Delhi)(DB)

- Conviction set aside for lack of proof

Suresh Kumar@ Shashi v/s State of Haryana, 2009(5) RCR(Criminal) 833(P&H).

ENVIRONMENT PROTECTION ACT (EPA), 1986

Definition : Is defined as an Act to provide for the protection and improvement of environment and for matters connected therewith.

Enactment : Enacted by the Parliament in 1986 (23/05/1986).

Jurisdiction : Extends to the whole of India.

Penalty: - Under Section 5 of EPA, State Pollution Control Board/Committee, has power to enforce the closure, prohibition or regulation of any unit or process or stoppage or regulation of the supply of electricity or water or any other service.

- Under Section 15 of EPA, whoever fails to comply with or contravenes any of the provisions of this Act, or the rules made or orders or directions issued thereunder, shall, in respect of each such failure or contravention, be punishable with imprisonment for a term which may extend to five years or with fine which may extend to ₹ one lakh, or with both, and in case the failure or contravention continues, with additional fine which may extend to ₹ 5000 for every day during which such failure or contravention continues after the conviction for the first such failure or contravention.

Bio-Medical Waste (Management and Handling) Rules, 1998

Notification: The Govt. of India has notified BMW (Management and Handling) Rules 1998, with a view to properly manage and stop indiscriminate disposal of hazardous waste/bio-medical waste vide Notification SO No. 630 (E) dt. July 20, 1998.

Amended Notification: Govt. of India in its Amended Notification SO 201 (E) dt. March o6, 2001, has authorised the State Pollution Control Committees for the purpose of granting authorisation for collection/ reception/storage/treatment and disposal of Bio-medical waste and to implement the aforesaid rules.

Jurisdiction : These Rules are applicable to all Institutions generating Bio-medical waste, which includes hospitals, nursing homes, clinics, dispensaries, veterinary hospitals, animal houses, research and pathological laboratories, blood banks.

Exhumption : Occupiers of institutes providing treatment to less than 1000 patients per month are however exempted from taking authorisation from State Pollution Control Comittee (SPCC).

Duties of Occupier :

- To take all steps to ensure that it is handled without any adverse effect to human health and environment.

  To ensure requisite treatment of waste in accordance to Schedule 1.

  To ensure that segregation into containers/bags at the point of generation is in accordance to Schedule 2, prior to its storage, transportation, and these containers are required to be labelled according to Schedule 2.

Schedule 1 (Categories of Bio-Medical Waste) :

- Human Wastes : body tissues, organs, wastes.
- Animal Wastes : body tissues, organs, parts, carcasses, body fluid, blood and blood products, surgical waste, autopsy waste, animal house for research work, veterinary hospital, livestock farms, hatcheries.

Laboratory (Microbiology and Bio-technology) Waste:

- Specimens of micro-organisms

- Culture stocks
- Vaccines : live and attenuated

Sharp Waste :

- Needles, syringes, knives, scalpels, blades, glass, autoclaving/microwaving.

Discarded Medicines :

- Expired, contaminated and discarded medicines.

Solid Waste :

- Discarded tubes, catheters, intravenous sets, urine packs.

Liquid Waste :

- Disinfectants: waste from laboratory, OT, cleaning, washing.

Soiled Waste :

- Soiled cotton, dressings, plaster casts, linens, beddings, contaminated soiled packaging materials.

Chemical Waste :

- Biological chemicals, disinfectants, insecticides

Schedule 2 : Color Coding and Type of Container for BMW (Table 7-1) :

TABLE 7.1: Schedule 2 (Colour Coding and Type of Container for BMW Disposal

Color	*Yellow*	*Red*	*Blue/White*	*Black*
Container	Plastic Bag	Plasic Bag	Plastic Bag	**Plastic Bag**
Waste	Human, Animal	Soiled, Microbiology, Biotechnology	Soiled, Sharp, Solid	**Discarded medicines**, **Cytotoxic drugs** **Incineration ash**
Treatment Options	Incineration/ Deep burial	Autoclave/ Microwave/ Chemical Destruction/ Shredding	Autoclave/ Microwave/ Chemical/	**Disposal in secured landfill**

(*Source* : ENVIS-CENTRE, Department of Environment, Chandigarh).

FATAL ACCIDENTS ACT, 1855

Definition : Is defined as an Act to provide compensation to families for the loss occasioned by the death of a person caused by actionable wrong.

Enactment : Enacted in 1855 (27th March, 1855).

Jurisdiction : Extends to the whole of India, except the State of Jammu and Kashmir.

Features : Under this Act, the context otherwise requires :-

- Suit for compensation to the family of a person's death by actionable wrong.
- Person : means, bodies politic and corporate.
- Parent : means, father, mother, grand-father and grand-mother.
- Child : means, son, daughter, grand-son, grand-daughter, step-son and step-daughter.

Section : Sections 1A of Fatal Accidents Act, 1855.

Offence : Causing death by actionable wrong.

Penalty : Recovery of damages proportioned to the loss resulting from such death to the affected parties (wife/husband, parent and child).

IMMORAL TRAFFIC (PREVENTION) ACT, 1956

Definition : Is defined as an Act to provide in pursuance of the International Convention signed at New York on the 9th day of May, 1950, for the prevention of immoral traffic.

Enactment : Enacted by the Parliament in 1956 (34th December, 1956).

Jurisdiction : Extends to the whole of India.

Features : Under this Act, the context otherwise requires :-

- Prostitution : means the sexual abuse/or exploitation of a person for the commercial purposes.
- Major : means, a person, having attained the age of 18 yrs.
- Minor : means, a person, having attained the age of 16 yrs., but having not attained the age of 18 yrs.
- Child : means, a person, who has not attained the age of 16 yrs.
- Brothel : means, a place e.g. a room, house or a portion of house, used for the purpose of sexual abuse/exploitation, as a monetary purpose by

another person, or by the personal gain of a group of prostitutes.

- Trafficking police officer : means a police officer, appointed under this Act –Section 13 (sub-section 4) by the Central Government.
- Special Police Officer (SPO) : means, a police officer appointed under this Act, by or on behalf of the State Government, to be In-charge of police duties, within a specified area (specific jurisdiction).
- Rehabilitation (Corrective) institution : means, an institution, including a shelter home (protective home), established/or licensed under Section 21, in which persons, in need of rehabilitation, may be detained under this Act.

Section : Sections 13 (sub-section 4).

Offence : Maintaining (Running) a brothel/or allowing a place to be used as a brothel.

Penalty : 1st conviction :

- Rigorous imprisonment for a term of not less than one year, that may be extended to three yrs., and with fine which may extend to ₹ 2000.

2nd or subsequent conviction :

- Rigorous imprisonment for a term of not less than two yrs., that may be extended to five yrs., and with fine which may extend to ₹ 2000.

Offence : Detaining a person (with or without consent) at a place used as a brothel.

Penalty : Rigorous imprisonment for a term of not less than seven yrs., that may be extended to ten yrs., or for life, and with fine.

Offence : Maintaining (Running) a brothel at a public place.

Penalty : Imprisonment for a term which may extend to three months.

Minor/Child case :

- Rigorous imprisonment for a term of not less than seven yrs., that may be extended to ten yrs., and with fine.

Offence : Seducing/Soliciting at a public place, for purpose of prostitution.

Penalty : 1st conviction :

- Imprisonment for a term which may be extended to six months, or with Fine which may extend to ₹ 500, or with both.

2nd or subsequent conviction :

- Imprisonment for a term which may extend to one yr., and with fine which may extend to ₹ 500.

Offence : Custodial seduction of a person for purpose of prostitution.

Penalty : Imprisonment for a term which shall not be less than seven yrs., that may be extended to ten yrs., or for life, and with fine.

MEDICAL TERMINATION OF PREGNANCY (MTP)

Definition : The act prohibits termination of pregnancy by an unauthorised person who is not an RMP for doing MTP.

Advantages/Benefits :

Aims to regulate and ensure access to safe abortion care and defines 'when','where' and under 'what' conditions, the abortion is permissible.

Recent amendments made to decentralise powers of abortion care to the District level, aims to encourage registration of abortion facilities by minimising administrative delays.

Disadvantages/Shortcomings :

- Non-compliance of Good Clinical Practice : majority of MTP providers have been utilising unsafe abortion practices e.g. sharp curettage, vacuum suction, eneral anesthetic, different drug schedules and protocols for MTP.
- Faulty implementation of MTP Act Rules : MTP Act Rules–clearly define 'person' and 'place' requirements, but fail to refer to any National/ International technical guidelines to provide safe abortion care, inspite of plethora of scientific

advances (reproductive technique and newer practices).

- Faulty contraceptive measures : the clause applies only to a married woman.

  This discrepancy demands correction on account of fast changing social and cultural scenario.

Offence : Terminating of pregnancy by a person who is not a Registered Medical Practitioner (RMP).

Punishment : Rigorous imprisonment for a term of two to seven yrs.

Registration : An RMP must :

- register herself/himself for doing MTP,
- register place for doing MTP,
- get specific registration–in case of doing MTP upto 20 weeks.

MEDICAL TRMINATION OF PREGNANCY (MTP) ACT, 1971 (Act No. 34 of 1971) (10th August 1971) :

Definition : Is defined as an Act to provide for the termination of certain pregnancies by Registered Medical Practitioners and for matters connected therewith or incidental thereto.

Enactment : Enacted by the Parliament in 1969 (34 of 1971).

Jurisdiction : Extends to the whole of India except State of Jammu and Kashmir.

Features : Subject to the provisions of Section 4 and sub-section (2) of Section 3, a pregnancy may be terminated by a Registered Medical Practitioner:-

- When the period of pregnancy does not exceed twelve weeks.
- When the period of pregnancy exceeds twelve weeks but doesn't exceed twenty weeks.
- When two or more Registered Medical Practitioners are of opinion, formed in good faith, that :-
- Continuation of pregnancy may endanger the life of the pregnant woman, or may lead to grave mental or physical injury, or
- There may be a substantial risk, that the born child may suffer from mental or physical disorders.

- Pregnancy caused by Rape–resulting in grave mental and physical injuries to the pregnant woman esp. an unmarried one.
- Pregnancy occurring as a result of failure of family planning measures (for the purpose of limiting the number of children).
- When the pregnant woman is < 18 yrs., the pregnancy is terminated only with the written consent of her guardian. :
- When the pregnant woman is > 18 yrs., the pregnancy is terminated only with the written consent of the pregnant woman.

Section : Sections 4 and sub-section (2) of Section 3.

Offence : Termination of pregnancy by any person, who is not a Registered Medical Practitioner.

Penalty : Rigorous imprisonment for a term of two years, that may be extended to seven years under the modified Code.

Offence : Termination of pregnancy at a place other than that specified in Section 4.

Penalty : Rigorous imprisonment for a term of two years, that may be extended to seven years under the modified Code.

Offence : Termination of pregnancy at an unapproved place, the owner of place shall be punishable under clause (b) of Section 4.

Penalty : Rigorous imprisonment for a term of two years, that may be extended to seven years under the modified Code.

Protection : Under this Act, a Registered Medical Practitioner shall not be held guilty of any offence e.g. any damage caused or likely to be caused by anything that is in good faith done or intended to be done.

Legal Opinion: A pregnancy may be terminated by a Registered Medical Practitioner, either at an established Government hospital or at a place approved by Government/or District Committee nominated by the Government.

MEDICAL TERMINATION OF PREGNANCY AMENDMENT ACT, 2002 (Act No. 64 of 2002) (18th December 2002) :

Definition : An Act to amend the Medical Termination of Pregnancy Act No. 34 of 1971.

It says that termination of pregnancy by a person who is not a Registered Medical Practitioner, shall be punishable with rigorous imprisonment for a term which shall not be less than two years, but which may extend to seven years under that Code, and that Code shall, to this extent, stand modified.

Whoever terminates any pregnancy in a place other than that mentioned in Section IV, shall be punishable with rigorous imprisonment for a term which shall not be less than two years but which may extend to seven years. Any person being owner of a place which is not approved Inder clause (b) of Section IV shall be punishable with rigorous imprisonment for a term which shall not be less than two years but which may extend to seven years.

MEDICAL TERMINATION OF PREGNANCY REGULATIONS, 2003 :

Definitions : Admission Register-means the register maintained by the Central Government or the Government of Union Territory.

Section-means a section of the Act every RMP who terminates any pregnancy shall, within three hours from the termination of the pregnancy certify such termination in Form 1.

The consent given by a pregnant woman for the termination of her pregnancy, together with the certified opinion recorded under Section 3 or 5, as the case may be and the intimation of termination of pregnancy shall be placed in an envelop which shall be sealed by the Registered Medical Practitioner/s by whom such termination of pregnancy was performed and until that envelop is sent to the head of the hospital or owner of the approved place or the Chief Medical Officer of the State, it shall be kept in the safe custody of the concerned Registered Medical Practitioner/s, as the case may be.

On every envelop referred to in sub-regulation (1), pertaining to the termination of pregnancy under Section 3, there shall be noted the serial number assigned to the pregnant woman in the Admission Register and the name of the Registered Medical Practitioner/s by whom the pregnancy was terminated and such envelop shall be marked "SECRET". Where the pregnancy is not terminated in an approved place or hospital, every envelop referred to in sub-regulation (6) shall be sent by registered post to the Chief Medical Officer of the State on the same day on which the pregnancy was terminated or on the next working day following the day on which the pregnancy was terminated.

Provided that where the pregnancy is terminated in an approved place or hospital, the procedure provided in sub-regulations (1) to (6) shall be followed.

Maintenance of Admission Register : every head of the hospital or owner of the approved place shall maintain a register in Form 3 for recording there in the details of the admissions of women for the termination of their pregnancies and keep such register for a period of five years from the end of the Calendar year it relates to. The entries in the Admission Register shall be made serially and a fresh serial shall be distinguished from the serial number of other years by mentioning the year against the serial number, for example, serial number 5 of 1972 and serial number 5 of 1973 shall be mentioned as 5/1972 and 5/1973.

Admission Register: shall be a secret document and the information contained therein as to the name and other particulars of the pregnant woman shall not be disclosed to any person. Admission Register not to be open to inspection. The

Admission Register shall be kept in the safe custody of the head of the hospital or owner of the approved place, or by any person authorised by such head or owner and save as otherwise provided in sub-regulation (5) of regulation 4 shall not be open for inspection by any person except under the Authority of Law. Provided that the Registered Medical Practitioner on the application of an employed woman whose pregnancy has been terminated, grant a certificate for the purpose of enabling her to obtain leave from her employer provided further that any such employer shall not disclose this information to any other person. Entries in the registers maintained in hospital or approved place, no entry shall be made in any case-sheet, operation theatre register, follow-up card or any other document or register other than the Admission Register maintained at any hospital or approved place indicating therein the name of the pregnant woman and reference to the pregnant woman shall be made therein by the serial number assigned to the woman in the Admission Register.

Maintenance of Forms :

Form I - is to be maintained under Regulaion 3,

Form II–is to be maintained under regulation 4 (5)

Form III – is to be maintained under regulation file.

Note : Admission Register–is to be destroyed on the expiry of five years from the date of the last entry in the Register.

Caution : Register yourself for :

- Doing MTP,
- Register place for MTP,
- Specific registration : in case of MTP upto 20 weeks.

MENTAL HEALTH ACT, 1987

Definition : Is defined as an act to consolidate and amend the law relating to the treatment and care of mentally ill persons, to make better provision with respect to their property and affairs and for matters connected therewith or incidental thereto.

Enactment : Enacted by the Parliament in 1987 (effective from 1st April, 1993)

Jurisdiction : Extends to the whole of India.

Features : Specified by the State Government by passing general/or special order made (notification) under the provision of this Act, for the admission and detention of a mentally ill person (in need of treatment of a mental disorder other than mental retardation) in a psychiatric hospital/nursing home.

Section : Admission and detention of a mentally-ill prisoner:-

- under Section 30 of the Prisoners Act, 1900, or
- Under Section 145 of the Army Act, 1950, or
- Under Section 143 or 144 of the Navy Act, 1957, or
- Under Section 144 of the Air Force Act, 1950, or
- Under Section 330 or 335 of the Code of Criminal Procedure, 1973(2/1974).

Admission and detention of a mentally-ill person, pending medical report :-

- Under section 23 or 25, authorise detention by a Magistrate for observation, for a period of 10-30 days.

Offence: - Whosoever establishes or maintains a Psychiatric hospital/nursing home in contravention of this Act.

Penalty : 1st conviction : shall be punishable with imprisonment for a period of three months, with a fine of ₹ 200, or with both.

2nd or subsequent conviction : imprisonment for a term–upto six months, with fine of ₹ 1000, or with both.

Offence: - Whosoever (post-conviction) under sub-section (1) continues to maintain a Psychiatric hospital/ nursing home in contravention of this Act.

Penalty : Shall be punishable with a fine of ₹ 100 per day, for the period of contravention (if contravention continued post 1st day).

Offence: - Whosoever makes improper admission or detention of mentally ill person in a Psychiatric nursing home in contravention of the provisions of this Act.

Penalty : Shall be punishable with imprisonment for a period of three months, with a fine of ₹ 200, or with both.

Offence: - Whosoever manages the property of mentally ill person) in contravention of Sections 60 and 69 of this Act.

Penalty : Shall be punishable with a fine of ₹ 2000.

Sanction for prosecution : As per Code of Criminal Procedure 1973 (2 of 1974), under Section 82, except with the pre-sanction of the Licensing Authority, no Court shall take cognisance of any punishable offence.

Repeal: - Indian Lunacy Act, 1912 (4 of 1912)
- Indian Lunacy Act, 1977.

MENTAL RETARDATION AND MULTIPLE DISABILITIES ACT, 1999

Definition : Is defined as an Act to provide protection/ support to mentally retarded and Mentally handicapped persons.

Features: - That most of the effects of these disorders can be minimised or avoided with adequate, timely medical care.
- That a very few mentally retarded children have multiple disabilities.
- That mentally retarded children, being slow learners, are to be managed by the parents, with extra understanding and patience.
- That mentally retarded children may be better off in a special home e.g. mental hospitals.

- That, the decision of placing such a child in a special home should be taken after consultation with psychologists and professional specialised in the problems of the mentally retarded children.

Offence : Neglecting mentally retarded person by the guardian.

Section : Punishable under Sections 14, 15 and 16.

Penalty : Imprisonment, with a fine, or with both.

MORAL TURPITUDE

Definition : Is not properly defined till date, yet the term is used legally for centuries.

Evidence:
- That there is no hard and fast rule for constitution of moral turpitude.
- That moral turpitude, may not be a question of fact and frequently circumstancial i.e. difficult to determine nature of crimes involving moral turpitude.
- That sexual crimes may fall within purview of definition. That an assault resulting in hurt, may fall within purview of definition.

NARCOTIC DRUGS AND PSYCHOTROPIC SUBSTANCES ACT, 1985

Definition : Is defined as an Act to prove the Conscious Possession of Narcotic Drugs and Psychotropic substances.

Evidence:
- Circumstantial evidence–accused found in possession of the contraband, charged under Section 15 of Act.
- Statements of material witnesses.
- Confessional statements recorded by police.
- Link evidence–deficient, neither reliable nor creditworthy e.g. unexplained delay in sending sample parcel to FSL and tampering with the sample parcels.

Narco-analysis :

Definition : Is defined as hypno-analysis when narcotics are used in producing the hypnotic state.

Evidence: - That Narco Analysis, Brain Mapping and similar tests undertaken to find out the truth from an accused/witness.

OATHS ACT, 1969

Definition : Is defined as an act to (promise to tell the truth in a court e.g. "I solemnly affirm that I shall give the truth, whole truth, nothing but truth and I conceal nothing, if anything given false, so God Almighty help me") consolidate and amend the law relating to judicial oaths and for certain other purposes.

Enactment : Enacted by the Parliament in 1967 (44 of 1969).

Jurisdiction : Extends to the whole of India, except the State of Jammu and Kashmir (J&K).

Power to Administer Oath :

- Any Court, Judge, Magistrate or person empowered by the law, shall have the power to administer oath, themselves, or under the provisions of sub-section (2) of Section 6, shall empower an officer on their behalf, to discharge the duties imposed (oaths and affirmations) or in exercising of the powers conferred upon them by law.
- The CO of Army, Naval or Air Force base, or a ship occupied by the Union.

Armed Forces, provided the administration of oath or affirmation is within its jurisdiction.

- Any Court, Judge, Magistrate or person empowered by the High Court, shall administer oath and affirmations, in respect of affidavits for the purpose of Judicial Proceeds.
- Any Court, Judge, Magistrate or person empowered by the State Govt. shall administer oath and affirmations, in respect of other affidavits for the purpose of Judicial Proceeds.

Exemption : Armed Forces Court Martial.

A child < twelve years old

Oath Taking: Oaths or affirmations to be taken/made by :-

- A witness – to be legally examined or may be required to give evidence before any court or person authorised to examine/or to receive evidence from such witness.
- Interpreters
- Jurors.

Exemption : Armed Forces Court Martial.

A child < twelve years old.

Affirmation : A witness, interpreter or Juror may make an affirmation, instead of making an oath.

Oaths and Affirmations Forms:

Form No. 1 (Witness/s) :

I do swear in the name of God/solemnly affirm, that what I shall state shall be the truth, the whole truth and nothing but the truth.

Form No. 2 (Juror/s) :

I do swear in the name of God/solemnly affirm, that I will well and truly try and true deliverance make between the State and the prisoner/s at the bar, whom I shall have in charge, and a true verdict give according to the evidence.

Form No. 3 (Interpreter/s) :

I do swear in the name of God/solemnly affirm, that I will well and truly interpret and explain all questions put to and evidence given by witness/s and translate correctly and accurately all documents given to me for translation.

Form No. 4 (Affidavits) :

I do swear in the name of God/solemnly affirm, that this is my name and signature (or mark) and that the contents of this my affidavit are true.

Serious :

Offence : Lying under oath is a serious offence (in contravention of this Act).

Penalty : Fine and/or imprisonment.

POISONS ACT, 1919

Definition : Is defined as an act to consolidate and amend the law regulating the importation, possession and sale of poisons.

Enactment : Enacted in 1919.

Jurisdiction : Extends to the whole of India, except the State of Jammu and Kashmir (J&K).

Power of State Government to regulate possession and sale of any poison :

The State Government may regulate the possession and sale of any poison (wholesale or retail) within its jurisdiction, under framed rules:

- To grant licences to possess any poison for sale (wholesale or retail) against payment of licence fee.
- To grant licences to specific persons for sale.
- To grant licences to specific persons for purchase.
- To inspect the registers of sales maintained by persons selling such poisons.
- To inspect the safe custody of such poisons by the selling persons.

Power of Central Government to prohibit import of any poison :

The Central Government, by notification prohibit import of any poison, except against a licence for any specified poison.

Offence:
- Violation of any rule made under Section 2.
- Violation of any rule made under Section 3 i.e. Imports without a licence.

Penalty : 1st conviction : with imprisonment for three months, or with fine of ₹ 500 or with both.

2nd or subsequent conviction : with imprisonment for six months, or with fine of ₹ 1000 or with both.

Plus confiscation of the stock of poison for sale.

PRE-NATAL DIAGNOSTIC TECHNIQUES (PNDT) ACT AND RULES

Definition : Is defined as an act to provide for the regulation of the use of pre-natal diagnostic techniques for the purpose of detecting genetic or metabolic disorders, or chromosomal abnormalities, or certain congenital malformations, or sex linked disorders, and for the prevention of the misuse of such techniques for the purpose of pre-natal sex determination, leading to female feticide; and, for matters connected therewith or incidental thereto.

Enactment : Enacted by the Parliament in 1994 (57 of 1994).

Jurisdiction : Extends to the whole of India.

Features:
- The PNDT (Regulation Act (1994) : enacted and brought into operation from 1st January 1996, in order to check female feticide. Also rules have been framed under the Act.
- The Act prohibits determination and disclosure of the sex of the fetus. It also prohibits any advertisements related to pre-natal determination of sex and prescribes punishment and fine.
- Amendments of PNDT Act and rules :
- PNDT (PRINCIPLE) ACT – 1994
- PNDT (PRINCIPLE) RULES – 1996
- PNDT ADVISORY COMMITTEE RULES - 1996
- PNDT AMENDMENT ACT – 2002
- PNDT AMENDMENT RULE - 2003

These amendments have been made, as per emerging technologies for selection of sex (pre and post conception) and subsequent problems faced in the working of implementation of the Act, and directions issued by the Hon'ble Supreme Court vide a PIL filed in 2000 by CEHAT and others, an NGO on delayed implementation of the Act. These amendments have become operative with effect from 14th February, 2003.

Offence : Misuse of the test for the purpose of pre-natal sex determination, thereby opting for female feticide.

Penalty : Imprisonment and fine.

PRE-NATAL DIAGNOSTIC TECHNIQUES (REGULATION AND PREVENTION OF MISUSE) ACT (1994) No. 57 (20th September 1994) :

Chapter I : It has two Sections. The Section 2 of the Act has definitions defining the appropriate authority:

- Genetic Counselling Centres,
- Genetic Laboratory,
- Pre-natal diagnostic procedures,
- Genetic Clinics.

Chapter II : It makes compulsory the registration of :

- Genetic Counselling Centres,
- Genetic Laboratories,
- Genetic Clinics.

It is important to note that all tests are to be conducted by the authorised person named in form B at the place mentioned in form B. Any change in address, persons conducting tests and sonography (ultrasound) apparatus, should be intimated (informed) to the appropriate authority within 30 days and seek their approval.

Chapter III : Sections 3 and 4 : Section 3 provides a list of conditions for which the genetic tests can be conducted in Section 4.

Section 5 : Mentions that it is necessary to obtain written consent of the pregnant woman and prohibition of communicating the sex of fetus.

Chapter IV : Is about Central Supervisory Board.

Chapter V : Is about Appropriate Authority and Advisory Committee.

Chapter VI : Is about registration of :

Genetic Counselling Centres,

Genetic Laboratories,

Genetic Clinics,

Cancellation or suspension of registration–by the :

Appropriate Authority–may suo motto, or on complaint

Chapter VII : Deals with offences and penalties and are punishable with imprisonment for a term which may extend to minimum three years and/or with a fine which may extend to ₹ ten thousand.

PRE-NATAL DIAGNOSTIC TECHNIQUES (REGULATION AND PREVENTION OF MISUSE) RULES (1996) :

Section IV : Is about registration of :

Genetic Counselling Centre,

Genetic Laboratories,

Genetic Clinics,

Where an application for registration shall be made to the Appropriate Authority, in duplicate, in Form A. The Appropriate Authority, or any person in his/her office authorised on his/her behalf, shall acknowledge receipt of the application for registration, vide the acknowledge slip provided at the bottom of Form A, immediately if delivered at the office of the Appropriate Authority, or not later than the next working day, if received by post.

Application Fee :

₹ 2000 for Genetic Counselling Centre,

₹ 3000 for Genetic Laboratories,

₹ 3000 for Genetic Clinic,

₹ 4000 for Institute, Hospital, Nursing home, or any place providing jointly the services of a Genetic Counselling Centre, Genetic Laboratories, Genetic Clinic, or any combination of such Centre, Laboratory or Clinic.

Section VI : A certificate of registration in Form B in duplicate. One copy of the certificate of registration shall be displayed by the registered Genetic Counselling Centre, Genetic Laboratory or Genetic Clinic at a conspicuous place at its place of business. In case of rejection, Form C is sent within a period of 90 days from the date of receipt of application. The Certificate of Registration, shall be non-transferable. In the event of Change of Ownership or Change of

Management or on ceasing to function as a Genetic Counselling Centre, Genetic Laboratory or Genetic Clinic, both copies of the Certificate of Registration shall be surrendered to the Appropriate Authority.

Validity of Registration : Is for a period of five years from the date of its issue.

Renewal of Registration : An applicant has to apply for the renewal of certificate of registration in duplicate in Form A, to the Appropriate Authority 30 days, prior to date of expiry of the Certificate of Registration. An acknowledgement receipt is issued by the Appropriate Authority.

Section IX : Is important regarding maintenance and preservation of records and amongst it filing of Form F, as per rules and verbatim (very essential), otherwise it may invite sealing of Ultrasound apparatus (machine) and initiating of prosecution against Genetic Counselling Centre, Genetic Laboratory and Genetic Clinic.

Section XIII : Under Section 13, it is essential to intimate about any changes in the place of apparatus and employees operating the apparatus. Every Genetic Counselling Centre, Genetic Laboratory or Genetic Clinic, is required to intimate about any change of place of operating apparatus, employees, address and equipment installed, to the Appropriate Authority within a period of 30 days of such changes.

PRE-NATAL DIAGNOSTIC TECHNIQUES (REGULATION AND PREVENTION OF MISUSE) AMENDMENT ACT (2002):

Definition : Is defined as an Act to provide information in detail of "conceptuous, embryo, fetus" . It also defines sex Slection, sonologist or imaging specialist meaning a person who possesses any one of the medical qualifications recognised under the Indian Medical Act, 1956 or who possesses a post-graduate qualification in ultrasonography or imaging techniques or radiology.

Offence : Any one having an Ultrasound machine, imaging machine, scanner or any other technology, capable of undertaking determination of sex of the fetus, or sex selection shall issue, publish, distribute, communicate or cause to be issued, published, distributed or communicated any advertisement, in any form, including internet.

Penalty : Imprisonment for a term which may extend to 3 yrs. and/or with fine which may extend to ₹ 10,000.

PRE-NATAL DIAGNOSTIC TECHNIQUES (REGULATION AND PREVENTION OF MISUSE) AMENDMENT RULE (2003):

Definition : Is defined as a Rule to specify essential qualifications and experience for persons related to PNDT :

- Gynecologist or a Pediatrician : should have six months experience or four weeks training in Genetic counselling,
- Laboratory technician : should possess a BSc. Degree in Biological Science or a degree or diploma in medical laboratory course and should have atleast one yr. experience.

Application Forms :

- Form A : is an application form for registration or renewal of registration of a Genetic Counselling Centre, Genetic Laboratory, Genetic Clinic, Ultrasound Clinic, and Imaging Centre.
- Form B : is an application form for Certificate of Registration.
- Form C : is an application form for rejection of application for grant/renewal of registration.
- Form D : is an application form for maintenance of records by the Genetic Counselling Centre.
- Form E : is an application form for maintenance of records by the Genetic Laboratory.
- Form F : is an application form for maintenance of records in respect to pregnant woman by the

Genetic Clinic, Ultrasound Clinic and Imaging Centre.

- Form G : is an application form for taking consent for invasive techniques.
- Form H : is an application form for maintenance of permanent records of applications for grant/ rejection of registration under the PNDT Act 1994.

Offence:
- Failure to submit Form F, as per format given,
- Failure to inform change in place/address, change in person/s or change in USG machine, to the Appropriate Authority and receiving their order in the subject within 30 days.

Penalty : Sealing of machine and initiating prosecution, post confirmation e.g. by sending a decoy patient for sex determination.

PREVENTION OF FOOD ADULTERATION ACT, 1954

Definition : Is defined as an Act to provide for the prevention of adulteration of food.

Enactment : Enacted by Parliament in 1954 (into force on 01-06-1955)

Jurisdiction : Extends to the whole of India.

Offence : Manufacture, store, sell or distribute an adulterated food, misbranded food, unlicenced food or prohibited food.

Section : Punishable under Section 14 or section 14A.

Penalty : Imprisonment, which may extend to three yrs. with fine, which may extend upto ₹ 1,000.

PREVENTION OF VIOLENCE AND DAMAGE TO PROPERTY ACT:

THE PUNJAB PROTECTION OF MEDICARE SERVICE PERSONS AND MEDICARE INSTITUTIONS (PREVENTION OF VIOLENCE AND DAMAGE TO PROPERTY) ACT, 2008 (Punjab Act No. 26 of 2008)

Department of Legal and Legislative Affairs, Punjab, Notification. The 30th October, 2008.

No. 29-Leg./2008.–The following Act of the Legislature of the State of Punjab received the assent of Governor of Punjab on the 10th October, 2008, and is hereby published for general information :

Definition : Is defined as an Act to provide for the protection of Medicare Service Persons and Medicare Service Institutions in the State of Punjab and for prevention of violence and damage to the property and for the matters connected therewith or incidental thereto.

Enactment : Enacted by the Legislature of the State of Punjab in 2008 (30-10-2008)

It shall come into force at once, vide notification dated 30th October 2008.

Jurisdiction : Extends to the whole of Punjab State.

Definitions : In this Act, unless the context otherwise requires,-

(a) "Medicare Service Institution" means an institution, providing Medicare service either in the Medicare Service Institution or through Mobile Medical Unit or by arranging medical camps, which is under the control of the Central Government or the State Government or a local body including any private hospital having facility of treatment of the sick and used for their reception or stay, any private maternity home, where women are usually received and accommodated for the purpose of confinement and ante-natal and post-natal care in connection with the child birth or anything connected therewith, and any private nursing home used or intended to be used for the reception and accommodation of persons suffering from any sickness, injury or infirmity whether of body or mind, and providing of treatment of nursing or both of them and includes convalescent home ;

(b) "Medicare Service Person" in relation to a Medicare Service Institution, shall include, -

Registered Medical Practitioner, Registered Practitioner and Practitioner, working in a Medicare Service Institution;

Nurse;

Auxiliary Nurse and Mid-wife;

Nurse-Dai;

Trained-Dai;

Medical Student;

Nursing Student;

Para Medical Worker; and Other staff or workers directly or indirectly engaged by a Medicare Service Institution for providing the required services;

Explanation–For the purpose of this Act, the expressions Registered Medical Practitioner, Medical Practitioner, Practitioner, Nurse, Auxiliary Nurse and Midwife and trained Dai, shall have the same meanings, as assigned to them in the Punjab Medical Registration Act, 1916, the Punjab Nurses Registration Act, 1932, the Punjab Ayurvedic and Unani Practitioners Act, 1963 and the Punjab Homeopathic Practitioners Act, 1965;

(c) "Medical Student" means a student, who is undergoing training or studies in medical profession;

(d) "Mobile Medical Unit" means an ambulance, equipped with medical equipment, used for providing medicare services;

(e) "Nursing Student" means a student, who is undergoing training or studies in nursing profession;

(f) "Offender" means any person, who either by himself or as a member or leader of a group of persons or organisation commits or attempts to commit or abets or incites the commission or violence;

(g) "Paramedical Worker" means a person, who assists the Medicare Service Person providing Medicare services;

(h) "Property" shall include both movable and immovable property; and

(i) "Violence" means any act, which causes or may cause any harm, injury or endanger life, obstruct or hinder any Medicare Service Person in the discharge of his duty in a Medicare Service Institution or damage to property in Medicare Service Institution.

Prohibition of : Any act of violence against a Medicare Service Person or Prohibition of Violence damage to property in a Medicare Service Institution, shall be prohibited.

Penalty : An offender, who commits any act in contravention of the provisions of this Act shall be punished with an imprisonment, which may extend to one year, or with fine, which may extend to ₹ 50,000/-, or with both.

Cognisance : Any offence committed under this Act, shall be cognisable and non-bailable of Offence and shall be triable by the Court of Judicial Magistrate of the First Class.

Recovery of : (1) In addition to the punishment as specified in Section 4, the offender Loss shall also be liable to pay a penalty of twice the amount of purchase price of medical equipment damaged or loss caused to the property, as may be determined by the Court referred to in Section 5.

(2) If the offender has not paid the penalty, imposed under sub-section (1) the same shall be recoverable as arrears of land revenue.

Derogation : The provisions of this Act shall be in addition to the provisions of any other law, for the time being in force.

THE HARYANA PROTECTION OF MEDICARE SERVICE PERSONS AND MEDICARE INSTITUTIONS ACT, 2009 (Haryana Act No. 14 of 2009)

Haryana Government, Law and Legislative Department, Notification, The 26th March, 2009

No. Leg. 18/2009.–The following Act of the Legislature of the State of Haryana received the assent of Governor of Haryana on the 19th March, 2009, and is hereby published for general information :

Definition : Is defined as an Act to prohibit violence against Medicare Service Persons and damage to property in Medicare Service Institutions and for matters connected therewith or incidental thereto.

Enactment : Enacted by the Legislature of the State of Haryana in 2009 (19-03-2009). It shall come into force at once, vide notification dated 26th March, 2009.

Jurisdiction : Extends to the whole of Haryana State.

Definitions : In this Act, unless the context otherwise requires,-

(a) "Medicare Service Institution" means an institution, used or intended to be used for the reception, accommodation, treatment and medicare of persons suffering from any sickness, injury or infirmity whether of body or mind and providing of treatment or nursing or both of them and includes maternity home, convalescent home, nursing home or hospital etc. owned or controlled either by the State Government or Central Government or any person or individual;

(b) "Medicare Service Person" in relation to a Medicare Service Institution, shall include, -

(i) Registered Medical Practitioners (including those having provisional registration);

(ii) Registered Nurses;

(iii) Medical Students;

(iv) Nursing Students;

(v) Para-Medical Workers.

Penalty : (1) Whoever, endangers the life of or causes any harm, injury, intimidation, obstruction or hindrance to any Medicare Service Person in the discharge of duty or damage to any property in Medicare Service Institution, commits an act of violence which shall be an offence under this Act.

(2) Whoever, either by himself or as a member or as a leader of a group of persons or organisation commits or attempts to commit or abets or incites the commission of offence, shall be

punished with imprisonment for a term of three years and shall also be liable to a penalty of actual amount of purchase price of medical equipment damaged and loss caused to the property as may be determined by the competent Court.

Cognisable offence. - The offence committed under Section 3 shall be cognisable and non-bailable.

Recovery as arrears of land revenue. If a person fails to pay the penal amount under Section 3, the said amount shall be recoverable as if it were arrears of land revenue.

Act not in derogation of any other law : The provisions of this Act shall be in addition to and not in derogation of the provisions of any other law, for the time being in force.

Power to make rules :

The State Government may, by notification in the Official Gazette, make rules for carrying out the purposes of this Act.

Every rule made under this Act shall be laid, as soon as may be, after it is made, before the House of State Legislative, while it is in session.

PROHIBITION OF CHILD MARRIAGE ACT, 2006

Definition : Is defined as an Act to provide for the prohibition of solemnisation of child marriages and for matters connected therewith or incidental thereto.

Enactment : Enacted by Parliament in 2007 (into force on 10-01-2007).

Jurisdiction : Extends to the whole of India, except the State of Jammu and Kashmir (J&K).

Offence : Marrying a child by an adult male above 18 yrs. of age.

Section : Notwithstanding anything contained in the Code of Criminal Procedure, 1973 (2 of 1974), an offence punishable under this Act shall be cognisable and non-bailable.

Penalty : Imprisonment, or fine or both.

Offence : Promoting or permitting solemnisation of Child marriage.

Penalty : Rigorous imprisonment, which may extend to two yrs. with fine, which may extend upto ₹ 1 lakh.

Offence : Solemnising a child marriage.

Penalty : Rigorous imprisonment, which may extend to two yrs. with fine, which may extend upto ₹ 1 lakh, unless he/she proves that he/she had reasons to believe that the marriage was not a child marriage.

Prohibition : A Judicial or a Metropolitan Magistrate can issue an injunction prohibiting child marriage on an application by a Child Marriage Prohibition Officer or on a complaint or suo motu.

PROTECTION OF HUMAN RIGHTS ACT, 1993

Definition : Is defined as an Act to provide for the constitution of a National Human Rights Commission, State Human Rights Commission in States and Human Rights Courts for better protection of human rights and for matter connected therewith or incidental thereto.

Enactment : Enacted by Parliament in 1993 (into force on 28-09-1993)

Jurisdiction : Extends to the whole of India, except the State of Jammu and Kashmir (J&K) where applicable to matters incld. In List I or III in the 7th Schedule of the Constitution.

NATIONAL HUMAN RIGHTS COMMISSION

Constitution: Constituted by the Central Government.

Headquarter: Delhi

Composition: Chairperson : Chief Justice of the Supreme Court

Secretary General : An officer of Secretary rank (Government of India) who shall be the Chief Executive Officer

Members: Judge of the Supreme Court (is/has been) Chief Justice of High Court (is/has been)

Two members – familiar with matters related to Human Rights

Chairperson of - National Commission for Minorities

- National Commission for Scheduled Cast
- National Commission for Scheduled Tribes
- National Commission for Women

Appointment: By the President, on the recommendation of a committee consisting of :

Chairperson – The Prime Minister

Members : Speaker of the House of People

Minister of Home Affairs

Leader of the Opposition in the House of People

Leader of the Opposition in the Council of States

Deputy Chairman of the Council of States.

Judge of the Supreme Court/or High Court – provisional, after consultation with Chief Justice of India.

Term : Five years or attains the age of seventy years– whichever is earlier.

Resignation: By written notice addressed to the President of India.

Removal : By the President of India :

- under sub-section (3) on the ground of confirmed misbehaviour
- under sub-section (2) on the ground of that :

  Is unfit (mentally or physically) to continue in office

  Is of unsound mind

Is convicted and imprisoned for an offence (moral turpitude)

Is engaged in a paid employment beside his official duties.

Vacancy : The President may authorise one of the members to act as the Chairperson, to discharge the duties of the Chairperson until the appointment of a new Chairperson.

Function:
- To exercise the powers conferred upon.
- To perform the assigned functions.
- To inquire a petition filed by a victim or anyone on his/her behalf into complaint of - Any Human Rights Violation.
- Any negligence by a Public Servant to prevent such violation.
- To intervene in any Court proceeding involving allegation of Human Rights Violation, pending before a Court, with the approval of such Court.
- To inspect/visit any State Government controlled jail/or institute, where inmates are detained/or lodged for treatment, reformation or protection, in order to study their living conditions and thereby make recommendations to the government.
- To review the safeguards provided for the protection of Human Rights.
- To review acts of terrorism, that hamper the Human Rights.
- To recommend effective implementation of treaties on Human Rights.
- To promote public awareness of Human Rights, by means of publication, electronic media, lectures, seminars, debates.
- To encourage the efforts of Non-Governmental Organisations (NGOs) for the promotion of Human Rights.

Powers : Shall have all the powers of a Civil Court trying a suit under the Code of Civil Procedure, 1908, pertaining to following :

- To summon and enforce the attendance of witnesses and examine them on Oath.
- To receive evidence on affidavits.
- To enforce discovery and production of any document.
- To requisite any public record/or copy from any Court or office.
- To summon any person to furnish information relevant to inquiry.
- To utilise the services of any officer or investigating agency of the Central Government or any State Government for the purpose of conducting any investigation pertaining to the inquiry.
- To visit/search any place, relevant to inquiry.
- To forward the case (after recording the facts pertaining to offence) to a Magistrate having jurisdiction to try the same under Section 346 of the Code of Criminal Procedure, 1973 (2 of 1974).
- To expedite disposal of any particular complaint pending before it, the Commission may transfer the complaint to the State Commission of the State, to which the complaint pertains to be.
- To dispose of any transferred complaint, the State Commission under sub-section (6), shall deal it as if it was a complaint initially filed before it.

Post-Inquiry Steps : **Subs. By Act 43 of 2006, Section 11, for Section 18 (w.e.f. 23-11-2006).**

Section 18, pre-substitution, stood as under : The Commission may take any of the following steps during or upon the completion of an inquiry held under this Act, namely :

- Where the inquiry discloses, the Commission of Violation of Human Rights or negligence in the prevention of violation of Human Rights by a public servant, it may recommend to the concerned Government or Authority the initiation of proceedings for prosecution or such other action as the Commission may deem fit against the concerned person/s ;

- Approach the Supreme Court or the concerned High Court for such directions, orders or writs as the Court may deem necessary :
- Recommend to the concerned Government or Authority for the grant of such immediate interim relief to the victim or the members of his family as the Commission may consider necessary :
- Subject to the provisions of clause (5) provide a copy of the inquiry report to the petitioner or his representative ; - The Commission shall send a copy of its inquiry report together with its recommendations to the concerned Government or Authority and the concerned Government or Authority shall, within a period of one month, or such further time as the Commission may allow, forward its comments on the report, including the action taken or proposed to be taken thereon, to the Commission ;
- The Commission shall publish its inquiry report together with the comments of the concerned Government or Authority on the recommendations of the Commission.

Procedure : Adopted with respect to Armed forces :

The Commission shall deal with complaints or violation of Human Rights by the members of the Armed Forces, in accordance with the procedure laid down in this Section.

Rules:

- It is incumbent on the Commission to submit an annual report as also special reports to the Central Government and the State Government concerned.
- The Central Government and the State Government shall have to lay the annual and special reports along with a memorandum of action or acceptance before each House of Parliament and before the House/s of the State Legislature.

STATE HUMAN RIGHTS COMMISSIONS

Constitution : Constituted by the State Government.

Headquarter: To be specified by the State Government's notification.

Composition: Chairperson : Chief Justice of High Court

Secretary : shall be the Chief Executive Officer of the State Commission

Members : Judge of the High Court (is/has been)

District Judge of that State (is/has been)

Two members–familiar with matters related to Human Rights.

Appointment: By the Governor, on the recommendation of a committee consisting of :

Chairperson–The Chief Minister of that State.

Members : Speaker of the Legislative Assembly

Minister of Home Affairs in that State

Leader of the Opposition in the Legislative Assembly

Chairman of the Legislative Council (if exists)

Leader of the Opposition in the Legislative Council of States.

Term : Five years or attains the age of seventy years–whichever is earlier.

Resignation : By written notice addressed to the Governor.

Removal : By the President of India :

- under sub-section (3) on the ground of confirmed misbehaviour
- under sub-section (2) on the ground of that :
- Is unfit (mentally or physically) to continue in office
- Is of unsound mind
- Is convicted and imprisoned for an offence (moral turpitude)
- Is engaged in a paid employment beside his official duties.

Vacancy : The Governor may authorise one of the members to act as the Chairperson, to discharge the duties of the Chairperson until the appointment of a new Chairperson.

Function:
- To exercise the powers conferred upon.
- To perform the assigned functions.
- To inquire a petition filed by a victim or anyone on his/her behalf into complaint of - Any Human Rights Violation.
- Any negligence by a Public Servant to prevent such violation.
- To intervene.

Function:
- To exercise the powers conferred upon.
- To perform the assigned functions.
- To inquire a petition filed by a victim or anyone on his/her behalf into complaint of - Any Human Rights Violation.
- Any negligence by a Public Servant to prevent such violation
- To intervene in any Court proceeding involving allegation of Human Rights Violation, pending before a Court, with the approval of such Court.
- To inspect/visit any State Government controlled jail/or institute, where inmates are detained/or lodged for treatment, reformation or protection, in order to study their living conditions and thereby make recommendations to the Government.
- To review the safeguards provided for the protection of Human Rights.
- To review acts of terrorism, that hamper the Human Rights.
- To recommend effective implementation of treaties on Human Rights.
- To promote public awareness of Human Rights, by means of publication, electronic media, lectures, seminars, debates.
- To encourage the efforts of Non-Governmental Organisations (NGOs) for the promotion of Human Rights.

Powers : Shall have all the powers of a Civil Court trying a suit under the Code of Civil Procedure, 1908, pertaining to following :

- To summon and enforce the attendance of witnesses and examine them on oath
- To receive evidence on affidavits
- To enforce discovery and production of any document
- To requisite any public record/or copy from any Court or office
- To summon any person to furnish information relevant to inquiry
- To utilise the services of any officer or investigating agency of the Central Government or any State Government for

Human Rights Courts

For the purpose of providing speedy trial of offences arising out of violation of Human Rights, the State Government may, with the concurrence of the Chief Justice of the High Court, by notification, specify for each district a Court of Session to be a Human Rights Court to try the said offences :

Provided that nothing in this Section shall apply if–

- A Court of Session is already specified as a Special Court ; or
- A Special Court is already constituted, for such offences under any law for the time being in force.

Public Prosecutor

For every Human Rights Court, the State Government shall, by notification, specify a Public Prosecutor or appoint an advocate who has been in practice as an advocate for not less than seven years, as a Special Public Prosecutor, for the purpose of conducting cases in Human Rights Court.

PROTECTION OF WOMEN FROM DOMESTIC VIOLENCE ACT, 2005

Definition : Is defined as an Act to provide for more effective protection of the rights of women guaranteed under the Constitution who are victims of violence of any kind occurring within the family and for matters connected therewith or incidental thereto.

Enactment : Enacted by Parliament in 2006 (26 Oct. 2006).

Offence:
- Harms, harasses, injures or endangers the aggrieved person, to coerce her or any other person related to her, to fulfil any illegal demand for dowry, property or valuable security; or
- Harms, injures or endangers the health, safety, life, limb or well-being, whether mental or physical of the aggrieved person or tends to do so and incls. causing abuse (verbal and emotional, physical, sexual and economical) ; or
- Threatens the aggrieved person or any person related to her.

Penality : under Section 12 sub-section (1) :
- Counselling : The Magistrate may direct the aggrieved person, singly or jointly to undergo counselling with a service provider at any stage of the proceedings.
- Right to reside in a shared household : The aggrieved person shall not be evicted or excluded from the shared household by the respondent except in accordance with the procedure established by law.
- Protection orders : The Magistrate may pass a protection order in favour of the aggrieved person and prohibit the respondent from committing, aiding or abetting any act of violence, or trespassing the places of aggrieved person, or attempting to communicate in any form with the aggrieved person.
- Residence orders : The Magistrate may pass a residence order–restraining the respondent from

dispossessing or disturbing the aggrieved person from the shared household.

- Monetary relief : The Magistrate may direct the respondent to pay monetary relief to the aggrieved person, to meet the expenses incurred and losses suffered by the aggrieved person and any child of the aggrieved person as a result of domestic violence.
- Compensation orders : The Magistrate may direct the respondent to pay compensation and damages for the injuries (incld. Mental torture and emotional distress (as a result of domestic violenc).
- Breach of protection order : Punishable with imprisonment of upto 1 yr., or with fine which may extend to ₹ 20,000, or with both.

PROTECTION OF WOMEN AGAINST SEXUAL HARASSMENT AT WORKPLACE BILL, 2007

Definition : Is defined as an Act to provide for the protection of women against sexual harassment at workplace.

Aims:

- To provide protection not only to women who are employed but also to any woman who enters the workplace as a client, customer, apprentice, and daily wage worker or in an ad-hoc capacity. It also covers students, research scholars in Colleges/Universities and patients in Hospitals. It seeks to cover workplaces in the unorganised sectors.
- To provide an effective complaints and redress mechanism.
- To be mandatory for every employer to constitute a Local (internal) Complaints Committee (LCC) to be constituted by the designated District Officer at the District/or Sub-district levels, depending on the need. The LCCs will enquire into the complaints of sexual harassment and recommend action to the employer or District Officer.

Enactment : Enacted by Parliament in 2007.

Jurisdiction : Extends to the whole of India.

Offence : Sexual harassment at workplace. Also the promise or threat to a woman's employment prospects or creation of hostile work environment as as 'sexual harassment' at the workplace and expressly seeks to prohibit such acts.

Flaws : Members of the complaints committee might not always be independent of the influences of the management which has instituted it, and this esp. becomes a tricky issue if the offender in question is part of the top management.

Security : Though the bill is not foolproof, it at least provides a starting point of security.

But yes, every working woman should take the onus of her personal security and well-being at the work place.

Safeguards : That the bill provides for safeguards in case of false or malicious complaint of sexual harassment. However, merely inability to substantiate the complaint or give adequate proof would't make the complaint liable for punishment.

Precautions:- That women should express strong resistance to the smallest inappropriate gesture, action, word or speech. Otherwise the offender will assume that he has her consent and will progress to bigger offences.

- That women should learn to discern friendly behaviour from inappropriate behaviour and maintain certain boundaries with men at all times.

Example : Laugh and joke may be fine, but crude jokes are unpardonable.

Penalty : Employers who fail to comply with the provisions, will be liable to punishment with a fine which may extend to ₹ 50,000.

Since there is a possibility that during the inquiry, the woman may be subject to threat and aggression, she has been given the option to seek relief in the form of transfer either of her own or the respondent or seek leave from work. The complaint committees are required to complete their inquiry within 90 days and a period of 60 days has been given to the Employer/ District Officer for the implementation of the recommendations of the committee.

Safeguards : The bill provides for safeguards in case of false or malicious complaint of sexual harassment. However, merely inability to substantiate the complaint or give adequate proof would't make the complaint liable for punishment.

Vox-Populi : **Ramesh Behl** (Sr. Manager MNC, Gurgaon): The problem stems at two levels :

1st: That some women, who think there is nothing wrong in talking loosely and dressing provocatively. This category of women, more often than not, is not conscious of the fact that their conduct is likely to attract unwanted attention from male colleagues. Needless to say, however they are courting risk.

2nd: That certain women, who have ambitions but lack efficiency and knowledge of the job, they have been assigned to do. There have been women, who used their feminine guiles to manipulate career moves and hence became very susceptible to sexual harassment.

Raina Bhattacharjee (Psychological Therapist and Wellness Counsellor): From the woman's point of view, this alleged manipulation usually starts and stops with flirting. This means that more often than not, most women in this scenario might be fine going for an occasional lunch date or receiving a few flirtatious compliments, but they are uncomfortable and unwilling when it comes to anything beyond this. Unfortunately, however, most men cannot comprehend this unspoken firewall in terms of permissiveness and consequently these women soon find themselves in sticky situations. That women should express strong resistance to the smallest inappropriate gesture, action, word or speech. Otherwise the offender will assume that he has her consent and will progress to bigger offences. That women should learn to discern friendly behaviour from inappropriate behaviour and maintain certain boundaries with men at all times.

Example : Laugh and joke may be fine, but crude jokes are unpardonable.

Flavia Agnes (Women's Rights Lawyer and Writer): The worst thing that may happen in such cases is that the women finds herself completely alone. She feels that if she complains, people will unduly and sceptically question her about her initial overtures. And when ther situation becomes unbearable, women often resort to extreme measures like Geetika Sharma suicide case.

Members of the complaints committee might not always be independent of the influences of the management which has instituted it, and this esp. becomes a tricky issue if the offender in question is part of the top management.

PROTECTION OF WOMEN AGAINST SEXUAL HARASSMENT AT WORKPLACE BILL, 2013

Definition : Is defined as an Act to provide for the protection of women against sexual harassment at workplace.

Aims:

- To provide protection not only to women who are employed but also to any woman who enters the workplace as a client, customer, apprentice, and daily wage worker or in an ad-hoc capacity. It also covers students, research scholars in Colleges/Universities and patients in Hospitals.

  It seeks to cover workplaces in the unorganised sectors.
- To provide an effective complaints and redress mechanism.
- To be mandatory for every employer to constitute a Local (internal) Complaints Committee (LCC)

to be constituted by the designated District Officer at the District/or Sub-district levels, depending on the need. The LCCs will enquire into the complaints of sexual harassment and recommend action to the employer or District Officer.

Enactment : Enacted by Parliament in 2013.

Jurisdiction : Extends to the whole of India.

Offence : Sexual harassment at workplace. Also the promise or threat to a woman's employment prospects or creation of hostile work environment as as 'sexual harassment' at the workplace and expressly seeks to prohibit such acts.

Flaws : Members of the complaints committee might not always be independent of the influences of the management which has instituted it, and this esp. becomes a tricky issue if the offender in question is part of the top management.

Security : Though the bill is not foolproof, it at least provides a starting point of security.

But yes, every working woman should take the onus of her personal security and well-being at the work place.

Safeguards : That the bill provides for safeguards in case of false or malicious complaint of sexual harassment. However, merely inability to substantiate the complaint or give adequate proof would't make the complaint liable for punishment.

Precautions:- That women should express strong resistance to the smallest inappropriate gesture, action, word or speech. Otherwise the offender will assume that he has her consent and will progress to bigger offences.

- That women should learn to discern friendly behaviour from inappropriate behaviour and maintain certain boundaries with men at all times.

Example : Laugh and joke may be fine, but crude jokes are unpardonable.

Penalty : Employers who fail to comply with the provisions, will be liable to punishment with a fine which may extend to ₹ 50,000.

Since there is a possibility that during the inquiry, the woman may be subject to threat and aggression, she has been given the option to seek relief in the form of transfer either of her own or the respondent or seek leave from work. The complaint committees are required to complete their inquiry within 90 days and a period of 60 days has been given to the Employer/ District Officer for the implementation of the recommendations of the committee.

Safeguards : The bill provides for safeguards in case of false or malicious complaint of sexual harassment. However, merely inability to substantiate the complaint or give adequate proof would't make the complaint liable for punishment.

Vox-Populi : **Ramesh Behl** (Sr. Manager MNC, Gurgaon): The problem stems at two levels :

1st : That some women, who think there is nothing wrong in talking loosely and dressing provocatively. This category of women, more often than not, is not conscious of the fact that their conduct is likely to attract unwanted attention from male colleagues. Needless to say, however they are courting risk.

2nd : That certain women, who have ambitions but lack efficiency and knowledge of the job, they have been assigned to do. There have been women, who used their feminine guiles to manipulate career moves and hence became very susceptible to sexual harassment.

Raina Bhattacharjee (Psychological Therapist and Wellness Counsellor): From the woman's point of view, this alleged manipulation usually starts and stops with flirting. This means that more often than not, most women in this scenario might be fine going for an occasional lunch date or receiving a few flirtatious compliments, but they are uncomfortable and unwilling when it comes to anything beyond this. Unfortunately, however, most men cannot comprehend this unspoken firewall in terms of permissiveness and consequently these women soon find themselves in sticky situations. That women should express strong resistance to the smallest inappropriate gesture, action, word or speech. Otherwise the offender will assume that he has her consent and will progress to bigger offences. That women should learn to discern friendly behaviour from inappropriate behaviour and maintain certain boundaries with men at all times.

Example : Laugh and joke may be fine, but crude jokes are unpardonable.

Flavia Agnes (Women's Rights Lawyer and Writer): The worst thing that may happen in such cases is that the women finds herself completely alone. She feels that if she complains, people will unduly and sceptically question her about her initial overtures. And when their situation becomes unbearable, women often resort to extreme measures like Geetika Sharma suicide case.

Members of the complaints committee might not always be independent of the influences of the management which has instituted it, and this esp. becomes a tricky issue if the offender in question is part of the top management.

REGISTRATION ACT

INDIA :

Enactment : Registration Act, 1956.

Jurisdiction : Applicable to all doctors (Medical Practitioners) practicing medicine.

Governing Body : Medical Council of India (MCI) is the governing body in India.

Powers : Limited powers, because health being a concurrent State subject, different States enact certain acts–application of these at times create confusion and Court interventions.

Aims:
- To approve, recognise, inspect and monitor the medical education.
- To define the code of conduct and medical ethics.
- To ensure that doctors are uptodate in their medical knowledge.
- To ensure that doctors are fit to practise medicine throughout their careers.

Renewal : Based on 50 hrs. of Continued Medical Education (CME) every five years.

UK :

Jurisdiction : Applicable to all doctors (Medical Practitioners) practicing medicine.

Options :

A. Registration with a Licence to practice (Fitness to practice), subjected to periodic revaluation.

Relicencing : subject to renewal every five yrs.

B. Registration without a Licence to practice : registered but not be able to practice.

C. Registered no longer : voluntary removal of name from the register.

Governing Body : General Medical Council (GMC).

Powers:
- To regulate doctors ensuring Good Medical Practice, effective on 13/11/06.
- Doctors are personally accountable for their professional practice and must always be prepared to justify their decisions and actions.

Aims:
- To ensure that doctors are uptodate in their medical knowledge.
- To ensure that doctors are fit to practise medicine throughout their careers.
- To make the care of patient as first concern.
- To protect and promote the health of patients and the public.
- To provide a good standard of practice and care.

To treat patients as individuals and respect their dignity.

- To work in partnership with patients.
- To be honest and open and act with integrity.

Revalidation: Periodic revalidation compulsory for a licence to practise.

REGISTRATION OF BIRTHS AND DEATHS ACT, 1969

Enactment : Registration of Births and Deaths Act, 1969.

Jurisdiction : Applicable to all citizens.

Governing : Registrar Births and Deaths, appointed by the State Governments.

Body

Powers: - To regulate census.

It seeks to cover workplaces in the unorganised sectors.

- To provide an effective.

Transplantation of Human Organs Act, 1994 (TOHO)

Definition : An Act to provide for the regulation of removal, storage and transplantation of human organs for the therapeutic purposes and for the prevention of commercial dealings in human organs and for matters connected therewith or incidental thereto.

Titles :

Appropriate Authority : Officer/s appointed by the Central or State Government by notification under Section 13, for implementing the Act.

Authorisation Committee : Constituted under Section 9(4) clause (a) or (b).

Duties: - To grant Registration under Section 15(1) or Renewal Registration under Section 15(3).

- To suspend/or cancel Registration under Section 16(2).
- To enforce prescribed standards for hospitals conducting the transplantation, storage or removal of human organ/s.
- To inspect periodically hospitals, clinics, medical institutes and medical centres, for evaluating

the standard of transplantation and medical care provided to the donor/s and recipient/s.

Hospital : Including Nursing Home, Medical Institute, Medical Centre or Clinic, for therapeutic purpose/s.

Donor : A person >18 yrs. of age, voluntarily permits the removal of his organs for therapeutic purposes, under Section 3(1or 2).

Human organ : Part of human body, that cannot be replaced by the body.

Recipient : A person receiving the transplanted organ.

Brain-stem death–the clinical stage at which all body functions cease permanently and irreversibly, declared under Section 3(6).

Deceased : A person in whom all evidence of life cease permanently, due to Brain-stem death or Cardio-respiratory failure, declared under Section 3.

Transplantation : Grafting of a human organ from a donor person (living or dead) into a recipient person, for therapeutic (life-saving) purpose.

Therapeutic purpose/s : Management (life-saving treatment) of a serious disease/disorder.

Authority for removal of Human organs :

Voluntarily: A person authorising removal of any human organ of his/her body before death.

Will : A person authorising (in writing) any person/s, anytime before his/her death, the removal of any part of his/her body, after his/her death.

No objection : A person before his/her death has neither authorised nor objected to removal of any organ of his/her body after death, the person/s lawfully in possession of the dead body, may authorise removal of any organ of the dead body, until and unless objection from any near relative/s of the deceased person.

Registered Medical Practitioner : Is the authorised person (Specialist, Incharge of the hospital where death occurred, or RMP treating the deceased person) to remove and transplant any human organ, under Section 3(1or 2).

The RMP is required to examine the dead body, in order to confirm the brain-stem death, before removal of any organ from the dead body.

Minor donor : Anyone of the parents of the deceased person (<18 yrs. of age), certified under sub-section (6), may authorise removal of any organ from the body of the deceased person.

Unclaimed bodies : Lying in a hospital or prison for >48 hrs., are authorised by the management of the hospital or prison, for removal of any human organ.

Post-mortem bodies : Are authorised by the competent authority for removal of an organ for translantation, and which was not required for the histo-pathological examination, as decided by the competent authority.

Restrictions imposed on removal of Human organs :

- No human organ transplantation by a donor allowed before his death, in case the recipient is not his/her near relative.
- No human organ transplantation by a donor allowed after his death, in case the recipient is not his/her near relative, until and unless the deceased person had authorised without any objection for removal of any organ from his dead body and donating it to any person, unrelated to him/her.
- No human organ transplantation allowed by the authorised person, in case of an inquest required to be held related to such body.
- No human organ transplantation allowed by the donor or authorised person, for any purpose other than therapeutic purpose.
- No human organ transplantation from the body of deceased is authorised by a person entrusted with the deceased body for the sole purpose of interment and cremation only.
- No removal or transplantation of any human organ should be conducted by an RMP, until

and unless the RMP explain fully possible implications (complications) that may occur as a result of transplantation, to the donor/near relatives (in case of deceased) and recipient.

Regulation of Hospitals conducting Transplantation of Human Organs :

- No Hospital, Clinic, Medical Institute or Medical Centre, until and unless is registered under the Act, shall conduct, aid or involve in, the removal, storage or transplantation of any human organ.
- No removal, storage or transplantation of any human organ, by an RMP, can be conducted at a place other than a registered place, as per Act.

Registration Certificate : Issued by the Appropriate Authority to the applicant (Hospital, Clinic, Nursing home, Medical Institute or Medical Centre), after fully satisfied that the applicant has fulfilled all the requirements of the Act.

Suspension/or cancellation of registration : The Appropriate Authority issues a notice on the basis of a complaint, to the hospital conducting organ transplantation, to show cause, why its registration should not be suspended/or cancelled on account of reasons mentioned in the notice.

The Appropriate Authority, after giving an opportunity to the hospital, realises that there has been a breach of Act's provisions, may initiate action against the defaulting hospital e.g. suspend/or cancel its registration under Section 15(2) or Section 16(2).

Appeals : An aggrieved person may appeal to :

- the Central Government against the order of Appropriate Authority under Section 9(4) or Section 13(1), or to :
- the State Government against the order of Authorised Committee under Section 9(4) or Section 13(2), for rejecting, suspending or cancelling the registration.

Offences and Penalities

Offence : Unauthorised removal of human organ/s :

An unauthorised person rendering his services to/or at a hospital, for purpose of transplantation, conducting, associating or helping in the removal of human organ/s, is convicted under sub-section (1).

Penality : Any person (non-RMP) :

- Imprisonment upto five yrs. plus fine upto ₹ 10,000

Registered Medical Practitioner (RMP) :

- Imprisonment upto five yrs.plus fine upto ₹ 10,000, plus :
- 1st offence : Suspension of Registration for two yrs.
- 2nd offence : Permanent erasing of his/her name from the Register of State Medical Council.

Offence : Commercial dealings in human organ/s : Any person that :

- seeks to find a willing donor for supply of his/ her body organ/s, against payment.
- supplies human organ/s against payment.
- supplies/or offers to supply his/her organ/s, against payment.
- initiates/or negotiates mode of payment for the supply of human organ/s.
- participates in the managing committee (firm, company or society) involved in the process of payment for removal of human organ/s.
- advertises or publishes – asking donors to supply and recipients to receive human organ/s against payment.

Penalty : Imprisonment for 2-7 yrs. plus fine ₹ 10000-20000.

State of West Bengal v/s Bhola Devi (1996) 1 (Crimes) 427 (Cal DB) :

Moral conviction must be replaced by legal conviction.

Cognisance of offence :

Cognisance of offence under this Act–not to be taken by any Court.

Exception : Appropriate Authority, Central or State Government, or a person who has filed a complaint (>60 days) to the concerned Appropriate Authority.

Only Metropolitan Magistrate or a Judicial Magistrate First Class, shall try any offence under this Act.

The Court may direct the concerned Appropriate Authority, to supply copies of the records in its possession, to a persion who has filed a complaint under sub-section (1) clause (b).

Making of Rules :

Step 1 : The Central Government by notification, makes the rules, for carrying out the Act in good faith, that :

Authorising donor for removal of his/her organ/s before his/her death under Section 3(1).

Certifying Brain-stem death, by fulfilling all the conditions and requirements required for the purpose under Section 3(6).

Authorising parent/s for removal of organ/s of the minor, following Brain-stem death under Section 3(7).

Authorising removal of organ/s of the unclaimed dead body, by the owner or management of the hospital under Section 5(1).

Preserving the removed human organ/s under Section 7.

Declaring jointly the declaration by the donor and recipient for removal and transplantation of human organ/s under Section 9(5).

Explaining possible side effects, complications, by the Registered Medical Practitioner to the donor and the recipient, about the removal and transplantation of human organs under Section 12.

Enforcing standards by the Authorised Authority for hospitals involved in the removal, storage or transplantation of human organ/s under Section13(iii)(3).

Applying for Registration and depositing of fee under Section 14(2).

Granting of Certificate of Registration for a period under Section 15(1).

Renewing Certificate of Registration under Section 15(3).

Preferring Appeal under Section 17.

Issuing notice to the Appropriate Authority of the alleged offence by a person and his/her intention of making a complaint to the Court under Section 22.

Step 2 : Parliament (Both Houses e.g. Lok Sabha and Rajya Sabha) : Any rule made under the Act, has to be laid ASAP, before each House of Parliament (to be in session) for :

Making the Act by passing the rule as such by both houses.

Making the Act after making any amendment (modification) in the rule, by both houses.

Rejecting the rule as such.

News : New Delhi : Saturday March 10, 2012 :

Dorso.org launched to facilitate organ donation in Brain Stem-Death cases :

The Delhi Government has launched dorso.org, an online registration system for voluntary organ donation in brain-death cases. Institute of Liver and Biliary Sciences has been given the responsibility of initiating and supervising the framework for Deceased Organ Retrieval Sharing Organisation (DORSO).

Dr. S.K. Sarin, Director ILBS : "The fact that registered hospitals of Delhi will have a user name and password to access this website (dorso.org) will be helpful in facilitating organ retrievals in the event of brain-death circumstances."

DORSO is a non-Government organisation, without any profit, that has been approved by the Delhi State Deceased Organ and Retrieval Transplant Authority (DORTA) as implementers of the Delhi State Deceased Organ and Retrieval Programme. (*Source :* DNA)

Repeal : Following Acts are hereby repealed :

Ear drums and Ear bones Act, 1982 (28) (Authority for use for Therapeutic Purposes)

Eyes Act 1982(29) (Authority for use for Therapeutic Purposes)

References :

1. Baldwa, M: Criminal liability of doctors and when doctors should inform police. The Doctor People. Vol. II, Issue-5, New Delhi.
2. Baldwa, M., Navarange, J : Law of Consent. The Doctor People. Vol. II, Issue-6, New Delhi.
3. Gupta, P : Doctor's vis-à-vis CPA. The Doctor People. Vol. II, Issue-4, New Delhi.
4. Halder S : Medical negligence – Indian Penal Code and CPA vis-à-vis medical profession.
5. Navarange, J.R : Medical negligence.The Doctor's People. Vol. II, Issue-4, New Delhi.
6. Sarin, SK : Organ Donation. The News, New Delhi.

PROMINENT LAWS RELATED TO MEDICAL PROFESSION:

Laws governing, controlling and regulating Medical Profession:

- Labour laws
- Nursing Home Registration Act
- Registration Act
- Shop and Establishment Act

Laws governing doctors as medical witness :

- Accident cases : to assess the nature, extent and type of injury

- Homicidal death
- Marital disputes : age of girl/woman, virginity, impotency and child paternity
- Mental defects–confirmation.
- Sedition law
- Sexual offences: rape, sodomy, brutality, molestation
- Special Acts: MTP Act, PNDT Act, Organ transplant Act, Lunacy Act
- Suicidal death.

NATIONAL COMMISSION FOR HUMAN RESOURCES FOR HEALTH-BILL – 2011 : to reduce the shortage and uneven distribution

UK LAWS (Medico-legal) :

- **Halisbury's Laws of England – Vol. 6 (3rd Edition) Pages 17-18,**
  Medical Negligence
- **Halisbury's Laws of England (Fourth Edition, Vol. 30, Para 35):-**
- **Black's Law (Negligence) :**
- **Decisions of British applicable and relied by Indian Judiciary**
- **Charles Worth and Percy on Negligence (10th Edition, 2001)**
- **Decision of five Law Lords in Maynard v/s West Midlands Regional Health Authority, (1985) 1 All ER 635 (HL)**
- **Lord Denning in Hucks v/s Cole and Another (1968) 118 New LJ 469**
- **Lord Scarman recording of speech**
- **Lord President (Clyde) in Hunter v/s Hanley**
- **BOLAM Rule (Test)**
- **Justice McNair's judgment**
- **Judgment of Lord Edmund Davies, Lord Fraser and Lord Russel**
- **TORT LAW**

HALISBURY'S LAWS of ENGLAND – Vol. 6 (3rd Edition) Pages 17-18, defines medical negligence in following terms:-

Negligence: "duties owed to the patient. A person who holds himself oat as ready to give medical (a) advice or treatment impliedly undertakes that he is possessed of skill and knowledge for the purpose. Such a person, whether he is a registered medical practitioner or not, who is consulted by a patient, owes him certain duties, namely, a duty of care in deciding whether to undertake the case; a duty of care in deciding what treatment to give: and a duty of care in his administration of that treatment, (b) A breach of any of these duties will support an action for negligence by the patient (c)".

HALISBURY'S LAWS of ENGLAND – Vol. 30 (4th Edition) Para 35), defines the degree of skill and care required by a medical practitioner as:-

"The practitioner must bring to his task a reasonable degree of care.

Neither the very highest nor a very low degree of care and competence, judged in the light of the particular circumstances of each case, is what the law requires, and a person is not liable in negligence because someone else of greater skill and knowledge would have prescribed different treatment or operated in a different way; nor is he guilty of negligence if he has acted in accordance with a practice accepted as proper by a responsible body of medical men skilled in that particular art, even though a body of adverse opinion also existed among medical men. Deviation from normal practice is not necessarily evidence of negligence. To establish liability on that basis it must be shown (1) that there is a usual and normal practice; (2) that the defendant has not adopted it; and (3) that the course in fact adopted is one, no professional man of ordinary skill would have taken had he been acting with ordinary care."

BLACK'S LAW (Negligence) : defines medical negligence per se as :-

"Conduct, whether of action or omission, which may be declared and treated as negligence without any argument or proof as to the particular surrounding circumstances, either because it is in violation of a statute or valid municipal ordinance, or because it is so palpably opposed to the dictates of common prudence that it can be said without hesitation or doubt that no careful person would have been guilty of it. As a general rule, the violation of a public duty, enjoined by law for the protection of person or property, so constitutes".

DECISION of BRITISH applicable and relied by INDIAN JUDICIARY As per Charles Worth and Percy on Negligence (Tenth Edition, 2001), in current forensic speech, negligence has three meanings. They are:

(i) a state of mind, in which it is opposed to intention;

(ii) careless conduct; and

(iii) the breach of duty to take care that is imposed by either common or statute law.

All three meanings are applicable in different circumstances but anyone of them does not necessarily exclude the other meanings (Para 1.01).

The essential components of negligence, as recognised, are three:

"duty", "breach" and "resulting damage", that is to say:-

(1) the existence of a duty to take care, which is owed by the defendant to the complainant;

(2) the failure to attain that standard of care, prescribed by the law, thereby committing a breach of such duty; and

(3) damage, which is both causally connected with such breach and recognised by the law, has been suffered by the complainant. (Para 1.23).

DECISION of five LAW LORDS in Maynard v/s West Midlands Regional Health Authority (1985) 1 All ER 635 (HL) :-

"Has been accepted as having settled the law on the point by holding that it is not enough to show that there is a body of competent professional opinion which considers that decision of the defendant professional was a wrong decision, if there also exists a body of professional opinion, equally competent, which supports the decision as reasonable in the circumstances. It is not enough to show that subsequent events show that the operation need never have been performed, if at the time the decision to operate was taken, it was reasonable, in the sense that a responsible body of medical opinion would have accepted it as proper".

LORD DENNING in Hucks v/s Cole and Another (1968) 118 New LJ 469 observed as :

" a medical practitioner was not to be held liable simply because things went wrong from mischance or misadventure or through an error of judgment in choosing one reasonable course of treatment in preference of another. A medical practitioner would be liable only where his conduct fell below that of the standards of a reasonably competent practitioner in his field".

LORD SCARMAN who recorded the leading speech with which other four Lords agreed Quoted by the following words of **Lord President (Clyde) in Hunter v/s Hanley 1955 SLT 213 at 217,** observing that the words cannot be bettered "In the realm of diagnosis and treatment there is ample scope for genuine difference of opinion and one man clearly is not negligent merely because his conclusion differs from that of other professional men. The true test for establishing negligence in diagnosis or treatment on the part of a doctor is whether he has been proved to be guilty of if acting with ordinary care."

Lord Scarman added "a doctor who professes to exercise a special skill must exercise the ordinary skill of his speciality. Differences of opinion and practice exist, and will always exist, in the medical as in other professions.

There is seldom any one answer exclusive of all others to problems of professional judgment. A court may prefer one body of opinion to the other, but that is no basis for a conclusion of negligence." His Lordship further added that a judge's 'preference' for one body of distinguished professional opinion to establish negligence in a practitioner whose actions have received the seal of approval of those whose opinions, truthfully expressed, honestly held, were not preferred."

BOLAM RULE (TEST) :

Definition : Is defined as the basic principle relating to medical negligence.

The rule is applied to establish negligence, on the basis of whether special skill or competence has been used or not, and is not the testing of the man on the top of a Clapham omnibus, because he has been lacking this special skill. The test is the standard used for assessing an ordinary skilled man exercising and professing to have that special skill i.e. It is a well established law, being sufficient to assess the ordinary skilled man exercising that particular art.

JUSTICE McNAIR's Judgment : This rule was laid down in the judgment of :

Bolam v/s Friern Hospital Management Committee (1957) 1 WLR 582 (1957) 2 All 118 (Queen's Bench Division) :

"A doctor is not negligent, if he is acting in accordance with a practice accepted as proper by a reasonable body of medical men skilled in that particular art, merely because there is a body of such opinion that takes a contrary view.

The direction that, where there are two different schools of medical practice, both having recognition among practitioners, it is not negligent for a practitioner to follow one in preference to the other accords also with American Law, See 70 Corpus Juris Secundum (1951) 952-953 para 44. Moreover, it seems that by American Law, a failure to warn the patient of dangers of treatment is not, of itself, negligence ibid 971, para 48.

Lord Justice McNair also observed : Before I turn that, I must explain what in law we mean by "negligence". In the ordinary case which does not involve any special skill, negligence in law means this : some failure to do some act which a reasonable man in the circumstances would do : or doing some act which a reasonable man in the circumstances would not do, and if that failure or doing of that act results in injury : then there is a cause of action. How do you test whether this act or failure is negligent ? In an ordinary case, it is generally said, that you judge that by the action of the man in the street. He is the ordinary man. In one case it has been said that you judge it by the conduct of the man on the top of a Clapham omnibus. He is the ordinary man. But where you get a situation which involves the use of some special skill or competence, then the test whether there has been negligence or not is not the test of the man on the top of a Clapham omnibus, because he has not got this man exercising and professing to have that special skill. A man need not possess the highest expert skill at he risk of being found negligent. It is well established law that it is sufficient if he exercises the ordinary skill of an ordinary competent man exercising that particular art".

Judgment of LORD EDMUND DAVIES, LORD FRASER and LORD RUSSEL–All ER 267 House of Lords in Whitehouse v/s Jordon and Another (1981)(1) (dictum of McNair Jo in Bolam v/s Friern Hospital Management Committee (1957) 2 All Er 118 (Queen's Bench Division) :

" The test whether a surgeon has been negligent is whether he has failed to measure up in any respect whether in clinical judgment or otherwise".

TORT

Definition : Is defined as an action that is wrong but not criminal and can be dealt with in a Civil Court of Law.

Judgment: W.E. Sathyanarayana v/s Vijaykumar (2009)(5) RCR(Criminal) 172 (Karnataka)

Tort–Malicious prosecution–Suit for damages– Defendant filed a complaint against plaintiff under Sections 324 and 506 IPC–Police registering a case and filing charge sheet–Case ended in discharge of accused–Plaintiff claiming damages from defendant for filing false complaint–Criminal Court has not given a finding that there was no offence committed by plaintiff and complaint is false–Closure of Criminal case cannot be held as a malicious prosecution–Defendant cannot be made liable for damages on ground of malicious prosecution.

TORT LAW

Definition : Is defined as any wrong, not arising out of contract, for which there is a remedy by compensation or damages.

Judgment: Malay Kumar Ganguly v/s Dr. Sukumar Mukherjee (2009)(4) RCR(Civil) 15(SC)(Short Note) : (2009)(4) RCR(Criminal) 3: (2009)(5) R.A.J. 405(SC) Tort law–Meaning of word "Negligence" –Held–

- Negligence is the breach of a duty caused by the omission to do something which a reasonable man, guided by those considerations which ordinarily regulate the conduct of human affairs would do, or doing something which is prudent and reasonable man would not do.

- Negligence means either subjectively a careless state of mind, or objectively careless conduct–It is not an absolute term but is a relative one.
- Negligence is strictly non-feasance and not malfeasance–It is the omission to do what the law requires, or the failure to do anything in a manner prescribed by law.

References :

1. Navarange, J.R : Medical negligence. The Doctor's People. Vol. II, Issue-4, New Delhi.
2. Halder, S : Medical negligence–Indian Penal Code and CPA vis-à-vis medical profession.
3. Gupta, P : Doctor's vis-à-vis CPA. The Doctor People. Vol. II, Issue-4, New Delhi.
4. Baldwa, M: Criminal liability of doctors and when doctors should inform police. The Doctor People. Vol. II, Issue-5, New Delhi.
5. Baldwa, M., Navarange, J : Law of Consent. The Doctor People. Vol. II, Issue-6, New Delhi.
6. Gupta, M.C. : Clinical Establishment Bill–A Critique. The Doctor's People. Vol. III, Issue-03, New Delhi.
7. Nagpal, N, Sharma, R : The Clinical Establishment (Registration and Regulation). Will it improve the Health Care ?, Chandigarh.

CHAPTER - VIII

SECTIONS

SECTIONS :

INDIA

Sections IPC (Indian Penal Code) :

2(1)(o)	Service of any description (consultation, diagnosis and treatment–medical or surgical), made available to potential patient/s by a doctor.
2(1)(d)	Consumer who hires/avails any service for a paid or promised service.
2(1)(g)	Any faulty, imperfect, inadequate or shortcoming in rendering service.
2(1)(1)	Refusal of treatment by the treating physician of a patient suffering from an ailment which is not within the range of his/her experience and may refer the patient to another physician.
2(c)	Clinical Establishment (CE) Act 2010–CE means– a hospital, maternity home, nursing home, clinic, dispensary, sanatorium, or a place established as an independent entity or part of an establishment referred to in sub-clause (i), in connection with the diagnosis, investigations or treatment of diseases, and shall incld. a CE owned, controlled or managed by the Government, a trust or a corporation, excluding the CE owned, controlled or managed by the Armed Forces under the Army Act, 1950, the Air Force Act 1950 and the Navy Act, 1957.

2(d)	Allopathic Medical Practitioner, excluding Veternity medicine or surgery, Ayurvedic, Unani, Homeopathic or Biochemic system of medicine.
2(8)	Bombay Homeopathic Practitioners Act (Homeopathy i.e. Homeopathic system of medicine incld. use of Biochemic remedies.
3	West Bengal Property Defacement Act.
3	Causing damage to public property.
3	Advertisements containing indecent representation of women.
4	Publication or sending by post, books, pamphlets etc; containing indecent representation of women.
6	Penalty of the Indecent Representation of Women Act 1986.
3,4,5	MTP Act
5,6	PNDT Act
8,20,23,29	Narcotics control
12	Domestic violence
12(1)	Employment of Trained (Qualified) staff by each and every hospital, to maintain the minimum standards e.g. to employ trained (qualified) staff and that every hospital having 1-25 beds, will have to employ atleast four MBBS doctors to provide 24 hrs. emergency care, besides provision of well equipped OT, labour rooms, monitors, ventilators, defibrillator, diathermy, laboratory, X-ray, canteen and pantry.
12(2)	Obligation to treat and stabilise every kind of emergency (The Clinical Establishment (Registration and Regulation) Act 2010).
13-A-3-67	Gambling Act
14(1)	Compensation to be awarded for loss or injury suffered by the consumer due to medical negligence.
18-19-20	Provision for the regulation of removal, storage and transplantation of human organs for therapeutic purposes and for the prevention of commercial dealings in human organs and for

	matters connected therewith or incidental thereto.
20(12)(a)	Homeopathy practice only.
20 and 22	Possession of Narcotic drugs and Psychotropic substances.
21 IPC	Force feeding of prisoners on hunger strike.
24	Contempt of court.
26	Juvenile Justice Act (employing child less than 14 yrs. old)
29	Document–used as an evidence.
31	Will–used as a legal declaration of a person after his/her death.
32(1)(a)	Non-compliance of conditions of the registration.
32(1)(b)	Cancellation of registration on the basis of conviction of the owner of the hospital.
32,33,36	"Act" of illegal "Omissions"
34	Acts done by several persons in furtherance of common intention.
39	Voluntarily act–knowingly or intentionally.
44	Injury–mentally, physically, defamation or to assets/property.
50(2)	Act by which the police is under legal obligation to inform the doctor for the grounds/reason of arrest.
52	"Good faith"–genuine effort to reach the truth provided by the doctor or his staff. Penalty : Negligence proved : Doctor liable for to compensate family of deceased.
66	Hacking.
66-A :	Sending abusive messages or adopting a menacing character over an electronic medium, is punishable with three yrs. imprisonment and a fine. That action is taken only when an individual complaint being lodged at the local police station (cumbersome - abuse generally generated from anonymous accounts).

67	Publication of information which is obscene in electronic form of the IT Act 2000.
80	Occurrence of Accident in doing lawful act.
81	Act done to avoid further harm.
87-91	Act under consent.
88	Act not intended to cause death, done by consent in good faith for person's benefit.
90	Consent known to be given under fear of misconception.
92	Bona fide act for another's benefit, done without consent.
105	Act of evidence.
120A-B	Definition of Criminal conspiracy.
161	Anticipatory bail that can be asked when summons issued by the police for investigation and interrogations.
176	Inquiry by a magistrate into the cause of dowry death.
191	False evidence given under oath.
197	Issuing or signing false certificate.
201	Act of disguising evidence of offence, or giving false information to defend an offender.
202	Act of intentional omission to provide information of offence by the person bound to inform.
211	False charge of an offence.
212-216	Harbouring an offender-providing shelter to an offender under the pretext of illness in a nursing home/hospital.
228A	Disclosure of identity of the victim of certain offence.
268	Illegal omission.
269-271	Spread of infectious disease and disobedience of a Quarantine rule.
272-273	Adulteration of food and drinks.
274-276	Adulteration of drugs.
277-278	Fouling water and vitiating atmosphere.
304	Homicidal death.
304-A	Death caused by a negligent act.

306-309	Abetment of suicide.
319-328	Causing hurt, grievous hurt, loss of vision, loss of hearing or disfigurement by dangerous mean
320	Grievous hurt.
321	Intentional omission to apprehend on the part of public servant bound to apprehend.
322	Voluntarily causing grievous hurt.
323	Punishment for voluntarily causing hurt.
324	Voluntarily causing hurt by dangerous weapons or means.
325	Punishment for voluntarily causing grievous hurt
326	Voluntarily causing grievous hurt by dangerous weapons or means.
327	Voluntarily causing hurt to extort property, or to constrain to an illegal act.
328	Causing hurt by means of poison, etc. with intent to commit an offence.
329	Voluntarily causing grievous hurt to extort property, or to constrain to an illegal act.
330	Voluntarily causing hurt to extort confession, or to compel restoration of property.
331	Voluntarily causing grievous hurt to extort confession, or to compel restoration of property.
332	Voluntarily causing hurt to deter public servant from his duty.
333	Voluntarily causing grievous hurt to deter public servant from his duty.
334	Voluntarily causing hurt on provocatiion.
335	Voluntarily causing grievous hurt on provocation.
336	Act endangering life or personal safety of others
337	Causing hurt by act endangering life or personal safety of others.
338	Causing grievous hurt by act endangering life or personal safety of others.
336-338	Causing hurt by rash or negligent act by dangerous means.
340-342	Wrongful confinement.

354	Assault or criminal force applied to a woman with intent to outrage her modesty.
376	Rape.
376-D	Sexual intercourse by any member of the management or staff of a hospital with any woman in that hospital.
405	Criminal breach of trust.
406	Punishment for criminal breach of trust.
415	Cheating .
420	Cheating and dishonestly inducing delivery of property.
438	Filling of FIR being not a condition precedent to the exercise of the power.
438(1)	Section that confers on the High Court and the Court of Sessions, the power to grant anticipatory bail if the applicant has reason to believe that he/she may be arrested on the accusation of having committed a non-bailable offence.
470	Forged document.
471	Using a forged document as genuine.
499	Defamation.
504	Intentional insult with intent to provoke breach of the peace.
506	Punishment for criminal intimidation.

PROMINENT SECTIONS

Sections 304 and 304-A

Section 304 :

Definition :	Related to homicidal death.
Section :	Is a non-bailable offence.
Offence :	Homicidal death. Professional negligence causing patient's death. Criminal negligence is the gross and culpable neglect/or failure to exercise reasonable care and precautions to guard against injury or mishap.
Penalty :	Life imprisonment or capital punishment (death) in rarest of rare cases.

Effects :	Causes lot of embarrassment, harassment, hardship, bad reputation and mental agony to the doctors.

Section 304 A :

Definition :	Related to death caused by a negligent act
Section :	Is a bailable offence.
Offence :	Professional negligence causing death of a patient. Mere inadvertence or some degree of want of adequate care and caution might create civil liability, but wouldn't suffice to hold him criminally liable.

Section 306 :

Definition :	Related to suicide.
Offence :	Abetement to suicide.
Section :	Under Section 306.
Penality :	Imprisonment of term, and a fine.

Section 312-315 :

Definition :	Related to unauthorised abortion.
Offence :	Criminal abortion.
Section :	Bailable/non-bailable.
Penalty :	Imprisonment of term, and a fine.

Section 332 :

Definition :	Related to voluntarily causing hurt to deter public servant from his/her duty.
Offence :	Voluntarily hurting to deter public servant from discharging his/her duty.
Section :	Bailable/non-bailable.
Penalty :	Imprisonment of term, and a fine.

Section 354-D :

Definition :	Related to stalking.
Offence :	Stalking.
Section :	Bailable/non-bailable.
Penalty :	Imprisonment of term, and a fine.

Section 363 :

Definition : Related to kidnapping.

Offence : Kidnapping.

Section : Bailable/non-bailable.

Penalty : Imprisonment of term, and a fine.

Section 376 :

Definition : Related to rape.

Offence : Rape of victim by an accused person.

Section : Bailable/non-bailable.

Penalty : Imprisonment of upto ten yrs, and a fine.

Section 376-G :

Definition : Related to gangrape.

Offence : Rape of victim by more than one person (accused).

Section : Bailable/non-bailable.

Penalty : Imprisonment of upto ten yrs, and a fine.

Section 376-E :

Definition : Related to repeated offence (rape).

Offence : Repeated rape.

Section : 376-E

Penalty : Death sentence.

Section 376-F :

Definition : Related to rape of a girl < 12 years old.

Offence : Rape of a girl < 12 years old by an accused person.

Section : Bailable/non-bailable.

Penalty : Imprisonment of upto ten yrs, and a fine.

Section 509 :

Definition : Related to using words to insult the modesty of woman.

Offence : Insulting modesty of woman.

Section : Bailable/non-bailable.

Penalty : Imprisonment of term, and a fine.

/non-bailable

Section 509 :

Definition :	Related to word, gesture or act intended to insult the modesty of a woman.
Offence :	Outraging modesty of a woman.
Section :	Bailable/non-bailable.
Penalty :	Imprisonment of term, and a fine.

USA

Sections :

125 :	Related to Homicide.
125.00 :	Related to Definition of homicide.
125.05 :	Related to Definition of homicide, abortion and related offences.
125.10 :	Related to Criminally negligent homicide.
125.11 :	Related to Aggravated criminally negligent homicide.
125.12 :	Related to Vehicular manslaughter in the 2nd degree.
125.13 :	Related to Vehicular manslaughter in the 1st degree.
125.14 :	Related to Aggravated vehicular homicide.
125.15 :	Related to Manslaughter in the 2nd degree.
125.20 :	Related to Manslaughter in the 1st degree.
125.21 :	Related to Aggravated manslaughter in the 2nd degree.
125.22 :	Related to aggravated manslaughter in the 1st degree.
125.25 :	Related to Murder in the 2nd degree.
125.26 :	Related to Aggravated murder.
125.27 :	Related to Murder in the 1st degree.
125.40 :	Related to Abortion in the 2nd degree.
125.45 :	Related to Abortion in the 1st degree.
125.50 :	Related to Self-abortion in the 2nd degree.
125.55 :	Related to Self-abortion in the 1st degree.
125.60 :	Related to Issuing abortional articles.
130 :	Related to Sexual Offenses.
130.00 :	Related to Definitions of terms.

130.05 :	Related to Lack of consent.
130.10 :	Related to Limitation ; Defences.
130.16 :	Related to Corroboration.
130.20 :	Related to Sexual misconduct.
130.25 :	Related to Rape in the 3rd degree.
130.30 :	Related to Rape in the 2nd degree.
130.35 :	Related to Rape in the 1st degree.
130.40 :	Related to Criminal Sexual Act in the 3rd degree.
130.45 :	Related to Criminal Sexual Act in the 2nd degree.
130.50 :	Related to Criminal Sexual Act in the 1st degree.
130.52 :	Related to Forcible touching.
130.53 :	Related to Persistent sexual abuse.
130.55 :	Related to Sexual abuse in the 3rd degree.
130.60 :	Related to Sexual abuse in the 2nd degree.
130.65 :	Related to Sexual abuse in the 1st degree.
130.65-a :	Related to Aggravated sexual abuse in the 4th degree.
130.66 :	Related to Aggravated sexual abuse in the 3rd degree.
130.67 :	Related to Aggravated sexual abuse in the 2nd degree.
130.70 :	Related to Aggravated sexual abuse in the 1st degree.
130.75 :	Related to Course of sexual conduct against a child in the 1st degree.
130.80 :	Related to Course of sexual conduct against a child in the 2nd degree.
130.85 :	Related to Female genital mutilation.
130.90 :	Related to Facilitating a sex offence with a controlled substance.
130.92 :	Related to Sentencing.
130.95 :	Related to Predatory sexual assault.
130.96 :	Related to Predatory sexual assault against a child.
263.00 :	Related to Definitions of terms.
263.05 :	Related to Use of a child in a sexual performance.

263.10 : Related to Promoting an obscene sexual performance by a child.

263.11 : Related to Possessing an obscene sexual performance by a child.

263.15 : Related to Promoting a sexual performance by a child.

263.16 : Related to Possessing a sexual performance by a child.

263.20 : Related to Sexual performance by a child affirmative defences.

263.25 : Related to Proof of age of child.

CHAPTER - IX

JUDGMENTS (MEDICO-LEGAL)

JUDGMENTS (MEDICO-LEGAL):

- Abetment to Suicide
- Academic Matters Read with Consumer Protection Act, 1986
- Advertisements Forbidden by Provisions of Drug and Magic Act, 1954
- Child Abuse/Vulnerable Childhood/No Country for Children
- Civil and Criminal Contempt
- Civil and Criminal Proceeding
- Civil Procedure Code, 1908
- Clinical Establishments (Registration and Regulation) Act, 2010
- Consent
- Constitution of India, 1950
- Consumer Disputes Redressal Commission Act, 1986
- Consumer Protection Act, 1986
- Contempt of Courts Act, 1971
- Copyright Act, 1957
- Criminal Procedure Code, 1973
- Domestic Violence
- Dowry Prohibition Act, 1961
- DNA Test
- Drugs and Cosmetics Act, 1940
- Drugs and Magic Remedies (Objectionable Advertisements) Act, 1954

- Dying Declaration
- Environment Protection Act, 1986
- Euthanasia
- Fatal Accidents Act, 1855
- Homicide
- Immoral Traffic (Prevention) Act, 1956
- Indian Medical Council Act, 1956
- Indian Penal Code, 1860
- Medical Negligence
- Mental Health Act, 1987
- Mental Retardation and Multiple Disabilities Act, 1999
- Moral Turpitude
- Narco Analysis
- Narcotic Drugs and Psychotropic Substances Act, 1985
- Oaths Act, 1969
- PNDT (Regulation and Prevention of Misuse) Act, 1994
- PNDT (Regulation and Prevention of Misuse) Rules, 1996
- Protection of Human Rights Act, 1993
- Protection of Women from Domestic Violence Act, 2005
- Protection of Women from Domestic Violence Rules, 2006
- Protection of Women against Sexual Harassment at Work Place Bill, 2007
- Registration of Births and Deaths Act, 1969
- Sedition Act
- Sexual Offences and Penalty in India
- Sexual Offences and Penalty in UK
- Shops and Commercial Establishments Act, 1948
- Transplantation of Human Organs Act, 1994

ABETMENT TO SUICIDE:

Judgment: **Kishangiri Mangalgiri Goswami v/s State of Gujarat (2009)(1) RCR**

(Criminal) 947: (2009) (1) R.A.J. 675(SC)

Section 306 – Abetment to Suicide:

Suit:

- That the accused (husband) sent letters to her parents, demanding ₹ 40K, for purchase of house

- That the accused (husband) tortured and harassment wife demanding dowry.

Defence:
- That the accused showed evidence by which he had purchased valuable silver ornaments for the deceased (wife) and in his insurance policy, the deceased was shown as his nominee
- That the accused himself had taken the deceased (wife) to the hospital
- That the letters were unsigned.

Order:
- Accused acquitted under Section 306 IPC, but convicted under Section 498-A IPC and Section 3 of Dowry Prohibition Act.

Judgment: Chitresh Kumar Chopra v/s State (Govt. of NCT of Delhi (2009)(4)

RCR (Criminal) 196: (2009)(5) R.A.J. 278(SC)

Section 107 – IPC, Section 306 – Abetment to suicide:

Suit:
- That the accused and the deceased were business partners.
- That the accused mentally tortured the deceased and forced the deceased to sign a settlement wherein the share of the deceased was reduced.
- That the accused pressurised the deceased to sign the agreement if desired to live in the society, otherwise commit suicide by taking poison.
- That the deceased committed suicide soon thereafter.

Framing of charge/issue:
- That Court may consider the material only keeping in view, whether there is sufficient ground for presuming that the accused has committed an offence, and not for the aim of arriving at the conclusion that it may not likely to lead to a conviction.

Order:
- To constitute an offence under Section 306 IPC, the prosecution has to establish:
- That a person committed suicide, and

- That such suicide was abetted by the accused.
- That an offence under Section 306 would stand only if there is an "abetment" for the commission of the crime.
- That parameters of "abetment" have been stated in Section 107 of the IPC.

Held:
- That each individual's suicidability pattern depends on his/her inner subjective experience of mental torture, fear and loss of self respect.
- That different individuals under the same situation behave and react differently because of adding personal meaning to each event.

Judgment: Darshan Singh v/s State of Punjab (2009)(5) RCR (Criminal) 766(P&H)

Section 306 – Abetment to Suicide:

Suit:
- That accused (husband) is a drunkard who used to harass and torture his deceased wife.
- That she (wife) committed suicide by consuming some poisonous substance.
- That it would be for the Trial Court to determine whether, per se, habit of drinking and thereafter causing harassment would constitute abetment to suicide.

Order:
- That the prosecution failed to produce evidence. Bail granted.

Judgment: Dammu Sreenu v/s State of A.P. (2009)(3) RCR(Criminal) 153: (2009)(3) R.A.J. 685(SC)

Section 306 – Abetment to suicide:

Suit:
- That accused having illicit open relations with wife of deceased.
- That on one occasion accused took away wife of deceased and returned after four days.
- That deceased (husband) felt insulted and humiliated.
- That husband committed suicide.

Section:
- That accused and wife of deceased charged under Section 306 IPC.

Order: - Accused sentenced to 3 yrs. In jail whereas wife of deceased to 1 yr. in jail.

Section 306 – Abetment to suicide:

Judgment: Gopal Goyal Kanda v/s State of UT, Delhi (2014)

Section 306 – Abetment to suicide:

Suit:
- That accused ex-Haryana Minister Gopal Goyal Kanda alleged to sexually exploited ex-air hostess Geetika Sharma.
- That accused and his aide Aruna Chadha were harassing Geetika Sharma.
- That Kanda and his aide Aruna accused of abetting the suicide of the 23 years old ex-air hostess Geetika Sharma, who had left behind a note accusing the duo of harassing her.

Section: - Under Section 306 IPC.

Order:
- That accused Gopal Goyal Kanda sentenced to jail by the Trial Court for abetting the suicide of ex-air hostess, Geetika Sharma.
- That the Trial Court on March 4, 2014 allowed the bail application of Kanda while observing that he was in judicial custody since August 2012.
- That Justice VP Vaish of Delhi High Court, sought response from Kanda by May 1, 2014, on plea of Geetika's brother and Police who also moved the Court for cancellation of Kanda's bail, who was in jail for the past 18 months after being accused of abetting her suicide, contending that Kanda is an influential person and while on bail, will try to tamper with evidence and influence the witnesses.They asked the High Court to cancel the bail, saying that the Trial Court has not taken into consideration all the aspects while granting bail.
- That High Court had earlier dropped the charge of sexual exploitation against Kanda.

Judgment: Arti and others v/s State of UT Chandigarh (2014):

Section 306 – Abetment to suicide: Acquitted:

Suit: - That Pradeep was found hanging from a ceiling fan in May 2013.

- That the complainant Hem Chander handed over to police the alleged suicide note by Pradeep and an SMS, whereby he had blamed his in-laws for death.
- That the complainant had alleged that Pradeep had returned from the house of his in-laws a few minutes prior to ending his life.
- That the police had arrested Avtar Singh, his wife Ash and daughters Aarti and Malti, in September 2013 for abetment to suicide.

Section: - Under Secion 306 IPC.

Held: - That the prosecution failed to prove the charges.

Order: - That the Additional District and Sessions Judge Najar Singh on May 5, 2014, acquitted four persons, including wife of deceased, of the charges of abetment to suicide.

ACADEMIC MATTERS READ WITH CONSUMER PROTECTION ACT, 1986

Judgment: Buddhist Mission Dental College and Hospital v/s Bhupesh Khurana (2009(2) RCR(Civil) 144: R.A.J. 164(SC)

Section 2(1)(g) – Deficiency in service:

Suit: - That a Dental College published advertisement in newspaper and falsely claimed that it was affiliated with a University and recognised by Dental Council of India.
- That students got admission by paying exorbitant fee and other charge and wasted two yrs.
- That their carrier ruined.

Framing of Charge/issue: Deficiency in service

Order: - College directed to pay compensation as under to each student –
- That refund of admission expense with interest at the rate of 12 per cent P.A. ₹ 20 thousand towards expense on purchase of books.
- That ₹ one lakh as compensation and ₹ one lakh towards cost of litigation.

Relied: - AIR 1978 SC 548.

ADVERTISEMENTS FORBIDDEN BY PROVISIONS OF DRUG and MAGIC ACT, 1954:

Judgment: Smt. Aarti v/s State of Punjab through Principal Secretary (2009)(3)

RCR(Civil) 844: 2009(3) RCR(Criminal) 785(P&H)(DB) AIR 1960 (SC).

Article 19(1)(a) of the Constitution

Suit: - That Advertisements forbidden by Provisions of Drug and Magic Act, 1954, are protected by the Right to Freedom of Speech guaranteed under this Article.

Order: - That Advertisements Forbidden by Provisions of Drug and Magic Act, 1954, are not protected by the Right to Freedom of Speech guaranteed under this Article.

- That advertising of prohibited drugs or commodities of which the sale is not in the interest of the general public cannot be speech within the meaning of freedom of speech and would not fall within Article 19(1)(a).
- That the main purpose and true intent and aim, object and scope of the Act is to prevent self-medication of self treatment and for that purpose advertisements commending certain drugs and medicines have been prohibited.
- That it cannot be said that this is an abridgement of the petitioner's right of free speech, AIR 1960 (SC).

Judgment: Dr Rama Sofat, Dr Amit Sofat and Dr Harpreet Singh v/s Punjab Medical Council (2014)

Suit: - That the accused Dr Rama Sofat of Ludhiana, and Dr Harpreet Singh of Jallandhar, advertised their services through various mediums.

Held: - That the Punjab Medical Council issued show-cause notices to three doctors for advertising their services through various mediums, in violation of ethics to be observed by RMPs.

- That notices served to Dr Rama Sofat and Dr Amit Sofat of Dr Rama Sofat Hospital, Ludhiana, and Dr Harpreet Singh, MD of Orthonova Hospital, Jallandhar, by the Registrar PMC, demanding clarification within fifteen days.
- That the actions of these doctors amounts to soliciting patients, which is against medical practitioners ethics.
- That the council also objected to the half-hour programme on Zee Punjabi by Dr Harpreet Singh.
- That the cases are sub-judicial.

CHILD ABUSE/VULNERABLE CHILDHOOD/NO COUNTRY FOR CHILDREN

Kidnapping/Rape/Sodomy/Murder:

Judgment: Sukhdev Singh, Gurvinder Singh, Nand Kishore v/s State of UT, Chandigarh (2014):

Suit: - That Khushpreet (5) was kidnapped on December 21, 2010 by the accused, and his body was recovered on January 5, 2011, from a pit in Phase X, SAS Nagar.

Section: - Under Sections 302 (murder), 364-A (kidnapping for ransom), 120 (conspiracy) and 291 (destruction of evidence) of the IPC.

Held: - That the Additional District and Sessions Judge Atul Kasana, on April 15, 2014, held three accused guilty of kidnapping for ransom and murder of minor helpless kid.

Order: - That the Court awarded life term to the three convicts for the murder of minor Khushpreet, plus the Court awarded compensation of ₹ 1.75 lakh to parents and the money to be generated from the fine imposed on the convicts.

Judgment: Mamta v/s State of UT, Chandigarh (2014):

Suit: - That Sonakshi (1) was murdered in May 2013, by her own mother Mamta.

Section: - Under Section 302 (murder).

Held: - That the District and Sessions Judge SK Aggarwal on April 22, 2014, held Mamta guilty of strangulating her own one year old daughter Sonakshi, allegedly born out of an affair before her marriage, after being threatened by her ex-boyfriend Vicky of disclosure.

- That the verdict relied on an extra-judicial confession to her Mewa Singh, owner of the house.

Order: - That the Court awarded life term to the convict Mamta for killing her daughter Sonakshi. Though gruesome, the Court did not find the murder to be treated among the "rarest of rare" cases, warranting the capital punishment.

Judgment: Ravinder Singh Gill v/s State of Haryana (2013):

Suit: - That the accused Ravinder Singh kidnapped Jiya, a two years old girl for ransom, from her house at Sector 7, Panchkula, on October 20, 2009.

Section: - Under Section 364-A (kidnapping for ransom).

Held: - That the District and Sessions Judge on January 21, 2013, held Ravinder Singh guilty of kidnapping two years old girl from Panchkula.

Order: - That the Court awarded life term to the convict Ravinder Singh Gill, for kidnapping two years old girl.

Judgment: Ravinder Singh Gill v/s State of Haryana (2014):

Suit: - That the accused Ravinder Singh kidnapped a one year old boy for ransom, from his house at Sector 7, Panchkula, on October 5, 2010.

Section: - Under Section 364-A (kidnapping for ransom).

Held: - That the District and Sessions Judge on February 27, 2013, held Ravinder Singh guilty of kidnapping one year old boy from Panchkula.

Order: - That the Court awarded life term to the convict Ravinder Singh Gill, for kidnapping one year old boy.

Judgment: Ravinder Singh Gill v/s State of Punjab (2014):

Suit: - That the accused Ravinder Singh kidnapped a five years old girl for ransom, from her house in Phase X, SAS Nagar, on February24, 2010.

Section: - Under Section 364-A (kidnapping for ransom).

Held: - That the District and Sessions Judge on April 24, 2014, held Ravinder Singh guilty of kidnapping five years old girl from SAS Nagar.

- That the verdict relied on statement of JS Chhina, victim's father – the accused had taken a ransom of ₹ ten lac, for returning the child though he had demanded ₹ 30 lakh.
- That victim's father identified the accused while he was in the custody of Panchkula's Police, where he was arrested in connection with the kidnapping of one year old boy, for that he had been awarded life term by a Panchkula Court.

Order: - That the Court awarded life term to the convict Ravinder Singh Gill, for kidnapping five years old girl.

Judgment: Sunil and Ajay v/s State of UT Chandigarh (2014):

Suit: - That the accused Sunil of Bhiwani and Ajay of Manimajra kidnapped a 13 years girl, resident of Manimajra, with intent to rape.

- That the verdict relied on the statement of victim's uncle.

Section: - Under Section 365 (kidnapping).

Held: - That the District and Sessions Judge on February 27, 2013, held Ravinder Singh guilty of kidnapping one year old boy from Panchkula.

Order: - That the Court awarded life term to the convicts Sunil and Ajay, for kidnapping 13 years old girl with intent to rape.

Judgment: Chand v/s State of Punjab (2014):

Suit: - That the accused Chand of Dera Bassi kidnapped a 15 years old boy from Kharar, had taken him to Rupnagar forcibly and indulged in an unnatural offence (sodomodised).

- That the verdict relied on the statement of victim's relative R/o Dera Bassi.

Section: - Under Sections 365 (kidnapping), 377 (consensual sexual acts of adults in private) and 506 (criminal intimidation).

Held: - That the Additional District and Sessions Judge on March 19, 2014, held Chand guilty of kidnapping one year old boy from Panchkula

Order: - That the Court awarded life term to the convicts chand, for kidnapping 15 years old boy with intent to unnatural offence.

Judgment: Rajnath v/s State of UT Chandigarh (2014):

Suit: - That the accused Rajnath of Colony No 4, kidnapped a 7 year old girl from outside the shop of convict on May 12,2013, had taken her to a nearby jungle area on the pretext of buying her chocolates, and raped her.

- That the verdict relied on the complaint of victim's mother.

Section: - Under Sections 365 (kidnapping), 376 F (raping girl less than 12 yrs.).

Held: - That the Additional District and Sessions Judge, Anshu Shukla, while presiding over a Special Court for crimes against women, on April 28, 2014, held Rajnath 55 yrs. old R/o Colony No. 4, guilty for raping a 7 yrs old girl after kidnapping her.

Order: - That the Court awarded ten years jail to the convict Rajnath for raping the minor girl after kidnapping her. The Court also imposed a fine of ₹ 35K on convict.

Judgment: Pradeep Kumar v/s State of Haryana (2014):

Suit: - That the accused Pradeep Kumar of Barwala kidnapped a 15 years old girl from same block in October 2013, had fled with the girl, were traced by Police from Haridwar a week later.

- That the verdict relied on the statements of victim.

Section: - Under Sections 365 (kidnapping).

Held: - That the Additional District and Sessions Judge Roopam Singh on April 15, 2014, held Pradeep Kumar guilty of kidnapping 15 years old girl from Barwala.

- That the girl had refused to undergo a medical examination and did not accuse Kumar of rape in her statement before the Magistrate, she did do so at the trial.

- That the Court noting the contradiction in victim's statements, acquitted Kumar of rape but convicted him of kidnapping.

Order: - That the Court sentenced Pradeep Kumar with five years of rigorous imprisonment for kidnapping the minor girl.

Judgment: Sukhbir Singh, Gaurav, Sonu Singh and three others v/s State of Punjab (2012):

Suit: - That the accused Gaurav, Avtar Singh, Sukhbir Singh alias Shoki kidnapped a minor girl from Maloya on November 13, 2010, had taken her forcibly to a farm house, where Sonu, Sukhbir and Jasbir were present.

- That while Sukhbir, Gaurav and Sonu raped the victim, Avtar, Shoki and Jasbir remained present.

- That the verdict relied on the statement of victim and medical examination of the victim including report of semen samples collected from the clothes and body of the victim.

Section: - That Sukhbir, Gaurav and Sonu held guilty under Sections 376 (2)(G) of IPC (gangrape), 363 (kidnapping), 366-A (procuring of a minor girl) while Avtar, Shoki and Jasbir, under Sections 368 of IPC for (wrongfully concealing and keeping the victim in confinement).

Held: - That the Additional District and Sessions Judge Preeti Sahni observed that the accused in order to fulfil their lustravished the victim and betrayed her faith that she reposed in accused Gaurav. He not only committed rape upon her, but also allowed others to rape her.

- That after-effects of such offence cannot be imagined which she (victim) would undergo. These offences not only shock the victim but society as a whole and should be dealt with strict hand.

Order:
- That the Court sentenced Sukhbir Singh, Gaurav and Sonu Singh to undergo rigorous imprisonment for ten years each and to pay fine of ₹ 10K.
- That the Court sentenced Avtar, Shoki and Jasbir to five-year jail terms for facilitating the crime.
- That the Court awarded five-year jail terms to all the accused, for wrongfully concealing and keeping the victim in confinement.
- That all the sentences would run concurrently.

Judgment: Sunil and Ajay v/s State of UT Chandigarh (2014):

Suit:
- That the accused Sunil of Bhiwani and Ajay of Manimajra kidnapped a 13-year girl, resident of Manimajra, with intent to rape.
- That the verdict relied on the statement of victim's uncle.

Section:
- Under Section 365 (kidnapping).

Held:
- That the District and Sessions Judge on February 27, 2013, held Ravinder Singh guilty of kidnapping 13-year old girl from Manimajra

Order:
- That the Court awarded life term to the convicts Sunil and Ajay, for kidnapping 13-year old girl with intent to rape.

Judgment: Chandan Sahni and Shiv Kumar alias Tamatar Sahni Ajay v/s State of UP (2013):

Suit:
- That the accused Chandan Sahni and Shiv Kumar kidnapped a minor girl, from Vaishali, Bihar, on May 24, 2010, forcibly taken her to a secluded place with them, and raped her before slitting her throat.

Section:
- Under Sections 376 (2)(G) of IPC (gangrape), 363 (kidnapping), 366-A (procuring of a minor girl).

Held:
- That the Additional District and Sessions Judge on May 24, 2013, held Chandan and Shiv for the rape and subsequent murder of the minor girl.

Order: - That the Court awarded death sentence to the convicts Chandan and Shiv for the rape and subsequent murder of a minor girl, because the case fell in the 'rarest of rare' category.

Judgment: Jiwan Singh v/s State of Punjab (2014):

Suit: - That on June 29, 2012, while victim was alone at her house, the accused entered and overpowered her, gagged her with a dupatta, tied her arms and legs, and then raped her.

Section: - Under Sections 376, 363 (kidnapping), 366-A (procuring of a minor girl).

Held: - That the Additional District and Sessions Judge on January 16, 2013, held Jiwan Singh for the rape of the minor girl.

Order: - That the Court awarded seven years of rigorous imprisonment and fine of ₹ 5K under Section 376 of IPC. The accused was also sentenced to three years jail and fine of ₹ 3K under Section 452 of IPC, a minor girl.

CIVIL and CRIMINAL CONTEMPT:

Judgment: Kanwar Singh Saini v/s High Court, 2009(2) RCR(Rent) 326:(2009)(4)

RCR(Civil) 574:(2009)(161) D.L.T. 466 (Delhi) (DB)

Civil and Criminal Contempt

Order: - That whether contempt of any Subordinate Court is committed or not and

- That whether the alleged contempt is civil or criminal, has to be decided by the High Court on the basis of facts which are brought to the notice of the High Court.

CIVIL and CRIMINAL PROCEEDING:

Judgment: Lakshmi v/s Chinnammal @ Rayyammal (2009)(2) RCR(Civil) 907: (2009)(1) RCR (Rent) 497(SC):

Order: - That the Court shall not create a situation wherein a criminal proceeding would remain stayed.

- That wherein a civil proceeding as well as a criminal proceeding is pending, the criminal proceeding shall get priority.

Judgment: Lakshmi v/s Chinnammal @ Rayyammal (2009)(1) RCR(Rent) 497: (2009)(2) RCR (Civil) 906(SC):

Order:
- That a decision by a Criminal Court does not bind the Civil Court while a decision by the Civil Court binds the Criminal Court.
- That an order passed by the Executive Magistrate in proceedings under Sections 145/146 of the Code is an order by a Criminal Court and that too based on a summary enquiry.
- That at the stage of final adjudication of rights by Civil Court, which would be on the evidence adduced before the Court, the order of the Magistrate is only one out of several pieces of evidence.

Relied:
- (2004)(2) RCR(Criminal) 881: (2004)(3) Apex Criminal 100(SC)

CIVIL PROCEDURE CODE, 1908:

DNA Test:

Judgment: Sathya Raj v/s Jayaprakash (2009)(1) RCR(Civil) 516 (Karala): Section 151 – DNA Test:

Suit:
- That respondent was father of petitioner.

Ruling:
- That, It is mandatory to have a DNA test, which is a conclusive test to fix paternity of a person.
- That Civil Court has power under Section 151 C.P.C. to issue direction for DNA test.
- That subjecting a person to a medical test in a civil case is not in violation of Article 21 of Constitution of India.

Non-service of Summons:

Judgment:Venkatesh v/s P. Subbaiah (2009)(5) RCR(Civil) 55 (Karnataka): Order 5 Rule 20(1A) – Civil Procedure Code, Order 9 Rule 13

Suit:
- That summons not served in accordance with law.
- That no summon for specific date was served upon the petitioner.

- That summons served without a copy of complaint.

Held: - That receipt of summons without a copy of complaint, held as insufficient.
- That Court ordered substituted service in daily newspaper.
- That words "daily newspaper" appearing in Order 5 Rule 20(1A) meant not only a newspaper which is circulated on all days of week but has to be a reputed newspaper, published as a morning edition, to the Court's satisfaction
- That Court should avoid permitting publication in all and sundry newspapers for mere asking.

Order: - Ex parte order set aside for want of procedural lapse.

Judgment: Mahadev Prasad v/s Mansa Ram 2009(5) RCR (Civil) 350 (Rajasthan) (Jaipur Branch):

Order 9, Rule 13 (proviso second) – Setting aside of Ex-parte decree:

Suit: - That the party had knowledge of proceedings in the Court.
- That no summon for specific date was served upon the petitioner.

Held: - That the party had the knowledge of the "date of hearing but not the knowledge of pendency of suit" which is necessary for the purpose of said proviso.
- That no summon for specific date was served upon the petitioner.

Order: - Ex-parte decree set aside.

Pleadings:

Judgment: K. Laxmanan v/s Thekkayil Padmini (2009)(1) RCR(Civil) 389 (SC): Order 6 Rule 1 – Pleadings:

Held: - That Pleading consist only of csmplaint and a written statement and replication to written statement if allowed by Court.

Judgment: Baljinder Kaur v/s Rajesh Kumar (2009)(5) RCR(Civil) 435 (P&H): Order 6 Rule 2 – Pleadings:

Suit: - That replication signed by counsel for plaintiff not illegal.

- That advocate appearing on behalf of client is authorised to plead his case.

Order: - That an omission or mistake in signatures is not fatal to the suit and such an irregularity is a mere defect of procedure and can be ignored.

Relied: - 1993(1) RCR 309.

Judgment: Mal Singh v/s Mohinder Singh (2009)(5) RCR (Civil) 702 (P&H): Order 6 Rule 2 – Pleadings:

Order: - That no amount of evidence can be considered if the same has not been specifically pleaded.

Amendment in pleadings:

Judgment: Vidyabai v/s Padmalatha, 2009(1) RCR(Rent) 121: 2009(1) RCR(Civil) 763: 2009(1) R.A.J. 449: 2009(1) Civ.C.C. 798(SC):

Order 6, Rule 17 proviso:

Suit: - Party seeking to amend written statement after filing of an affidavit.

Held: - That Court has no jurisdiction to allow amendment after commencement of trial.

- That Court may allow amendment only in case wherein such an amendment is necessary to decide the real controversy among the disputed parties.

Relied: - 2005(2) RCR(Civil) 379 (SC).

Trial of Civil Suit:

Judgment: Nalini Janardhanan v/s Elamana Chinnammu (2009)(5) RCR(Civil) 544 Kerala:

Order 17 Rule 3 – Trial of Civil Suit:

Suit: - That plaintiff failed to produce evidence on the fixed date.

Held: - That party failed to produce evidence on the fixed date.

- That an advocate appeared on behalf of an absent party, for seeking adjournment only, and not to conduct or defend the case.
- That appearance of such an advocate on behalf of party not to be considered for in terms of Order 17 Rule 3(a).

Order:
- Decision given by the Court in such a case is invalid and set-aside.

CLINICAL ESTABLISHMENTS (Registration and Regulation) Act, 2010:

Judgment: RS Bedi and Another v/s Union of India and Others (2011), Panjab and Haryans High Court, Chandigarh: Clinical Establishment:

Suit:
- That the Clinical Establishments (Registration and Regulation) Act 2010, is ultra vires the Constitution.
- That the case of the petitioners is that they are medical practitioners having their clinics.
- That the Act lays down the requirement of seeking registration, providing for penal consequences in absence of registration.
- That Registration can be granted only on fulfilment of conditions lays down under the Act.
- That Section 12(2) of the Act requiring facilities to stablise the emergency medical condition of any individual who is brought to clinical estabilishment.

Defence:
- That requirement of providing for facilities for stabilisation of emergency medical condition of an individual is arbitrary and interference with the right of the petitioners to carry on their profession.
- That the petitioners are only running their clinics and they may not be able to provide for facilities for stabilising the emergency medical condition of individuals who are brought to such clinics.
- That those who cann't provide such facilities cann't be debarred from carrying on their medical profession.

- That we are unable to accept the submission.

Held:
- That Clinical establishment as defined under Section 2(C) covers various types of clinical establishments.
- That facilities for stabilising, expected to be provided in each such establishment, will obviously mean facilities expected from the type of clinical establishment run, by an institution or an individual.
- That an individual medical practitioner may not be expected to do something impossible by providing facilities at par with a big hospital.
- That interpretation of a statutory provision depends upon situation which may arise.
- That the provisions of the Act do not create any impossible situation, so as to affect the right of the petitioners to practice the medical profession.
- That there is, thus, no ground to interfere at this stage. The individual fact situation can be considered as and when the same arises.

Order:
- That writ petition is dismissed.

CONSENT:

Legal issues pertaining to consent:

Informed Consent:

1. Inadequate explanation/information prior to treatment:

Judgment: Gray v/s Grunmagle (1966) 223 A 2d 663 Pa: Medical negligence:

Suit:
- That the patient consented for Laminectomy operation.
- That the patient was not explained about what is laminectomy.
- That the patient was not informed about post-operative complications.
- That the patient suffered post-operative paralysis.

Held:
- The Court observed that the patient did not understand about what is laminectomy.
- That there was no evidence that the patient was explained about the laminectomy operation.

- That it was not an informed consent.

Order:
- The patient was awarded compensation for post-operative paralysis.

Judgment: Ms. Ins. Malhotra v/s Dr. A. Kriplani (2009)2 RCR(Civil) 79: (2009) 3 R.A.J. 88(SC): Medical negligence –

Suit:
- That the patient was admitted in hospital as a case of renal failure.
- That the patient was put on hemodialysis.
- That the hemodialysis was stopped due to persistent demands from the sister of the deceased.
- That doctors were negligent.

Defence:
- That the patient examined by a team of expert doctors and informed relatives of patient that patient was critical and kidney transplantation could not be done nearly for one year and also the consequence of the renal failure suffered by the patient.
- That sister of patient instructed the doctors to stop haemodialysis treatment to the patient.
- That because of the persisting demand of the appellant, haemodialysis was stopped which according to the respondents resulted in the untimely death at risk of complainant.

Observation: Professional may be held liable for negligence on one of two findings:
- That either he was not possessed of the requisite skill which he professed to have possessed, or
- That he did not exercise, with reasonable competence.
- That in the given case, the skill which he did possess.
- That the standard to be applied for judging, whether the person charged has been negligent or not, would be that of an ordinary competent person exercising ordinary skill in that profession.

- That the doctor cannot be held liable per se by applying the doctrine of 'res ipsa loquitor.

Relied: - 2005(3) RCR(Criminal) 836: 2005(2) Apex Criminal 649 (SC).

Order: - No case of medical negligence or deficiency in service made out against doctors.

2. Failure to inform inherent risks:

Laws in: USA- The doctor is required to inform the patient about inherent risks.

UK- Only substantial risks are to be informed/ disclosed.

India- Only substantial risks are to be informed/ disclosed i.e.

- Patient - is to be informed about the high risk of unpleasant result, ignoring the resulting psychological effect on him/her.

Judgment: Cobbs v/s Grant (1972) 8 Cal 3d 229 SC California: Medical Negligence

Suit: - That the patient consented for operation for gastric ulcer.

- That the patient was not informed about risks involved during and after surgery.
- That the patient had injury to spleen during operation, resulting in post-operative bleeding.

Held: - That there was no evidence that the patient was explained about the risks involved during and after the surgery.

Order: - The surgeon was held liable.

Judgment: Denning LJ. In Hatcher v/s Black (1954) The Times:

Suit: - That the patient had toxic goitre

- That the Surgeon told patient not to opt for prolonged conservative treatment and rather surgery to be preffered for better results.
- That the patient was not informed about risks involved during and after the surgery.

- That the patient suffered impairment of her voice during surgery.

Defence: - That surgeon did not explain to the patient about the risks involved during and after surgery, in good faith of not to worry the patient.

- That the incidence happened as an unfortunate surgical complication.

Held: - The Court observed that law does not condemn the doctor so placed would do.

- That none of the doctors called as witnesses have suggested that the surgeon was wrong. All agreed that it was a matter for his own judgment. If they do not condemn him, why should you ?".

Relied: - Denning LJ.

Order: - The surgeon was held liable.

Judgment: Malay Kumar Ganguly v/s Dr. Sukumar Mukherjee (2009) 4 RCR(Civil) 16(SC)(Short Note): (2009) 4 RCR (Criminal) 3: (2009) 5 R.A.J. 405(SC): Medical Negligence

Suit: - That it was not an informed consent.

- That the hospital did not have basic facilities like oxygen cylinders.
- That the hospital knowingly faied to provide certain amenities – fundamental for the patient.
- That the patient was not informed about the admitted risks.

Held: - That an error of judgment by a professional is not negligence per se.

- That mere deviation from normal professional practice should not be concluded as negligence.
- That mere accident is not necessarily be an evidence of negligence.
- That whether a patient not responded to a standard treatment or the surgery failed, the treating doctor cannot be held liable as per the doctrine of 'res ipsa loquitor'

Order: - The doctor was not held liable.

Judgment: Atma Singh Lt. Col. (Retd.) v/s The Managing Director, Fortis Healthcare Ltd. and Others (2010): Section 2(1)(g), 2(1)(r) &14(1)(d): Medical service deficiency: – Unfair trade practice – Compensation:

Suit: - That the patient was admitted in an advanced stage of cancer.
- That the patient was not explained about risks involved during and after surgery.
- That the patient died after few days.

Held: - The respondent hospital held liable jointly and severely with two doctors.

Order: - Compensation of ₹ ten lacks (₹ 10,00,000) awarded to the complainant.

Relied: - AIR (2005) Supreme Court 3280 in State of Punjab v/s Shiv Ram and Others.

3. Failure to provide adequate standard of care:

Judgment: Radha Ujjainkar v/s State of M.P. (2009) 5 RCR (Civil) 266(M.P.) (Gwalior Bench)(DB):

Medical negligence – Tort:

Suit: - That the patient undergone LTT operation, as already having three children.
- That the appellant became pregnant again post-LTT operation.

Held: - That the appellant failed to prove that a reasonable standard surgery not being performed.
- That although sterilisation operation is highly effective as a method of contraception and successful but failure may occur even without negligence of the doctor. That a reasonable standard of care was taken in the operation.

Order: - The surgeon was not held liable.

Judgment: Gold v/s Harngey Health Authority (1987) 2 All ER 888: Medical negligence – Tort:

Suit: - That the patient undergone LTT operation, as already having three children.
- That the appellant became pregnant again post-LTT operation.

Held: - That the appellant failed to prove that a reasonable standard surgery not being performed.
- That although sterilisation operation is highly effective as a method of contraception and successful but failure may occur even without negligence of the doctor.
- That a reasonable standard of care was taken in the operation and there was a responsible medical opinion that would not have given any signal of failure.

Order: - The surgeon was not held liable.

Judgment: Dr. Narayana K. Swamy v/s A. Nazir Ahamad Khan (2009) 3 AICJ 589 (Karnataka): Medical Negligence:

Suit: - That the patient was admitted with severe headache and vomiting.
- That the doctor incharge suggested angiography, which was not done.
- That lumbar puncture test done thrice.
- That the patient passed into stage of coma and died.

Held: - That the Trial Court held the doctor negligent.
- That the High Court upheld the award by observing that an imperative angiography was not done while tests not required were conducted thrice, and that the patient was not provided with elementary hospital facilities.
- That the Doctor and Hospital liable to pay compensation.

Order: - The surgeon and hospital held liable and fined.
- The patient was awarded compensation.

Judgment: Thake v/s Maurice (1986) QB 644: Medical negligence – Tort:

Suit: - That the husband undergone vasectomy operation.
- That the wife became pregnant and gave birth to a child.

Held: - That the operation of vasectomy failed.

- That the surgeon failed to inform the patient about the reversibility.
- That a reasonable standard of care was not taken in the operation.

Order: - The surgeon was held liable and fined

- The patient was awarded compensation of GB 9677 for upcoming of the child.

Express consent

Judgment: Pala Ram v/s State of Punjab (2009) 2 RCR (Criminal) 628(P&H):

Medical Evidence and Ocular Evidence:

Held: - That if there is variance between the medical and ocular evidence, latter has to be accepted, provided it stands the test of Judicial scrutiny in the crucible of probability.

CONSTITUTION OF INDIA, 1950:

Judgment: Parvesh v/s State of Haryana (2009) 4 RCR (Criminal) 470(P&H): Moral turpitude:

Suit: - That petitioner was selected as Police constable.

- That petitioner was denied the appointment as being charged with offence under Section 307.

Held: - That person charged with an offence under Section 307 IPC, cannot be held for moral turpitude.

- That conduct and character of petitioner were normal, without any evidence of wickedness, lacking honesty, morality or modesty.
- That person cannot be denied appointment in the Government Service.

Order: - Acquitted by the High Court of charge of moral turpitude.

- Authority directed to consider petitioner's appointment.

Relied: - AIR 1959 Allahabad 71.

Judgment: Samepatraoe R Arvelli v/s State of Maharashtra (2009) 5 RCR (Criminal) 607 (Bombay) (Nagpur Bench):

Narco Analysis, Brain Mapping and Analogous tests:

Suit: - That petitioner challenged permission for Narco analysis, brain mapping and other analogous tests.

Held: - That petitioner cannot refuse giving consent/ willingness for undertaking of Narco analysis, Brain mapping and other analogous tests.

- That larger interests to outweigh personal liberties and fundamental rights.

Order: - Dismissed.

Judgment: Dalbir Singh v/s State of U.P. (2009) 5 RCR (Criminal) 847(SC): Custodial Death:

Suit: - That the deceased committed suicide in lock up of Police station.

FOC: - An FIR registered.

Police officials charged for offences under Sections 330, 342 and 306.

Held: - That cognizance of offences taken

That no further direction necessary.

Order: - Sanction for prosecution granted.

Judgment: Anil Kumar Jain v/s Maya Jain (2009) 4 RCR (Civil) 310: (2009) 5 R.A.J. 428(SC):

Divorce by Mutual Consent:

Suit: - That divorce petition filed by husband wife on ground of irretrievable breakdown of marriage.

- That parties living separately for more than 7 yrs.

- That wife withdrew her consent for divorce later on.

Held: - That under Section 13B(2) Trial Court and High Court cannot pass decree of divorce prior to expiry of six months period.

- That under Article 142) SC can pass decree of divorce even before six months period, based on any ground not provided in Section 13 and 13B.

Order: - Divorce granted.

Judgment: D.S. Grewal v/s Vimmi Joshi (2009) 2 RCR (Criminal) 92: (2009) 1 S.C.T. 773: (2009) 2 R.A.J. 73(SC):

Protection of Women against Sexual Harassment at Work place Bill 2007:

Suit: - Hostile working environment.

Held: - That no complaint committee constituted.

- That no set up for redressal of victim's complaint.
- That management of the school found guilty of violating the guidelines laid down by the SC.

Order: - Management to pay the total cost of the !st respondent and Council fee assessed at ₹ 50 KA.

CONSUMER DISPUTES REDRESSAL COMMISSION ACT, 1986:

Judgment: Ms. Ins. Malhotra v/s Dr. A. Kriplani (2009)2 RCR(Civil) 79: (2009) 3 R.A.J. 88(SC):

Medical negligence –

Suit: - That the patient was admitted in hospital as a case of renal failure.

- That the patient was put on hemodialysis.
- That the hemodialysis was stopped due to persistent demands from the sister of the deceased.
- That doctors were negligent.

Defence: - That the patient examined by a team of expert doctors and informed relatives of patient that patient was critical and kidney transplantation could not be done nearly for one year and also the consequence of the renal failure suffered by the patient.

- That sister of patient instructed the doctors to stop haemodialysis treatment to the patient.
- That because of the persisting demand of the appellant, haemodialysis was stopped which

according to the respondents resulted in the untimely death at risk of complainant.

Observation:- Professional may be held liable for negligence on one of two findings:

- That either he was not possessed of the requisite skill which he professed to have possessed, or
- That he did not exercise, with reasonable competence.
- That in the given case, the skill which he did possess.
- That the standard to be applied for judging, whether the person charged has been negligent or not, would be that of an ordinary competent person exercising ordinary skill in that profession.
- That the doctor cannot be held liable per se by applying the doctrine of 'res ipsa loquitor.'

Relied: - 2005(3) RCR(Criminal) 836: 2005(2) Apex Criminal 649 (SC).

Order: - No case of medical negligence or deficiency in service made out against doctors.

CONSUMER PROTECTION ACT, 1986:

Judgment: Malay Kumar Ganguly v/s Dr. Sukumar Mukherjee, 2009(4) RCR(Civil) 14(SC) (Short Note): 2009(4) RCR(Criminal) 1: 2009(5) R.A.J. 405(SC): Medical Negligence:

Suit: - That patient admitted with rashes all over her body – case of dermatologist.

- That the patient was not referred to a dermatologist.
- That patient was prescribed overdose of 'Depmedral'.
- That patient died after few days of treatment.

Held: - That negligence must be of a very high degree that amount to Criminal Negligence.

- That for amounting to negligence an element of mens rea is mandatory.

- That prior to conclusion of medical negligence is made, the Court should hold not only evidence of negligence but also omission/or commission on his/her part upon going into the competency of the doctor as well his/her nature of the job.
- That to prosecute a doctor for medical negligence, it must be proved that the accused doctor did something wrong or failed to do something that under the same circumstances, no doctor in his/her normal senses and prudence would have done or failed to do.

Order:
- Medical negligence on part of doctor and hospital
- Under Section 304A IPC, Doctor not guilty of criminal negligence.
- Case remitted to Consumer Commission for fixing amount of compensation.

Judgment: Malay Kumar Ganguly v/s Dr. Sukumar Mukherjee, 2009(4) RCR(Civil) 14(SC) (Short Note): 2009(4) RCR(Criminal) 1: 2009(5) R.A.J. 405(SC):

Medical Negligence:

Law of Tort - Deficiency Service - Guidelines to determine compensation:

Held:
- That it is based on the principle of restitution in integrum.
- That the principle entitles a person to get compensation equivalent to his earning, at the earliest possible.
- That the money given to him would help him to retain the same position but not sustained the wrong one.

Order:
- Relied (1880)5 AC 25 J.

Judgment: Malay Kumar Ganguly v/s Dr. Sukumar Mukherjee, 2009(4) RCR(Civil) 14(SC) (Short Note): 2009(4) RCR(Criminal) 1: 2009(5) R.A.J. 405(SC): Medical Negligence:

Criminal medical negligence and Civil medical negligence – Deficiency Service:

Held:
- That patient admitted in hospital with rashes all over her body – a case of dermatology –
- That the doctor had not referred her to a Dermatologist, and rather prescribed "Depmedral" in higher dose superseding the maximum recommended dose, overseeing its implications.
- That condition of patient deteriorated and died after few days of treatment.

Order:
- Medical negligence on part of doctor and hospital but under Section 304A IPC, Doctor not guilty of criminal negligence.
- Deficiency of service - Case remitted to Consumer Commission for fixing the amount of compensation.

Judgment: Malay Kumar Ganguly v/s Dr. Sukumar Mukherjee, 2009(4) RCR(Civil) 15(SC) (Short Note): 2009(4) RCR(Criminal) 2: 2009(5) R.A.J. 405(SC): Medical Negligence – Section 2 IPC – Cost:

Held:
- That patient admitted in hospital.
- That death of patient due to negligence of hospital and doctor.
- That proceedings against the hospital and doctor.

Order:
- Doctor directed to pay a cost of ₹ 5 lakh and hospital to pay cost of ₹ 1 lakh for their conduct and stand taken in the proceedings.

Judgment: Dr. B. Reghupathi v/s B. Vasantha, 2009(5) RCR (Criminal) 226: 2009(5) RCR(Civil) 281 (Allahabad) (DB):

Medical Negligence – Section 2(1)(g) – Tort:

Held:
- That deceased was not a heart patient and the ECG taken before the biopsy was normal.
- That doctor liable for to compensate deceased's family.
- That no evidence to prove that deceased was weak or was suffering from any heart trouble, he died due to cardiac arrest.

- That cardiac arrest being the consequence of deficiency in service in administering anesthesia.
- That principle of res ipsa loquitur applies.

Order:
- Doctor liable for to compensate deceased's family.

Judgment: Martin F. D'souza v/s Mohd. Ishfaq, 2009(2) RCR(Civil) 1: 2009(2) RCR(Criminal) 65: 2009(2) R.A.J. 39: 2009(157) D.L.T. 391(SC):

Medical Negligence – Sections 11, 14, 21 and 2 IPC, Section 304-A

Suit:
- That patient suffered from various ailments like renal failure, kidney swelling, blood and urinal tract infection and running high fever.
- Doctor administered him life saving injections which impaired hearing of patient.

Held:
- Doctor not guilty of negligence.
- Life was more important than saving function of ear. 2005(3) RCR(Criminal) 836: 2005(2)
- 2005(3) RCR(Criminal) 836: 2005(2) Apex Criminal 649(SC) relied.

Judgment: Martin F. D'souza v/s Mohd. Ishfaq, 2009(2) RCR(Civil) 1: 2009(2) RCR(Criminal) 65: 2009(2) R.A.J. 39: 2009(157) D.L.T. 391(SC):

Medical Negligence – Sections 11, 14, 21 and 2 IPC, Section 304-A –

Held:
- That whenever a Court or Consumer Forum receives a complaint against any doctor it should refer the matter to a panel of experts.
- That a notice should be issued to concerned doctor only after the committee finds there was prima facie case of medical negligence.
- That Police should not arrest or harass the doctor.
- That it should obtain competent medical opinion.
- 2005(3) RCR(Criminal) 836: 2005(2) Apex Criminal 649(SC) relied.

Judgment: Martin F. D'souza v/s Mohd. Ishfaq, 2009(2) RCR (Civil) 2: 2009(2)

RCR(Criminal) 66: 2009(2) R.A.J. 39: 2009(157) D.L.T. 391(SC):

Medical Negligence – Sections 11, 14, 21 and 2 IPC, Section 304-A –

Suit: - That a child is born to a woman even after she had undergone a sterilisation operation by a surgeon.

Held: - That the doctor was not liable because there cannot be a 100 per cent certainty that no child will be born after a sterilisation operation.

- 2005(4) RCR(Criminal) 175: 2005(4) RCR (Civil) 169: 2005(3) Apex Criminal 320(SC) relied.

Suit: - That patient died a day after surgery and the relatives found a pair of scissors utilised by the surgeon while collecting the last remains.

Held: - The doctor was held liable and a compensation of ₹ 1.2 lakh was awarded by the State Consumer Forum.

- 1996 CPJ 112 relied.

Suit: - That a minor child was admitted by his parents to a diagnosed typhoid and gave medicines for typhoid fever.

- That an injection Lariago which was administered by the nurse to the patient who immediately collapsed.

Held: - That the doctor was negligent in performing his duty because instead of administering the injection himself he permitted the nurse to give the injection.

- That there was clear dereliction of duty on the part of the nurse who was not even a qualified nurse and was not registered with any nursing council of any State.

- That the doctor, nurse and the hospital were found liable.

- That compensation of ₹ 12.5 lakh was awarded.
- 1996 CPJ 112 relied.

Order:
- The following acts are declared negligent:
- Removal of the wrong limb.
- Performance of an operation on the wrong patient.
- Giving injection of a drug to which the patient is allergic without looking into the out-patient card containing the warning.
- Use of wrong gas during the course of an anesthetic.
- 1995(6) SCC 651 relied.

Judgment: Post Graduate Institute of Medical Education and Research, Chandigarh v/s Jaspal Singh, 2009(3) RCR(Civil) 873: 2009(4) R.A.J. 556(SC):

Medical Negligence – Section 21 –

Held:
- That in the medical negligence actions, the burden is on the claimant to prove breach of duty, injury and causation – The injury must be sufficiently proximate to the medical practitioner's breach of duty.

Judgment: Post Graduate Institute of Medical Education and Research, Chandigarh v/s Jaspal Singh, 2009(3) RCR(Civil) 873: 2009(4) R.A.J. 556(SC):

Medical Negligence – Section 23 –

Suit:
- That Patient admitted with 50 per cent burn injuries in P.G.I.
- That mismatched blood transfused.
- That patient died after 40 days.

Held:
- That such an error is not an error of professional judgment but in the very nature of things a sure instance of medical negligence.
- That PGI to pay compensation of ₹ 2 lakh.

IMPORTANT JUDGMENTS OF INDIAN COURTS:

Judgment: Malay Kumar Ganguly v/s Dr. Sukumar Mukherjee (2009) 4 RCR (Civil) 14 (SC) (Short Note): (2009) 4 RCR (Criminal) 1: (2009) 5 R.A.J. 405 (SC): Section 2 IPC, Section 304-A: Medical

negligence – Criminal medical negligence and Civil Medical negligence – Deficiency Service:

Suit:
- That a patient admitted in hospital who had rashes all over her body.
- That it was a case of dermatology.
- That the doctor did not refer her to dermatologist.
- That instead he prescribed "Depmedral" in higher dose beyond maximum recommended dose without foreseeing its implications.
- That condition of patient deteriorated and died after some days of treatment.

Held:
- That it was medical negligence on part of doctor and hospital but doctor not guilty of criminal negligence under Section 304-A IPC.
- That it is deficiency of service.
- That case remitted to consumer commission for determination of quantum of compensation.

Order:
- **SC: Medical negligence** – Cost: Doctor directed to pay a cost of ₹ 5 lakhs and to pay cost of one lakh for their conduct and stand taken in the proceedings.

Judgment: Dr. B. Reghupathy v/s B. Vasantha (2009) 5 RCR (Criminal) 226: (2009) 5 RCR (Civil) 281 Allahabad (DB):

Section 2 (1)(g) – Medical negligence – Tort:

Suit:
- That deceased was not a heart patient and the ECG taken before the biopsy was normal
- That doctor liable for to compensate family of deceased.
- That no evidence that deceased was weak or was suffering from any heart trouble.
- That he died due to cardiac arrest.

Held:
- That cardiac arrest is the consequence of deficiency in service in administering anesthesia.
- That Principle of **res ipsa loquitur applies.**
- That doctor liable for to compensate family of deceased.

Judgment: Nizam Institute of Medical Sciences v/s Prasnath S. Dhananka (2009) 3 RCR (Civil) 174: (2009) 3 RCR (Criminal) 125: (2009) 3 R.A.J. 634 (SC):

Section 11,14,21 - Tort – Medical negligence:

Held:
- That, It is impossible for a doctor to guarantee a successful result and the only assurance that he can give or can be understood to have given by implication is
- That he is possessed of the requisite skill in that branch of profession which he is practicing and while undertaking the performance of the task entrusted to him he would be exercising his skill with reasonable competence.

Judgment: Martin F.D' Souza v/s Mohd. Ishfaq (2009) 2 RCR (Civil) 1: (2009) 2 RCR (Criminal) 65: (2009)(2) R.A.J. 39: (2009)(157) D.L.T. 391 (SC):

Section 11,14,21 and 2 – IPC, Section 304-A – Medical negligence:

Suit:
- That a patient suffered from various ailments like renal failure, kidney swelling, blood and urinal tract infection and running high fever.
- That doctor administered him life saving injections which impaired hearing of patient.

Held:
- That doctor not guilty of negligence.
- That life was more important than saving function of ear.

Judgment: Martin F.D' Souza v/s Mohd. Ishfaq (2009)(2) RCR(Civil) 1: (2009)(2) RCR (Criminal) 65: (2009)(2) R.A.J. 39: (2009)(157) D.L.T. 391 (SC):

Section 11,14,21 and 2 – IPC, Section 304-A – Medical negligence:

Held:
- That whenever a Court or Consumer forum receives a complaint against a doctor it should refer the matter to a panel of experts.
- A notice should be issued to concerned doctor only after the committee finds there was prima facie case of medical negligence.
- That Police should not arrest or harass the doctor.

- That, It should obtain competent Medical opinion.
- (2005) 3 RCR (Criminal) 836: (2005)(2) Apex Criminal 649 (SC) relied.

Judgment: Post Graduate Institute of Medical Education and Research, Chandigarh v/s Jaspal Singh (2009) (3) RCR (Civil) 873: (2009)(4) R.A.J. 556 (SC):

Section 21 – Medical negligence:

Held:
- That, In the medical negligence actions, the burden is on the claimant to prove breach of duty, inquiry and causation.
- That the inquiry must be sufficiently proximate to the medical practitioner's breach of duty.

Judgment: Post Graduate Institute of Medical Education and Research, Chandigarh v/s Jaspal Singh (2009) (3) RCR (Civil) 873: (2009)(4) R.A.J. 556 (SC):

Section 21 – Medical negligence:

Suit:
- That patient admitted with 50 per cent burn injuries in P.G.I.
- That mismatched blood transfused.
- That, patient died after 40 days.

Held:
- That, In the medical negligence actions, the burden is on the claimant to prove breach of duty, injury and causation.
- That the injury must be sufficiently proximate to the medical practitioner's breach of duty.
- That such an error is not an error of professional judgment but in the very nature of things a sure instance of medical negligence.
- That PGI to pay compensation of ₹ 2 lakhs.

NATIONAL CONSUMER DISPUTES REDRESSAL COMMISSION, NEW DELHI

Judgment: B. Sreekanth v/s N.N. Shiva Kumar (Dr.) (2010) 2 (NC)

Medical negligence – Compensation:

Suit:
- That respondent/OP doctor did not display the level of current knowledge expected of a surgeon of ordinary skills in prescribing the application

of magsulph dressing to the affected leg and foot of the complainant.

- That standard protocol of diagnostic test not followed.
- That the doctor unable to diagnose the onset of gangrene in the affected limb of the complaint.
- That valid consent of the complainant not taken though complainant was very much in a position to give valid consent.

Held:
- That a case of medical negligence.
- That lump sum compensation of ₹ 1 lakh awarded to the appellant/ complainant.

Reference:
- **Bolam v/s Friern Hospital Management Committee (1957) Queens Bench Division.**
- **Eckersley v/s Binnie (1998) 10: 18 Con LR.**
- **Jacob Mathew v/s State of Punjab and Another (2005) 6 SCC 1.**
- **Samira Kohli v/s Dr. Prabha Manchanda and Another (2008) 2 SCC 1.**

PUNJAB STATE CONSUMER DISPUTES REDRESSAL COMMISSION, CHANDIGARH

Judgment: Atma Singh Lt. Col. (Retd.) v/s The Managing Director, Fortis Healthcare Ltd. and Others (2010) 2 (Pb):

Section 2(1)(g), 2(1)(r) &14(1)(d) – Medical service – Deficiency in service

– Unfair trade practice – Compensation:

Suit:
- That Patient in advanced stage of cancer.
- That as per medical literature she was to survive for six months without any treatment.
- That surgery performed by doctors of respondent hospital and patient died within one month.

Held:
- That no option for first surgery obtained.
- That no document placed on file to prove if the patient was made aware about the post-operative consequences.
- That it was for the respondent Hospital and its doctors to explain as to how the patient came to

die so soon particularly when she was allegedly operated by the doctors to enhance her life from six months onwards.

- That the respondents have not taken any specific plea about the internal or external factors which were unknown and which suddenly appeared and which caused the death.
- That the respondent hospital held liable jointly and severely with two doctors.
- That compensation of ₹ Ten Lacs (₹ 10,00,000) awarded to the complainant.

Reference: **AIR(2005) SC 3280 in State of Punjab v/s Shiv Ram and Others.**

Judgment: Talwar Nursing Home (Dr.) v/s Manjit Singh and Others (2010) 2 (Pb):

Medical negligence – **Compensation:**

Suit:

- That patient suffering from carcinoma stomach.
- That admitted by appellant in his own hospital instead of referring her to a higher specialised hospital for medically treated by more expert doctors.
- That by admitting and operating the patient in his own hospital the appellant precipitated the death of the patient by own medical negligence as he lacked management in case of complications.
- That the patient was 58 years old and suffering from cancerous disease which was fatal in itself.
- That the medical negligence committed by the appellant only precipitated death of the patient.
- That the amount of compensation reduced from ₹ 2.5 lakh to ₹1 lakh @ of interest from 18 per cent to 7.5 per cent.

Reference: **AIR (2005) Supreme Court 2312 in Dharampal and Others v/s U.P. State Road Transport Corporation.**

Judgment: Nivedita Singh v/s Asha Bharti (Dr.) and Ors. (2010)(2) (UP):

(i) CCPA 1986, Section 2(1)(o) – Service – Medical Service – Government Hospital:

Held:
- That complainant deposited registration fees and maintenance charges, but failed to prove that due to non-production of any receipt of any fees having been deposited by her for her delivery.
- That since it was a free service rendered to her by the Government Hospital the complaint held not maintainable.
- That excessive bleeding after the delivery could not be proved with support of any kind of evidence nor the injury to her toes had any connection with her post-delivery treatment.
- That neither the gangrene had developed at the time of the appellant discharged from the Hospital nor the post-discharge complications had any connectivity with her delivery in the Government Hospital.
- That the appellant has completely failed to prove her case of medical negligence attributed to the respondents.

Reference:
- **Savita Garg v/s Director National Heart Institute (2004)(4) AWC 3699 SC.**
- **Shanta v/s State of Andhra Pradesh (1998) AIR 51 (A.P.).**
- **H.S. Sharma v/s Indraprastha Apollo Hospital and Anr. (2007) II CPJ21 (NC).**
- **Shantaben Muljibhai Patel and Ors. v/s Breach Candy Hospital and Research Centre and Ors. (2005) CTJ 501 (CP) (NCDRC).**

Judgment: **National Insurance Co. Ltd. and Anr. v/s Anita (2010)(2) (HR):**

Consent: Medical negligence – Delivery case– Surgery – Removal of uterus:

Held:
- That uterus of the complainant was removed to save the life of the complainant when there was excessive bleeding after delivery of a female child by way of caesarean operation and that too with the consent of the complainant's husband.

- That the written consent placed on record.
- That it cannot be said that the operation of uterus was conducted without any consent of the complainant/her husband. (Para 16).
- That no expert witness has been examined by the complainant to prove any negligence on the part of OP No. 1-Doctor.
- That OP No. 1-Doctor has filed a detailed written statement which is supported by affidavits of Medical Experts.
- That it was established on record that the operation of the complainant was performed under Spinal Anaesthesia.
- That had it been delayed it would have led to several complications and even the death of the complainant due to excess bleeding which was possible as per norms of 'Abnormalities of the Third Stage of Labour.'
- That proved on record that the OP No. 1-Doctor had performed her duties with due care and caution and by her wisdom decided to remove the uterus of the complainant and save complainant's life, because it was for the treating doctor to decide as to what treatment appropriate to be given at that critical moment.
- That OP No. 1 - the treating doctor has been held guilty by the District Forum only on the sympathetic ground that the complainant would not be able to give birth to a child in future for which she has been rebuked by her-in-laws.
- That such an approach of the District Forum not sustainable in the eyes of law and liable to be set aside. (Paras 19 to 21).

Reference:
- **Manjulaben Vinod Bhai Patel v/s Dr. Harshida K. Patel and Anr. (1998)II CPJ 660 (Gujarat).**
- **Bolam v/s Friern Hospital Management Committee (1957)(1) WLR 582.**
- **Martin F.D.' Souza v/s Mohd. Ishfaq (2009) II SLT 20.**

- **Jacob Mathew v/s State of Punjab (2005)(6) SCC 1.**
- **Vinitha Ashok v/s Lakshmi Hospital and Ors. (1992) II CPJ 372 (NC).**

Judgments Favouring Doctors (Dentists):

Judgment: R.K. Trika v/s Dr. Karamjeet Singh - Haryana SCDRC - Pg. No. 472, CPJ 2007, Vol. II:

CPA 1986, Section 2(1)(g) and Section 15 - Medical negligence - Proof of:

Suit:

- That complainant's daughter received Orthodontic treatment from OP.
- That OP advised treatment from Periodontist before starting treatment with headgear.
- That patient refused to wear headgear.
- That patient contacted OP for treatment after three months.
- That complainant took patient to Goa instead of getting necessary treatment.
- That patient developed swollen gums.
- That OP gave treatment as per well-accepted norms required for ailment.
- That no evidence to prove negligence.
- That burden to prove negligence on part of OP lies on complainant.
- That failure of – Effect of – No medical negligence proved.
- That Forum justified in dismissing complaint.

Judgment: Shalan S. Jadhav v/s Dr. Prakash Choukwale - Maharashtra SCDRC - Pg. No. 28, CPJ 2008, Vol I:

CPA 1986, Section 2(1)(g) – Medical negligence –Operation:

Suit:

- That tooth extracted without bothering to take pre-extraction tests.
- That extraction improper.
- That it resulted in swelling and unabated bleeding.

- That patient shifted from one hospital to another, and ultimately expired.

Held:
- That allegations not proved.
- That patient expired due to multiple causes/ diseases.
- That only dental treatment was not responsible for death of patient.
- That Pre-extraction tests conducted by Dr. Singh before operation for extracting tooth.
- That no negligence or deficiency in service proved
- That no relief entitled.

Judgment: **Dr. Sandeep Verma v/s Krishan Lal Nandwani – Chandigarh CDRC – Pg.**

No. 184, CPJ 2009, Vol. IV:

CPJ 2007, Vol. II:

CPA 1986, Section 15 – Medical negligence – Dental treatment:

Suit:
- That dental problems suffered by complainant.
- That uneasiness in implanted teeth alleged stating gums not properly fixed by OP.
- That treatment taken from another doctor to fill the void.
- That deficiency in services alleged.

Held:
- That complaint allowed.
- That OP directed to pay ₹ 15,750 along with ₹ 15,000 as compensation.
- That costs awarded.

Appeal:
- That contention - no treatment accorded to complainant.
- That mere advice given in respect of tablets, gum paint and extraction.
- That no extraction ever made.
- That pleadings of complainant relate to implant, however estimate relates to bridge.
- That evidence contrary to pleadings.
- That contentions allowed.
- That no record produced by complainant to substantiate that any implants were got fixed from OP.

- That no proof of complainant having paid consideration for alleged bridging procedure.
- That document relied upon by Forum scored out, not reliable.
- That deficiency in services not proved.
- That order set aside.
- That no relief entitled.

Judgment: Dr. Rasik M. Shah v/s Dr. A.R. Kalra – Maharashtra SCDRC – Pg. No. 232, CPJ 2007, Vol. II:

CPA 1986, Section 2(1)(g) – Medical negligence – Dental:

Suit:
- That negligence in treatment alleged.
- That two methods available to relieve pain of offending tooth.
- That offending tooth extracted by OP.
- That aspiration method as suggested by complainant not followed.

Held:
- That Surgeon has to decide for which method or procedure to be followed in given circumstances.
- That simply because complainant's suggestion turned down, does not mean OP guilty of medical negligence.
- That complaint dismissed by Forum.
- That Order upheld in Appeal.

Judgments Favouring Doctors (Anesthetists):

Judgment: Varsha Priya v/s Dr. Sushma Pandey - NCDRC – Pg. No. 371, CPJ 2007, Vol. II:

CPA 1986, Section 2(1)(g) – Medical negligence – Delivery:

Suit:
- That spinal anesthesia administered by Gynecologist, without assistance of Anesthetist.
- That condition of patient deteriorated.

Held:
- That no expert evidence produced in support of allegations.
- That spinal anesthesia administered by Anesthetist proved by certificate produced on record.

- That certificate given by Anesthetist not challenged by Complainant.
- That proper care taken by OPs while attending patient proved by detailed notes of doctors.
- That stand taken by complainant completely falsified by medical record.
- That medical negligence not proved.
- That no relief entitled.

Judgment: Mini v/s Dr. G. Mohan – NCDRC – Pg. No. 201, CPJ 2008, Vol I: CPA 1986, Section 21) – Medical negligence – Operation:

Suit:
- That respiratory failure, resulted in death of deceased due to overdosage of anesthesia.
- That chest X-ray not taken to ascertain problems in lungs.

Held:
- That allegations not proved.
- That pre-operative and pre-anesthesia tests conducted.
- That factum of not taking Chest X-ray in minor operation of patient less than 40 yrs. not amount to medical negligence.
- That no expert evidence/medical literature produced by the complainant to contradict expert evidence supported by medical literature brought on record by OPs.
- That onus to prove negligence not discharged by the complainant.
- That no relief granted.

Judgment: Sadanand Rawal v/s State of UP - NCDRC – Pg. No. 173, CPJ 2007, Vol I: CPA 1986, Section 2(1)(g) – Medical negligence – Operation:

Suit:
- That removal of stones from gall bladder.
- That death occurred soon thereafter.
- That alleged overdosage of drugs by anesthetist, leading to brain damage.
- That as per evidence from various Authorities, standard drugs used.

- That wrong use of drugs or overdosage, not been proved.
- That present case is unfortunate development of pulmonary embolism which is rare but major hazard of any surgery.
- That every effort made to control same.
- That no medical negligence proved.
- That OPs not liable.

Judgment: Kamalakar Dhyaneshwar Male v/s Ranade Hospital Organisation –NCDRC – Pg. No. 238, CPJ 2009, Vol. IV:

CPA 1986, Section 2(1)(g) – Medical negligence – Surgery:

Suit:
- That improper/overdosage of anesthesia administered.
- That complainant developed pyogenic meningitis.
- That complainant admitted to clinic, later developed right hemipresis and dysarthria.

Held:
- That allegations not proved by produced evidence in support.
- That meningitis can occur within 48 hrs. of operation and not after many days.
- That complainant operated on 2nd July, complained fever, headache on 16th.
- That meningitis cannot develop after such a long gap.
- That adequate care taken to prevent any infection during operation.
- That development of meningitis, not related to administration of anesthesia, in absence of expert evidence.
- That onus to prove medical negligence lies on complainant.
- That onus not discharged.
- That no relief entitled.

Judgments Favouring Doctors (Cardiologists):

Judgment: Gulnaz S. Malik Mini v/s Dr. Prakashvir Parikh – Gujarat – SCDRC - Pg. No. 140, CPJ 2007, Vol. I:

CPA 1986, Section 2(1)(g) – Medical negligence – Angioplasty:

Suit:
- That complications occurred during procedure.
- That patient died.
- That procedural part by OP, not violative of normal principle of treatment and documentation.
- That documents indicate due care and diligence shown in management of case
- That no evidence to indicate act of omission or commission on part of OP.
- That technical details brought out in oral depositions.
- That documents do not indicate any technical or material flaw in time or procedure of angioplasty.
- That complications occurred were dully recognised.
- That appropriate remedial measures instituted.
- That OP a qualified cardiologist with enough experience in procedure of angioplasty.
- That said procedure carried out after due written consent and after explaining all its pros and cons.
- That mere unfortunate outcome, without evidence, not sufficient to conclude deficiency in service or negligence.
- That complainant failed to prove her case.
- That OP not liable.

Judgment: Srikant v/s Wockhardt Hospital and Heart Institute - Karnataka – SCDRC – Pg. No. 383, CPJ 2007, Vol. I:

CPA 1986, Section 2(1)(g) – Medical negligence – Treatment for Carotid

Angioplasty and stent followed by CABG operation:

Suit:
- That treatment not very much successful.
- That contention of complainant, adverse effects of treatment neither revealed, nor accepted.
- That complainant known diabetic, aged 67 yrs., with history of hypertension, ITP.
- That complained of fatigue on exertion.
- That cannot be said hale and hearty man.

Held:
- That no previous medical records to show exact state of health prior to taking treatment from OP.
- That treatment records show action plan discussed and five per cent risk of stroke explained to wife of complainant.
- That risk not revealed cannot be said.
- That no expert evidence to show steps taken by OP were against accepted procedure for treatment.
- That simply because treatment not very much successful, cannot mean doctor negligent.
- That complainant failed to prove any negligence of OP.

Judgment: Martin F.D.' Souza v/s Mohd. Ishfaq (2009) 2 RCR (Civil) 1: (2009) 2 RCR (Criminal) 65: (2009)(2) R.A.J. 39: (2009)(157) D.L.T. 391 (SC):

Section 11,14,21 and 2 – IPC, Section 304-A – Medical negligence:

Suit:
- That patient suffered from various ailments like renal failure, kidney swelling, blood and urinal tract infection and running high fever.
- That doctor administered him life saving injections which impaired hearing of patient – Doctor not guilty of negligence –

Held:
- That life was more important than saving function of ear. Examples:

(i) CPA 1986, Section 2(1)(g) – Service – Medical Service – Government Hospital:

- That complainant simply proved that she deposited registration fees and maintenance charges.
- That there is no receipt of any fees having been deposited by her for her delivery.
- That since it was a free service rendered to her by the Government Hospital the complaint held not maintainable.

(ii) Medical negligence:

- That excessive bleeding after the delivery could not be proved with support of any kind of evidence nor the injury to her toes had any connection with her post-delivery treatment.
- That neither the gangrene had developed at the time of the appellant discharged from the Hospital nor the post-discharge complications had any connectivity with her delivery in the Government Hospital.
- That the appellant has completely failed to prove her case of medical negligence attributed to the respondents.

CONTEMPT OF COURTS ACT

Civil and Criminal Contempt:

Judgment: In the Matter of Contempt Proceedings v/s Kanwar Singh Saini (2009)(2)

RCR(Rent) 326: (2009)(4) R.C.R. (Civil) 574: (2009)(161) D.L.T. 466 (Delhi)(DB):

Civil and Criminal Contempt:

Held:

- That the question whether contempt of any Subordinate Court is committed or not and whether the alleged contempt is civil or criminal to be decided by the High Court on the basis of facts which are brought to the notice of the High Court.

Judgment: Rajesh Kumar Singh v/s High Court of Judicature of M.P., AIR 2207 SC 2725:

Held: - That purpose of imposing punishment to ensure faith, trust and confidence in administration of justice.

Judgment: Noorali Babul Thanewala v/s K.M.M. Shetty, AIR 1990 SC 564:

Held: - That breach of an injunction, or breach of an undertaking given to a Court by a person in a civil proceeding amounts to contempt.

Judgment: Supreme Court Bar Association v/s Union of India, AIR 1998 SC 1895:

Held: - That the power of the Supreme Court to punish for contempt of Court, though quite wide, is yet limited and cannot be expanded to include the power to determine whether an advocate is also guilty of "professional misconduct" in a summary manner.

COPYRIGHT ACT, 1957

Judgment: Fateh Singh Mehta v/s O.P. Singhal (1990) AIR 8 (RAJ):

Held: - That copyright in a work is deemed to be infringed when any person, without a licence granted by the owner of the copyright does anything, which is the exclusive right to do, conferred by the Act upon the owner of the copyright. Where a person has copyright in a literary work, and any other person produces or reproduces the work or any substantial part thereof in any material form, he is committing an infringement of copyright.

Judgment: Academy of General Education, Manipal v/s Manini Mallya (2009)(2) RCR (Civil) 67: (2009)(2) R.A.J. 91 (SC): Section 2(h) and 2(o):

Held: - That a literary work with dramatic elements in it would also be a literary work i.e. dramatic literature.

- That copyright act makes a distinction between the "literary work" and "dramatic work."

- That copyright in respect of performance of "dance" would not come within the purview of literary work but would come within the purview of definition of "dramatic work."

Judgment: R.G. Anand v/s Delux Film (1978) AIR 1613 (SC):

Held:
- That, It is not necessary that the alleged infringement should be an exact or verbatim copy of the original but its resemblances with the original in a large measure is sufficient to indicate that it is a copy.

CRIMINAL PROCEDURE CODE, 1973

Judgment: Dr. Ajay Madan v/s State of Haryana, 2009(4) RCR(Criminal) 983(P&H):

Medical Negligence – Section 482 IPC, 1860 Section 304-A – Quashing – Framing of charges:

Suit:
- That patient went to accused doctors for abortion.
- That accused found her case serious, admitted her but ultimately she died.
- That– accused stated that Court ignored the question that whether it is a case of medical negligence or of any penal offence.

Order:
- That Medical profession needs protection from frivolous prosecution.
- That charges set aside.
- That matter remitted back.

Held:
- That private complaint not maintainable unless complainant produce opinion of another competent doctor preferably Government doctor.
- That opinion of competent doctor must apply Bolam's test.
- That doctor must not be arrested in routine manner simply because a charge levelled against him unless arrest is necessary for prosecution case.
- Relied upon 2005(3) RCR(Criminal) 836: 2005(2) Apex Criminal 649(SC).

Judgment: Jeewan Kumar Raut v/s Central Bureau of Investigations (2009)(3) RCR(Criminal) 587: (2009) (4) R.A.J. 336 (SC): Section 4-Transplantation of Human Organs Act, 1994, Sections 18 &19: Investigation of offence under Transplantation of Human Organs Act (TOHO):

Held:

- That report lodged with SHO regarding to commission of offence under TOHO.
- That SHO is not empowered to investigate the offence.
- That investigation in terms of Section 13(3)(iv) of TOHO, thus, must be conducted by an authorised officer.
- That nobody else could do it.
- That TOHO being a special Act and the matter relating to dealing with offences there under having been regulated by reason of the provisions thereof, there cannot be any manner of doubt whatsoever that the same shall prevail over the provisions of CrPC.
- That, If a special statute lays down procedures, the ones laid down under the general statutes shall not be followed.

Judgment: Jeewan Kumar Raut v/s Central Bureau of Investigations (2009)(3)

RCR(Criminal) 586: (2009)(4) R.A.J. 336 (SC): Section 167(2):

Transplantation of Human Organs Act, 1994, Sections 18, 19, 20 and 22:

Held:

- That arrest of accused under transplantation of Human Organs Act, (TOHO) and under Section 307 IPC.
- That CBI investigating the offence and filing complaint under Section 22 of TOHO
- That separate Police report under Section 173(2) Cr.P.C. in respect of offences under IPC not filed – Expiry of 90 days.
- That accused not entitled to bail under Section 167(2) Cr.P.C. as complaint was filed in the

Court within 90 days in terms of Section 22 of TOHO.

Judgment: M.P./Peter v/s State of Kerala, 2009(3) RCR(Criminal 459: 2009(4) R.A.J. 215(SC): Section 145 – Criminal and Civil proceedings:

Held:
- That a decision by a Criminal Court does not bind the Civil Court while a decision by the Civil Court binds the Criminal Court.
- That an order passed by the Executive Magistrate in proceedings under Sections 145, 146 of the code is an order by a Criminal Court.

DOMESTIC VIOLENCE

Judgment: Milan Kumar Singh v/s State of U.P. (2009)(5) RCR(Criminal) 124 (Allahabad)

Domestic Violence:

Suit:
- That complaint lodged under the Act.

Held:
- That use of words as nearly as possible here to in Section 12 and Rule 6 show that intention of Legislature was not to reject complaint for not filing in the prescribed Form II.

Judgment: Kulwinder Singh v/s State of Punjab (2009)(5) RCR(Criminal) 784(P&H) Domestic Violence – Quashing of proceedings:

Held:
- That on the intervention of the respectable, a compromise has been arrived at.
- That a joint petition for mutual divorce under Section 13-B of the Hindu Marriage Act, has been filed.
- That where a compromise has been effected between the parties, continuation of proceedings would be an abuse of the processing of Court.
- That impugned FIR and all subsequent proceedings quashed.

Judgment: Ajit Sekhon v/s Crown Court, Sheffield, UK (2014) RCR(Criminal) 124: Domestic Violence:

Suit:
- That accused Ajit Sekhon attacked his wife Manjit Kaur and son Paul during a row over watching a TV soap opera Emmerdale.

- That he attacked his son Paul with a metal bowl, battering him repeatedly on the head.
- That Ajit then beat his wife Manjit with an ornament, riping the skin off her head.
- That Ajit pleaded guilty to two counts of grievous bodily harm with intent at a previous court hearing.
- "That this was a sustained and brutal assault and this type of violence won't be tolerated within the criminal justice system. The victims are still recovering from their injuries, both physically and mentally", detective sergeant Stuart Hall of South Yorkshire Police said

Held:
- That the Judge at Crown Court Sheffield, held Ajit for assault on his wife Manjit and son Paul.
- "That this was a sustained and brutal assault and this type of violence won't be tolerated within the criminal justice system. The victims are still recovering from their injuries, both physically and mentally," detective sergeant Stuart Hall of South Yorkshire Police said.

Order:
- That the Judge awarded Ajit a robust sentence – nine years for the attack on Manjit and a further six years and nine months for the assault on his son Paul. The sentences are to run consecutively.

DOWRY PROHIBITION ACT, 1961

Judgment: Satbir Singh v/s State of Punjab (2001) AIR 2828(SC) –

Held:
- That the word "dowry" should be any property or valuable given or agreed to be given in connection with the marriage. The customary payments in connection with birth of child or other ceremonies are not involved within ambit of dowry.

Judgment: Rajeev v/s Ram Kishan Jaiswal (1994) Cri. LJ NOC 255(ALL) –

Held:
- That any property given by parents of the bride need not in consideration of the marriage, it

can even be in connection with the marriage and would constitute dowry.

Judgment: Prem Kumar v/s State of Rajasthan (2009) (1) RCR(Criminal)850:(2009)(1)

R.A.J. 524(SC): Section 2 – Dowry death:

Held:
- That to prove an offence under Section 304-B IPC, it is not required to be shown that there was agreement with regard to giving of dowry as mention under Section 304-B IPC.
- That offence under Section 304 B makes demand of dowry itself punishable.
- That when Section 304-B refers to "demand of dowry", it refers to the demand of property or valuable security as referred to in the definition of "dowry" under the Act.

Judgment: K.U. Mariambi v/s P.A. Abdul Khader (2009)(5) RCR(Criminal) 889(Karnataka): Sections 3, 4 and 5 – IPC (1860), Sections 498-A and 506 – Com-plaint case – Demand of dowry Investigation:

Suit:
- That private complaint filed by the wife on the allegations of dowry harassment.
- That, It is the duty of the Magistrate to record the statement of the complainant and her other witnesses to find out as to whether there is any prima facie case made out to proceed against the accused by investigating the same as per the provisions of Section 202 of the Cr.P.C.
- That complainant is to be allowed to prove her case.

Judgment: K.U. Mariambi v/s P.A. Abdul Khader (2009)(5) RCR(Criminal) 889 (Karnataka): Sections 3, 4 and 5 IPC (1860), Sections 498-A and 506 – Demand of dowry:

Suit:
- That Magistrate referred the matter to the police under Section 156(3) Cr.P.C.
- That accused agreed to repay amount before investigating officer and issued cheque.

- That Magistrate recorded a finding that amount paid to the husband was only a financial help to him and dismissed the complaint.

Held:
- That Order set aside.
- That Magistrate was required to see only the prima facie case against the accused, not the evidence for conviction.
- That order passed by the Magistrate amounts to an order of acquittal by discarding the evidence of the complainant.
- That such a course is not permissible in law.
- That order of the Magistrate set aside.

Judgment: Kishangiri Mangalgiri Goswami v/s State of Gujarat (2009)(1) RCR (Criminal) 947: (2009)(1) R.A.J. 675(SC): Section 3 – Abetment of Suicide:

Suit:
- That accused (husband) sent letters to in-laws demanding ₹ 40,000 for purchase of house.
- That allegation of torture and harassment to wife demanding dowry.
- That defence evidence showed that accused had purchased valuable silver ornaments for the deceased and in his insurance policy, the deceased was shown to be his nominee.
- That accused himself had taken the deceased to the hospital.
- That letters were unsigned.

Held:
- That accused acquitted under Section 306 IPC, but convicted under Section.

Judgment: Ram Singh and Kanta Devi v/s State of Punjab (2014)(1) RCR (Criminal): Section 3 – Abetment of Suicide:

Suit:
- That accused Ram Singh (father-in-law) and his wife Kanta Devi (mother-in-law) of the deceased Manpreet Kaur, used to torture and harass the deceased demanding dowry.
- That victim Manpreet Kaur committed suicide by consuming poison in September 2012.
- That the complaint of abetment to suicide was filed by the victim's father.

Held: - That accused Ram Singh and wife Kanta Devi were held for abetment to suicide of their daughter-in-law Manpreet Kaur.

Order: - That Jaswinder Sheemar awarded seven years jail to the couple for holding them guilty of dowry death of their daughter-in-law Manpreet Kaur.

Judgment: Sudesh Rani, Sunil and Snehlata v/s State of Haryana (2014)(5) RCR (Criminal): Section 2 – Dowry death:

Suit: - That accused Sudesh Rani (mother-in-law), Sunil (brother-in-law) and Sneh Lata (sister-in-law) of the deceased Suman Rani, used to torture and harass the deceased demanding dowry.

- That the parents of the deceased alleged that the accused had poured kerosene on their daughter and had set her on fire on September 6, 2012.
- That the complaint of dowry death was filed by the victim's parents.
- That the deceased, in her dying declaration at PGI, Chandigarh, had said her mother-in-law, brother-in-law and sister-in-law, had poured kerosene on her, while sparing her husband not being involved.

Held: - That accused Sudesh Rani, Sunil and Snehlata were held for dowry death of Suman Rani.

Order: - That Vimlesh Tanwar, Additional Sessions Judge, awarded life imprisonment to the accused Sudesh Rani (mother-in-law), Sunil (brother-in-law) and Snehlata (sister-in-law) for holding them guilty of dowry death of their daughter-in-law Suman Rani.

DNA TEST

CIVIL PROCEDURE CODE, 1908:

Judgment: Sathya Raj v/s Jayaprakash (2009)(1) RCR(Civil) 516 (Kerala: Section 151

498-A IPC and Section 3 of Dowry Prohibition Act.

DNA TEST

CIVIL PROCEDURE CODE, 1908:

Judgment: Sathya Raj v/s Jayaprakash (2009)(1) RCR(Civil) 516 (Karala:

Section 151 – DNA Test:

Suit: - That whether respondent was father of petitioner.

Held: - That, It is necessary to have a DNA test.

- That DNA test is a conclusive test to fix paternity of a person.
- That Civil Court has power under Section 151 C.P.C. to issue direction for DNA test.
- That subjecting a person to a medical test in a civil case is not in violation of Article 21 of Constitution of India.

Judgment: Raj Devi v/s Ram Lakhan (2009)(5) RCR (Criminal) 155 (Allahabad)

DNA Test: CRIMINAL PROCEDURE CODE, 1973:

Suit: - That husband turned out his wife.

- That wife claiming maintenance.
- That contention of husband that his wife was living in adultery and child born to her was illegitimate.

Held: - That husband however, did not apply for DNA Test to identify of father.

- That no evidence that wife was living in adultery when she filed application for maintenance.
- That maintenance could not be refused.
- That maintenance of ₹ 500 P.M. granted.

Judgment: Amar Sharma v/s Seema Sharma (2009)(5) RCR(Criminal) 71(M.P.) (Gwalior Bench):

DNA Test:

Suit: - That dispute with regard to parentage of minor girl.

- That DNA test conducted at centre for DNA Finger Printing and Diagnostic (CDFD).
- That serious allegations levelled against technical officer who took blood sample of the parties.

Held: - That second DNA Test ordered.
- That DNA Test, however, cannot be ordered at choice place of one of the parties.

Judgment: Pawan Kumar v/s Mamta, 2009(3) RCR(Criminal) 71(M.P.):

Section 125 – Evidence Act, Section 45 – DNA test:

Suit: - That man having illicit relations with a woman
- That a child born to them.
- That the man denying paternity, but refusing to undergo DNA test.

Held: - That the man was the father.
- That the child entitled to claim maintenance from her father.

Judgment: Pawan Kumar v/s Mamta, 2009(3) RCR(Criminal) 71(M.P.): Section 125:

Suit: - That illegitimate child entitled claim maintenance from her father.
- That man having illicit relation with a woman.
- That child born to them.

Held: - That Illegitimate child entitled to claim maintenance from her father under section 125 Cr. P.C.

DRUGS and COSMETICS ACT, 1940

Judgment: Balkar Singh and Parwinder Singh v/s UT, Chandigarh (2014)

Held: - That on June 4, 2011, the Narcotic Control Bureau (NCB) arrested Balkar and Parwinder for possessing one Kg heroin.
- That the consignment was to be delivered to two customers in Chandigarh, who however escaped.
- That apart from the recovery, Balkar's statement wherein he admitted to regularly supplying narcotics became the basis of conviction.
- That drug trafficking, trade and consumption has assumed alarming proportions - the Court must endeavour for a drug-free society and drug trafficking must be dealt with heavy hands,

observed the Court while awarding the jail term to convicts Balka and Parwinder Singh.

- That Additional district and Sessions Judge Shalini S Nagpalon awarded eleven years jail to the convicts Balkar Singh, a dismissed constable of the Punjab Police, and Parwinder Singh, for possessing one Kg heroin.

Judgment: D. Ramakrishnan v/s Intelligence Officer Narcotic Control Bureau, 2009 (1) RCR (Criminal) 315: 2009(5) R.A.J. 652: 2009 A.I.R. (SC) 2404

Drugs and Cosmetics Act, 1940 – Narcotics Drugs and Psychotropic Substances Act, Section 80:

Held: - That provisions of NDPS Act or the Rules thereunder are in addition to, and not in derogation of the Drugs and Cosmetics Act, 1940 or the rules made thereunder.

Judgment: Swaran Singh v/s State of Punjab, AIR (1987) 81 (P&H)

Held: - That the practitioners of the Indian system of medicine (AUSH), that is Ayurveda, Unani, Sidha and Homeopathy, are not entitled to keep allopathic drugs for administering to the patients.

Judgment: Paramjit Singh v/s State of Punjab (2012)

Suit: - That on November 30, 2007, the NCB had arrested Paramjit and Benson (foreigner), from a car parked in sector 39, Chandigarh and recovered ten Kg of heroin from them, during delivery by Paramjit to Benson.

- That Paramjit was already undergoing a ten years sentence for carrying 1.02 Kg of heroin, and was on parole when the NCB arrested him in Chandigarh.

- That Benson had come to India on a student visa, and was based in Mumbai and regularly used to visit Delhi, where he met Paramjit.

Held: - That Additional District and Sessions Judge Shalini Singh Nagpal, held Paramjit Singh guilty of selling drugs.

- That Paramjit Singh had earlier also been convicted under the same act.

Order: - That the Judge awarded Paramjit Singh, capital punishment, considering the fact that he had earlier also been convicted under the same act.

- That the Judge awarded Festus Benson, a native of Burundi, Africa, sentence of fifteen years in jail, besides being slapped a fine of ₹ 1.5 lakh.

Judgment: Jaskaran Singh, Gurwant Singh, Bhag Singh v/s State of Punjab (2014)

Suit: - That on July 8, 2011, the accused brothers Jaskaran and Gurwant were arrested, and about eight Kg of heroin was seized from them.

Held: - That Additional District and Sessions Judge Balwant Singh held Jaskaran Singh, Gurwant Singh and Bhag Singh, guilty of selling drugs.

Section: - Under Sections 21, 61 and 85 of the Narcotic Drugs and Psychotropic Substances (NDPS) Act.

Order: - That the Judge awarded Jaskaran Singh, Gurwant Singh and Bhag Singh ten years imprisonment and imposed a fine of ₹ one lakh on them, failing that, they would have to undergo one year extra imprisonment.

DRUGS and MAGIC REMEDIES ACT, 1954

Judgment: T.K. Kuppuswamy v/s Union of India, AIR (1991) 17 (Mad)

Held: - That the Act is within Legislative Powers of Parliament and falls under Entry 97 of List I of 7th Schedule of the Constitution.

Judgment: A.S.P. Kurup v/s Union of India, FAJ (1984) 36 (Ker)

Held: - That a drug unless it is intended as preventive or curative, itself has no meaning.

DYING DECLARATION ACT,

Judgment: Jitender Kumar v/s State NCT Delhi (2009) (5) RCR (Criminal) 931 Delhi (SC) - Dying declaration:

Suit: - That deceased categorically stated that her mother-in-law poured kerosene oil over her.

Held:
- That kerosene residues not detected in the clothes.
- That no kerosene dropping on the floor.
- That doctor did not note smell of kerosene from the person of deceased.
- That no evidence to prove that mother-in-law was at all in the house at the time of incident.
- That possibility of deceased suffering accidental burn injuries while preparing food cannot be ruled out.
- That accused acquitted giving benefit of doubt.

Judgment: Jitender Kumar v/s State NCT Delhi (2009)(5) RCR(Criminal) 931 Delhi (SC) Dying declaration: Necessity of corroboration for basing conviction on:

Held:
- That to sustain a conviction on a dying declaration, Court has to record a satisfaction that the same contains a nugget of truth.
- That a dying declaration is a piece of evidence and has to be considered along with other relevant and admissible evidence on record.
- That where evidence on record casts a doubt on a factual aspect disclosed in the dying declaration, unless satisfactorily explained.

Judgment: Arjun v/s State of U.P. (2009)(5) RCR(Criminal) 642 (Allahabad)

Dying declaration – Section 302:

Held:
- That accused convicted on the basis of dying declaration.
- That plea of accused that a known person would not commit such a crime in the night without concealing his identity.
- That heinous crime like murder etc. are being committed in the day and night without concealing identity of culprits.
- That accused had come in the house of complainant or deceased to take revenge from a person, who in the garb of friendship, had developed illicit relation with his wife.

- That dying declaration of deceased cannot be discarded on the ground that accused did not conceal his identity.

Environment Protection Act (EPA), 1986

Judgment: M.C. Mehta v/s Union of India (1992) AIR, 382 (SC)

Power of Central Government:

Held: - That the Central Government is empowered to take all such measures as it deems necessary or expedient for the purpose of protecting and improving the quality of the environment and preventing, controlling and abating environmental pollution.

Judgment: Municipal Corporation of India v/s Dev Raj (1985) FAJ 156 DEL (DB) Vicarious Criminal Liability:

Held: - That, It is well settled principle of Law that vicarious criminal liability cannot be attached unless all the conditions for fastening such liability are proved.

Judgment: Sat Priya Mehamia Memorial Education Trust (Regd.) v/s State of Haryana (2009)(2) RCR (Civil) 495 (P&H)(DB)

Environment (Protection) Act, 1986 – Municipal Solid Wastes

(Management and Handling) Rules 2000, Rule 6 – Dumping site – Disposal of solid waste:

Suit: - That petitioner's school at a short distance from dumping site of solid waste

- That petitioner praying for their shifting/closing of dumping site.

Held: - That as the master plan permits use of the site as dumping site and for disposal of solid waste, no violation of master plan.

EUTHANASIA:

Judgment: Supreme Court of India in the case of Aruna Shanbaug:

Suit: - That petition filed by social activist Pinki Virani

who sought euthanasia for former Mumbai hospital nurse Aruna Shanbaug, 60, who has been living in a vegetative state for 37 yrs., after being raped and strangulated by a sweeper in the hospital premises.

Held:

- That the bench laid down a procedure to be followed in case a patient or his/her family opt for passive euthanasia. The guidelines include seeking a declaration from a medical board and State Government.
- That "If a person consciously and voluntarily refuses to take life-saving medical treatment, it is not a crime," the bench said.
- That In the absence of any legislation on passive euthanasia, the Supreme Court said its ruling would be the law until Parliament legislates on the matter.
- That the Court rejected the Centre's contention that euthanasia should not be permitted in any form as India is still a "backward and emotional country". It referred to various international judgments on the subject and said passive euthanasia should be allowed if a patient wishes for it.
- That, In case its non-voluntary application, the patient's close relative or a friend should give his/her consent.
- That the Court, however, dismissed Virani's petition saying she has no locus standi in the case. Though the Court praised Virani for espousing the cause, it said she could not be considered Shanbaug's friend and did not have the right to move such a petition.
- That the Court, however, said that in the absence of a family, the petition could be filed by the KEM Hospital's nursing staff that has been looking after her for 37 yrs. and ensured that not even a single bedsore was reported.
- That the Court had constituted a medical board of three doctors from Mumbai to examine

Shanbaug and submit a report on her physical condition.

Legal Fraternity divided on Passive Euthanasia:

ARGUMENTS FAVORING EUTHANASIA:

Legal Fraternity:

Held:

- The Supreme Court of India: "Active euthanasia declared illegal by the Supreme Court of India, while allowing passive euthanasia vide SC Bench's verdict on 7th March 2011. The SC in its judgment had specified guidelines for High Courts to follow before giving a final go-ahead for withdrawal of life-sustaining drugs and life support systems in cases of patients who are brain-dead or in a permanently vegetative state, after obtaining the consent of relatives& the opinion of medical experts. It had made it clear that its judgment would hold good until the Parliament enacts a law on this issue, but the government is not ready to enter into any fresh controversy and wants the Courts to decide and monitor such cases if they want to.
- Delhi High Court Judge RS Sodhi (Retd): "India allows capital punishment and the State is allowed to take one's life. Then why an individual who suffers extensively should not be allowed to say I have had enough?"
- Delhi High Court Judge JD Kapoor (Retd): "Expressed similar views".
- Sr. SC lawyer KTS Tulsi: "The SC ruling with in-built safeguards has made the right to live more meaningful."
- Legal expert Subash Kashyap: "It is good that the Apex Court has laid down certain guidelines and each plea for mercy killing will be decided on a case-by-case basis. If there was a general rule, there would have been misuse.

Amicus Curiae (Friend of the Court):

- "Passive euthanasia should be allowed. Right to

life does not include right to live in a vegetative state."

- "End of violation of one`s right to live with dignity."

ARGUMENTS OPPOSING EUTHANASIA:

Legal Fraternity:

Held:

- The Supreme Court of India: "is not in favour of active euthanasia that involves the use of lethal substances to end a patient's life."
- SC lawyer Anand Grover: "Courts cannot decide such a sensitive issue. As per the Constitution, no one can take away anyone's life without a procedure established by law. It means there has to be a proper statute on the issue..."
- Advocate Pinky Anand: "I cannot countenance a position where one is allowed to end one's life. It is an area which must be left alone. Courts cannot take on such a difficult task..."

Legislator:

Held:

- "Euthanasia cannot be allowed in our country as it is still backward and emotional. It would lead to misuse". Understandably, for the legislators, euthanasia, like life itself, is a grey area with too many conflicting views. Rejecting the SC legalised passive euthanasia (mercy killing), allowing withdrawl of life support for patients living in a permanent vegetative condition, the Government has decided to stay out of the issue and not make any law on the subject.
- The Law Ministry, which has been treading cautiously on the controversial matter since last year, has sought a response on four specific queries from the Law Commission of India, which advises the Government on complex legal issues.
- The Law Commission is not in favour of conducting any fresh study on the subject. "Since the Supreme Court has already made it clear that High Courts can decide on cases of

passive euthanasia based on medical advice, there is no need for the Government's opinion," said a top Commission official.

Points to consider:

- Whether a new law as desired by the SC could have a negative impact on social values and be prone to misuse ?
- Is it correct to let the relatives of a patient in a permanently vegetative state decide about his/her life ?
- Why should the Govt. make a law on the basis of an SC judgment when not a single case has come up before any HC a year after the judgment?
- What will be the effect of allowing euthanasia to be regulated as per the SC directions ?

FATAL ACCIDENTS ACT, 1855

Judgment: Dhyan Singh v/s Union of India (2009)(2) RCR (Civil) 27(P&H)(DB) Section 2:

Suit:

- That death of two sisters in Railway Accident.
- That both were unmarried.

Held:

- That their minor brother entitled to claim compensation.
- That provisions of Section 2 of the Fatal Accidents Act, 1855, cannot be deemed to be superseded by enactment of Railway Act, 1855, cannot be deemed to have been curtailed in any manner by the enactment of the aforesaid Acts.

Judgment: Fizabai v/s Nemi Chand, AIR (1993) MP (79): Section 1A:

Held:

- Compensation awarded for loss of dependency, worked out by applying the principle of multiplier is a part of damages "proportioned to the loss resulting from the death".

HOMICIDE

Judgment: Mamta v/s State of Haryana, (2014):

Held:

- That convict Mamta strangulated her one yr. old daughter, Sonakshi, allegedly out of an affair before her marriage, after being threatened by her ex-boyfriend of disclosure, in May 2013.

- That Mamta was convicted by District and Sessions Judge, SK Aggarwal, on April 18, 2014, as found guilty of strangulating daughter, Sonakshi, to death.
- That the verdict relied on her extra-judicial confession before Mewa Singh, her landlord and complainant in the case.
- That District and Sessions Judge, SK Aggarwal, awarded life imprisonment to the convict Mamta for killing her one yr. old daughter Sonakshi.

Judgment: Cops v/s State of UT, Delhi (2014):

Held:

- That convicts (18 cops) were arrested for the cold blooded murder of Ranbir Singh R/o Ghaziabad, in a fake shoot-out in Dehradun in 2009.
- That following the staged shoot-out, the Uttarakhand Police, claimed to have caught Ranbir and his companions on July 3, 2009.
- That CBI had asked for death penalty for the convicted policemen.
- That CBI Special Judge JPS Malik awarded life terms to the 17 cops, and said that the case did not fall in the "rarest of rare" category as being based on circumstantial evidence. The Judge acquitted 18th cop of the murder charge while convicting him for falsifying records.
- That the Court slapped seven cops (Bhat, Bisht, Neeraj Kumar, Chauhan, Chandra Mohan and Ajeet Singh) with a fine of ₹ 50K, while the remaining ten were asked to pay ₹ 20K.

Judgment: Sukhdev Singh, Gurvinder Singh, Nand Kishore v/s State UT, Chandigarh (2011):

Held:

- That Khushpreet, a KG student was kidnapped and murdered by accused Sukhdev Singh, his brother Gurvinder Singh and a labourer Nand Kishore, on January 5, 2011.

- That Aditional District and Session Judge, Atul Kasana, Chandigarh, held all three accused guilty.
- That Additional District and Sessions Judge, Atul Kasana Chandigarh, awarded life imprisonment to all three convicts for killing five yrs. old Khushpreet, and awarded compensation of ₹ 1.75 lakh to parents. The money to be generated from the fine imposed on the convicts.

Judgment: ASI Ram Kumar, Head Constable Ramfal, Constables Karambir and Balram v/s State of Haryana, (2012):

Held:
- That the convicts found guilty of shooting Kuldeep Singh in a fake encounter on November 3, 2008.
- That the verdict relied on Hukam Singh's statement.
- That Additional District and Session Judge, Sarita Gupta, Bhiwani, Haryana, awarded life imprisonment to the four policemen for killing Kuldeep Singh.

Judgment: Shera Singh v/s State of Haryana, (2012):

Held:
- That convict Shera Singh pushed his wife and two daughters into Bhalra Canal on December 25, 2010.
- That District Sessions Court, Sirsa, Haryana, awarded life imprisonment to the convict Shera Singh, for killing his wife and daughter.

Judgment: RK Chaudhary MLA v/s State of Haryana, (2012):

Held:
- That Jyoti, a dalit girl R/o Bhunga village in Hoshiarpur was found dead on a road in sector 21, Panchkula, on November 22, 2012, with her head smashed.
- That doon MLA Ram Kumar Chaudhary is a prime accused in the case.
- That members of SIT, DSP Suresh Kaushik and ACP K Hooda, probing Jyoti murder case, recorded their statements in the Court of Additional District and Sessions Judge Roopan

Singh, Panchkula, Haryana, on May 07, 2014. Both supported prosecution in the case.

- That ACP Hooda had recorded the statements of toll plaza for furnishing entries of different vehicles incld. those allegedly used by Chaudhary and his accomplices for the crime from 6 pm on November 21, 2012, till 6 am on November 22, 2012.
- That the police had alleged that Jyoti was bearing the child of Chowdhary, and that Jyoti was taken to the nursing home by Chowdhary for MIT.
- That the matter is subjudicial till-date (July 2014).

Judgment: Neel Kumar @ Anil Kumar v/s State of Haryana, (2009):

Held:

- That accused committed rape on his four yrs. old daughter.
- That he kept her in a critical condition without imparting any medical aid to her, and thereafter committed her murder.
- That the verdict relied on ocular evidence corroborated by medical evidence – disclosure made by the accused and blood-stained bedsheet recovered from his jhuggi.
- That District Sessions Court, Sirsa, Haryana, awarded life imprisonment to the convict Shera Singh, for killing his wife and daughter.
- That the Judge observed that accused deserves no mercy and leniency.
- That death sentence upheld (confirmed).

Judgment: Surinder Koli and Mohinder Pandher v/s State of Uttar Pradesh, (2014):

Held:

- That during Feb. 2005 to Nov. 2006, accused Surinder Koli allegedly murdered and sexually abused sixteen women and children and disposed off their bodies.

- That during investigation it was revealed that Koli dismembered parts of victim' bodies which he cooked and ate.
- That Koli's land-lord Mohinder Singh Pandher was arrested as co-accused for murder and rape.
- That CBI charge sheeted Koli in sixteen cases of murder and rapes, while Pandher was charge sheeted in a single case under provisions of Immoral Trafficking Act.
- That in February 2009, CBI Court Ghaziabad, awarded death penalty to Koli and Pandher.
- That on appeal, Pandher was acquitted of all charges, while Koli's sentence was upheld by the Allahabad High Court.
- That in 2010 Koli awarded death penalty in a case related to murder of an eight eight yrs. old minor.
- That Koli was awarded death penalty in three more cases.
- That in August 2014 Allahabad High Court granted bail to Mohinder Singh Pandher in the sensational Nithari murders.

IMMORAL TRAFFIC (PREVENTION) ACT, 1956

Judgment: Renu Bansal v/s U.T. Chandigarh (2009)(3) RCR(Criminal) 218(P&H)

Section 2(f) – Meaning of word Prostitute:

Held:

- That the word "Prostitute" means a female who offers her body for promiscuous sexual intercourse for hire, whether in money or kind.
- That a female having a paramour is not a prostitute.
- That the real meaning of prostitution is that a woman who surrenders her body for monetary consideration to some one who is not in law entitled to have sexual intercourse with her for consideration in money or kind.

- That a female who frequently lives in houses of ill fame or at a house which men of bad character frequently associate with women of bad character for chastity may be deemed a prostitute. However, it excludes the intercourse which a person may have with a permanently kept concubine or with a woman without paying any consideration either in cash or in kind.

Judgment: Guria, Swayam Savisansthan v/s State of U.P. (2009)(3) RCR(Criminal) 963: (2009)(5) R.A.J. 97(SC)

Section 5,6 and 9 – Criminal Procedure Code, Section 439(2)

Held:
- That bail in an offence under Immoral Traffic (Prevention) Act, 1956 granted to accused by High Court.
- That SC found that it was not a fit case to grant bail.
- That Supreme Court, however, did not cancel the bail on the grounds that bail was granted long time back and in some cases trials have also been concluded, it would not be proper to cancel the bail at this stage.

INDIAN MEDICAL COUNCIL Act, 1956

Judgment: Dr Barinder Singh, President Ludhiana MWA v/s State of Punjab (2009)(4) RCR(Civil) 117: (2009)(5) RCR(Criminal) 565(P&H)(DB) – Drugs and Cosmetics Act, 1940, Sections 26 and 32 – Self styled doctor and quacks in the States of Punjab, Haryana and UT Chandigarh – Medical Negligence

Suit:
- That PIL filed in the High Court that self-styled doctors and quacks are practicing n the States of Punjab, Haryana, UT Chandigarh, which is a non cognizable offence under Section 15(3) of IPC.

Held:
- That to curb this offence High Court passed the directions to the State Governments.

- That State Governments to authorise Civil Surgeons for filing of complaints under Section 32 of Drugs and Cosmetics Act and for offences punishable under Section 15(3) of IPC.
- That Civil Surgeons be authorised to verify the registration and qualification of medical practitioners.

INDIAN PENAL CODE, 1860

Judgment: Muralidhar v/s State of Karnataka (2009)(2) RCR(Criminal) 469: (2009)(2) R.A.J. 513(SC) – Quantum of Sentence

Held:
- That exemplary punishment may be awarded where offences are committed against woman, dacoity, kidnapping, misappropriation of public money, treason and offences incld. moral turpitude or moral delinquency.
- That taking liberal or sympathetic view due to lapse of time will be result-wise counter-productive and against social interest.

Judgment: Mohindra v/s Secretary Health Services (2009)(1) RCR(Civil) 735(P&H) - Failure of Tubectomy Operation

Suit:
- That twins born after sterilisation operation.
- That abortion not advised by the doctor.
- That allegations of negligence and dereliction of duty.
- That compensation claimed.

Held:
- That no full proof gurantee of success of sterilisation operation.
- That no evidence on record to even suggest negligence.
- That no evidence as to whom she approached for abortion.
- That no liability can be imposed on respondents.

Judgment: Hemraj v/s State of Rajasthan (2009)(3) RCR(Criminal) 357: (2009)((4) R.A.J. 84(SC) – Gang rape

Held:
- That a group of persons having common intention to commit rape, but only one of them committed the rape.
- That a person who has not actuallycommitted rape is deemed to have committed rape.

Judgment: Chitresh v/s State Govt. of NCT of Delhi (2009)(4) RCR(Criminal) 196: (2009)(5) R.A.J. 278(SC) – Abetment to Suicide

Held:
- That to constitute an offence under Section 306 IPC, the prosecution has to establish (i) that a person committed suicide and (ii) that such suicide was abetted by the accused.
- That an offence under Section 306 would stand only if there is an "abetment" for the commission of the crime.
- That the parameters of "abetment" have been stated in Section 107 of the IPC.

Judgment: Dr. Saroj Sethi v/s State of Punjab (2009)(1) RCR(Criminal) 66(P&H) – Medical negligence

Suit:
- That a young lady aged 38 yrs was operated for tonsillitis.
- That deceased died within 2-3 hrs – That Board of doctors of Govt. Medical College opined that death occurred due to asphyxia as a result of aspiration of blood into respiratory tract.

Held:
- That the Trial Court held that the petitioners had followed a practice acceptable to medical profession on that day.
- That the Doctor cannot be held liable for negligence.

MEDICAL NEGLIGENCE

HISTORICAL INDIAN JUDGMENTS/RULINGS (Medico-legal):

RECENT SUPREME COURT RULINGS (JUDGMENTS):

Judgment: Before the case of Jacob Mathew v/s State of Punjab 2005(6)SCC page 1 the Supreme Court of India delivered two different opinions on doctors' liability:

- **Mohanan v/s Prabha G Nair and another** (13):

Held:
- That it ruled that a doctor's negligence could be ascertained only by scanning the material and expert evidence that might be presented during a trial.

- **Suresh Gupta's case in August 2004:**

Held:
- That the standard of negligence had to be proved to fix a doctor's or surgeon's criminal liability was set at "Gross negligence" or recklessness."
- That the Supreme Court distinguished between an error of judgment and culpable negligence.
- That criminal prosecution of doctors without adequate medical opinion pointing to their guilt would do great disservice to the community.
- That a doctor cannot be tried for culpable or criminal negligence in all cases of medical mishaps or misfortunes.
- That a doctor may be liable in a civil case for negligence but mere carelessness or want of due attention and skill cannot be described as so reckless or grossly negligent as to make him/her criminally liable. The courts held that this distinction was necessary so that the hazards of medical professions being exposed to civil liability may not unreasonably extend to criminal liability and expose them to the risk of imprisonment for alleged criminal negligence. Hence the complaint against the doctor must show negligence or rashness of such a degree as to indicate a mental state that can be described as totally apathetic towards the patient. Such gross negligence alone is punishable.

Judgment: Justice Arijit Pasayat and CK Thakker on 9, September 2004:

Held: Referred the question of medical negligence to a larger Bench of the Supreme Court. They observed that words such as "gross, reckless, incompetence, and indifference" did not occur anywhere in the definition of "negligence" under Section 304-A of the IPC and hence they could not agree with the judgement delivered in the case of Dr. Suresh Gupta.

Judgment: Jacob Mathew v/s State of Punjab (14):

Held:
- That *the issue was decided in the Supreme Court.*
- That *the court directed the central government to frame guidelines to save doctors* from unnecessary harassment and undue pressure in performing their duties. It ruled that until the government framed such guidelines, the following guidelines would prevail:
- That as per law laid down by Hon'ble Supreme Court in India in "Samira Kohli v/s doctors case" The Hon'ble Court held that consent-can be implied in some circumstances from the citation of the patient. (2008(1) CLT 426.

Judgment: Bolam's Rule (test) has been approved by the Supreme Court in the case of Jacob Mathew:

Judgment: Supreme Court in Jacob Mathew v/s State of Punjab (Supra):

This Court heavily relied on the case of Bolam (supra). The Court referred to the opinion of McNair J, defining negligence as under:

- That in a situation which involves the use of some special skill or competence, then the test as to whether there has been negligence or not the test of the man on the top of a Clapham omnibus, because he has not got this special skill.
- That the test is the standard of the ordinary skilled man Ercising and professing to have that special skill.
- That a man need not possess the highest expert skill: it is well established law that it is sufficient if he exercises that particular art".

- That this Court observed that higher the acuteness in emergency and higher the complication, more are the chances of error of judgment. The Court further observed as under:

  (25) That at times, the professional is confronted with making a choice between the devil and the deep sea and he has to choose the lesser evil. The medical professional is often called upon to adopt a procedure which involves higher element of risk, but which he honestly believes as providing greater chances of success for the patient rather than a procedure involving lesser risk but higher chances of failure. Which course is more appropriate to follow, would depend on the facts and circumstances of a given case. The usual practice prevalent now-a-days is to obtain the consent of the patient or of the person in-charge of the patient, if the patient is not be in a position to give consent before adopting a given procedure. So long as it can be found that the procedure which was in fact adopted was one which was acceptable to medical science as on that date the medical practitioner cannot be held negligent merely because he chose to follow one procedure and not another and the result was a "failure".

SECTIONS 304 and 304-A (Related to professional negligence):

Judgment: Martin F.D'Souza v/s Mohd. Ishfaq (2009)(2) RCR(Civil)(2): (2009)(2)

RCR(Criminal) 66: (2009)(2) R.A.J. 39: (2009) 157 D.L.T. 391(SC):

Section 304-A - Medical negligence:

Held:

- That basic principle relating to law of medical negligence is the Bolam Rule
- That the test in fixing negligence is the standard of the ordinary skilled doctor exercising and professing to have that special skill, but a doctor need not possess the highest expert skill. (1957) (1) WLR 582 relied.

Judgment: Martin F.D'Souza v/s Mohd. Ishfaq (2009)(2) RCR(Civil)(2): (2009)(2)

RCR(Criminal) 66: (2009)(2) R.A.J. 39: (2009) 157 D.L.T. 391(SC):

Section – 304-A – Medical negligence: Examples:

Suit: - That a child born to a woman even after she had undergone a sterilisation operation by a surgeon.

Held: - That the doctor was not liable because there cannot be a 100 per cent certainity that no child will be born after a sterilisation operation. (2005(4) RCR(Criminal) 175: (2005)(4) RCR(Civil) 169: (2005)(3)

Relied: - Apex Criminal 320(SC).

Suit: - That patient died a day after surgery and the relatives found a pair of scissors utilised by the surgeon while collecting the last remains.

Held: - That the doctor was held liable and a compensation of ₹ 1.20 lakhwas awarded by the State Consumer Forum.

Relied: - (1966) CPJ 112.

Suit: - That minor child was admitted by his parents to a diagnosed typhoid and gave medicines for typhoid fever.

- That nurse asked the father of the patient to get an injection Lariago which was administered by the nurse to the patient who immediately collapsed.
- That the doctor was negligent in performing his duty because instead of administering the injection himself he permitted the nurse to give the injection.
- That there was clear dereliction of duty on the part of the nurse who was not even a qualified nurse and was not registered with any nursing council of any State.
- That both the doctor and nurse and the hospital were found liable and ₹ 12.5 lakh was awarded as compensation.

Relied: (1996) CPJ 112.

Suit:
- That the following acts are negligence:-
- Removal of the wrong limb.
- Performance of an operation on the wrong patient.
- Giving injection of a drug to which the patient is allergic without looking into the Out-Patient (OPD) card containing the warning.
- Use of wrong gas during the course of an anaesthetic, etc.

Relied: (1995)(6) SCC 651.

Judgment: Martin F. D'Souza v/s Mohd. Ishfaq (2009)(2) RCR(Civil)(2): (2009)(2)

RCR(Criminal) 66: (2009)(2) R.A.J. 39: (2009) 157 D.L.T. 391(SC):

Section 304-A – Medical negligence:

Held:
- That doctors who cause death or agony due to medical negligence should certainly be penalised, it must also be remembered that like all professionals doctors too can make errors of judgment but if they are punished for this no doctor can practice his/her vocation with equanimity.
- That indiscriminate proceedings and decisions against doctors are counter-productive and serve society no good.
- That they inhibit the free exercise of judgment by a professional in a particular situation.

Judgment: Martin F. D'Souza v/s Mohd. Ishfaq (2009)(2) RCR(Civil)(1): (2009)(2)

RCR(Criminal) 65: (2009)(2) R.A.J. (39): (2009)(157) D.L.T. 391(SC):

Section 304-A – Medical negligence: Examples:

Held:
- That the professional may be held liable for negligence on the ground that he was not possessed of the requisite skill which he professes to have – Thus, a doctor who has a qualification in Ayurvedic or Homeopathy medicine will be liable if he/she prescribes Allopathic treatment

which causes some harm.

- That a private complaint should not be entertained unless the complainant has produced prima facie evidence before the court in the form of a credible opinion given by another competent doctor to support the charge of rashness or negligence on the part of the accused doctor.
- That the investigating officer should, before proceeding against the doctor accused of rash or negligent act or omission, obtain an independent and competent medical opinion preferably from a doctor in government service qualified in that branch of medical practice who can normally be expected to give an important opinion applying the Bolam test.
- That doctor accused of negligence should not be arrested in a routine manner simply because a charge has been levelled against him unless his arrest is necessary for furthering the investigation or for collecting evidence or unless the investigating officer feels satisfied that the doctor proceeded against would not make himself/ herself available to face the prosecution unless arrested.
- That medical practitioner is not liable to be held negligent simply because things went wrong from mischance or misadventure or through an error of judgment in choosing one reasonable course of treatment in preference to another.
- That he would be liable only where his conduct fell below that of the standards of a reasonably competent practitioner in his field.
- That he would be liable if he leaves a surgical gauze inside the patient after an operation.
- That to fasten liability in criminal proceedings e.g. under Section 304-A IPC, the degree of negligence has to be higher than the negligence which is enough to fasten liability in Civil proceedings.

Judgment: Martin F. D'Souza v/s Mohd. Ishfaq (2009)(2) RCR(Civil)(1): (2009)(2)

RCR(Criminal) 65: (2009)(2) R.A.J. 39: (2009) 157 D.L.T. 391(SC):

Section 304-A – Medical negligence:

Held:
- That whenever a court or consumer forum receives a complaint against a doctor it should refer the matter to a panel of experts.
- That a notice should be issued to concerned doctor only after the committee finds there was prima facie case of medical negligence.
- That Police should not arrest or harass the doctor, rather it should obtain competent medical opinion, prior to any arrest.

Relied: **(2005)(3) RCR(Criminal) 836 and (2005)(2) Apex Criminal 649 (SC)**

Judgment: Malay Kumar Ganguly v/s Dr. Sukumar Mukherjee (2009)(4) RCR(Civil)

15(SC)(Short Note): (2009)(4) RCR(Criminal)(2): (2009)(5) R.A.J. 405(SC):

Section 304-A – Medical negligence and Criminal medical negligence:

Held:
- That Criminal medical negligence is governed by Section 304-A of IPC.
- That Criminal negligence is the failure to exercise duty with reasonable and proper care and employing precautions guarding against injury to the public generally or to any individual in particular.
- That to prove negligence under criminal law, the prosecution must prove:
- The existence of duty.
- A breach of the duty causing death.
- The breach of the duty must be characterised as gross negligence.

Judgment: Malay Kumar Ganguly v/s Dr. Sukumar Mukherjee (2009)(4) RCR(Civil) 14(SC)(Short

Note): (2009)(4) RCR(Criminal)(1): (2009)(5) R.A.J. 405(SC):

Section 304-A – Medical negligence: Criminal medical negligence and Civil Medical negligence – Deficiency Service:

Suit:
- That patient admitted in hospital who had rashes all over her body.
- That, It was a case of dermatology.
- That the doctor did not refer her to dermatologist.
- That rather he prescribed "Depmedral" in higher dose beyond maximum recommended dose without foreseeing its implications.
- That condition of patient deteriorated and died after some days of treatment.

Held:
- That it was medical negligence on part of doctor and hospital but doctor not guilty of criminal negligence under Section 304-A IPC – It is deficiency of service.
- That case remitted to Consumer Commission for determination of quantum of compensation.

Important Decisions of the Court

Code of Medical Ethics

Drawn up with the approval of the Central Government under Section 33 of the Indian Medical Council Act:

Judgment: Bolam's Rule (test) has been approved by the Supreme Court in the case of Jacob Mathew:

The Supreme Court in Jacob Mathew v/s State of Punjab (Supra):

This Court heavily relied on the case of Bolam (supra). The Court referred to the opinion of McNair J, defining: Negligence as under:

1. Surendra Chauhan v/s State of M.P. (2000) 4 SCC 110:
2. State of Haryana and others v/s Raj Rani (2005) 7 SCC 22:
3. P.N. Rao v/s G. Jayaprakasu AIR (1990) AP 207:

4. Dr. Laxman Balkrishna Joshi v/s Dr. Trimbak Bapu Godbole and another AIR (1969) SC 128:
5. Dr. Suresh Gupta v/s Government of N.C.T. of Delhi and another AIR (2004) SC 4091:
6. Nihal Kaur v/s Director, P.G.I. M.S.R. (1996) CPJ 112:
7. Spring Medows Hospital and another v/s Harjol Ahluwalia thr' K.S. Ahluwalia and another (1998) CPJ 1:
8. Sethuraman Subramaniam Iyer v/s Triveni Nursing Home and another (1998) CPJ 110.
9. A.S. Mittal and another v/s State of U.P. and others JT (1989) 3 SCC 223:
10. Indian Medical Association v/s V.P.Shantha (1995) 6 SCC 651 (vide para 37)
11. New India Assurance Co. Ltd. v/s Rajesh Kumar and Ors. (2010-11-03)(2)

References:

1. Martin F.D'Souza v/s Mohd. Ishfaq (2009) CPJ 32 (SC).
2. Jacob Mathew v/s State of Punjab and Anr. (2005) 6 SCC 1.
3. Pushkar Dutt v/s Christian Medical College and Hospital, Ludhiana and Anr. (2010-11-03) 2: Medical negligence.
4. Kusum Sharma and Ors. v/s Batra Hospital and Medical Research Centre and Ors. (2010-11-03) 2 (SC):

Medical negligence – Surgery:

References:

1. Bolam v/s Friern Hospital Management Committee (1957) 2 All ER 118.
2. Roe and Woolley v/s Minister of Health (1954) 2 QB 66.
3. R. v/s Lawrence (1981) 1 All ER 974 (HL).
4. R. v/s Caldwell (1981) 1 All ER 961 (HL).
5. Jacob Mathew v/s State of Punjab and Anr. (2005) 6 SCC 1.

6. Hucks v/s Cole and Anr. (1968) 118 New LJ 469.
7. Hunter v/s Hartley (1955) SLT 213.
8. John Oni Akerele v/s The King AIR (1943) PC 72. Andrews v/s Director of Public Prosecutions (1937) A.C. 576.
9. Ram Singh Rai (Dr.) v/s Ranno Bai Barkade (2010-11-03)(2):

   Medical negligence – Compensation – Drug reaction:

References:

1. Poonam Verma (1986) 4 SCC 332.
2. Peoples Clinic and Hospital v/s Deepa Satheesh and Anr. (2010-11-03)(2) Kerala.
3. Cherothe Suhara v/s Dr. K.K. Subramoniam and Anr. (1995)(i) CPR 258.
4. Geetha Kumari v/s Dr. Mrs. Anitha Rajan (1995)(ii) CPR 393.
5. Talwar's Nursing Home (Dr.) v/s Manjit Singh and Ors. (2010)(2) (Pb).
6. B. Sreekanth v/s H.N. Shiva Kumar (Dr.) (2010)(2) (NC).
7. Santokh Nursing Home and Anr. v/s Jaswinder Singh and Ors. (2010)(2) (NC).
8. Balkrishna Mahadev Kare v/s P.N.Nagpal (Dr.) and Anr. (2010)(2) (MH).

IMPORTANT JUDGMENTS/RULINGS of SUPREME COURT:

Judgment: The Supreme Court in Santra case

Held:
- That liability in civil law is based upon the amount of damages incurred.
- That liability in criminal law is based upon the amount and degree of negligence. However, certain elements must be established to determine criminal liability in any particular case, the motive of the offence, the magnitude of the offence, and the character of the offender.

Judgment: The Supreme Court in Poonam Verma v/s Ashwin Patel case - distinguished between negligence, rashness, and recklessness:

Held:
- That a negligent person is one who inadvertently commits an act of omission and violates a positive duty.
- That a person who is rash knows the consequences but foolishly thinks that they will not occur as a result of his/her act. A reckless person knows the consequences but does not care whether or not they result from his/her act. Any conduct falling short of recklessness and deliberate wrongdoing should not be the subject of criminal liability.
- That a doctor can not be held responsible for a patient's death unless it is shown that he/she was negligent or incompetent, with such disregard for the life and safety of his patient that it amounted to a crime against the state.

Judgment: The Supreme Court in Malay Kumar Ganguly v/s Dr. Sukumar Mukherjee (2009)(4) RCR(Civil) 15(SC) (Short Note): (2009)(4) RCR(Criminal)(2): (2009)(5) R.A.J. 405(SC):

Section 304-A – Death of a patient caused by Doctor due to negligence – Whether it is criminal negligence or civil negligence.

Held:
- That to constitute negligence, simple lack of care or an error of judgment is not sufficient.
- That negligence must be of a gross or a very high degree to amount to Criminal negligence.
- That before an inference of medical negligence is drawn, the court must hold not only existence of negligence but also omission or commission on his part upon going into the depth of the working of the professional as also the nature of the job.
- That for negligence to amount to an offence the element of res ipsa loquitur, must be shown to exist.

- That to prosecute a medical professional for negligence under criminal law it must be shown that the accused did something or failed to do something which in the given facts and circumstances no medical professional in his ordinary senses and prudence would have done or failed to do.

Judgment: The Supreme Court in Malay Kumar Ganguly v/s Dr. Sukumar Mukherjee (2009)(4) RCR(Civil) 15(SC) (Short Note): (2009)(4) RCR(Criminal) (2): (2009)(5) R.A.J. 405(SC):

Section 304-A – Consumer Protection Act (1986) – Medical negligence –

Held:

- That Tort in Criminal negligence and Civil negligence – as standard of proof.
- That an act which may constitute negligence of even rashness under torts may not amount to same under Section 304-A.

Judgment: The Supreme Court in Malay Kumar Ganguly v/s Dr. Sukumar Mukherjee (2009)(4) RCR(Civil) 15(SC) (Short Note): (2009)(4) RCR(Criminal)(2): (2009)(5) R.A.J. 405(SC):

Section 304-A – Medical negligence and Criminal Medical negligence –

Held:

- That Criminal Medical negligence is governed by Section 304-A of IPC.
- That Criminal negligence is the failure to exercise duty with reasonable and proper care and employing precautions guarding against injury to the public generally or to any individual in particular.
- That to prove negligence under criminal law, the prosecution must prove:
- The existence of duty
- A breach of the duty causing death
- The breach of the duty must be characterised as gross negligence.

Judgment: The Supreme Court in B. Jagdish v/s State of A.P. (2009)(1) RCR (Criminal) 447: (2009)(1) R.A.J. 88(SC):

Section 304-A – Medical negligence:

Suit:
- That child under treatment died.
- That two view by media experts, i.e. one view there was negligence of doctor, other view that there was no negligence.
- That, It is no ground to quash criminal complaint.
- That which opinion would ultimately prevail is essentially a question to be determined by the learned Trial Judge upon considering the evidence adducted by the parties hereto in their entirety.

Judgment: The Supreme Court in B. Jagdish v/s State of A.P. (2009)(1) RCR (Criminal) 447: (2009)(1) R.A.J. 88(SC): Section 304-A – Criminal offence - Magistrate taking cognizance and issuing process:

Suit:
- That petition for quashing the proceedings.

Held:
- That at the stage of quashing of an order taking cognizance, an accused cannot be permitted to use the material which would be available to him only as his defence.

IMPORTANT JUDGMENTS/RULINGS of INDIAN COURTS:

Judgment: Martin F.D'Souza v/s Mohd. Ishfaq (2009) 2 RCR (Civil) 1: (2009) 2 RCR (Criminal)65: (2009) 157 D.L.T. 391 (SC):

Section 11,14,21 and 2 – IPC, Section 304-A – Medical negligence:

Suit:
- That patient suffered from various ailments like renal failure, kidney swelling, blood and urinal tract infection and running high fever.
- That doctor administered him life saving injections which impaired hearing of patient.

Held:
- That doctor not guilty of negligence.
- That life was more important than saving function of ear.

- That whenever a Court or Consumer forum receives a complaint against a doctor it should refer the matter to a panel of experts.
- That a notice should be issued to concerned doctor only after the committee finds there was prima facie case of medical negligence.
- That Police should not arrest or harass the doctor.
- That, It should obtain competent medical opinion.

Relied: - (2005) 3 RCR (Criminal) 836 and (2005) 2 Apex (Criminal) 649 (SC).

Judgment: Sosamma Kuriau v/s State of Kerala (2009) 5 RCR (Criminal) 238(Kerala) Medical negligence:

Suit:

- That woman delivered twin children in a private clinic.
- That woman died sometime post delivery.
- That criminal complaint against doctor lodged under Section 304 IPC.
- That as per complaint some complication had developed during surgical procedure due to negligence of doctor.

Held:

- That these are vague allegations and do not prima facie show that the accused had done any act which could be termed as rash or negligent.
- That even if it is assumed that there were some lapses or any omission or commission on part of accused it will make out a civil negligence.
- That an act to amount to criminal negligence under Section 304-A IPC, the degree of negligence should be much higher. Negligence which is neither gross nor of a higher degree may provide a ground for action in civil law, but it cannot form the basis for criminal prosecution.
- That concept of negligence differs in Civil law and Criminal law.

Order: - That summoning order against the doctor quashed.

Judgment: Dr. Neena Gupta v/s State of Punjab (2009)(1) RCR(Criminal) 744(P&H):

Section 304-A – Medical negligence:

Suit: - That criminal complaint for death of patient due to negligence of doctor.

Held: - That complaint may be entertained only after prima facie evidence is produced before the Court in the form of credible opinion given by another competent doctor to support the charge of rashness or negligence on the part of the accused doctor.

Judgment: Dr. Neena Gupta v/s State of Punjab (2009)(1) RCR(Criminal) 744(P&H):

Section 304-A – What is Medical negligence:

Held: - That a professional would be liable for negligence on one of the two findings either he was not possessed of the requisite skill which he professed to have possessed, or, he did not exercise with reasonable competence in the given case, the skill which he did possess.

- That a practitioner must bring to his task a reasonable degree of skill and knowledge, and must exercise a reasonable degree of care.
- That deviation from normal practice is not necessarily evidence of negligence.
- That mere accident is also not evidence of negligence.
- That an error of judgment on the part of a professional would not per-se be negligence.
- That as long as it can be found that the procedure which was adopted was one which was acceptable to medical science as on that date, the medical practitioner cannot be held negligent merely because he chose to follow one procedure and not another and the result was a failure.

Judgment: Nizam Institute of Medical Sciences v/s Prasnath S. Dhananka (2009) 3 RCR (Civil) 174: (2009) 3 RCR (Criminal) 125: (2009) 3 R.A.J. 636 (SC):

Section 11,14,21 &2 – IPC, Section 304-A – Medical negligence:

Held: - That is impossible for a doctor to guarantee a successful result and the only assurance that he can give or can be understood to have given by implication is that he is possessed of the requisite skill in that branch of profession which he is practicing and while undertaking the performance of the task entrusted to him he would be exercising his skill with reasonable competence.

Judgment: Post Graduate Institute of Medical Education and Research, Chandigarh v/s Jaspal Singh (2009) 3 RCR (Civil) 873: (2009) 4 R.A.J. 556 (SC):

Section 21 – Medical negligence:

Suit: - That patient admitted with 50 per cent burn injuries at P.G.I. Chandigarh.

- That transfusion of mismatched blood administered.
- That patient died after 40 days.

Held: - That in the medical negligence actions, the burden is on the claimant to prove breach of duty, injury and causation.

- That the injury must be sufficiently proximate to the medical practitioner's breach of duty.
- That such an error is not an error of professional judgment but in the very nature of things a sure instance of medical negligence

Penalty: - That PGI to pay compensation of ₹ 2 lakh.

Judgment: Dr. B. Reghupathi v/s B. Vasantha (2009) 5 RCR (Criminal) 226 (Allahabad) (DB):Medical negligence – Tort:

Suit: - That deceased was not a heart patient and the ECG taken prior to normal biopsy.

- That doctor liable to compensate family of deceased.
- That no evidence that deceased was weak or was suffering from any heart ailment.

Held:
- That patient died due to cardiac arrest.
- That cardiac arrest is the consequence of deficiency in service in administering anesthesia.
- That Principle of res ipsa loquitur applies.
- That standard reasonable care of an average but prudent doctor and not cure is expected by law (Tindal J).
- That one must remember 'Ignorance of law' is un-excusable.

Penalty:
- That doctor liable for to compensate family of deceased.

Judgment: The National Consumer Disputes Redressal Commission applied this principle in Kantimathi Dr. Janak Nathan v/s Murlidhar Eknath Masane (8):

Held:
- That the principle of res ipsa loquitur comes into operation only when there is proof that the occurrence was unexpected.
- That the accident could not have happened without negligence and lapses on the part of the doctor.
- That the circumstances conclusively show that the doctor and not any other person was negligent.
- **Examples:**
- **Gross unskill or unreasonable carelessness:**
- That amputating wrong limb.
- That leaving a swab inside abdomen/wound.
- That administering wrong anaesthetic gas.
- That administerting a drug to a patient with known H/o allergy to it.
- That Overstepping one's limitations as per knowledge and facilities concerned.
- **Performing illegal acts or misuse of rights and duties:**
- That issuing false medical certificates, reports or altering medical documents.

- **Medical examination/or giving treatment without any consent:**
- That under pressure from the higher authorities incld. Police or Court.
- **Performing criminal abortion**:
- That is forbidden and punishable by law.

IMPLIED UNDERSTANDING:

Negligence: Duties owed to the patient:

Held:
- That a person who holds himself oath as ready to give medical advice or treatment impliedly undertakes that he is possessed of skill and knowledge for the purpose. Such a person, whether he is a registered medical practitioner or not, who is consulted by a patient, owes him certain duties, namely, a duty of care in deciding whether to undertake the case; a duty of care in deciding what treatment to give: and a duty of care in his administration of that treatment.
- That a breach of any of these duties will support an action for negligence by the patient.
- That persons who offer medical advice and treatment implicitly state that they have the skill and knowledge to do so, that they have the skill to decide whether to take a case, to decide the treatment, and to administer that treatment. This is known as an "implied understanding" on the part of a medical professional.

Judgment: Supreme Court in the case of the State of Haryana v/s Smt. Santra:

Held:
- That every doctor "has a duty to act with a reasonable degree of care and skill".

Subtle/Complicated negligence:

Judgment: Supreme Court in the case of Dr. Laxman Balkrishna Joshi v/s Dr. Trimbak Bapu Godbole:

Held:
- That if a doctor has adopted a practice that is considered "proper" by a reasonable body of professionals who are skilled in that particular field, he/or she will not be held negligent only

because something went wrong. Doctors must exercise an ordinary degree of skill.

- That they can not give a warranty of the perfection of their skill or a guarantee of cure.
- That, If the doctor has adopted the right course of treatment, he/she is skilled and has worked with a method and manner best suited to the patient, he/she can not be blamed for negligence if the patient is not totally cured.

ACT OF OMISSION:

Judgment: - Bryth v/s Birmingham Waterworks Co. (Lord Justice Clyde)

- Governor in Council v/s Mt Saliman (1949).

VICARIOUS LIABILITY:

Judgment: Dr. N.K. Sengupta v/s State of NCT Delhi (2009)(5) RCR(Criminal) 967 (Delhi): Vicarious liability:

Held: – That a person who was neither the chairman nor the director of the company nor was responsible for the day-to-day affairs in any manner at the time of deposit by the complainant or on the date of issuance of the cheque by the company, cannot be made liable for an offence under Section 138 of N.I. Act.

NATIONAL CONSUMER DISPUTES REDRESSAL COMMISSION, NEW DELHI:

Judgment: Dinesh Jaiswal (Deceased) Through L.Rs. and Ors. v/s Bombay Hospital and Medical Research Centre and Another (2010) 2 (NC):

Medical negligence – res ipsa loquitur – Compensation:

Suit:

- That surgery for urgent surgical repair of aneurysm as gangrene was impending.
- That doctor OP No. 2 delegated his responsibility to his inexperienced junior doctor especially when it was known to be a case which had necessitated second surgery and expert post-operative care and timely decision on amputation of gangrene affected legs.

- That due to negligence of the surgeon in the first operation, a corrective surgery was required to be performed emergently on the next date, which got delayed due to late arrival of OP No. 2, non-functioning of the DSA machine and non-availability of operation theatre.
- That incidence of paraplegia in such case is only 0.2 per cent, but in the case paraplegia occurred immediately resulting in numbness of feet, non-movement of legs and setting in of gangrene.
- That OP No. 2 has not placed on records to prove that he has made best efforts
- That in fact, prior to going abroad for about one month he did not meet the patient till his departure though he was admitted under his care.
- That three surgeries performed in this case.
- That, It does not mention that the treating surgeons have informed the risks involved in the surgeries and the chances of success and failure of the same.
- That by no stretch of imagination, the consent obtained can be considered to be an informed consent.

Held:

- That the hospital held vicariously liable for the acts of commission and omission by the doctors and para-medical staff, whether they are employed on permanent basis or as consultants or visiting doctors.
- That deceased was aged 42 years and was bus operator.
- That would have been reasonable expected to earn till the age of 62 years.
- That taking ₹ 4000 p.m. for determination of compensation and multiplier of 18 years ₹ 8,64,000 and total of ₹ 14,18,941 under all heads with interest@ 9 per cent allowed.

References:

- Martin D'Souza v/s Mohd. Lshfaq (2009) 3 SCC 1.

- Jacob Mathew v/s State of Punjab and Another (2005) 6 SCC 1.
- Samira Kohli v/s Dr. Prabha Manchanda and Another (2008) AIR 1385.
- Spring Meadows Hospital and Anr. v/s Harjot Ahluwalia and Anr. (1998) 4 SCC 39.
- Nizam Institute of Medical Sciences v/s Prasnath S. Dhananka and Ors. (2009) 11 SC.

NATIONAL CONSUMER DISPUTES REDRESSAL COMMISSION, NEW DELHI:

Judgment: B. Sreekanth v/s N.N. Shiva Kumar (Dr.) (2010) 2 (NC)

Medical negligence – Compensation:

Held:
- That Respondent /OP doctor did not display the level of current knowledge expected of a surgeon of ordinary skills in prescribing the application of magsulph dressing to the affected leg and foot of the complainant.
- That standard protocol of diagnostic test not followed.
- That unable to diagnose the onset of gangrene in the affected limb of the complainant.
- That valid consent of the complainant not taken though complainant was very much in a position to give valid consent.
- That a case of medical negligence.

Penalty:
- That compensation of ₹ 1 lakh awarded to the appellant-complainant.

References:
- Bolam v/s Friern Hospital Management Committee (1957) Queens Bench Division.
- Eckersley v/s Binnie (1998) 10: 18 Con LR.
- Jacob Mathew v/s State of Punjab and Another (2005) 6 SCC 1.
- Samira Kohli v/s Dr. Prabha Manchanda and Another (2008) 2 SCC 1.

PUNJAB STATE CONSUMER DISPUTES REDRESSAL COMMISSION, CHANDIGARH

Judgment: Atma Singh Lt. Col. (Retd.) v/s The Managing Director, Fortis Healthcare Ltd. and Others (2010) 2 (Pb): Section 2(1)(g), 2(1)(r) &14(1)(d) – Medical service – Deficiency in service – Unfair trade practice – Compensation:

Suit:
- That patient in advanced stage of cancer.
- That as per medical literature she was to survive for six months without any treatment.
- That surgery performed by doctors of respondent hospital.
- That patient died within one month.
- That no option for first surgery obtained.

Held:
- That no document placed on file to prove if the patient was made aware about the post-operative consequences
- That it was for the respondent hospital and its doctors to explain as to how the patient came to die so soon particularly when she was allegedly operated by the doctors to enhance her life from six months onwards.
- That the respondents have not taken any specific plea about the internal or external factors which were unknown and which suddenly appeared and which caused the death.
- That the respondent hospital held liable jointly and severely with two doctors.

Penalty:
- That compensation of ₹ Ten Lacs (₹ 10,00,000) awarded to the complainant.

Reference:
- AIR (2005) Supreme Court 3280 in State of Punjab v/s Shiv Ram and Others.

Judgment: Talwar Nursing Home (Dr.) v/s Manjit Singh & Others (2010) 2 (Pb): Medical negligence – Compensation

Suit:
- That patient suffering from carcinoma stomach.
- That patient admitted by appellant in his own hospital instead of referring her to a higher

specialised hospital for medically treated by more expert doctors.

- That by admitting and operating the patient in his own hospital the appellant precipitated the death of the patient by own medical negligence as he lacked management of complicated cases.

Held:
- That the patient was 58 years old and suffering from cancerous disease which was fatal in itself.
- That medical negligence committed by the appellant only precipitated death of the patient.
- That the amount of compensation reduced from ₹ 2.5 lacs to ₹ 1 lakh @ of interest from 18 per cent to 7.5 per cent.

Reference:
- AIR (2005) Supreme Court 2312 in Dharampal and Others v/s U.P. State Road Transport Corporation.

Judgment: Nivedita Singh v/s Asha Bharti (Dr.) and Ors. (2010) (2) (UP): CCPA 1986, Section 2(1)(o) – Service – Medical Srevice – Government Hospital:

Held:
- That complainant simply proved that she deposited registration fees and maintenance charges.
- That there is no receipt of any fees having been deposited by her for her delivery.
- That since it was a free service rendered to her by the Government Hospital the complaint held not maintainable.
- That excessive bleeding after the delivery could not be proved with support of any kind of evidence nor the injury to her toes had any connection with her post-delivery treatment.
- That neither the gangrene had developed at the time of the appellant discharged from the hospital nor the post-discharge complications had any connectivity with her delivery in the Government Hospital.
- That the appellant has completely failed to prove her case of medical negligence attributed to the respondents.

References: - Savita Garg v/s Director National Heart Institute (2004)(4) AWC 3699 SC.

- Shanta v/s State of Andhra Pradesh (1998) AIR 51 (A.P.).
- H.S. Sharma v/s Indraprastha Apollo Hospital and Anr. (2007) II CPJ 21 (NC).
- Shantaben Muljibhai Patel and Ors. v/s Breach Candy Hospital and Research Centre and Ors. (2005) CTJ 501 (CP) (NCDRC).

Judgment: National Insurance Co. Ltd. and Anr. v/s Anita (2010)(2) (HR): Consent: Medical negligence – Delivery case – Surgery – Removal of uterus

Held:

- That uterus of the complainant was removed to save the life of the complainant when there was excessive bleeding post-delivery of a female child by means of Caesarean section.
- That it cannot be said that the operation of uterus was conducted without any consent of the complainant/her husband. (Para 16).
- That the written consent of the complainant's husband placed on record.
- That no expert witness has been examined by the complainant to prove any negligence on the part of OP No. 1-Doctor.
- That OP No. 1-Doctor has filed a detailed written statement which is supported by affidavits of Medical Experts.
- That as per records the operation of the complainant was performed under Spinal Anaesthesia.
- That had it been delayed it would have led to many complications and even the death of the complainant due to excessive bleeding which was possible as per norms of 'Complications of the Third Stage of Labour.'
- That proved on record that the OP No. 1-Doctor had performed her duties with due care and caution and by her wisdom decided to remove the uterus of the complainant and save

complainant's life, because it was for the treating doctor to decide as to what treatment appropriate to be given at that critical moment.

- That OP No. 1-the treating doctor has been held guilty by the District Forum only on the sympathetic ground that the complainant would not be able to give birth to a child in future for which she has been rebuked by her-in-laws.
- That such an approach of the District Forum not sustainable in the eyes of law and liable to be set aside.

References:
- Manjulaben Vinod Bhai Patel v/s Dr. Harshida K. Patel and Anr. (1998) II CPJ 660 (Gujarat).
- Bolam v/s Friern Hospital Management Committee (1957)(1) WLR 582.
- Martin F.D.'Souza v/s Mohd. Ishfaq (2009) II SLT 20.
- Jacob Mathew v/s State of Punjab (2005)(6) SCC 1.
- Vinitha Ashok v/s Lakshmi Hospital and Ors. (1992) II CPJ 372 (NC).

Judgment: Santokh Nursing Home and Anr. v/s Jaswinder Singh and Ors. (2010) 2 NC Medical negligence – Compensation

Held:
- That Surgical procedure for removal of uterine fibroid.
- That wavering stand taken by appellant.
- That doctor has not denied the factum of pieces of swabs/mops having been left inside the abdomen of the deceased at the time of surgical procedure
- That ample material, in the form of ultrasound report and the subsequent treatment/surgical procedure of the patient underwent to show that a foreign body, like a mop was left inside the abdomen of the deceased at the time of surgery which led to infection and septicaemia which ultimately led to her death despite the best

possible treatment the patient could be given in other upgraded hospitals.

- That order of the State Commission holding the doctor and the hospital guilty of negligence/ deficiency of service upheld.
- That compensation of ₹ 12,34,414.50/- awarded by the State Commission held to be excessive and reduced to ₹ 8 lakh.

Reference: - Martin F.D'Souza v/s Mohd. Ishfaq (2009) 3 SCC (1).

Contributory Negligence:

Important Decisions of the Court

Code of Medical Ethics:

Drawn up with the approval of the Central Government under Section 33 of the Indian Medical Council Act:

Observation:

- That every doctor whether at a Government Hospital or otherwise has the professional obligation to extend his services for protecting life.
- That the obligation being total, absolute and paramount, laws of procedure whether in statutes or otherwise cannot be sustained and therefore, must give way."
- That It is the duty of the doctor in an emergency to begin treatment of the patient and he should not await the arrival of the police or to complete the legal formalities.
- That the life of a person is far more important than legal formalities.
- That this view is in accordance with the Hippocratic oath of doctors as mentioned in George Bernard Shaw's play:The Doctor's Dilemma."
- That the medical profession is a noble profesion and it should not be brought down to the level of a simple business or commerce. The truth of the

matter, sadly, is that today in India many doctors (though not all) have become totally money-minded, and have forgotten their Hippocratic oath.

- That since most people in India are poor, the consequence is that for them proper medical treatment is next to impossible, and hence they have to rely on quacks. This is a disgrace to a noble profession.

Judgment: Surendra Chauhan v/s State of M.P. (2000) 4 SCC 110:

Held:

- That the appellant was having a degree of Bachelor of Medicine in Electro-homeopathy from the Board of Electrohomeopathy Systems of Medicines, Jabalpur (M.P.).
- That he did not possess any recognised medical qualification as defined in the Indian Medical Council Act, 1956.
- That he performed an operation to terminate the three month pregnancy in a woman, who died in the clinic due to shock due to non-application of anesthesia.
- That the Supreme Court confirmed his sentence but reduced it to one and a half years rigorous imprisonment under Section 314/34 IPC and a fine of ₹ 25K, payable to the mother of the deceased.

Judgment: State of Haryana and others v/s Raj Rani (2005) 7 SCC 22:

Held:

- That if a child is born to a woman even after she had undergone a sterilisation operation by a sugeon, the doctor was not liable because there cannot be a 100 per cent certainty that no child will be born after a sterilisation operation.
- That the Court relied on another three Judge Bench in state of Punjab v/s Shiv Ram and others (2005) 7 SCC.
- That these decisions will be deemed to have overruled the two Judge Bench decision in state

of Haryana and others v/s Smt. Santra AIR 2000 SC 1888 in which it was held that if a child is born after the sterilisation operation the surgeon will be liable for negligence.

Judgment: P.N. Rao v/s G. Jayaprakasu AIR (1990) AP 207:

Suit:
- That the plaintiff was a brilliant young boy, getting a monthly scholarship.
- That he suffered from chronic nasal discharge.
- That was diagnosed as nasal allergy by a consulted RMP, who suggested operation for removal of tonsils.
- That he was admitted in the Government General Hospital, Guntur and the operation was performed.
- That he did not regain consciousness even after three days and thereafter for another 15 days he was not able to speak coherently.
- That on discharge from hospital, he could only utter a few words and could not read or write and lost all his knowledge and learning.
- That his was taken to Vellore, examined by a Professor of Neuro Surgery and it was found that his brain had suffered due to cerebral anoxia, as a result of faulty induction of anaesthetics and failure to take immediate steps to reduce anaesthesia.

Held:
- That defendants were clearly negligent in discharging their duties and the State Government was vicariously liable.

Judgment: Dr. Laxman Balkrishna Joshi v/s Dr. Trimbak Bapu Godbole and another AIR (1969) SC 128:

Suit:
- That patient had fracture of the femur.
- That the accused doctor while putting the leg in plaster used manual traction and used excessive force for this purpose, with the help of three men, although such traction is never done under morphia alone but done under proper general anaesthesia.

- That resulted in shock causing the death of the boy.

Held:
- That the doctor was liable to pay damages to the parents of the boy.

Judgment: Dr. Suresh Gupta v/s Government of N.C.T. of Delhi and another AIR (2004) SC 4091:

Suit:
- That the accused doctor caused death of his patient.
- That the operation performed by him was for removing nasal deformity.

Held:
- That the Magistrate charged the appellant while conducting the operation for removal of the nasal deformity gave a wrong incision causing seepage of blood into the respiratory tract, resulting in asphyxia.
- That patient collapsed and died.
- That the High Court upheld the order of the Magistrate observing that adequate care was not taken to prevent seepage of blood resulting in asphyxia.
- That the Supreme Court held that from the medical opinions adducted by the prosecution the cause of death was stated to be not introducing a cuffed endotracheal tube of proper size so as to prevent aspiration of blood from the wound into the respiratory passage.
- That the Supreme Court held that this act attributed to the doctor, even if accepted to be true, can be described as a negligent act as there was a lack of care and precaution.
- That for this act of negligence he was held liable in a civil case, but it cannot be described to be so reckless or grossly negligent as to make him liable in a criminal case.
- That for conviction in a criminal case the negligence and rashness should be of such a high degree which can be described as totally apathetic towards the patient.

Judgment: Nihal Kaur v/s Director, P.G.I. M.S.R. (1996) CPJ 112:

Suit: - That patient died a day after surgery and the relatives found a pair of scissors utilised by the surgeon while collecting the last remains.

Held: - That the doctor was held liable and a compensation of ₹ 1.20 lakhs was awarded by the State Consumer Forum, Chandigarh.

Judgment: Spring Medows Hospital and another v/s Harjol Ahluwalia thr' K.S. Ahluwalia and another (1998) CPJ 1:

Suit:
- That minor child was admitted by his parents to a nursing home as he was suffering from fever.
- That the patient was admitted and the doctor diagnosed it as typhoid and gave medicines for typhoid fever.
- That Lariago injection was administered by the nurse to the patient.
- That the patient collapsed immediately.
- That the doctor testified that the child suffered a cardiac arrest on account of the medicine having being injected which led to brain damage.
- That the National Commission held that the cause of cardiac arrest was Intravenous injection of Lariago of such a high dose.
- That the doctor was negligent in performing his duty.
- That instead of administering the injection himself he permitted the nurse to give the injection.
- That there was clear dereliction of duty on the part of the nurse who was not even a qualified nurse and was not registered with any nursing council of any State.
- That both the doctor and nurse and the hospital were found liable

Penalty: - That ₹ 12.5 lakhs was awarded as compensation to the parents.

Judgment: Sethuraman Subramaniam Iyer v/s Triveni Nursing Home and another (1998) CPJ 110:

Suit:
- That the complainant's wife suffered from Sinusitis and was advised surgery by the doctor.
- That she had suffered a massive heart attack while in the operation theatre, resulting in death.

Held:
- That the State Commission found that necessary precautions and effective measures were taken to save the deceased and dismissed the complaint.
- That the complainant had not given any expert evidence to support his allegation and in these circumstances it was held that no case was made out against the doctor.
- Relied: Affidavits of four doctors who opined that there was no negligence.

Judgment: A.S. Mittal and another v/s State of U.P. and others JT (1989) 3 SCC 223:

Suit:
- That a free eye camp was organised for ophthalmic surgical treatment to patients.
- That the eyes of many patients irreversibly damaged, due to post-operative infection of the eyes, caused by normal saline used at the time of surgery.

Held:
- That the Supreme Court directed the State Government to pay ₹ 12,500 as compensation to each victim as there was a clear negligence.

Judgment: Indian Medical Association v/s V.P. Shantha (1995) 6 SCC 651 (vide para 37):

Held:
- That the following acts are clearly due to negligence:
- Removal of the wrong limb;
- Performance of an operation on the wrong patient;
- Giving injection of a drug to which the patient is allergic without looking into the out-patient card containing the warning.
- Use of wrong gas during the course of an anaesthetic, etc.

Judgment: New India Assurance Co. Ltd. v/s Rajesh Kumar and Ors. (2010-11-03)(2): Medical negligence

Suit:
- That a little hole had formed in small intestine of complainant due to wrong treatment given by the OP No. 1 and OP.
- That No. 2 had not operated the complainant for not arranging the operation fee.

Held:
- That there is nothing on record to prove that there was any lack of medical facility.
- That in the hospital of OP No. 1 while providing treatment to the complainant, It is not the case of the complainant that OP No. 1 is not a qualified doctor.
- That there is nothing on record that the complainant was brought to OP No. 2 in a serious condition and he was refused to provide treatment.
- That as per records, the operation of complainant was a routine operation and was not an emergency necessitating immediate surgery.
- That no deficiency in service on the part of OP No. 2.
- That the District Forum wrongly granted relief to the complainants and complaint deserves dismissal.

References:
1. Martin F.D'Souza v/s Mohd. Ishfaq (2009) CPJ 32 (SC).
2. Jacob Mathew v/s State of Punjab and Anr. (2005) 6 SCC 1.

Judgment: Pushkar Dutt v/s Christian Medical College and Hospital, Ludhiana and Anr. (2010-11-03) 2: Medical negligence:

Held:
- That as per angiography report there was blockage of 70 per cent and 50 per cent of the two arteries.
- That no medical expert or medical literature produced to show that the operation was not necessary at that stage.

- That in the absence of any evidence to show that the blood in pericardium can be detected without opening the heart.
- That, In the absence of such evidence it cannot be held that the respondent were guilty of medical negligence and deficiency in service.
- Relied: That term 'medical negligence' explained on the basis of Texts and case law.

Reference: 1. Jacob Mathew v/s State of Punjab and Anr. (2005) 6 SCC 1.

Judgment: Kusum Sharma and Ors. v/s Batra Hospital and Medical Research Centre and Ors. (2010-11-03) 2 (SC):

Medical negligence – Surgery – For removal of left adrenal tumor:

Suit:
- That 'anterior' approach adopted at the time of first surgery was not the correct approach, surgery should have been done by adopting 'posterior' approach.

Held:
- That besides medical literature the evidence of two eminent doctors of AIIMS supported 'anterior' approach in view of inherent advantage of the approach.
- That doctor who performed the operation had reasonable degree of skill and knowledge.
- That the appellants have failed to make out any case of medical negligence against the respondents.
- That the National Commission was justified in dismissing the complaint of the appellant.

References:
- Bolam v/s Friern Hospital Management Committee (1957) 2 All ER 118.
- Roe and Woolley v/s Minister of Health (1954) 2 QB 66.
- R. v/s Lawrence (1981) 1 All ER 974 (HL).
- R. v/s Caldwell (1981) 1 All ER 961 (HL).
- Jacob Mathew v/s State of Punjab and Anr. (2005) 6 SCC 1.

- Hucks v/s Cole and Anr. (1968) 118 New LJ 469.
- Hunter v/s Hartley (1955) SLT 213.
- John Oni Akerele v/s The King AIR (1943) PC 72. Andrews v/s Director of Public Prosecutions (1937) A.C. 576.

Judgment: Ram Singh Rai (Dr.) v/s Ranno Bai Barkade (2010-11-03)(2): Medical negligence – Compensation – Drug reaction:

Suit:
- That allopathic injection administered by a homeopath.
- That as per appellant's own averments, homeopathic drugs do not cause any reaction, then he had no business to give allopathic injection or any drug other than homeopathic medicines.

Held:
- That as per documents the respondent was treated for drug reaction.
- The respondent deserves to be compensated for the medical expenses incurred in her treatment and for the mental agony suffered.
- That compensation of ₹ 50 K by the District Forum held to be on higher side and reduced to ₹ 35 K.

Reference:
- Poonam Verma (1986) 4 SCC 332.

Judgment: Peoples Clinic and Hospital v/s Deepa Satheesh and Anr. (2010-11-03)(2) Kerala: Medical negligence – Compensation - Drug reaction:

Held:
- That there is nothing to suggest that the hospitals treated the complainant were aware of the nature of the drug that was injected on the complainant.
- That the same would have helped the treatment of the complainant who was in serious state of affairs.
- That the attitude of the staff of the OP hospital testified by PW1 mentioned in the complaint is really unhelpful.
- That drugs reaction stands established.

- That order of the District Forum directing appellant/OP to pay a sum of ₹ 10 K as compensation upheld.

References:
- Cherothe Suhara v/s Dr. K.K. Subramoniam and Anr. (1995)(i) CPR 258.
- Geetha Kumari v/s Dr. Mrs. Anitha Rajan (1995)(ii) CPR 393.
- Talwar's Nursing Home (Dr.) v/s Manjit Singh and Ors. (2010)(2) (Pb).
- B. Sreekanth v/s H.N. Shiva Kumar (Dr.) (2010)(2) (NC).
- Santokh Nursing Home and Anr. v/s Jaswinder Singh and Ors. (2010)(2) (NC).
- Balkrishna Mahadev Kare v/s P.N. Nagpal (Dr.) and Anr. (2010)(2) (MH).

Application of the general principles to particular cases:

Judgment: Jacob Mathews Case - A landmark judgment of medical negligence of the Indian Judiciary

Held: **Law of Torts:** Negligence is the breach of a duty caused by omission to do something which a reasonable man guided by those considerations which ordinarily regulate the conduct of human affairs would do, or doing something which a prudent and reasonable man would not do.

(Ratanlal and Dhirajlal edited by Justice G.P. Singh, referred to hereinabove, holds good).

- That negligence becomes actionable on account of injury resulting from the act or omission amounting to negligence attributable to the person sued. The essential components are three: 'duty', 'breach' and 'resulting damage'.
- That negligence in the context of medical profession necessarily calls for a treatment with a difference. To infer rashness or negligence on the part of a professional, in particular a doctor, additional considerations apply.
- That a case of occupational negligence is different from one of professional negligence. A simple lack of care, an error of judgment or an accident,

is not proof of negligence on the part of a medical professional.

- That as long as a doctor follows a practice acceptable to the medical profession of that day, he cannot be held liable for negligence merely because a better alternative course or method of treatment was also available or simply because a more skilled doctor would not have chosen to follow or resort to that practice or procedure which the accused followed.
- That when it comes to the failure of taking precautions what has to be seen is whether those precautions were taken which the ordinary experience of men has found to be sufficient ; a failure to use special or extraordinary precautions which might have prevented the particular happening cannot be the standard for judging the alleged negligence.
- That the standard of care, while assessing the practice as adopted, is judged in the light of knowledge available at the time of the incident, and not at the date of trial. Similarly,
- That when the charge of negligence arise out of failure to use some particular equipment, the charge would fail if the equipment was not generally available at that particular time (that is, the time of the incident) at which it is suggested it should have been used.

A professional may be held liable for negligence on 1 of the 2 findings:

- That either he was not possessed of the requisite skill which he professed to have possessed, or, he did not exercise, with reasonable competence in the given case, the skill which he did possess.
- That the standard to be applied for judging, whether the person charged has been negligent or not, would be that of an ordinary competent person exercising ordinary skill in that profession. It is not possible for every professional to possess the highest level of expertise or skills in that branch which he practices.

- That a highly skilled professional may be possessed of better qualities, but that cannot be made the basis or the yardstick for judging the performance of the professional proceeded against an indictment of negligence.

The test for determining medical negligence as laid down in:

Bolan's case (1957) 1 W.L.R. 582, 586 holds good in its applicability in India.

The Jurisprudential concept of negligence differs in civil and criminal law

- That negligence in Civil Law may not necessarily be negligence in Criminal Law.
- That for negligence to amount to an offence, the element of mens rea must be shown to exist. For an act to amount to criminal negligence, degree of negligence should be much higher - gross/or of a very high degree negligence which is neither gross nor of a higher degree may provide ground for action in civil law but cannot form the basis for prosecution.

The word 'gross' has not been used in Section 304-A of IPC:

- That in criminal law negligence or recklessness, to be so held, must be of such a high degree as to be 'gross'. The expression 'rash or negligent act' as occurring in Section 304-A of the IPC has to be read as qualified by the word 'grossly'.

To prosecute a medical professional for negligence under criminal law:

- That it must be proved that the accused did something or failed to do something which in the given facts and circumstances no medical professional in his ordinary senses and prudence would have done or failed to do.
- That the hazard taken by the accused doctor should be of such a nature that the injury which resulted was most likely imminent.

res ipsa loquitur:

- That is only a rule of evidence and operates in the domain of Civil law specially in cases of torts and helps in determining the onus of proof in actions relating to negligence.
- That, It cannot be pressed in service for determining per se the liability for negligence within the domain of Criminal law.
- That res ipsa loquitur has a limited application in trial on a charge of Criminal negligence.

Judgment: Martin F.D'Souza v/s Mohd. Ishfaq. (2009) 2 CLT 395 (SC):

Held:

- That the practitioner must bring to his task a reasonable degree of skill and knowledge, and must exercise a reasonable degree of care.
- That neither the very highest nor a very low degree of care and competence is what the law requires.
- That medical negligence needs to be understood. The Court observed that before dealing with these principles two things have to be kept in mind:
- That Judges are not experts in medical science, rather they are lay men. This itself often makes it somewhat difficult for them to decide cases relating to medical negligence.
- That Judges have usually to rely on testimonies of other doctors which may not necessarily in all cases be objective, like in all professions and services, doctors too sometimes have a tendency to support their own colleagues who are charged with medical negligence.
- That the testimony may also be difficult to understand, particularly in complicated medical matters, for a layman in medical like a Judge; and a balance has to be struck in such cases.
- That doctors who cause death or agony due to medical negligence should certainly be penalised

- That like all professionals doctors too can make errors of judgment but if they are punished for this no doctor can practice his vocation with quanimity.
- That indiscriminate proceedings and decisions against doctors are counter productive and serve society no good.
- That these inhibit the free exercise of judgment by a professional in a particular situation.

Judgment: Achutrao Haribhau Khodwa and others v/s State of Maharashtra and others AIR (1996) SC 2377:

Held:

- That a medical practitioner is not liable to be held negligent simply because things went wrong from mischance or misadventure or through an error of judgment in choosing one reasonable course of treatment in preference to another.
- That he would be liable only where his conduct fell below that of the standards of a reasonably competent practitioner in his field. For instance, he would be liable if he leaves a surgical gauze inside the patient after an operation (Achutrao Haribhau Khodwa).
- That the standard of care has to be judged in the light of knowledge available at the time of the incident not at the date of the trial.
- That where the charge of negligence is of failure to use some particular equipment, the charge would fail if the equipment was not generally available at that point of time.
- That there may be few cases where an exceptionally brilliant doctor performs an operation or prescribes a treatment which has never been tried before to save the life of a patient when no known method of treatment is available.
- That the doctor should not be held liable, in case the patient dies or suffers seriously.
- That experiments sometime end in failure e.g. the operation on the Iranian twin sisters who

were joined at the head since birth, or the first heart transplant by Dr. C. Bernard in South Africa.

- That in such cases it is advisable for the doctor to explain the situation to the patient and take his/her written consent.
- That simply because a patient has not favourably responded to a treatment given by a doctor or a surgery has failed, the doctor cannot be held liable for medical negligence by applying the doctorine of res ipsa loquitur.
- That no sensible professional would intentionally commit an act or omission which would result in harm or injury to the patient since the professional reputation of the professional would be at stake. A single failure may cost him dear in his lapse.

Supreme Court in Jacob Mathew's case:

- That, A medical practitioner faced with an emergency ordinarily tries his best to redeem the patient out of his suffering. He does not gain anything by acting with negligence or by omitting to do an act.
- That it will be for the complainant to clearly make out a case of negligence before a medical practitioner is charged with or proceeded against criminally.
- That a surgeon with shaky hands under fear of legal action cannot perform a successful operation and a quivering physician cannot administer the end-dose of medicine to his patient. If the hands be trembling with the dangling fear of facing a criminal prosecution in the event of failure for whatever reason.
- That whether attributable to himself or not, neither can a surgeon successfully wield his life-saving scalpel to perform an essential surgery, nor can a physician successfully administer the life-saving dose of medicine.

- That discretion being the better part of valour, a medical professional would feel better advised to leave a terminal patient to his own fate in the case of emergency where the chance of success may be 10 per cent (or so), rather than taking the risk of making a last ditch effort towards saving the subject and facing a criminal prosecution if his effort fails.
- That such timidity forced upon a doctor would be a disservice to society.

Judgment: Dr. Shiv Kumar Gautam v/s Alima, Revision Petition No. 586 of 1999 decided on 10.10.2006:

Held:
- That the National Consumer Commission held a homeopath liable for negligence for prescribing allopathic medicines and administering glucose drip and giving injections.

Judgment: Postgraduate Institute of Medical Education and Research, Chandigarh v/s Jaspal Singh and others (2009) 7 SCC 330:

Held:
- That the Court held that mismatch in transfusion of blood resulting in death of the patient after 40 days, is a rare case of medical negligence.
- That the learned Judges did not use the expression res ipsa loquitur.
- That a case of mismatch blood transfusion is one of the illustrations given in various textbooks on medical negligence to indicate the application of res ipsa loquitur.

Medical Evidence v/s Ocular Evidence

Judgment: Pala Ram v/s State of Punjab (2009) 2 RCR (Criminal) 628 (P&H):

Held:
- That, If there is varience between the medical and ocular (eye) evidence, later has to be accepted, provided it stands the test of judicial scrutiny in the crucible of probabilities.

References:
- Manjulaben Vinod Bhai Patel v/s Dr. Harshida K. Patel and Anr. (1998) II CPJ 660 (Gujarat).
- Bolam v/s Friern Hospital Management Committee (1957)(1) WLR 582.

- Martin F.D.'Souza v/s Mohd. Ishfaq (2009) II SLT 20.
- Jacob Mathew v/s State of Punjab (2005)(6) SCC 1.

Protection to Doctors in Criminal Cases

Judgment: Supreme Court in Jacob Mathew's case:

Held:

- That doctors have to be protected from frivolous complaints of medical negligence, laid down certain rules in this connection:
- That a private complaint should not be entertained unless the complainant has produced prima facie evidence before the court in the form of a credible opinion given by another competent doctor to support the charge of rashness or negligence on the part of the accused doctor.
- That the investigating officer should, before proceeding against the doctor accused of rash or negligent act or omission, obtain an independent and competent medical opinion, preferably from a doctor in government service, qualified in that branch of medical practice who can normally be expected to give an impartial opinion applying the Bolam test.
- That a doctor accused of negligence should not be arrested in a routine manner simply because a charge has been leveled against him.
- That unless his arrest is necessary for furthering the investigation or for collecting evidence or unless the investigating officer feels satisfied that the doctor proceeded against would not make himself available to face the prosecution unless arrested, the arrest should be withheld.

Precautions which Doctor/Hospitals/Nursing Homes should take:

- That current practices, infrastructure, para-medical and other staff, hygiene and sterility should be observed strictly. Examples:

Judgment: Sarwat Ali Khan v/s Prof. R. Gogi and others Original Petition No. 181 of 1997, decided on 18.7. 2007 by the National Consumer Commission:

Held:

- That the facts were that out of 52 cataract operations performed between 26th and 28th September, 1995 in an eye hospital 14 persons lost their vision in the operated eye.
- That an enquiry revealed that in the operation theatre two autoclaves were not working properly. This equipment is absolute necessary for sterilisation of instruments, cotton, pads, linen, etc., and the damage occurred because of its absence in working condition.
- That the doctors were held liable.
- That no prescription should ordinarily be given without actual examination.
- That tendency to give prescription over the telephone, except in an acute emergency should be avoided.
- That a doctor should not merely go by the version of the patient regarding his symptoms, but should also make his own analysis including tests and investigations where necessary.
- That a doctor should not experiment unless necessary and even then he should ordinarily get a written consent from the patient.

An expert should be consulted in case of any doubt. Examples:

Judgment: Decision of National Insurance Commission on 9.8. 2007 in case of Smt. Indrani Bhattacharjee, Origional Petition No. 233 of 1996:

Suit:

- That the patient was diagnosed as having 'Mild Lateral Wall Ischemia'. The doctor prescribed medicine for gastro-enteritis, but he expired.

Held:

- Held that the doctor was negligent as he should have advised consulting a cardiologist in writing.

Full record of the diagnosis, treatment, etc. should be maintained:

Judgment: V. Kishan Rao Appellant (s) v/s Nikhil Super Speciality Hospital and another Civil Appeal No. 2641 Of 2010 decided on 8.3. 2010 by the Hon'ble Supreme Court:

Held:

- That the test of medical negligence which was laid down in Bolam v/s Friem Hospital Management Committee reported in 1957 (2) All England Law Reports 118, has been accepted by this Court as laying down correct tests in cases of medical negligence.
- That Bolam was suffering from mental illness of the depressive type and was advised by the doctor attached to the defendants' hospital to undergo electro-convulsive therapy.
- That prior to the treatment Bolam signed a form of consent to the treatment but was not warned of the risk of fracture involved.
- That even though the risk was very small and on the first occasion when the treatment was repeated for the second time he sustained fractures.
- That no relaxant drugs or manual control were used except that a male nurse stood on each side of the treatment couch throughout the treatment.
- That about this treatment there were two bodies of opinion, one of which favoured the use of relaxant drugs or manual control as a general practice, and the other opinion was for the use of drug that was attended by mortality risks and confined the use of relaxant drugs only to cases where there are particular reasons for their use and Bolam case was not under that category.
- That on these facts the expert opinion of Dr. J.de Bastarrechea, consultant Psychiatrist attached to the Hospital was taken.
- That the Court held the Doctors not negligent.

- That in this context the following principles have been laid down:
- That a doctor is not guilty of negligence if he has acted in accordance with a practice accepted as proper by a responsible body of medical men skilled in that particular art.
- That in the realm of diagnosis and treatment there is ample scope of genuine difference of opinion and a doctor is not negligent merely because his conclusion differs from that of other professionally men.
- That the true test for establishing negligence in diagnosis or treatment on the part of a doctor is whether he has been proved to be guilty of such failure as no doctor of ordinary skill would be guilty of acting with extra-ordinary care.

Observation: Michael Jones on Medical Negligence:

- That, It is felt "to do this would set us on the slippery slope of excusing carelessness when it happens often enough".
- That the directions in D'Souza (supra) are also inconsistent with the principles laid down in another three-Judge Bench of this Court rendered in Indian Medical Association (supra) wherein a three-Judge Bench of this Court, on an exhaustive analysis of the various provisions of the Act, held that the definition of 'service' under Section 2(1) (o) of the act has to be understood on broad parameters and it cannot exclude service rendered by a medical practitioner.

Observation: Indian Medical Association makes the following position clear

- That there may be simple cases of medical negligence where expert evidence is not required.
- That those cases should be decided under the said Act on the basis of the procedure which has been prescribed under the said Act.

- That, In complicated cases where expert evidence is required the parties have a right to go to the Civil Court.
- That right of the parties to go to Civil court is preserved under Section 3 of the Act.
- That the decision in Indian Medical Association has been further explained and reiterated in another three-Judge Bench decision in Dr. J.J. Merchant and others v/s Shrinath Chaturvedi reported in (2002) 6 SCC 635.
- That the three-Judge Bench in Dr. J.J. Merchant accepted the position that it has to be left to the discretion of Commission to examine experts if required in an appropriate matter.
- That it is equally true that in cases where it is deemed fit to examine experts, recording of evidence before a Commission may consume time.
- That the Act specifically empowers the Consumer Forums to follow the procedure which may not require more time or delay the proceedings.
- That the only caution required is to follow the said procedure strictly.

LIABILITIES:

Vicarious Liability:

Judgment: Dr. N.K. Sengupta v/s State of NCT Delhi (2009)(5) RCR(Criminal) 967 (Delhi): Vicarious liability:

Held: - That a person who was neither the chairman nor the director of the company nor was responsible for the day-to-day affairs in any manner at the time of deposit by the complainant or on the date of issuance of the cheque by the company, cannot be made liable for an offence under Section 138 of N.I. Act.

Medical Negligence:

NATIONAL CONSUMER DISPUTES REDRESSAL COMMISSION, NEW DELHI:

Judgment: Dinesh Jaiswal (Deceased) Through L.Rs. and Ors. v/s Bombay Hospital and Medical Research Centre and Another (2010) 2 (NC):

Medical negligence – res ipsa loquitur – Compensation:

Suit:

- That surgery for urgent surgical repair of aneurysm as gangrene was impending.
- That doctor OP No. 2 delegated his responsibility to his inexperienced junior doctor especially when it was known to be a case which had necessitated second surgery and expert post-operative care and timely decision on amputation of gangrenous legs.
- That due to negligence of the surgeon in the first operation, a corrective surgery was required to be performed emergently on the next date, which got delayed due to late arrival of OP No. 2, non-functioning of the DSA machine and non-availability of operation theatre.
- That incidence of paraplegia in such case is only 0.2 per cent, but in the case paraplegia occurred immediately resulting in numbness of feet, non-movement of legs and setting in of gangrene.
- That OP No. 2 has not placed on records to prove best efforts made.
- That, In fact, prior to going abroad for about one month he did not meet the patient till his departure though he was admitted under his care.
- That three surgeries performed in this case.
- That, It does not mention that the treating surgeons have informed the risks involved in the surgeries and the chances of success and failure of the same.
- That by no stretch of imagination, the consent obtained can be considered to be an informed consent.

Held:

- That the hospital held vicariously liable for the acts of commission and omission by the doctors and para-medical staff, whether they are employed on permanent basis or as consultants or visiting doctors.

- That deceased was aged 42 years and was bus operator.
- That would have been reasonable expected to earn till the age of 62 years.
- That taking ₹ 4000 p.m. for determination of compensation and multiplier of 18 years ₹ 8,64,000 and total of ₹ 14,18,941 under all heads with Interest @ 9 per cent allowed.

References:
- Martin D'Souza v/s Mohd. Lshfaq (2009) 3 SCC 1.
- Jacob Mathew v/s State of Punjab and Another (2005) 6 SCC 1.
- Samira Kohli v/s Dr. Prabha Manchanda and Another (2008) AIR 1385.
- Spring Meadows Hospital and Anr. v/s Harjot Ahluwalia and Anr. (1998) 4 SCC 39.
- Nizam Institute of Medical Sciences v/s Prasnath S. Dhananka and Ors. (2009) 11 SC.

Judgment: Abhishek Ahluwalia through mother Anuradha v/s Dr Saluja and Inscol Hospital, Chandigarh (2014) 2 (NC):

Medical negligence – res ipsa loquitur – Compensation:

Suit:
- That surgery for urgent surgical repair of aneurysm as gangrene was impending.
- That doctor OP No. 2 delegated his responsibility to his inexperienced junior doctor especially when it was known to be a case which had necessitated second surgery and expert post-operative care and timely decision on amputation of gangrenous legs.
- That due to negligence of the surgeon in the first operation, a corrective surgery was required to be performed emergently on the next date, which

got delayed due to late arrival of OP No. 2, non-functioning of the DSA machine and non-availability of operation theatre.

- That incidence of paraplegia in such case is only 0.2 per cent, but in the case paraplegia occurred immediately resulting in numbness of feet, non-movement of legs and setting in of gangrene.
- That OP No. 2 has not placed on records to prove best efforts made.
- That In fact, prior to going abroad for about one month he did not meet the patient till his departure though he was admitted under his care.
- That, three surgeries performed in this case.
- That, It does not mention that the treating surgeons have informed the risks involved in the surgeries and the chances of success and failure of the same.
- That by no stretch of imagination, the consent obtained can be considered to be an informed consent.

Defence:

- That the line of treatment rendered by Dr Saluja was prompt, adequate and correct, as per clinical conditions of Abhishek, throughout the period.

Held:

- That the hospital held vicariously liable for the acts of commission and omission by the doctors and para-medical staff, whether they are employed on permanent basis or as consultants or visiting doctors.
- That deceased was aged 42 years and was bus operator.
- That would have been reasonable expected to earn till the age of 62 years.

Order: District Forum held (2003):

- That taking ₹ 4000 p.m. for determination of compensation and multiplier of 18 years ₹ 8,64,000 and total of ₹ 14,18,941 under all heads with Interest @ 9% allowed.

State Consumer Disputes Redressal Commission (2003) held:

- That the sum total of the relief which could be considered by it amounted to ₹ 15 lakh, less than ₹ 20 lakh. The complaint was ordered to be returned to be filed before the District Forum. Anuradha, mother of Abhishek, filed an appeal against the order of the State Commission before the National Commission.

National Commission (2004): set aside the order of the State Commission and said that case must be taken on merit.

State Commission (2005): dismissed the complaint.

National Commission (2014): directed Dr Sanjay Saluja to pay ₹ 70 lakh as compensation for negligent treatment that lead to the amputation of a young man (then teenager) in 2003.

References:
- Martin D'Souza v/s Mohd. Lshfaq (2009) 3 SCC 1.
- Jacob Mathew v/s State of Punjab and Another (2005) 6 SCC 1.
- Samira Kohli v/s Dr. Prabha Manchanda and Another (2008) AIR 1385.
- Spring Meadows Hospital and Anr. v/s Harjot Ahluwalia and Anr. (1998) 4 SCC 39.
- Nizam Institute of Medical Sciences v/s Prasnath S. Dhananka and Ors. (2009) 11 SC.

Judgment: CHL Apollo Hospital Indore v/s Reena (deceased) through Ashish Sanyal Medical Negligence:

Held:
- That the National Consumer Disputes Redressal Commission (NCDRC) directed Indore-based CHL Apollo Hospital to pay over ₹ 4 lakh as compensation to the husband of a patient who had died due to blood loss after undergoing heart surgery there.
- That the bench headed by Justice Ashok Bhan also held the hospital and the concerned doctors guilty of negligence as they failed to explain as to

how the 37 yrs. old woman's blood count had dropped drastically after surgery.

- That in the absence of any explanation, it would be reasonable to assume that the haemoglobin test was done prior to the surgical procedure on August 22, 2003 and without for this report which would have indicated the low haemoglobin count, the surgery, which proved to be fatal, was undertaken.
- That in his complaint, Ashish Sanyal had alleged that the hospital was negligent in the treatment of his wife Reena Sanyal as the surgery was done even though her haemoglobin (blood count) was very low and the concerned doctors were not present either when her condition became serious.
- That CHL Apollo Hospital directed to pay ₹ 4 lakh for Negligence.
- Relied:- Indian Express, Category: NEWS, New Delhi, June 24, 2012:

Judgment: Dr Amita Srivastava of Chhapra, Bihar v/s Poonam Devi

Held:

- That the National Consumer Disputes Redressal Commission (NCDRC) ordered Dr. Amita Srivastava of Chhapra in Bihar to pay ₹ 2.75 lakh as compensation to a woman for damaging the veins of her right forearm during a blood transfusion, leading to its amputation.
- That the NCDRC bench, presided by Justice VB Gupta, dismissed Dr. Srivastava's appeal against the concurrent rulings of the State Consumer Commission and the District Forum, which held the doctor negligent and ordered her to pay the compensation.
- That according to the State and District Consumer Forums, the patient Poonam Devi, had approached the doctor in December 2002 with an 'abdominal complaint' and the veins of her right forearm was damaged during blood

and saline transfusion and became septic, leading to amputation of her arms.

- That the complaint petition gives details of not only the medical consequences of the alleged negligence, but also resultant financial cost to the complainant.
- That for this, a total compensation, of ₹ 3.46 lakh, was sought against which ₹ 2.75 lakh has been awarded (Para 2).
- Relied: BS, New Delhi, June 16, 2012.

Observations of the State Commission:

- That the State Commission has observed in the impunged order dated 18/08/2011, that there is no dispute on the fact that the complainant had undergone abnormal surgery (hysterectomy).
- That there is no dispute that during the course of the treatment, transfusion of blood and saline had been given to the complainant in the clinic of Dr. Amita Srivastava (opposite party).
- That it is also an admitted fact that swelling & discolouration of the arm was first noticed on 11/12/2012.
- That, It is also admitted that at the time of her admission, complainant Poonam Devi had no problem with her right arm (Para 3).

SCDRC observation on District Forum findings:

- That the State Commission also referred to the findings of District Forum that the blood flow in the right arm was normal and the problem of discolouration and swelling was noticed only on 11/12/2002 after transfusion of blood and saline in between.

SCDRC decision:

- That the State Commission finally arrived at the following conclusion:
- That in the present case, we also find that the chain of incident and circumstances under which the complication took place to the patient started under the care of appellant-doctor, on the basis

of which there is only one inference of negligence of the appellant is drawn. Therefore, the respondent does not required to provide any further opinion of expert on the subject. The complainant succeeded to make out a case of negligence whereas the appellant failed to prove her innocence." (Para 4)

Revision Petition before NCDRC:

- Ground and scope of revisional jurisdiction:
- Jurisdictional error
- Material irregularity or
- Illegality in the impunged order of lower Court.

NCDRC observation on Jurisdiction error:

- That NCDRC observed that "A perusal of the revision petition and the grounds raised therein clearly shows that it is a mere attempt to challenge the concurrent finding of fact by the NCDRC, Bihar and District Consumer Forum, Chhapra.
- That it needs to be pointed out at the very outset that the scope of revisional jurisdiction is a limited one in terms of the provision in Section 21(b) of the Consumer Protection Act, 1986 intervention of this Commission is contemplated only when there is case of jurisdictional error material, irregularity or illegality in the impunged order".
- Relied: SC judgement: "While considering the scope of this provision, Hon'ble SC of India observed in Rubi (Chandra) Dutta v/s United India Insurance Co. Ltd. (2011) 11 SCC 269, that powers under Section 21(b) of the CPA 1986 can be exercised only if there is some prima facie jurisdictional error appearing in the impunged order.
- That in the matter before the Apex Court it was observed that there was no jurisditional error or miscarriage of justice, which could have warranted the National Commission to take a view different from what was taken by the two Forums.

- That the decision of the National Commission was based not on some legal principle, which was ignored by the Lower Court, but on different interpretation of the same set of facts. Therefore, the order of the National Commission was quashed and set aside by the Apex Court (Para 5).
- That during the hearing of the present revision petition, learned counsel for the petitioner confined himself to the details of the treatment given to the complainant i.e. the facts (Para 6).
- That no case made out for revisional jurisdiction:
- That neither the petition nor the petitioner's counsel made out any case for exercise of revisional jurisdictional, as contemplated under Section 21(b) of the Act and as enunciated by the Apex Court in the decision mentioned above (Para 6).
- That case dismissed for the want of merit.
- That the revision petition therefore, dismissed for want of merit and the impunged order of Bihar State Consumer Disputes Redressal Commission (SCDRC) in FA No. 921 of 2006 (Para 7).

Reference: - Dr. Mukesh Yadav, Editor Journal of Indian Academy of Forensic Medicine (JIAFM). *Source:* Yahoo Groups (Quality of Medical Education), Categories: NEWS.

STATE CONSUMER DISPUTES REDRESSAL COMMISSION, CHANDIGARH:

Judgment: Santokh Nursing Home and Anr. v/s Jaswinder Singh and Ors. (2010) 2 NC Medical negligence – Compensation:

Suit:
- That surgical procedure for removal of uterine fibroid.
- That wavering stand taken by appellant – doctor at different stages.
- That of the complaint – Doctor has not denied the factum of pieces of swabs/mops having been

left inside the abdomen of the deceased at the time of surgical procedure.

- That ample material, in the form of ultrasound report and the subsequent treatment/surgical procedure of the patient underwent to show that a foreign body, like a mop was left inside the abdomen of the deceased at the time of surgery which led to infection and septicaemia which ultimately led to her death despite the best possible treatment the patient could be given in other upgraded hospitals.

Held: - That order of the State Commission holding the doctor and the hospital guilty of negligence / deficiency of service upheld.

- That compensation of ₹ 12,34,414.50 awarded by the State Commission held to be excessive and reduced to ₹ 8 lakh.

References: - Martin F.D'Souza v/s Mohd. Ishfaq (2009) 3 SCC (1).

- Relied:- Indian Express, Category: NEWS, New Delhi, June 24, 2012:

The Haryana State Consumer Disputes Redressal Commission, Chandigarh

Judgment: Dr Kulbhushan Jain of Jain Nursing Home, Kurukhetra v/s Shingara Singh, June 27, 2012: Medical negligence:

Held: - That the Haryana State Consumer Disputes Redressal Commission, ordered Dr. Kulbhushan Jain of Jain Nursing Home, Kurukhetra to pay a compensation of ₹ 5 lakh to a patient whose kidney was removed without his consent and without any reason despite the fact that it was functioning properly.

- That the complainant, Shingara Singh, a resident of Kurukshetra, was operated in the nursing home for removal of stones from his right kidney, for which he was charged ₹ 30 K. When even after the operation, his pain persisted an X-ray from a hospital revealed the missing kidney while the stone was still unremoved.

- That the Commission ruled that the doctor had acted in an inhuman manner by depriving the complainant of an important body organ and expressed surprise that a criminal case was not registered against him.
- Relied:- Indian Express, Category: NEWS, New Delhi.

Judgment: Dr Rajanna Sreedhara and Dr Ramcharan Thiagarajan v/s Pankaj Rai Medical Negligence:

Suit:

- Will the Doctor fraternity recommend illegal transplantation surgeries ?

  Maj Pankaj Rai (Retd): June 10, 2012:
- That Major (Retd) Pankaj Rai, wrote a rejoinder (in response to 'A letter from Dr. R Sreedhara to Aamir Khan') in which he had tried to present his version of the story involving the death of his wife Seema Rai, who expired on May 6, 2010 after kidney-pancreas transplant surgery at Fortis Hospital, Bangalore.
- That the incident was featured in the fourth episode, 'Every life is precious', of the TV programme Satyamev Jayate aired on May 27, 2012.
- That complained to Karnataka Medical Council (KMC) and Appropriate Authority (AA) for Organ Transplantation of medical negligence and violation of Transplantation of Human Organs Act (THOA) by Fortis Hospital and its doctors.
- That Fortis' doctors – Dr. Rajanna Sreedhara and Dr. Ramcharan Thiagarajan, did not report the death of his wife within the stipulated period of 7 days but after 10 months.
- That they did not recommend post-mortem even though she died on the 6th day of hospitalisation.
- That the cause of death mentioned (natural death) in Form No. 4 'Medical Certificate' of the hospital sighned by Dr. Ananda.

Held:

- That AA accepted two of the three points in the complaint viz surgery without licence and post-operative infection but not 'informed consent'.

- That KMC exonerated doctors/hospital of violation of THOA, while issued warning a warning to Fortis Hospital for post-operative infection (a violation of the terms and conditions of the Transplantation licence) unchallenged by the hospital.
- That Hon'ble SC had observed, "it is the duty of the doctors to prevent further spreading of infections. Hospitals or Nursing homes where a patient is taken for better treatment should not be a place for getting infection".
- That the Division Bench of Karnataka High Court orders:
- 19/03/2012 observed that Fortis was trying to protract litigation since they got a stay order.
- 17/04/2012: Fortis is restrained from doing any Transplant surgery.
- 30/08/2012: Fortis cannot do organ transplant surgery.

Vox-populi:
- That in this case a surgery was done without any consent and also without a need to do it.
- That if the intent here was to save the patient then why was such a surgery even done ? Abha Rai, 11/06/2012.
- That Dr. Siddharth, 11/06/2012: In this particular case, it was a high grade infection which only occurs when the immune system is suppressed by the chemotherapy drugs. It is a well known, though rare complication. Had the treating team warned me of this? Some complications are expected, others unexpected and yet others that may occur for the first time and be reported in the literature as 'case reports'. Does that mean that rare complications should be viewed as criminal actions on part of the treating doctor ? Absolutely no.
- That Anil Kumar, Kochi: Aamir Khan is doing a great duty towards the country by all means. He is doing whatever myself and all Indians wish to do but can't. However, he will get threats from

all the culprits who are doing wrong practices. But he will get support from all the Indians."

- That Dr. Davare VR, a GP, Ahmednagar: Whatever Aamir projected through his show is true. "There is no reason IMA or any other medical association should blame him. He is doing social work, indirectly exposing the bad elements in the medical profession. And it is equally true that 40 per cent of the medical practitioners are looting the population.
- That Dr. Mohmmed Irfan H Momin: There is no doubt that medical profession is noble profession. Many of the doctors are honest. Aamir Khan has tried to highlight malpractices in the medical profession. And his message is for those doctors who are indulging in unethical practices and not for all. He has exposed the bad elements in the medical profession. He will get threats from all the culprits who are doing wrong practices.

DISTRICT CONSUMER FORUM, PANCHKULA:

Judgment: Dr. Renu Chakarwarti v/s District Consumer Forum Panchkula (2014) 2 (NC):

Medical negligence - res ipsa loquitur - Compensation:

Suit:

- That patient admitted for delivery at Chakarwarti Nursing Home, Panchkula.
- That doctor Renu Chakarwarti suspected problem on ultrasound findings.
- That Dr Chakarwarti advised Level II ultrasound alongwith triple-test.
- That ultrasound conducted at civil hospital, Mohali – no congenital abnormality.
- That no triple test performed – as per records.
- That another ultrasound advised by the suspecting Dr Chakarwarti conducted – hydrocephalus and meningocele seen.
- That police registered a case against Dr. Chakarvati as medical negligence.

- That a medical board formed by the civil surgeon, Panchkula.

Held:
- That the Medical Board held that Dr Chakarwarti can't be held responsible for medical negligence.
- That District Forum observed that the Medical Board's report is biased – to save Dr Chakarvarti, being a professional colleague.
- That another expert opinion sought from PGI, Chandigarh, headed by its Director – held Dr Chakarwarti not responsible for any medical negligence

References:
- Martin D'Souza v/s Mohd. Lshfaq (2009) 3 SCC 1.
- Jacob Mathew v/s State of Punjab and Another (2005) 6 SCC 1.
- Samira Kohli v/s Dr. Prabha Manchanda and Another (2008) AIR 1385.
- Spring Meadows Hospital and Anr. v/s Harjot Ahluwalia and Anr. (1998) 4 SCC 39.
- Nizam Institute of Medical Sciences v/s Prasnath S. Dhananka and Ors. (2009) 11 SC.

Judgment: Medical Council of India, New Delhi v/s Dr Jayanarayan Naik June 19, 2012: Medical Negligence

Held:
- That the Medical Council of India (MCI) removed the name of Dr. Jayanarayan Naik, Director Cardiology and Cath Lab services Medical Superspecialty Hospital, Kolkata from the medical register for a period of three months starting from June 1, holding him guilty of being a negligent physician.
- That the MCI order based on an appeal against the order of Odisha Medical Council filed by Jayeeta Verma Sarkar, daughter of the patient RS Verma, a retd. Air Force Officer, who died following Dr. Naik's treatment.
- That the issue was taken up by the MCI Ethics Committee, which decided to award punishment to the doctor.

- That the ethics committee after hearing both the parties and going through the available records, unanimously decided that Dr. Jayanarayan Naik, cardiologist, had not given the high risk information form to the patient or the attendant, which was a necessary procedure in this case," MCI said.

Order:
- MCI cancels registration of Dr. Jayanarayan Naik for three months.
- Relied:- Deccan Herald, PBT, Category: NEWS, New Delhi.

HISTORICAL UK JUDGMENTS/LAWS/RULINGS (Medico-legal)

Halisbury's Laws of England – Vol. 6 (3rd Edition) Pages 17-18, defines:

Medical Negligence: Duties owed to the patient:

- That a person who holds himself oath as ready to give medical advice or treatment impliedly undertakes that he is possessed of skill and knowledge for the purpose.
- That such a person, whether he is a registered medical practitioner or not, who is consulted by a patient, owes him certain duties, namely, a duty of care in deciding whether to undertake the case; a duty of care in deciding what treatment to give: and a duty of care in his administration of that treatment.
- That a breach of any of these duties will support an action for negligence by the patient.

Halisbury's Laws of England (Fourth Edition, Vol. 30, Para 35):-

The degree of skill and care required by a medical practitioner is stated as:

- That the practitioner must bring to his task a reasonable degree of care.
- That neither the very highest nor a very low degree of care and competence, judged in the light of the particular circumstances of each case, is what the law requires, and a person is

not liable in negligence because someone else of greater skill and knowledge would have prescribed different treatment or operated in a different way; nor is he guilty of negligence if he has acted in accordance with a practice accepted as proper by a responsible body of medical men skilled in that particular art, even though a body of adverse opinion also existed among medical men.

- That deviation from normal practice is not necessarily evidence of negligence.
- That to establish liability on that basis it must be shown
- there is a usual and normal practice
- the defendant has not adopted it; and
- the course in fact adopted is one no professional man of ordinary skill would have taken had he been acting with ordinary care."

Black's Law on Negligence: defines:

Medical Negligence:

- That negligence per se is defined as "Conduct, whether of action or omission, which may be declared and treated as negligence without any argument or proof as to the particular surrounding circumstances, either because it is in violation of a statute or valid municipal ordinance, or because it is so palpably opposed to the dictates of common prudence that it can be said without hesitation or doubt that no careful person would have been guilty of it.
- That as a general rule, the violation of a public duty, enjoined by law for the protection of person or property, so constitutes.

Michael Jones in his treaties on Medical Negligence (Sweet and Maxwell), 4th ed.): Observation:

- That it criticised the Bolam test as it opts for the lowest common denominator. The learned author noted that opinion was gaining ground in England that Bolam test should be restricted to those cases where an adverse result follows a course of treatment which has been shown to benefit other patients previously.

- That this should not be extended to certain types of medical accident merely on the basis of how common they are.

Charles Worth and Percy on Negligence (Tenth Edition, 2001):

Decisions of British applicable and relied by Indian Judiciary:

- That in current forensic speech, negligence has three meanings.
- a state of mind, in which it is opposed to intention;
- careless conduct; and
- the breach of duty to take care that is imposed by either common or statute law.
- That all three meanings are applicable in different circumstances but anyone of them does not necessarily exclude the other meanings (Para 1.01).
- That the essential components of negligence, as recognised, are three: duty, breach and resulting damage, i.e.
- the existence of a duty to take care, which is owed by the defendant to the complainant;
- the failure to attain that standard of care, prescribed by the law, thereby committing a breach of such duty; and
- damage, which is both causally connected with such breach and recognised by the law, has been suffered by the complainant. (Para 1.23).

Judgment: Decision of Five Law Lords in Maynard v/s West Midlands Regional Health Authority, (1985) 1 All ER 635 (HL):

- That it has been accepted as having settled the law on the point by holding that it is not enough to show that there is a body of competent professional opinion which considers that decision of the defendant professional was a wrong decision, if there also exists a body of professional opinion, equally competent, which supports the decision as reasonable in the circumstances.

- That, It is not enough that subsequent events show that the operation need never have been performed, if at the time the decision to operate was taken.
- That it was reasonable, in the sense that a responsible body of medical opinion would have accepted it as proper.

Judgment: Lord Denning in Hucks v/s Cole and Another (1968) 118 New LJ 469: Observation:

- That a medical practitioner was not to be held liable simply because things went wrong from:
- mischance or misadventure or
- through an error of judgment in choosing one reasonable course of treatment in preference of another.
- That a medical practitioner would be liable only where his conduct fell below that of the standards of a reasonably competent practitioner in his field.

Judgment: Lord President (Clyde) in Hunter v/s Hanley 1955 SLT 213 at 217: Observation:

- That Lord Scarman who recorded the leading speech with which other four Lords agreed, quoted the following words of Lord President (Clyde) that the words cannot be bettered in the realm of diagnosis and treatment there is ample scope for genuine difference of opinion and one man clearly is not negligent merely because his conclusion differs from that of other professional men.
- That the true test for establishing negligence in diagnosis or treatment on the part of a doctor is whether he has been proved to be guility of if acting with ordinary care.

- Lord Scarman added that a doctor who professes to exercise a special skill must exercise the ordinary skill of his speciality. Differences of opinion and practice exist, and will always exist, in the medical as in other professions. There is seldom any one answer exclusive of all others to problems of professional judgment.
- That a court may prefer one body of opinion to the other, but that is no basis for a conclusion of negligence.
- His Lordship further added that a judge's 'preference' for one body of distinguished professional opinion to establish negligence in a practitioner whose actions have received the seal of approval of those whose opinions, truthfully expressed, honestly held, were not preferred.

BOLAM Rule (Test):

Definition : Is defined as the basic principle relating to medical negligence.

- That the rule is applied to establish negligence, on the basis of whether special skill or competence has been used or not, and is not the testing of the man on the top of a Clapham omnibus, because he has been lacking this special skill.
- That the test is the standard used for assessing an ordinary skilled man exercising and professing to have that special skill i.e. It is a well established law, being sufficient to assess the ordinary skilled man exercising that particular art.

Judgment: Justice McNair's judgment: This rule was laid down in the judgment of: Bolam v/s Friern Hospital Management Committee (1957)1 WLR 582 (1957)2 All 118 (Queen's Bench Division):

- That a doctor is not negligent, if he is acting in accordance with a practice accepted as proper by a reasonable body of medical men skilled in that particular art, merely because there is a body of such opinion that takes a contrary view.

- That the direction where there are two different schools of medical practice, both having recognition among practitioners, it is not negligent for a practitioner to follow one in preference to the other accords also with American Law (See 70 Corpus Juris Secundum (1951) 952-953 para 44).
- That moreover, it seems that by American Law, a failure to warn the patient of dangers of treatment is not, of itself, negligence ibid 971 (Para 48).

Lord Justice McNair also observed:

- That, before I turn, I must explain what in law we mean by "negligence".
- That In the ordinary case which does not involve any special skill, negligence in law means this:
- some failure to do some act which a reasonable man in the circumstances would do, or
- doing some act which a reasonable man in the circumstances would not do, and if that failure or doing of that act results in injury, then there is a cause of action.
- How do you test whether this act or failure is negligent ?
- That, in an ordinary case, it is generally said, that you judge that by the action of the man in the street. He is an ordinary man.
- That in one case it has been said that you judge it by the conduct of the man on the top of a Clapham omnibus. He is the ordinary man.
- That in a situation which involves the use of some special skill or competence, then whether there has been negligence or not is not the test of the man on the top of a Clapham omnibus, because he has not got this man exercising and professing to have that special skill.
- That a man need not possess the highest expert skill at he risk of being found negligent.

- That it is sufficient if he exercises the ordinary skill of an ordinary competent man exercising that particular art.

Judgment: Lord Edmund Davies, Lord Fraser and Lord Russel – All ER 267 House of Lords in Whitehouse v/s Jordon and Another (1981)(1) (dictum of McNair Jo in Bolam v/s Friern Hospital Management Committee (1957) 2 All Er 118 (Queen's Bench Division):

Held:
- That the test whether a surgeon has been negligent is:
- That whether he has failed to measure up in any respect, whether in clinical judgment or otherwise, to the standard of the ordinary skilled surgeon exercising and professing to have the special skill of a surgeon.

Judgment: Privy Council in Chin Keow v/s Government of Malaysia and Anr. (1967) WLR 813 - applied these words of McNair, J. In Bolam v/s Friern Hospital Management Committee:

Held:
- That in a situation which involves the use of some special skill or competence, then the test as to whether there has been negligence or not the test of the man on the top of a Clapham omnibus because he has not got this special skill.
- That the test is the standard of the ordinary man exercising and professing to have that special skill.

Judgment: Eckersley v/s Binnie (1988) 18 Con LR 1: defines the Bolam test as:

Held:
- That a professional man should command the corpus of knowledge which forms part of the professional equipment of the ordinary member of his profession.
- That he should not lag behind other ordinary assiduous and intelligent members of his profession in the knowledge of new advances, discoveries and developments in his field.

- That he should have such an awareness as an ordinarily competent would have of the deficiencies in his knowledge and the limitations on his skill.
- That he should be alert to the hazards and risks in any professional task he undertakes to the extent that other ordinarily competent members of the profession would be alert.
- That he bring to any professional task he undertakes no less expertise, skill and care than other ordinarily competent members of his profession would bring, but need bring no more.
- That the standard is that of the reasonable average.
- That the law does not require of a professional man that he be a paragon combining the qualities of a polymath and prophet.

Judgment: Lord Clyde stated in Hunter v/s Hanley 1955 SLT 213:

Held:
- That in the realm of diagnosis and treatment there is ample scope for genuine difference of opinion and one man clearly is not negligent merely because his conclusion differs from that of other professional men.
- That the true test for establishing negligence in diagnosis or treatment on the part of a doctor is whether he has been proved to be guilty of such failure as no doctor of ordinary skill would be guilty of it acting with ordinary care.

Judgement: Privy Council in John Oni Akerele v/s The King (1943) PC 72:

Conviction:
- That the doctor was accused of manslaughter, reckless and negligent act and he was convicted.

Held:
- That conviction was set aside by the House of Lords and it was held:
- That a doctor is not criminally responsible for a patient's death unless his negligence or incompetence went beyond a mere matter of compensation between subjects and showed such

disregard for life and safety of others as to amount to a crime against the State.

- That the degree of negligence required is that it should be gross, and that neither a Jury nor a Court can transform negligence of a lesser degree into gross negligence merely by giving it that appellation.
- That there is a difference in kind between the negligence which gives a right to compensation and the negligence which is a crime.
- That it is impossible to define culpable or criminal negligence, and it is not possible to make the distinction between actionable negligence and criminal negligence intelligible, except by means of illustrations drawn from actual judicial opinion.
- That the most favourable view of the conduct of an accused medical man has to be taken, for it would be most fatal to the efficiency of the medical profession if no one could administer medicine without a halter round his neck.

Judgement of Lord Denning in Roe and Woolley v/s Minister of Health (1954)(2) QB 66:

Held:

- That it is so easy to be wise after the event and to condemn as negligence that which was only a misadventure. We ought to be on our guard against it, especially in cases against hospitals and doctors.
- That medical science has conferred great benefits on mankind but these benefits are attended by unavoidable risks.
- That every surgical operation involves risks, and one cannot take the benefits without taking the risks.
- That every advance in technique also involves risks.
- That doctors, have to learn by experience, and experience often teaches in a hard way.

- That it is a disservice to the community at large if liability to be imposed on hospitals and doctors for all the wrong that happened.
- That doctors would be forced to consider their own safety, than of the welfare of their patients, initiative would be stifled and confidence shaken.
- That a proper sense of proportion requires to have regard to the conditions in which hospitals and doctors have to work.
- That with due care for the patient at every stage, refrain from condemning the negligence which is only a misadventure.

Judgment of Lord Atkin in Andrews v/s Director of Public Prosecutions (1937) AC 576:

Held:
- That simple lack of care – such as will constitute civil liability is not enough for purposes of the criminal law.
- That there are degrees of negligence, and a very high degree of negligence is required to be proved before the felony is established.
- That a clear distinction exists between simple lack of care incurring civil liability and very high degree of negligence which is required in criminal cases.

Lord Porter said in his speech in the same case:
- That a higher degree of negligence has always been demanded in order to establish a criminal offence than is sufficient to create civil liability.

Reference:
- Charlesworth and Percy on Negligence, 10th Ed. 2001, (Para 1 13).

Guidelines:The Secretary General United Nations sub-mitted draft guidelines for consumer protection to the Economic and Social Council in 1983:
- That on an extensive discussions and negotiations among various countries on the scope and content of such impending legislation certain guidelines were arrived at:
- That taking into account the interests and needs of consumers in all countries, particularly those

in developing countries, recognising that consumers often face imbalances in economic terms, educational level and bargaining power, and bearing in mind that consumer should have the right of access to non- hazardous products, as well as importance of promoting just, aquitable and sustainable economic and social development.

- That these guidelines for consumer protection have the following objectives:
- To assist countries in achieving or maintaining adequate protection for their population as consumers.
- To facilitate production and distribution patterns responsive to the needs and desires of consumers.
- To encourage high levels of ethical conduct for those engaged in the production and distribution of goods and services to consumers.
- To assist countries in curbing abusive business practices by all enterprises at the National and International levels which adversely affect consumers.
- To facilitate the development of independent consumer groups.
- To further International cooperation in the field of consumer protection.
- To encourage the development of market conditions which provide consumers with greater choice at lower prices.

Judgment: Spring Meadows case of Medical Negligence the Hon'ble Court:

Held:

- That in cases of gross medical negligence the principle of res ipsa loquitur can be applied.

Principle of res ipsa loquitur: Author Michael Jones:

- That the principle is intended to assist a claimant who, for no fault of his/her own, is unable to adduce evidence as to how the accident occurred.

- That where negligence is evident, the principle of res ipsa loquitur operates and the complainant does not have to prove anything as the thing (res) proves itself. In such a case it is for the respondent to prove that he has taken care and done his duty to repel the charge of negligence.
- That, If the general directions in D'souza case are to be followed then the doctrine of res ipsa loquitur which is applied in cases of medical negligence by this Court and also by the Courts in England would be redundant.
- That the principle has been explained by the author's illustrations based on following decided cases of medical negligence:

Judgment: Coyne v/s Wigan Health Authority (1991) 2 Med. L.R. 301, QDB:

Held: - That where, following an operation under anaesthesia, a patient in the recovery ward sustained brain damage caused by hypoxia for a period of 4 to 5 mts.

Judgment: Lindsay v/s Mid-Western Health Board (1993) 2 I.R. 147 at 181 ;

Held: - That where, following a routine appendisectomy under general anaesthesia, an otherwise fit and healthy girl suffered a fit and went into a permanent coma.

Judgment: Clarke v/s Warboys, The Times (1952)18 March, CA:

Held: - That where a patient sustained a burn from a high frequency electrical current used for "electric coagulation" of the blood.

Judgment: Cavan v/s Wilcox (1973) 44 D.L.R. (3rd) 79 SCC:

Held: - That where gangrene developed in the claimant's arm following an intramuscular injection.

Judgment: Eady v/s Tenderenda (1974) 51 D.L.R. (3rd) 79 SCC:

Held: - That patient underwent a radical mastoidectomy and suffered partial facial paralysis.

Judgment: Rietz v/s Bruser (No. 2) (1979) 1 W.W.R. 31, Man QB:

Held: - That where the defendant filed to diagnose a known complication of surgery on the patient's hand for Paget's disease.

Judgment: Bull v/s Devon Area Health Authority (1989) 4 Med. L.R. 117 at 131:

Held: - That where, there was a delay of 50 mts., in obtaining expert obstetric assistance at the birth of twins when the medical evidence was that at the most no more than 20 mts. should elapse between the birth of the 1st and the 2nd twin.

Judgment: Brazier v/s Ministry of Defence (1965) 1 L.I.Law Rep. 26 at 30:

Held: - That when a needle broke in the patient's buttock while he was being given an injection.

Judgment: Roe v/s Minister of Health (1954) 2 Q.B. 66: and:

Brown v/s Merton, Suton and Wandesworth Area Health Authority (1982) 1 All E.R. 650:

Held: - That where a spinal anaesthetic became contaminated with disinfectant as a result of the manner in which it was stored causing paralysis to the patient.

Judgment: Hajgato v/s London Health Association (1982) 36 Q.R. (2d) 669 and 682

Held: - That where an infection following surgery in a "well-staffed and modern hospital" remained undiagnosed until the patient sustained crippling injury.

Judgment: Crits v/s Sylvester (1956) 1 D.L.R. (2d) 502:

Held: - That where an explosion occurred during the course of administering anaesthetic to the patient when the technique had frequently been used.

References: - Navarange, J.R: Medical negligence.The Doctor's People. Vol. II, Issue-4, New Delhi.

- Halder, S: Medical negligence – Indian Penal Code and CPA vis-à-vis medical profession.

- Gupta, P: Doctor's vis-à-vis CPA. The Doctor People. Vol. II, Issue-4, New Delhi.
- Baldwa, M: Criminal liability of doctors and when doctors should inform police. The Doctor People. Vol. II, Issue-5, New Delhi.
- Baldwa, M., Navarange, J: Law of Consent. The Doctor People. Vol. II, Issue-6, New Delhi.
- Chawla, B.S: Consumer Protection Act, 1986 Total Digest 2009 Year Book. Chawla Publications (P) Ltd., Chandigarh, 2010.
- Universal Law Publishing Co. Pvt. Ltd.: Universal's Criminal Minor Acts. Delhi, 2009.

MENTAL HEALTH ACT, 1987

Judgment: Ezlinda Fernandes v/s Chetan Sanghi, Sub-Divisional Magistrate (1977)(4) Bom CR 641:

Held:

- That Magistrate acting mechanically on Police report without applying mind in ordering detention of an alleged lunatic found on medical observation to be a normal person amounts to wrongful detention and violation of Article 21 of the Constitution.

Judgment: Dial Singh v/s Inspector General of Prison (1998) GLJ 661:

Held:

- That where the Magistrate not only failed to examine the alleged insane person but on the contrary recorded in the Reception Order that he had not personally seen him at all.
- That it was a serious dereliction of duty.

Judgment: Abdul Kareem v/s T. Gopala Krishnan Nambisan (1990) Cri LJ 742 – Section 28(1):

Held:

- That the Act confers jurisdiction on Magistrate to deal with a person who is alleged to be a lunatic when he is brought before the Magistrate.
- That such a person can be detained by an order of the Magistrate for such time not exceeding ten days as may be in his opinion, necessary to enable the Medical Officer to determine whether such alleged lunatic is a person in respect of

whom a Medical Certificate may be properly given.

Judgment: Ms. Asha Shamandas Bajaj v/s Mrs. Meeran Barwankar (2009)(3) RCR (Criminal) 48 Bombay (DB): Section 23:

Held:
- That a mentally ill person harassing other persons by continuously sending SMS and letters.
- That Police taking into protection mentally ill person.
- That order of Police illegal under Section 23 and set aside.
- That under Section 23 the person can be taken into protection by a Police Officer when he has reason to believe that the person was mentally ill as to be mentally incapable of taking care of himself.
- That he should have found him wandering at large within the limits of his jurisdiction under sub-section (1)(b) of Section 23.
- That the person can be taken into protection if the Officer has reasons to believe that the person was dangerous by reason of his mental illness.

Judgment: Ms. Asha Shamandas Bajaj v/s Mrs. Meeran Barwankar (2009)(3) RCR (Criminal) 48 Bombay (DB): Section 23 – Mentally ill person:

Suit:
- That Police taking a mentally ill person into protection.

Held:
- That action of Police illegal on following grounds:
- That the petitioner was not found wandering at large.
- That there was no material before the Police Officer to believe that petitioner was incapable of taking care of herself.
- That there was no material also to suggest that there was any reason for the Police Officer to believe that presence of petitioner was dangerous by reason of her mental illness.

- That the record does not show that the reasons of taking into protection were communicated to the petitioner or her mother.

MENTAL RETARDATION AND MULTIPLE DISABILITIES ACT, 1999

Judgment: Narayanankutty Menon v/s State of Kerala (2009)(5) RCR (Civil) 887 (Kerala): Section 14: appointment of a person as guardian of mentally retarded person:

Held:
- That duties of a person appointed as a guardian under Sesction 14 are governed by Sections 15 and 16.
- That such a person is empowered to act as the guardian with regard to the property of the mentally retarded persons.

MORAL TURPITUDE

Judgment: Parvesh v/s State of Haryana (2009)(4) RCR (Criminal) 470 (P&H) Moral turpitude:

Held:
- That the term 'Moral Turpitude' is not defined anywhere
- That the term used in law for centuries.
- That sexual crimes would fall within scope of moral turpitude, but sexual offences are not the only offences involving moral turpitude.
- That there are other offences also which within term moral turpitude.

Judgment: Parvesh v/s State of Haryana (2009)(4) RCR (Criminal) 470(P&H) Moral turpitude:

Held:
- That homicide may or may not involve moral turpitude depending upon the degree of the crime and so would be the position regarding attempted homicide.

NARCO ANALYSIS

Judgment: Samepatraoe R. Arvelli v/s State of Maharashtra (2009)(5) RCR (Criminal) 607 Bombay (Nagpur Bench): Narco Analysis, Brain mapping and other analogous tests:

Suit:
- That permission challenged by Petitioner.

- That whether narco analysis, brain mapping and similar tests could be undertaken in the absence of consent/willingness of accused/ witness.

Held:
- That narco analysis, brain mapping and similar tests could be undertaken in the absence of consent/willingness of accused/witness.
- That larger interest should outweigh the individual liberties and fundamental rights and balance can be struck by considering the perspective of reasonable restrictions.

NARCOTIC DRUGS and PSYCHOTROPIC SUBSTANCES ACT, 1985

Judgment: Jitendra Panchal v/s Intelligence Officer, NCB (2009)(3) RCR(Criminal) 381(SC): Section 15 – IPC Sections 3 and 4:

Suit:
- That seizure of narcotic from accused (Indo-US-Citizen) in possession of narcotic is an offence under Indian Law.
- That accused prosecuted and sentenced in India.

Held:
- That a person liable by any Indian Law to be tried for any offence committed outside India is to be dealt with under the provisions of the code, having regard to the fact that the provisions of the code would also apply to any offence committed by any citizen of India in any place within and beyond India.

Judgment: Jaskaran Singh, Gurwant Singh and Bhag Singh v/s State of Punjab (2014): RCR(Criminal): Sections 21, 61 and 85 - IPC:

Suit:
- That acting on a tip, accused were arrested on July 8, 2011, in Jallandhar, by the State Special Operation Cell of Counter Intelligence.
- That about 8-Kg heroin was seized from the Tata-Safari, accused were travelling in. The vehicle was impounded and a case was registered.

Held:
- That the accused were held on charges of drug peddling, the Narcotic Drugs and Psychotropic Substances (NDPS) Act.

- That Balwant Singh, Additional District and Sessions Judge (Fast Track Court) on May 03, 2014, awarded ten years imprisonment to all the three accused persons. The Court also imposed a fine of ₹ 1 lakh on them, failing which they would have to undergo one year extra imprisonment.

OATHS ACT, 1969

Judgment: M. Veerabhadra Rao v/s Tek Chand (1985) AIR 28 (SC): Section 3:

Held:
- That any Court, Judge, Magistrate or person have the power to administer oaths, as far as affidavits are concerned.
- That they have the power to do so only if they are empowered by the High Court or the State Government, in respect of affidavits.

Judgment: Chotan Prasad v/s Hari Dusadh (1977) AIR 407 (SC)

Held:
- That evidence of a witness can be received by the courts or persons only on oath and this can be done only when these courts or persons are acting in the discharge of the duties or in exercise of the powers imposed or conferred upon them by law.

Judgment: Rouben Isreal Pattar v/s Mamta (1983) AIR 10 (Kant)

Held:
- That an oath cannot be administered to a child, who is below the age of 12 years and by any person, who is not authorised to examine the child or who is not a court of law.

PRE-NATAL DIAGNOSTIC TECHNIQUES (PNDT) ACT and RULES

Judgment: Ferozepur District Forum on 28/12/2009 in Bachan Singh and anr. v/s Punjab Health System Corporation and others:

Held:
- That the permissible qualifications for sonologist mentioned in the PNDT Act are meant only for

the purposes and circumstances related to the Act and the concerned Pre-natal Diagnostic Techniques.

- That the licence granted under the PNDT Act for ultrasonography doesn't mean that the person so licenced is competent to perform ultrasonography in all other patients of diverse nature in a hospital.

Observation:

Saikumar G: July, 2012:

- That public attacks on doctors have become more mainly as a result of grief once the patient dies and the relatives have to pay hefty amount as hospital charges.
- That, In some cases, attacks are planned in such a way to frighten the hospital management and get the hospital charges waived or demand money as compensation.
- That in case the patient belongs to a dominant local caste or political party, then the hospital staff will have horrid time.

PROTECTION OF HUMAN RIGHTS ACT, 1993

Judgment: Puthuppan P.K. v/s K.S. Girija (2009) (5) RCR (Criminal) 93: (2009) (5)

RCR(Civil) 339(Kerala): Section 2(d): Protection from sexual harassment of women at work places:

Held: - That existing Civil and Penal laws do not adequately make specific provision or protection of women at work places.

Reference: - That Guidelines issued for the purpose by Supreme Court in the case of Vishaka case (1997)(4) RCR(Crl.) 187(SC) relied.

PROTECTION OF WOMEN FROM DOMESTIC VIOLENCE ACT, 2005

Judgment: Nand Kishore v/s State of Rajasthan (2009)(2) RCR(Criminal) 909: (2009)(1) RCR(Civil) 773: (2009)(1) HLR 226 (Rajasthan) (Jaipur Bench) Section 2(q), 12 and 23 – Domestic violence:

Held:
- That under proviso of Section 2(q) of the Act, wife can file complaint against any male or female relative of the husband.
- That in the said proviso the word is "relative" and not male relative.
- That a female relative is not excluded from the definition of respondent contained in Section 2(q) of the Act.

Judgment: Milan Kumar Singh v/s State of U.P. (2009)(5) RCR(Criminal) 124 (Allahabad): Section 12 - Procedure to file Complaint to Magistrate:

Held:
- That complaint cannot be rejected merely on basis that it does not contain verification note on complaint itself.
- That complaint filing affidavit swearing contents of complaint.
- That amounts to sufficient compliance of prescribed procedure.

Judgment: Anilkumar v/s Sidhu (2009)(5) RCR(Criminal) 343(Kerala): Sections 12, 14: Trial of offence under Protection of Women from Domestic Violence Act:

Held:
- That provisions in the Cr.P.C. relating to the inquiry of offences are applicable to the inquiries under the Act.
- That Chapter XIII Cr.P.C. dealing with the jurisdiction of the Criminal Courts with regard to inquiries and trials is applicable to the proceedings under Act.

PROTECTION OF WOMEN AGAINST SEXUAL HARASSMENT AT WORK PLACE BILL, 2007

Judgment: D.S. Grewal v/s Vimmi Joshi (2009)(2) RCR (Criminal) 93: (2009) (1) S.C.T. 773: (2009)(2) R.A.J. 73(SC): Section 2(d): Sexual harassment: Working lady:

Suit:
- That Vice chairman allegedly wrote a letter to principal.
- That complaint Committee not constituted by the Army Public School.
- That Constitution of Complaint Committee is imperative.

Held:
- That High Court may appoint a Three Members committee headed by a lady in the event it is found that the writ petitioner was subjected to sexual harassment.
- That the report thereof may be sent to the Army Authorities for initiation of a disciplinary action against the appellants.
- That all the expenditures which may be incurred in this behalf may be borne by the Army Authorities.

REGISTRATION OF BIRTHS AND DEATHS ACT, 1969

Judgment: Arpanaben Krunal Shah v/s Regional Passport Office, Ahmedabad, 2009(5) RCR(Civil) 923 (Gujarat): Sections 11, 13 and 14:

Proof of date of birth:

Held:
- That entry of birth date in the Register maintained under the Act is presumed to be correct unless otherwise declared by a Civil Court.
- That entry of birth date in the Register has to be given primacy over that of School Leaving Certificate.

SEDITION ACT

Judgment: Simranjit Singh Mann v/s State of Punjab, (2005) (SC):

Held:
- That Punjab politician Simranjit Singh Mann was slapped with four cases of sedition after

he raised pro-Khalistan slogans in the Golden Temple complex on the 21st anniversary of Operation Blue Star, in June 2005.

- That the SC dismissed the charges against him.

Judgment: Binayak Sen v/s State of Chhattisgarh, Haryana (2011) (SC):

Held:

- That Paediatrician and activist Binayak Sen was arrested in May 2007, for waging war against the Nation with the help of Maoists in Chhatisgarh.
- That he was convicted in December 2010 and granted bail by the SC in April 2011, pending an appeal of the vedict in the Chhatisgarh High Court. "The Sedition law in India is being utilised in a very direct way to suppress legitimate dissent," he says.

Judgment: Kashmiri Students v/s State of Uttar Pradesh (2014):

Held:

- That 67 Kashmiri scholarship students were suspended and sent home by the Vice-Chancellor of Swami Vivekanand Subharti University in Meerut, after they cheered Pakistan's victory over India in a cricket match, on March 2, 2014.
- That charges of sedition, a colonial law that carries a life term, were also filed against them the SC dismissed the charges against him.
- That amid an uproar in Kashmir over the treatment, J&K Chief Minister Omar Abdullah, contacted UP Chief Minister Akhilesh Yadav, for dropping charges, since the students had not technically broken any laws.
- That eventually, the sedition charges were dropped, and the Versity says it plans to revoke the suspension.

SEXUAL OFFENCES/PENALTY/JUDGMENTS:

SEXUAL OFFENCES IN INDIA:

Offence: - Adultery

Penalty: - That under Section 497, man is held guilty of adultery (sexual intercourse with another man's wife), and for that imprisonment of either description for a term which may extend to five yrs., or with fine, or with both. The wife of another man's involved, shall not be punishable as an abettor.

Offence: - Rape.

Penalty: - That under Section 376, rigorous imprisonment for a term extended to 10 yrs. with fine.

Offence: - That assault by penetration.

- That the Act makes it an offence for any male or female to penetrate the vagina or anus of another person without their consent.
- That the offence is committed where the penetration is by a part of the body e.g. a finger or anything else e.g. a bottle for sexual intent.
- That even an attempt is an offence.

Penalty: - That a person found guilty of this offence could be sent to prison along with fine.

Offence: - Assault/Molestation.

- That the Act makes it an offence for any male or female to intentionally touch/fondle another person sexually without his or her consent.

Penalty: - Under Section 3 of the Act, a person found guilty of this offence could be sent to prison for a maximum of ten years.

ADULTERY:

Judgment: Kalyani v/s Sailja, SC:

Suit: - Sailja alleged that her husband was in illicit relationship with another woman Kalyani.

Held: - SC quashed the case of adultery registered against Andhra woman Kalyani at the instance of another woman Sailja who alleged that her husband was in illicit relationship with the former. While absolving Kalyani of criminal charges of adultery, the SC said:the provision is currently under criticism from certain quarters for showing a strong gender bias for it makes the position of a married woman almost as a property of her husband. But in terms of the law as it stands, it is evident from a plain reading of the Section 497 IPC that only a man can be prosecuted against and punished for the offence of adultery.

Judgment: Navy Commander KM Nanavati v/s businessman P Ahuja: April 27, 1959,

Suit: Nanavati shot dead Ahuja, for his illict relationship with his wife Sylvia.

Held: - That while Nanavati faced prosecution, Sylvia went scot free.

Judgment: Corporal HS Dhillon v/s AOC Indian Air Force: March November 28, 2013:

Suit: - A complaint was filed against Dhillon by victim's husband on March 17, 2013, for having sexual intercourse' with his wife, pre-medicated sedation, and extorting money by threatening to circulate her defamatory MMS.

Held: - That the Court of inquiry indicted him, and was dismissed from service under Section 20(3) of the Air Force Act. His appeal for relief to the Armed Forces Tribunal (AFT) was rejected.

RAPE:

Judgment: Chenthamara v/s State of Kerala (2009)(1) RCR (Criminal) 793 (Kerala): Sections 375 and 376, Explanation to Section 376 – Rape – Actual entry of penis through vagina essential to constitute rape under Section 375:

Held: - That to constitute offence of rape actual entry of penis through vagina resulting in rupture of hymen is not must.

- That, It will constitute offence if during process penis gets contact with any of the external portions of female genital organ.

Judgment: Chenthamara v/s State of Kerala (2009)(1) RCR (Criminal) 793 (Kerala):

Sections 375 and 376 – Rape – Meaning of expression "penetration":

Held: - That "Penetration" referred to in Section 375 IPC is something lesser in extent, nature and degree than what is ordinarily understood by the word "penetration", in common parlance, in the context of sexual intercourse

- That by virtue of the explanation to Section 375 IPC, in legal parlance for the sexual intercourse which is necessary for the offence of "rape", penile-vaginal entry is not a must, but even in the absence of such entry or rupture of hymen, offence of "rape" can be committed.

Judgment: S. Balaraman v/s State (2009)(4) RCR (Criminal) 724: (2009) Cri.i.j. 3603 (Madras)(DB): Section 376 – Rape:

Suit: - That girl aged 16 yrs., raped, while she was grazing sheep on the field.

Held: - That her testimony is natural, cogent and convincing and is corroborated by testimony of other witnesses and medical evidence.

- That conviction upheld.
- That the evidence of a victim of sex offence is entitled to great weight and there exist no circumstances which cast a shadow of doubt over her veracity.

Judgment: Jarnail Singh v/s The State of Haryana (2009)(2) RCR (Criminal) 544(P&H)

Section 376 – Rape with Consent - Prosecutrix above 16 yrs. of age

Suit: - That accused after alluring her took her away, to some other place, and he alongwith his co-accused, committed rape with her.

Held: - That prosecutrix above 16 yrs. of age.

- That did not mean that the prosecutrix was a consenting party.

Judgment: MQ Shaikh, V Jadhav and MS Ansari v/s The State of Maharashtra (2014) RCR (Criminal) Section 376 – Rape:

Suit: - That the accused had allegedly gangraped a telephone operator on July 31, 2013 and a photo journalist on August 22, 2013 at the Shakti Mills compound, Mumbai.

- That the Court framed a charge of repeat offence against the accused persons.

Section: - Under Sections 376 and 376E for repeat offenders in rape cases.

Held: - That Principal Sessions Judge observed that the accused had previous history of committing sexual acts presumed that they must have committed the present offence.

- That the Judge observed that the prosecution had made sufficient ground for framing of the charge.
- That the crime was not one committed in a moment of passion, but was pre-meditated...one has to respond to the cry of the victim for justice and that of the collective conscious of society.
- That the manner of offence was brutal. They sexually ravished the girl and left her in a pathetic state.
- That the Court held five accused persons guilty in both the gang rape cases.

Order: - Awarded life imprisonment in the telephone operator case.

- That in the photo journalist gang rape case, Special Public Prosecutor filed an application to add Section 376E, for awarding punishment for repeat offenders in rape cases in which the punishment can range from life imprisonment to death.

Order: - April 2014:-That convicts Shaikh, Jadhav and Ansari, common to both Shakti Mill gangrape cases, sentenced to death, while Khan and Ashfaque, convicts in one each case, sentenced to life imprisonment.

- July 2014: Juvenile Justice Board: awarded correctional sentence for 3 yrs to two juveniles, common to both Shakti Mill gangrape cases.

Judgment: Ranjodh Singh Gurvinder Singh, Virender Singh v/s State of Haryana (2014) RCR (Criminal) Section 376, 302 – Rape and Murder:

Suit: - That Ranjodh Singh alias Jodha, Gurvinder Singh alias Ginder and Virender Singh alias Vickey, allegedly abducted a teen, raped and then murdered her.

Section: - Under section 376-G, 302 of IPC.

Held: - That Additional District and Sessions Judge, Poonam Suneja awarded life imprisonment to the convicts after holding him guilty for raping the helpless teenage for gangrape as well as murder.

- That the verdict relied on the statements of the cyber experts victim's relatives and forensic science evidence.

Judgment: Davinder Singh v/s State of Punjab (2014): RCR (Criminal) Section 376: 302 – Rape:

Suit: - That Davinder Singh allegedly raped a mentally challenged girl.

- That the accused was caught by victim's relatives and neighbours, while trying to flee the spot, after committing the crime.

Section: - Under section 376.

Held: - That Additional District and Sessions Judge, Jaswinder Shhimar, awarded ten yrs. Jail to the convict after holding him guilty for raping the helpless mentally challenged girl.

- That the verdict relied on the statements of the victim's relatives and neighbours.

Judgment: Ram Kumar v/s State of UT, Chandigarh (2014):RCR (Criminal) Sections 376, 366-A – Rape and Procreation of minor girl:

Suit: - That Ram Kumar allegedly entered the house of the victim and sexually harassed her (a ten year old neighbour) by outraging her modesty.

- That the accused was arrested by the police on the complaint of the victim's mother.

Section: - Under Sections 376 and 366-A.

Held: - That Additional District and Sessions Judge presiding over the special court for crime against women, Anshu Shukla convicted Ram Kumar of sexually harassing a ten years old neighbour.

- That the Judge awarded ten yrs. Jail to the convict after holding him guilty for raping the helpless girl.

- That the verdict relied on the statements of the victim's mother.

Judgment: Shiva Verma v/s State of Punjab, SAS Nagar (2014):RCR (Criminal) Sections 376(i), 323 , 341 and 506 – Rape, beating, restraining and intimidating:

Suit: - That Verma had forcibly taken the victim to an abandoned house and raped and thrashed her (a 13-year old girl).

- That the accused was arrested by the police on the complaint of the victim's mother

Section: - Under Sections 376(i), 323, 341 and 506.

Held: - That Additional District and Sessions Judge presiding over the special court for crime against women, convicted Shiva Verma of sexually harassing a 13-year old girl.

- That the Judge awarded ten yrs. rigorous imprisonment to the convict after holding him guilty for raping the helpless girl.

- That the verdict relied on the statements of the victim's mother.

Judgment: Rahul, Ravi and Vinod v/s State (2014) RCR (Criminal) Section 376 – Rape:

Suit: - That the accused had allegedly gangraped a 19-year old woman, brutalised the victim, poured acid into her eyes and shoved a broken bottle inside her before killing her.

- That the Court framed a charge of rape and murder offences against the accused persons.

Section: - Under Sections 376 and 302 for rape and murder offences.

Held: - That Additional Sessions Judge of Delhi Court V Bhat, observed that the Rape and murder of a girl in her teens are a distinct class of offences and cannot be eduated to cases involving only rape or only murder. It is combination of two distinct heinous crimes that deserve capital punishment, adding, "The perpetrators of crime like rape and murder forfeit their right to live. Life imprisonment is highly inadequate in these cases. These criminals are a menace to the society and they don't deserve to be kept alive. Time has come when Courts should deal with such heinous crimes sternly in order to send a strong message...so that nobody dares to engage in such brutal crimes."

Order: - Awarded the death penalty to all three convicts for abduction, gangrape and murder, and imposed a fine of ₹ 1.6 lakh each on the convicts.

SODOMY:

Judgment: Shakalu v/s State (2009)(5) RCR(Criminal) 941(Delhi)(DB): Sodomy and murder:

Held: - That Sessions Judge observed that the accused had previous history of committing sexual acts both natural and unnatural, and presumed that he must have committed the present offence.

- That bad character of an accused is irrelevant in criminal trial unless and until he tries to prove his good character.
- That character of an accused would be relevant only for the purpose of deterrence of punishment.

Judgment: Pardeep Kumar v/s State (2014) RCR (Criminal) Panjab:

Sodomy and Murder:

Suit: - That the accused admitted to having sexually exploited the minor boy before suffocating him to death.

- That on the basis of accused's statement the police exhumed the body in the presence of a magistrate and a medical officer.

Section: - Under Sections 377, 365, 506 and 302 for unnatural sexual acts, kidnapping, criminal intimidation and murder.

Held: - That Additional Session Judge, Hoshiarpur, observed that it is a settled provision of law that the accused can be held guilty in case of circumstantial evidence, provided the prosecution proves its point beyond doubt.

- That the accused had previous history of committing sexual acts and murder of another minor in October last year, the trial is pending, thus presumed had committed the present offence.
- That the chain of events is complete and the allegations stand proved.
- That it is one of the most heinous crimes against children. The accused does not deserve any leniency.

Order: - Awarded imprisonment in jail till remainder of natural life and a fine of ₹ 50K.

Judgment: Chand v/s State (2014) RCR (Criminal) Panjab: Sodomy:

Suit: - That in September 2012, the accused alleged to having abducted minor boy (13 yrs old).

- That the accused indulged in an unnatural sex with the victim.

Section: - Under Sections 377, 365 and 506 IPC, for unnatural sexual acts, kidnapping and criminal intimidation.

Held: - That Additional District and Session Judge, SAS Nagar, observed that it is a settled provision of law that the accused held guilty of committing unnatural offence with a minor boy.

Order: - Awarded 3 yrs. imprisonment in jail and a fine of ₹ 3K, failing to pay which, the imprisonment would further be extended for three months.

Judgment: Dharambir v/s State UT, Chandigarh (2014) RCR (Criminal):

Sodomy:

Suit:
- That on September 28, 2013, the accused Dharambir waylaid the victim – a six years old boy, and then committed an unnatural offence on him.
- That the accused was arrested by the police on the complaint of the six years old's grandmother

Held:
- That Additional District and Sessions Judge presiding over the special court for crime against women, Anshu Shukla, awarded five years jail term to the convict and also imposed a fine of ₹ 5K.

Judgment: Shakalu v/s State (2009)(5) RCR(Criminal) 941(Delhi) (DB):

Sodomy and murder:

Held:
- That Sessions Judge observed that the accused had previous history of committing sexual acts both natural and unnatural, and presumed that he must have committed the present offence.
- That bad character of an accused is irrelevant in criminal trial unless and until he tries to prove his good character.
- That character of an accused would be relevant only for the purpose of deterrence of punishment.

SEXUAL OFFENCES IN UK:

Offence:
- That the Sexual Offences Act 2003 governs sex laws in the UK.
- That under this Act, it is an offence for any male to penetrate with his penis the vagina, anus or mouth of a female or male without their consent.

Penalty:
- That a person found guilty of this offence could be sent to prison for life.

Offence:
- That assault by penetration.
- That the Act makes it an offence for any male or female to penetrate the vagina or anus of another person without their consent.

- That he offence is committed where the penetration is by a part of the body e.g. a finger or anything else e.g. a bottle for sexual intent.

Penalty: - A person found guilty of this offence could be sent to prison for 10 yrs.

Offence: - Assault/Molestation.

The Act makes it an offence for any male or female to intentionally.

Touch/fondle another person sexually without his or her consent.

Penalty: - Under Section 3 of the Act, a person found guilty of this offence could be sent to prison for a maximum of ten years.

Offence: - Causing sexual activity without consent.

It is an offence to cause or encourage another person to engage in sexual activity without his or her consent.

Penalty: - If penetration is involved then a person found guilty of this offence could be sent to prison for life.

If no penetration is involved then a person found guilty of this offence could be sent to prison for upto ten years.

SHOPS and COMMERCIAL ESTABLISHMENTS Act, 1948

Judgment: Dr. Shubhada Mohwani v/s State of Maharashtra (2014), June 12, Bombay High Court 901-wp-1731-2002, of Judicature at Bombay.

Suit: - That case filed under Article 226 of Constitution of India.

- That petitioner challenged Section 7(1) of Bombay Shops and Establishments Act 1948.
- That petitioner is an RMP.
- That show cause notice served on petitioner for not obtaining a licence under the Bombay Shops and Establishments Act 1948 and criminal prosecution was launched against her for contravention of Section 7(1) of said Act.

- That prior to 1997 – legal and medical practitioners were not incld. under the definition of commercial establishment.
- That by filing a petition, legal professionals were excluded from definition of commercial establishment, by the Court.

Held: - That criminal prosecution against the petitioner is quashed.
- That petition is disposed of.

Relied: - Judgment: Dr. DM Surti vs State of Gujarat 1 AIR (1969) SC 63:

Held: That private dispensary of doctor is not a commercial establishment.

- Judgment: NK Fuladi and Anr. v/s State of Maharashtra: Maharashtra Law Journal (1985) page 1: Division Bench of Bombay High Court:

Held: That a legal practitioner having a office doesn't fall in definition of commercial establishment.

Reference: - PD Kode J and VM Kanade J.

TRANSPLANTATION OF HUMAN ORGANS Act, 1994

Criminal Procedure Code, 1973:

Judgment: Jeewan Kumar Raut v/s Central Bureau of Investigations (2009)(3)

RCR(Criminal) 587: (2009)(4) R.A.J. 336 (SC): Section 4:

Transplantation of Human Organs Act, 1994, Sections 18 and 19:

Investigation of offence under Transplantation of Human Organs Act (TOHO).

Suit: - That report lodged with SHO regarding to commission of offence under TOHO.

Held: - That SHO is not empowered to investigate the offence.
- That investigation in terms of Section 13(3)(iv) of TOHO, thus, must be conducted by an authorised officer.

- That nobody else could do it.
- That TOHO being a special Act and the matter relating to dealing with offences there under having been regulated by reason of the provisions thereof, there cannot be any manner of doubt whatsoever that the same shall prevail over the provisions of CrPC.
- That, If a special statute lays down procedures, the ones laid down under the general statutes shall not be followed.

Judgment: Jeewan Kumar Raut v/s Central Bureau of Investigations (2009)(3)

RCR(Criminal) 586: (2009)(4) R.A.J. 336 (SC):

Section 167(2) – Transplantation of Human Organs Act, 1994, Sections 18, 19, 20 and 22:

Suit:
- That accused arrested under transplantation of Human Organs Act (TOHO) and under Section 307 IPC.
- That CBI investigating the offence and filing complaint under Section 22 of TOHO.
- That separate Police report under Section 173(2) Cr.P.C. in respect of offences under IPC not filed (expiry of 90 days).
- That accused not entitled to bail under Section 167(2) Cr.P.C. as complaint filed in the Court within 90 days in terms of Section 22 of TOHO.

Judgment: Poonam Gupta v/s State of Punjab (2009) 3 RCR (Civil) 568 (P&H): Sections ((3) and 2(i): Bar on donation of Human Organs by strangers – "Near relatives" – "Commercial dealing in human organs":

Held:
- That the act categorically prohibits transplantation of human organ unless the donor is a near relative of the recipient except as per Section 9(3), by reason of affection or attachment or any other special reasons subject to prior approval of Authorisation faction or attachment or any other special reasons subject to prior approval of Authorisation Committee after holding an inquiry and its satisfaction.

- That, If the donor is found to be misrepresenting the facts, the authority can draw an inference:
- that he is not a bona fide donor
- that there can be no direct evidence of commercial dealings
- that the appreciation of facts and circumstances of each case would be required by the authorities to draw a logical inference
- that mere a remote and old intimacy between the parties cannot be construed their such an affection and attachment that the donor would outrightly beome ready to donate his body organs
- that approval of Authority held rightly refused.

Judgment: Hitesh Kishorechand Raithatha v/s State of Maharashtra (2009) 1 RCR (Criminal) 699 (Bombay) (Aur. Bench): Section 18:

Held:

- That removal of human organ is punishable if it is done for purpose of transplantation without authority.
- That removal of human organ during course of medical treatment or the operation without any kind of nexus with misuse of the same for transplantation will not come within ambit of Section 18.
- That in the instant case uterus of patient removed during operation without his consent.
- That no evidence on record to show that removal was done with a view to misuse it commercially for transplantation.
- That, It would not come with Section 18.

Judgment: Linda v/s Central Bureau of Investigation (2009) 1 RCR (Criminal) 808 (P&H): Sections 18,19, 20 and 22: Offence under Transplantation of Human Organ (TOHO) Act cognizable and non-bailable:

Held:

- That the cognizance of the offence under the TOHO Act in terms of Section 22 is to be taken on the basis of a complaint filed by concerned Appropriate Authority.

Judgment: Linda v/s Central Bureau of Investigation (2009) 1 RCR (Criminal) 807 (P&H): Sections 20,18 and 19: Criminal Procedure Code, Section 167(2): Offence of Kidney removal against the accused:

Held:

- That accused arrested under Sections 20, 18 and 19 of Transplantation of Organ (TOHO) Act.
- That offence is cognizable and non-bailable.
- That Police post-investigation not submitting challan under Section 173(2).

  Cr.P.C., but filed a complaint under Section 22 of TOHA Act within 90 days of arrest.
- That accused not entitled to bail under Section 167 Cr.P.C.AIR (1965) HP 37 and AIR (1963) Calcutta 191 Distt.

MEDICAL JURISPRUDENCE

VOLUME - 3

P. S. Kapoor
MBBS, MS, PCMS (Ex)

KALPAZ

©Author

All rights reserved. No part of this work may be reproduced, stored, adapted, or transmitted in any form or by any means, electronic, mechanical, photocopying, microfilming recording or otherwise, or translated in any language, without the prior written permission of the copyright owner and the publisher. The book is sold subject to the condition that it shall not, by way of trade or otherwise, be lent, resold, hired out, or otherwise circulated without the prior publisher's written consent in any form of binding or cover other than that in which it is published.

The views and opinions expressed in this book are author(s) own and the facts reported by them have been verified to the extent possible, and the publishers are not in any way liable for the same.

First Published, 2018

Published by

Kalpaz Publications
C-30, Satyawati Nagar,
Delhi – 110052
E-mail: kalpaz@hotmail.com
Ph.: 9212142040

Printed at: G. Print Process, Delhi

Cataloging in Publication Data—DK
Courtesy: D.K. Agencies (P) Ltd. <docinfo@dkagencies.com>

Kapoor, P. S., author.
Medical jurisprudence / Dr P.S. Kapoor.
volumes cm
Includes bibliographical references.
ISBN 9789386397584 (set : HB)
ISBN 9789386397614 (Vol-III :HB)

1. Medical laws and legislation—India. I. Title.

KNS1520.K37 2018 | DDC 344.54041 23

Contents

PART - II

MEDICAL JURISPRUDENCE

PART - III

STATE MEDICINE

PART - IV

APPENDIX

Part - III

STATE MEDICINE

CHAPTER - X

STATE MEDICINE

STATE MEDICINE

Definition: Is defined as field of medical practice pertaining to its social and legal aspects. As such the medical practice has become systematised and regulated under rules and regulations of current Medical Council, infringement of which will invite explanation, if not punishment. The modern medical science has made phenomenal advancement and stride forward in all its branches and sub-branches. People at large have become more conscious about their rights and privileges, and are aware of consumer rights to claim damage for the trauma suffered, which is assessed in terms of compensation awarded.

Medical Practitioners have got to be aware of their duties and responsibilities encompassing the legal aspect of the medical practice in their own interest. Their duties and responsibilities can be described vis-à-vis its legal aspect of medical practice as following:

- Duties to sick patient.
- Duty to offer proper regime of treatment and proper direction to the patient.
- Unwarranted delegation of duty of treating a patient to another doctor without express permission of the patient.
- Failure to properly attend and examine an accident patient in a hospital.

- Notification of infectious disease.
- Duties in respect of consultation with a specialist.
- Duties with regard to surgical operations.
- Duty of a doctor when he detects involvement of the patient in any criminal matter during the treatment.
- Doctor's duty in case of poisoning.
- Professional negligence or medical malpraxis.

Conclusion:

State Medicine envisages proper code of conduct of Registered Medical Practitioners, to guide and regulate their professional activities, to protect the community at large from quacks and charlatans against malpractice.

Doctor's medical practice is in many ways interlinked with legal implications which can be summarised as below:

- His/her duty towards the child and adult cannot be the same.
- Doctor's duty in emergency department is not only to render immediate treatment and relief to the patient and take life saving measures, but also to record dying declaration, etc, from the dying patient as part of his duty towards the State, as an insight into the circumstances relating to present moribund state of the patient; more to see that no crime goes undetected.
- An injured patient in the doctor's chamber may be injured victim or even an assailant in a case of crime – as per law, he is to be looked by the police and the attending doctor is duty bound to inform the police accordingly at the cost of himself getting booked or made liable under various sections of penal code.
- The GP need be aware of his duty to accord best of care and attention to his patient and issue fit certificate on cure and never to issue false certificate of illness at the cost of loosing his registration number, so also he is duty bound to

issue death certificate of the patient when he dies a natural death under his care and treatment, but the doctor is not to issue any death certificate of a patient:

(i) when he was not under his care and attention in his last illness

(ii) so also when the doctor is not sure about his cause and nature of death or

(iii) when there is any suspicion of foul play in the cause and nature of his death.

- The doctor is not to examine any female patient without a female attendant or without her consent in writing.
- The doctor is not to divulge any professional secrecy confided to him by the patient except on demand of trial court or of privileged communication. The doctor must be very careful and serious about negligence in care and treatment of the patient.
- More so in respect of criminal negligence than civil negligence
- The doctor need be aware about vicarious liability, contributory negligence, therapeutic misadventure, etc, as all the topics have some indirect relationship, with medical practice by one way or other.

Hence medical practice of today is intimately interlinked with legal need medico-legal implications by one way or other. The practising physician can only ignore this aspect of medical practice at the risk of getting himself involved in litigations and prosecution in courts of law – the serious outcome of these may be "professional death sentence with loss of registration number" or even imprisonment for varying periods by order of the courts of law.

Author: It is for the practising doctor to ponder and decide - 'What to do?' To be a law abiding dutiful doctor looking after his patients with due care and attention or be a carefree, charlatan oblivious of his duties and obligations as a doctor. He is to decide if to lead a life of shame as a guilty person all through rest of life or to have a dignified, respectful life of a senior citizen for the rest of life.

Precautions to be taken by Doctors/Hospitals/Nursing Homes:

Behaviour: Avoid rude, rough, temperamental behavoiour.

Consent: Informed consent to be taken for procedures in presence of witness.

Criticism: Avoid criticising colleagues

Examination: Always examine a female patient in presence of a female attendant/or female relative.

Monetary: Always explain to the patient and relatives, about the appx. cost of treatment.

Limitaions: Always know one's professional limitations.

Malpractice: Avoid referring the patient for unwanted laboratory test/X-rays etc. Avoid referring the patient to a particular laboratory/diagnostic centre for investigations.

Avoid using substandard drugs/materials.

Experimentation: Avoid experiments on a patient.

Secracy: Avoid disclosing medical information of the patient to any other third person Medical Records: Avoid manipulating/tampering/changing of medical records of the patient.

Certificates: Avoid issuing bogus certificates.

TORTURE

Definition: An act of deliberate hurting someone in order to compel them to confess:

"Deliberate systematic or wanton infliction of physical/or mental injury or damage by one or more persons acting alone or on the orders of the higher authority, to force another person to disclose information/to make a forced confession, or for any other reason".

(*Source:* World Medical Association in its Tokyo Declaration, 1975)

Violation: Global issue of Concern - Human Rights Violation:

Torture is considered as an important human rights violation – a worldwide misuse of power. "Any act by which severe pain or suffering (physical or mental) inflicted intentionally on a person for purposes e.g. obtaining information or a confession, punishing him for an act he/ she or a third person has committed/or is suspected of having committed, or intimidating/ or coercing him for any reason based on discrimination of any kind, when such pain or suffering is inflicted by/or at the instigation of/ or with the consent/or acquiescence of a public official/or another person acting in an official capacity, excluding pain of suffering inflicted from, inherent in or incidentals to lawful sanctions."

(*Source:* United Nations Convention, December 1991).

Motives:
- To extort a confession – misused as legal proof.
- To extract information.
- To punish a person.
- To suppress persons associated with tortured person (violent distortion).
- To torture/torment - prisoners, political opponents, by methods incld. water boarding etc.

Rehabilitation: Anti-torture and rehabilitation centre is in Copenhagen, Denmark, where torture victims are rehabilitated and studies are carried out on the effects of torture. So many works are done but many objectives are still to be fulfilled.

Sexual Torture

Sexual torture/assault is as old as human civilisation and has been prevalent since ancient times in one form or other.

Types:
- Mental: forced nakedness, humiliations, abuses, threats and forced to witness others being sexually tortured/assaulted.

- Physical: molestation/assault of victim by the tormentor or by using an Animal for physical contact with the victim.

Objectives/Motives:

- Forceful confession – misused as legal proof.
- Personal vendetta - by torturing individual or his family members.
- To pollute (defile) the race.
- To satiate - sexual starvation of soldiers at war by assaulting women of enemy.
- Ethnic conflicts.
- Personality disorder - sexual assault of men/ women in custody by a mentally deranged person.
- Misuse of custodial power - by sexual assault of victims in custody.
- Distortion of the personality - victim tortured to develop helplessness, loss of self-confidence, and worthlessness.
- To extract information.
- Family violence (domestic/or marital violence), child abuse, sexual harassment, rape, kid-napping, hostage taking and terrorist act and pornography etc. Should also be viewed as human right violation as its repercussions are far reaching in society.

Modus operandi:

: Psychological:

- Verbal abuses, threats, and humiliation, publically.
- Undressing (nudity) in front of opposite sex esp. fair sex.
- Being photographed in compromising positions.
- Forced to masturbate in front of others.
- Forced to watch sexual torture/assault of others.
- Forced to perform sexual torture/assault on other collegue victims.

Physical:

- Introduction of chillies, irritants etc. into eyes, mouth, vagina, or anus.

- Introduction of ants, rats, insects, etc. into vagina, or anus.
- Penetration of vagina, anus by batons, rods, handle bars, candles etc.
- Plucking of nails, fingers, teeth, toes by instruments.
- Use of burning cigarettes on sensitive parts (genitals, breasts etc.).
- Electrical shocks – given to sensitive parts.
- Mutilation of breasts, genitals, buttocks etc.

Sexual:

- Fondling, squeezing, kissing/sucking of breasts, buttocks, genitalia.
- Raped by person of same/opposite sex.
- Sexual assault (Rape etc.) by animals e.g. trained dogs, monkeys.

Prevention:

- Public awareness - to condemn these barbarous, uncivilised acts and fight against torture.
- Media support – esp. for women's rights, curbing domestic violence.
- Police and administration's support – for implemen-tation of law strictly.
- Motivation of National Commission for Women and ILO.
- Medical organisations participation - should spread the ethical principles that address human right and their violations.
- Motivation of Employers (Public and Private) – to set up women cells in order to curb sexual exploitation at their working places.
- Motivation of every physician to realize his/her duty to protest his/her fellow citizen against violation of his right.

(*Source:* Tokyo declaration, 1975)

Doctors and Torture:

Definition: A doctor may be involved illegally in the process of torture/assault directly or indirectly, either voluntarily (a human right activist) or under compulsion from the society, government or terrorists. He may participate unwillingly or unintentionally or may participate directly with malafide intentions.

Motives:
- To assess victim's threshold to tolerate pain/suffering.
- To provide professional knowledge and skill to the tormentor.
- To monitor torture/assault by means of medical therapy.
- To suppress medical information deliberately while issuing medical certificates esp. death certificates, surgical or autopsy reports etc.
- To conceal/withhold information about incidence of abuses.
- To participate actively in administering torture/assault.

Role of Doctors:

Ethical: Doctors in the government and military services are most vulnerable (under compulsions) to pressure from seniors, for these illegal acts.

Criminal Liability of Doctors

Definition: During the last decade doctor-patient relationship has deteriorated and criminal complaints against doctors esp. medical negligence have increased alarmingly.

Factors:
- Medical negligence.
- Behaviour of doctors/staff – rude, rough and unbearable.
- Cost factor – exorbitant rates of treatment.
- Lack of awareness among the masses about inherent risk.

Liability: Criminal law (u/s 304 and 304-A) is applicable to all. Doctors are no exception to it.

When Doctors Should Inform Police

Duty: Police must be informed in following cases, and failure to inform may result in legal penalties.

Cases
- of homicidal death
- of suicidal death
- of operational death (during or post-operative)
- of unnatural death
- of sudden, unexpected death
- of instant death post-treatment/or medicine reaction
- of undiagnosed death within 24 hrs. of admission
- of accidental deaths
- of poisoning, burns, tetanus, aids death
- of married woman dying within 7 yrs. of marriage
- of sexual offences:
  - Rape
- marriage related offences e.g. mock marriage, bigamy, adultery, criminal elopement, husband/ relatives subjecting wife to cruelty.
- of violence against Medical Services.

Procedure: Information to police should preferably be in writing, and a written acknowledgement to be obtained. If the information is telephonic, then note down name, belt no. and designation of the police.

Can a Doctor be Arrested and Bailed

Doctors have no immunity against arrest for the various criminal acts.

Offence: Cognizable (non-bailable under Section 304).

Examples:
- criminal negligence in treating, causing grievous injury/death, as per an F.I.R. filed by the patient/ relatives in the police station.
- dealing in illegal organ trading.
- dealing in unlawful sex-determination test (PNDT).

Offence: Non-cognizable (bailable under Section 304-A).

Examples:
- Criminal negligence in treating, causing simple injury.
- The police are reluctant/or refuse to register an F.I.R. The complaint has to be filed in the court of Judicial Magistrate.

Bail: Doctor is entitled to be released at the police level, by executing a personal release bond of sureties, or by orders of the Magistrate.

Anticipatory bail: In case of likelihood of a criminal complaint being filed against a doctor, he/she can apply for a anticipatory bail under Section 438(1), in order to avoid arrest by the police.

Limitation of Each Pathy and Speciality

- Graduates/GP (MBBS) can not perform Major Surgeries.
- General Surgeons can not perform CS and Hysterectomies.
- Gynecologist can not perform Ultrasonographies.
- Physician/Surgeons can not give General/Spinal Anesthesia.
- Specialist to restrict to his/her speciality.
- Dentist can not issue death certificate.
- Homeopath can not prescribe allopathic drugs.

Q. Can a Gynecologist with no formal training in Surgical Oncology perform Cancer Surgery on Breast ?

Ans: The situation is surprising. The following actions can be taken: A complaint can be lodged with the State Medical Council (SMC), against the gynaecologist, either by the patient, or by another doctor, under the the Medical Council of India (MCI) Regulations 2002. The MCI is likely to hold the gynaecologist guilty.

- A consumer complaint can be lodged with the Consumer Court, by a patient, alleging negligence, stating in the complaint that the treating doctor did not take the informed consent in the sense that she did not inform the patient, that she had no qualification in general surgery, plastic surgery, or oncology surgery. The Consumer Court, depending on the facts of the case, may award compensation. The doctor's indemnity insurance co. May refuse to pay the compensation on the ground that she exceeded her scope of risk by performing oncological surgery while she declared herself to be a gynecologist while buying the policy.

- A complaint can be lodged with the State Health Directorate (or to the Authority established under the Clinical Establishment Act, or the Nursing Home Act, as applicable) against the hospital concerned for employing not fully qualified persons and thereby exposing patients and public to health hazards and also for violating the provisions of the act concerned. The Authorities are likely to hold the hospital guilty.

Dr. MC Gupta (Advocate)

MD (Medicine) LLM, Health and Medico-legal Consultant, New Delhi.

CHAPTER - XI

MEDICAL ETHICS

HIPPOCRATIC OATH

Definition: Is defined as the promise made by the medical students, at the time of graduation, that they will obey the principles of the medical profession.

Oath: "I will look upon him who shall have taught me this Art even as one of my parents. I will share my substance with him, and I will supply his necessities, if he be in need. I will regard his offspring even as my own brethren, and I will teach them this Art, if they would learn it, without fee or covenant. I will impart this Art by precept, by lecture and by every mode of teaching, not only to own sons, but to the sons of him who taught me, and to disciples bound by covenant and oath, according to the Law of Medicine the regimen I adopt shall be for the benefit of my patients according to my ability and judgment, and not for their hurt or for any wrong. I will give no deadly drug to any, though it be asked of me, nor will I counsel such, and especially, I will not aid a woman to procure abortion.

"Whatever house I enter, there will I go for the benefit of the sick, refraining from all wrongdoing or corruption, and especially from any act of seduction, of male or female, of bond or free. Whatsoever things I see or hear concerning the life of men, in my attendance on the sick, or even apart therefrom, which ought not to be noised abroad, I will keep silence thereon,

counting such things to be as sacred secrets."
(Hippokrates......born about 460 B.C.)

CODE of MEDICAL ETHICS

Drawn up with the approval of the Central Government under Section 33 of the Indian Medical Council Act:

Observation: Every doctor whether at a Government Hospital or otherwise has the professional obligation to extend his services for protecting life. The obligation being total, absolute and paramount, laws of procedure whether in statutes or otherwise cannot be sustained and therefore, must give way. "It is the duty of the doctor in an emergency to begin treatment of the patient and he should not await the arrival of the police or to complete the legal formalities. The life of a person is far more important than legal formalities. This view is in accordance with the Hippocratic oath of doctors as mentioned in George Bernard Shaw's play: The Doctor's Dilemma." The medical profession is a noble profesion and it should not be brought down to the level of a simple business or commerce. The truth of the matter, sadly, is that today in India many doctors (though not all) have become totally money-minded, and have forgotten their Hippocratic oath. Since most people in India are poor, the consequence is that for them proper medical treatment is next to impossible, and hence they have to rely on quacks. This is a disgrace to a noble profession.

Medical Ethics for Doctors:

Definition: Defined as the special rules and regulations from the point of view of morality (as per Hippocratic oath), which a doctor should follow, although its violation is not an offence legally, but is shameful and disgraceful from the point of view of medical profession (plethora of stigmata associated with medical profession).

Principles: To follow the principles in Good Medical Practice e.g.:

- To make the patient's care, doctor's first concern.
- To protect and promote the health of patients and the public.
- To provide a good standard of practice and patient's care.
- To raise concern about patient's safety with the employing body.
- To avoid treating a close personal relation.
- To provide emergency treatment, wherever required, taking account of their own's safety, their competence and the availability of other options for care.
- To upgrade their knowledge and skill regularly.
- To maintain and improve their performance.
- To be willing to contribute to activities e.g. teaching, training, appraising and assessing doctors.
- To provide the patients the information they want or need in a way they can understand.
- To maintain healthy doctor-patient relationship.
- To communicate effectively with the patients.
- To safeguard and protect the health and well-being of children and young people.
- To be considerate to relatives, carers, partners and others close to the patient and be sensitive and responsive in providing required information and support, esp. after a patient has died.
- To have consent prior to undertake any examination or investigation, provide any form of treatment.
- To treat information about patients as confidential, including after a patient's death.
- To respect the skills and contributions of your colleagues.
- To avoid malicious and unfounded criticism of their colleagues, that may undermine patients'

trust in the care or treatment they receive, or in the judgement of those treating them.

- To share information with other healthcare professionals is important for safe and effective patient care.
- To be honest and trustworthy and acting with integrity: this is at the heart of medical professionalism.
- To be honest and trustworthy when writing reports, and when completing, signing or issuing forms, reports and other documents e.g. certificates etc.
- To inform patients about their fees and charges, wherever possible prior to asking for their consent to treatment.
- To act in their patients' best interests when making referrals and when providing or arranging treatment or care. They must not ask for or accept any inducement, gift or hospitality which may affect or be seen to affect the way they prescribe for, treat or refer patients. They must not offer such inducements to colleagues.

DO's and DON't for DOCTORS

Do's:

- Provide First aid medicare to an emergency case, even if it is ML case
- Provide immediate medicare to serious cases on priority basis (Triage)
- Provide medicare to HIV/AIDS patients without any reservation
- Provide medicare without any Ethnic discrimination
- Provide medicare at-par to poor and rich patients
- Record precisely the history of illness and physical examination
- Record history of any drug allergy
- Consult senior/specialist in case of any difficulty in diagnosis or treatment

- Mention clearly your name, qualification, designation and registration number on your prescription slip
- Listen attentively and look carefully
- Write prescription, discharge slip, certificates/ documents clearly
- Always confine to your own speciality
- Always respect the interests of your colleague
- Record precisely the history of illness and physical findings -

Don't:

- Don't examine, when you are sick, exhaust or under influence of alcohol or Intoxicated
- Don't be overconfident – do anything beyond your competence
- Don't hesitate to consult your senior/specialist, while not sure what to do
- Don't refuse the patient's right to examine, to know diagnosis and treatment
- Don't withhold information
- Don't examine a female patient without a female nurse/or attendant
- Don't argue with an annoyed patient
- Don't scold attendants
- Don't insist for the history of illness or examination in presence of others
- Don't prescribe without examining the patient
- Don't adopt experimental method
- Don't advise unnecessary investigations/tests
- Don't over prescribe drugs
- Don't leave dead body unattended at the time of death
- Don't hesitate to extend your condolences and sympathies
- Don't issue death certificate without verification
- Don't issue/divulge false, misleading reports/ information
- Don't refuse first aid treatment to an emergency case

- Don't refuse medicare to an HIV/AIDS patient
- Don't perform MTP without possessing the required permission
- Don't perform MTP at an unauthorized place
- Don't talk loose of your colleagues
- Don't overstep your speciality – better restrict to your speciality:
- GP (MBBS) can't perform major surgeries
- General Surgeon can't perform hysterectomy, Caesarean section
- Gynecologist can't perform herniectomy, ultrasonography
- Surgeon/Physician can't give general and spinal anesthesia
- Dentist can't issue the death certificate
- Homeopath and Ayurved can't prescribe Allopathic drugs.

GOOD MEDICAL PRACTICE

Definition: Good Medical Practice sets out the principles & values on which good practice is founded; these principles together describe medical professionalism in action. The guidance is addressed to the doctors, but it is also intended to let the public know what they can expect from doctors.

Aim:
- That patient should be able to trust doctors with their lives and health.
- That to justify trust, doctors must have respect for human life.

Duties: Of a Doctor registered with the Medical Council:
- Make the care of your patient your first concern
- Protect and promote the health of patients and the public
- Provide a good standard of practice and care
- Keep your professional knowledge and skills up to date
- Recognise and work within the limits of your competence

  - Work with colleagues in the ways that best serve patients' interests
  - Treat patients as individuals and respect their dignity
  - Treat patients politely and considerately
  - Respect patients' right to confidentiality
  - Work in partnership with patients
  - Listen to patients and respond to their concerns and preferences
- Give patients the information they want or need in a way they can Understand
- Respect patients' right to reach decisions with you about their treatment and care
- Support patients in caring for themselves to improve and maintain their health
- Be honest and open and act with integrity
- Act without delay if you have good reason to believe that you or a colleague may be putting patients at risk
- Never discriminate unfairly against patients or colleagues
- Never abuse your patients trust in you or the public's trust in the profession.

Principles: How Good Medical Practice applies to you:

It is responsibility of all registered doctors to be familiar with Good Medical Practice and to follow the guidance it contains. The doctor must be prepared to explain and justify his/her decisions and actions.

Terms used: 'You must' is used for an overriding duty or principle.

'You should' is used when we are providing an explanation of how you will meet the overriding duty.

Serious or persistent failure to follow this guidance will put your registration at risk.

Good doctors:

1. Patients need good doctors. Good doctors make the care of their patients their first concern: they are competent, keep their knowledge and skills

up-to- date, establish and maintain good relationships with patients and colleagues.

(Those a doctor works with or not they are also doctors) are honest and trustworthy, and act with integrity.

Good Clinical Care:

Providing good clinical care:

2. Good clinical care must incld.:

(a) adequately assessing the patient's conditions, taking account of the history, (incld. the symptoms, and psychological and social factors), the patient's views, and where necessary examining the patient.

(b) providing or arranging advice, investigations or treatment where necessary

(See paragraph 21b and GMC consent guidance)

(c) referring a patient to another practitioner, when this is in the patient's best interests.

3. In providing care you must:

(a) recognise and work within the limits of your competence

(b) prescribe drugs or treatment, incld. repeat prescriptions, only when you have adequate knowledge of the patient's health, and are satisfied that the drugs or treatment serve the patient's needs

(See GMC prescribing guidance paragraph 38)

(c) provide effective treatments based on the best available evidence

(d) take steps to alleviate pain and distress whether or not a cure may be possible

(See paragraph 21b)

(e) respect the patient's right to seek a second opinion

(f) keep clear, accurate and legible records, reporting the relevant clinical findings, the decisions made, the information given to patients, and any drugs prescribed or other investigation or treatment

(g) make records at the same time as the events you are recording or as soon as possible afterwards

(h) be readily accessible when you are on duty

(i) consult and take advice from colleagues,when appropriate

(j) make good use of the resources available to you.

(See GMC management guidance).

Supporting self-care:

4. You should encourage patients and the public to take an interest in their health and to take action to improve and maintain it. This may incld. advising patients on the effects of their life choices on their health and well-being and the possible outcomes of their treatments.

   (See endnote 1)

Avoid treating those close to you:

5. Wherever possible, you should avoid providing medical care to anyone with whom you have a close personal relationship.

   (See paragraph 77)

Raising concerns about safety:

6. If you have good reason to think that patient safety is or may be seriously compromised by inadequate premises, equipment, or other resources, policies or systems, you should put the matter right if that is possible. In all other cases you should draw the matter to the attention of your employing or contracting body. If they do not take adequate action, you should take independent advice on how to take the matter further. You must record your concerns and the steps you have taken to try to resolve them.

   (See GMC management guidance and GMC guidance on raising concerns)

Decisions about access to medical care:

7. The investigations or treatment you provide or arrange must be based on the assessment you and the patient make of their needs and priorities, and on your clinical judgement about the likely effectiveness of the treatment options. You must not refuse or delay treatment because you believe that a

patient's actions have contributed to their condition. You must treat your patients with respect whatever their life choices and beliefs. You must not unfairly discriminate against them by allowing your personal views (This includes your views about a patient's age, colour, culture, disability, ethnic or national origion, gender, lifestyle, marital or parental status, race, religion or beliefs, sex, sexual orientation, or social or economic status) to affect adversely your professional relationship with them or the treatment you provide or arrange. You should challenge colleagues if their behaviour does not comply with the guidance.

(See GMC guidance on valuing diversity).

8. If carrying out a particular procedure or giving advice about it conflicts with your religious or moral beliefs, and this conflict might affect the treatment or advice you provide, you must explain this to the patient and tell them they have the right to see another doctor. You must be satisfied that the patient has sufficient information to enable them to exercise that right. If it is not practical for a patient to arrange to see another doctor, you must ensure that arrangements are made for another suitably qualified colleague to take over your role.

9. You must give priority to the investigation and treatment of patients on the basis of clinical need, when such decisions are within your power. If inadequate resources, Plicies or systems prevent you from doing this, and patient safety is or may be seriously compromised, you must follow the guidance in paragraph 6.

   (See paragraph 6).

10. All patients are entitled to care and treatment to meet their clinical needs. You must not refuse to treat a patient because their medical condition may put you at risk. If a patient poses a risk to your health or safety, you should take all available steps to minimise the risk before providing treatment or making suitable alternative arrangements for treatment.

Treatment in emergencies:

11. In an emergency, wherever it arises, you must offer assistance, taking account of your own safety, your competence, and the availability of other options for care.

Maintaining good medical practice:

Keeping uptodate:

12. You must keep your knowledge and skills up-to-date throughout your working life. You should be familiar with relevant guidelines and development s that affect your work. You should regularly take part in educational activities that maintain and further develop your competence and performance.

    (See endnote 2 and GMC guidance on continuing professional development).

13. You must keep up-to-date with, and adhere to, the laws and codes of practice relevant to your work.

Maintaining and improving your performance:

14. You must work with colleagues and patients to maintain and improve the quality of your work and promote patient safety.

    In particular you must:

(a) maintain a folder of information and evidence, drawn from your medical practice

(b) reflect regularly on your standards of medical practice in accordance with GMC guidance on licencing and revalidation

(c) take part in regular and systematic audit

(d) take part in systems of quality assurance and quality improvement

(e) respond constructively to the outcome of audit, appraisals and performance reviews, undertaking further training where necessary

    (See endnote 3)

(f) help to resolve uncertainties about the effects of treatments

(g) contribute to confidential inquiries and adverse event recognition and reporting, to help reduce risk to patients

    (See endnote 4)

(h) report suspected adverse drug reactions in accordance with the relevant reporting scheme (See endnote 5 and GMC prescribing guidance)

(i) co-operate with legitimate requests for information from organisations monitoring public health – when doing so you must follow the guidance in Confidentiality: Protecting and providing information. (See GMC confidentiality guidance)

Teaching and training, appraising and assessing

15. Teaching, training, appraising and assessing doctors and students are important for the care of patients now and in the future. You should be willing to contribute to these activities.
16. If you are involved in teaching you must develop the skills, attitude and practices of a competent teacher.
17. You must make sure that all staff for whom you are responsible, incld. locums and students, are properly supervised.
18. You must be honest and objective when appraising or assessing the performance of colleagues, incld. locums and students. Patients will be put at risk if you describe as competent someone who has not reached or maintained a satisfactory standard of practice. are properly supervised.
19. You must provide only honest, justifiable and accurate comments when giving references for, or writing reports about, colleagues. When providing references you must do so promptly and incld. all information that is relevant to your colleague's competence, performance or conduct.

    (See paragraph 63)

Relationships with patients:

The doctor-patient partnership:

20. Relationships based on openness, trust and good communication will enable you to work in partnership with your patients to address their individual needs.

21. To fulfil your role in the doctor-patient partnership you must:
(a) be polite, considerate and honest
(b) treat patients with dignity
(c) treat each patient as an individual
(d) respect patients' privacy and right to confidentiality
(e) support patients in caring for themselves to improve and maintain their health
(f) encourage patients who have knowledge about their condition to use this when they are making decisions about their care.

Good communication:

22. To communicate effectively you must:
(a) listen to patients, ask for and respect their views about their health, and respond to their concerns and preferences
(b) share with patients, in a way they can understand, the information they want or need to know about their condition, its likely progression, and the treatment options available to them, incld. associated risks and uncertainties

(See GMC consent guidance paragraphs 4-13)

(c) respond to patients' questions and keep them informed about the progress of their care
(d) make sure that patients are informed about how information is shared within teams and among those who will be providing their care.

(See GMC confidentiality guidance paragraphs 8, 10-15 and FAQ 3)

23. You must make sure, wherever practical, that arrangements are made to meet patients language and communication needs.

(See GMC consent guidance paragraph 13)

Children and young people:

24. The guidance that follows in paragraphs 25-27 is relevant whether or not you routinely see children and young people as patients. You should be aware of the needs and welfare of children and young

people when you see patients who are parents or carers, as well as any patients who may represent a danger to children or young people.

(See GMC consent guidance paragraphs 23-24 and Appendix A. See endnote 6)

25. You must safeguard and protect the health and well-being of children and young people.
26. You should offer assistance to children and young people if you have reason to think that their rights have been abused or denied.
27. When communicating with a child or young person you must:

(a) treat them with respect and listen to their views

(b) answer their questions to the best of your ability

(c) provide information in a way they can understand.

28. The guidance in paragraphs 25-27 is about children and young people, but the principles also apply to other vulnerable groups.

Relatives, carers and partners:

29. You must be considerate to relatives, carers, partners and others close to the patient, and the sensitive and responsive in providing information and support, incld. after a patient has died. In doing this you must follow the guidance in Confidentiality: Protecting and providing information.

(See endnote 7 and GMC confidentiality guidance)

Being open and honest with patients if things go wrong:

30. If a patient under your care has suffered harm or distress, you must act immediately to put matters right, if that is possible. You should offer an apology and explain fully and promptly to the patient what has happened, and the likely short-term and long-term effects.

(See endnote 8)

31. Patients who complain about the care or treatment they have received have a right to expect a prompt, open, constructive and honest response incld. an explanation and, if appropriate, an apology. You

must not allow a patient's complaint to affect adversely the care or treatment you provide or arrange.

Maintaining trust in the profession:

32. You must not use your professional position to establish or pursue a sexual or improper emotional relationship with a patient or someone close to them.

    (See GMC guidance on maintaining boundaries)

33. You must not express to your patients your personal beliefs, incld. political, religious or moral beliefs, in ways that exploit their vulnerability or that are likely to cause them distress.

34. You must take out adequate insurance or professional indemnity cover for any part of your practice not covered by an employer's indemnity scheme, in your patients' interests as well as your own.

35. You must be familiar with your GMC reference number. You must make sure you are identifiable to your patients and colleagues, for example by using your registered name when signing statutory documents, incld. prescriptions. You must make your registered name and GMC reference number available to anyone who asks for them.

    (See GMC guidance on registration numbers)

Working with colleagues:

Working in teams

41. Most doctors work in teams with colleagues from other professions. Working in teams does not change your personal accountability for your professional conduct and the care you provide. When working in a team, you should act as a positive role model and try to motivate and inspire your colleagues. You must:

(a) respect the skills and contributions of your colleagues

(b) communicate effectively with colleagues understand your role and responsibilities in the team, and who is responsible for each aspect of patient care

(c) participate in regular reviews and audit of the standards and performance of the team, taking steps to remedy any deficiencies.

(d) support colleagues who have problems with performance, conduct or health.

42. If you are responsible for leading a team, you must follow the guidance in Management for doctors.

(See GMC management guidance).

Conduct and performance of colleagues

43. You must protect patients from risk of harm posed by another colleague's conduct, performance or health. The safety of patients must come first at all times. If you have concerns that a colleague may not be fit to practice, you must take appropriate steps without delay, so that the concerns are investigated and patients protected where necessary. This means you must give an honest explanation of your concerns to an appropriate person from your employing or contracting body, and follow their procedures.

(See confidentiality FAQ 16 and the following GMC guidance on referring a doctor, raising concerns, and management).

44. If there are no appropriate local systems, or local systems do not resolve the problem, and you are still concerned about the safety of patients, you should inform the relevant regulatory body. If you are not sure what to do, discuss your concerns with an impartial colleague or contact your defence body, a professional organisation, or the GMC for advice. (See GMC guidance on raising concerns)

45. If you have management responsibilities you should make sure that systems are in place through which colleagues can raise concerns about risks to patients, and you must follow the guidance in Management for doctors.

(See GMC management guidance)

Respect for colleagues

46. You must treat your colleagues fairly and with respect. You must not bully or harass them, or

unfairly discriminate against by allowing your personal views (about a colleague's age, colour, culture, disability, ethnic or national origion, gender, lifestyle, marital or parental status, race, religion or beliefs, sex, sexual orientation, or social or economic status) to affect adversely your professional relationship with them. You should challenge colleagues if their behaviour does not comply with this guidance.

(See GMC guidance on valuing diversity)

47. You must not make malicious and unfounded criticism of colleagues that may undermine patients trust in the care or treatment they receive, or in the judgement of those treating them.

Arranging cover

48. You must be satisfied that, when you are off duty, suitable arrangements have been made for your patients' medical care. These arrangements should incld. effective hand-over procedures, involving clear communication with healthcare colleagues. If you are concerned that the arrangements are not suitable, you should take steps to safeguard patient care and you must follow the guidance in paragraph 6.

(See paragraph 6)

Taking up and ending appointments

49. Patient care may be compromised if there is not sufficient medical cover. Therefore, you must take up any post, incld. a locum post, you have formally accepted, and you must work your contractual notice period, unless the employer has reasonable time to make other arrangements.

Sharing information with colleagues

50. Sharing information with other healthcare professionals is important for safe and effective patient care.

51. When you refer a patient, you should provide all relevant information about the patient, incld. their medical history and current condition.

(See GMC confidentiality guidance paragraph 10)

52. If you provide treatment or advice for a patient, but are not the patient's general practitioner, you should tell the general practitioner the results of the investigations, the treatment provided and any other information necessary for the continuing care of the patient, unless the patient objects.
53. If a patient has not been referred to you by a general practitioner, you should ask for the patient's consent to inform their general practitioner before starting treatment, except in emergencies or when it is impractical to do so.

    If you do not inform the patient's general practitioner, you will be responsible for providing or arranging all necessary after-care.

Delegation and referral

54. Delegation involves asking a colleague to provide treatment or care on your behalf. Although you will not be accountable for the decisions and actions of those to whom you delegate, you will still be responsible for the overall management of the patient, and accountable for your decision to delegate.

    When you delegate care or treatment you must be satisfied that the person to whom you delegate has the qualifications, experience, knowledge and skills to provide the care or treatment involved. You must always pass on enough information about the patient and the treatment they need.
55. Referral involves transferring some or all of the responsibility for the patient's care, usually temporarily and for a particular purpose, such as additional investigation, care or treatment that is outside your competence.

    You must be satisfied that any healthcare professional to whom you refer a patient is accountable to a statutory regulatory body or employed within a managed environment. If they are not, the transfer of care will be regarded as delegation, not referral. This means you remain responsible for the overall management of the patient, and accountable for your decision to delegate.

Probity:

Being honest and trustworthy

56. Probity means honest and trustworthy, and acting with integrity: this is at the heart of medical professionalism.

57. You must make sure that your conduct at all times justifies your patients' trust in you and the public's trust in the profession.

58. You must inform the GMC without delay if, anywhere in the world, you have accepted a caution, been charged with or found guilty of a criminal offence, or if another professional body has made a finding against your registration as a result of fitness to practice procedures.

    (See GMC guidance on reporting convictions)

59. If you are suspended by an organisation from a medical post, or have restrictions placed on your practice you must, without delay, inform any other organisations for which you undertake medical work and any patients you see independently.

Providing and publishing information about your services

60. If you publish information about medical services, you must make sure the information is factual and verifiable.

61. You must not make unjustifiable claims about the quality or outcomes of your services in any information you provide to patients. It must not offer guarantees of cures, not exploit patient' vulnerability or lack of medical knowledge.

62. You must not pressure on people to use a service, for example by arousing ill-founded fears for their future health.

Writing reports and CVs, giving evidence and signing documents

63. You must be honest and trustworthy when writing reports, and when completing or singing forms, reports and other documents.

64. You must always be honest about your experience, qualifications and position, particularly when applying for posts.
65. You must do your best to make sure that any documents you write or sign are not false or misleading. This means that you must take reasonable steps to verify the information in the documents, and that you must not deliberately leave out relevant information.
66. If you have agreed to prepare a report, complete or sign a document or provide evidence, you must do so without unreasonable delay.
67. If you are asked to give evidence or act as a witness in litigation or formal inquiries, you must be honest in all your spoken and written statements.

    You must make clear the limits of your knowledge or competence.

    (See paragraph 3a)
68. You must co-operate fully with any formal inquiry into the treatment of a patient and with any complaints procedure that applies to your work. You must disclose to anyone entitled to ask for it any information relevant to an investigation into your own or a colleague's conduct, performance or health.

    In doing so, you must follow the guidance in Confidentiality: Protecting and providing information.

    (See GMC confidentiality guidance)
69. You must assist the coroner or procurator fiscal in an inquest or inquiry into a patient's death by responding to their enquiries and by offering all relevant information. You are entitled to remain silent only when your evidence may lead to criminal proceedings being taken against you.

    (See GMC confidentiality guidance)

Research

70. Research involving people directly or indirectly is vital in improving care and reducing uncertainty for patients now.

71. If you are involved in designing, organising or carrying out research, you must:

(a) put the protection of the participants interests first

(b) act with honesty and integrity

(c) follow the appropriate national research governance guidelines and the guidance in Research: The role and responsibilities on doctors.

(See GMC research guidance and endnote 10)

Financial and commercial dealings

72. Research involving people directly or indirectly is vital in improving care and reducing uncertainty for patients now and in the future, and improving the health of the population as a whole.

73. You must be honest in financial and commercial dealings with employers, insurers and other organisations or individuals.

In particular:

(a) before taking part in discussions about buying or selling goods or services, you must declare any relevant financial or commercial interest that you or your family might have in the transaction

(b) if you manage finances, you must make sure the funds are used for the purpose for which they were intended and are kept in a separate account from your personal finances.

Conflicts of interest

74. You must act in your patients' best interests when making referrals and when providing or arranging treatment or care. You must not ask for or accept any inducement, gift or hospitality which may affect or be seen to affect the way you prescribe for, treat or refer patients. You must not offer such inducements to colleagues.

(See GMC guidance on conflicts of interest and endnote 11)

75. If you have financial or commercial interests in organisations providing healthcare or in pharmaceutical or other biomedical companies, these

interests must not affect the way you prescribe for, treat or refer patients.

(See GMC prescribing guidance paragraphs 10-12)

76. If you have a financial or commercial interest in an organisation to which you can to refer a patient for treatment or investigation, you must tell the patient about your interest. When treating NHS patients you must also tell the healthcare purchaser.

Health

77. You should be registered with a general practitioner outside your family to ensure that you have access to independent and objective medical care. You should not treat yourself.

78. You should protect your patients, your colleagues and yourself by being immunised against common serious communicable diseases where vaccines are available.

(See endnote 12)

79. If you know that you have, or think that you might have, a serious condition that you could pass on to patients, or if your judgement or performance could be affected by a condition or its treatment, you must consult a suitably qualified colleague. You must ask for and follow their advice about investigations, treatment and changes to your practice that they consider necessary. You must not rely on your own assessment of the risk you pass to patients.

(*Source:* Good Medical Practice, 2006, General Medical Council, UK)

References:

1. An Experienced Teacher: Medical Jurisprudence and Toxicology. Current Publishers, 7, Indian Mirror Street, Calcutta, 1965.
2. Chawla, B.S., Advocate: Total Digest 2009, Year Book Chawla Publications (P) Ltd., Chandigarh, 2010.
3. General Medical Council: Good Medical Practice. Guidance for Doctors. London, 2006.

4. Gupta, M.C.: Clinical Establishments Bill – A Critique. The Doctor's People, Vol. III, Issue 03, 05-09, AICL, New Delhi, 2010.
5. Gupta, MC: Can a Gynecologist with no formal training in surgical oncology perform cancer surgery on breast ? ARTICLE.
6. Halder, S.: Medical negligence – Indian Penal Code and vis-à-vis medical profession. Journal of Indian Medical Association, Vol. 108, No. 07, Kolkata, 2010.
7. Universal Law Publishing Co. Pvt. Ltd.: Criminal Minor Acts. Universal Law Publishing Co. Pvt. Ltd., New Delhi, 2009.

CHAPTER - XII

ISSUES

ISSUES:
- Abetment to Suicide
- Acid Attacks Trauma
- Advertising Medical Services
- Agony of Senior Citizens
- Alcohol Abuse
- All India Bar Examination (AIBE)
- Article 370
- Batchelor of Rural Medicine (BRM)
- Child Abuse / Vulnerable childhood / No Country for children
- Clinical Establishment Act (CEA)
- Consumer Protection Act (CPA)
- Domestic Violence (Intimate-partner violence)
- Dowry Menace
- Eve-teasing
- Euthanasia
- Honour Killing
- Homicide
- Indecent Portrayal of Women
- Judicial Moralism
- Medical Education
- Medical Negligence
- Medical Profession
- Mandatory Rural Posting for PG Examination Entry

- National Commission for Human Resources for Health
- Pre-natal Sex Determination
- Rape
- Sexual Harassment at working place
- Torture:
  - Physical Torture
  - Psychological Torture: Trolls and Sadists
- Violence Against Medical Establishments
- Violence against Women

ABETMENT TO SUICIDE (Decriminalise suicide attempts)

Preface: Is to incite by encouragement or aid someone to commit suicide, which is wrong or illegal. In India-2011 (National Crime Records) about 1.35 lakh people took their own lives (372 suicides/day i.e. 16 suicides/hr.). While social and financial factors have been the major causes to commit suicide, in case of females, emotional and personnel being the primary reasons. Although the actual numbers may be much higher than these as the statistics only pertain to reported cases. Recently, an increasing trend of enacting publically, suicide threats (pressurising tactics) on minor subjects, in order to gain cheap publicity. Many a times, jilted lovers climb high rise buildings/water tanks, threatend to end their lives, thereby disturbing public's peace and tranquility. That in cases of hunger strikes, incld. fast-unto-death, these tactics are resorted to pressurise concerned authority to concede to agitator/s demand/s. Mostly the intention of agitator n't to kill him/herself. Only in case of agitator's refusal to take meals and fluids and in case of imminent danger to life, he/she may be held under the Attempt to Suicide Act.

Courting trouble (social and financial):

That the lust for power and everything that comes with it has been driving women to disaster.

Lured by the majestic ways of the rich world of the high and mighty, many of them have been entering into forbidden liaisons only to realise, much later, that they have tied the knot with trouble. Some of them had to pay with their lives for attempts to break free from the shackles of a mundane middle-class existence.

Cases:

- Anuradha Bali, alias Fiza, who entered into a murky relationship with a Deputy CM Haryana, Chander Mohan, and hit the headlines, was just one of them whose love story ended in tragedy. Their marriage lasted only forty days, and nobody realised that she would end up like so many other victims of "forbidden love". Her maggot-infested body was found in a highly decomposed state in her house in SAS Nagar.
- Shivani Bhatnagar, Monika Kapila and Madhumita met the fatal end with hardly any difference, while Monica Bedi is the only exception..
- Shivani Bhatnagar murder: Shivani, a journalist who went beyond the call of her duty and entered into a relationship with IPS officer RK Sharma, the prime accused in her murder, was acquitted by the High Court after spending ten years in jail. Nothing substantial came out of the allegations, but Shivani Bhatnagar's life and death have brought out the dangers of associating with the high and mighty. Shivani was killed by two men in her East Delhi flat on January 23, 1999.
- Monika Kapila and DSP Balraj Gill, could have carried on with their clandestine relationship, but for their brutal murder on February 1, 2012 at a farmhouse, near Ludhiana, by three robbers. The robbery brought to fore the forbidden relationship Monika and the DSP were sharing, and were frequent visitors to the farmhouse. Though both were already married, they entered into a relationship which did not see the light of the day.

- Madhumita Shukla killing: Poetess Madhumita's life turned topsy-turvy after she allegedly entered into a relationship with UP Minister Amarmani Tripathi. Madhumita was six months pregnant when she was shot dead at her house in Lucknow in May, 2003. Tripathi is still in jail.
- Geetika Sharma suicide: Airhostess Geetika of the now defunct MDLR Airlines had a perilous association with her boss, a Haryana Minister Gopal Goyal Kanda. Sharing a relationship that went beyond the association a boss has with an employee, Geetika claimed in her suicide note that she was pushed to the wall and forced to end her life. Geetika committed suicide on August 5, 2012, accusing Kanda of mental harassment. Kanda was booked for abetment to suicide. Kanda, a married man claimed innocent, but resigned hours after he was booked.
- Monica Bedi an actress – only exception, who managed to come out of the underworld after her alliance with don Abu Salem, and is now struggling to again find a foothold in Bollywood after serving her jail sentence.

Criminal conspiracy:

- Ranjit Singh ETO ended his life following his arrest by the SP Amandeep Kaur on trumped-up bribery charges. Inquiry by IAS Officer Manasvi Kumar and IPS Officer Harpreet Sidhu had revealed the trap as fake, and recommended that the SP and the co-accused be booked for abetment to suicide.

Emotional and Personal (Depression / failures in examinations or love affairs/Dowry):

- Shubhneet, a Dentist who was undergoing treatment for depression at PGI, Chandigarh, allegedly hanged herself to death at her house on June 12, 2014. She did not leave behind any suicide note. Inquest proceedings have been Initiated under Section 174 IPC.

- Anjali, a teenaged girl hanged herself to death at her house in PGI campus on June 10, 2014. She had left behind a suicide note holding no one responsible, and the note reading "please forgive me I am going to my father (died last year)". Inquest proceedings have been initiated under Section 174 IPC.
- Divya, MSc girl student PU,jumped off the 6th floor of hostel on the campus on June 11, 2014. In her suicide note, she blamed herself for some "wrong things" and did not hold anyone responsible for the extreme step. Inquest proceedings have been initiated.
- Ankrita Tripathi, a Dental Sciences student, committed a suicide at her home on November 30, 2013, and had blamed her teacher for taking the extreme step (abetment).
- Harjit Kaur, a 30 year old woman, allegedly committed suicide by jumping before a train at Barara railway station on June 12, 2014. A suicide note recovered from the deceased blamed her mother-in-law Rupinder Kaur, sisters-in-law Satwant Kaur and Krishna, and Krishna's husband Deep, for taking the extreme step. The note mentioned constantly harassment by them, while her husband was caring and innocent. The accused had been booked on the complaint of deceased's mother Kamlesh for abetment to suicide under Section 306 IPC.
- Anjali (14), Class X student, hangs herself at her house, on June 11, 2014. She was under depression.
- Charu, a young girl (25) consumed poison and died on June 9, 2014. She was a working girl and was under depression.
- Vinod Kumar (57), DPI, Punjab, ended his life by jumping into Sukhna Lake, on June 3, 2014. He was under depression.
- Kalawat (29) alias Kirti, Call Centre executive, ended her life by jumping into Sukhna Lake, on May 28, 2014. She was under depression.

- Sandeep (18), a student, depressed over prolonged illness, hanged himself to death. He was under depression.

Legally: Punishable under Section 306-309 IPC: that whoever attempts to commit suicide and does any act towards the commission of such offence shall be punishable with simple imprisonment for a term which may extend to one year or with fine or with both. Thus, technically, suicide as such not a crime under the IPC Act, but it is only an attempt to commit suicide that is punishable.

- SC in case of P Rathinam (1994): The Bench held that Section 309 of IPC deserves to be effected (void) from the statute book as it violates Article 21.
- SC in case of Gian Kaur (1996): The Constitutional Bench held that Article 21 of Constitution guarantees the right to life but not the right to die. The SC had only upheld the Constitutional validity of Section 309 of IPC, and did not consider the desirability of retaining the same in the IPC.
- Law Commission of India (18th): Humanisation and Decriminalisation of Attempt to Suicide 210th report (2008): also advocated for penalising the suicide attempt.

Expert:

- GS Bhullar, SSP, SAS Nagar: Those who are into extra-marital affairs have high expectations from such relationships, which, when not fulfilled, leads them to take the extreme step.
- P Rajput, Women's Rights Activist: Women entering into extra-marital affairs, esp. With the high and mighty, reflects poorly on the Dociety. The society may advocate of women's freedom, but then women should know where to draw the line. They should not do something that spoils their reputation.
- R Gill, HOD Deptt. of Sociology and Women's Studies, PU: Fiza entered into the relationship

willingly. Going by media reports, it appears she tried to manipulate things for mileage and personal benefits. It is not a case of gender discrimination.

- BS Chavan, HOD Deptt. of Psychiatry, GMCH 32, Chandigarh: The trend of an increase in number of suicide cases during the summer months is being observed for more than decade now. During May, June and July incidence of suicide is found to have increased.

International scenario:

- That in many countries, attempt to commit suicide, regarded more as a manifestation of a perverted (diseased) mind, deserving treatment and care rather than an offence attracting punishment:

  UK: The British Parliament in 1961, enacted the Suicide Act, whereby attempt to commit suicide ceased to be an offence.

  India, Pakistan, Bangladesh, Malaysia, Singapore etc.: persisted with this undesirable law.

Vox-populi: H Kumar, Advocate: That an attempt to suicide indeed merits decriminalisation and hence omission from the penal statute. It is really unfortunate that attempt to commit suicide continues to be a penal offence under the IPC, despite the fact that when distressed people decide to terminate life prematurely, they require sympathy, counselling and appropriate treatment, and certainly not any punishment.

Refernces:

1. H Kumar: Decriminalise suicide attempts, HT, July, 2012.
2. M Sharma: Dangerous liaisons courting trouble, HT, August, 2012.
3. H Rao: Booked for abetting suicide, Kanda resigns as Minister, HT, August, 2012.
4. M Sharma: Girls taking extreme step a disturbing trend, HT June, 2014.

ACID ATTACKS TRAUMA

Preface: Is a barbarian, monstrous, uncivilised, unpardonable crime, committed by accused on helpless victims mostly young innocent girls/women. This inhuman crime has to be condemned forcefully by the society and deserves stringent punishment to the accused while full medical aid (free) and financial compensation to the victim and affected family.

Legal: Acid attacks are registered under Section 307 (attempt to murder) or Section 326 (voluntarily causing grievous hurt) of the IPC. Under both sections maximum punishment is life sentence, but there is no minimum sentence.

- V Ghai (Sr. Advocate Punjab and Haryana High Court, Chandigarh): "There should be a provision for such cases under Section 307 and a minimum sentence of seven years. Law should be amended to match social reality."
- V Dadwal (Advocate Punjab and Haryana High Court, Ludhiana): touched upon the delay in conviction, usually adding to trauma of the victim. Witnesses do not come for hearings due to social pressures. That is a big problem."
- T Singh (Advocate District Courts, Chandigarh): Courts rarely order compensation for victims in criminal cases. Victims families have to file separate petitions to avail of the benefit.

The IPC was amended in 2013 to incld. a new section 326A which deems acid attack as being punishable by imprisonment which shall not be less than 10 yrs but which may extend to life and with fine which may extend to ₹ 10 lakh, provided that any fine levied under this section shall be given to the person on whom acid has been thrown or administered.

Etiology: Jealousy:- dejected lovers, family members (relatives), business rivals

Revenge:- sexual exploitations e.g. rape, molestation

Violence:- fights

Cheating:- financial frauds

Dowry: family members – mostly greedy husband and in-laws Property disputes

Errors: tragedy of errors

Psychological: Schizophrena, antisocial, sadism.

Risks: Acids easily available in the market, without any licence. Easily thrown over the victim/s

Accused/s mostly go unnoticed after committing the crime

Legal flaws:-long legal procedures,

- lack of evidence/witness
- little penalty
- bail provision to accused
- family pressures – mostly family reputation.

Media: "Scarred Bodies, Wounded Souls":

It is the most insidious face of violence against women. Yet the scourage of acid attacks, an alarming trend in Punjab, Haryana and Himachal, remains invisible and hardly provokes the public outrage that dowry deaths and female feticide do. Victims of these revenge-wit-acid dedations, invariably by jilted lovers, are young and unmarried girls. Scarred, both physically and mentally, the survivors are condemned to a life-long horror of disfigured faces and limbs. As an HT investigation reveals, the victims are left to fend for themselves and need prolonged and expensive treatment. Worse, while some give up the fight against their tormentors altogether out of fear or frustration over the slow-moving wheel of justice, others are fighting a losing legal battle. Their searred bodies – images of which may be disturbing to some readers – capture the searing trauma that words could never describe. It's time to faceup to the horrific reality and take steps to stamp out this diabolic crime.

(Ramesh Vinayak, Resident Editor, Hindustan-Times, June 8, 2012)

Case: "Our legal system is crippled. I have given up":

Jyoti, Ambala: After loosing her father at the age of 12, Jyoti had somehow managed to rebuild her life by getting a job in a telecom company by the time she turned 19. By 22, she seemed to have found real love with a colleague.

"He put forth a marriage proposal, that was rejected by both's families. This angered the jilted lover, who threw acid on her on February 14, Valentine's day. Jyoti suffered burns on her face. Main problem is financial as well as disturbed family. So far, she has spent around ₹ 1.5 lakh, but there are boils on the face again.

"The Deputy Commissioner had promised me a job, but it has been more than a year and no assistance has come. Not even the Red Cross Society has helped. A private hospital in Karnal where I go for treatment had told me that ₹ 10,000, is the cost for the laser treatment per week. Her cousion's husband, helped, but still, they would not be able to afford the treatment." A case was registered, but the attacker is out on bail at present. "With a salary of ₹ 6,000 from a private job in a telecom company, I have to get myself treatment, fend for the family and bear legal expenses. I have lost fath in the government, society and the media too. The legal system in this country is crippled." I even thought of ending my life initially, but I can't leave my mother alone," she said, not morose but confident, having just completed her graduation through distance education.

(Monica Sharma, HT)

Case: "jailed culprits live better":

Mamta, Mandi: A jilted lover, Mahmud Magrub, threw acid on her on May 27. Mamta suffered burns on her face and lost her vision, dashing her hopes of becoming a teacher. The main problem is financial as well as disturbed family. The family of six is surviving on the pension of her ex-serviceman father Khem Chand, who said, "Even life imprisonment is no deterrent. The jailed culprit lead a better life as compared to the victims."

The culprit has been lodged in the Nahan jail, serving a seven years sentence, his bail plea has been rejected by the HP High Court.

(Bhawani Negi, HT)

Case: "Seeing her in such pain, we wished for her death":

Prerna, Rohtak: The target was someone else, but a tragedy of errors led to Prerna suffering 40 per cent burns and being left with a severely disfigured face. Her friends – Yashika, the actual target, and Urwashi – too suffered burns but were lucky to escape severe injuries that have made Prerna an outcast of sorts.

Prerna's mother, Monika, said "Just those vital two minutes made all the difference." Wrapped in a bandage around her chin, Prerna has hardly any structured features, words don't come out of her mouth, but her eyes scream, anguished, searching for your face from behind thick glasses to see whether you are just another sympathiser from the neighbourhood. Those eyes tell a story, the story of June 18, 2011, when acid was thrown on Prerna, Yashika, both 14 at the time, and Urwashi, who was 15 then, by two boys in Sector 3 of Rohtak.

Yashika's family believes one of their jealous relatives hired the acid throwers to disfigure her. Yashika's aunt is among the three arrests made so far in the case. After the State Police exonerated Rohan, one of the attackers identified by Prerna, the High Court ordered a CBI investigation on a petition by the victims on May 22. The HC has also directed the Haryana Government to pay ₹ 5 lakh as compensation to Prerna "too little too late". Her father said, more than ₹ 19 lakh has been spent on her 10 skin grafting surgeries, while nine more surgeries (each costing ₹ 2 lakh) being required to restore her face. "No one from the Government, media and public helped," said Monika, revealing in distress.

But why does she have to suffer ? She just happened to come in the line of fire," cried Prerna's mother.

Prerna (mistaken target) suffered burns on her face, chest and arms, while Yashika (actual target) got her back and arms badly burnt, and Urvashi suffered from the spills.

A year has lapsed since Prerna, a keen dancer and Kho-kho player, faced the horror. But troubles continue. Even now, she has to constantly remain indoor to avoid heat outside. Can't afford hospitalisation (₹ 6000 per day).

"Fast track Courts should be set up and a policy should be framed for the treatment as well," she added sobbing. And then came the anger. "For us, justice will be done when acid is poured on the culprits."

(Monica Sharma, HT)

Case: "Life finished for volleyball player":

Ritu Saini, Rohtak: Ritu's cousion Ram Niwas, out of jealousy is alleged to have hatched the conspiracy by hiring men, who threw acid on her on May 27.

Ritu suffered 20 per cent burns on her face, arms and chest. Her eye is endangered. The main problem is lacking money. Lakhs of rupees are required for skin graftings. For Ritu, it is a one sentence verdict: "My life is finished." Police has arrested all the attackers and the conspirators.

Case: "I can make you pretty, not myself":

Amandeep Kaur, Bathinda: A jitlted lover, Daljinder Singh, Aman's brother-in-law, alleged to have hatched the conspiracy by hiring men, who threw acid on her on January 31. Aman suffered 90 per cent burns on her face and lost her vision, now a living, walking life lesson (To be the object of someone's affection is a compliment. But when it turns to obsession, don't ignore the obvious signs of impending paranoia). The main problem is financial as well as disturbed family. Aman's future depends on donations. "The treatment will cost ₹ 20 lakh more, beyond their reach," rued Aman's father.

Police arrested the culprit, inspite of protests by both the families, to save the reputation as well as the sensitive relationships. Aman's family requested the Court to drop the case, but the Judge said, he would first like to see if Daljinder helps in Aman's treatment.

(Kamaldeep Singh Brar, HT)

Case: "From beauty business to a life of loneliness":

Sharanjit Kaur, Amritsar: A jealous sister-in-law, masterminded the attack – two unknown persons threw acid her on August 18. Sharanjit suffered burns on her face and right arm, dashing her hopes of running her business (beauty parlour). The main problem is financial as well as disturbed family. The incident left the family hapless. The beauty parlour closed down, the family took loans to pay for Sharanjit's treatment.

Police case continued for nearly two yrs. But the societal pressures forced a compromise. "The family decided to consider a settlement, as continuation of the case would spoil the life of their seven yrs. old niece." After the compromise everybody else has settled in their lives, but for Sharanjit, whose life has been spoiled by the unfortunate incidence.

(Archna Matharui, HT)

Case: "Let me throw acid on him. That will be justice"

Rajwant Kaur, Ludhiana: Balkar Singh, a jealous, threw acid on Sandeep and Rajwant on April 1, 2007. While Sandeep (main target) succumbed on June 28, Rajwant suffered burns on her face and lost her eyesight. The main problem is financial (her father and sisters are daily wagers) as well as disturbed family – her parents have given up hope of a normal life for her.

The police arrested Balkar, who is in jail facing trial for attempt to murder, but the case lingers. "This delay is rubbing salt on our wounds. We want justice," sobbed her mother. Rajwant burst out, "I'll tell you what justice is. I should be given permission to throw acid on Balkar's face. Only then he will realise what it's like to be a lifeless being, who just breathes, eats and drinks, and just exists, does not live."

(Anshu Seth)

Case: "No clue who attacked me and why":

Anu Bhola, Ropar: An unknown, masked man threw acid on her on January 27. Anu suffered burns on her face, neck, arms and back. The main problem is financial as well as disturbed family – her mother is the lone financial support as her father died four yrs. ago. With a meagre monthly income of ₹ 2,500. In reality, it was to support her mother that she had dropped out after BA-I and taken up a job as a helper in a hospital. "False promises of justice or medical aid were made but not a single person has helped.

The police used to come to her house initially but never made any breakthrough, blaming it a case of mistake identity.

(Monica Sharma, HT)

Medical: Dr. Bholeshwar Prasad Mishra (Psychologist, DMCH, Ludhiana): Acid attacks are "the most heinous" crime against women. "We need to inculcate tolerance in youngsters. Most attacks are by jilted lovers." Young victims go into deep depression. Due to high costs, not everyone can afford cosmetic surgery. Thus, counselling plays an important role in making them believe in themselves and took beyond the disfiguring."

Dr. Sanjeev Uppal (Cosmetic Surgeon, DMCH, Ludhiana):

"In most cases, the victims suffer 3rd degree burns, which even char bones.

Reconstruction is possible but complicated and expensive. It requires 8-12 surgeries and each costs around ₹ 50,000."

Police: Ishwar Singh (Police Commissioner, Ludhiana):

Blamed the attackers 'criminal mentality'. "Their prime aim is to disfigure the faces of the victims, which leaves them scarred for life." On action he said,

"We immediately register cases under the relevant sections, though I personally feel that these cases should be decided in fast-track Courts to expedite convictions. That will be an effective deterrent."

Government: Administration to aid of acid attack and rape victims:

Notification: The Chandigarh Administration has notified a new scheme for providing financial assistance to acid attack victims, rape victims and to those who have suffered loss of life or injury in any criminal act.

Provision: The scheme would have a provision to provide maximum financial assistance of ₹ 5 lakh for loss of life, ₹ 3 lakh to victims who suffer loss of any body part resulting in permanent disability above 40 per cent, ₹ 3 lakh to those whose faces are disfigured in acid attacks and ₹ 2 lakh for rape victims.

Eligibility: Only those victims and their dependents would be eligible for grant of assistance who have not received any assistance for loss of life and injury under any other scheme of the central government or the administration.

Moreover, the scheme would also empower the State Legal Service Authority and the District Legal Services Authority, Chandigarh, to order for immediate first-aid facility or any other interim relief to the victim.

"The benefit will be made available free of cost and would not be adjustable against the amount of assistance. However, no request would be entertained after a period of three yrs. from the date of commission of crime." said MM Sabharwal, the Director Department of Public Relations, UT, Chandigarh.

Remedy: In order to check this heinous crime, following measures are suggested:

- Immediate filing of the FIR against the accused.
- Non-bailable warrants against the accused/s.
- Fast-track Courts, to decide the case at the earliest.
- Stringent punishment to the accused/s (Imprisonment plus fine).
- Full payment to the victim/s and their families incld. total cost of treatment and compensation for the disability or loss of life, to be recovered from the accused/s.
- Government to provide full protection to the victim and family.
- Public awareness and support in preventing this crime and providing help to the victim and affected family.
- Media exposure of this crime till the punishment to the accused as well as full compensation to the victim.

References: 1. A Sethi: Drunk driving on the rise, HT, February, 2014.

2. D Raza: Catching them young, HT December, 2013.

ADVERTISING MEDICAL SERVICES

Preface: That advertising medical services through various mediums is considered as violation of medical ethics to be observed by the Registered Medical Practitioners (RMPs). Guidelines: DO's:

- That information in the press can be released on starting practice, change of type of practice, changing address, temporary absence from duty, resumption of another practice, succeeding to another practice, public declaration of charges or acquiring new equipment or starting a new procedure or operation.
- That the advertisement in the press should not be more than 15 cm x 10 cm and should be black and white.
- That doctors can deliver lectures/talks of mass awareness on television without giving their address.
- That there should not be request to consult the particular doctor.

DON'Ts:

- That the advertisement should not carry photograph of the doctor / building / equipment/ procedure. It should not appear that the advertisement seems to solicit patients.
- That there should not be hoardings of any size/ shape along the roadside or on buildings, anywhere in India.
- That advertisements in radio and electronic media in the form of strips on cable television are considered as violation of medical rules/ ethics.

AGONY OF SENIOR CITIZENS

Preface: In the past, elderly citizens usually lived with their children and grandchildren ; currently this has changed, and the reality of today's children abandoning their parents is a common sight. It is agonising to think of the heartbreak elderly parents, who must have gone through when their children turned away and forsook them. With the gradual erosion of the joint family system, there have been many unfortunate cases of senior citizens facing lack of basic needs such as housing, as many instances of seniors being forcibly evicted from their own properties or being wrongfully denied unhindered access and enjoyment of their property by their children and/or relatives. Finally their hopes were crushed to the point that they breathed their last.

Factors: Children's point of views:

- That their working schedule hinders them sparing time for attending to elderly.
- That they have to look after the interests of their own wife and children.
- That they have to face the financial constraint, for looking after the elderly.
- That they have to take the side of their wives and children over their parents in family disputes.

Elderly's point of views:

- That they feel dejected in family disputes, when their children take the sides of their own wives and children, even while the elderly feel themselves on the right side.
- That they suffer financially after handing over property etc. to their children, and thereafter almost request/beg for money for their common needs.
- That they feel loneliness as their children don't spare time to chat/gossip etc with them esp. those living abroad.

Remedy: Legal option:

- Under Maintenance and Welfare of Parents and Senior Citizens Act 2007:

  Seeks to ensure that the elderly are not deprived of basics esp. housing. One of the main objects of the Act is to provide an institutional framework for the protection of life and property of elderly persons. There's a legal responsibility on children and relatives to maintain the senior citizen or elderly parent, in order to facilitate them with a normal life. This obligation applies to all Indian citizens, including those who lived abroad. Making matters worse is the fact that much of the elderly population doesn't know what they can do to procure sufficient support needed for themselves.

Section 23 of Act 2007: essentially enables an aggrieved senior citizen to reclaim ownership and/or possession of his/her property that had been earlier transferred by him/her. The term 'property' includes:

- both immovable and movable property
- both ancestral and self-acquired property – both tangible and intangible property.

Eligibility: to seek relief under the Act, certain points to be kept in mind:

- senior citizens should have made the transfer of his/her property in favour of his/her offspring/ relative, post-enactment of Act 2007.
- mode of transfer of the property can be gift, sale or long-term lease.
- senior citizen should have transferred his/her property to his/her offspring/relative, subject to the condition that the transferee would provide basic amenities and fulfil the essential needs of the senior citizen. For that, senior citizen may certainly include an explicit clause for setting out this condition in the gift/sale or lease deed.

Maintenance Tribunals: failure/refusal to comply: this clause in future by the transferee, the senior citizen may approach the special maintenance tribunals established under this Act, to seek legal relief. The Tribunal would first assess whether the requirements set out are fulfilled or not, in a particular case.

- In case requirements are fulfilled, then the transfer of property in question would be deemed as a transfer made by fraud, coercion or under undue influence due to the transferee's subsequent failure in fulfilling the clause of providing basic amenities to the senior citizen.

- An earlier transfer of property made by senior citizen in favour of his/her offspring/relative may also be declared void, in case the senior citizen desires so, and the transfer of property made by him/her shall be deemed to never have taken effect.
- In case senior citizen is unable to contact the maintenance tribunal, action may be taken on his/her behalf by voluntary organisations/ associations, or may be represented by a specially designated maintenance officer during the proceedings.
- Appeal: an appeal may be filed against the order of a maintenance tribunal, by an aggrieved senior citizen, within 60 days from the date of the order. To curb prolonged litigation, the appellate tribunal endeavours to decide the case within one month from the receipt of the senior citizen's appeal.

Non-legal option:

- Elderly parents and senior citizens, who don't like the legal option can reduce stress by concentrating on their hobbies and interests, like indulging in yoga, studying, playing cards or field games, music, visiting friends, watching movies, TV plays/movies. They can travel together or resume working life. The purpose is to make an effort to remain happy and stand firmly on their own feet, sparing their children venture into their own life.
- Senior citizen homes: Some elderly persons prefer/under compulsion, opt for senior citizen homes, where they live peacefully amongst other elderly persons, sharing their grief / joys, till the end of their lives. This may help in solving the problem of loneliness.

References: 1. R Krishan: The agony of loneliness. Sunset Boulevard, HT, February, 2014.

2. S Tyagi: Who will protect the rights of Senior Citizens, HT, March, 2014.

3. S Tyagi: Regret transferring your property ? Get it back, HT, March, 2014.

ALCOHOL ABUSE

Preface: That alcohol abuse is a menace, particularly amongst the youth. Increase in underage drinking is a problem that needs to be curbed with participation of society. Law alone can't be enough to tackle the problem. That parents with drinking or drug abuse problems are a high risk factor for child sex abuse. The biggest problem about abuse/dependence is that those esp. Youngsters addicted to alcohol, smoking or drugs rarely want to quit. A common scene is that friends and family members take them kicking and screaming to the de-addiction centres/ clinics. De-addiction is achievable but only with the help of family members and friends.The helping people's aim not to be critical, as the addicted persons need acceptance, not criticism, experts said.

Vox- populi:- RP Upadhyaya, UT IGP, Chandigarh: That whatever help can be extended to women who are found drunk is always provided. They should also remain careful and refrain from being vulnerable.

- V Kumar, UT DSP Traffic, Chandigarh: That cases of drunk driving in the city are on the rise, and those convicted under Section 185, were having alcohol level exceeding 30 ml per dl of blood, and the Court slapped penalty ranging from ₹ 1200 to ₹ 4500 on offenders, and some offenders were awarded sentence 'till rising of the Court' (TRC) – making them stand in the Court for nearly eight hrs.

Law: Under Section 185 of the Motor Vehicle act, if alcohol content is found more than 30 ml per dl of blood, a driver can be booked for drunk driving.

Anyone found guilty of drunk driving faces imprisonment up to six months or a fine of ₹ 2K, or both. A repeat offender can be jailed up to two yrs and fined ₹ 3K or more.

- A Gupta, Panchkula: That legally drinking age variable from State to State, and ranges from 18 to 25 yrs. while nobody cares about it. States cann't ban alcohol sale on account of revenue earned. Through surrogate advertising they are adopting tactics to lure vulnerable segment of customers, which is youth and women, keeping in their mind, profit as the only motive, Young boys and girls have given a new meaning to socialising. Taking advantage of this, pubs and night clubs keep on serving them till they are over-drunk and then uncontrolling their senses they create ruckus publically on roads or lie on roadside unattended, most often indulging in road accidents. Here arises the need for introspection.
- S Negi, Panchkula: Drinking menace among teenagers – a blot on society:

  Youths under the influence of alcohol wandering on streets in the night has become commonplace. "It's my life" attitude, not only deteriorating their health but also degrading society culture and their lifestyle. The drunken teenagers often end up creating ruckus on roads by shouting, quarrelling or misbehaving with by-standers. The discotheque too indulges in marketing of alcohol by offering free drinks for girls and ladies, and on misbehaviour, they are left to fend for themselves on the roads by the bar-managers.
- NGOs: That there is a direct link between child sex abuse and problem of drug addiction or alcoholism in parents.
- Dr B Bharti, PGI, Chandigarh: That drug abuse and alcoholism are closely linked to sexual

offences as the person loses inhibition. An alcoholic person or drug addict does not know what he is doing. But sexual abuse cases come occasionally to hospitals as families prefer to be silent on them.

- Dr Harshminder: That though the cases reported to government hospitals are mostly from lower income strata, incest is rampant in all sections of society. "Mother is part of the conspiracy of silence. Such is the social stigma attached to the abuse that mothers bury it till the physical or emotional symptoms become telling. Even doctors do not probe this angle if a minor girl comes with obvious symptoms of sexual abuse. While an infant runs a risk to her life in case she develops septicaemia in her private parts, young girls can suffer other physical complications, such as fibrosis, making them unable to bear children. The psychological implications are equally damaging, resulting in extreme sexual behaviours – they can either become too sexually active or fear even a touch – or they grow into adults incapable of having normal sexual relations. The trauma lasts a lifetime.
- S Salaria, Chairman, Punjab Child Rights Commission (PCRC): That the problem of liquor and drug abuse is on the rise in Punjab. There are bound to be social implications. But there is a social stigma attached to sexual abuse.

  When the father is an abuser, it becomes a bigger taboo. They also fear further harassment/ victimisation by the police.

Remedy: Alcohol abuse is one of the most common addictions, that causes health issues, such as liver damage, heart disease, stroke and cancers. Drinking, the bane of society. Alcohol has potential to ruin a generation. The remedial modalities are:

- Detoxification: must be done under professional care. In certain cases, even hospital admission is required to curb withdrawal symptoms incld.

severe anxiety and poor sleep. The addict is put on anti-anxiety drugs.

- Rehabilitation: The addict is given medicines (disulfiram, topiramate and acamprosate) and counselling to maintain sobriety. Done at the OPD level but in extreme cases the addict may require hospitalisation.
- Avoiding relapse: to maintain self-motivation, the addict should join active self-help groups.

Remedial measures are:

- Need for introspection
- Need for counselling and awareness amongst teenagers
- Need for awareness amongst youth about ill-effects of drinking
- Need for pragmatic laws
- Need for society's curb underage drinking
- Need for saving youth from drinking menace
- Need for banning teenage drinking
- Need for parents acting as role models
- Need for parents and teachers playing their part
- Need for parents and Police saving youth from alcohol's blazing inferno
- Need for collective effort
- Availability of alcohol must be controlled
- Prevention programmes must be encouraged
- Matter of concern
- Collective effort.

References: 1. A Sethi: Drunk driving on the rise, HT, February, 2014.

2. D Raza: Catching them young, HT December, 2013.

3. A Gupta: Need for introspection, HT February, 2014.

4. R Kaul: Alcohol dependence a growing menace, HT June, 2014.

All India Bar Examination (AIBE)

Preface: That to ensure maintenance of standards in the legal profession, the Supreme Court made it mandatory for each and every law graduate to clear the test before practising law. Since the Bar Council of India, started this examination (AIBE) four years back, the result has been quite positive. Legal experts are of the view that the AIBE, is encouraging a lot of students to take study of law more seriously. It has certainly raised the standards of legal education in India (Chairman Bar Council of India).

Aim: To raise the standards of legal education in India.

Requirement: That the AIBE was started when the Supreme Court, while hearing a matter related to affiliation of a college with the Bar Council of India, expressed concern over the low standards of legal education in India. The Apex Court constituted a three-member committee under the chairmanship of senior lawyer G Subramanium, which recommended that "qualifying a bar examination should be made a pre-requirement to admission to the Bar by all State Bar Councils (SBCs) across the country."

Examination: That the examination held biannually, using multiple-choice questions. The examination, which is held in forty cities all over India, covers the same subjects as are prescribed by the Bar Council of India for the three-year and five-year LLB courses at Law schools/colleges in the country. A student gets four chances to clear the examination. After clearing the examination, he/she is awarded Licence (Certificate) to Practice by the Bar Council of India (BCI).

Since 2010, the pass per cent has gone up because candidates can take reference from previous question papers. Besides that BCI provides preparatory material (Guide) two weeks after submission of application form by the candidate, thereby an advocate can also revise what they have learnt at the beginning of their law school career (B Gowda, vice-chairman BCI).

Legal:
- That I feel now, when students take up the study of law seriously, they know that they can't practice law in any Indian Court until and unless they clear the AIBE. It has certainly raised the standards of legal education in India (BS Sinsinwar), chairman BCI).
- That the purpose is to test the reasoning and analytical ability of a student using multiple-choice questions and not the ability to memorise big answers. (B Gowda, vice-chairman BCI).

Reference: JP Sharma: Why the All India Bar Examination is a must for lawyers, HT May, 2014.

Article 370

Preface: Article 370 is a provision of the Indian Constitution that accords special autonomous status to the State of Jammu and Kashmir. In 1947, the then Maharaja of Jammu and Kashmir, Hari Singh, had agreed to accede to India by signing the Instrument of Accession, after Pakistan prevented essential supplies, and its troops/tribesmen entered Kashmir. But the accession was pre-conditioned. Article 370 was the basis of the accession (a temporary provision). Article says that except for defence, foreign affairs, communications and ancillary matters (specified in Instrument of Accession), Parliament needs J&K Govt's concurrence for applying all other laws. In 1954, J&K Constituent Assembly ratified accession. That J&K residents have separate laws, incld. on citizenship and ownership of property.

Repeal of Article 370:

Reviving an old debate:

- That Article 370 has several aspects to it and all should receive attention. The statement of the Minister of State in the PMO, that Article 370 of the Constitution, giving special status to J&K,

will be the subject of a debate with stakeholders. The Minister's statement provoked an angry reaction from J&K Chief Minister Omar Abdullah. What is getting lost in the jumble is a picture of the Constitutional development of the State.

Can it be repealed/amended ?:

Scenario - I: under Article 370(3), President of India, may declare that the Article shall cease to exist, provided State's Constitutent Assembly recommends it. But the Constituent Assembly lapsed in 1957.

Scenario -II: under Article 368, notwithstanding anything in constitution (read Article 370), Parliament may amend/repeal any provision in accordance with procedure laid down in this article. But: Amending/repealing any provision of Constitution requires two-thirds majority in each House of Parliament. Since current new Government (BJP/NDA) does not have this kind of majority in both Lok Sabha and Rajya Sabha, it does not appear possible to repeal Article 370 using Article 368.

What if repealed ?:

J&K would become like any other Indian State. All laws made by would apply and people from other States could buy property there.

Arguments: - That on May 27, 2014, Dr Jitendra Singh, Minister of State in the PMO, set off the controversy with his remark that the process of abrogating Article 370 – that provides J&K special status, had started and the Government was speaking to "Stakeholders" (J Singh, MOS in PMO).

- That we will oppose the move tooth and nail, being one of the stakeholder as Chief Minister of J&K State. Either J&K won't be part of India or Article 370 will still exist (Omar Abdullah, CM J&K).
- That J&K won't be part of India? Is Omar thinking it is his parental estate? Article 370 or no 370. J&K has been and will always be an

integral part of India (Ram Madhav, RSS leader).

- That Article 370 is an integral part of the Constitution and it can neither be amended nor abrogated by any authority in the Country unless the people of J&K themselves want it. Any debate on Article 370 is illogical, but RSS will continue to pressurise the Central Government for its abrogation. If it was an achievable goal, the BJP Government led by then Prime Minister AB Vajpayee would have done it. The fact is, it will always remain a dream. That for the past 25 yrs or more, the BJP has been making abrogation of Article 370, adoption of Common Civil Code and construction of Ram Mandir as their main political issues (Saifuddin Soz, PCC Chief J&K).
- That the Centre must strengthen rather than revoke Article 370. It is an unfortunate statement from newcomer MOS Jitendra Singh (Mehbooba Mufti, PDP Chief J&K).
- That Article 370(3) read with Article (2) clarifies that Article 370 can't be repealed without consent of Constituent Assembly, which does not exist. No briner (Manish Tewari, Congress spoke-person).
- That abrogating Article 370, was not appropriate and called for restraint on the issue, as the whole question is extremely sensitive and must be handled coolly and in a mature fashion (Karan Singh S/o Maharaja Hari Singh).
- That revoking and repealing Article 370 was not possible for any government. But nothing is impossible, if people in power decide to abrogate the provision, they might even pierce through the mountains, but where will it leave Kashmir, needs to be seen. That even debate about revocation can lead to increased sense of security among people. Kar and KD Sethi are the only two surviving members of the seventy five member Constituent Assembly, which ratified

Article 370 in 1951. (GR Kar, member J&K Constituent Assembly).

- That defeated, Omar (party lost Lok Sabha seats) has no right to speak for J&K State, and must not make irresponsible and provocative statements on the political status of Jammu, Kashmir and Ladakh. Article 370 is part of the Indian Constitution and the Parliament, the highest legislative body in the Country invested with the power to amend the statute book. By using Article 368, it can amend or repeal any of the provisions of Indian Constitution as and when needed by the exigency of the situation. Even the President of India can amend or abrogate Article 370. The Indian Constitution does not give the right to secede to any State (Hari Om, BJP leader).
- That the statement of the MOS in the PMO that Article 370 of the Constitution giving special status to J&K State, will be the subject of a debate with the stakeholders. The statement provoked an angry reaction from J&K Chief Minister Omar Abdullah, who said the State would not be part of India if the Article ceased to exist – a response reminiscent of what his father and National Conference (NC) Chief, Farooq Abdullah, said about Kashmir leaving India if a "communal" Government came to power in New Delhi. What is getting lost in the jumble is a picture of the Constitutional development of the State. The J&K State became part of the Indian Union because the then Maharaja Hari Singh of J&K State, had signed the Instrument of Accession with the Indian Government in 1947, the Centre's control remained confined to defence, foreign affairs and communication, and the Indian Government had given an assurance that the accession would finally have to be confirmed by the people, without involvement of any third party. Subsequently, the Constituent Assembly of the State ratified the accession to India, and

through the Constitution (Application to J&K) Order in 1954, the Centre's jurisdiction had extended to all items on the Union List of the Constitution. Apart from the fact of Article 370, the State has a separate Constitution, effective from January 26, 1957, and which too recognised the accession to India. Article 370 has several aspects to it and all should receive attention. Any discussion (debate) on abrogating the Article must take into account these facts of history (Editor HT).

References: 1. T Rashid, J&K Constituent Assembly Member: Article 370 can't be abrogated, HT, May 2014.

2. K Singh, Sr Congress leader: Calls for restraint on issue, HT, May 2014.

3. T Rashid, H Baweja, K Uttam: Article 370 row gets bigger, RSS jumps in, HT, May 2014.

4. HT Correspondents: PMO Minister attacks Article 370, Omar and Mehbooba fume, HT, May 2014.

5. Editorial: Reviving an old debate, HT, May 2014.

Bachelor of Rural Medicine (BRM)

Preface: That to overcome the acute shortage of modern medical professionals in rural area, resulting in risky life of people living in rural areas, the Central Government has implemented the need for staring Bachelor of Rural Medicine Course.

Debate:

IMA Spanner in 3.5 yrs. Degree course:

News: New Delhi: A day after Times of India, reported on the Union Health Ministry's plans to roll the three and a half (3.5) yrs. Medical degree course, the Indian Medical Association (IMA) asked the Medical Council of India (MCI) not to compromise on patient's safety.

IMA: Reacting to Union Health Minister Ghulam Nabi Azad's three week ultimatum to MCI on BRM, the IMA National President Dr. Vijay Aggarwal said MCI would not bend before the Government and refused to endorse the course. "IMA is willing to cooperate with the Government to find a solution on rural health" his letter said.

It added "There are better ways to overcome the shortage of modern medicine professionals in rural area. Lowering the standard of medical education and producing low-quality professionals is not the solution" Aggarwal said MCI is "duty bound to consider patient safety and cannot obviously reverse a process initiated by Bhore Committee report of 1946, to abolish such mediocre short-term courses.

This notion that over 30 per cent of primary health centres do not have an MBBS doctor is not supported by statistics. Only 5.3 per cent of PHCs are without a qualified doctor. Compulsory rural health posting of MBBS graduates for one yr. After internship would make available 30,000 MBBS graduates every yr. NHRC has come out against such a course" IMA said.

Suggestions by IMA:

- Incentives for rural posting in form of special increments, to be made.
- Provision of all facilities, as being provided to IAS and IPS officers, posted in rural areas.
- Special provisions for Postgraduation courses for doctors working in rural areas.
- Declaring certain areas as difficult terrain for posting of doctors, who should be compensated with added benefits.

Petition: Petitioner Meenakshi Gautam, through advocate Prashant Bhushan, filed the contempt of Court in Delhi High Court:

- That on November 10, 2010, a Division Bench of this Court, had ordered the MCI to implement by March 2011, the Bachelor of Rural Health Care (BRHC) Degree Course, approved by the Health Ministry, but no action has been taken so far. She contended that life of people living in rural areas is in risk because of lack of qualified medical practitioners there.

- That the Court had given the MCI two months time to finalise the curriculum and syllabus of the three and half years, Primary Health Care Practitioner Course, the implementation of the introduction of which was approved by the Union of India. The Course was named Bachelor of Rural Health Care (BRHC).
- That a further period of two months was given to the Ministry of Health and Family Welfare for the enforcement of the same.
- That, by seeking the Court's direction to implement the course, it said the course should have been introduced by March 2011, as per the timeline stipulated by the Court in its order, but no such course has been introduced as of February 2012.
- That the MCI apparently opposed the course in 2011 and is not willing to notify it, the petition said.
- That the continual delays and lack of initiative by the respondents in implementing a proposal which promises a headway in the realisation of our Country's long held dream of providing at least Primary Health Care to all, is extremely worrisome, the petition said. The petitioner expressed fear that if despite the Court's order specifying the timelines for implementing the course, the Ministry is not in a position to introduce it after more than a year: from the time directed then left to itself, it would never do so.

(*Source:* IANS) Categories: NEWS, New Delhi.

Court: Court questions Centre on Rural Medical Course: New Delhi:

- That Justice SK Mishra of the Delhi High Court told the Central Government to file its reply on the contempt plea filed against it for alleged failure to start a three-year course for non-MBBS people to practice medicine in rural health centres.

- That Justice SK Mishra sought a detailed affidavit indicating if steps had been taken to start the course, within eight weeks and posted the matter for December 5.
- That petitioner Meenakshi Gautam, filing the contempt petition through advocate Prashant Bhushan, said on November 10, 2010, a Division Bench of this court had ordered the Medical Council of India (MCI) to introduce by March 2011, the Bachelor of Rural Health Care (BRHC) course, approved by the Health Ministry, but no action taken so far. "The MCI apparently opposed the course in 2011 and is not willing to notify it," the petition said. The Court had earlier given the MCI two months to finalise the curriculum and syllabus of the three-and-half-year primary healthcare practitioner course, approved by the Central Government, she added (IANS).

(Category: NEWS)

MCI: MCI approves 3-and-a-half-year medical course, BSc in Community Health:

New Delhi: Monday, September 24, 2012: The Medical Council of India (MCI) has cleared introduction of the three-and-a-half-year medical course, called BSc in Community Health. The new course is likely to be open to students who have completed class 12 with physics, chemistry and biology.

According to MCI chairman Dr. KK Talwar, this special cadre of health workers to be trained mainly in District Hospitals, be placed in Sub-Centres or Primary Health Centres and will be taught some module of clinical work. "We intend to introduce the course from April next year," Dr. Talwar has said.

The Health Ministry has been pushing for the introduction of this cadre, in order to address the shortage of doctors in rural areas. Only 26 per cent of doctors in India reside in rural areas, serving 72 per cent of India's population.

(*Source.* TOI)

Vox populi:

Narpat Charan: September, 2012: "Government and MCI must think course of General medicine after BDS or relaxation of one or two-year in MBBS, person having BDS degree or BSc in Community Health course having minimum qualification like BDS, BHMS, BAMS or BSc Nursing, so that right person goes to rural belt of India and right person get right line of their field for future and after that they can do their master degree as MBBS person."

Drd: September, 2012: MCI certified quacks to treat rural, patients now........

Dr Alexander John: September, 2012: These people can be very useful in Public Health if employed under supervision of the Medical Officers. They definitely should not be treating patients but can assist the doctors. Dr Pankaj Jain: September, 2012: It is a good step to serve rural people they may be posted at subcentre as a community health advisor.

CHILD ABUSE/VULNERABLE CHILDHOOD/NO COUNTRY FOR CHILDREN

Preface: Child abuse is a catastrophe. It can only function as the end of one story and the beginning of another.

Issue: Safety of youngsters.

Abuse::

- Kidnapping for ransom of money, jealousy or revenge.
- Murders for jealousy or revenge.
- Kidnapping and murder for ransom of money, jealousy or revenge.
- Assault: physical torture or inflicting burn injuries.
- Monitory: making children blind or physically handicapped, for purpose of forced begging, and selling girls to brothels for illict purposes.
- High on drugs and liquor, prey on infant/young daugters.
- Greed and Poverty.

Cases: **Kidnapping and Murder:**

- Gurkirat Singh (10) kidnapped on November 7 from Verka. Body found on November 16. As the Amritsar police struggle to crack the case, incidents of kidnapping and subsequent murder of minor children, which have been coming to light at a regular interval, have put a question mark on the safety of children. In majority of cases parents of kidnapped children got ransom calls, and later on brutally murdered by the perpetrators for not fulfilling their unjustified/ hefty demands.
- Sushant (11) kidnapped on June 12. Body found on June 20.
- Mohit Kapoor (11) kidnapped on October 26. Body found on October 27.
- Jagjit Singh (14) kidnapped on April 28. Body found at Bhuchchar village.

Assault:

- Roshan Lama (4) hospitalised with 20 per cent burns, inflicted by his neighbour by pouring a pot of boiling hot soup on his back. The reason – ongoing bickering with Roshan's father. (HTC)
- Raipur teen (12) committed suicide, after pinning blame on her allegedly cruel school teacher of frequently tormenting her. (HTC)
- Tripura girl, stripped and tied up for hrs.
- Patiala teen (3 months old), hospitalised with vaginal bleeding, inflicted by her alcoholic father by pushing a toothbrush into her vagina, just half-an-inch in size. The mother refused to lodge a police complaint to save the accused, and left the hospital, refusing even medication for the child.
- Patiala teen (9 months old), hospitalised with vaginal bleeding, inflicted by her drug-addict father by pushing a carrot into her vagina, just half-an-inch in size. The mother refused to lodge a police complaint to save the accused, and

left the hospital, refusing even medication for the child.

Sexual abuse: By close relatives, friends, or unknown persons luring teens:

- Bhilwara teen (14) raped by her adoptive father for more than three yrs.
- Kerala teen (13) raped by drug addict and alcoholic. dad, uncle and brother. The elder sister committed suicide after being similarly abused.
- Bangalore teen (4) allegedly sexually abused by her father's friend, has 17 bite marks on her body. ((HTC)
- Patiala teen (5), hospitalised with vaginal tear inflicted by her alcoholic father by trying to penetrate her. The mother refused to lodge a police complaint against the accused in order to save the family honour, and the father is the only bread-winner.

Greed and Poverty: Forced to send their children away to some Kerala orphanages by close relatives, friends, or unknown persons luring teens. For eight years, these orphanages have been raising funding by enrolling children from impoverished States. Few are actually orphans though all are poor. HT traces the trail from destitution to profiteering, from Jharkhand to Kerala. The Railway authorities and the District Administration rounded up six hundred children at the Palakkad station, travelling without tickets, many had starved, barely clothed, aged between 3 and 12, had no idea where they were being taken by the Ustad, had been sent away from home in the hope that they would get three meals per day and an education. Jharkhand's Ameena and her six years old brother had been sold by her parents for ₹ 10K. Most of the papers seized from persons accompanying children were fudged. There are 1K odd orphanages in Kerala, most of them, do good business by accepting generous donations from across the country and abroad, by citing these 'orphans'. "To raise funds from the Government or from donors in the Gulf Countries, these orphanages started getting kids from remote areas when many of the 'rescued children from Godda have returned, but many more are still in orphanages in Kerala. Several organisations, incld. Christian missionaries, Muslim madrasas and Hindu groups also get children from this region.

Though many agents have been booked under Section 23 (Juvenile Justice Act) and Section 370(5) IPC, liable to punishment for cruelty to juveniles or children, not even a single child reported any cruelty or abuse, as the facilities provided at these orphanages are much more than non-existing at their homes (abject poverty and lack of education).

(*Source:* R Babu, Kozhikode/ Malappuram (Kerala) HT, June, 2014).

Media:

- Kidnapping incidents are on the rise because of growing greed among people. Lust among people to get rich faster is leading to such crimes.

  People must go back to the old style of living and shun greed.

  (Dr. Inderjit Kaur, president, All India Pingalwara Charitable Society)

- In most kidnapping cases, personal enmity is involved. It is not a social problem but a law and order issue. Children are the easiest& most sensitive targets and incidents involving kidshurt parents emotionally the most. The police need to handle such cases in a better way.

  (Dr. BL Goel, Director,Vidya Sagar Institute of Mental Health)

- Security of children needs to be ensued. To ensure safety of children, people should remain vigilant whether they are in the house or outside. Police personnel need to reactive and they should increase patrolling outside schools.

(A Mehra, principal, Spring Blossoms School)

- This is a serious law and order problem. The notorious persons have no fear of police and they commit such crimes. There is an urgent need that police instill fear among anti-social elements and then only such heinous crimes can be brought under control.

(A Singh, investigator with PHRO)

- That there is a direct link between child sex abuse and problem of drug addiction or alcoholism in parents (NGOs):
- That drug abuse and alcoholism are closely linked to sexual offences as the person loses inhibition. An alcoholic person or drug addict does not know what he is doing. But sexual abuse cases come occasionally to hospitals as families prefer to be silent on them.

  (Dr B Bharti, PGI, Chandigarh).

- That though the cases reported to government hospitals are mostly from lower income strata, incest is rampant in all sections of society.

  "The mother is part of the conspiracy of silence. Such is the social stigma attached to the abuse that mothers bury it till the physical or emotional symptoms become telling. Even doctors do not probe this angle if a minor girl comes with obvious symptoms of sexual abuse. While an infant runs a risk to her life in case she develops septicaemia in her private parts, young girls can suffer other physical complications, such as fibrosis, making them unable to bear children. The psychological implications are equally damaging, resulting in extreme sexual behaviours – they can either become too sexually active or fear even a touch – or they grow into adults incapable of having normal sexual relations. The trauma lasts a lifetime. (Dr Harshminder).

  S Salaria, Chairman, Punjab Child Rights Commission (PCRC): That the problem of liquor and drug abuse is on the rise in Punjab. There are bound to be social implications. But there is a social stigma attached to sexual abuse. When the father is an abuser, it becomes a bigger taboo. They also fear further harassment/ victimisation by the police.

Remedy: Child abuse, the bane of society.

Alcohol and drug abuse have potential to ruin a generation.

Need for introspection.

Need for counselling and awareness amongst parents.

Need for awareness amongst addicts youth about ill-effects of drinking and drugs.

Need for pragmatic laws.

CLINICAL ESTABLISHMENT ACT (CEA)

CLINICAL ESTABLISHMENT (REGISTRATION and REGULATION) Act 2010

Preface: The Clinical Establishment Act 2010 (passed by both the houses of Indian Parliament) was enacted under Article 252 of the Constitution.

Definition: The Clinical Establishment is defined under Section 2(c) of the Act as:

(i) A hospital, maternity home, nursing home, dispensary, clinic, sanatorium or an institution by whatever name called that offers services, facilities requiring diagnosis, treatment or care for illness, injury, deformity, abnormality or pregnancy in any recognised system of medicine (Allopathy, Homeopathy, Ayurveda, Unani or Siddha), except the establishments run by the Armed Forces.

Explanation: That for the purpose of this clause "Armed Forces" means the forces constituted under the Army Act, 1950, and the Navy Act, 1957.

(ii) A place established as an independent entity or part of an establishment referred to in sub-clause (i), in connection with the diagnosis or treatment of diseases where pathological, bacteriological, genetic, radiological, chemical, biological investigations or other diagnostic or investigative services with the aid of laboratory or other medical equipment, are usually carried on, and established and administered or maintained by any person or body of persons, whether incorporated or not, and shall include a clinical establishment owned, controlled or managed by:

(a) The government or a department of the government;

(b) A trust, whether public or private;

(c) A corporation (including a society) registered under a Central, Provincial or State Act, whether or not owned by the government;

(d) A local authority

(e) An individual doctor.

Jurisdiction:- That the Act was enacted by the Central Government under Article 252 of the Constitution for implementation in the:

- States of Arunachal Pradesh, Himachal Pradesh, Mizoram and Sikkim.
- Union Territories.
- Other States have a choice of implementing this legislation or enacting their own legislation on the subject.
- That any place where a patient is examined or advised treatment, is a Clinical Establishment (CE) and has to be registered under this Act.
- That no free medical camps or eye camps can be held - as the place will not be registered;
- That no home visits can be made;
- That no home deliveries can be performed;
- That no mobile health clinics can be run – as the particular area may not be registered for the Act.

Aims:

- That registration is mandatory.
- That the purpose of the Act is to provide for the registration and regulation of clinical

establishments with a view to prescribe minimum standards of facilities and services, which may be provided by them i.e.:

(a) To prevent quackery:

- That under the Act, only qualified persons will be able to practice medicine.
- That under the Act, even single practitioner shall be covered by CE.
- That under the Act, registration of all clinical establishments, shall be mandatory.
- That to run an unregistered clinical establishment, shall be an offence.

(b) To abide by the principles of Good Medical Practice.

- That Good Medical Practice sets out the principles and values on which Good practice is founded; these principles together describe medical professionalism in action.

Registration:- That as per the Act, registration is mandatory for all clinical establishments.

- That the CE Act is governed by Sections 12(1), 12(2), 2(o) and 10:

Section 12(1): under this section:

- That for registration and re-registration, it would be mandatory for all clinical establishments to fulfil the following criteria:
- That to prescribe the minimum standards of facilities and services.
- That to prescribe the minimum requirement of personnel.
- That to prescribe provisions for maintenance of records and reporting.
- That to prescribe such other conditions.

Section 12(2): The clinical establishment shall undertake to provide within the staff and facilities available, such medical examination and treatment as may be required to stabilise the emergency medical condition of any individual who comes or is brought to such clinical establishment.

Conclusion: The Act provides that every CE will have to treat all types of emergency cases and provide treatment in order to stabilise it before referring to other hospital/institute.

Section 2(o): Under this section stabilisation has been defined in the Act as:

"to stabilise (with the grammatical variations and cognate expressions)" means, with respect to an emergency medical condition specified in clause (d), to provide such medical treatment of the condition as may be necessary to assure, within reasonable medical probability, that no material deterioration of the condition is likely to result from or occur during the transfer of the individual from a clinical establishment".

Conclusion: The Act provides that every CE will have to treat all types of emergency cases and provide treatment in order to stabilise it before referring to other hospital/institute

Section 10: The State Government by notification, shall appoint the District Registering Authority for each district for registration of clinical establishments.

Composition of District Registration Authority:

Chairperson: District Collector

Convenor: District Health Officer

Members (3): On terms and conditions prescribed by Central Government.

Doctor's point of view: To avoid arbitrary punishment, one of the three nominated members of the District Registering Authority, should be a member from the legal profession on the lines of the similar provision under Section 21 of the Delhi Medical Council Act, 1997, and under Section 17(6) of the PNDT Act, 1994.

Procedure for Registration:

- That registration is done by the District Registering authority (District Health Officer).

- That the Provisional registration issued within ten days of submission of application as prescribed, without any inquiry or inspection.
- That Provisional registration is renewable yearly.
- That the establishments existing before commencement of the Act will have to apply within a year and those started after the commencement of the Act, within six months of the date of their establishment.
- That the registration will be non-transferable.
- That Provisional registration will not be granted beyond two years from the date of notification of standards in case of establishments that existed before the notification of standards, and beyond six months of notification of standards in case of those established after the notification of standards.
- That Permanent registration will be granted for a period of five years, on submission of application along with fees and evidence of compliance with prescribed standards. The particulars of the applicant will be published for information and for any objections by the public within 30 days. If objections are received, the same will be communicated to the clinical establishment for a response within 45 days.

Penalty: - A fine of up to ₹ 5,00,000 (0.5 million) may be imposed by the District Registration Authority (notified by the State Government vide Section 10) meant for registration of clinical establishments.

Cancellation of Registration:

Section 32: - That the registration can be cancelled in case of any violation of:

32(1)(a) - the conditions of the registration are not being complied with; or 32(1)(b) - the person entrusted with the management of the clinical establishment has been convicted of an offence punishable under this Act.

- That means any offence even a minor one for which a monetary penalty is imposed will be a valid ground for cancellation.
- That the District Registering Authority is vested with quasi judicial powers and will decide about the punishment for offences under this Act and punishment is imposing of the monetary penalty and naturally penalty can only be imposed if one is convicted of the offence. This effectively means that if a penalty is levied that means conviction under the Act and it will be a valid ground for cancellation.

Doctor's point of view:

- That there is no room for even a single offence howsoever minor one.
- That the Act makes the practicing of medicine a zero margin profession.
- That a doctor commits even a minor non-clinical error like some short coming in record keeping and he/she is gone!
- That can a doctor work with free mind under such stressful conditions with a gun pointed to his/her head.
- That to compound the matters further, there is no provision for revocation of the cancellation, so once cancelled the doctor who is running his own hospital will have no alternative but to join some other hospital or start doing something else.

Offences and Punishments:

Section 42: - That running a clinical establishment without registration would be punishable for:

1st offence: a fine of ₹ 50 KA

2nd offence: a fine of ₹ 2 lac

Subsequent offence: 5 lac.

Serving in an unregistered clinical establishment: a fine of upto ₹ 25 KA. Wilful disobedience of any lawful direction or obstruction to lawful authority or refusal to submit any information asked for or living false information knowingly: a fine of upto ₹ 5 lakh.

Section 44: - That contravention by a company (hospital) the person in charge of the operations/management: liable for action.

Section 45: - That the provisions of Section 44 and punishments would be equally applicable to Government Departments: liable for action.

Critical Analysis:

- That the old Acts for registration of hospitals/ nursing homes in nine States (mentioned in the Act's Schedule), made registration mandatory only for the hospitals and nursing homes (excluding private clinics, clinical laboratories, blood banks, imaging centres etc.) to get registered with the State Health Authorities.
- That the old Acts applicable only to the Allopathic establishments.
- That AYUSH – Ayurveda, Unani, Siddha, Homeopathy establishments were not covered by these old Acts.
- That the new Central Act is a blanket legislation making it mandatory for all establishments i.e. hospitals, nursing homes, private clinics, clinical laboratories, blood banks, imaging centres etc. of all systems – Allopathic as well as AYUSH), to get registered by a common single Registering Authority (District Registering Authority).
- That the Defence Services establishments (Army, Naval, Airforce, Police, BSF, CRPF) exempted from registration for unknown reasons.
- That some of the States allowed to continue with their old Legislations, thereby exempting registration to the private clinics, clinical laboratories, imaging centres of all systems and hospitals/ nursing homes/dispensaries of non-allopathic systems (controversial/disputable part of the Act).
- That the Central and State Councils incld. the members from non-allopathic systems for

dealing with non-allopathic (AYUSH) establishments.

- That the District Registration Authority does not incld. representation from non-allopathic systems.

Confirmity to the Standards:

- That conformity to the standards: time consuming factor to lay down the standards for so many different types of establishments pertaining to different systems of medicine.
- That monitoring the compliance with standards by millions of establishments requires a fleet of officials.
- That implementing/enforcing the standards to millions of establishments: a very cumbersome procedure.
- That fear of inspector raj and undue harassment: main resentment.

Schedule of Charges:

- That schedule of charges for services: to be decided by the State – a provision not palpable to the clinical establishments at all. The State can not and should not dictate the fees for the services/procedures provided by the clinical establishments.
- That every clinical establishment should have the right to determine the charges for the services provided by it.
- That while confirming to the prescribed minimum standards, there may be a lot of difference between the standards of facilities and expertise provided by the establishments, catering to the different locations, clients, standards/tastes/ expectations and paying capacity of clients.
- That every clinical establishment should have the right to determine the charges for the services provided by it.

Standard Treatment Guidelines issued by the Central Government:

- That the standard treatment protocols, in principle, help to ensure certain basic standards of treatment.
- That these protocols can be acceptable only as long as they are limited to broad principles, life threatening emergencies (CPR, anaphylactic shock, poisoning, treatment of snake-bite etc.) or treatment of major public health problems (such as AIDS, malaria, pulmonary tuberculosis).
- That physicians should have adequate freedom to decide as per their learning and experience, which modality of treatment to use in which situation in broad compliance with the protocols practised by the professional community – nationally and internationally.

Maintenance of EHR and EMR of every patient:

- That may be determined and issued by the Central or State Government. A good idea in principle, but a requirement, which is likely to be resented by the private clinics because of the added cost (of the system, software and the salary of the computer operator) as well as additional workload for busy clinicians.
- That many physicians esp. of Indian System of Medicine (ISM), may not be computer savvy at all.

Fear of Scrutiny:

- That physicians are worried most about scrutiny and exposure of their professional inadequacies, shortcuts, poor facilities, and mistakes as well as the harassment caused by the inspecting officials.
- That millions of private clinics, nursing homes/ hospitals, clinical laboratories etc. have been operating throughout the country, unknown, unregistered, thereby not subject to any scrutiny/ inspection/questioning by authorised authorities. There is no check over their facilities or standards and many of them giving care and treatment of dubious quality to the patients, often in utter disregard of the rules and regulations.

- That their fear is, once registered, they would no more be able to hide from the legal and professional scrutiny.

Public notice:

- That publishing the particulars of the clinical establishment for public comments is not a palpable idea.
- That purpose of publishing not clear, as the public will have no clue about the technical aspects/standards of the hospital esp. In case of the newly commissioned establishments. Also the local community or the rival establishments are unlikely to come forward with any meaningful comments.
- That periodic feedback/comments from public about the quality of services provided by the establishments can be important in case of already permanently registered establishments as their renewal due after five long ears.

Cancellation of Registration (Section 32):

- That cancellation of registration in case of private clinics, clinical laboratories, nursing homes etc. may be possible, but in case of hospitals it may not be practically feasible idea in view of patients admitted for indoor treatment.
- That in case of repeated violations and reckless disregard for the safety of patients, exemplary penalties, to the tune of a yearly profit amount and/or imprisonment for the trustees/CEO/COO (if found negligent), may be more practical.

Treatment of life-threatening emergencies:

- That treatment in case of life-threatening emergencies remain the prime duty of every doctor, wherever, in whatever position or location. Shirking this responsibility or refusal to render necessary assistance in timely transportation of patient will be viewed as medical negligence liable to punishment.
- That non-payment of medical bills of treatment of emergency cases is a point of serious and

genuine concern of the medical community. The Act is silent on this aspect.

- That the concerned Authorities must redress the grievance to the satisfaction of medical professionals by following a mechanism of ensuring problem free reimbursement of bills. The liability may be borne by the insurance sector or by the government itself.

Opposition/Resentment to Act by the Medical Fraternity (Doctor's point of view):

The Act has evoked strong resentment from the medical fraternity. It opines:

- That It is doubtful that this will improve the health care dramatically or that It will prove to be boon for the patients.
- That, it will result in many fold escalation in cost of treatment which an average person will find difficult to afford.
- That an ordinary person will suffer the most.
- That there are many objectionable clauses in the Clinical Establishment Act 2010, which will make the medical practice esp. by single or couple doctors in small setups almost impossible. The Act appears motivated to promote flourishing of only large corporate hospitals. Given the diversity of Indian Population, and clustering of medical facilities in different areas this appears to be a retrograde step which will in one stroke kill medical entrepreneurship.
- That no free medical camps or eye camps can be held, as the place will not be registered.
- That no home deliveries can be done.
- That no mobile health clinics can be run without registration in the particular area.
- That no provision has been made in the Act, stating that who will pay for the treatment ? Worst hit will be small clinics run by a single practitioner or a couple managing small hospitals/nursing homes.

- That doctors attain specialisations in very limited areas of their respective specialty. They are specialists in their own field and have a right to practice in their specialty. They cannot stabilise the patients of other specialties 'within the staff and the facilities available' in their clinical establishment.

  They cannot be forced to engage another specialist for emergency cases. The doctor will be caught in a Catch-22 situation i.e. if he treats the emergency case which he is not qualified to treat and God forbid, the patient dies, the doctor will be held guilty of negligence and if he doesn't treat, he will be liable for action under this Act.
- A General surgeon may have operated and established his practice only by managing haemorrhoids. Forcing him to stabilise a case of acute pancreatitis or to close down his establishment may deny the society of services of a competent surgeon.
- What will a Medical specialist do in case of a surgical emergency ?, or
- What will an Eye specialist do in case of a heart attack ?, or
- What will an Orthopaedic surgeon do in case of obstetric emergency ?
- That a patient who has suffered a heart attack requires primary angioplasty as best mode of treatment. Similarly a patient with vomiting of blood (Haemoptysis) is best handled by a facility providing endoscopy.

  Even very good medical centres will not have facilities for all the procedures. There will always be a risk of deterioration when patient is being sent to higher centre. But the risk of not doing angioplasty or endoscopy in appropriate situation is greater. This law will be a hindrance in good medical practice.
- That even, if the emergency case happens to be his own speciality, but the patient cannot be

stabilised, "within the staff and the facilities available" then what to do ? Patient cannot be referred because he is not 'stabilised' as per the Act. So what do you do?, just let the patient die? without giving him a remote chance of survival if he could have been sent to a hospital better equipped to deal with such cases.

- That how can a single or couple doctors doing their practice in their own specialities in small centres, provide 24 hrs. emergency care in any other speciality? After notification of this Act, everyone will have to manage multi-specialities in his clinical establishment. For that huge investments required and the cost will have to be passed on to the patient. Forcing them to provide round the clock emergency care; free of cost, means they have to bear expenditure to hire minimum of four MBBS doctors, nurses, OT technicians, radiographers and lab technicians to provide round the clock services. That makes smaller hospitals/nursing homes unviable and it is a certainty that many smaller clinical establishments will close down.
- That to make it mandatory for all hospitals including OPD clinics to make arrangements to give guaranteed treatment to all emergency cases round the clock and that too without any provisions for recovering the cost of the treatment is neither feasible nor desirable and not acceptable. Accepting this will mean that all these small to medium hospitals/nursing homes will close down and only big corporate sector hospitals which can provide round the clock emergency services in all specialities will survive and then those will charge at exorbitant rates that even middle and upper middle class will find difficult to afford. Why not an emergency patient, approach a hospital that advocates providing 24 hr. Emergency services.
- That there are retired professors and senior doctors of medical/surgical specialities, who are

doyens in their field and now wish to practice in a limited fashion, providing only consultation or wish to operate on limited number of specialised cases. By bringing this Act, we force all doctors to become unpaid bonded labourers of the society with no freedom to regulate their working hrs. Effectively all establishments which desire to provide only limited services of their own speciality and within their resources will be forced to close down. This draconian law in effect states that an individual doctor cannot practice medicine unless he/she invests crores (millions) and works 24 hrs. For which patients may or may not pay.

- That a highly skilled doctor suffers a heart attack and is advised restricted professional activity and no stress. Under this Act, he/she has to retire by closing his/her clinical establishment because he/she will no longer be able to provide round the clock medical services to all emergencies. That again is society's loss, as it may deprive services of a trained professional who would have provided services – may be for a limited hrs.
- That the Act will become another avenue for corruption, because the punishments of far reaching consequences including cancellation of registration with no provision for its revocation will be awarded not by the courts but by the District Registration Authority, that will be inspecting prosecuting and Judging authority, all rolled into one !

  "Too much power is being vested into this Authority and Absolute power always corrupts"
- That the State has to provide right to health to all its citizens. The right to health of any citizen is against the State and not against fellow citizen even if he is a doctor.
- That this ill conceived idea will destroy the private healthcare sector which has so long been filling the vacuum created by the Government

abdicating its own fundamental duties to provide affordable and accessible healthcare facilities to its citizens.

Does it help remove quackery ?

- That Para 34 allows inspection of unregistered premises only after giving proper notice (and adequate time for the quack to close shop and disappear). However, as per Para 33(1) no such notice is required to inspect a registered (legal) clinical establishment.

Section 2.1.1. of the Code of Ethics Regulations, 2002:

(Indian Medical Council Professional conduct, Etiquette and Ethics):

"However for good reason, when a patient is suffering from an ailment which is not within the range of experience of the treating physician, the physician may refuse treatment and refer the patient to another physician". It is of paramount importance to provide life-saving emergency treatment to citizens, such treatment is costly and does not come free and the treatment giver needs to be compensated through an appropriate mechanism that needs to be worked out by the government before the bill is made operative.

Advantages (Benefits) of the Act:

- That the Act is a positive development, if implemented in all the States in the form, broadly in line with the Central Act and Rules.
- That it would act as the first ever factual census of the number, category, speciality and location of all the physicians and all the medical establishments of all the systems of medicine in the country.
- That helpful in the countrywide planning and posting of physicians as well as healthcare establishments.
- That uptil now the Authorities do not know exactly how many of what category are available in a particular area.

- That Registration without any inspection or inquiry, based on the documents submitted by the establishment, should be encouraging for many private clinics, nursing homes to come forward and opt for registration.
- That it helps in isolating and identifying millions of quacks, playing havoc with the lives of people all over the country.
- That the system of registration will necessarily help in improving the standards of healthcare establishments within few years.
- That the system of registration will bring about some uniformity in the standards of care all over the country.
- That for maximum benefits and uniform effects, the Central Act should have been made applicable in all the States and Union Territories.
- That being a State subject, mandatory application is not possible. As most of the States enact their own legislations, there are variations in the provisions from State to State.
- That the important aspect is the speed of enactment and enforcement of legislation in the States. There should be no delays on any account.
- That for better implementation, lacunae are to be addressed and removed and the legislations made more friendly to the medical community.
- That the medical professionals also rise above the individual interests and keep in mind of larger public as well as professional interests.

Reference: 1. Dr. SK Joshi, Clinical Establishment Act, 2010.

CONSUMER PROTECTION ACT (CPA):

Preface: Over the ages, man's greed to have more and more, increased many fold and he started using available sources without any accountability. Since industrialisation, natural resources, incld. man-power have been used and consumed very drastically, thereby creating problems e.g. global warming, scarcity of water and food, pollution, inadequate medical aids, poor education system, un-employment, recession, violence, crime and exploitation etc., have emerged, while quality of life is lost. That we talk about survival of the fittest, meaning 'more profit more efficient'. Those who are not having good health, quality, technology and money can't exist. To prove him/ herself 'Fittest One' every one is in the race to increase profit by hook and crook and thus adopting illicit and unethical methods e.g. by using new technologies without knowing their side effects, hybrid variety of raw materials with deteriorating ingredients, reducing manpower with increased work pressure, adulteration, malpractices used in marketing, misleading the consume through luring advertisements and evasion of tax, corruption and many more. Over all the ultimate sufferer is consumer who is paying higher cost for sub-standard products. That consumer is unaware of the actual cost of the product due to faulty system. That pharmaceutical sector is worst affected where cost charged to patient for life saving medicines is much higher by the unethical professionals. That the best remedy available is determination of actual 'cost of production' of a product or service. That cost accountancy is still a profession with perfection and doing justice to the consumer.

(A Sharma, Secretary ICWAI, Chandigarh).

Rights of patients:

The rights of patients flow from the Universal Declaration of Human Rights adopted by the United Nations General Assembly in 1948 and since then, several countries around the world have recognised the rights of patients through specific laws or charters. The European Charter of Patients Rights, recognises fourteen rights of patients incld. right to choice, right to information, right to consent, right to privacy and confidentiality, right to compensation and the right to participate in policymaking in the area of health. That Israel has a Patients Rights Act, while Japan has Patients' Rights Ombudsman. In India, even though the government is yet to turn its attention to this crucial aspect pertaining to doctor-patient relationship, the Courts esp. the Consumer Courts, have stepped in to protect the patients. Their orders have helped define the rights of patients and it is imperative that consumers be aware of Consumer Protection Act (CPA) 1986 and Consumer Protection Act (CPA) 1995, related to medical profession. (P Girimaji).

CONSUMER PROTECTION ACT (CPA) - 1986

Preface:

- That CPA is to protect the interest of the user/or purchaser (consumer) of goods/or service, from exploitation by the seller/or service provider.
- That the act was passed by the Indian parliament in 1986.

Aims:

- To protect the interest of the consumer (purchaser/or consumer) of the goods/or service, from exploitation by the seller/or service provider.

CONSUMER PROTECTION ACT (CPA) - 1995

Preface

- That to protect the interest of the consumer (purchaser/or consumer) of the goods/or service, from exploitation by the seller/or service provider.
- That currently the doctor-patient relationship has been commercialised to a great extent, resulting in rising trend in medical negligence.

Necessity:

- That Medical services were brought into the purview of CPA in 1995.
- That prior to CPA enactment, the aggrieved patient/or relatives had three alternatives for redressal of grievances i.e. to approach:
- the Civil Courts
- the Criminal Courts
- the Medical Councils.
- That so far justice to the patients has been denied due to reasons:

- Enormous delays.
- Hectic and cumbersome Court procedures.
- Medical Councils have practically become toothless (powerless) and corrupt (malpractices).
- That is why the aggrieved and unsatisfied patients or their relatives demanded and have been approaching the Consumer Courts (established) these days with great expectations.

Expectations: That to expect Good Medical Practices from doctors e.g.:

- To make the patient's care, doctor's first concern.
- To protect and promote the health of patients and the public.
- To receive a good standard of practice and patient's care from doctors.
- To provide the patients the information they want or need in a way they can understand.
- To maintain healthy doctor-patient relationship.

Benefits:

- No Court fee or stamp duty.
- No enormous delays and without any hectic and cumbersome procedures.
- Simple procedure i.e. complaint can be filed in a specific format.
- Speedy disposal of the case i.e. less time consuming.

Forums:

- District Consumer – at the lowest level.
- State Consumer Commission – at the middle level.
- National Consumer Commission – at the highest level.
- Supreme Court – a final order passed by the National Consumer Commission is appealable to the Supreme Court.

Litigations: Medical Negligence is the base of all litigations against doctors under CPA.

Burden of Proof: The burden of proof is always on the complainant. He/she has to prove that the damage has been done due to the doctor's negligence and such negligence is the direct and proximate cause of the damage.

Resistance (Resentment) posed by Medical Profession:

Apprehension: A perceptible sense of fright is common amongst majority of the doctors due to following factors/reasons:

- Frivolous complaints may be lodged against the doctors either to harass or to black-mail them.
- Inherent risk may always be there in any form of treatment.
- Response of an individual may be variable from patient to patient e.g. a drug may be effective in one patient, while ineffective in another patient.
- Speed of recovery is variable amongst each individual and may/or may not be dependant upon treatment alone, but also on the patient's strength.
- Basic infrastructures e.g. Clinical laboratoty, X-ray, Ventillator etc. may not be made available at every placel (mainly due to cost factor).

Defensive medicine:

- As a precautionary measure (safety purpose) many doctors have been opting for defensive medicine – aimed at avoiding medical negligence suits and hefty compensation claims, resulting in wastage of time and energy, besides wastage of financial and medical resources and delayed treatment of the patient (by advising investigations – many a times are not absolutely required).

Insurance coverage:

- These days many doctors (GPs and Specialists) esp. in the private sector have been opting for insurance cover, in order to prevent financial loss besides mental tension, resulting from various litigations relating to the medical negligence charges brought against them at Consumer Courts (Consumer Redressal Forum) and in Criminal Courts under Section 304-A of IPC Act.

Conclusion:- That there is hardly any reason for any honest doctor to entertain any fear if they are doing their jobs properly with amicable attitude towards their patients and their relatives.

- That Consumer Protection Act (CPA) has changed only the procedure of Law and not the principles of Law.
- That the doctors should rather welcome CPA.
- That doctors are also the consumers of various goods and professional services.

DOMESTIC VIOLENCE

Preface: - Domestic violence against women is a tradition of sorts. This system of relegating the women to the status of slaves has been evolved by men. Politicians are least bothered about the problems faced by these women in distress.

Act: - That domestic violence is punishable under Act 2006:

- That the Centre promulgated the Domestic Violence Act 2006, for protection of women facing regular domestic violence.
- That the Act was enacted in October 2006.

Aims: - To protect the interest of the women from domestic violence by the husband or his family members (mother/father-in-law, sister/brother-in-law.

Vox-populi: - That Rajit Tandi, a Dalit woman in Pithora, Chhatisgarh: walked out of her marriage, as her husband was an alcoholic and wife-beater, like most other in her village. She decided to realise women in her community speak up against domestic violence and turned activist. Today her women's groups put together plans to help sisters in distress (facing similar issues).

Reference: E Kaiser: Telling them not to tolerate domestic violence, HT March, 2014.

DOWRY MENACE

Preface: - That young married/un-married girls are being killed for money, a piece of land, a motorcycle/ scooter, a car etc.

Incidence:
- That dowry related crimes are on the rise.
- That in year 2013, 793 dowry death cases were registered across 53 Indian Cities, and Delhi topped the list with 125 cases.
- That number of cases registered between January 1 to May 31 on dowry related crimes against women in Mumbai (Table XII-1):

TABLE XII-1: Cases registered between 1/1/14 to 31/5/14 in Mumbai*

Crime	*2013*	*2014*
Dowry deaths (u/s 304B IPC)	5	10
Dowry-suicides (u/s 306 IPC)	19	16
Dowry Prohibition Act, 1961	5	4
Cruelty by husband/relatives (u/s 498A IPC) (5-6% conviction rate)	236	238

* (*Source:* Mumbai Police, HT)

Cases:
- Nitesh Yadav, May 2014: That soon after the marriage, the boy's family started troubling Nitesh for dowry. They taunted her, threatened her, beat her and would even throw her out of the house. She kept shuttling between her father's home and her in-laws. One month after delivery, she was burnt by her in-laws. In her statement to the Magistrate, Nitish accused her husband and in-laws for setting her on fire. She passed away after enduring a month of unbearable pain and discomfort as her burnt flesh rotted away.

  Case status: Police arrested her husband and mother-in-law, and after her death arrested her father-in-law and the elder brother-in-law, leaving the younger brother-in-law for lack of evidence. LK Jain, State Women's Commission Chief said that until the people's mindset changes, the situation will not improve.
- Sanjana Kolwanker, February 2014: That she had set herself on fire after enduring years of harassment at the hands of her in-laws.

Her husband saw her set herself on fire but did nothing to stop her and took her to the hospital only on the insistence of neighbours. She succumbed to her injuries four days later.

Case status: Sanjana's family alleged that her husband Sanjay and his family would cerbally and physically assault her as they deemed her family incapable of helping her and made indirect dowry demands.

Police registered an FIR following Sanjana's death, and arrested her husband and in-laws under Sections 498A and 306. They were eventually granted bail.

- Sonika, July 2014: That barely a month after marriage her in-laws started torturing her for dowry. Sonika's in-laws wanted ₹ 2 lakh more despite being paid a handsome amount during wedding. Sonika was burnt alive by her in-laws. Except her charred body found in one corner of a room, not a single item in the room was burnt.

  Case status: Police arrested Sonika's husband and father-in-law. Other members of her in-laws family are still on the run, incld. her mother-in-law and two sisters-in-law. Her family has vowed to bring the people responsible for her death to justice.

Act: - That dowry death is punishable under Section 304B IPC.

Aims: - To protect the interest of the women from dowry related crimes by the husband or his family members (mother/father-in-law, sister/brother-in-law.

Vox-populi: - Build public opinion: It is really tragic that in today's progressive world, the evil of dowry continues to exist. In order to root out dowry from the society, we need to build strong public opinion against it. We must make citizens sensitive towards the issue. Children in schools and colleges should be made to take a pledge that they would neither seek nor give dowry.

- Support daughters: Parents must support their daughters by providing them good education, and encourage them to raise their voice against the greedy in-laws demands of dowry.
- Make girls independent: In order to rid the society of dowry menace, merely making women aware of their rights is not enough, they need to be truly independent. There is need to make laws more stringent, to see changes.

EVE-TEASING

Preface: The menace of eve-teasing has reached to an alarming level. What to talk about public places, the offenders even reach the girls house in order to physically harm the family. Whether she confronts the eve teaser or complains to the police, the hapless female finds herself at cross-roads and always at the receiving end.

Incidence: Such is the extent of sexual harassment, that even in a modern and educated society, the numbers only underline an ugly reality. For this campaign, institutional changes to ensure a safer placeare to be major aim.

That in the current era, more girls are working and move freely, yet majority of them face sexual harassment, and only minority find their work place safe. Sexual harassment is rising in spite of new laws and public outrage. Girls are being sexually harassed in the public domain, yet this misbehaviour is not under public scrutiny.

That public

Risk factors:

- To use deserted roads, esp. late at night.
- To walk alone and not in groups.
- To ignore indescent remarks by the boys, as the girls prefer to suffer in silence. This way they embolden the eve-teasers and thereby encourage them to strike again.
- To avoid reporting to police about the eve-teasing.

- Mushrooming PG business.
- Discotheque culture.
- Vulnerable areas: Most of these incidents take place outside schools, colleges, university campuses and premises for private tutorials. Rehri markets (overcrowded) too are prone to eve-teasing incidents, with miscreants passing obscene remarks and even touching/molesting girls and young women in busy markets. Festivals and shopping fairs also witness eve-teasing incidents.

Eve-teasers profile:

Most eve-teasers are outsider students from neighbouring areas. The miscreants mostly zip around in their cars/motorbikes and pass lewd remarks at passing girls/women. In certain cases, colony residents too indulge in harassing girls/women esp. moving at late night hrs. Many men still view women as inferior to them and cannot tolerate any reactions from them, as it hurts their male ego and the miscreants end up assaulting the victims. Senior citizens too indulge in eve-teasing. Cops too found guilty of act. Girls often fear backlash.

Grouse:
- Harassment of family post complaint.
- Fear of character assassination.
- Indecent cops.
- Senior citizens teasing girls.
- Financial status should not hinder action.

Legal: Punishable under Section 294 of IPC, if they sing, recite or utter any obscene song or word in or near any public place to the annoyance of others.

Misuse: Male students voiced their apprehension that law could be misused, which in reality is very remote, as no sane girl/woman would like to involve herself unnecessarily and be under stress by lodging a false complaint. Also the case can't be registered without proper verification of the complaint.

Police: Fighting the menace of eve-teasing:

SSP, during an interaction with college students on eve-teasing, motivated the girls to become strong – physically and psychologically to combat the problem. He sought cooperation and alertness from girls to minimise the incidence of crime against women and exorted them to fight for their right to dignified existence and fear-free atmos-phere. He ensured that the offender would be dully punished, irrespective of his social or political stature. About the right reaction to a situation, he advised: Use intuition, couple it with intelligence and inform the police accordingly.

Q. One of the male students asked the SSP on what their reaction should be if girls pass comments ?

Ans. Responding to the question in a lighter way, the SSP said the boy should consider himself lucky if he received comments from a girl.

(Naunihal Singh, SSP UT, Chandigarh)

* Case: October 16: Police have arrested 3 miscreants, on the charge of eve-teasing and intimidation.
* Case: Police have arrested 20 miscreants, incld. a home guard volunteer, on charge of eve-teasing from different parts of Chandigarh, in the past more than a week, while the PCR received more than 30 calls from victims of eve-teasing during this period.
* Case: August 10: Satpal, a resident of Dadumajra colony, booked for eve-teasing and outraging modesty of a girl at dividing road of Sectors 37 and 38.
* Case: August 23: Shekhar, a resident of Maloya village, booked for making obscene gestures and singing vulgar songs in front of a woman.
* Case: September 16: Manoj Kumar and Ajay, residents of Vikas Nagar, Mauli Jagran, were arrested from Sector 17 Inter-state bus stand, for eve-teasing.

* Case: September 30: Ranjit Singh, a resident of Sector 22, working as a driver, was arrested under Section 294 of IPC, after being spotted passing obscene remarks at girls near the Tribune roundabout by a police control room vehicle (PCR) deployed in the area.

Vox populi: While many feel the need for a stringent law to punish eve-teasers, most say police presence should be increased around educational institutions and other vulnerable points – Cops need to step up vigil.

Supportive of Police efforts:

* Principal Dr Puneet Bedi was supportive of the efforts being made by the authorities to ensure safety of women. She said such endeavours enthuse in the public the spirit of oneness against crime, thereby making society fraternal, stronger and more goal-oriented.

  (Dr P Bedi, Chandigarh)

* Take strict action against eve-teasers:

  The incidents of all types of crimes against women are on the increase because of the fast diminishing fear of law and police among the youths. The police officials should hold periodical interaction with the girls, provide necessary protection and security to them and increase patrolling at strategic points. The cops should also take strict action against eve-teasers to inspire confidence among the girls. The police top-brass should introspect as to what has gone wrong in policing, resulting into spurt in crimes and decreasing fear of law.

  (PC Sanghi, Chandigarh)

Introduce helpline for women to report eve-teasing:

* It is high time that the menace of eve-teasing is curbed. The police and local administration need to pull up their socks and take measures to check this heinous crime against women. Apart from increasing security near schools, college and bus stops, the police should introduce a

quick response helpline for women so that they can promptly report such incidents. Undoubtedly, this will give a feeling of security and self-defence to girls, and encourage them to report such incidents. In addition to this, there is a need to ensure that eve-teasers are dealt with an iron hand, so that they feel ashamed of their doing and do not think about repeating their disgraceful act.

(MB Dhamrait, Kharar)

* Girls' dressing sense provokes boys:

  One cannot blame the boys only. They are provoked because of girls' modern dressing sense.

  (B Bitu, Chandigarh)

* Society should support police initiative:

- Apart from encouraging women to come forward to report such incidents to the police, orientation programme for boys' colleges are also required to motivate them to desist from the evil and to make aware of consequences.

  (registration of an FIR is sufficient to ruine one's carrier).

  (SL Soni, Chandigarh).

* Need for social change:

- Social change is taking place fast in some spheres while traditional practices continue to be part of multifaceted persona. There have been living-in relationships, women are heading offices and industries, single women are adopting children, men take pride in looking after household activities like cooking and decorating their homes etc. Best friends are no longer of the same gendre, groups of boys and girls are travelling out together. Simultaneously, Indian culture is booming e.g. Karva Chauth richly drapes the markets and women, Raksha Bandhan load the brothers' wrists and honour Tikka (Bhai Dooj) marks the fore-heads with responsibility, and the bride ushers in her lavish Sangeet with

'Sheela ki Jawani'. Add to this mix the migrants, Industrial workers and traditionalists who enjoy the item number, but maintain that female respectability is bound to her conduct and distance from men. What is a right in one setting becomes an invitation in another. But, neither the modernity nor the traditional challenges, the growing market for sexuality, the expression of power or the overriding individual needs collective responsibility. (Dr Rainuka Dagar, Chandigarh).

Author: Do's and Don'ts for Girls: Avoid use of deserted roads, esp. Late at night –

- Avoid walking alone and walk in groups, outside schools/colleges.
- Avoid ignoring indescent remarks by the boys, and prefer not to suffer in silence. This way do not embolden the eve-teasers and thereby encourage them to strike again.
- Girls must speak up and report to the police about eve-teasers' vehicle registration number.
- Girls to wear helmets for more safety.
- Avoid taking lift while walking alone.
- Dress up properly, in order to avoid lewd remarks from offenders with low thinking personality

Countering the menace (Young women more assertive):

- That the 1st move to secure women is the nature and extent of abuse must be understood and people sensitised that it is not just the brutal or the physical that is abuse, but its many forms included indecent behaviour, leering, kerb crawling and stalking. All of these are a violation, and should be unacceptable to any male or female.
- That reaction continues to remain focussed on brutalities of rape and molestation, while condoning abusive, intrusive misconduct and even legitimising offensive violation as part of a natural sexuality.

- That if the culture of silence continues, accepting abuse of others and blaming modernity, media and victims themselves, an epidemic awaits.
- That Desperate situations demand desperate measures. So would it seem going by the rising number of eve-teasing incidents, and the way some of the city girls are countering the menace. Gone are the days when they would ignore obscene remarks or bear the insult quietly. The gen-next women like late-night partying, are well equipped to have their following ways:
- Some girls react to eve-teasing by raising voice or even using abusive language against miscreants.
- Carry products e.g. chilli powder, pepper spray, Swiss knives, needles, steel batons (short thin stick) or deodorants. These are some of the 'weapons' that are gaining popularity amongst the college-going girls.
- Carry a 'stungun', a weapon that momentarily disablews a person with an electric shock.
- Martial art: gaining popularity amongst the teenagers. In fact, martial art to be made a compulsory subject for school &college girls and for all working girls, as one of the best safety measure.

Do's and Don'ts for Boys:

- Avoid eve-teasing as the punishment (registration of an FIR is sufficient to ruine one's carrier.
- Be a responsible citizen and behave like a Gentel-man (one who behaves proper in presence of women). Always think the victim girl/woman to be someone's daughter or sister like yours own.

Stop the offenders from eve-teasing, by adopting:

- To persuading them not to indulge in this indescent behaviour.
- To note down the registration number of the offender's vehicle and report to the police for immediate action

- To support the victim rather than the offenders.
- To accompany the girl walking alone at odd hrs. In a descent manner, to her destination.

EUTHANASIA (MERCY KILLING)

Preface: Is defined as an act or practice of putting painless death to people, who are very sick, especially in cases of incurable suffering, or very old, in order to stop them from suffering (the intentional killing by act or omission of a dependant human being for his/or her alleged benefit. (The key word here is "intentional").

Note: If death is not intended, it is not an act of euthanasia.

Classification:

- Active Euthanasia: Intentionally causing a person's death by performing an action such as by giving a lethal injection.

  Example: A lethal injection given to a patient with a terminal disease.

  Active euthanasia declared illegal by the Supreme Court of India, while allowing passive euthanasia vide SC Bench's verdict on 7th March 2011.

  Active euthanasia is permitted in countries such as Netherlands, Belgium and Switzerland.
- Passive Euthanasia: Intentionally causing death by withholding medical care, food and water of terminally ill patients.

  Example: Removing the Heart-Lung machine (Ventilator) from a patient in coma. The Supreme Court of India allows passive euthanasia.

  Passive euthanasia is allowed in:

USA: In the States of Oregon, Montana and Washington

- Voluntary euthanasia: When the person who is killed has requested to be killed.
- Non-voluntary: When the person who is killed made no request and gave no consent.
- Involuntary euthanasia: When the person who is killed made an expressed wish to the contrary.

- Assisted suicide: Someone provides an individual with the information, guidance, and means to take his or her own life with the intention that they will be used for this purpose. When it is a doctor who helps another person to kill themselves it is called "physician assisted suicide."

What Euthanasia is NOT: There is no euthanasia unless the death is intentionally caused by what was done or not done. Thus, some medical actions that are often labeled "passive euthanasia" are no form of euthanasia, since the intention to take life is lacking. These acts include not commencing treatment that would not provide a benefit to the patient, withdrawing treatment that has been shown to be ineffective, too burdensome or is unwanted, and the giving of high doses of pain-killers that may endanger life, when they have been shown to be necessary. All those are part of good medical practice, endorsed by law, when they are properly carried out.

Factors Favouring Euthanasia:

Factors:
- Unbearable pain
- Right to commit suicide
- Forced to stay alive.

Unbearable pain:

- May be the major argument in favour of euthanasia.
- Euthanasia advocates stress the cases of unbearable pain as the top criterias for euthanasia.
- Drawback: people are driven into a painless drugged (undignified) state and for that reason may require euthanasia (on demand).

Solution:
- Almost all types of pain can be eliminated fully and in unrelieved cases can be reduced significantly by providing adequate treatment &:
- By upgrading medical knowledge to healthcare professionals on these vital issues,

- By enlarging access to healthcare.
- By making aware patients about their consumer rights (to pain relief).
- By referring the patient to a specialist in pain management, for relief of pain as well as to alleviate emotional suffering and depression that may accompany pain.

Right to commit suicide factor:

- Euthanasia is not about the right to die. It's about the right to kill.
- Euthanasia is not about giving rights to the person who dies but, instead, is about changing the law and public policy to support the doctors, relatives and others, to end another person's life, directly and intentionally.
- People do have the power to commit suicide. Suicide and attempted suicide are not criminalised. Suicide is a tragic, individual act.
- Euthanasia is not about a private act. It's about letting one person facilitate the death of another. That is a matter of very public concern since it can lead to tremendous abuse, exploitation and erosion of care for the most vulnerable people among us.
- Supreme Court of India on 7th March, 2011, recommended to the Parliament to consider decriminalising attempt to suicide, saying the provision had become anachronistic and the time has come when Section 309 IPC (attempt to commit suicide) should be deleted by the Parliament.
- US Supreme Court Backs Oregon Assisted Suicide Law (2006):
  - Supreme Court Holds Hearing on Assisted Suicide Dispute:
  - Gonzales v/s Oregon (2005)
  - Washington v/s Glucksberg Supreme Court Ruling (1997)
  - Vacco v/s Quill Supreme Court Ruling (1997)

Forced to stay alive factor:

- That neither the law nor medical ethics permit force to keep a person alive against his/her wishes.
- That postponing death by any available means is violation of law and being cruel and inhumane.
- That at certain stage, continuing treatment on compassionate base, may be considered medically unwise.

Solution: That is the deciding time when all efforts should be made:

- To make the patient's remaining time comfortable, by alleviating pain and other discomforts (emotional suffering and depression).

ARGUMENTS FAVOURING EUTHANASIA:

Legal Fraternity:

- The Supreme Court of India: "Active euthanasia declared illegal by the Supreme Court of India, while allowing passive euthanasia vide SC Bench's verdict on 7th March 2011. The SC made it clear that the guidelines for passive euthanasia (withholding medical treatment for terminally ill patients) would be in force until Parliament enacts a proper law."
- **Delhi High Court Judge RS Sodhi (Retd):** "India allows capital punishment and the State is allowed to take one's life. Then why an individual who suffers extensively should not be allowed to say I have had enough?"
- **Delhi High Court Judge JD Kapoor (Retd):** "Expressed similar views".
- **Sr. SC lawyer KTS Tulsi:** "The SC ruling with in-built safeguards has made the right to live more meaningful."
- Legal expert Subash Kashyap: "It is good that the Apex Court has laid down certain guidelines and each plea for mercy killing will be decided on a case-by-case basis. If there was a general rule, there would have been misuse.

- **Legal Panel: Right to die:**
- **Justice PV Reddi, The Law Commission's Chairman:**

  In April 2011, the Govt. sought the Law Commission's views after the Supreme Court (SC) legalised passive euthanasia in the Shanbaug case and said its verdict will be the Law of the land until Parliament enacted a Law on the issue.

  The Law Commission has sent a draft "Medical Treatment of terminally-ill patients (Protection of Patients and Medical Practitioners) Bill" to the Government, to initiate measures to enact a comprehensive law on passive euthanasia, subject to certain safeguards. "A competent adult patient has the right to insist that there should be no invasive medical treatment by way of artificial life-sustaining measures/treatment and such a patient, provided that the doctor is satisfied that the patient has taken an 'informed decision' based on free exercise of his/her will," the panel said. Should the patient not be in a position to take healthcare decisions due to an irreversible coma or is in a persistent vegetative state, the doctor's or relatives' decision to with-hold or withdraw medical treatment is not final, the report stated.

  But, active euthanasia remains a crime under Section 303 (murder) or 304 (culpable homicide not amounting to murder) of the Indian Penal Code (IPC), along with physician-assisted suicide under Section 306 IPC (abetment to suicide).

Medical fraternity: The divide is sharp.

- There are many experienced doctors who insist that:

  'Quality' is more important than 'right to life' esp. in the case of Aruna Shanbaug, who has been living in a permanent vegetative state for the last 38 yrs.

Right to Die Organisations:

Amicus Curiae (Friend of the Court):

- "Passive euthanasia should be allowed. Right to life does not include right to live in a vegetative state."
- "End of violation of one's right to live with dignity."

EUTHANASIA SQUADS: NVVE "RIGHT TO DIE": NEDERLANDSE VERENIGING VOOREEN VRIJWILLIG LEVENSEINDE (NVVE)

London: Euthanasia squads offer death by delivery:

- A controversial mobile euthanasia programme has been launched in the Netherlands, sending specialised teams door-to-door to help patients end their lives, reports the Independent. The project which has provoked sharp criticism from doctors, is the brainchild of the Dutch's largely donor-funded pro-mercy killing group "Right to Die" NL (NVVE in Dutch). It follows the Government's 2002 decision to legalise euthanasia, making the Netherlands the first Country in the world to do so. Right to Die-NL, said it had received seventy phone calls from potential assisted suicide patients since the scheme was announced in early February, 2012. It said that its six tems expected to receive around 1,000 requests each yr. The organisation stressed that its mobile units were comprised of doctors and nurses, specially trained in performing assisted suicide at its clinic. It said the procedure involved injecting the patient with a sleep inducing drug and then with barbiturates to stop heart and lung function, according to the newspaper.

(*Source:* ANS) Categories: NEWS Tags: Euthanasia Squads, NVVE, Right to Die.

Right to Die Families:

- **AIIMS data:** "Families of 10 out of 200 patients in a vegetative state have asked for active euthanasia. Many families, in fact, have refused to take such patients back."

Vox Populi:

- **Actor Hrithik Roshan:** "Euthanasia must be allowed in cases that merit it. But a strong system needs to be set in place." The actor recently played the role of a paraplegic magician Ethen, whose plea for euthanasia, only to be turned down by the court.

FACTORS OPPOSING EUTHANASIA:

Factors:
- Terminally ill factor
- Cost factor
- Involuntary factor
- Human life factor.

Terminally ill factor:

The definition of "terminal" is controversial in case of Euthanasia i.e.:

- That a terminal illness may be any disorder, restricting life even for a day.
- That a terminal condition may be any disorder, resulting in death within a "relatively short time."
- That a terminal may be any disorder, resulting in death within a couple of months.
- That a terminally ill patient may not die for months/years, from the diagnosed disorder.
- That to simplify, terminal illness may be replaced with such titles as desperately ill, hopelessly ill, incurably ill, hopeless condition, or useless life.
- That assisted suicide may be a suicidal impulse resulting from terminal illness, unbearable pain, emotional stress or depression.

Cost factor - That recently greater emphasis has been placed on healthcare providers to curtail costs, thereby projecting euthanasia a means of cost containment, as many people have no medical insurance coverage.

- That the poor and minorities generally lack access to available pain control.
- That doctors are being offered cash incentives by the managed-care facilities for not providing required treatment to terminally ill patients.
- That by legalising euthanasia, doctors may be financially sound, by forcing/counselling, a seriously ill or disabled person, to choose to die rather than receive a long-term medical care.
- That the government may also have a cost consideration i.e. govt. may cut back on paying for medical care and treatment, thereby consider for choosing euthanasia.

Examples:

- That the State of Oregon announced plans to cut back on healthcare coverage for poor state residents.
- That In Canada, hospital stays are being shortened while, at the same time, funds have not been made available for home care for the sick and elderly.
- That Registered nurses are being replaced with less expensive Practical nurses.
- That patients are forced to endure long waits for many types of needed surgery.

Involuntary factor:

- That depressed/or dependant persons may be pressurised by financial, emotional and psychological factors to opt for euthanasia or assisted suicide, rather than to receive medical care.
- That persons favouring euthanasia, insist that voluntary euthanasia may not result in involuntary euthanasia.

Human life factor:

For Euthanasia:

- That it is better for terminally ill, depressed, emotionally stressed and financially unsound persons to opt for voluntary euthanasia, instead of guility feeling of burden on dependants (cost and care factors).

Against Euthanasia:

- That with euthanasia no one's life is being saved-life is only taken.
- That euthanasia has been considered a crime since ages.
- That it is better help those suffering from unbearable pain, depression, emotional stress and financial crisis, by all available means, instead of pressurising them to opt for horrible/ disgusting euthanasia.

Vox Populi: - That "Nazi legislation and Hitler's ideas are reemerging in Europe via Dutch euthanasia laws and the debate on how to kill ill children."

Carlo Giovanardi. Italian Parliamentary Affairs Minister, March 2006

- That "Experience in The Netherlands, where there has been relatively little effort to improve pain and symptom treatment, suggests that legalisation of physician-assisted suicide might weaken society's resolve to expand services and resources aimed at caring for the dying patient."

Foley, 1995; Hendin, 1994...from "Treatment of Pain at the End of life: A Position Statement from The American Pain Society."

- That "I can understand at the individual level that in some cases you wish it was all over with, but the problem is as a society you have to chose what's going to be your norm."..."We have this idea that what happens to me is nobody's business. The problem with euthanasia is it requires another person to do it, and it requires a complicit society to authorise it."

Margaret Somerville, founding director of the McGill Centre for Medicine, Ethics and Law

- That "physician-assisted suicide, if it became widespread, could become a profit-enhancing tool for big HMOs." "...drugs used in assisted suicide cost only $ 40, but that it could take $ 40,000 to treat a patient properly so that they don't want the "choice" of assisted suicide. **Wesley J. Smith,** Sr. fellow at the Discovery institute.

ARGUMENTS OPPOSING EUTHANASIA:

Legal Fraternity:

- **The Supreme Court of India:** "Is not in favour of active euthanasia that involves the use of lethal substances to end a patient's life."
- **SC lawyer Anand Grover:** "Courts cannot decide such a sensitive issue. As per the Constitution, no one can take away anyone's life without a procedure established by law. It means there has to be a proper statute on the issue..."
- **Advocate Pinky Anand:** "I cannot countenance a position where one is allowed to end one's life. It is an area which must be left alone. Courts cannot take on such a difficult task..."

Legislators: "Euthanasia can't be allowed in our country as it is still backward and emotional. It would lead to misuse" Understandably, for the legislators, euthanasia, like life itself, is a grey area with too many conflicting views.

Example: The view of religious leaders.

Medical Fraternity:

Most of doctors, who publically, swear by the Hippocratic Oath:

"I will give no deadly medicine to anyone if asked, nor suggest any such counsel", oppose euthanasia.

Organisations:

- "No one had the right to take one's life without a proper law on euthanasia in the country."

References: 1. Nair, HV: Legal fraternity divide on passive euthanasia. Hindustan Times, March 08,.Top of Form Click here to cancel "reply".

2. Prakash, S: 'DECRIMINALISE SUICIDE BIDS'. Hindustan Times, March 08, 2011.
3. Prakash, S: Legislators dither, apex court steps in. Hindustan Times, March 08, 2011 of Form Click here to cancel "reply".
4. Sinha, B: Passive euthanasia allowed. Hindustan Times, March 08, 2011.

HONOUR KILLING

Preface: "The Government has been engaged in the process to make changes in the criminal law, to deal with growing incidents of honour killings across the Country. However, its efforts so far seem to have failed to convince nearly half the States in the country". 13 States yet to send views on proposed changes in the criminal laws laws to curb honour killings, esp. In Haryana, Rajasthan and UP. These three States have admitted in the Supreme Court that they have not prepared any specific legal framework to curb the menace. "There was no specific legal framework to address the problem of honour killings, but top police officials have issued directions to treat such cases seriously," the UP Government informed the Supreme Court. Rajasthan and Haryana cited administrative circulars issued by the state Governments to address the problem of honour killings. Another problem faced by the Centre is the lack of official data on honour killings.

"Cases of honour killings are registered under the offence of murder, therefore not possible to exactly pinpoint such cases," said a government official.

States in favour: Assam, Bihar, Chhattisgarh, Delhi, Goa, J&K, Madhya Pradesh, NE States, Rajasthan and UP.

Non-committed: Andhra, Gujarat, Jharkhand, Karnataka, Kerala, Maharashtra, Odisha, Punjab, Uttarakhand.

Opposed: Haryana.

JUDICIAL MORALISM

Preface: French philosopher Montesquieu in 'Spirit of the Laws' published in 1748 pronounced "Civil Laws are not an appropriate tool for enforcing the religious norms of conduct." In India, many Courts that attempt to enforce religious norms and what are assumed to be widely accepted standards of morality haven't yet imbibed the great man's commonsensical dictum. Judges who include comments on morality and religion in Court orders may be encouraging the use of coercive power to enforce the moral attitudes of the majority.

Sitting in Judgement:

Case Studies (When Judges get Moralistic):

Judgment: Justice Srivastava of the Allahabad High Court:

- **Every Indian must follow Gita Dharma (September 12, 2007):** In August 2007, while hearing a petition filed by a priest of a Varanasi temple over a disput involving a temple property, the Judge held that:
- the Bhagvad Gita should be made the National "Dharma Shastra."
- the Bhagvad Gita had greatly inspired those involved in the freedom struggle and continued to inspire people from all walks of life. "Hence, it is the duty of every Indian citizen under Article 51-A of the Constitution of India, irrespective of caste, creed or religion, to follow dharma as propounded by the Gita."

Judgment: Justice VS Sirpurkar and Justice Deepak Verma of the SC:

- **Inter-caste Union defeat of Family (February 27, 2010):** In February 2010, while commuting the death sentence slapped on three accused in a multiple murder case to life imprisonment, a Division Bench, noted murders were the outcome of an inter-caste marriage. The Bench held that: in the case of inter-caste or inter-community marriages resulting from secret love affairs, society holds the woman's elder brother responsible. "It is held as the defeat of the family. At times, he has to suffer taunts and snide remarks even from persons who really have no business to poke their nose into the affairs of the family." The brother of the victim must have been a prey of the so-called insult which his younger sister had imposed upon his family and that must have been in his mind," the bench held while commuting the death sentence upheld by the Bombay High Court for the three convicts to life imprisonment.

Judgment: Justice Markandey Katju and Justice TS Thakur of the SC:

- **It's like Setting the clock back (October 22, 2010):** In October 2010, while delivering a judgment on live-in relationships, the Division Bench mentioned the words "keep" and "one night stand". The Bench held that:
- If a man has a "keep" whom he maintains financially and uses mainly for sexual purpose and/or as a servant, it would not be a relationship in the nature of marriage.
- merely spending weekends together or a one-night stand would not make it a 'domestic relationship.'

Additional Solicitor-General (a woman) Indira Jaising, attached to the Supreme Court said:

- she and several women in the country opposed the expression "keep" and the use of the phrase "one night stand".
- It is like setting the clock back after the SC has passed the historic judgment in the Vishaka case. "That judgment is cited in Courts all over the World," the ASG had said.

Judgment: Justice K Bhaktavatsala of the Karnatka High Court:

- **Women suffer in all marriages (August 31, 2012):** In August 2012, while hearing a petition filed by a woman alleging domestic violence against her husband, Justice councelled the victim saying:

- "women suffer in all marriages."

- you are married with two children, and know what it means to suffer as a woman. Your husband is doing good business, he will take care of you.

- Why are you still talking about his beatings?" "I know you have undergone pain. But that is nothing in front of what you undergo as a woman."

Judgment: Justice K Bhaktavatsala of the Karnataka High Court:

- **Spinsters unfit for Family cases (September 5, 2012):** In September 2012, while hearing a petition filed by an estranged wife alleging domestic violence against her husband, Justice told the female advocate that:
- she was "unfit" to take up a case on behalf of the estranged wife because she was unmarried.
- while the lady advocate was citing allegations against the husband, Justice Bhaktavatsala stopped her midway and asked, "Are you married?"
- when she replied in the negative, he commented: "You are unfit to know real life. Why are you arguing like this? He is your (client's) partner, not a stranger.
- family matters should be argued only by married people, not spinsters. You should only watch.
- bachelors and spinsters watching family court proceedings will start thinking whether there is any need to marry at all. Marriage is not like a public transport system.
- you better get married and you will get very good experience to argue such cases.

Judgment: Justice K Bhaktavatsala and Justice S Govindarajulu of the Karnataka High Court:

- **Parents of Girls should approve (September 6, 2012):** In September 2012, while hearing a habeas corpus petition filed by a 21 yrs old man alleging that the girl he married had gone missing, the Bench held that:
- girls below 21 yrs of age suffered from hormonal imbalances, resulting in falling prey to boys, falling in love, marry and repenting at leisure.
- girls below 21 yrs of age are not capable of forming a rational judgement as to the suitability of the boy she is in love with.
- girls below 21 yrs of age, having love affair and opting for love marriage, may be considered as a condition for parents approval of the marriage, otherwise such marriages should be declared void or voidable.

Judgment: Justice N Kirubakaran of the Madras High Court:

- **Rape victim chose wrong travel time (September 2, 2013): In September 2013, while at the inauguration ceremony of a Fast Track Mahila Court in Ramanathapuram in Tamil Nadu, Justice Kirubakaran, reported to have said that:**
- **women were equally responsible for the crimes committed against them.**
- **while interacting with the media, the Judge allegedly commented that the December 16, 2012 Delhi gang-rape victim had chosen the wrong time to travel.**

  AIDWA (All India Democratic Women's Association): Rattled by such words coming from an officer of the higher judiciary, the AIDWA, had written to Justice Kirubakaran urging him to rise above such regressive views.

Judgment: Additional Sessions Judge V Bhat of a Delhi Court:

- **No sex for Girls before marriage (October 7, 2013):** In October 2013, while acquitting a man of raping a woman by deceitfully making her believe that she was his legally wedded wife, the Judge said that:

- girls voluntarily elope with their lovers but thereafter lodge false cases to escape a scolding from their parents.
- girls voluntarily elope with their lovers to explore the greener pastures of bodily pleasure and on return to their homes, they conveniently fabricate the story of kidnap and rape in order to escape harsh treatment by their parents.
- girls are morally and socially bound to not indulge in sexual intercourse before a proper marriage, and if they do so, it would be to their peril and they cannot be heard to cry later on that it was rape.
- the complainant must understand that she is engaging in an act which not only is immoral but also against the tenets of every religion. No religion in the world allows pre-marital sex.

Vox-populi: **Justice AP Shah (former Chief Justice of Delhi High Court) Chairman Law Commission of India:** Does not approve of such behaviour of the Judges.

India is a secular country and secularism is part of the basic structure of our constitution. When the Judges try to preach morality, they should keep in mind that it does not violate various freedoms guaranted to an individual under the constitution. Judges should confine themselves to the issues involved in a particular case. Unnecessary and excessive comments not germane to the issue at hand should be avoided.

Sr. Advocate S Bhushan (former Law Minister): Has a nuanced view on the issue. Law is not always divorced from morality and every Judge has his own understanding of law and morality. While a Judge decides a case on the basis of law, he should be free to make comments, and his freedom of speech can't be curtailed. One is free to criticise him if not agreed with him. Ulti, something better will emerge from the churning.

Eminent Sociologist Dipankar Gupta: Believes there should be a check on unwarranted comments by Judges. Judges quoting scriptures to prescribe a moral code of conduct cannot be acceptable in a liberal democratic setup. A Judge studied law books and interprets statutes to decide cases, and moreover The Bhagawad Gita, The Quran or The Old Testament are not taught at law schools. If a Judge makes comments based on religious scriptures, it is a clear aberration. It is against the call of his duty, which is to decide cases on the basis of law, and it's certainly not talking about religion and morality.

Indeed, the mention of "the tenets of every religion" itself is uncalled for in a court of law of a secular nation.

Author:

- That better turn to the wise Montesquieu once again to understand the danger of conforming to religious laws: "When Judges attempt to enforce God's laws for Him, or to cast themselves as His protectors, they make religion an instrument of fanaticism and oppression; this is a service neither to God nor to their country."
- That currently, India is witnessing a phenomenon described by many jurists as 'judicial moralism', where the distinction between law and morality gets blurred or even obliterated altogether.
- That can happen when a Judge thinks all 'moral wrongs' should also be treated as judicial wrongs. It implies that it is permissible for the State or for Judges to use coercive power to enforce the moral attitudes accepted by the majority.
- That unwanted comments from Judges be checked by prescribing a maximum limit on the size of a judgment. In India, Judges write judgments running into hundreds of pages. In contrast, the 1954 landmark verdict in Brown v/s Board of Education in which the US Supreme

Court declared State laws establishing separate public schools for black and white students unconstitutional, was barely 25-30 pages.

Why can't Indian Judges be precise and to the point ?

References: 1. S Prakash: Sitting in Judgment, HT, February, 2014.

2. SR Singh: Case Studies – When Judges get moralistic, HT, February, 2014.

MEDICAL EDUCATION – Need Globally Compatible Medical Skills

Preface: That, It is imperative that there should be continuous assessment of the quality of teaching and training being imparted to the students, in order to achieve a status level in the competitive world arena.

International scenario:

- That news about medical education at Indian Medical Institutions not featuring in top International rankings or Indian Medical Students found wanting in International examinations have been frequent in the recent past. Although these cannot be construed as a verdict on the Indian education system, it does reflect some of its lacunae.

Overseas Doctors:

- That developed countries do not experience brain drain, but there is a brain waste phenomenon in the medical profession when doctors move from one country to another.When doctors and other medical professionals migrate to developed countries, they find it hard to clear mandatory examinations to acquire a licence to practice. That in Canada it is necessary to get one of the 22 medical licences (II Bourgeault, Professor University of Ottawa).

UK: That recently highest number of overseas doctors barred from practising or suspended from work in NHS, following complaints were those who qualified in India. That 93 Indian doctors were struck off the medical register following 'fitness to practice' hearings, while 88 more Indian doctors were suspended following complaints and similar hearings during the last five years (GMC).

- That Indian doctors working in NHS, reacted with dismay, blaming there is institutional racism in NHS. That often, the Indian and other overseas doctors working in NHS, are given far harsher punishment than the locals for the same mistakes. Fewer local doctors are referred to the GMC, who also get off lightly (R Mahta, President BAPIO of Indian origion).
- That several Indian doctors who came to the UK years ago told that conditions had become increasingly difficult. That there has been a major decline in the number of Indian doctors coming to the UK since 2004. That from 3,640 in 2004 to 340 in 2013. That Indian doctors, it seems, are increasingly keeping away from the healthcare system they were once the 'mainstay' of. It is mainly due to a booming private health sector in India, better career prospects – salaries were equal to or better than those paid by NHS - and a chance to be with their aging parents, immigration restrictions in the UK and a perception of unfair treatment at workplace in NHS.
- That the number of overseas doctors who have returned to India, or moved to better conditions in the US, Canada or Australia, is said to be in the hundreds, and growing. Currently of the 259,777 NHS doctors, 68,116 got their primary medical education and training in countries outside Britain and the European Union. They include 25,092 doctors who qualified in India and passed the mandatory test to register with GMC and work in the NHS.

(A new study that questions the competence of overseas doctors hasn't helped)

- That International medical graduates make a huge contribution to healthcare in the UK and the vast majority of them provide excellent care for their patients (N Dickson, CEO GMC).

US: That there is long slog for immigrant (overseas) doctors intending to practise in US. That thousands of foreign trained overseas doctors are living in US with life saving skills that are going unused because they stumbled over one of the many hurdles in the pathway of becoming a licenced doctor here e.g.:

- That 1st of all these doctors must meet the US's high quality standards. Some development experts are also loath to make it too easy for overseas doctors to practice here on account of the risk involved of a 'brain drain' abroad.
- That many overseas doctors and their advocates argue that the process is unnecessarily restrictive and time consuming, esp. since America's need for doctors will expand sharply within a short period under President Barack Obama's healthcare law.
- That US already faces a shortage of doctors in many States of the country, esp. in specialties where overseas (foreign-trained) doctors are most likely to practice, like primary care.
- That immigrant advocates and some economists point out that the medical labour force could be ramped up much faster if the country tapped the underused skills of the overseas doctors who are already here, but are not allowed to practice. "That it doesn't cost the taxpayers a penny because these doctors come fully trained" (N R Rao, ex-chairman of AMA International Medical Graduates Governing Council (IMGGC). That for decades the US has been training small numbers of doctors to meet its own needs, because of industry- set-limits on the number of medical school slots available. Currently about one in four doctors practising in the US were trained abroad.

- That overseas doctors, no matter how experienced and well trained, must run a long, costly and confusing gauntlet before they can actually practice here.

(1) That the pathway starts with submitting of an application to a NGO that verifies medical school transcrits and diplomas.

(2) That overseas doctors must prove they speak English.

(3) That they pass three steps of the US Medical Licencing Examination.

(4) That they get US recommendation letters; and be permanent residents.

(5) That the biggest hurdle is that an overseas doctor must obtain one of the coveted slots in American's Medical residency System, which typically involves grueling 80-hr. work/week, mandatory whether the doctor did his/her residency overseas. That only exception is for doctors who did their residencies in Canada. That argument against recruitment of overseas doctors to practice in US is to discourage inflow of overseas doctors from poor countries like India, Pakistan etc. (paid for their medical teaching/training from public funds). That there is need to wean from extraordinary dependence on overseas doctors from the poor developing countries (F Mullan, Professor of Medicine at GW University, Washington DC). That each year ECFMG, clears about 8K overseas doctors to apply for the National Residency Match System, about 3K of them successfully match to a residency slot – mostly least desired residencies in community hospitals, unpopular locations and in less lucrative specialties like primary care. That during last five years about 42.1 per cent of overseas doctors succeeded in winning over the least desired residencies, compared to 93.9 per cent for seniors at America's mainstream medical schools. That is because the number of accredited US medical schools and thereby

US trained medical students, has increased substantially in the last decade, while the number of residency slots has barely budged since Congress effectively froze residency funding in 1997. (C Rampell, NYT).

India: That recently majority of Indian doctors, being taught and trained in Russia, Ukrain and Uzbekistan etc. failed repeatedly to clear the entry test mandatory for registration by the MCI – aim is to assess the quality of teaching and training being imparted to the students, in order to achieve a status level in the Indian medical stream.

MCI: - That in India there is an acute shotage of doctors and nurses, must try to re-innovate medical education to make it globally compatible. (KK Talwar, Chairman MCI)

IMA: That, It is the quality of Medical Education imparted today that would determine the Health status of our citizens tomorrow and in fact that of the whole world as many of our medical graduates continue to excel in almost all the developed countries.

- That IMA does play the key role in shaping the Medical Education of our Country and for over three decades the IMA has been proposing the setting up of medical colleges at each District, where in meritorious students from the local areas can be admitted with a uniform policy in distribution of seats to be implementable throughout the Country, while also fulfilling the Constitutional Obligations which could vary from State to State.
- That, It is imperative that all states should implement the three language formula which would enable the students to excel in higher education.
- That would ensure streamlining of medical College admission throughout the Country and pave the way for uniformity in curriculum, syllabi

and examination resulting in quality Medical Professionals, graduating from our Universities.

- That IMA welcomes banning of capitation in Medical Education and instead is in favour of a "Fee Structure" which would enable the colleges to function efficiently and should also be acceptable to the government.
- That such a move will ensure financial transparency, which should become the buzz word of all Educational Institutions in our Country.
- That, It is imperative that there should be continuous assessment of the quality of teaching and training being imparted to the students and that can be effected by "Surprise Visits to ensure quality teaching and training" by the MCI, or any other accredited body.
- That, Post Graduate Students should be appropriately groomed to develop adequate teaching and clinical skills.
- That evaluation of teachers by students is an effective way of assessing the quality of Medical Education in any Institution.
- That IMA strongly favours National Eligibility and Entrance test for all Medical Graduate and Post Graduate Courses with due weightage for Rural Service and fulfilling all Constitutional Obligations which may vary from State to state.
- That having ensured that the quality of Medical Education is not compromised for any reason whatsoever, since 1928, IMA vehemently opposes the short sighted and immature decision of the Government of India to introduce the short course of B.R.M.S. (Bachelor of Rural Medical Service).
- That letting loose such half baked, ill informed Medical Professionals into the Rural Community is much against the fundamental rights of an Indian citizen, where in discrimination is being

made on the basis of the geographical status of the area concerned in providing health care.

- That, IMA with its vast efficient network has been the pioneer in conducting Continuiting Medical Education Programmes for over three decades and IMA calls upon the government to fund these educational programmes and the MCI to implement Re-Registration through mandatory "CME credit hours". In fact, Government support to CME programmes would be a boon to improve Healthcare in the villages.
- That, IMA calls upon the MCI to recognise the National Board Examinations on par with the recognised Master Degree of the Universities.
- That, IMA welcomes the move of Government of India to take a re-look at the status of deemed universities and IMA appeals to all State Governments to upgrade all State-run Health Science Universities and Medical Institutions to enable them to become "Centres of Excellence" both in Education and Healthcare Services.
- That, IMA has submitted the draft of IMA National Health Policy – 2010 to the Prime Minister of India, keeping in view the fact that 70 per cent of India's population resides in the villages and as per the dream of the Mahatma, effective and scientifically acceptable Healthcare, should be provided to the rural masses from "Womb to Tomb" free of cost for those below the poverty line and at a minimal cost for others.
- That effective Healthcare delivery can be ensured only by a team of well qualified support staff - Paramedics. IMA calls upon the government to evolve a "National Policy" on Para Medical Courses and lay down standards for colleges imparting such courses.
- That, IMA at this point in the "Time Continuum" of the Worlds Largest Non Governmental Organisation (NGO), will continue to tackle the current/pending issues, and the newer issues

will also be addressed appropriately, keeping in view the interest of the common man as a matter of prime concern, while upholding the dignity and honour of our nation.

Conclusion:

- That the Indian Medical Association is the only protector and spokesman of the entire lot of practitioners of the Modern Scientific system of medicine in our Country and hereby sincere appeal to every medical practitioner of India possessing a registrable qualification in modern scientific medicine, to lend a helping hand, by practicing the profession ethically adhering to the motto of "service before self".

(Prof. Dr. G.K. Ramachandrappa (National President IMA)

Author: That, It is imperative that there should be continuous assessment of the quality of teaching and training being imparted to the students, in order to achieve a status level in the competitive world arena.

MEDICAL NEGLIGENCE

Preface: Is defined as perceived and actual dereliction of duty e.g. deficient care/or attention, by a medical professional, causing injury or death of a patient.

Medical negligence or medical malpractice comes under the purview of law of contracts e.g. breach of a legal duty to patient's care – meaning carelessness in a matter for which the law mandates carefullness. Any breach of this duty gives the patient/or relatives, a right to initiate legal action against the negligent doctor/hospital.

Charles Worth and Percy on Negligence (Tenth Edition, 2001):

That as per current forensic speech, negligence has three meanings:

- a state of mind, in which it is opposed to intention;
- careless conduct; and

- the breach of duty to take care that is imposed by either common or statute law.

That all three meanings are applicable in different circumstances but anyone of them does not necessarily exclude the other meanings (Para 1.01).

That the essential components of negligence, as recognised, are three: **"duty", "breach"** and **"resulting damage"** i.e.:

- the existence of a duty to take care, which is owed by the defendant to the complainant;
- the failure to attain that standard of care, prescribed by the law, thereby committing a breach of such duty; and
- damage, which is both causally connected with such breach and recognised by the law, has been suffered by the complainant (Para 1.23).

Vox Populi: That doctor-patient trust depleting. People in general blame it on the commercialisation of healthcare services, lack of standard treatment guidelines and regulatory body, absence of grievance redressal system responsible for doctor-patient souring relationship, they say.

Doctor-patient ties souring: That trust is a two-way path:

- Doctors in government hospitals are overworked and the doctor-patient ratio is severely skewed. With so much workload, where is the time to develop a doctor-patient relationship?, Patients have to wait in long queues for hours for a few mts. consultation, whereas in private sector setups the scene is no better, here the doctors behave business like Robots, rather than healers.
- Patients are equally guilty, for deteriorating relationships. They feel that by paying, they are entitled to trouble the doctors as much as possible, never realise that doctors are also humans, being held responsible for errors of judgment. CPA has led to unnecessary medical litigation

cases filed by patients/relatives/attendants, to earn fast money.

- Media: often responsible for defaming doctors (yellow journalism).
- Insurance companies: also contribute in deteriorating relationships, by dictating policies (V Kapoor, PKL).

Every incident is termed medical negligence: That patients keep hopping from one doctor to another, which further complicates the issues. Every incident is termed as medical negligence. One must realise that doctors treat patients to cure them. R Bhalla, SMO CH, SAS Ngr.)

Patient can't bear negligence: That with increasing awareness, patients are becoming more health conscious, and cannot bear any type of negligence, ignoring the doctor's work (Dr. JS Thakur, PGI, Chandigarh).

Breach of faith glaring: That greedy doctors get unethical financial favours by referring patients to diagnostic centres, clinical labs etc, unnecessarily. The aim is to get referral commission, resulting in loosing people's faith in doctors.

Doctors should keep in mind that patients are fully aware of these mishappenings, media is proactive, and the medical treatment is under the survey of consumer forums and covered by RTI Act, thereby chances of full transparency (AJ K, SAS Ngr.).

Need to develop mutual tryst: That some RMPs have been maligning the medical profession's image. They are interested in safeguarding their own interests, at the cost of patient's welfare. That the relatives/attendants of patients pretend to have superior medical knowledge then the treating doctors, and if results are not upto their liking, they resort to protests/agitation/ verbal abuses and physical violence. Medical professionals (public and private sector) to look after the deficiencies in their areas of operation, lest India becomes like certain other countries , where court cases involving RMPs are mind boggling (A Sharma, Chandigarh).

Negligence can't be ignored: That mistakes do occur, but carelessness and Negligence cannot be ignored. The doctor-patient relationship is one of most unique and privileged relation based on mutual trust and faith, which should not be spoiled, and to be maintained by both sides.

Restore trust: That treating patients with care will restore trust in caring Doctors. Awareness amongst people resulted in rise in number of complaints of medical negligence, while doctors have lost faith and respect. To restore the confidence of people in doctor, the medical fraternity has to take a lead by treating patients with compassion and love (R Chhabra, Chandigarh).

Lack of communication: That unrest against medical fraternity is neither due to more awareness nor due to loss of faith, whereas most of the times it is due to lakh of communication between patient's kin and doctors. A patient and his kin should be counselled on treatment plans and the scientific basis of doing it frequently and all the queries should be answered with patience. No doctor on earth can save 100 per cent of his/her patients and compli-cations for any given procedures are known and reported in literature. No doctor wants to lose his/her patient but Nature has its own rule to play. Government has done a big wrong by bringing medical profession under ambit of consumer forum. Medical care is not a saleable commodity and should be looked upon as a most pious service to humanity both in public as well as private sector (Dr V Sarwal, I/c Cardiothoracic and Vascular Surgery, Fortis Hptl, SAS Ngr).

Legal remedies: That quite a handful of doctors are there who try to make handsome money out of a patient's misery, thereby forcing patients and their relatives/attendants resort to legal help (Monika).

Need to implement law with strictness: That the Government should ensure to implement law with strictness and effective checking by the department concerned (S Singh, Chandigarh).

That the current unsavoury scenario of patient-doctor relationship has arisen because the medical fraternity does not have any effective regulatory body of its own. There is a Medical Council Act and the Indian Medical Council (Professional Conduct, Etiquette and Ethics) Regulations, 2002 but these have seldom been brought into action against a practicing doctor. Moreover the maximum punishment which can be given hereunder is the removal of the name of the doctor from the Register of Medical Practitioners. This action fails to give any relief to the patient who has suffered (P Chandgothia, President, Chandigarh Consumer Courts Bar Association).

Guilty doctors must be punished: That currently medical care is a commodity that can be purchased. Both doctors and patients are equally businesslike in their dealings. Attitude of patients/relatives/attendants, has become demanding, threatening and hostile. CPA has led to unnecessary medical litigation cases, filed by patients who want to make a fast buck. That media are instrumental in ensationalisation of unfortunate incidents. The trend must be stopped and incompetent doctors found genuinely guilty must be punished (Dr SK Chawla, Chandigarh).

Growing materialism to blame: That growing materialism in the mindsets of medical professionals/institutions is coming heavily on humanity. If the system is deteriorating, public too is becoming aware and active against irregularities, aggressiveness, however on both counts is detrimental to public. Medical profession is most pious and dedication oriented to humanity but unfortunately becoming over corruptive, not a good sign indeed (MPS Chadha, SAS Ngr).

Hostile hospital staff: That often the hospital staff are hostile towards the relatives/attendants of the patients. There is communication gap, resulting in unfortunate developments (resentments/agitations). Besides there were instances of doctors/staff carelessness, resulting in avoidable complications and loss of lives (A Sarkar F/o deceased Anupama).

IMA can play a vital role: That IMA should be empowered to redress medical negligence complaints, and the culprit could be punished (AK Sharma).

Doctors on safer side legally: That as per the criminal liability for alleged negligence and the fear of Police action, the doctors are on safe ground, vide the settled law that no doctor can be booked or arrested under IPC, unless the Police receive a clear and categorical opinion regarding his/her culpability from a medical board or magistrate inquiry (P Chandgothia).

Doctors must be protected: That patients/ relatives/attendants expectation levels have increased with rise in income, thereby thinking of buying doctors.

Hospitals are overcrowded and it is the concerned doctor, who has to decide about prioritising patients esp. in Accident and Emergency units. Blaming doctors unnecessarily should be stopped, and let the doctors perform their emergency duties fearlessly. Doctors/staff must be protected by the governing authorities and the culprits must be dealt firmly.

(Dr S Aggarwal, Deputy CS, Pkl).

Charges of negligence often framed: That even if the patient is critical and there are no chances of his/her survival, even then relatives/

attendants blame the doctors/hospitals for negligence. Often these allegations are levelled to prepare a ground to make the case strong in consumer courts, so that hefty compensation can be granted, irrespective of the condition of the patient. The authorities should take serious note of the situation, otherwise difficult for the clinics/hospitals to function fearlessly (Dr P Garg, Pkl).

Introduce doctors protection bill: That with the increasing cost of treatment there is a need to ensure transparency in the costs and the parents should be clearly told about the charges without any hidden costs. The administration should also impose doctors' protection bill to safeguard the doctors from being ill-treated (Dr G Singh, SAS Ngr).

Nobody should break the law: That the number of patients has increased manifold in hospitals though the facilities remained more or less the same. The patients' conditions in majority of hospitals are pathetic, laboratories and diagnostic facilities are either lacking or there is a long queue of patients, instead the doctors are blamed for not providing quality service. Recently a new trend has emerged where doctors/staff are beaten up and the clinic/hospital smashed by unruly crowds, as if the doctor is mainly responsible for the mishappening/or death of the patient. Nobody should take law and order in his/her hand (MP Singh, SAS Ngr).

Understanding of health system is poor: That little knowledge is always dangerous. That in India, patients understanding about health system is poor.

Doctors are overburdened and are paid poorly, while in Western countries patients are fully aware of health system i.e. they are covered under insurance and bills are settled between hospitals and insurance companies.

(Dr P Aggarwal).

That the high compensation claims awarded by various Commissions and Courts in cases of medical negligence has a negative impact on the doctor-patient relationship in general. Ultimately, these unlimited compensations are going to increase healthcare costs for everyone as the doctor has to recover it from his other patients. Commercialisation of healthcare is not in anyone's interest. If a doctor begins to think that a negligent act while treating the rich will result in compensation worth crores, he/she will shift his/her focus on treating the rich properly. In a poor country, this could have dangerous repercussions (Dr N Nagpal, ex-president, IMA Chandigarh).

Observation:

- That a doctor is not guilty of negligence if he has acted in accordance with a practice accepted as proper by a responsible body of medical men skilled in that particular art.
- That in the realm of diagnosis and treatment there is ample scope of genuine difference of opinion and a doctor is not negligent merely because his conclusion differs from that of other professionally men.
- That the true test for establishing negligence in diagnosis or treatment on the part of a doctor is whether he has been proved to be guilty of such failure as no doctor of ordinary skill would be guilty of acting with twelve ordinary care.
- That Consumer Forum Panels should have eminent medical professionals, so that neither the doctor nor the patient gets a raw deal. Justice has to be ensured to both the sides without discrimination of any kind.
- That a panel of medical experts may be roped in by the Consumer Forums to fix the amount of compensation, depending upon the extent of damage.

MEDICAL PROFESSION...TESTING TIMES (IN TROUBLED WATERS)

Preface: In the past Medical Profession was considered as a noble profession – next only to the God Almighty. With the passing times, this image has been eroded on account of many factors e.g. malpractices, negligence, patient's mistrust, rude behaviour of doctors/paramedics towards patients/attendants, leading to the enactment of Acts (harsh measures) like CPA etc., opposed/ resented by the medicos en-masse.

Good Medical Practice:

Every doctor whether at a Government Hospital or otherwise has the professional obligation to extend his services for protecting life. The obligation being total, absolute and paramount, laws of procedure whether in statutes or otherwise cannot be sustained and therefore, must give way." It is the duty of the doctor in an emergency to begin treatment of the patient and he should not await the arrival of the police or to complete the legal formalities. The life of a person is far more important than legal formalities. This view is in accordance with the Hippocratic oath of doctors as mentioned in George Bernard Shaw's play: "The Doctor's Dilemma." The medical profession is a noble profesion and it should not be brought down to the level of a simple business or commerce. The truth of the matter, sadly, is that today in India many doctors (though not all) have become totally money-minded, and have forgotten their Hippocratic oath. Since most people in India are poor, the consequence is that for them proper medical treatment is next to impossible, and hence they have to rely on quacks. This is a disgrace to a noble profession.

Medical Ethics for doctors:

Definition: Defined as the special rules and regulations from the point of view of morality (as per

Hippocratic oath), which a doctor should follow, although its violation is not an offence legally, but is shameful and disgraceful from the point of view of medical profession (plethora of stigmata associated with medical profession).

Code of Medical Ethics:

Drawn up with the approval of the Central Government under Section 33 of the Indian Medical Council Act:

Principles: To follow the principles in Good Medical Practice e.g.:

Do's for Doctors:

- To make the patient's care, doctor's first concern
- To protect and promote the health of patients and the public
- To provide a good standard of practice and patient's care
- To raise concern about patient's safety with the employing body
- To avoid treating a close personal relation
- To provide emergency treatment, wherever required, taking account of their own's safety, their competence and the availability of other options for care
- To upgrade their knowledge and skill regularly
- To maintain and improve their performance
- To be willing to contribute to activities e.g. teaching, training, appraising and assessing doctors
- To provide the patients the information they want or need in a way they can understand
- To maintain healthy doctor-patient relationship
- To communicate effectively with the patients
- To safeguard and protect the health and well-being of children and young people
- To be considerate to relatives, carers, partners and others close to the patient and be sensitive and responsive in providing required information and support, esp. after a patient has died

- To have consent prior to undertake any examination or investigation, provide any form of treatment
- To treat information about patients as confidential, including after a patient's death
- To respect the skills and contributions of your colleagues
- To avoid malicious and unfounded criticism of their colleagues, that may undermine patients' trust in the care or treatment they receive, or in the judgement of those treating them
- To share information with other healthcare professionals is important for safe and effective patient care
- To be honest and trustworthy and acting with integrity: this is at the heart of medical professionalism
- To be honest and trustworthy when writing reports, and when completing, signing or issuing forms, reports and other documents e.g. certificates etc.
- To inform patients about their fees and charges, wherever possible prior to asking for their consent to treatment
- To act in their patients' best interests when making referrals and when providing or arranging treatment or care. They must not ask for or accept any inducement, gift or hospitality which may affect or be seen to affect the way they prescribe for, treat or refer patients. They must not offer such inducements to colleagues.

Don't for Doctors:

- Don't examine, when you are sick, exhaust or under influence of alcohol or intoxicated
- Don't be overconfident – do anything beyond your competence
- Don't hesitate to consult your senior/specialist, while not sure what to do
- Don't refuse the patient's right to examine, to know diagnosis and treatment

- Don't withhold information
- Don't examine a female patient without a female nurse/or attendant
- Don't argue with an annoyed patient
- Don't scold attendants
- Don't insist for the history of illness or examination in presence of others
- Don't prescribe without examining the patient
- Don't adopt experimental method
- Don't advise unnecessary investigations/tests
- Don't over prescribe drugs
- Don't leave dead body unattended at the time of death
- Don't hesitate to extend your condolences and sympathies
- Don't issue death certificate without verification
- Don't issue/divulge false, misleading reports/ information
- Don't refuse first aid treatment to an emergency case
- Don't refuse medicare to an HIV/AIDS patient
- Don't perform MTP without possessing the required permission
- Don't perform MTP at an unauthorised place
- Don't talk loose of your colleagues
- Don't overstep your speciality – better restrict to your speciality:
- GP (MBBS) can't perform major surgeries
- General Surgeon can't perform hysterectomy, Caesarean section
- Gynecologist can't perform herniectomy, ultrasonography
- Surgeon/Physician can't give general and spinal anesthesia
- Dentist can't issue the death certificate
- Homeopath and Ayurved can't prescribe Allopathic drugs.

MANDATORY RURAL POSTING FOR PG EXAMINATION ENTRY

Preface: Medical Council of India in its notification made it mandatory one year rural posting of PHC (Primary Health Centre) after completing MBBS for medical students prior to seeking admission to PG course examination.

Doctors: Agitating medical students (Save the doctor):

- That thousands of undergraduate, postgraduate and senior doctors across the country are aggrieved with the Health Ministry's recent decision to make one-year rural posting mandatory for medical graduates.
- That the move, will not help much in achieving the aim of providing good healthcare facilities to the rural people.
- That there are not enough facilities in the villages for providing quality healthcare (incld. proper infrastructure, equipment, laboratories, regular power supply, medicines, security, good living conditions and support paramedical staff for the doctors) to the people.
- That according to Dr Narendra Saini, secretary general, IMA, representing the

  "Save the Doctor campain," the posting should not be mandatory, but voluntary and students should be given points or credits for this so that they can easily get a seat at the postgraduate level.
- That doctors are also wondering how this move will be implemented.
- That as per the right to information (RTI) there are about 23,887 Primary Health Centres (PMC) functioning in the Country as on March 2011, out of which there are just 2866 vacant seats. Then how can this be implemented with more medical students at the undergraduate level.
- That there is a huge gap between the number of undergraduate and postgraduate seats for medical students in the country.

- That pursuing postgraduation in any stream of medicine is essential for a doctor to become a specialist. Currently, India lacks specialist doctors because of fewer number of clinical PG seats in medical institutions. Nine out of the top ten diseases in the world can't be treated without specialist doctors.
- That the doctor-patient ratio in India is 1:2K, which is 40 per cent less than the world average.
- That although India has the largest number of medical institutions, the disparity in the number of seats allotted for PG and UG students along with the mandatory rural posting will affect young doctors and they will end up spending 13 yrs. just studying,
- That there are about 12K PG seats and about 45K UG seats, and the number of students taking the PG entrance tests keeps on increasing every year. In comparison, in the US, there are 19K UG seats and 32K PG and Fellowship seats. That with a pass rate of 80 to 90 per cent, nearly 40K doctors graduate every year and compete for 12K seats with their batch mates and over 100K seniors.
- That the mismatch in the number of UG and PG seats is one of the major reasons of brain drain.
- That there are so many students from rural areas who come to cities to study for their MBBS. They would want to go back to the villages and serve the people.

Suggestions:

- That every PG student must do six months of rural posting as part of their course during internship and PG.
- That every medical officer during their tenure is entitled to at least 4-5 promotions. For every promotion, one-year rural posting can be made mandatory. Also simultaneously, opening more medical colleges in rural areas, upgrading district hospitals into medical colleges, giving incentives

along with housing facilities, security and improving infrastructure in the rural areas will be other additional factors which will attract medical graduates to join rural services. As there are fewer PG seats, it should also be increased in a paced manner to provide affordability and quality healthcare for all including rural population.

Rural posting not mandatory for current batch (NEWS, February 14, 2014) Health Minister Ghulam Nabi Azad, New Delhi: Allayed the fears of agitating medical students, regarding the Medical Council notification in respect of one-year mandatory rural posting at PHC (Primary Health Centre) after completion of MBBS, prior to their seeking admission to PG course. "The Minister has directed the concerned officials of the Ministry to keep the notification in abeyance," it said. He also stated that rural posting will not be mandatory for appearing in PG examination for the year 2015-16, the statement said.

The statement issued by the Health Ministry has, in the meanwhile, given a great reprieve to the current batch of MBBS students. What lies in store for future students remain to be seen.

Agitating MBBS students: However, the statement did not give much satisfaction to the agitating students as the relief related to rural posting has been given only for the current batch. The students are exploring legal options now to deal with the situation.

Students were demanding that instead of increasing the MBBS course duration, the compulsory one-year rural posting be either incorporated within the existing MBBS course structure or included as a part of the PG curriculum and the MBBS course duration should be brought back to the original five and a half years.

References:

Dr. N Saini, secretary general, IMA (save doctor campaign)

Dr. N Motreja, coordinator, IMA (save doctor campaign)

Dr. M Maiti, National joint secretary, IMSA

Dr. N Nagesh, IMA (save doctor campaign).

(*Source*: Indian Express)

NEWS, New Delhi (agitating MBBS students against mandatory rural posting)

NATIONAL COMMISSION FOR HUMAN RESOURCES FOR HEALTH BILL, 2011

Preface: That to reduce shortage, standardise quality and bridge the uneven distribution of existing work force in the health sector, the Central Government proposed for centralisation of powers by forming National Commission for Human Resources for Health, thereby curtailing the autonomy of all the concerned Boards, Councils and other wings of the Union Government for Health.

Government:

Aims:

- To reduce the shortages and uneven distribution.
- To ensure uniform augmentation of trained specialist and superspecialist.
- To constitute a fund to be called the National Commission for Human Resources for Health fund.
- To repeal the INC Act, Pharmacy Act 1948, Dentist Act 1948 and IMC Act 1956.
- To audit the accounts of State Councils by the CAG of Central Government, and not by the State Councils.
- To make the decisions of the Commission unquestioned in the Court of Law, and prevent the agreed persons from seeking legal remedies.
- To prohibit doctors from engaging in any business/occupation, other than health

profession. Any violation to be considered as misconduct.

- To propose Common Entrance Examination for Plus Two Examinations.
- To exempt foreign graduates from appearing in Screening test, and to provide equivalency to persons holding Certificate with Foreign National Course.
- To hand over the role of Medical Education, to seven members of National Board of Health Education, from Democratic National Medical Council.
- To evaluate and assess health institutions by an external evaluation agency.
- To register in the National Council, thereby allowing a doctor to practice anywhere in India, instead of practicing only in the State of Registration (existing practice).

IMA:

Objections:

- That decentralisation is a slogan of the Union Government for better organisation and achievements. But it is unfortunate to learn that the benign government is proposing for centralisation of powers by forming National Commission and by taking away the autonomy of all the concerned Boards, Councils and other wings of the Union Government for Health.
- That the Medical Council of India, constituted by Indian Medical Act 1956, has been an autonomous body regulating medical education in the country.
- That the majority of the members were elected and represented different States, they were able to give unbiased opinion regarding medical institutions and medical courses.
- That the new Commission is constituted by Central Government appointed members. They will act like a department of Union Ministry of Health and Family Welfare and will not be able to give unbiased opinion.

- That as per the clause 105 (1) and (2), the Commission, the Board, Committee or the National Council will be bound by the directions of the Central Government.
- That the Commission, the Committee and the Council will execute the orders given by the Central Government.
- That in the circumstances, it will not be possible for the Commission, Board, Committee or the Council to provide fair assessment of the medical education or healthcare delivery.
- That there is no provision for the representation from the professional organisations, like the Indian Medical Association or Health Universities in the Commission, Board/Council, shunning the voice of the health care providers.
- That Section 100, that bars challenging of removal of name from State Register should be deleted. It is unconstitutional and is against the fundamental principles of Constitution. No law can bar the citizen of India from seeking a judicial recourse for getting relief against the decision of a regulatory body.
- That a single body can't be investing, prosecuting, judging and then final super punishing authority whose decision is un-challengeable in the Court of Law. It is against natural justice.
- That the bill fails to talk about the Rehabilitation Council of India Act 1991, Delhi Council for Physiotherapy and Occupational Therapy Act 1997, Maharashtra.
- That State Council for Occupational Therapy and Physiotherapy Act 2002, Gujarat State Council for Occupational Therapy and Physiotherapy Act 2011, Tamil Nadu State Physiotherapy Order etc.
- That Modern medicine is not defined properly. It is defined only as medicine. Health professionals are not properly defined to discharge their duties.

Without defining properly the objectives of the bill will not be accomplished.

- That Section 2 (u) of the Bill: defines Modern medicine as provided under the Indian Medical Council Act 1956. The definition of Modern medicine when defined in this Bill should clearly specify it as Modern medicine and not as medicine. Hence the word "medicine" at the beginning of the definition should be replaced as "Modern medicine".
- That Section 2 (t) of the Bill: defines Medical practitioner as "Modern Medical Practitioner".
- That the Bill fails to define Dentistry, Dentists, Nursing, Nurses, Pharmacy, Pharmacists, Paramedics and Paramedical Personals.
- That the Indian Medical Association (IMA) totally rejects the proposed

  "National Commission for Human Resources for Health Bill 2011".
- That Section 2 page (1) says: Supervision and regulation is not by dissolving the Bill in its preamble says "......to supervise and regulate Professional Councils in various disciplines of health sector". However, subsequently it dissolves all the existing Councils and takes away all their duties and fund autonomy is lost.
- That Section 4(j) page says: "to empower the Central Government to supersede Commission, Board, Committee or National Council". It gives autocratic power to Central Government to make the Commission to dance to its tunes.
- That Clause (2) page 115 says: "If the Commission, Board, Committee or National Council, as the case may be, fails/or neglects to comply with such order, Central Government may make, amend or revoke the regulations made by the Commission,......as the Central Government thinks fit.
- That National Commission, Board, Committee, all will have only appointed or nominated

members by the Central Government and no elected person will be there.

- That Clause 12 says: Central Government may by order remove from offices the Chairperson or any members of the Commission.

· Reduce the shortage and uneven distribution:

- That Section (2) page 53 says: "to reduce shortage, standardise quality and bridge the uneven distribution of existing work force in the health sector".
- That without roadmap, how the government is going to reduce the shortage of manpower by forming this Commission is said without statistical evidence based input. Using attractive words will not solve the problem.
- That need not to dissolve the existing Health Councils to achieve this purpose.
- That Health is a State subject and resources cannot be redistributed by the Central Government.
- That there is acute shortage of water and electricity in various parts of Country. Will the Central Government constitute the Commission to make even distribution?

Do we need more Specialist (or) Family physicians:

- That Prime Minister of India said: "India needs more Family physicians and efforts will be taken to increase the importance of Family physician.
- That Section 4 (c) page 53 says: "The bill does not talk about this but says:

  "to ensure uniform augmentation of trained Specialist and Superspecialist" as Its priority".

Fund transfer is the vision:

- That Section 4 (g) says: "to constitute a fund to be called the National Commission for Human Resources for Health Fund" and

- That Section 4 (h) says: "to transfer the assets, liabilities, rights, duties etc., of the existing Council to the Commission".
- That there are different Councils with age old registered members and their fees as assets and transferring them to common pool and vesting the authorities with Central Government appointed Commission is not acceptable.
- That funds of democratic Councils cannot be transferred to autocratic body.

Ayush Council and Rehabilitation Council:

- That Section 4 (k) page 54 says: "to repeal the INC Act 1947, Pharmacy Act 1948, Dentist Act 1948 and IMC Act 1956 and to dissolve the respective Council. However, AYUSH Council is dealing with Health Care and Rehabilitation Council of India Act 1991. What will happen to this Council ?

Audit and Accounting:

- That Clause 77 says: "even the accounts of State Councils will be audited only by the CAG of Central Government. State will have no role on this".

Bill above the existing laws:

- That Clause, 100 and 101 (page 34) says: "the decisions of the commission cannot be questioned in the Court of Law and the alleged persons cannot seek legal remedies".

Doctor doing any other occupation a misconduct:

- That Section 68 in Part 1 (10) page 50 says: "engage in any business/or occupation other than Health profession is a misconduct. This prohibits all career opportunities for Health professionals".
- That no elected members from Professional Associations in National Commission.
- That National Commission – the proposed supreme body with vested powers will have no elected members and State representatives to represent their needs and demands.

- That Professionals from other discipline of Management technology and law are given place in this Commission will pave way for dilution and nepotism.
- That in a democratic country, it is unfortunate that elected Representative Council is brought under appointed non-democratic body.

Common Entrance Examination by National Board of Health Education:

- That Clause 31 page 15 says: "entry level Common Entrance is not a viable option".
- That the proposed Common Entrance Examination by National Board, without providing common syllabus for Plus 2 Examinations, will affect the students not having opportunity to study CBSE syllabus.
- That will imbibe the social fabric and reservation systems in each State, as many students study Plus 2 in their regional language. Hence entry level Common Entrance is not a viable option.
- That Clause 33 (4) page 16 says: "power of commission to exempt persons (foreign graduates), from appearing in screening test will jeopardize the system.
- That power of National Board for Health Education to give Equivalency Certificate with Foreign National Course is objectionable.
- That role of Democratic National Medical Council responsible for Medical Education is taken away and handed over to seven members of National Board of Health Education. It is strange that no representative of Council/or State is included in the Board.
- That distance education mode without hands on training is a dangerous move for licensing a human handler.
- That Clause 30(z) says: "vision to promote cross disciplinary programmes in Health Sector will enhance quackery".

National Evaluation and Assessment Committee:

- That Clause 37 (e) says: National Evaluation and Assessment Committee with only six members and quorum of two, will be a mess to evaluate & take decision on the nearly 20,000 Health Institutions in all disciplines.

National Council:

- That the vision and objective with which the National Councils constituted are thrown into dust bin and only the power of registration is restored with Councils.
- That State Concils are made mere the branches of Central Council. The membership pattern is unacceptable.
- That instead of one member for each State, one member for 5,000 doctors must be emphasised.
- That Registration in State Council valid only for the State.
- That Clause 57 (4) says: "In contrary to the existing practice as per Clause 57 (4) a candidate who has registered in State Council can practice only in the State of Registration, and if registered in the National Council, can practice anywhere in India. That will negate the State Councils and no one will opt for registration in the State Council.

Medical Education is a specified area:

- That NCHRH is of the Government, by the Government, for the Government, and not for the Health Profession and Education.
- That NCHRH will definitely affect the Health Education and Health scenario of India.
- That independent Council is the need of the Medical Profession.

(*Source:* Prof. Dr. G.K. Ramachandrappa (National President IMA) and Dr. D.R. Rai (Hony. Secretary General IMA):

PRE-NATAL SEX DETERMINATION TESTS (PCPNDT) ACT

Preface: In the past Medical Profession was considered as a noble profession – next only to the God Almighty. With the passing times, this image has been eroded on account of many factors e.g. malpractices, commercialisation leading to negligence, patient's mistrust, enforcing authorities to enact the PNDT Act. opposed/ resented by the medicos.

Judgment: Rajasthan Medical Council suspends 12 doctors, Jaipur, July, 2012:

Complaint: Sri Ganganagar's SDM filed cases against 11 doctors, in the Court of Chief Judicial Magistrate, for conducting sex determination tests in their clinics and hospitals.

RMC: Rajasthan Medical Council (RMC) suspended licences of 12 doctors allegedly conducting sex determination tests.

Vox populi: Chiranjeeb Kakoty, July, 2012:
shame, shame:

"Suspension of licences is a vague phrase. Patients do not ask for licence of doctors prior, during or after consultation – at least I have never heard of it so far !!".

Doctors: Dr. Shambhu N Gupta: July, 2012: No one knows the causes of suspension of the Registration of doctors, by the RMC. The Appropriate Authority (AA) neither given the notice nor heard the alleged doctors and the Court framed charges on basis of AA's complaint only.

Vox-populi: - That the medical profession has become a profit-making business, with many bureaucrats and politicians also in connivance. The authorities have failed to keep a check on such errant doctors and hospitals. (SP Kansal, Chandigarh)

- That commercialisation and deteriorating moral standards in the society have had their effect on the medical profession too. Patients are equally guilty for the current scenario, by filing unnecessary medical litigation cases, in order to make a fast buck. The media has been instrumental in sensationalising and exaggerating incidents (SK Chawla, Chandigarh).

RAPE

Preface: Is a barbarian, monstrous, uncivilised, unpardonable crime, committed by accused on helpless victims mostly young innocent girls/women.

This inhuman crime has to be condemned forcefully by the society and deserves stringent punishment to the accused while full medical aid (free) and financial compensation to the victim and affected family.

- That rape is a catastrophe. It can only function as the end of one story and the beginning of another (Germaine Greer – feminist).
- That "Violence against women must never be accepted, never excused, never tolerated. Every girl and woman has the right to be respected, valued and protected. The Secretary General calls for steps and reforms to deter such crimes and bring perpetrators to justice (Ban Ki-Moon, UN Secretary General)".

Indian scenario:

Where rapists roam free:

"The chances of an Indian woman being raped have nearly doubled over the past two decades, but the probability of conviction has been denied by a third.

Every 20 mts., a woman is raped in India. Every 3rd victim of rape is a child, according to 2011 figures from the NCRB. The NCRB numbers capture only those cases that are reported to police, but officials agree that many rapes go unreported due to social stigma, political pressure and status inequality. Also the police, in certain cases discourage victims from pressing charges The message is clear: India is a dangerous place for women.

(*Source:* National Crime Records Bureau (NCRB).

Rapes (90 per cent) by known persons:

- That in majority of reported rape cases (90 per cent) the perpetrators (relatives, neighbours and colleagues) are known to victims (Police data). That women incld. a majority of minors, raped by known persons, and faced danger not from outside, but within the close confines of their homes and neighbourhood.

  In majority of cases, minors living in colonies subjected to sexual assault by their neighbours. That in certain cases, women exploited on the pretext of marriage (*Source*: M Sharma).

Rapes by minors (Juveniles):

The Indian Govt. had, in accordance with the United Nations Child Convention modified The Juvenile Justice Act, and brought children between 16-18 yrs. Under the protection of the law – which offers them the opportunity to reform. Rapes by juveniles have increased fivefold in a decade since 2000, when definition of "Juveniles" was modified (HT) .

That law and order, judicial reforms, punishments meted out to assaulters and patriarchal Indian mindsets are being addressed in the public domain.

KHAPS not in favour of death penalty for rapists:

- Hisar KHAP panchayats in Haryana have opposed the demand for death penalty for rapists, saying such laws may be misused. Amending the law and introducing death penalty for the rapists can lead to negative consequences (SS Samain KHAP leader). Instead, KHAPS demanded that rapists must be boycotted socially and their right to property scrapped. The guilty should be behind the bars for at least twenty yrs. without parole (HTC).

Crime Graph:

Hall of Shame: Numbers tell the truth:

2011's disturbing figures on the heinous crime:

Cases: 24,206 rape cases reported in India.

Judgment: Wait for justice long, often in vain Conviction: 26.6 per cent.

(*Source:* HT Bureau)

2012's Shocking incidents of rape:

- That West Bengal reported the highest number of crimes against women in India in 2012. Kolkata was reported to be the third most dangerous city for women.
- Delhi, December 16: A 23-yr- old physiotherapist gangraped brutally in a moving Delhi bus by four people for about 25 mts., besides beaten with a blunt object resulting in injuries to private parts, stomach and intestine, and ultimately succumbed to injuries and multiple organ failure in Singapore hospital (being shifted in critical condition for organ transplantation). The incidence led to public furor at a large scale, and majority demand capital punishment for all the accused for committing this heinous crime.
- Delhi, October 7: A 14-yr. old girl, working as a domestic help at a doctor's residence, alleged that her employer raped her for a year.
- Delhi, September 24: Two Delhi University students were allegedly raped by three men after being offered drinks laced with sedatives at a get-together in Bawana.
- Kolkata, December 24: A lawyer intern S James was sexually molested in a hotel room, by a recently retired SC Judge, old enough to be her grandfather. That a SC Judge, in a blatant abuse of power, had taken advantage of an intern, the lowest, most defenceless person in any professional pecking order. That the Judge was so sure of his power and so bereft of a sense of justice, that he was willing to harass a young woman who could not retaliate and hope to escape with her career intact. James revealed that other interns had also been harassed by the same Judge and had chosen to remain silent (to avoid social stigma).

- Kolkata, September 25: An 18-month old infant, allegedly raped by her uncle, was found covered in blood by her mother at Royal Street.
- Kolkata, December 29: A 45-yr old woman was allegedly gang-raped by six men and thereafter bludgeoned her to death. Her husband accompanying her, was forced to drink acid, battling for life at Kolkata's Medical College Hospital.
- Kolkata, February: Suzette Jordan, allegedly gang-raped in Kolkata's Park Street. The case is sub-judicial. Her only request to every political party is not use incidents of rape or murder for their own profit. When a woman is raped, she is not from any political party, she is just a woman.
- Haryana, September 9: A 16-yr old dalit girl was gang-raped and an MMS was circulated. In another incident on September 21, A 30-yr old mother of two was gang-raped and filmed in Jind. These incidents were among the twelve cases reported in Haryana in last one month.
- Haryana: A Delhi Court, awarded the death penalty to three men for abduction, gangrape and murder of a 19 yrs. old woman whose mutilated and decomposed body was recovered from a Haryana village in 2012.
- Mumbai, August 9: A 25-yrs old lawyer was killed in her Wadala flat by security guard, when she resisted his attempt to rape her at knife point.
- Patna, June 14: A school girl was gang-raped by her boyfriend and his classmates, who shot a video of the act 7 circulated an MMS to blackmail the victim.
- Delhi, April 13: A 14-yr old girl was raped and sodomised by her employer for two yrs before she was rescued.
- Kolkata, February 5: A 37-yr old woman was raped at gunpoint by a man and his associates she had befriended in a pub at Park Street.

- Chandigarh, November 13: A minor girl was gang-raped by her boyfriend and two associates. All the three rapists were awarded ten yrs jail term each, while their three accomplices were sentenced to five yrs jail terms.
- Bathinda, December 20: Two minors, allegedly raped by 50 yrs old neighbour, arrested under Sections 376 and 506.
- Panchkula/Ambala, December 13: Excise inspector gets 7-yrs. RI for rape under Section 376 of IPC, as he concealed his first marriage to his 2nd wife.

2013's Shocking incidents of rape:

Mumbai: July 31: An 18-yr old telephone operator, was gang-raped at the abandoned Shakti Mill. All the five rapists were awarded jail sentence for the rest of their life.

Mumbai: August 22: A 22-yr old telephone operator, was gang-raped at the abandoned Shakti Mill, by the same convicts involved in the gang-rape of the telephone operator on July 31. All the three rapists were awarded death sentence, under Section 376E of IPC, meant for repeat offenders.

Goa: November 7-8: Tarun Tejpal, Tehelka co-founder, alleged to have sexually assaulted and raped a young journalist colleague working for his magazine Tehelka. Tejpal was arrested by the Goa Police, and has been in jail since November 30, 2013. The case is subjudicial.

2014's Shocking incidents of rape:

There isn't a day that goes by in India without rape:

- Two teenage girls were raped and murdered in village Badaun, UP. Their bodies were found hanging from the tree.
- Three minor Dalit girls were allegedly gangraped by seven men for opposing eve-teasing in village Singauli, UP, on July 08.

- A 22-yr old woman was allegedly kidnapped and raped by four men in a moving car in Ghaziabad on July 07. The victim was dumped in Noida around midnight with her hands and legs tied and an alcohol bottle shoved inside her. The accused also made an MMS prior to dumping her.
- A dalit girl being gang-raped by upper-caste men in her Haryana village.
- A professional being raped by an acquaintance becase she dared say no, in Mumbai.
- A girl student being dragged away from a parked car and gang-raped by a group of men believing that because she is making out with one man, she must be 'up for it' with them as well.
- Two minor girls were raped after being abducted by a priest's son and a woman, who were arrested by the police, in SAS Nagar.
- A 40 yrs old father R/o Mauli-Jagran, was arrested for sexually assaulting his 16 yrs old daughter for past 5-months. The police arrested the accused on the basis of complaint lodged by the mother of the victim.
- A 19 yrs old college student was raped by her father several times for the past 2-months. The Police arrested the accused on the basis of complaint lodged by the girl's teacher.
- A girl set herself on fire because she couldn't live with the stigma of being a rape victim.
- A father kills himself when shown video clips of his daughter being gang-raped by a group of men.

Given the staggering number of rape stories that emerge from India every day, there really isn't much more than we can learn about this crime, is there? We know that it is not so much about sex as it is about power. We know that such is the aura of shame that surrounds the crime that the victim ends up feeling much more at fault than the perpetrator. And we know that society plays into that feeling of guilt by effectively telling the woman that, in one way or the other, she asked for it.

Marrying late causes rape:

Young men and women have sexual desires, so as soon as they reach puberty, they should be married off so that they do not 'stray'. In other words, the best way of ensuring that rape does not occur is by making sure that girls and boys are married off as minors. Because, as we know married women never get raped, and married men only ever have sex – consensual or forced – with their wives.

(*Source:* Sube Singh, KHAP Panchayat leader in Haryana. View endorsed by OP Chautala, ex-Chief Minister, Haryana)

Naughty trouble makers:

Around 90 per cent of rapes occur when women go along willingly with their rapists.

When what starts off as consensual sex goes wrong, these women start crying rape.

(*Source:* D Goyat, Congress party spokesperson, Haryana)

Bizarre theory:

The consumption of fast food causes rape, due to hormonal imbalance in men making their animal instincts veer out of control, and their increased sexual desire manifests itself as rape.

(*Source:* J Chander, KHAP Panchayat leader, Haryana)

Instigating rape (Social life):

Going to a nightclub and there drinking too much and mixing with strangers (men), and then later on complaining about rape. Honestly, what were you doing there in the first place?

(*Source:* M Mitra, Minister, West Bengal).

Mobiles causing spurt in rapes:

The Anjuman Muslim Panchayat in Rajasthan, issued a diktat banning girls from using mobile phones and singing and dancing at weddings. That mobiles are spoiling girls (Habib-ur-Rahman). A cross-section of women denounced the edict. Why should restrictions not apply to boys (Adv. R Rizvi).

(*Source:* UD Rawal).

Rape of grown-up women understandable, but not of minors:

Barabari ya bade logo ke sath balatkar samajh me ata hai, lekin nabalig bachhiyon ke sath is tarah ka jaghanya apradh karna... Inko to fansi par latka dena chahiye (R Bais, BJP's chief whip in the Lok Sabha). S Sitharaman BJP spokes person said, "This could be Bais's personal view".

(*Source:* E Kaiser).

Boys make mistakes, Why hang them?:

"Phansi dena ghalat hai (for rape). Ladkon se ghalti ho jaati hai. Hum satta mein aaye to kanoon mein badlav karenge (Handing out death penalty for rape is not fair. Boys make mistakes. There will be changes in the law if we come to power)" (MS Yadav, SP Chief), while addressing an election rally in Moradabad, UP.

Irresponsible remark:

- That while the entire country demands stern action against the rapists, a National leader putting to shame the National sentiment and insulting the collective wisdom of Parliament and the public who instituted a strict law for the safety of women. MS Yadav, cannot label a heinous act just "a mistake for boys" (A Sethi).
- That politicians like Yadav, think of women as objects, and no crime is worse than rape (P Kaur).

Rape sometimes right, sometimes wrong

- That "It is a social crime which depends on the man and the woman. It is sometimes right and sometimes wrong". Babulal Gaur (Home Minister

MP State), told press reporters, that the crime of rape can only be considered to have been committed if it is reported to police.

Showing their ugly colours:

- That all parties must crack the whip on those leaders within their ranks who express hateful justifications of rape. If it is beyond some of political worthies to be sensitive or sympathetic to the plight of women who have been subjected to sexual violence, the least they can do is keep quite. Whatever their misguided views, the least these elected public officials should ensure is that the culprits are brought to book. Once they realise that they can't get away with perpetrating violence on women, such incidents will come down (Editor, HT).
- **From the KHAP** – dominated Haryana to progressive Bengal, rape is a grim reality in India with triggers that are as diverse as the socio-economic and cultural fabric of the country.

Need of the hour, to give ruthless punishment:

- That the need of the hour is to give ruthless punishment to rapists. That why cover faces of criminals in public? Their families should be disgraced as they are the ones whon did not give right upbringing to them. That steps are taken for gender equality and strive to make the Judicial system effective".

  (U Singh, Actress).

Sensitivity towards women: Insensitive crude joke:

"When rape is unavoidable, better enjoy it", advocated by an agricultural scientist (Anita Shukla at a police workshop in MP, in response to the brutal rape-cum-murder of a Delhi girl, saying that "it is the women who provoke men. What was the girl doing outside home at 10 in night?" And if that was not enough, she added, "After being surrounded by six rapists, why didn't she surrender? At least, that could have prevented the pulling out of her intestines."

(*Source:* HTC, Indore)

Inequality – It's time to get real:

Why are we so outraged by the view that the recent rash of rapes in India has something to do with public displays of intimacy? There are many poor and middle-class people in India who don't have a normal conjugal life. Thanks to lack of living space, we pay lip service to low-income Urban Housing, but do nothing about it. Rape is correlated to uncontrollable male urges – a physical and psychological given, with a 'men will be men' sigh of resignation.

(*Source:* A Banerjee, HT)

Rape – A risky formulation:

The argument that unequal access to space is leading to rapes relies on an entrenched sense of male entitlement to women's bodies. The image of the lonely deprived boy ogling the unavailable woman and then raping her goes too far down the garden path to argue, for there is no such thing as men's right to equal sexual access to women. Rape also gets coded as a matter of family honour, the 'besmirching' of a woman's name more shameful than the mental and physical violence she suffers. Marital rape, on the other hand, is not considered punishable, and family sexual abuse is almost always unreported, meaning that these ubiquitous private spaces of rape (conjugal beds, homes, families) are invisible to the law. It is the male sense of entitlement to non-consensual sex that is the crux of the problem, and not the presence of women as obscure objects of desire for them, who then need to be trundled off to marital bedrooms for everybody's peace and fulfilment.

(*Source:* S Basu, B Bose, HT).

International forum:

* In India, it is often the women who are blamed

after rape, not just by ordinary people but by politicians and influential figures (The Independent).

* In India, rapes are appalling, says Angelina Jolie, UN Envoy, used the closing session of the Global Summit at London, on June 13, 2014, seeks urgent action to End Sexual Violence in Conflict.
* There is deeply entrenched patriarchy and widespread misogyny in vast swathes of the Country, esp. in the north (BBC).
* Acceptance of domestic violence, stigmatising rape victims to compromise and low status of women are among reasons for problem of sexual violence in India (The Washington Post).
* India as a Country "which basks in its success as a growing business and technological mecca but tolerates shocking abuse of women. Many victims, shamed into silence and callously disregarded by a male-dominated power structure, never go to the authorities to seek justice. Women are routinely blamed for inciting violence against them. (The New York Times).
* Rape political tool in India: Rape is often used as a tool for political and social subjugation of Dalit women, doomed to the lowest rungs of society due to caste-based prejudices. Sexual violence against Dalit women is a systemic way of enforcing status quo of the Dalits. Dalit women constitute the worst victims of sexual violence in India, along with rapes committed by security forces. Despite circumstancial evidence, often "probes are thwarted to facilitate their exoneration". The review noted that two women are raped every hour, and every six hrs, a married woman is found beaten to death, burnt or driven to suicide. Abduction of Scheduled Caste women are rampant in Utttar Pradesh, which account for 58.8 per cent of the cases in 2011, the year assessed.

  (UN REPORT).

World scenario:

God's Will:

If you do get pregnant as a consequence of rape, then abortion is not an option, but consider it as a 'gift from God' (God's intention).

(*Source:* R Mourdock, US Senate candidate).

Penalty:

Some rapes are more serious than others. In the case of an 18 yr old man having sex with an underage girl, or in cases of date rape, the crime is less serious than other rapes and deserves a lesser punishment.

(*Source:* K Clarke, Justice Secretary, UK).

- Jimmy Savile, late BBC star, one of Britain's most prolific sex offenders, had sexually abused hundreds of victims, mainly youngsters, at hospitals and at BBC premises, incld. dead bodies in the mortuary of a hospital where he worked as a volunteer.

Conclusion: This is what political leaders across the world – not just in backward, obscurantist Haryana but in such developed, enlightened countries such as USA and UK – believe about rape. One may either laugh or cry: at the ignorance; the insensitivity; and the sheer stupidity of it all.

(*Source:* S Goswami, HT).

Trials and tribulations:

"Humiliating questions, insensitive defence layers and open courts that do nothing to make a rape victim comfortable. For a victim who decides to go ahead and fight for justice in the court of law, the trauma of rape has to be lived till the trial is over. "The initial trauma of rape has to be relived over and over again at the time of getting the initial statement recorded and thereafter in the cross-questioning, which is usually brutal. Even though the Courts have said that rape victims' past should not be brought up to justify the rape, defence lawyers use it regularly to malign the victim".

(Nilanju Dutta, lawyer Violence Intervention Team at NGO Jagori)

"While the initial statement of the victim can be recorded on tape, if requested, cross-questioning has to be done face to face. A proactive judge is very important to ensure that the defence lawyer does not harass the victim as the ordeal of the girl does not end with the rape. It continues from the time the act is committed right through to filing the complaint and the trial.

(Monica Arora, advocate SC)

Questionnaire:

Q. Why do rapes happen and why do groups of men attack a woman ?

Ans: That as per psychologists, gangrape is a manifestation of certain psychodynamics in a patriarchal society i.e. false appraisal of masculinity, peer approval, boredom, joblessness combined together can lead to such sort of psychopathic gang behaviour. Gangrape is a part of negative group dynamics, is an urban malaise (ultimate terror in metros). Mostly gang rapists are either rich/or powerful, poor/or unemployed or drug addicts/alcoholics. (Zofeen Maqsood)

Q. Why has it come to this and is the problem even bigger than we know of ?

Ans: That as per statics, in 2002, reported cases of rape: New York City 1468, London 2731, Delhi 383 (misleading as large no. of cases unreported). That a patriarchal culture where a woman is seen as a source who can bring potential shame to the family, is responsible. It is because of this fear that many women choose to bear the trauma silently.

(Nirmala Venkatesh, Ex-member National Commission of Women).

That social stigma is global: US: 54 per cent of sexual assaults unreported and 97 per cent of rapists roam freely as a result of delayed trials, hostile witnesses and often delayed/denied justice, society's apathy discouraging a girl from reporting.

(Adv. Pinky Anand).

Q. Why are people feeling so helpless and angry, even though it's yet another case ?

Ans: That violent incidents of rape/and murder, being viewed as a result of the State's complete indifference toward its citizens. That widespread protests could be an attempt to activate the State from its moral lethargy (Radhika Chopra, Professor Sociology, DU). That violent incidents have shaken the conscience of the Country (Dr. Sandeep Vohra, Psychiatrist, Apollo hospital).

(Furquan Siddiqui).

Q. Why even lowly criminals and muderers look down on the rape accused ?

Ans: That a rape accused is ostracized, not given work or position of responsibility by co-inmates or even jail authorities (BK Gupta, Ex-Police Commissioner, Delhi). A rapist is deemed filthy and at the bottom of the pile as per this hierarchy as he's seen to have targeted a vulnerable girl, part of somebody's family. Even a murderer cares about his family. Rape accused fear co-inmates in the US and some European Countries too. Jails there segregate them.

(Abhishek Sharan).

Q. Why is the incident our Sandy Hook in terms of the shockwaves and how do we explain it ?

Ans: That when a gunman walked into the Sandy Hook elementary school in US in December 2013, and shot dead 22 children, it shocked the entire world and led to the US rethinking its gun laws. The Delhi gang-rape has been as shocking. Besides the anger and helplessness, the gory nature of the crime makes it difficult to explain to kids. Schools can be helpful in communicating such issues to children (Dr. Sunir Parikh, Psychiatrist, Fortis Healthcare).

Furquan Siddique).

Q. Why were male politicians silent, leaving women MPs to make emotional speeches ?

Ans: That male MPs were relatively mum on the issue, leaving the female MPs to make emotional speeches (MS Aiyar, MP). It is a patriarchal thing. On women's issues, men MPs can be extremely ill-mannered. In fact, few MPs have spoken about it even on TV (KM Chenoy, Professor Political Theory, JNU).

(Somar Khurshid).

Q. Why is a woman's voice and her vote not seen as being heard in the Country ?

Ans: That during elections, appeals are often made to caste/religion vote banks but gender issues are not prominent, the reason being very strong patriarchy and masculinity factors. The perception of traditional gender roles still exists. Women are seen as commodities, not independent thinkers (KM Chenoy, Professor Political Theory). That even though there has been a demographic change in women, men do not see them as equal (A Sharma, Sociologist). That no dominant political party is willing to challenge patriarchal attitudes (K Krishan, Secretary AIPWA).

(Somar Khurshid).

Q. Why was there such lax security to begin with for such a crime to take place ?

Ans: That while Police has come under criticism, there has been talk of forces been underdeployed. With shortage of staff, the Police move from one crisis to another.

(Faizan Haider)

Suggested solutions:

* Ban Ki-Moon, UN Secretary General: Violence against women must never be accepted, never

excused, never tolerated. Every girl and woman has the right to be respected, valued and protected. The Secretary General calls for steps and reforms to deter such crimes and bring perpetrators to justice.

* VN Khare, former Ex-CJI: Suggests a special police cell to be installed.
* Amodh Kanth, former Joint Commissioner of Delhi Police: Provisions to protect the victim in the Court already exist.
* Satyapal Singh, Police Commissioner Mumbai: Suggested measures:
  - Police stations to report immediately cases of crimes against women to the respective DCPs.
  - DCPs to superwise investigations of these cases. Probes to be time-bound.
  - Police to instal complaint boxes for women to drop complaints without revealing their identities.
  - Police stations to have at least five women constables and officers.
* Khushwant Singh, Sr. Journalist: Punishment should be a deterrent and not the outcome of public outrage. Death sentence imposed on murderers has not brought down the incidence of murders – nor will it have any impact on the incidence of rape. The rapist should be castrated and once for all be unable to repeat his crime.

SC: Justice KS Radhakrishnan and Justice V Sen: Rape is a reprehensible act and every perpetrator of the crime should be punished severely and strictly, but only after the accused's guilt has been proved beyond doubt.

Remedy: Suggested measures to be followed are the urgent need:

* Parents/guardians: to be fully aware of the whereabouts of the girls esp. at odd hrs. duties, and if possible to be escorted by close relative/ friends.

* Girl students and working women: mandatory to learn judo/karate, and to carry pepper sprays – for self protection.
* Modest dressing – to avoid provoking immature minded persons.
* Entertainment (TV and Films): to be responsible towards public showings.
* Media: doing the excellent job by making the public aware of the misdeeds of the wrong-doers.
* Police: to be sensitive towards the victims and should file the complaint/FIR, immediately, irrespective of the accused's status.That more personnel would allow Police to have better trained manpower, posting more women staff at PCRs and Police Stations, raising visibility of uniformed personnel at night.
* Technology as force: installation of a web of CCTV cameras with face recognition, although the project hasn't progressed.
* Legal: setting up of Fast-track Courts: to expedite the cases pertaining to the violence against women. Until the justice is able to deliver convictions within a reasonable time, the law loses its deterent value.
* Government: to expedite changes in criminal law dealing with crimes against women – so far tough molestation law remains a non-starter.
* Punishment: majority suggested tough measures may eradicate/control the menace of violence against women, while some persons suggest that punishment should be a deterrent and not the outcome of public outrage.

- Capital punishment (Death sentence): for each and every proven case of rape-cum-murder (as rarest of rare).
- Life imprisonment: for rape esp. of minors.
- Imprisonment: current limit of 7-10 yrs to be raised alongwith hefty fine.

- Juvenile accused: criminal law to be changed for raising the sentence period and may be death sentence in rarest of rare cases.
- Castration: to render the rapist incapable of repeating his crime for ever. But he may become a more dangerous evil, by resorting to more violent evil acts like molestation, physical torture of victims and even resort to murders, in retaliation (revenge) for his castration punishment. Mere castration may not be justified punishment esp. in case of rape-cum-murder.

Rapes by minors (Juveniles):

Concern: Rapes by juveniles have increased five fold in a decade since 2000, when its definition was modified to incld. children of 16 to 18 yrs. Under the category.

2000: The Indian Government had, in accordance with the United Nations Child Convention, modified The Juvenile Justice Act 1986, and brought Children between the age group of 16-18 yrs., under the protection of the law which offers them the opportunity to reform.

National Crime Records Bureau (NCRB): also indicated that crimes being committed by juveniles are on the rise. The inclusion of children in the age group of 16-18 in 2000 accounted for the spurt in cases under the juvenile- delinquency head. NCRB states that the trend is worsening with each passing year, and that about 65 per cent of such juveniles booked under the Indian Penal Code are between 16 and 18 yrs. of age (2010-11), while 94 per cent of juvenile crimes are committed by boys.

World scenario:

UK:

- That anyone who has attained the age of 17 yrs, being considered as adult.
- That Special Youth Courts try cases involving those under 18 yrs old.

- That a juvenile under 17, involved in heinous offences like sexual assault, he/she can be tried as an adult.
- That capital punishment (death penalty) is not allowed.
- That if a youth offender is jointly charged with an adult, the charge is heard and tried by a regular Court.

France:

- That Special Juvenile Courts to try those under 18 yrs old.
- That may be awarded tougher punishment but no capital punishment. That Juvenile Assize Courts to try juveniles (16-18) for heinous offences.

USA:

- That Special Juvenile Courts deal with those under 18 yrs old.
- That no capital punishment for juveniles.
- That about twenty States allow juveniles to be tried as adults and in case found guilty, sentenced to life imprisonment.

(*Source:* MD Gupta, HT 2014).

Punishment: As per the modified Juvenile Justice (Care and Protection of Children) Act, 2000 the maximum punishment for a crime committed by a juvenile is three yrs as compared to imprisonment of upto life for the same offence committed by adults.

Vox-populi: After the horrifying Delhi gangrape case where a juvenile was also involved, there is growing anger and demand that juveniles between 16-18 yrs. be punished like adults for heinous crimes. Of the six accused, the 17 yrs old had purportedly abused the 23-yr old woman in the most inhuman manner.

SEXUAL HARASSMENT OF WOMEN AT WORKPLACE (PREVENTION, PROHIBITION AND REDRESSAL) ACT, 2013

Preface: Is defined as an Act to provide for the protection of women against sexual harassment at workplace. Sexual harassment results in violation of the fundamental rights of a woman to equality under Articles 14 and 15 of the Constitution of India and her right to life and to live with dignity under Article 21 of the Constitution and right to practice any profession or to carry on any occupation, trade or business which incld. A right to a safe environment free from sexual harassment. The Act has replaced Vishaka guidelines.

International scenario:

- That the protection against sexual harassment and the right to work with dignity are universally recognised Human Rights by International Conventions and Instruments such as Convention on the Elimination of all Forms of Discrimination against women, which has been ratified on 25 June, 1993 by the Government of India.

  Navi Pillay (UN High Commissioner for Human Rights):

Aims:

- To provide protection not only to women who are employed but also to any woman who enters the workplace as a client, customer, apprentice, and daily wage worker or in an ad-hoc capacity. It also covers students, research scholars in Colleges/Universities and patients in Hospitals.

  It seeks to cover workplaces in the unorganised sectors.
- To provide an effective complaints and redress mechanism.
- To be mandatory for every employer to constitute a Local (internal) Complaints Committee (LCC) to be constituted by the designated District Officer at the District/or Sub-district levels, depending on the need. The LCCs will enquire

into the complaints of sexual harassment and recommend action to the employer or District Officer.

Forms: That sexual harassment at workplace constitutes:

- physical contact and advances
- a demand or request for sexual favours
- making sexually coloured remarks
- showing pornography
- any other unwelcome physical, verbal/non-verbal conduct of sexual nature.

Enactment: Vishaka case verdict (1997): A three Judge bench headed by the then Chief Justice of India, JS Verma, had laid down a set of detailed guidelines mandating setting up of internal complaints committee headed by a woman in every organisation – government or private – to address the issue of sexual harassment of women employees at workplace. But the SC held that these directions (Vishaka guidelines) would be binding and enforceable in law until suitable legislation is enacted to occupy the field.

The Sexual Harassment of Women at Workplace (Prevention, Prohibition and Redressal) Act, 2013: The Parliament passed the new law, that is an improvement over the Vishaka guidelines as it also covers unorganised sector and domestic workers and expands the definition of 'workplace' to include many public and private organisations incld. educational institutions, sports institutes, stadium, hospitals employing more than ten workers, and even a house.

The Act provides for a mechanism in terms of internal and local complaints committees to be established by the employer and the appropriate government.

Jurisdiction: Extends to the whole of India.

Offence: Sexual harassment at workplace. Also the promise or threat to a woman's employment prospects or creation of hostile work environment as 'sexual harassment' at the workplace and expressly seeks to prohibit such acts.

Flaws: Members of the complaints committee might not always be independent of the influences of the management which has instituted it, and this esp. becomes a tricky issue if the offender in question is part of the top management.

Security: Though the bill is not foolproof, it at least provides a starting point of security. But yes, every working woman should take the onus of her personal security and well-being at the work place.

Safeguards: That the bill provides for safeguards in case of false or malicious complaint of sexual harassment. However, merely inability to substantiate the complaint or give adequate proof would't make the complaint liable for punishment.

Precautions:- That women should express strong resistance to the smallest inappropriate gesture, action, word or speech. Otherwise the offender will assume that he has her consent and will progress to bigger offences.

- That women should learn to discern friendly behaviour from inappropriate behaviour and maintain certain boundaries with men at all times.

Example: Laugh and joke may be fine, but crude jokes are unpardonable.

Penalty: Employers who fail to comply with the provisions, will be liable to punishment with a fine which may extend to ₹ 50K.

Since there is a possibility that during the inquiry, the woman may be subject to threat and aggression, she has been given the option to seek relief in the form of transfer either of her own or the respondent or seek leave from work. The complaint committees are required to complete the inquiry within 90 days and a period of 60 days has been given to the Employer/

District officer for the implementation of the recommendations of the committee.

Accused person: held guilty:

- deduction of his salary @ 10% PM for a period of one year or in lumpsum, or
- withdrawal of privileges and perks, or
- termination of service.

Safeguards: The bill provides for safeguards in case of false or malicious complaint of sexual harassment. A fine of ₹ 500 or 5 per cent of the salary of the complainant PM for a year. However, merely inability to substantiate the complaint or give adequate proof would't make the complaint liable for punishment.

Vox-Popul: Ramesh Behl (Sr. Manager MNC, Gurgaon): The problem stems at two levels:

1st: That some women, who think there is nothing wrong in talking loosely and dressing provocatively. This category of women, more often than not, is not conscious of the fact that their conduct is likely to attract unwanted attention from male colleagues. Needless to say, however they are courting risk.

2nd: That certain women, who have ambitions but lack efficiency and knowledge of the job, they have been assigned to do. There have been women, who used their feminine guiles to manipulate career moves and hence became very susceptible to sexual harassment.

Raina Bhattacharjee (Psychological Therapist and Wellness Counsellor): From the woman's point of view, this alleged manipulation usually starts and stops with flirting. This means that more often than not, most women in this scenario might be fine going for an occasional lunchdate or receiving a few flirtatious compliments, but they are uncomfortable and unwilling when it comes to anything beyond this. Unfortunately, however, most men cannot comprehend this unspoken firewall in terms of permissiveness and consequently these women soon find themselves in sticky situations. That women should express strong resistance to the smallest inappropriate gesture, action, word or speech. Otherwise the offender will assume that he has her consent and will progress to bigger offences. That women should learn to discern friendly behaviour from inappropriate behaviour and maintain certain boundaries with men at all times.

Example: Laugh and joke may be fine, but crude jokes are unpardonable.

Flavia Agnes (Women's Rights Lawyer and Writer): The worst thing that may happen in such cases is that the women finds herself completely alone. She feels that if she complains, people will unduly and sceptically question her about her initial overtures. And when the situation becomes unbearable, women often resort to extreme measures like Geetika Sharma suicide case.

Members of the complaints committee might not always be independent of the influences of the management which has instituted it, and this esp. becomes a tricky issue if the offender in question is part of the top management.

Gauri Sharma (Journalist): I couldn't believe I was being harassed.

Legal Speak: That accused's comments and embracing would fall within the definition of inappropriate conduct at workplace. A woman/ man in the organisation has a right to expect their company to be in compliance with the law (Adv. Naina Kapur).

Tania Banerjee (Journalist): I left the publication disheartened.

Legal Speak: That feeling uncomfortable, she could have asked her boss to stop criticising her dress, or spoken to the HR (Adv. Seema Misra).

Mahima Singh (IT Professional): I didn't complete my internship.

Legal Speak: That the actions of the team leader could fall within the definition of prohibited conduct under the law as an unwelcome and direct physical advance (Adv. Naina Kapur).

Preeti (HR Professional): The girl's reputation is tarnished.

Legal Speak: That the unwelcome attempt by the organisation head to hug.

Preeti would fall within prohibited unwelcome physical conduct as per Vishaka guidelines for Sexual harassment of Working Women (prevention, prohibition and redressal) Act, 2013 (Adv. Naina Kapur).

Judgment: SC: Medha Kalwal Lele: October 20, filed a PIL, seeking its direction to expand the ambit of the historic 1997 verdict (Vishaka case) to include various other institutions. A bench headed by Justice RM Lodha said "lip service and hollow statements" are not enough to uplift the condition of women and asked the Governments to put in place law to tackle the problem. The Court thus expanded the ambit of its historic 1997 Vishaka verdict, by directing regulating bodies and all the institutions affiliated to them to implement the guidelines framed in the Vishaka case of 1997 within two months.

Remedy: In orfer to check this heinous crime, following measures are suggested:

- Immediate filing of the FIR against the accused.
- Non-bailable warrants against the accused/s.
- Fast-track Courts, to decide the case at the earliest.
- Stringent punishment to the accused/s (Imprisonment plus fine).
- Full payment to the victim/s and their families incld. total cost of treatment and compensation for the disability or loss of life, to be recovered from the accused/s.

- Government to provide full protection to the victim and family.
- Public awareness and support in preventing this crime and providing help to the victim and affected family.
- Media exposure of this crime till the punishment to the accused as well as full compensation to the victim.

TORTURE: PHYSICAL TORTURE

Preface: That deliberate systematic or wanton infliction of physical/or mental injury or damage by one or more persons acting alone or on the orders of the higher authority, to force another person to disclose information/to make a forced confession, or for any other reason.

(*Source:* World Medical Association in its Tokyo Declaration, 1975)

Violation: Global issue of Concern-Human Rights Violation:

- That Torture is considered as an important human rights violation–a worldwide misuse of power. "Any act by which severe pain or suffering (physical or mental) inflicted intentionally on a person for purposes e.g. obtaining information or a confession, punishing him for an act he/she or a third person has committed/or is suspected of having committed, or intimidating/or coercing him for any reason based on discrimination of any kind, when such pain or suffering is inflicted by/or at the instigation of/or with the consent/or acquiescence of a public official/or another person acting in an official capacity, excluding pain of suffering inflicted from, inherent in or incidentals to lawful sanctions."

(*Source:* United Nations Convention, December 1991).

Motives:

- To extort a confession–misused as legal proof.
- To extract information.
- To punish a person.

- To suppress persons associated with tortured person (violent distortion).
- To torture/torment-prisoners, political opponents, by methods incld. water boarding etc.

Forms:
- Slapping
- Pushing
- Shoving
- Hair pulling
- Hitting with fist or rod.

Rehabilitation:
- That anti-torture and rehabilitation centre is in Copenhagen Denmark, where torture victims are rehabilitated and studies are carried out on the effects of torture. So many works are done but many objectives are still to be fulfilled.

TORTURE: PSYCHOLOGICAL TORTURE:

TROLLS /SADISTS

Preface: That both trolls and sadists feel glee at the distress of others. That they just want to have fun, and Internet is their playground, although it's just not funny anymore. That with increasing death and rape threats, bitter and incessant abuse and psychological torture that has even led some to suicides, and that hate trolling is currently a menacing activity carried out by the positively twisted, and the only way to fight back is to stand up to them. Trolls have always found place in popular culture since the later Nineties, and till recently was endured as a kind of pungent kick that came with the enriching, particularly experience that is the Internet. But anyone who has been remotely active online, will know that TBAT just doesn't cut it anymore for the invective-laden, violent, hate-filled and often deeply terrifying comments that are doing the rounds these days. That troll is an imaginary creature in the ancient Scandinavian stories, like a very large or very small ugly person.

Vulnerabile: That persons seen to sway opinion e.g. journalists, film critics, activists, stand-up comics, Twitter celebrities or public figures, are often the most vulnerable to it. Perhaps those who indulge in this derive a fake sense of power, aided by the anonymity the Internet provides (R Sardesai, editor-in-chief IBN7 network)

- Gender: while men are abused too, trolling is not entirely gender neutral and women get the rawest end of the deal. Men too mostly get abused with regard to their mothers and sisters, displaying a deep-seated patriarchal mindset. That men go after women with a sense of powerlessness because they feel unfulfilled somewhere. That with the changing social scenario, women are no longer dependent on men the way their mothers were. That's unsettling for them and thereby reacting with violence, both in real life and online. (S Bhaduri, Psychoanalyst).

Celebrity Trolls: That celebrities evoke scary levels of devotion among their fans, which translate into troll armies online. International: That different. Equally aggressive or sometimes more so, these fan bases work in unison against anyone, even other public figures, for what they feel is best for their idol. Examples:

- Justin Bieber: Believers-a rabid fan base, defend the teen idol's every action (DUIs, arrests, public fights etc.) and thrash anyone suggesting otherwise.
- Lady Gaga; during TV show, host Kelly Osborne criticised Gaga for missing a red carpet appearance, and Gaga's fans routinely called her fat and asked her to kill herself.
- Beyonce: her fan base often miffed with the singer for actions, they think she shouldn't do e.g. her recent friendship with Kim Kardashian, which drew ire.

Web without name:-That same anonymity lies at the centre of abusive trolling. That in real life, interaction is aided by biological cues e.g. hurt, shame or anger which prevent us from being abusive in person. But this connect is missing in the online world. That it brings out the worst in human behaviour when a person is behind a computer or tablet screen. "The real world bears consequences.

That the rules of good behaviour (whether formed), have't been implemented firmly (HK Arora, Psychologist).

- That absence of social cues also fails to generate empathy online, because that's what essentially enables people to identify with the pain and discomfort of others. That there is nothing to jolt his/her (Troll's) consciousness or tell how hurt one could be from his/her comments, which in turn makes one crueller, aggressive and animal like. That there is a delusional control over the medium where the abuser often feels that he/ she can exit anytime without any harm.

  (S Bhaduri, Psychoanalyst).

- That democracy at home and school is important, as childen need to be made aware that there could be legal implications of their internet use. That enough emotional contact and sufficient education about the law can curb the misuse of Internet (H Shetty, HTC).

Checks and Controls:

- That Internet abuse is a global phenomenon, many Countries have evolved active laws to counter it. Young Internet users should guard against putting up content that could lead them in trouble under the IT Act. Parents should supervise net use.

  UK: apart from running several campaigns against cyber bullying, recently arrested two men, threatening rape and violence to a woman on twitter.

  Winnipeg: online trolling correlates to narcissism, Machiavellianism (being deceitful and cunning), psychopathy, and sadism, with sadism being the most robust link (EE Buckels, University of Manitoba).

India: inspite of the law being fairly toothless, when it comes to online abuse, it does lay the responsibility on the agency to moderate the comments hosted on it. As per Section 75 of the IT Act, an agency hosting such abuse does become complicit in it, and has to exercise due diligence to remove it (P Duggal, SC lawyer). That while most news websites monitor comments, on Twitter a lot of vulgar hate speech continues to thrive. Currently the social network has a 'report tweet' feature, under which one can report abusive tweets, and for which there is a round-the-clock team to take care of the grieveances. However, abuse continues to proliferate.

- Facebook: comparatively sees the least trolling, owing to the presence of a wide network of friends, pictures and family ready to judge you.
- Twitter: offers a lower degree of personalisation.
- Reddit: requires nothing more than an email ID to join, sees greater degree of abuse and hate speech.
- 4chan: public bulletin board, where anyone can post anonymously, is the dark space of Internet, where users goad others into suicide and serious self-harm e.g. 4chan users organised groups to goad teenaged girls to cut themselves in the name of teen pop musician Justin Bieber.

Caught in the act:

- Thane: Jealous, a school girl created a fake online profile of her classmate, and posted obscene pictures of her on it.
- Mumbai: a 22-yr. old chartered student, hacked into the e-taxation accounts of Anil Ambani, Salman Khan, Shah Rukh Khan, Sachin Tandulkar and MS Dhoni and others, out of curiosity. That he was booked under Sections of the IT Act.

(*Source:* HTC).

Act: Indian IT Act does make provisions to prevent online abuse.

Section: Under Section 66-A, sending abusive messages or adopting a menacing character over an electronic medium is punishable with three yrs. imprisonment and a fine. That action is taken only when an individual complaint being lodged at the local police station (cumbersome - abuse generally generated from anonymous accounts).

DOs:
- That children must consult their parents/ guardians prior to posting pictures online.
- That parents/guardians to be informed prior to downloading or uploading software or indulging in an activity that may hurt the computer or mobile phone, or disturbs the family's privacy.
- That the children's spending online should be time-bound.

DONTs:
- That don't post any pictures which parents/ guardians consider inappropriate.
- That personal information (address and telephone number), not to be shared without parents/ guardian's permission.
- That don't shre your password with anyone.
- That don't post hostile things hurting anyone.
- That don't select passwords which can be easily guessed.
- That don't believe anything seen/or read on the web.
- That don't respond to any messages which are mean or uncomfortable.
- That don't do anything costing money unless having prents/guardians permission.
- That don't click on pop-up ads. might be installing spyware, adware, or malware on your computer.
- That don't fill out information to win a free-gift

Reference: M Thaver, HTC.

VIOLENCE AGAINST MEDICAL ESTABLISHMENTS

Preface: Public attacks on doctors have become more mainly as a result of grief once the patient dies and the relatives have to pay hefty amount as hospital charges.

In some cases, attacks are planned in such a way to frighten the hospital management and get the hospital charges waived or demand money as compensation. If the patient belongs to a dominant local caste or political party, then the hospital staff will have horrid time.

Legal: Prevention of Violence and Damage to Property Act 2012

Indian scenario:

"Any offence committed under the section shall be cognisable and non-bailable." Attack on doctors in Kerala may invite 3 yrs. in jail, a fine of ₹ 50K, July, 2012. Thiruvananthapuram: The State Assembaly passed an Act, by which any attack against a duty bound doctor, a hospital or its staff would invite an imprisonment of upto 3 yrs. and a fine of ₹ 50K. The offender will also be liable to pay to the hospital a compensation of twice the amount of the purchase price of medical equipment damaged and loss caused to the property as determined by the Court trying the offender.

Act: **PREVENTION OF VIOLENCE and DAMAGE TO PROPERTY ACT:**

THE PUNJAB PROTECTION OF MEDICARE SERVICE PERSONS AND MEDICARE INSTITUTIONS (PREVENTION OF VIOLENCE AND DAMAGE TO PROPERTY) ACT, 2008

(Punjab Act No. 26 of 2008) Department of Legal and Legislative Affairs, Punjab, Notification. The 30th October, 2008.

No. 29-Leg./2008.–The following Act of the Legislature of the State of Punjab received the assent of Governor of Punjab on the 10th October,

2008, and is hereby published for general information:

Definition: defined as an Act to provide for the protection of Medicare Service Persons and Medicare Service Institutions in the State of Punjab and for prevention of violence and damage to the property and for the matters connected therewith or incidental thereto.

Enactment: Enacted by the Legislature of the State of Punjab in 2008 (30-10-2008) shall come into force at once, vide notification dated 30th October 2008.

Jurisdiction: Extends to the whole of Punjab State.

Definitions: In this Act, unless the context otherwise requires, -

(a) "Medicare Service Institution" means an institution, providing Medicare service either in the Medicare Service Institution or through Mobile Medical Unit or by arranging medical camps, which is under the control of the Central Government or the State Government or a local body including any private hospital having facility of treatment of the sick and used for their reception or stay, any private maternity home, where women are usually received and accommodated for the purpose of confinement and ante-natal and post-natal care in connection with the child birth or anything connected therewith, and any private nursing home used or intended to be used for the reception and accommodation of persons suffering from any sickness, injury or infirmity whether of body or mind, and providing of treatment of nursing or both of them and includes convalescent home ;

(b) "Medicare Service Person" in relation to a Medicare Service Institution, shall include, -

Registered Medical Practitioner, Registered Practitioner and Practitioner, working in a Medicare Service Institution:

- Nurse
- Auxiliary Nurse and Mid-wife
- Nurse-Dai, Trained-Dai
- Medical Student. Nursing Student
- Para Medical Worker; and
- Other staff or workers directly or indirectly engaged by a Medicare Service Institution for providing the required services;

  Explanation–For the purpose of this Act, the expressions Resitered Medical Practitioner, Medical Practitioner, Practitioner, Nurse, Auxiliary Nurse and Midwife and trained Dai, shall have the same meanings, as assigned to them in the Punjab Medical Registration Act, 1916, the Punjab Nurses Registration Act, 1932, the Punjab Ayurvedic and Unani Practitioners Act, 1963 and the Punjab Homeopathic Practitioners Act, 1965;

(c) "Medical Student" means a student, who is undergoing training or studies in Medical in medical profession;

(d) "Mobile Medical Unit" means an ambulance, equipped with medical equipment, used for providing medicare services;

(e) "Nursing Student" means a student, who is undergoing training or studies in nursing profession;

(f) "Offender" means any person, who either by himself or as a member or leader of a group of persons or organisation commits or attempts to commit or abets or incites the commission or violence;

(g) "Paramedical Worker" means a person, who assists the Medicare Service Person providing Medicare services;

(h) "Property" shall include both movable and immovable property; and

(i) "Violence" means any act, which causes or may cause any harm, injury or endanger life, obstruct or hinder any Medicare Service Person in the discharge of his duty in a Medicare Service Institution or damage to property in Medicare Service Institution.

Prohibition of violence: Any act of violence against a Medicare Service Person or damage to property in a Medicare Service Institution, shall be prohibited.

Penalty: An offender, who commits any act in contravention of the provisions of this Act shall be punished with an imprisonment, which may extend to one year, or with fine, which may extend to ₹ 50,000, or with both.

Cognizance: Any offence committed under this Act, shall be cognizable and non-bailable and shall be triable by the Court of Judicial Magistrate of the First Class.

Recovery of: (1) In addition to the punishment as specified in Section 4, the Offender shall also be liable to pay a penalty of twice the amount of purchase price of medical equipment damaged or loss caused to the property, as may be determined by the Court referred to in Section 5.

(2) If the offender has not paid the penalty, imposed under sub-section (1) the same shall be recoverable as arrears of land revenue.

Derogation: The provisions of this Act shall be in addition to the provisions of any other law, for the time being in force.

THE HARYANA PROTECTION OF MEDICARE SERVICE PERSONS AND MEDICARE INSTITUTIONS ACT, 2009

(Haryana Act No. 14 of 2009) Haryana Government, Law and Legislative Department, Notification, The 26th March, 2009

No. Leg. 18/2009.–The following Act of the Legislature of the State of Haryana received the assent of Governor of Haryana on the 19th March, 2009, and is hereby published for general information:

Definition: defined as an Act to prohibit violence against Medicare Service Persons and damage to property in Medicare Service Institutions and for matters connected therewith or incidental thereto.

Enactment: Enacted by the Legislature of the State of Haryana in 2009 (19th March, 2009), shall come into force at once, vide notification dated 26-3-2009.

Jurisdiction: Extends to the whole of Haryana State.

Definitions: In this Act, unless the context otherwise requires:

(a) "Medicare Service Institution" means an institution, used or intended to be used for the reception, accommodation, treatment and medicare of persons suffering from any sickness, injury or infirmity whether of body or mind and providing of treatment or nursing or both of them and includes maternity home, convalescent home, nursing home or hospital etc. owned or controlled either by the State Government or Central Government or any person or individual;

(b) "Medicare Service Person" in relation to a Medicare Service Institution, shall include, -

(i) Registered Medical Practitioners (including those having provisional registration);

(ii) Registered Nurses;

(iii) Medical Students;

(iv) Nursing Students;

(v) Para-Medical Workers.

Penalty: (1) Whoever, endangers the life of or causes any harm, injury, intimidation, obstruction or hindrance to any Medicare Service Person in the discharge of duty or damage to any property in Medicare Service Institution, commits an act of violence which shall be an offence under this Act.

(2) Whoever, either by himself or as a member or as a leader of a group of persons or organisation

commits or attempts to commit or abets or incites the commission of offence, shall be punished with imprisonment for a term of three years and shall also be liable to a penalty of actual amount of purchase price of medical equipment damaged and loss caused to the property as may be determined by the competent Court.

Cognizable offence: The offence committed under Section 3 shall be cognizable and non-bailable.

Recovery as arrears of land revenue. If a person fails to pay the penal amount under Section 3, the said amount shall be recoverable as if it were arrears of land revenue.

Act not in derogation of any other law: The provisions of this Act shall be in addition to and not in derogation of the provisions of any other law, for the time being in force.

Power to make rules:

The State Government may, by notification in the Official Gazette, make rules for carrying out the purposes of this Act.

Every rule made under this Act shall be laid, as soon as may be, after it is made, before the House of State Legislative, while it is in session.

VIOLENCE AGAINST WOMEN

Preface: That is defined as any act of gender-based violence that results in, or is likely to result in, physical, sexual, or psychological harm or suffering to women, incld. threats of such acts, coercion or arbitrary deprivation of liberty, whether occurring in public or private life. It encompasses, but is not limited to, “physical, sexual and psychological violence occurring in the family, incld. battering, sexual abuse of female children in the household, dowry related violence, marital rape, female genital mutilation and other traditional practices harmful to women, non- spousal violence and violence related to exploitation; physical, sexual and psychological violence occurring within the general community, incld. rape, sexual abuse, sexual harassment and intimidation at work, in educational institutions and elsewhere; trafficking in women and forced prostitution; and physical, sexual and psychological violence perpetrated or condoned by the state, wherever it occurs.

(Declaration on the Elimination of Violence against Women, adopted by the United Nations General Assembly, 1993).

Forms: Violence against women takes many forms, from the overt to the subtle.

WHO has adopted the following definitions of physical and sexual violence to aid in research and programming, concentrating on identifiable acts:

* Physical violence: perpetrators are looking for weak and easily submissive Victims. A woman has been slapped, pushed, shoved, or had something (acid or foreign body) thrown at her, or had her hair pulled; hit with a fist or something else that could hurt; choked or burnt; threatened with or had a weapon used against her.
* Sexual violence: a woman has been physically forced to have sexual intercourse; had sexual intercourse because she was afraid of what her partner might do; or forced to do something sexual she found degrading or humiliating.
* Psychological violence: though recognised as a serious and pervasive problem, emotional violence does not yet have a widely accepted definition.

  Example: a woman has been humiliated or belittled; been scared or intimidated purposefully.
* Domestic (Intimate-partner) violence: a woman has encountered any of the above types of violence, at the hands of an intimate partner or ex-partner; this is one of the most common and universal forms of violence experienced by women.

Indian scenario:

- That while many women made giant strides in their own fields, the issue of violence against women remains an enduring blot on Indian society.
- That the girl who died after that horrific gang-rape in Delhi seemed, for a while to bring about a real change in attitudes towards women, but only short-lived.

  The attacks on women in the Capital have not abated one bit, even little girls have not been spared. In many cases, the perpetrators of rape and murder are those known to the victims. But the increasing violence against women is not only a Delhi phenomenon.
- That in Kolkata, ruled by a woman Chief Minister, there have been instances of many rapes and murders of young women, including a tribal panchayat sanctioned gang-rape. Each time the Chief Minister dismissed the allegations of rape as political plot against her government by her political opponents.
- That in UP, almost daily there have been incidents of violence against women incld. rapes and murders of very young girls. Many women were raped during the Muzaffarnagar riots and live in fear in the relief camps, while their assailants walk about scot-free. The rapes and murders of young women on their way home from work have risen manyfold.
- That in short, women's vulnerability has increased manyfold, while the strengthened laws have not really been a deterrent.
- That by and large, the safety of women has not been debated by our lawmakers who are too busy squabbling among themselves.
- That mushrooming of khap panchayats, which invariably pass anti-women verdicts, seems to have political sanction, although those passing such retrograde orders should have been behind bars.

- That the only hope, when the women will be able to make political parties listen through their franchise votes.
- That India ratified the United Nations Convention on Elimination of All Forms of Discrimination against Women (CEDAW) in 1993.
- That, The Protection of Women from Domestic Violence Act, 2005, tries to be in line with this convention.

International scenario:

WHO multi-country study on women's health and domestic violence against women in 10 developing countries found that among women aged 15-49:

* 20 per cent of women and 5-10 per cent of men are victims of sexual violence as children.
* Intimate-partner and sexual violence are mostly perpetrated by men against girls and women. Child sexual abuse affects boys and girls.
* 0.3-11.5 per cent of women reported experiencing sexual violence by a non-partner since the age of 15 yrs.
* 15 per cent of women in Japan and 71 per cent of women in Ethiopia reported physical and/or sexual violence by an intimate partner.
* First sexual experience for many women was reported as forced–7 per cent in rural Tanzania, 24 per cent in rural Peru and 30 per cent in rural Bangladesh.

(Prashant Chaudhary, HT January 06, 2013)

Remedy:

- That given the impression of a confident and strong person may catch the perpetrators off guard and the victim may be able to run away. Pushing him off (if he's closer than desirable), saying NO and STOP are setting boundaries.
- That the voice should be assertive and loud and words such as sorry, please, can you, could you, etc. have to be avoided. No smiling either! Most women try to be polite and smile when they feel uncomfortable. Always present yourself as a

resolute, strong and unintimidated person. Your facial expression and body language should portray that as well.

- That for bystanders help, yell and tell them that you are being attacked. Many times the bystanders are reluctant to intervene fearing the attacker's motives.

  Failure to intimidate the attacker, change your tactic. Reason with him, for not ruining his career by rusting in a jail. That failure to convince him by reasoning, may force you to fight–by serious shouting, yelling, kicking, punching, elbowing, kneeing, scratching, eye gouging, bitting, well pretty much using everything you can do and what you have been practicing. The aim is to fight him hard, even if that means getting hurt in the process.

- That mandatory training of martial arts for self-protection for girls, women.

References: 1. VP Jacob: Fight your attacker tooth and nail, HT, March, 2014.

2. The Editor: She will be heard through the ballot, HT, March, 2014.

PART - IV

APPENDIX

CHAPTER - XIII

QUESTIONNAIRE

QUESTIONNAIRE (SECTION-WISE)

A. Introduction:

1. Define Medical Jurisprudence
2. Define Forensic Medicine
3. Define Medico-legal aspect
4. Define Autopsy
5. Define Benefits of Medical Jurisprudence
6. Define Principles of Forensic Medicine
7. Define DNA Fingerprinting
8. Define Application of DNA
9. Define Circumstantial Evidence
10. Define Narco Test

B. Legal Criminal Procedures:

11. Define Judicial Inquest
12. Define Police Inquest
13. Define Exhumation
14. Define PM Examination
15. Define Summon
16. Define Subpoena
17. Define Oath-Taking
18. Define Evidence Recording
19. Define Examination-in-Chief
20. Define Cross-Examination
21. Define Re-Examination
22. Define Medical Evidence

23. Define Oral/Verbal Evidence
24. Define Direct Evidence: Sensory - Visual (Eye-witness),
    - Audible
    - Olfactory
25. Define Indirect Evidence:-Circumstantial/Associated Evidence
    -Documentary Evidence:
26. Define Dying Declaration
27. Define Dying Deposition
28. Define Medical Certificate of Illness, Insanity and Fitness
29. Define Medical Certificate of Death
30. Define Medico-legal Reports:- Accident/Injury Report
    - Post-Mortem Report
    - Age-Evidence Report
    - Rape, Abortion, Molestatyion Reports
    - Poisoning Report
31. Define Witness: - Common/Ordinary Witness
    - Professional Witness:
    - Medical Professionals,
    - Finger-Print Experts
    - Hand-Writing Experts
    - Chemical Examiner Experts
    - Arms and Ammunition Experts
    - Skilled Witness
32. Define Identity: - Indications
    - Identifying (ID) factors

C. Medical Aberrations:

33. Define Death
34. Define Wounds
35. Define Sexual and Allied Disorders
36. Define Sexual Perversions
37. Define Sexual Offences
38. Define Pregnancy (Medico-legal Aspect)
39. Define Delivery (Medico-legal Aspect)
40. Define Abortion (Medico-legal Aspect)

41. Define Infanticide
42. Define Psychiatric Disorders

D. Poisoning:

43. Define poisoning
44. Define Types of poisons
45. Define Medico-legal classification of poisoning
46. Define Rules observed in a poisoning case
47. Define Classification of Poisons:
48. Define Corrosives:
    - Acids (Corrosive)
    - Alkalies (corrosive)
49. Define Irritants:
    - Irritants (Chemical):
    - Oxalic Acid
    - Carbolic Acid (Phenol)
    - Salicylic Acid
    - Mercury
    - Copper Sulphate
    - Lead
    - Phosphorus
    - Arsenic
    - Irritants (Animal):
    - Snake poisoning
    - Scorpion poisoning
    - Wasp and Bees poison
50. Define Neurotics

    Define Cardiac Glycosides:
    - Digitalis poisoning
    - Anticoagulants poisoning
    - Cytotoxic drugs poisoning:
    - Alkylating agents poisoning
    - Antimetabolites poisoning
    - Antihormonal poisoning
    - Vinca alkaloids
    - Antineoplastic antibiotics poisoning

Define Miscellaneous poisonings:

- Detergents poisoning:
- Soaps, detergents, antiseptics poisoning
- Disinfectants and Germicides poisoning
- Formaldehyde poisoning
- Chlorine poisoning
- Iodine poisoning
- Boric acid poisoning
- Insecticides and Arachnicides (Pesticides) poisoning
- Chlorophenothane (DDT) poisoning
- Fluorides (Insect powder) poisoning
- Phosphates (Organic) poisoning
- Rodenticides poisoning
- Barium poisoning
- Fluoroacetate poisoning
- Antihelminthics poisoning
- Carbon tetrachloride poisoning
- Aspidium (Mali-Fern, poisoning
- Amebicidal agents poisoning
- Emetine poisoning

Define Industrial poisoning:

- Heavy metals
- Arsenic poisoning
- Antimony poisoning
- Mercury poisoning
- Lead poisoning
- Cadmium poisoning
- Manganese poisoning
- Zinc poisoning
- Gold poisoning
- Silver poisoning
- Bismuth poisoning
- Thallium poisoning
- Beryllium poisoning
- Paint thinner poisoning

Define Household poisoning:

- Food poisoning

E. Legal System:

51. Define Indian Legal System

52. Define UK Legal System

53. Define USA Legal System

F. OFFENCES (MEDICO-LEGAL ASPECT):

54. MEDICAL NEGLIGENCE:

Define:

- Medical negligence
- Civil negligence
- Criminal negligence
- Implied understanding
- Subtle/ Complicated negligence
- Act of Commission
- Act of Omission
- Actionable Negligence
- Vicarious Liability
- Contributory Negligence

Questionnaire and response by Doctors encountering medico-legal problems:

Q.: Do you maintain records of your patients ?

Ans: Yes: No.

Q.: What type of language used in your written documents ?

Ans: English: Vernacular.

Q.: Do you use assistants to communicate with patient ?

Ans: Yes: No.

Q.: How much time spent with the patient ?

Ans: Yes: No.

Q.: What has been the attitude of your patient in general ?

Ans: Co-operative: aggressive: hostile.

Q.: What type of consent form used ?

Ans: Blanket: informed: explained.

Q.: Have you ever faced any medicolegal problem ?

Ans: Yes: No.

Q.: What type of problem have you faced ?

Ans: No problem: negligence: criminal case: threats of suit: legal/political Pressure.

Q.: Most likely person from patient's side to create problem ?

Ans: Patient himself/herself: relative (s): friend (s): social workers: press: other doctor (s): advocate (s): police.

Q.: What do you do, in case of a trouble, after death of the patient ?

Ans: Had no trouble: call police: advise post-mortem: waive fees.

Q.: Do you have any Court case pending against you ?

Ans: Yes: No.

Q: Are you aware of any law (s) protecting you in your practice ?

Ans: Yes: No.

Q.: What is your opinion about attitude of Judiciary in medicolegal cases ?

Ans: Friendly: callous: unfriendly: accusing: arrogant: unaware of medical issues.

55. Define Medical Termination of Pregnancy (MTP):
   - Abortion Policy in India
   - Critique of MTP Act
56. Define Torture:
   - Doctors and Torture
   - SEXUAL OFFENCES:
   - Sexual offences in India
   - Sexual offences in UK
   - Sexual abuse
   - Sexual Torture
   - Doctor's and Torture
57. Define Moral Turpitude
58. Define Sodomy

59. Define Rape
60. Define Euthanasia:
    - Factors favouring euthanasia
    - Arguments favouring euthanasia
    - Factors opposing euthanasia
    - Arguments opposing euthanasia
61. Define Environment Pollution

G. Acts and Laws/Acts (Civil and Criminal) Related to Medical Profession:

62. Define:
    - Civil and Criminal Proceeding
    - Civil Procedure Code, 1908
    - Consumer Protection Act, 1986
    - Clinical Establishment (Registration and Regulation) Act, 2010
    - Consent
    - Contempt of Courts Act, 1971
    - Copyright Act, 1957
    - Divorce Act, 1869
    - Dowry Prohibition Act, 1961
    - Drugs and Cosmetics Act, 1940
    - Drugs and Magic Remedies (Objectionable Advertisements) Act, 1954
    - Dying declaration
    - Environment Protection Act, 1986
    - Fatal Accidents Act, 1855
    - Immoral Traffic (Prevention) Act, 1956
    - Medical Termination of Pregnancy (MTP) Act, 1971
    - Medical Termination of Pregnancy (MTP) Rules, 1975
    - Mental Health Act, 1987
    - Mental Retardation and Multiple Disability Act, 1999
    - Narcotic Drugs and Psychotropic Substances Act, 1985
    - Oaths Act, 1969
    - PNDT (Regulation and Prevention of Misuse) Act, 1994

- PNDT (Regulation and Prevention of Misuse) Rules, 1996
- Poisons Act, 1919
- Prevention of Food Adulteration Act, 1954
- Prevention of Violence and Damage to Property Act, 2008 (The Punjab Protection of Medicare Service Persons and Medicare Institutions)
- Prevention of Violence and Damage to Property Act, 2009
- The Haryana Medicare Service Persons and Medicare Service Institutions
- Prohibition of Child Marriage Act, 2006
- Protection of Human Rights Act, 1993
- Registration Act, 1908
- Registration of Births and Deaths Act, 1969
- Suicide (Abetment to Suicide.
- Transplantation of Human Organs Act, 1994

H. Sections (Related to Medical Profession)

63. Define section :

Q. : 12 IPC ?

Ans : Related to Domestic violence.

Q. : 12(2) IPC ?

Ans : Related to Obligation to treat and stabilise every kind of emergency.

Q. : 24 IPC ?

Ans : Related to contempt of court.

Q. : 29 IPC ?

Ans : Related to document – used as an evidence.

Q. : 31 IPC ?

Ans : Related to Will – used as a legal declaration of a person after his/her death.

Q. : 32,33,36 IPC ?

Ans : Related to an "Act" of illegal "Omissions."

Q. : 34 IPC ?

Ans : Related to acts done by several persons in furtherance of common intention.

Q. : 39 IPC ?

Ans: Related to voluntarily act–knowingly or intentionally.

Q. : 44 IPC ?

Ans : Related to injury–mentally, physically, defamation or to assets/property.

Q. : 50(2) IPC ?

Ans : Related to act by which the police is under legal obligation to inform the doctor for the grounds/reason of arrest.

Q. : 52 IPC ?

Ans : Related to "Good faith"–genuine effort to reach the truth.

Q. : 80 IPC ?

Ans : Related to Occurrence of Accident in doing lawful act.

Q. : 81 IPC ?

Ans : Related to act done to avoid further harm.

Q. : 87-91 IPC ?

Ans : Related to act under consent.

Q. : 88 IPC ?

Ans : Related to act not intended to cause death, done by consent in good faith for person's benefit.

Q. : 90 IPC ?

Ans : Related to consent known to be given under fear of misconception.

Q. : 92 IPC ?

Ans : Related to bona fide act for another's benefit, done without consent.

Q. : 105 IPC ?

Ans : Related to act of evidence.

Q. : 120A IPC ?

Ans : Related to definition of Criminal conspiracy.

Q. : 161 IPC ?

Ans : Related to anticipatory bail that can be asked when summons issued by the police for investigation and interrogations.

Q. : 176 IPC ?

Ans : Related to failure to inform police whenever essential.

Q. : 191 IPC ?

Ans : Related to false evidence given under oath.

Q. : 197 IPC ?

Ans : Related to Issuing or signing false certificate.

Q. : 201 IPC ?

Ans : Related to act of disguising evidence of offence, or giving false information to defend an offender.

Q. : 202 IPC ?

Ans : Related to act of intentional omission to provide information of offence by the person bound to inform.

Q.: 211 IPC ?

Ans : Related to false charge of an offence.

Q.: 212-216 IPC ?

Ans : Related to harboring an offender-providing shelter to an offender under the pretext of illness in a nursing home/hospital.

Q. : 268 IPC ?

Ans : Related to illegal omission.

Q. : 269-271 IPC ?

Ans : Related to spread of infectious disease and disobedience of a Quarantine rule.

Q. : 272-273 IPC ?

Ans : Related to adulteration of food and drinks.

Q. : 274-276 IPC ?

Ans : Related to adulteration of drugs.

Q. : 277-278 IPC ?

Ans : Related to fouling water and vitiating atmosphere.

Q. : 304 IPC ?

Ans : Related to homicidal death.

Q. : 304-A IPC ?

Ans : Related to death caused by a negligent act.

Q. : 306-309 IPC ?

Ans : Related to abetment of suicide.

Q. : 319-328 IPC ?

Ans : Related to causing hurt, grievous hurt, loss of vision, loss of hearing or disfigurement by dangerous mean.

Q. : 336-338 IPC ?

Ans : Related to causing hurt by rash or negligent act by dangerous means.

Q. : 340-342 IPC ?

Ans : Related to wrongful confinement.

Q. : 354 IPC ?

Ans : Related to assault or criminal force applied to a woman with intent to outrage her modesty.

Q. : 376 IPC ?

Ans : Related to rape.

Q. : 376-D IPC ?

Ans : Related to sexual intercourse by any member of the management or staff of a hospital with any woman in that hospital.

Q. : 405 IPC ?

Ans : Related to criminal breach of trust.

Q. : 406 IPC ?

Ans : Related to punishment for criminal breach of trust.

Q. : 415 IPC ?

Ans : Related to cheating.

Q. : 420 IPC ?

Ans : Related to cheating and dishonestly inducing delivery of property.

Q. : 438 IPC ?

Ans : Related to filling of FIR being not a condition precedent to the exercise of the power.

Q. : 438(1) IPC ?

Ans : Related to section that confers on the High Court and the Court of Sessions, the power to grant anticipatory bail if the applicant has reason to believe that he/she may be arrested on the accusation of having committed a non-bailable offence.

Q. : 470 IPC ?

Ans : Related to forged document.

Q. : 471 IPC ?

Ans : Related to using a forged document as genuine.

Q. : 499 IPC ?

Ans : Related to defamation.

Q. : 504 IPC ?

Ans : Related to intentional insult with intent to provoke breach of the peace.

Q. : 506 IPC ?

Ans : Related to punishment for criminal intimidation

I. Judgment Related to Medical Profession :

64. Judgments related to :

Q. : Medical Negligence ?

Q. : Consumer Protection Act, 1986 ?

Q. : Clinical Establishment (Registration and Regulation) Act, 2010 ?

Q. : Consent ?

Q. : Contempt of Courts Act, 1971 ?

Q. : Copyright Act, 1957 ?

Q. : Divorce Act, 1869 ?

Q. : Dowry Prohibition Act, 1961 ?

Q. : Drugs and Cosmetics Act, 1940 ?

Q. : Drugs and Magic Remedies (Objectionable Advertisements) Act, 1954 ?

Q. : Dying declaration ?

Q. : Environment Protection Act, 1986 ?

Q. : Fatal Accidents Act, 1855 ?

Q. : Immoral Traffic (Prevention) Act, 1956 ?

Q. : Medical Termination of Pregnancy (MTP) Act, 1971 ?

Q. : Medical Termination of Pregnancy (MTP) Rules, 1975 ?

Q. : Mental Health Act, 1987 ?

Q. : Narcotic Drugs and Psychotropic Substances Act, 1985 ?

Q. : Oaths Act, 1969 ?

Q. : PNDT (Regulation and Prevention of Misuse) Act, 1994 ?

Q. : PNDT (Regulation and Prevention of Misuse) Rules, 1996 ?

Q. : Poisons Act, 1919 ?

Q. : Prevention of Food Adulteration Act, 1954 ?

Q. : Prevention of Violence and Damage to Property Act, 2008 (The Punjab Protection of Medicare Service Persons and Medicare Institutions) ?

Q. : Prevention of Violence and Damage to Property Act, 2009 ?

Q. : The Haryana Medicare Service Persons and Medicare Service Institutions ?

Q. : Protection of Human Rights Act, 1993 ?

Q. : Registration Act, 1908 ?

Q. : Protection of Women from Domestic Violence Act, 2005 ?

Q. : Protection of Women from Domestic Violence Rules, 2006 ?

Q. : Registration Act, 1908 ?

Q. : Registration of Births and Deaths Act, 1969 ?

Q. : Abetment to Suicide ?

Q. : Transplantation of Human Organs Act, 1994 ?

J. State Medicine :

Q. : Define State Medicine ?

Q. : Define Torture ?

Q. : Define Sexual Torture ?

Q. : Define Doctors and Torture ?

Q. : Define Criminal Liability of Doctors ?

Q. : Define When doctors should inform Police ?

Q. : Define Can a doctor be arrested and bailed ?

Q. : Define Limitations of each pathy and speciality ?

Q. : Can a Gynecologist with no formal training in surgical oncology perform surgery on breast ?

K. Medical Ethics

Q. : Define Medical Ethics ?

Q. : Define Hippocratic Oath ?

Q. : Define Code of Medical Ethics ?

Q. : Define Medical Ethics for doctors ?

Q. : Define Do's and Don't for doctors ?

Q. : Define Good Medical Practice ?

Q. : Define Principles of Good Medical Practice ?

L. Issues

Q. : Define Abetment to Suicide ?

Q. : Define Acid Attacks Trauma ?

Q : Define Advertising Medical Services ?

Q. : Define Agony of Senior Citizens ?

Q. : Define Alcohol Abuse ?

Q. : Define Bachelor of Rural Medicine (BRM) ?

Q. : Define Child Abuse/Vulnerable Childhood/No Country for Children ?

Q. : Define Clinical Establishment Act (CEA) ?

Q. : Define Consumer Protection Act (CPA) ?

Q. : Define Domestic Violence ?

Q : Define Dowry Menace ?

Q. : Define Eve Teasing ?

Q. : Define Euthanasia ?

Q. : Define Honour Killing ?

Q. : Define Homicide ?

Q. : Define Judicial Moralism ?

Q. : Define Medical Education ?

Q. : Define Medical Negligence ?

Q. : Define Medical Profession ?

Q. : Define Mandatory Rural Posting for PG Examination Entry ?

Q. : Define National Commission for Human Resources for Health Bill 2011 ?

Q. : Define Pre-Natal Sex Determination Tests (PSDT) Act ?

Q. : Define Rape ?

Q. : Define Juvenile Rape ?

Q. : Define Sexual Harassment of Women at Working Place Act 2013 ?

Q. : Define Physical Torture ?

Q. : Define Troll / Sadist ?

Q. : Define Violence Against Medical Establishments?

Q. : Define Violence Against Women ?

Index

B

C

D

J

K

L

M

N

O

P

Q

R

S

T

U

V

W

X

Y

Z